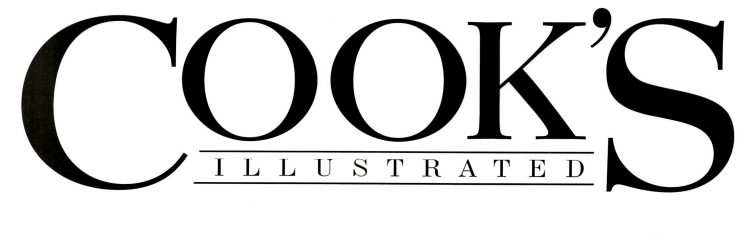

COOK'S

ILLUSTRATED

~ 2013 ~

Published by
America's Test Kitchen
17 Station Street
Brookline, MA 02445

ISBN-13: 978-1-936493-66-1
ISBN-10: 1-936493-66-7
ISSN: 1933-639X

To get home delivery of Cook's Illustrated magazine, call 800-526-8442 inside the U.S., or 515-247-7571 if calling from outside the U.S., or subscribe online at www.cooksillustrated.com.

In addition to Cook's Illustrated Annual Hardbound Editions available from each year of publication (1993–2013), America's Test Kitchen offers the following cookbooks and DVD sets:

THE COOK'S ILLUSTRATED COOKBOOK SERIES
The Cook's Illustrated Cookbook
The Cook's Illustrated Baking Book
The Science of Good Cooking
The America's Test Kitchen Menu Cookbook
Soups, Stews & Chilis
The Best Skillet Recipes
The Best Slow & Easy Recipes
The Best Chicken Recipes
The Best International Recipe
The Best Make-Ahead Recipe
The Best 30-Minute Recipe
The Best Light Recipe
The Cook's Illustrated Guide to Grilling and Barbecue
Best American Side Dishes
The Best Cover & Bake Recipes
The New Best Recipe
Steaks, Chops, Roasts, and Ribs
Baking Illustrated
Perfect Vegetables
Italian Classics
The Best American Classics
The Best One-Dish Suppers
The America's Test Kitchen Menu Cookbook

AMERICA'S TEST KITCHEN ANNUALS
The Best of America's Test Kitchen (2007–2014 Editions)
Cooking for Two (2009–2013 Editions)
Light & Healthy (2010–2012 Editions)

THE AMERICA'S TEST KITCHEN SERIES DVD SETS
(featuring each season's episodes from our hit public television series)
The *America's Test Kitchen* 4-DVD Set (2002–2013 Seasons)
The *America's Test Kitchen* 2-DVD Set (2001 Season)

THE AMERICA'S TEST KITCHEN SERIES COMPANION COOKBOOKS
America's Test Kitchen: The TV Companion Cookbook (2013)
America's Test Kitchen: The TV Companion Cookbook (2012)
America's Test Kitchen: The TV Companion Cookbook (2011)
The Complete America's Test Kitchen TV Show Cookbook (2010)
America's Test Kitchen: The TV Companion Cookbook (2009)
Behind the Scenes with America's Test Kitchen (2008)
Test Kitchen Favorites (2007)
Cooking at Home with America's Test Kitchen (2006)
America's Test Kitchen Live! (2005)
Inside America's Test Kitchen (2004)
Here in America's Test Kitchen (2003)
The America's Test Kitchen Cookbook (2002)

THE AMERICA'S TEST KITCHEN LIBRARY SERIES
The America's Test Kitchen Do-It-Yourself Cookbook
Slow Cooker Revolution
Slow Cooker Revolution 2: The Easy Prep Edition
Comfort Food Makeovers
The Best Simple Recipes
Best Grilling Recipes
The Six Ingredient Solution
From Our Grandmothers' Kitchens

ADDITIONAL BOOKS FROM AMERICA'S TEST KITCHEN
The America's Test Kitchen Quick Family Cookbook
The America's Test Kitchen Healthy Family Cookbook
The America's Test Kitchen Family Cookbook
The America's Test Kitchen Family Baking Book
The America's Test Kitchen Cooking School Cookbook
Pressure Cooker Perfection
The Complete Cook's Country TV Show Cookbook
Cook's Country Annual Hardbound (2005–2013 Editions)
1993–2013 Cook's Illustrated Master Index

Visit our online bookstore at www.cooksillustrated.com to order any of our cookbooks and DVDs listed above. You can also order subscriptions, gift subscriptions, and any of our cookbooks and DVDs by calling 800-611-0759 inside the U.S., or at 515-246-6911 if calling from outside the U.S.

BC = Back Cover

NUMBER 120

JANUARY & FEBRUARY 2013

COOK'S
ILLUSTRATED

Truly Foolproof Soft-Cooked Eggs
We Made More than 1,000

Butterscotch Pudding
A New Way to Make Pudding

Best Roasted Shrimp
The Secret to Intense Flavor

Testing Pressure Cookers
Why You Should Own One

French-Style Chicken with Stuffing

How to Cook Grains
Everything You Need to Know

Crispy Orange Beef
Winter Citrus Salads
Tasting Store-Bought Hummus
Better Oatmeal Muffins
Pasta all'Amatriciana

www.CooksIllustrated.com
$5.95 U.S./$6.95 CANADA

0 74470 62805 7

0 2>

CONTENTS
January & February 2013

Founder and Editor Christopher Kimball
Editorial Director Jack Bishop
Editorial Director, Magazines John Willoughby
Executive Editor Amanda Agee
Test Kitchen Director Erin McMurrer
Managing Editor Rebecca Hays
Senior Editors Keith Dresser
Lisa McManus
Senior Editor, Features Elizabeth Bomze
Associate Editor, Features Molly Birnbaum
Copy Editors Nell Beram
Megan Chromik
Associate Editors Andrea Geary
Amy Graves
Andrew Janjigian
Chris O'Connor
Dan Souza
Test Cook Lan Lam
Assistant Editors Hannah Crowley
Shannon Friedmann Hatch
Taizeth Sierra
Assistant Test Cooks Dan Cellucci
Sara Mayer
Celeste Rogers
Executive Assistant Christine Gordon
Test Kitchen Manager Leah Rovner
Senior Kitchen Assistant Meryl MacCormack
Kitchen Assistants Maria Elena Delgado
Ena Gudiel
Andrew Straaberg Finfrock
Executive Producer Melissa Baldino
Associate Producer Stephanie Stender
Production Assistant Kaitlin Hammond
Contributing Editor Dawn Yanagihara
Consulting Editor Scott Brueggeman
Science Editor Guy Crosby, Ph.D.
Managing Editor, Web Christine Liu
Associate Editors, Web Eric Grzymkowski
Mari Levine
Roger Metcalf
Senior Video Editor Nick Dakoulas

Design Director Amy Klee
Art Director Julie Cote
Deputy Art Director Susan Levin
Associate Art Director Lindsey Timko
Designer, Marketing/Web Mariah Tarvainen
Staff Photographer Daniel J. van Ackere
Photo Editor Steve Klise

Vice President, Marketing David Mack
Circulation Director Doug Wicinski
Circulation & Fulfillment Manager Carrie Fethe
Partnership Marketing Manager Pamela Putprush
Marketing Assistant Joyce Liao
Customer Service Manager Jacqueline Valerio
Customer Service Representatives Megan Hamner
Jessica Haskin

Chief Operations Officer David Dinnage
Production Director Guy Rochford
Senior Project Manager Alice Carpenter
Production & Traffic Coordinator Brittany Allen
Workflow & Digital Asset Manager Andrew Mannone
Production & Imaging Specialists Heather Dube
Lauren Pettapiece
Lauren Robbins
Systems Administrator Marcus Walser
Business Analyst Wendy Tseng
Web Developers Chris Candelora
Cameron MacKensie
Human Resources Director Adele Shapiro

VP New Media Product Development Barry Kelly

Chief Financial Officer Sharyn Chabot
Director of Sponsorship Sales Anne Traficante
Retail Sales & Marketing Director Emily Logan
Client Services Associate Kate May
Publicity Deborah Broide

PRINTED IN THE USA

GERMAN SAUSAGES Germany produces more than 1,500 varieties of sausage. Brühwurst is a category of sausage that is heated during production to achieve a firm consistency. Golden-cased GELBWURST is eaten cold. WEISSWURST, a Bavarian white sausage made with veal, pork, spices, and parsley, is typically a morning meal paired with pretzels. FRANKFURTERS, smoked all-pork sausages (different from Austrian pork-beef wieners), date back to the Middle Ages. Originally from Hungary, paprika-spiced DEBRECZINER look like stretched frankfurters. Rotund KNACKWURST, whose name is inspired by its snappy casing (*knacken* means "to crack" in German), is usually served grilled. Rohwurst is a category of raw sausage similar to salami that is dried at low temperatures. This process gives HOLSTEINER and LANDJÄGER a long shelf life. In contrast, Kochwurst, such as LEBERWURST and BLUTWURST, is made from cooked offal—such as liver, tongue, diced fat, and blood—and doesn't require reheating.

CORNER (Garlic): Robert Papp; BACK COVER (German Sausages): John Burgoyne

RECIPES THAT WORK®

America's Test Kitchen is a very real 2,500-square-foot kitchen located just outside Boston. It is the home of *Cook's Illustrated* and *Cook's Country* magazines and is the workday destination of more than three dozen test cooks, editors, and cookware specialists. Our mission is to test recipes over and over again until we understand how and why they work and until we arrive at the best version. We also test kitchen equipment and supermarket ingredients in search of brands that offer the best value and performance. You can watch us work by tuning in to *America's Test Kitchen* (AmericasTestKitchenTV.com) on public television.

LOST AND FOUND

Six years ago, I went hiking in the Pyrenees and, on the last day, chose a 23-kilometer walk on the border between Spain and France headed down to Banyuls-sur-Mer. I had a map (the kind printed on paper), no compass, and no GPS. I did have water, an apple, a *jambon* sandwich, a raincoat, and a plastic flashlight. The one thing I did not have was common sense. Instead of following the rickety slatted fence line straight east to the Mediterranean and my destination, I took a sharp left north based on a series of particularly small but bad decisions that overwhelmed a rather simple fact: I was supposed to be traveling east, not north. Late in the afternoon, after traveling for miles through the rough, dark Massane Forest on wild boar paths and backtracking around steep river gorges, I finally hitchhiked to a small town that, thankfully, had an open café. Three beers later, I called a cab that had to drive for half an hour to Banyuls—I wasn't even on the front side of my map.

Every honest Vermonter admits to getting lost. One might track a deer until twilight, end up on an unfamiliar ridge, head downhill, find a stream, and follow it out to a road. The difference between Vermonters and the rest of us is that Vermonters are used to being lost; they expect it.

Last year I was hiking just over a ridge that was part of a wildlife refuge. It was steep, the slope was heavy with dying shagbark hickory, and I was headed down looking for deer paths. I eventually backtracked, and when I reached high ground, I looked out and saw not my hunting cabin across the hollow as I had expected but, instead, an unfamiliar vista.

In that moment of being lost, I noticed the milky sun suspended above the far western ridge, the distant train whistle of the wind, the composted scent of wet leaves, and a spearmint blast of black birch. I heard the scuttling of a chipmunk and then watched a red squirrel sail from one oak to the next and then spiral up the trunk to his nest above. Assumptions about place and direction had been disproved; I was alone and no longer attached to the way back home.

I sat down on a stretch of log and took out a brisket sandwich and an apple, enjoying the sunny, cool afternoon. I stopped looking for the familiar—the spot where I had seen a six-pointer the year before or a rocky outcropping high above the valley. I was on safari in wild, unfamiliar country. The world was fresh and alive.

As the woods around my cabin become more familiar, as I venture out farther and farther, I seek the joy of cutting one's moorings, of walking through a dark, haunted forest, happy for the temporary dislocation.

Christopher Kimball

Robert Frost must have had this in mind when he wrote his most famous poem. His horse thinks it odd that Frost is stopping at a place "between the woods and frozen lake / The darkest evening of the year." The only other sound is "the sweep / Of easy wind and downy flake." The stanzas carry a quiet satisfaction, a rootedness in the middle of nowhere, on a dark night, lost to all things familiar.

Sometimes I am a swinger of birches but, recently, a quiet beckons. In "Going for Water," Frost writes about children who run through the woods during a fall evening to fetch water and, in so doing, uncover another world. "We ran as if to meet the moon / That slowly dawned behind the trees, / The barren boughs without the leaves, / Without the birds, without the breeze."

In "A Boundless Moment," Frost finds truth in the woods by shaking off his preconceptions about the way he wants the world to be. He at first believes that he has come across a splendid "Paradise-in-bloom" in March but instead admits that it is nothing more than a beech "clinging to its last year's leaves."

We must lose what we think we know so that we can come to see what we least expect.

FOR INQUIRIES, ORDERS, OR MORE INFORMATION

CooksIllustrated.com

At CooksIllustrated.com, you can order books and subscriptions, sign up for our free e-newsletter, or renew your magazine subscription. Join the website and gain access to 20 years of *Cook's Illustrated* recipes, equipment tests, and ingredient tastings, as well as companion videos for every recipe in this issue.

COOKBOOKS

We sell more than 50 cookbooks by the editors of *Cook's Illustrated*, including *The Cook's Illustrated Cookbook* and *The Science of Good Cooking*. To order, visit our bookstore at CooksIllustrated.com.

COOK'S ILLUSTRATED MAGAZINE

Cook's Illustrated magazine (ISSN 1068-2821), number 120, is published bimonthly by Boston Common Press Limited partnership, 17 Station St., Brookline, MA 02445. Copyright 2012 Boston Common Press Limited Partnership. Periodicals postage paid at Boston, Mass., and additional mailing offices, USPS #012487. Publications Mail Agreement No. 40020778. Return undeliverable Canadian addresses to P.O. Box 875, Station A, Windsor, ON N9A 6P2. POSTMASTER: Send address changes to *Cook's Illustrated*, P.O. Box 6018, Harlan, IA 51593-1518. For subscription and gift subscription orders, subscription inquiries, or change-of-address notices, visit us at AmericasTestKitchen.com/customerservice, call us at 800-526-8442, or write us at *Cook's Illustrated*, P.O. 6018, Harlan, IA 51593-1518.

FOR LIST RENTAL INFORMATION Contact Specialists Marketing Services, Inc., 777 Terrace Ave., 4th Floor, Hasbrouck Heights, NJ 07604; 201-865-5800.

EDITORIAL OFFICE 17 Station St., Brookline, MA 02445; 617-232-1000; fax 617-232-1572. Subscription inquiries, visit AmericasTestKitchen.com/customerservice or call 800-526-8442.

POSTMASTER Send all new orders, subscription inquiries, and change-of-address notices to *Cook's Illustrated*, P.O. Box 6018, Harlan, IA 51593-1518.

Doing the Cocktail Twist

Do the different ways of using citrus peel to garnish cocktails produce different tastes?

SAMUEL SHERRY
SOMERVILLE, MASS.

➤There are three common citrus garnishes for cocktails: The first is a "twist," a simple disk of citrus peel that is squeezed into the drink to release essential oils and then rubbed around the rim of the glass and discarded. The second is a "flamed twist," in which a flame is held between the drink and the peel so that when the peel is squeezed, its oils ignite briefly. The third type is a "swath," a band of zest with a little pith attached that is twirled and placed in the drink. We made all three types of garnishes with orange peel and tasted each in a simple Negroni cocktail. We found that the twist contributed bright orange notes that enlivened the drink. The flamed twist offered sulfurous undertones and had a somewhat subdued orange fragrance. The swath added citrus notes along with mild bitterness from the pith. In sum, fancy citrus garnishes are more than just ornamental: Your choice should hinge on the flavor profile you're trying to create. –L.L.

TWIST

FLAMED TWIST

SWATH

The Truth About Truffle Oil

I recently visited a gourmet shop that carried several different types of truffle oil, some of which were labeled "natural." Should I seek out natural truffle oil?

PETER FOSTER
HONOLULU, HAWAII

➤First, it helps to know that truffle oil isn't typically made by steeping the fungus in oil, a process that doesn't provide a shelf-stable product or extract enough of the more than 100 aromatic compounds in the truffle to provide reliably potent results. Instead, truffle oil is made by adding flavor molecules to oil (often olive oil). Some manufacturers harvest these compounds from fresh truffles, but many others choose cheaper organic sources to extract some of the same molecules to add to oil. Still other manufacturers create synthetic versions of flavors, most often 2,4-dithiapentane, the dominant flavor compound present in real truffles.

But the label "natural" on a bottle is no guarantee that the flavors you're tasting came from actual truffles—or even from some other natural foodstuff—versus being manufactured in a lab. This is because the U.S. Department of Agriculture regulates the term "natural" only when applied to cuts of meat and poultry, rendering the term meaningless on most other foods.

When we sampled 16 different truffle oils, seven of which were marketed as "natural," we found no correlation between tasters' preferences and this label. Prices ranged from $2.50 to $10.35 per ounce, and expensive oils didn't necessarily translate into a better product either. In fact, most of the oils were disappointing, with a flat, one-dimensional flavor when compared with that of real truffles. Of the brands we tasted, Antica ($8.26 per ounce) and Urbani ($6 per ounce) had the best—if somewhat mild—flavor. –C.R.

Measuring Flour

Your recipes list 1 cup of flour as weighing 5 ounces, but I've noticed that different sources list the same cup of flour as weighing slightly more or less. Why the discrepancy?

RANDY MACDONALD
PHILADELPHIA, PA.

➤The weight of a cup of flour depends on how it is measured. In the test kitchen, we favor the dip-and-sweep method—we dip a measuring cup into a container of flour and then level the flour with a straight edge—but some bakers prefer to spoon flour directly into the cup. Since these techniques—along with the heavy- or light-handedness of the baker—incorporate different amounts of air, we've found that there can be up to a 20 percent difference in the weight of a cup of flour, a variance that can easily ruin a recipe.

To determine our standard weight for flour, we had dozens of volunteers measure out 1 cup, weighed the results, and took the average (5 ounces) as our standard.

The bottom line: We provide volume measurements for readers who don't have access to a food scale, but measuring by weight is the only way to guarantee accuracy. If you have a food scale and a weight measurement is provided in a recipe, ignore the volume measurement. And since weighing standards vary depending on the recipe author, do not be tempted to transfer the weight conventions from one recipe to another. –A.G.

Rainy Day Meringues

Is there a way to store meringues in a humid environment without ruining their crisp texture?

GRACE ANDERSON
CARROLLTON, TEXAS

➤Many cooks believe that storing meringues on a rainy or humid day is futile because the confections contain a lot of sugar, and sugar is hygroscopic—meaning that it attracts moisture from the air, which causes the cookies to turn sticky and marshmallowy. Disproving this theory took just a simple test. We waited for a rainy day and baked up several batches of meringues. As soon as the cookies cooled (after about 10 minutes), we placed them in airtight plastic containers with tight-fitting lids. We put one container in the fridge (a relatively humid environment), one on the counter, and, as a control, one in the freezer (which tends to be arid). Two weeks and several rainy days later, we opened the containers. The cookies stored in the more humid refrigerator and on the counter were every bit as dry and crisp as those stored in the freezer. The upshot: As long as you pack meringues in an airtight container immediately after cooling them, any humidity in the air doesn't matter. –A.G.

WEATHERPROOF IT
To maintain crispness, pack meringues in an airtight container as soon as they're cool.

Rescuing Oversoftened Butter

I was recently softening butter in the microwave to make cookies when part of the stick melted. It was my last stick, so I tried to harden it a little in the fridge, but my cookies didn't turn out right. Could I have done something different?

ROXANNE REIMNEITZ
KAMLOOPS, BRITISH COLUMBIA

➤The fat in butter is partially crystalline and highly sensitive to temperature changes. When butter is properly softened to 65 or 70 degrees, the tiny crystals can effectively surround and stabilize the air bubbles that are generated during creaming. When heated to the melting point, however, these crystals are destroyed. They can be reestablished but only if the butter is rapidly chilled. (Returning it to the refrigerator will cool it too slowly and fail to reestablish the tiny crystals.)

To quickly cool down partially melted butter, we mixed in a few ice cubes. After less than a minute of stirring, the butter had cooled to a softened stage—right below 70 degrees—so we extracted the ice and prepared a couple of recipes. (The amount of icy water that leaked into the butter was negligible.)

Our fix worked: Sugar cookies made with our rehabilitated butter were nearly identical to those made with properly softened butter, and buttercream frosting was also acceptable, if slightly softer than a control batch. –C.R.

Freezing Cream Cheese

Does cream cheese freeze well?

ALLISON NEILL
SAN ANTONIO, TEXAS

➤To find out, we placed several blocks of cream cheese in the refrigerator and freezer. Two days later, we thawed the frozen samples and began our comparison.

As we unwrapped the defrosted cream cheese, the first thing we noticed was its crumbly, grainy texture, which stood in stark contrast to the smooth, dense, refrigerated cream cheese. Why the grittiness? Since cream cheese is about half water, it is especially sensitive to the formation and melting of ice crystals that happens during freezing and thawing. When ice crystals form, the previously emulsified water separates from the cheese curds, causing the thawed cheese to turn grainy and ricotta-like.

With its unappealing texture, spreading thawed cream cheese on bagels was out. To see if it might work for baking, we used it in pound cake, biscuits, and cheesecake. While the pound cake and biscuits turned out fine, the cheesecake was flawed, with a gritty texture. Our conclusion: If you're going to freeze cream cheese, use it only in applications in which its grainy texture won't stand out. –C.R.

Duck versus Chicken

I occasionally see duck eggs at Asian markets. Do they differ in flavor or texture from chicken eggs?

BEVERLY HOLT
BOSTON, MASS.

➤We purchased duck eggs ($4.49 per half-dozen) and eyeballed them next to large chicken eggs. In the carton, the eggs looked similar, but when we cracked open a few, we noticed that the yolks of the duck eggs were proportionally larger than those of the chicken eggs. In fact, when we separated the duck egg yolks from the whites and weighed each component, we found that the yolks contributed 42 percent of the total weight. When we ran the corresponding numbers for chicken eggs, we found that the yolks made up only 32 percent of the total weight.

Next, we made scrambled eggs and found more differences. The duck egg scramble was decidedly richer, with earthy, grassy flavors that weren't present in the chicken eggs. These traits can probably be

WHAT IS IT?

I purchased these ornate utensils from an antiques market, but I'm not sure what they are. Can you help?

CARRIE SHAFER, BOSTON, MASS.

SWEET SPOON
An absinthe spoon holds a sugar cube to sweeten the potent liqueur.

These are absinthe spoons, or *cuillères à absinthe*. Absinthe—an emerald-toned, herbal spirit distilled from wormwood leaves—was used as a medical cure-all in France until the late 19th century, when bohemian poets and artists claimed the spirit as their muse, asserting that it incited delirium. (Although potent, absinthe is not hallucinogenic.) Around that time, perforated spoons were manufactured to aid in its preparation.

The serving ritual for absinthe evolved to temper its bitterness and bring out flavor nuances. First, about 1 ounce of the elixir is poured into a tall, cone-shaped glass. Next, the spoon is laid across the rim and a sugar cube is placed on top. Ice water is slowly poured over the sugar, and the sweet liquid drips through the spoon's holes. The diluted absinthe, which turns from green to opaque and milky, is then stirred with the spoon.

There are many absinthe spoon designs. Yours appear to be reproductions of a Losange (with a diamond pattern), a Toulouse-Lautrec (the artist was rumored to have a hollow compartment in his cane for an absinthe flask), and a Feuille (which depicts a wormwood leaf). Reproductions sell for a few dollars; originals run in the hundreds. –SHANNON FRIEDMANN HATCH

attributed to the facts that the birds have different diets and that duck eggs have a higher fat content than chicken eggs do.

But the scrambled duck eggs also had a dense, resilient texture that some tasters objected to. That's because the duck egg whites contain more of the structure-building protein albumen than the whites of chicken eggs do. Because of this difference in composition, we don't recommend swapping duck eggs for chicken eggs in recipes. But if you're fond of yolks, duck eggs make a great breakfast. –A.G.

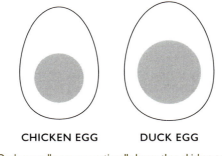

CHICKEN EGG   DUCK EGG

Duck egg yolks are proportionally larger than chicken egg yolks and have a different flavor. What's more, their whites are a different texture, so we don't recommend substituting.

Clarifications

➤In "The Whole Chicken Story" (September/October 2012), we mentioned a study conducted by Johns Hopkins researchers that found traces of arsenic and caffeine as well as the active ingredients in Benadryl, Tylenol, and Prozac in feather meal. Our story stated that these chemicals "had been fed to chickens to alter their moods." However, the authors of the Johns Hopkins study offered no conclusions about how trace amounts of these compounds ended up in the feather meal samples they tested. The industry denies that poultry processors are adding these chemicals to chicken feed. Instead, they point to the water supply and note that modern testing methodologies can detect trace amounts of almost anything.

In the same story, we placed the American Humane Certified label under the heading "Buyer Beware" in a sidebar on decoding chicken labels. We did not mean to imply that the American Humane Certified label attempts to mislead consumers. American Humane Certified is a program intended to promote animal health and reduce stress. To earn the seal, a producer must undergo annual audits and carry out self-policing of agreed-upon standards. To read the full text of the American Humane Certified regulations, go to americanhumane.org.

SEND US YOUR QUESTIONS We will provide a complimentary one-year subscription for each letter we print. Send your inquiry, name, address, and daytime telephone number to Notes from Readers, *Cook's Illustrated*, P.O. Box 470589, Brookline, MA 02447, or to NotesFromReaders@AmericasTestKitchen.com.

Quick Tips

COMPILED BY SHANNON FRIEDMANN HATCH

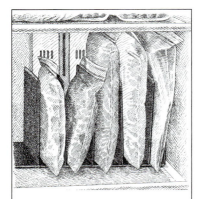

Ice Advice

Long-term freezer storage comes with a downside: Even if food is clearly labeled, it often gets buried—and then risks being forgotten. To keep track of her inventory, Norma Bozzini of San Mateo, Calif., offers a simple solution: Freeze food flat in labeled zipper-lock bags and then arrange the bags in a desktop file organizer. This system keeps her freezer tidy and takes up much less space.

Bread Crumbs in a Flash

Rather than discarding the heels of bread or extra hamburger or hot dog buns, Martin Brown of Atlanta, Ga., tears them into pieces and freezes them in a zipper-lock freezer bag until he needs fresh bread crumbs. Ten to 20 pulses in the food processor turns the leftovers into ready-to-use crumbs, no thawing necessary.

Another Way to Chunky Granola

The secret to producing chunky clusters in our Almond Granola with Dried Fruit recipe (March/April 2012) is pressing the oat mixture firmly into the rimmed baking sheet prior to baking. You can use a stiff metal spatula for the task, or you can follow the advice of Mike Lajczok of Wilmington, Del.: Place a second rimmed baking sheet on top of the one holding the granola and press down firmly.

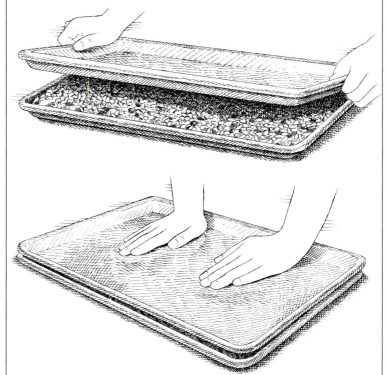

A Grate Idea for Hard Brown Sugar

When Gloria Lynch of Colorado Springs, Colo., finds that her brown sugar has turned from granular into a solid brick, she pulls out her grater. Running the block along the tool's sharp holes quickly breaks down the hard sugar into a measurable state.

Label Maker

Lauren Threadgill of Augusta, Ga., is an avid baker and stocks multiple kinds of flour in clear plastic storage containers. To keep track of what's inside, she came up with a crafty solution: She cuts the labels out of the flour bags and tapes them to the outsides of the containers. Now there's no second-guessing about whether she's grabbing cake, bread, or all-purpose flour.

Preserving Leftover Wine

Allowing red wine to "breathe," or briefly exposing it to air, can enhance its flavor. But prolonged exposure causes it to over-oxidize and take on an unpleasant, vinegar-like taste. Gadgets like vacuum pumps minimize air exposure to preserve the flavor of leftovers, but Andrea Pepicelli of Cumberland, R.I., gets the job done with this homemade solution: Completely fill an airtight container, like a small mason jar or an empty water bottle, with leftover wine (the wine must reach the very top of the container to eliminate all air). Screw on the top and refrigerate for up to one week.

SEND US YOUR TIPS We will provide a complimentary one-year subscription for each tip we print. Send your tip, name, and address to Quick Tips, *Cook's Illustrated*, P.O. Box 470589, Brookline, MA 02447, or to QuickTips@AmericasTestKitchen.com.

ILLUSTRATION: JOHN BURGOYNE

A Cool Trick for Rolling Out Pie Dough

Temperamental pie and tart doughs can't take the heat: In order to bake up flaky, the fat in the dough must stay cool, which is problematic, since working the dough warms it up. Rebecca Webber of Cambridge, Mass., uses this method to keep it cool.

1. While the dough is chilling in the refrigerator, fill two gallon-size zipper-lock bags halfway with ice and lay them on the rolling surface for 20 minutes.

2. When ready to roll out the dough, remove the ice bags and wipe any condensation from the surface. Work quickly with the dough in a cold space as directed in the recipe.

Handle Potholder

Bill Chatto of Parrish, Fla., found that a silicone garlic peeler is a great stand-in for a handle potholder. The tube slides right over the handle of most pots, and the silicone protects his hand just as well as a bulky mitt does.

Saving Cake

Noreen Awan of Seattle, Wash., uses this method to prevent leftover layer cake from staling: She arranges a folded piece of parchment paper to fit over the exposed edges. Pressing the parchment onto the cake lessens air exposure and keeps the next slices as good as the first.

Ring Around the Baking Mat

Rather than securing her rolled-up non-stick silicone baking mat with a rubber band for storage, Marcia Hestand of St. Joseph, Mo., uses a canning jar band to keep it from unrolling. Using the mat is as easy as sliding off the band, and the metal band is sturdier than a rubber band, which can tear and break.

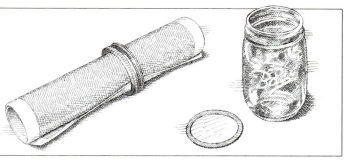

The Lowdown on Cooling Soups

For food safety reasons, soups and stews should be cooled to 40 degrees and stored within 4 hours of cooking, but placing large containers of the hot liquid directly in the refrigerator raises the appliance's temperature to an unsafe level. Joni Patrici of Cleveland, Ohio, uses a smarter approach: Fill a large cooler or the sink with cold water and ice packs. Place the saucepan or stockpot in the cooler or sink until the contents register about 80 degrees, 30 to 45 minutes, stirring the pot occasionally to speed the chilling process. Refill the cooler or sink with cold water if necessary.

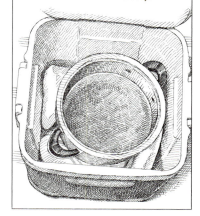

The Best Slice

Although Jenn Sheridan of Providence, R.I., uses our Thin-Crust Pizza recipe (January/February 2011) as her go-to recipe for New York–style pizza, one thing was missing: She craved the long, foldable slices typical of New York City pizzerias, not the 6-inch-long pieces that are produced by making multiple cuts through the center of a round pizza. With a few quick adjustments, she now has the perfect slice.

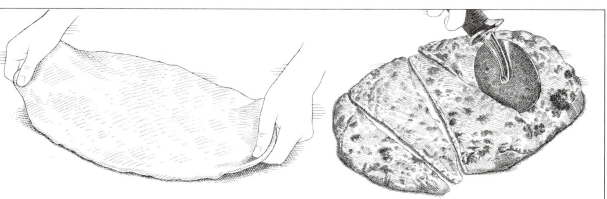

1. Instead of forming a 13-inch round on the pizza peel, stretch the dough into an oblong shape. Bake as directed.

2. Slice the pizza using a zigzag pattern across the width of the pie.

French-Style Chicken with Stuffing

The French have a curious take on stuffed chicken: Rather than roasting it, they braise it and add vegetables to make a one-pot meal. Sound odd? We thought so—until we tried it.

≥ BY LAN LAM ≤

In America, we tend to roast whole chickens, but French cooks like to put them in a pot, add vegetables and a little broth, and simmer them until tender and juicy. There are countless takes on *poule au pot*, but the one that intrigues me most hails from southwest France. For this traditional Sunday dinner, cooks stuff the bird with bread crumbs and some form of pork before cooking it in the pot with vegetables. To serve, the stuffing is removed from the cavity, the bird is carved, and both components are placed in bowls with the vegetables, a ladle of the rich broth, and accompaniments like crusty bread, cornichons, and mustard.

The dish's hearty profile appealed to me, but the handful of recipes I tried produced dismal results: Most of the birds were dry, the broths washed-out, and the stuffings loose and damp. Still, the concept was interesting, so I decided to refine poule au pot, with the following goals: juicy chicken, tender vegetables, a hearty stuffing, and a clean, concentrated jus.

Stuffing on the Side

Throughout the next several days, I stuffed and stewed several birds according to various methods: simmered high, low, on the stove, and in the oven. But no matter what approach I took, the white meat had cooked up dry and stringy by the time the stuffing was cooked through. Plus, cramming the stuffing inside the bird and then extracting it was a pain. It was time to separate the two components.

The idea wasn't entirely mine. One recipe I'd tried from Linda Arnaud's *The Artful Chicken* skipped the stuffed-bird route and instead called for forming the bread-sausage mixture into cylinders, wrapping them in foil or parchment paper, and steaming the packages in the pot until the meat had cooked through. The stuffing cylinders came out lightly springy, sliceable, and much tidier than the usual inside-the-bird stuffing. This seemed promising.

A savory pork-and-bread stuffing, rolled into sliceable logs, adds earthy dimension to the clean flavors of the poached chicken and vegetables.

The only problem was where to fit a pair of stuffing "logs" in a Dutch oven already crowded with a whole chicken and a pile of vegetables (for now, carrots, celery, and potatoes). But as I thought more about the space issue, an idea occurred to me: Since I no longer needed the chicken's cavity to house the stuffing, why not work with chicken parts instead? That way I could arrange the chicken pieces, vegetables, and stuffing logs as needed. Using parts would also speed up the cooking time for the meat, and it would save me the trouble of carving the chicken.

I gave it a try, seasoning two leg quarters and two breasts with salt and pepper and placing them in the pot, nestling the vegetables and stuffing logs around the chicken. I poured in just enough chicken broth to partially submerge the meat and vegetables, brought the liquid to a simmer, and transferred the vessel to a low (300-degree) oven, hoping the gentle heat would help prevent the white meat from drying out.

Now the chicken and stuffing were done in about an hour, but the flavor of the dish was thin and the white meat was still dry. Brainstorming ways to prevent the lean meat from overcooking, I recalled solving a similar problem when I developed our recipe for Red Wine–Braised Pork Chops (January/February 2012). I had propped the chops above the cooking liquid on top of meat scraps and vegetables, which allowed them to cook more gently, since air conducts heat less efficiently than water. With that in mind, I rearranged the pot's contents and came up with the following stacking order (from the bottom up): vegetables, leg quarters, stuffing logs (on either side of the dark meat), and breasts. I added just enough broth to partially submerge the vegetables, making sure that the white meat sat above the liquid, and then slid the pot into the oven.

After about an hour, I pulled the lid off the pot and sampled both the white and dark meat, which were, just as I'd hoped, equally tender and juicy. Now all I had to do was tune up the flavors.

Flavor Finesse

My original stuffing was bread-heavy, so I upped the sausage from 12 ounces to a full pound to help build savory depth, and I mixed in whole-grain mustard, garlic, and shallot. This meatier batch was also juicier and firmer and thus easier to form into sturdy logs.

The broth, however, was still weak, so though it went against tradition, I browned the chicken pieces before adding the liquid, which considerably boosted the savory flavor. (I removed the skin before serving, since it lost its appealing crispness as it

See How It Stacks Up

Video available FREE for 4 months at CooksIllustrated.com/feb13 simmered.) Some recipes called for adding a bouquet garni (herbs and aromatics tied together with twine) to flavor the pot, so I did the same. And to insert some fresh sweetness, I turned to a classic sausage mate: fennel. The quartered bulb went in with the other vegetables, the minced fronds into the stuffing.

Serving the mustard and cornichons alongside was fine, but the dish came together nicely when I mixed those bold-flavored accoutrements (along with more aromatics) into an olive oil–based dressing, which I passed at the table along with bread.

As I set out my final batch of poule au pot, I found myself thinking that, although I'd strayed from the classic recipes, I couldn't be more pleased by this package of juicy meat, savory stuffing, tender vegetables, and rich-tasting jus.

FRENCH-STYLE CHICKEN AND STUFFING IN A POT
SERVES 4 TO 6

A neutral bulk sausage is best, but breakfast or sweet Italian sausage can be used. You'll need a Dutch oven with at least a 7¼-quart capacity. Use small red potatoes, measuring 1 to 2 inches in diameter. Serve this dish with crusty bread and cornichons and Dijon mustard or Herb Sauce (recipe follows).

Sausage Stuffing
2	slices hearty white sandwich bread, crusts removed, torn into quarters
1	large egg
1	shallot, minced
2	garlic cloves, minced
2	tablespoons minced fresh parsley
2	tablespoons minced fennel fronds
2	teaspoons whole-grain mustard
1	teaspoon minced fresh marjoram
¼	teaspoon pepper
1	pound bulk pork sausage

Chicken
2	celery ribs, halved crosswise
8	sprigs plus 1 tablespoon minced fresh parsley
6	sprigs fresh marjoram
1	bay leaf
2	teaspoons vegetable oil
2	(12-ounce) bone-in split chicken breasts, trimmed
2	(12-ounce) bone-in chicken leg quarters, trimmed
	Salt and pepper
1½	pounds small red potatoes, unpeeled
2	carrots, peeled and cut into ½-inch lengths
1	fennel bulb, stalks trimmed, bulb quartered
8	whole peppercorns
2	garlic cloves, peeled
3–3½	cups low-sodium chicken broth

1. FOR THE SAUSAGE STUFFING: Adjust oven rack to middle position and heat oven to 300 degrees. Pulse bread in food processor until finely

SLICEABLE STUFFING

Though many traditional *poule au pot* recipes call for cramming a bread-sausage stuffing inside a whole chicken, we took the less-messy route and made a compact, sliceable stuffing by rolling the bread-sausage mixture in parchment paper. The pair of sausage-shaped logs cook right alongside the chicken pieces and vegetables.

ground, 10 to 15 pulses. Add egg, shallot, garlic, parsley, fennel fronds, mustard, marjoram, and pepper to processor and pulse to combine, 6 to 8 pulses, scraping down sides of bowl as needed. Add sausage and pulse to combine, 3 to 5 pulses, scraping down sides of bowl as needed.

2. Place 18 by 12-inch piece of parchment paper on counter, with longer edge parallel to edge of counter. Place half of stuffing onto lower third of parchment, shaping it into rough 8 by 2-inch rectangle. Roll up sausage in parchment; gently but firmly twist both ends to compact mixture into 6- to 7-inch-long cylinder, approximately 2 inches in diameter. Repeat with second piece of parchment and remaining stuffing.

3. FOR THE CHICKEN: Using kitchen twine, tie together celery, parsley sprigs, marjoram, and bay leaf. Heat oil in large Dutch oven over medium-high heat until just smoking. Pat chicken breasts and leg quarters dry with paper towels, sprinkle with ½ teaspoon salt, and season with pepper. Add chicken, skin side down, and cook without moving it until browned, 4 to 7 minutes. Transfer chicken to large plate. Pour off and discard any fat in pot.

4. Remove Dutch oven from heat and carefully arrange celery bundle, potatoes, carrots, and fennel in even layer over bottom of pot. Sprinkle peppercorns, garlic, and ¼ teaspoon salt over vegetables. Add enough broth so that top ½ inch of vegetables is above surface of liquid. Place leg quarters on top of vegetables in center of pot. Place stuffing cylinders on either side of leg quarters. Arrange breasts on top of leg quarters. Place pot over high heat and bring to simmer. Cover, transfer to oven, and cook until breasts register 160 degrees, 60 to 75 minutes.

5. Transfer chicken and stuffing cylinders to carving board. Using slotted spoon, transfer vegetables to serving platter, discarding celery bundle. Pour broth through fine-mesh strainer into fat separator; discard solids. Let stand for 5 minutes.

How Perfectly Cooked Chicken and Vegetables Stack Up

To guarantee that the various components cook up properly, we pack the pot in a specific order: Hardy vegetables sit in the broth at the bottom because water conducts heat more efficiently than air. Longer-cooking dark meat and stuffing sit above them; as the meat and vegetables cook and release juices, they will become almost completely submerged. The delicate white meat rests on top, out of the liquid.

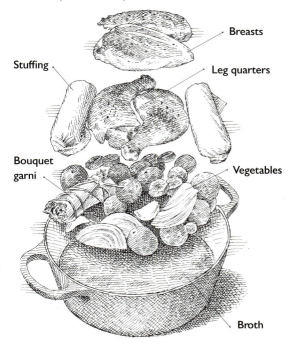

Breasts
Stuffing
Leg quarters
Bouquet garni
Vegetables
Broth

6. Unwrap stuffing cylinders and slice into ½-inch-thick disks; transfer slices to platter with vegetables. Remove skin from chicken pieces and discard. Carve breasts from bone and slice into ½-inch-thick pieces. Separate thigh from leg by cutting through joint. Transfer chicken to platter with stuffing and vegetables. Pour ½ cup defatted broth over chicken and stuffing to moisten. Sprinkle with minced parsley. Serve, ladling remaining broth over individual servings.

HERB SAUCE
MAKES ABOUT ½ CUP

⅓	cup extra-virgin olive oil
6	cornichons, minced
2	tablespoons minced fresh parsley
1	tablespoon minced fennel fronds
2	teaspoons minced shallot
2	teaspoons whole-grain mustard
1	teaspoon minced fresh marjoram
½	teaspoon finely grated lemon zest plus 2 tablespoons juice
¼	teaspoon pepper

Whisk all ingredients together in bowl. Let stand for 15 minutes before serving.

Great Roast Shrimp

Peeling shrimp before roasting them keeps things neat and tidy at the table— but are you throwing away the best part?

≽ BY ANDREW JANJIGIAN ≼

When I set out to find the best way to make roasted shrimp, I thought I'd hit the jackpot. Quick-cooking shrimp make an easy weeknight dinner, and the idea of roasting them until they develop deep, flavorful browning seemed so natural that I figured there were plenty of good recipes out there to learn from.

Imagine my surprise, then, when the handful I tried produced pale, insipid shrimp that looked as though they'd been baked, not roasted. Some of the missteps seemed obvious, such as crowding lots of small shrimp (tossed with oil and aromatics) on a sheet pan or in a baking dish, where their exuded moisture caused them to steam and prevented browning. Some of the oven temperatures were also strangely low—around 300 degrees. I was sure I could do better, while keeping the technique simple enough for an easy weeknight meal.

The Heat Is On

My challenge was clear from the start: The goals of roasting—a juicy interior and a thoroughly browned exterior—were impeded by the fact that lean shrimp cook through very quickly. Knowing that, I made two immediate decisions: First, I would crank the oven temperature very high to get good browning on the exterior of the shrimp—500 degrees seemed like a fine place to start. Second, I would use the biggest shrimp I could get. That meant skipping right past even the extra-large size and reaching for the jumbo (16 to 20 per pound) shrimp, which would be the least likely to dry out in the heat. Using larger shrimp would also mean that there would be fewer pieces crowding the pan, and their smaller total amount of surface area would mean that less steam would be created—therefore making browning possible. As a test run, I oiled and seasoned 2 pounds of peeled shrimp with nothing more than a little salt and pepper (I'd explore flavorings once I'd nailed down a cooking method) and slid them into the oven on a sheet pan.

I thought the 500-degree blast would get the shrimp good and brown in a hurry, so I hovered around the oven and checked on their color every

Butterflying the shrimp allows the heady flavors of garlic and spices to thoroughly coat the flesh.

couple of minutes. Trouble was, the color never came—and while I waited and waited for the browning to kick in, the shrimp turned from tender and slightly translucent to fully opaque. I knew before I plunged a fork into them that they were overcooked. Clearly, high heat alone wasn't going to cut it, so I started experimenting. "Searing"

them by preheating the baking sheet in the 500-degree oven helped, but only a little, since the pan's temperature plummeted as soon as the shrimp hit. Blasting the next batch under the broiler finally delivered some decent browning to the topsides of the shrimp, but their undersides were still damp and utterly pale.

Part of the problem was air circulation. When we roast beef or pork, we often elevate them on a rack so that hot air can surround them, drying out and browning even the underside of the meat. With that in mind, I tried broiling my next batch of shrimp on a wire rack set in the baking sheet—and finally started to see some real progress.

But the approach wasn't perfect. The heat of my broiler, as with all broilers, was uneven, which meant that I had to rotate the baking sheet halfway through cooking to prevent the shrimp from scorching under the element's hot spots, and even then I got a few desiccated pieces. In addition to using jumbo shrimp, the situation demanded a foolproof buffer against the heat, and the obvious answer was to brine the shrimp. The extra moisture that gets pulled into the lean flesh with the salt helps it stay moist even in a hot oven. Thanks to the shrimp's relatively small size, just a 15-minute soak in brine ensured that inside they stayed nice and plump—not to mention well seasoned throughout. Outside, however, they still shriveled under the broiler's heat before they had a chance to develop deep, "roasted" color and flavor.

Keys to Shrimp That Brown Deeply—but Don't Dry Out

USE JUMBOS
Bigger shrimp are less likely to dry out in the heat. Plus, there are fewer pieces to crowd the baking sheet and thwart browning.

16/20 PER POUND

LEAVE SHELLS ON
Cooking the shrimp shell-on helps protect their lean, delicate flesh from dehydrating before the exterior develops good browning.

BRINE BRIEFLY
Plumping up the shrimp with a quick saltwater soak further buffers them from the oven's heat and also seasons them throughout.

BROIL ON RACK
Broiling the shrimp on a wire rack set in a baking sheet allows the hot air to circulate around them for deep, even color.

SCIENCE | The Surprising Power of Shrimp Shells

We found that cooking shrimp in their shells kept them juicier, but our shell-on roasted shrimp boast such savory depth that we wondered if there wasn't more to this outer layer than we thought. Our science editor confirmed our suspicions. First, shrimp shells contain water-soluble flavor compounds that will get absorbed by the shrimp flesh during cooking. Second, the shells are loaded with proteins and sugars—almost as much as the flesh itself. When they brown, they undergo the flavor-enhancing Maillard reaction just as roasted meats do, which gives the shells even more flavor to pass along to the flesh. Third, like the flesh, the shells contain healthy amounts of glutamates and nucleotides, compounds that dramatically enhance savory *umami* flavor when present together in food. These compounds also get transferred to the meat during cooking, amplifying the effect of its own glutamates and nucleotides. Bottom line: Shrimp shells not only protect the meat during cooking but also significantly enhance its flavor. This also proves that those of us who enjoy eating the roasted shell along with the meat are onto something. –A.J.

An A-peeling Solution

I hoped that a thorough coat of olive oil (I'd been lightly glossing my shrimp) might stave off evaporation, but while the extra fat did keep the shrimp a bit more moist, it did nothing to even out browning. The idea of giving the shrimp a protective layer inspired another idea, though: What if I took advantage of the shrimp's natural protective coating and roasted them in their shells? Surely their "jackets" would prevent the surface of the meat from shriveling and, being drier than the meat, would probably brown quickly, too. The downside would be that shell-on shrimp are messier to eat, but if the results were good, having to peel them at the table would be worth it.

To make deveining and (later) peeling the shrimp easier, I used a pair of kitchen shears to split their shells from end to end without removing them from the flesh, and then I proceeded with my brine-and-broil technique. The results were stunning: shrimp that were moist and plump inside and evenly browned outside. In fact, the depth of the shrimp's "roasted" flavor exceeded my expectations and prompted me to mention the results to our science editor, who replied with some surprising intel. Turns out that the shells were doing much more than protecting the crustaceans' flesh: They are loaded with sugars, proteins, and other flavor-boosting compounds that amplify the rich seafood flavor. (For more information, see "The Surprising Power of Shrimp Shells.")

Juicy, deeply browned shrimp complete, I moved on to tackle flavorings. I was already splitting the shells across the back and deveining the shrimp, so I took the technique one step further and butterflied the exposed flesh, cutting through the meat just short of severing it into two pieces. Then, to jazz up the oil-salt-pepper base, I added spices (anise seeds and red pepper flakes), six cloves of garlic, parsley, and melted butter (a natural pairing with briny seafood) and worked the flavorful mixture deep into the meat before broiling. Just as brining had seasoned the shrimp throughout, butterflying the pieces and thoroughly coating them with the oil-spice mixture made for seriously bold flavor. And since my tasters instantly gobbled up the shrimp—some of them shell and all—I developed two equally quick, flavorful variations: a Peruvian-style version with cilantro and lime and an Asian-inspired one with cumin, ginger, and sesame.

A great-tasting dish that requires almost no prep work and goes from the oven to the table in fewer than 10 minutes? I knew I'd be making this one year-round.

GARLICKY ROASTED SHRIMP WITH PARSLEY AND ANISE
SERVES 4 TO 6

Don't be tempted to use smaller shrimp with this cooking technique; they will be overseasoned and prone to overcook.

- ¼ cup salt
- 2 pounds shell-on jumbo shrimp (16 to 20 per pound)
- 4 tablespoons unsalted butter, melted
- ¼ cup vegetable oil
- 6 garlic cloves, minced
- 1 teaspoon anise seeds
- ½ teaspoon red pepper flakes
- ¼ teaspoon pepper
- 2 tablespoons minced fresh parsley
  Lemon wedges

1. Dissolve salt in 1 quart cold water in large container. Using kitchen shears or sharp paring knife, cut through shell of shrimp and devein but do not remove shell. Using paring knife, continue to cut shrimp ½ inch deep, taking care not to cut in half completely. Submerge shrimp in brine, cover, and refrigerate for 15 minutes.

2. Adjust oven rack 4 inches from broiler element and heat broiler. Combine melted butter, oil, garlic, anise seeds, pepper flakes, and pepper in large bowl. Remove shrimp from brine and pat dry with paper towels. Add shrimp and parsley to butter mixture; toss well, making sure butter mixture gets into interior of shrimp. Arrange shrimp in single layer on wire rack set in rimmed baking sheet.

3. Broil shrimp until opaque and shells are beginning to brown, 2 to 4 minutes, rotating sheet halfway through broiling. Flip shrimp and continue to broil until second side is opaque and shells are beginning to brown, 2 to 4 minutes longer, rotating sheet halfway through broiling. Transfer shrimp to serving platter and serve immediately, passing lemon wedges separately.

TECHNIQUE | BUTTERFLYING
SHELL-ON SHRIMP

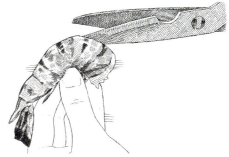

Starting at head of shrimp, snip through back of shell with kitchen shears. (This can also be done with very sharp paring knife: Cut from tail end of shell toward head.) Devein shrimp but do not remove shell.

Using paring knife, carefully continue to cut ½-inch slit in shrimp, making sure not to split it in half completely.

GARLICKY ROASTED SHRIMP WITH CILANTRO AND LIME

Annatto powder, also called achiote, can be found with the Latin American foods at your supermarket. An equal amount of paprika can be substituted.

Omit butter and increase vegetable oil to ½ cup. Omit anise seeds and pepper. Add 2 teaspoons lightly crushed coriander seeds, 2 teaspoons grated lime zest, and 1 teaspoon annatto powder to oil mixture in step 2. Substitute ¼ cup minced fresh cilantro for parsley and lime wedges for lemon wedges.

GARLICKY ROASTED SHRIMP WITH CUMIN, GINGER, AND SESAME

Omit butter and increase vegetable oil to ½ cup. Decrease garlic to 2 cloves and omit anise seeds and pepper. Add 2 teaspoons toasted sesame oil, 1½ teaspoons grated fresh ginger, and 1 teaspoon cumin seeds to oil mixture in step 2. Substitute 2 thinly sliced scallion greens for parsley and omit lemon wedges.

Watch Every Crucial Step
Video available FREE for 4 months at
CooksIllustrated.com/feb13

Savory Citrus Salads

For a winter salad that doesn't taste like an austere version of dessert, befriend the bitter side of citrus.

⇒ BY ANDREA GEARY ⇐

Call it fate: Smack in the middle of the coldest part of the year, just as the hefty braises of winter begin to pall on us, citrus season begins, swooping in with brilliant hues and bracing flavors. But we rarely take full advantage, usually limiting ourselves to eating oranges out of hand and grapefruits only at breakfast. A more impressive setting for these seasonal fruits is a salad, and savory versions—augmented with crisp greens, crunchy nuts, and dried fruit—provide a particularly nice context.

For maximum color, I decided to use both red grapefruits and navel oranges, the latter of which could easily be switched out for other varieties like blood oranges or tangelos. Painstakingly trimming the citrus into slim, membrane-free segments (or supremes) was too time-consuming, and simply dicing the flesh into chunks left diners contending with large, chewy pieces of membrane. I compromised and sliced the halved, peeled fruit into delicate half-moons that were easy on the eye—and on the teeth.

But when I dressed the citrus with a simple vinaigrette of olive oil, vinegar, mustard, and shallot and tossed it with the other components—for now, peppery watercress, chopped pecans (toasted in butter for extra richness), and sweet dried cranberries—the results were disheartening. The assertive grapefruits overpowered even these hearty flavors, and the heavier ingredients sank to the bottom of the bowl while the dressed greens sat irrelevantly on top.

To temper the grapefruits' sourness, I seasoned them with a bit of sugar and also salt—a trick we use to tone down bitterness in foods like eggplant and coffee. Rather than attempt to defy gravity's influence on the weighty fruit and nuts, I embraced it by composing the salad instead of tossing it: I arranged the citrus slices on a platter, dressed the watercress, and set the greens on top of the fruit. Finally, I scattered the nuts and dried cranberries over the top.

This attempt was better, but now the citrus juice pooled so heavily at the bottom of this salad that it threatened to overflow the platter. That's because the salt had exerted its osmotic force on the fruit, pulling out much of its liquid. Other problems: The fruit and greens seemed like two distinct

salads connected only by proximity, and there were issues with the vinaigrette. The oil had caused the watercress to wilt, and the vinegar combined with the grapefruit made the salad way too sour.

To remove excess liquid, I treated both the sliced grapefruits and oranges with salt, let their tangy juices drain off, and reserved them before plating the citrus. Since the olive oil had caused the watercress to droop, I drizzled it over the citrus instead, tossing the greens only with mustard, shallot, and some reserved juice instead of the vinegar. I mixed half of the nuts and cranberries into the greens and sprinkled the remainder on top.

This salad was pleasantly juicy but not swimming in liquid, and the flavors and textures were well integrated and complementary. As a last step, I devised a few variations, trading the watercress for radicchio, arugula, or napa cabbage; the cranberries for dates, golden raisins, or dried cherries; and the pecans for rich smoked almonds, walnuts, or cashews. Now citrus salads can light up my table all winter long.

CITRUS SALAD WITH WATERCRESS, DRIED CRANBERRIES, AND PECANS
SERVES 4 TO 6

You may substitute tangelos or Cara Caras for the navel oranges. Valencia and blood oranges can also be used, but since they are smaller, increase the number of fruit to four. For our free recipe for Citrus Salad with Napa Cabbage, Dried Cherries, and Cashews, go to CooksIllustrated.com/feb13.

2	red grapefruits
3	navel oranges
1	teaspoon sugar
	Salt and pepper
1	teaspoon unsalted butter
½	cup pecans, chopped coarse
3	tablespoons extra-virgin olive oil
1	small shallot, minced
1	teaspoon Dijon mustard
4	ounces (4 cups) watercress, torn into bite-size pieces
⅔	cup dried cranberries

1. Cut away peel and pith from grapefruits and oranges. Cut each fruit in half from pole to pole, then slice crosswise into ¼-inch-thick pieces. Transfer fruit to bowl and toss with sugar and ½ teaspoon salt. Set aside for 15 minutes.

Salting the citrus and draining the excess liquid keeps sogginess at bay.

2. Melt butter in 8-inch skillet over medium heat. Add pecans and ½ teaspoon salt and cook, stirring often, until lightly browned and fragrant, 2 to 4 minutes. Transfer pecans to paper towel–lined plate and set aside.

3. Drain fruit in colander, reserving 2 tablespoons juice. Transfer fruit to platter, arrange in even layer, and drizzle with oil. Whisk reserved juice, shallot, and mustard in medium bowl. Add watercress, ⅓ cup cranberries, and ¼ cup reserved pecans and toss to coat. Arrange watercress mixture over fruit, leaving 1-inch border around edges. Sprinkle with remaining ⅓ cup cranberries and remaining ¼ cup reserved pecans. Season with salt and pepper to taste. Serve immediately.

CITRUS SALAD WITH ARUGULA, GOLDEN RAISINS, AND WALNUTS

Substitute coarsely chopped walnuts for pecans, arugula for watercress, and ½ cup golden raisins for cranberries.

CITRUS SALAD WITH RADICCHIO, DATES, AND SMOKED ALMONDS

Substitute coarsely chopped smoked almonds for pecans, omitting butter and step 2. Substitute 1 small head radicchio, halved, cored, and sliced ¼ inch thick, for watercress, and chopped pitted dates for cranberries.

Watch Salads Take Shape
Video available FREE for 4 months at
CooksIllustrated.com/feb13

Foolproof Soft-Cooked Eggs

The usual approach is hit or miss. We cooked more than 1,000 eggs to develop a truly reliable method that delivers a tender, set white and a fluid yolk every time.

⇛ BY ANDREA GEARY ⇚

In retrospect, I can see why some stages of my quest for the perfect soft-cooked egg caused my coworkers to think I had gone off the deep end. I can understand why they were surprised and even alarmed to see me furtively slipping into a darkened restroom armed with a high-powered flashlight, an empty toilet paper roll, a permanent marker, and two cartons of U.S. grade A eggs, size large. (For the record, I was trying to determine the precise location of the yolk within each egg, because I was convinced that it influenced the way the egg cooked.) And I concede that it was a mistake to spend five weeks vigorously shaking raw eggs in their shells in an effort to encourage even cooking; the fact that 25 percent of the shaken eggs exploded in the saucepan probably should have tipped me off.

But I figured that achieving my goal would be worth a little embarrassment along the way. A soft-cooked egg—its smoothly gelled white encasing a sphere of warm liquid yolk—is every bit as satisfying to eat as a poached egg, but it looks tidier, and preparing it requires less equipment. It's a one-ingredient recipe; how hard could it be to get it right?

Turns out that soft-cooked eggs are a bit of a crapshoot because you can't rely on any visual cues to monitor the eggs' progress. You don't know if you've succeeded or failed until you're already seated at the breakfast table.

Granted, many people successfully make soft-cooked eggs every day, but here's the thing: Those folks have precisely tailored their individual methods to suit their kitchens. They use the same saucepan, the same amount of water, the same burner, and the same number of eggs every time. If any one of these variables changes, all bets are off.

That wasn't good enough for me. I wanted a method that would produce consistent results for any cook, in any kitchen, using any equipment, whether he or she was cooking one egg, four eggs, or even a half-dozen.

Taking Their Temp

The problem with eggs is that they *aren't* just one ingredient. Tucked within that porous shell

With our recipe, you can create an egg that looks this good no matter what pan you use or how many eggs are in the pot.

are really two very distinct ingredients: the white and the yolk. Each is composed of different types and ratios of proteins, fats, and water, which means that they react differently to heat. Most important: The white and the yolk begin to coagulate, or solidify, at very different temperatures. The egg white begins to coagulate at 142 degrees and is fully solid at around 180 degrees, while the yolk solidifies at about 158 degrees.

What does this mean? When cooking an egg that we want to be ultimately both solid (the white) and liquid (the yolk) at once, we have to bring the whites up to a much higher temperature—and do so carefully.

To begin, I figured that I had two choices for cooking: aggressively high heat or low-and-slow heat. The test kitchen's go-to method for making hard-cooked eggs is the epitome of a low-heat cooking method: Place the cold eggs in a saucepan, cover them with cold water, bring them to a boil, and then turn off the heat. Cover the saucepan and let the eggs finish cooking in the cooling water for 10 minutes. A quick chill in ice water, and *voilà*! Eggs with fully set whites and firm yolks. Could the key to soft-cooked eggs be as simple as halting the process a little earlier, before the heat penetrates to the center and sets the yolk?

No such luck. I followed our hard-cooked egg method, but to monitor the progress of the eggs, I cracked one open as soon as the water came to a boil and then another at each 1-minute interval after that. Sure, that first egg boasted a beautifully fluid yolk, but it was accompanied by a lot of slippery, transparent white. After 1 minute, part of the yolk of the next egg had started to solidify, but there was still a lot of undercooked white. By the time the white was fully set at the 3-minute mark, about half of the yolk had already coagulated and was beginning to turn chalky.

High heat it was. So I would simply take cold eggs from the fridge, drop them into boiling water, and then remove them as soon as the whites were

What Does Perfectly Cooked Mean?

The proteins in egg whites and egg yolks solidify at different temperatures, making the perfect soft-cooked egg an exercise in precision. Whites that are firm yet tender must reach 180 degrees, while the yolk must stay below 158 degrees to remain runny. To achieve this temperature differential, it's essential to start cooking your eggs in hot water (versus the cold-water start that we've proven conclusively works best for hard-cooked eggs) so that the whites will be blasted with enough heat to solidify before the heat has time to penetrate to the yolks.

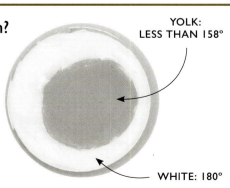

YOLK: LESS THAN 158°

WHITE: 180°

cooked but before the heat penetrated all the way to the yolks.

Admittedly, this is your basic soft-cooked egg recipe, and folks have been doing it this way for millennia. It took a bit of testing to find the timings and quantities that worked for me in the test kitchen, but after some trial and error, I landed on the following method: I placed two large, cold eggs in 4 cups of boiling water in a small, heavy saucepan and fished them out after 6½ minutes. After running cold water over them for 30 seconds, I peeled them and sliced them open to reveal set whites and warm, liquid yolks.

However, this was not a flexible method. When I added extra eggs, there were still some watery whites in evidence after 6½ minutes. That's because adding the cold eggs to the saucepan temporarily lowers the temperature of the water. With more eggs, the water's temperature dipped lower and took longer to return to 212 degrees; with fewer eggs, the water recovered more quickly. So changing the number of eggs changed the amount of time that it took for the eggs to cook perfectly.

Full Steam Ahead

If only I could somehow use boiling water to cook the eggs without actually submerging them in it, I thought. That seemed like an absurd idea—until it occurred to me to try a steamer basket. I brought 1 inch of water to a boil in a large saucepan while I loaded the steamer basket with two large, fridge-cold eggs. I lowered the steamer into the saucepan, covered it, and let the eggs steam for 6½ minutes, after which I transferred the steamer to the sink and ran cold water over the eggs before breaking them open. They were perfect. Eggs cooked in steam took exactly the same amount of time as eggs that were submerged in an ample amount of boiling water.

When I tested batches of one to six eggs with exactly the same cook time and got exactly the same results, I was sure I had cracked the case: The key to a perfect yet still flexible recipe for soft-cooked eggs was not to boil them but to steam them. But could I simplify it even more?

I wondered about steamerless steaming. If an egg cooked in steam takes the same amount of time to cook as an egg that is submerged in boiling water, doesn't it follow that if you cook the same egg partially in water and partially in steam, it will still cook evenly?

This time I brought a mere ½ inch of water to a boil in my saucepan, and then I placed two cold eggs directly on the bottom of the pot, covered it, and steamed/boiled them. Because of the curved exterior of the eggs, I reasoned, they wouldn't make enough contact with the water to lower the temperature significantly, so the cook time would remain the same as it did with the steamer. At the end of 6½ minutes, I cooled the eggs by transferring the whole pot to the sink and running cold water into it for 30 seconds. I peeled the eggs and cut each one in half,

The Problem: A Pot of Boiling Water

The biggest problem with the most widely used soft-cooked egg technique—dropping cold eggs into boiling water—is that you can perfect the cook time for a set number of eggs, but every time you add or subtract an egg (or even use a different pan), that timing is thrown off. That's because the number of eggs added to the pot (and how well that pot can hold heat) affects how little—or how much—the water temperature drops from the boiling point of 212 degrees. Even a 1- or 2-degree drop significantly influences the cook time. Here's how much the temperature changed immediately after we added one egg, four eggs, and six eggs to a quart of boiling water.

STEADY BOILING
The water temperature was unchanged by one egg.

NOT BOILING
With four eggs, the water took a full minute to return to a boil.

NOT BOILING
With six eggs, the water took 2 minutes to get back to 212 degrees.

The Solution: A Pot of Steam

Steaming eggs over ½ inch of boiling water cooks them in exactly the same way as a pot of boiling water, allowing us to create tender yet firm whites with luscious runny yolks. It also removes the big problem with the boiling technique: Because steaming involves so little liquid, the water returns to a boil within seconds, no matter how many eggs you add to the pot. By steaming your eggs, you can cook up one, two—even six—perfect soft-cooked eggs every time.

revealing two beautifully tender yet fully set whites cradling warm, fluid yolks.

Subsequent tests with different-size batches (from one to six eggs) worked equally well using exactly the same timing. And with only ½ inch of water to heat, this recipe was not only the surest and most flexible but also the quickest. Just in time, my reputation as a serious and sane test cook was restored. Never again would I stress about producing perfect soft-cooked eggs for breakfast anytime, anywhere, under any conditions.

SOFT-COOKED EGGS
MAKES 4

Be sure to use large eggs that have no cracks and are cold from the refrigerator. Because precise timing is vital to the success of this recipe, we strongly recommend using a digital timer. You can use this method for one to six large, extra-large, or jumbo eggs without altering the timing. If you have one, a steamer basket does make lowering the eggs into the boiling water easier. We recommend serving these eggs in eggcups and with buttered toast for dipping, or you may simply use the dull side of a butter knife to crack the egg along the equator, break the egg in half, and scoop out the insides with a teaspoon.

4 large eggs
   Salt and pepper

1. Bring ½ inch water to boil in medium saucepan over medium-high heat. Using tongs, gently place eggs in boiling water (eggs will not be submerged). Cover saucepan and cook eggs for 6½ minutes.

2. Remove cover, transfer saucepan to sink, and place under cold running water for 30 seconds. Remove eggs from pan and serve, seasoning with salt and pepper to taste.

Yes, You Can Peel a Soft-Cooked Egg

Though it seemed unlikely to us, soft-cooked eggs are actually easier to peel than are hard-cooked eggs. This is because the soft-cooked white is more yielding. Start by cracking

CRACK THE BROAD END

the broad end of the egg against a hard surface and then peel away both the shell and the inner membrane. A quick rinse in warm water removes any remaining wisps of membrane and shards of eggshell. Split the egg in half and serve it over toast, or have it your usual way.

Soft-cooked eggs turn a simple green salad into a meal.

SOFT-COOKED EGGS WITH SALAD
SERVES 2

Combine 3 tablespoons olive oil, 1 tablespoon balsamic vinegar, 1 teaspoon Dijon mustard, and 1 teaspoon minced shallot in jar, seal lid, and shake vigorously until emulsified, 20 to 30 seconds. Toss with 5 cups assertively flavored salad greens (arugula, radicchio, watercress, or frisée). Season with salt and pepper to taste, and divide between 2 plates. Top each serving with 2 peeled soft-cooked eggs, split crosswise to release yolks, and season with salt and pepper to taste.

SOFT-COOKED EGGS WITH SAUTÉED MUSHROOMS
SERVES 2

Heat 2 tablespoons olive oil in large skillet over medium-high heat until shimmering. Add 12 ounces sliced white or cremini mushrooms and pinch salt and cook, stirring occasionally, until liquid has evaporated and mushrooms are lightly browned, 5 to 6 minutes. Stir in 2 teaspoons chopped fresh herbs (chives, tarragon, parsley, or combination). Season with salt and pepper to taste, and divide between 2 plates. Top each serving with 2 peeled soft-cooked eggs, split crosswise to release yolks, and season with salt and pepper to taste.

SOFT-COOKED EGGS WITH STEAMED ASPARAGUS
SERVES 2

Steam 12 ounces asparagus (spears about ½ inch in diameter, trimmed) over medium heat until crisp-tender, 4 to 5 minutes. Divide between 2 plates. Drizzle each serving with 1 tablespoon extra-virgin olive oil and sprinkle each serving with 1 tablespoon grated Parmesan. Season with salt and pepper to taste. Top each serving with 2 peeled soft-cooked eggs, split crosswise to release yolks, and season with salt and pepper to taste.

TESTING Egg Toppers

Egg toppers neatly slice off the tops of soft-cooked eggs, claiming to be faster, neater, and more precise than the standard method of cracking the shell with the back of a butter knife. We put four models to the test, priced from nearly $6 to more than $26.

The designs fell into two categories: scissor-style and spring-loaded. Not surprisingly, scissor-style toppers look like a pair of scissors that end in a loop instead of straight blades. The loop goes over the tapered end of an egg; when you squeeze the handle, metal teeth emerge to bite into the shell and remove the top ½ inch of the egg. Spring-loaded toppers look like little metal plungers: The bowl fits over the end of the egg like a dunce cap. Two pulls on the spring-loaded lever in the handle punctures a circle around the top of the egg that can be gently pried off.

Scissor-style models were faster and did the job, but their shell-puncturing teeth left a jagged edge flecked with shell shards. One model's flimsy handles bent after only a few uses. Spring-loaded versions fared better. We sliced a dozen eggs with each of these models; while neither perfectly topped every egg, the Rösle Egg Topper was faster than a butter knife and is a worthwhile purchase if you enjoy soft-cooked eggs. For complete testing results, go to CooksIllustrated.com/feb13.
                                        —Hannah Crowley

TOP TOPPER
RÖSLE Egg Topper
Price: $22
Comments: This sturdy, plunger-shaped model was the most precise, quickly topping eggs with neat, even breaks.

MID TOP
PADERNO WORLD CUISINE
Stainless-Steel Egg Top Cutter
Price: $26.18
Comments: This spring-loaded model occasionally created perfectly topped eggs but too often cracked the bottom shell.

BOTTOM OF THE TOPS
FOX RUN Egg Topper
Price: $6.02
Comments: This scissor-style egg topper worked, but its handles were flimsy and it left behind jagged shards.

See the Perfection
Video available **FREE** for 4 months at CooksIllustrated.com/feb13

Crispy Orange Beef

Most versions of this Chinese restaurant standard are better dubbed "Soggy Orange Beef."
We wanted genuinely crispy results—and without heating up a full pot of oil.

≽ BY LAN LAM ≼

When I hear the words "crispy orange beef," I expect just that: a dish of shatteringly crisp strips of battered beef coated in a sweet, savory, and tangy citrus sauce. Unfortunately, this is a dish that rarely lives up to its name, especially in the home kitchen. All too often it has neither crispiness nor any kind of orange flavor. That's because genuinely crispy results usually involve deep-frying in copious amounts of oil—something I think we'd all rather leave to the restaurant world. And who has dried tangerine peels, which give authentic versions their bright "orange" taste, just lying around the kitchen? My goal: to successfully bring this traditionally Sichuan, vibrantly flavored dish into my own kitchen without all that oily mess.

A quick search brought up dozens of recipes based on the Americanized version of the dish, first popularized by Manhattan's Shun Lee Palace in the early 1970s. These recipes call for coating the beef in a mixture of cornstarch and egg whites before cooking and then tossing it with a sweet orange sauce. Many, I noticed, were more stir-fry than anything else—not a lot of oil there. But not a lot of crispiness either, I discovered after a few tests. I would have to start at square one.

Fear of Frying

I began the testing process with the simplest step: the cut of beef. I tried both flank and flap steak, cutting them into thin, wide strips and using a basic recipe I cobbled together from the Web. Each cut was plenty beefy, but my tasters unanimously preferred the looser-grained flap meat to the flank, which wasn't as tender. This easy decision out of the way, I turned to the more difficult matter at hand: frying.

Traditionally, crispy orange beef is made by deep-frying the strips of lightly battered beef in a full pot of oil—as much as 8 cups. During frying, water in the starchy crust turns to steam, leaving little crispy

Our recipe calls for just 3 cups of oil instead of the typical full pot.

pockets in its wake. In the name of research, I tried a version cooked in this abundant amount of oil. Not surprisingly, it worked, producing crispy strips of perfectly cooked beef. But these traditional recipes call for painstakingly placing each piece of meat in the oil, one by one, and then removing each piece individually when fully cooked. All of that? A pain. I tried throwing in all of the beef together, but that yielded a sticky mess. The egg white and cornstarch batter acted as a glue, fusing the strips of meat together as soon as they hit the oil—and no amount of stirring could separate them. Between the large amount of oil and the persnickety frying technique, this method was out of the question.

I already knew that the few tablespoons of oil used in the stir-fry methods also didn't work, but what if I struck a compromise? I decided to try frying in 3 cups of oil—an amount that seemed manageable for the home kitchen and yet was still enough volume (I hoped) to produce truly crispy beef. This lesser amount of oil would certainly mean frying in batches, since dropping all the beef into the pot at once would cause the oil temperature to

plunge dramatically, and if the oil wasn't hot enough, a crisp crust wouldn't have time to form before the beef overcooked. Fortunately, I found that three batches did the trick, allowing me to fry up nicely crisp pieces. But my problems weren't over. Even in these relatively small batches, the strips of beef still stuck together.

I had to try something new. I thought about other ways to create a crispy crust, and a classic bread-crumb coating jumped to mind. True, this type of coating is more typical of pan- or oven-fried foods, but why not give it a shot? I dipped the beef in flour, then egg wash, and then bread crumbs (panko, in this case) before frying. Sticking was not a problem with these strips of beef, and they looked bronzed and beautiful when they came out of the pot—I was ready to celebrate. But when we tasted them, we found that the large size of the crumbs relative to the size of the beef meant that the breading was actually thicker than the strips of meat themselves. To add insult to injury, this substantial crust contained deep crevices that sucked up the sauce, turning it soggy. Failure again.

I was feeling dejected and, for lack of any better ideas, decided to try simply dredging the meat in cornstarch alone. I was delighted to find that the cornstarch, which absorbed some of the juices at the surface of the beef, crisped up delicately

Turning Orange into Tangerine

Traditionally, crispy orange beef is made with dried tangerine peels, which have a pungent and complex flavor but can be tricky to find. We mimic this flavor by leaving some bitter pith on orange peel that we brown in oil.

PURPOSELY PITHY
Leaving some pith on fresh orange peel helps to mimic the flavor of dried tangerine peel.

PHOTOGRAPHY: CARL TREMBLAY

A BETTER CUT FOR FRYING

To prevent beef from folding over on itself while frying, cut flap meat steaks into 3-inch-wide lengths, then into ½-inch-thick slices, and the slices into ½-inch-wide strips.

in the hot oil, batch after batch. But I couldn't do a victory dance just yet. The beef pieces were still sticking together here and there. Plus, with this new, delicate coating, the thin but wide pieces of beef were folding over on themselves as they hit the oil, so that some of the cornstarch coating never fully cooked, leaving a pasty residue. Stirring did not help this situation; I had to tediously pick through the beef and unfold individual pieces. It was clear: I'd have to change the shape. Instead of flat little rectangles, I began slicing the beef into matchsticks. And when I dropped them in the oil, these pieces didn't fold up on themselves at all. They also had more surface area and more pointy edges and crags, further increasing crispiness. Even better, my tasters also raved at how remarkably ungreasy the meat seemed. Curious, I fried up a new batch, measuring the oil before and after cooking, and found that all of that beef had absorbed a total of just 2 tablespoons from the 3 cups of oil (see "Deep-Fried Doesn't Have to Mean Greasy").

As good as my results were, I couldn't resist one more tweak, which I borrowed from our Argentine grilled steak recipe (July/August 2010): I spread out the pieces of beef on a rack set in a rimmed baking sheet and placed the sheet in the freezer for 45 minutes. The very cold, very dry air of the freezer removed moisture from the surface of the meat, further boosting crispiness and eliminating any residual sticking.

Better (Bitter) Flavor

Now that I was satisfied with the cooking method, I went back to flavor. I decided to keep things very simple and began by seasoning the beef in a tablespoon of soy sauce before dredging it in cornstarch.

I had been tossing my crispy beef in a sauce made with a few difficult-to-find ingredients including Chinese rice wine and sweet dark soy sauce. I looked for more-common pantry ingredients to replace

these two. A combination of dry sherry, regular soy sauce, and molasses did the trick. But I had more trouble when it came to the orange flavor.

American versions of crispy orange beef call for orange zest, but traditional recipes use rehydrated tangerine peel. When I experimented with leaving fresh tangerine peel to dry for a few days in a sunny window, my tasters were wowed by the pungent depth it brought to the sauce—but this method took way too long. Dried orange peel is easy to find in the supermarket but has barely any flavor. This left me experimenting with fresh oranges. Instead of zesting the oranges, I used my vegetable peeler to pare away the peel as well as a portion of the bitter pith, which I sliced into slivers and tossed in the microwave to dry. While the pith added a subtle bitterness, the stint in the microwave robbed the peel of its volatile aromatic oils, diminishing its flavor. I decided to throw the strips of peel into a sauté pan. Letting the orange peel brown slightly introduced deeper, caramelized notes that came closer to the complex flavors of dried tangerine peel. Jalapeño added to the pan at the same time brought extra brightness.

After weeks of experimenting with crusts and sauce, here at last was a bright and flavorful, truly crispy orange beef worthy of the name.

CRISPY ORANGE BEEF
SERVES 4

Use a vegetable peeler on the oranges and make sure that your strips contain some pith. Do not use low-sodium soy sauce. Serve this dish with steamed rice.

- 1½ pounds beef flap meat, trimmed
- 3 tablespoons soy sauce
- 6 tablespoons cornstarch
- 10 (3-inch) strips orange peel, sliced thin length-wise (¼ cup), plus ¼ cup juice (2 oranges)
- 3 tablespoons molasses
- 2 tablespoons dry sherry
- 1 tablespoon rice vinegar
- 1½ teaspoons toasted sesame oil
- 3 cups vegetable oil
- 1 jalapeño chile, stemmed, seeded, and sliced thin lengthwise
- 3 garlic cloves, minced
- 2 tablespoons grated fresh ginger
- ½ teaspoon red pepper flakes
- 2 scallions, sliced thin on bias

1. Cut beef along grain into 2½- to 3-inch-wide lengths. Slice each piece against grain into ½-inch-thick slices. Cut each slice lengthwise into ½-inch-wide strips. Toss beef with 1 tablespoon soy sauce in bowl. Add cornstarch and toss until evenly coated. Spread beef in single layer on wire rack set in rimmed baking sheet. Transfer sheet to freezer until meat is very firm but not completely frozen, about 45 minutes.

2. Whisk remaining 2 tablespoons soy sauce,

orange juice, molasses, sherry, vinegar, and sesame oil together in bowl.

3. Line second rimmed baking sheet with triple layer of paper towels. Heat vegetable oil in large Dutch oven over medium heat until oil registers 375 degrees. Carefully add one-third of beef and fry, stirring occasionally to keep beef from sticking together, until golden brown, about 1½ minutes. Using spider, transfer meat to paper towel–lined sheet. Return oil to 375 degrees and repeat twice more with remaining beef. After frying, reserve 2 tablespoons frying oil.

4. Heat reserved oil in 12-inch skillet over medium-high heat until shimmering. Add orange peel and jalapeño and cook, stirring occasionally, until about half of orange peel is golden brown, 1½ to 2 minutes. Add garlic, ginger, and pepper flakes; cook, stirring frequently, until garlic is beginning to brown, about 45 seconds. Add soy sauce mixture and cook, scraping up any browned bits, until slightly thickened, about 45 seconds. Add beef and scallions and toss. Transfer to platter and serve immediately.

Beyond Rice: A Guide to Other Grains

These days, supermarkets offer an entire universe of grains—and with the right method they're as easy to cook, and as versatile, as rice. Here are six of our favorites.

BY SHANNON FRIEDMANN HATCH

GREAT GRAINS, GUARANTEED

Properly storing grains to retain freshness and choosing the right pot are the first steps toward ensuring top-notch results.

Mind the Store(age)
To prevent open boxes and bags of grains from spoiling in the pantry, store them in airtight containers and, if you have space, in the freezer. This is especially important for whole grains like wheat berries that turn rancid with oxidation.

The Right Pot
A sturdy, heavy-bottomed saucepan with a tight-fitting lid is a must for cooking any grain via the absorption or pilaf method.

Barley

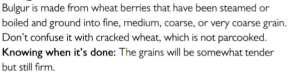

Best known in this country as a staple used in soups, this high-fiber grain's nutty, subtly sweet flavor makes it an ideal accompaniment to meat, chicken, and fish. Both hulled and pearl barley (the most widely available varieties) are stripped of their tough outer covering, but we prefer quicker-cooking pearl barley, which has been polished to remove the bran layer as well.
Knowing when it's done: The grains will be softened and plump but still somewhat firm in the center.
TIP: For a hearty alternative to risotto, substitute pearl barley for the Arborio rice typically used. Like rice, the barley will release starches when stirred, creating a creamy consistency. Be sure to add extra liquid since barley takes a bit longer to cook.
Try it in: Barley Risotto with Roasted Butternut Squash*

Bulgur

Bulgur is made from wheat berries that have been steamed or boiled and ground into fine, medium, coarse, or very coarse grain. Don't confuse it with cracked wheat, which is not parcooked.
Knowing when it's done: The grains will be somewhat tender but still firm.
TIP: Instead of simmering it in water, we often reconstitute fine- or medium-grain bulgur by soaking it in water flavored with lemon, lime, or tomato juice (use ⅔ cup of liquid for 1 cup of bulgur and soak for 60 to 90 minutes).
Try it in: Bulgur with Red Grapes and Feta*

Farro

A favorite ingredient in Tuscan cuisine, these hulled whole-wheat kernels boast a sweet, nutty flavor and a chewy bite. In Italy, the grain is available in three sizes—*farro piccolo, farro medio,* and *farro grande*—but the midsize type is most common in the United States.
Knowing when it's done: The grains will be tender but have a slight chew, similar to al dente pasta.
TIP: Although we usually turn to the absorption method for quicker-cooking grains, farro takes better to the pasta method because the abundance of water cooks the grains more evenly.
Try it in: Farro with Mushrooms and Thyme*

Millet

The mellow corn flavor and fine texture of these tiny seeds make them extremely versatile in both savory and sweet applications, including flatbreads, polenta-like puddings, and pan-fried cakes. We particularly like them in pilafs or even just mixed with a pat of butter.
Knowing when it's done: All of the cooking liquid will be absorbed and the grains will be fully tender.
TIP: Slightly overcooking millet causes the seeds to burst and release starch, creating a creamy consistency that makes this grain ideal for breakfast porridge.
Try it in: Millet Porridge with Maple Syrup*

Quinoa

Though actually a seed, quinoa is often referred to as a "super-grain" because it's a nutritionally complete protein. We love the pinhead-size seeds (which can be white, red, black, or purple) for their faint crunch and mineral taste.
Knowing when it's done: The grains will unfurl and expand to about three times their size.
TIP: Toast quinoa in a dry (no oil or butter) pot before adding water; we've found that toasting it in fat gives the grain a slightly bitter flavor.
Try it in: Quinoa Salad with Red Bell Pepper and Cilantro*

Wheat Berries

These are not berries at all but whole, husked wheat kernels with a rich, earthy flavor and firm chew. Because they're unprocessed, they remain firm, smooth, and distinct when cooked, which makes them great for salads.
Knowing when it's done: The grains will be softened but still quite chewy, smooth, and separate.
TIP: Though not typically done when boiling grains, we toast wheat berries in oil before adding them to the water, which brings out their nutty flavor.
Try it in: Wheat Berry Salad with Orange and Scallions*

Grain Recipes
*Recipes available FREE for 4 months at CooksIllustrated.com/feb13

TIMES, METHODS, AND MEASUREMENTS

1 cup raw	BARLEY	BULGUR	FARRO	MILLET	QUINOA	WHEAT BERRIES
Method(s)	Pasta	Absorption	Pasta	Absorption/Pilaf	Absorption/Pilaf	Pasta
Water	4 quarts	1 cup	4 quarts	2¼ cups	1 cup	4 quarts
Time	20–25 min	13–18 min	15–20 min	25–30 min	16–18 min	1 hour
Yield	3½–4 cups	2¼ cups	3 cups	2¼ cups	2¾ cups	3 cups

THREE COOKING METHODS

Most grains not only follow the same familiar cooking methods as rice but are actually more forgiving because they don't break down and turn mushy as easily.

Absorption

The grains are simmered slowly in a measured quantity of liquid until tender.
Best for: Tender grains like bulgur, millet, and quinoa

1. Combine 1 cup grains, water, and ½ teaspoon salt in saucepan.
2. Bring mixture to simmer, then reduce heat to low, cover, and simmer until grains are tender and liquid is absorbed. Off heat, let sit, covered, for 10 minutes. Fluff with fork and serve.

➤ **TIP:** A clean dish towel, placed between the pot and the lid before the cooked grains rest off heat, will absorb excess moisture and prevent the grains from turning gummy.

Pilaf

In this variation on the absorption method, the grains are toasted to impart a nutty flavor before the liquid is added.
Best for: Tender grains like millet and quinoa

1. Heat 1 tablespoon butter or oil in saucepan over medium-high heat until shimmering. Add 1 cup grains and toast until lightly golden and fragrant, about 3 minutes. Add ½ teaspoon salt and water.
2. Bring mixture to simmer, then reduce heat to low, cover, and simmer until grains are tender and liquid is absorbed. Off heat, let sit, covered, for 10 minutes. Fluff with fork and serve.

➤ **TIP:** For a more complex-tasting pilaf, sauté spices and aromatics like onions and garlic before adding the grains, swap in chicken broth for the water, and stir in fresh chopped herbs before serving.

Pasta

The grains are cooked like pasta in an abundant quantity of boiling water.
Best for: Firm grains like barley, farro, and wheat berries

1. Bring 4 quarts water to boil in Dutch oven. Stir in 1 cup grains and 1 tablespoon salt. Return to boil, reduce heat, and simmer until grains are tender.
2. Drain in strainer set in sink. Let sit in strainer for 5 minutes before using (or pat dry with a paper towel) to remove any excess moisture.

➤ **TIP:** To quickly cool down boiled grains for a cold salad, rinse them with cold water while they are in the strainer.

➤ **RINSE AND DRY BEFORE COOKING**
Most grains should be rinsed before cooking to remove excess starch, detritus, or bitter coatings. (Some quinoa comes conveniently "prewashed," but if you're unsure, rinse it to remove its saponin coating, which is mildly toxic.)

1. Rinse grains in fine-mesh strainer until water runs clear. Drain briefly.

2. Spread grains on rimmed baking sheet lined with clean dish towel. Let dry for 15 minutes.

3. To remove grains from towel, pick up towel by corners and gently shake grains into bowl.

SPEEDING UP THE PROCESS

The earthy flavor and chew of firm grains like wheat berries (and others like rye berries, spelt, and kamut) make them ideal for side dishes, but their cooking time (at least 1 hour) is an obstacle. Soaking overnight or adding baking soda to the cooking water will cut down the cooking time. (We don't recommend soaking or adding baking soda to grains cooked according to the absorption or the pilaf method; these shortcuts will throw off the amount of measured water the grains absorb.)

SOAK OVERNIGHT

Covering the grains with water for 8 hours (for safety, store them in the refrigerator) will shave 10 to 20 minutes off their cooking times—and ensure that they cook more evenly. Drain the grains before adding the cooking water.

ADD BAKING SODA

Adding ½ teaspoon of baking soda to 4 quarts of water will speed the grains' cooking time by 5 to 10 minutes.

MAKE AHEAD AND FREEZE

All types of cooked grains freeze well for at least three months, so making a large batch to freeze in smaller portions is a timesaver. To reheat the grains, thawing isn't necessary.

1. Place 2 cups cooled grains in zipper-lock bag. Lay bag flat and press out air. (To save space, freeze bags flat and stack once frozen.)

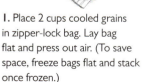

2. To warm, transfer grains to bowl and microwave until grains are hot, 2 to 3 minutes.

➤ **AVOIDING STUCK-ON GRAINS**
Before cooking:
To prevent grains from sticking to the pot, coat the bottom and sides of the vessel with vegetable oil spray before adding the grains.

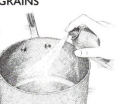

After cooking: If cooking still leaves behind a stubborn residue on the pan, try this trick: Fill the pan 2 inches high with water. Add ¼ cup of baking soda and ¼ cup of distilled white vinegar (the mixture will foam vigorously). Bring to a boil and cook for 15 minutes. Turn off the heat and let sit until cooled. Drain the water and clean the pot as usual. If any sticky patches remain, repeat.

Ultimate Butterscotch Pudding

Our goal was to develop a fail-safe method for producing this dessert's signature bittersweet flavor. While we were at it, we stumbled upon a better way to make pudding.

> BY DAN SOUZA

Most butterscotch pudding is synonymous with a powdered mix or those hermetically sealed small plastic cups from the supermarket. Rarely do we take the time to cobble it together from scratch—unfortunate, since we're sacrificing flavor for convenience. Real butterscotch gets its rich, nuanced, slightly bitter character from the complex reactions that take place when brown sugar and butter are cooked together into a caramel; when it's combined with custard, the result is miles away from the painfully sweet puddings produced commercially. And yet, it comes with a price of admission: Before you even get to the point of making pudding, you've got to successfully cook that caramel, which isn't easy. With this in mind, I set myself a high bar: Take the scare out of making caramel, simplify the pudding-making process, and ultimately bring the flavor of true butterscotch back into the American repertoire.

Butterscotch Breakdown

I started with a recipe Ruth Wakefield (of Toll House chocolate chip cookie fame) developed in the 1936 edition of *Toll House Tried and True Recipes*—a time well before fake butterscotch came on the scene. Unfortunately, I found it easy to under- or overcook the butterscotch, resulting in pudding that was either too sweet or unpalatably bitter, respectively. The problem revolved around visual cues: I never knew whether I'd reached the critical "dark brown" (read: properly caramelized) stage of making butterscotch because the brown sugar–butter mixture is already quite dark. I needed more precision, and that meant breaking out the thermometer.

I tried again, melting butter with equal amounts of granulated and brown sugars, salt, and a little water. I boiled batches of this mixture, aiming for 300 degrees—the peak of flavor development—before adding ¼ cup of cream to halt the cooking process. But I couldn't consistently nail that

With our deeply flavored caramel, there's no mistaking this dessert for the snack-pack version—in terms of either taste or color.

temperature. The window of doneness, which lasted only a few seconds somewhere between the 6- and 7-minute mark, was simply too narrow. If it was even a couple of degrees over, the caramel burned.

I needed to slow things down, so I switched gears and tried simmering a couple of batches over a low flame. Indeed, this afforded me a much wider window (minutes, not seconds) in which to check the temperature of the mixture and add the cream. The trade-off was time: This approach took 30 minutes—triple the amount that I had been spending. But maybe I could have it both ways. In the name of compromise, I tried a hybrid method in which I boiled the butterscotch hard at first to get the caramelization going and then dropped the heat and gently simmered it to the finish line. Bingo. A 5-minute boil brought the mixture to 240 degrees, at which point I lowered the heat for another 12 to 16 minutes of simmering to climb the final 60 degrees. The method was foolproof—and surprisingly, it produced a richer-tasting butterscotch than the high-heat method did.

Curious about the pudding's better flavor, I did a little digging and discovered that the flavor of butterscotch is highly dependent on the Maillard reaction. While we normally think of Maillard in relation to browning meat, the same reaction takes place when milk proteins in butter react with reducing sugars (fructose and glucose) to develop hundreds of new flavor compounds. This reaction depends on time and temperature: The longer the pudding cooks and the higher the temperature it cooks at, the more flavor that develops. By bringing the pudding to 240 degrees—a relatively high temperature—and then letting it slowly increase to 300 degrees, I was allowing the pudding to spend more time at higher temperatures, which translated into deeper flavor. It was a great side effect of my relatively quick, foolproof method.

Feeling confident about making the butterscotch, I wondered if there weren't other ways to nudge along the browning process and get even deeper flavor. I had been using a combination of white sugar (sucrose) and dark brown sugar (mostly sucrose, with a little glucose and fructose from the molasses). Because the Maillard reaction is fueled by simple sugars like glucose and fructose, I cast about for other sources of these sugars and made two additions to the butterscotch mixture: corn syrup, which is loaded with glucose, and lemon juice, which, through a process called inversion, promotes the breakdown of sucrose, a complex sugar, into simple glucose and fructose molecules. As the butterscotch simmered away, more and more sucrose inverted, providing extra fuel for the flavorful reaction.

Losing My Temper

With my rich-flavored, foolproof butterscotch in place, I moved on to streamlining my pudding approach. The classic method of cooking an egg- and starch-thickened custard goes as follows: Bring the liquid (here the butterscotch caramel thinned with milk and cream) to a simmer; stir a portion of it into a mixture of egg yolks, cornstarch, and a little liquid such as milk—a process known as tempering; return everything to the pot; and bring it up to a full boil. Finally, strain the mixture into a separate bowl to remove the inevitable bits of overcooked egg,

PHOTOGRAPHY: CARL TREMBLAY

A NEW WAY TO CONSISTENTLY PERFECT CARAMEL

The rich flavor of our butterscotch pudding depends on cooking the caramel mixture to 300 degrees before adding the cream, but it's easy to over- or undercook that mixture when it's boiled from start to finish (the usual approach). Our more forgiving method: Boil the caramel over medium heat until it reaches 240 degrees, then reduce the heat to medium-low, and gently simmer it until it reaches 300 degrees. The simmer phase takes about 12 to 16 minutes—plenty of time in which to grab a thermometer and the cream.

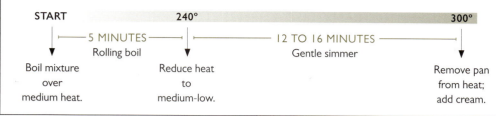

START	240°		300°
	⟵ 5 MINUTES ⟶	⟵ 12 TO 16 MINUTES ⟶	
	Rolling boil	Gentle simmer	
Boil mixture over medium heat.	Reduce heat to medium-low.		Remove pan from heat; add cream.

cover, and chill until set. Looking for a less fussy alternative, I paged through a number of cookbooks and stumbled upon a technique in which the liquid is brought to a full boil, immediately poured over the thickening mixture (egg yolks, cornstarch, and milk), and simply whisked until combined.

Having always known tempering as a slow, gentle method, I thought this approach sounded reckless. But for the sake of convenience, I cooked another batch of butterscotch; whisked together my yolks, cornstarch, and milk in a separate bowl; and—cringing—poured the hot butterscotch mixture over the yolk mixture and whisked vigorously. The result shocked me: Rather than a lumpy mess of curdled yolks, the pudding was smooth and glossy. Why did the mixture thicken properly—and why didn't it curdle?

It turns out that I'd misunderstood pudding making—and tempering—all along. Boiling pudding guarantees that it will thicken, but it's akin to ordering an airstrike when a single grenade will do. Why? Because the two components that thicken pudding—cornstarch and egg yolks—do so at temperatures well below the boiling point of 212 degrees. (For more information, see "Smoother Route to Pudding?")

As for why the pour-over method didn't cause the eggs to curdle, the explanation was twofold: First, the yolks were protected by the cornstarch, which absorbs water, swells, and slows down the binding of the egg proteins. Second, the pour-over approach removes the custard from direct heat, thereby eliminating any risk of curdling. (Some sources claim that the yolks must be boiled to prevent an active enzyme in them from liquefying the thickened custard, but I never encountered this problem.)

Pleased with my revamped caramel and pudding methods, I had one last tweak to make: I added 2 teaspoons of vanilla extract and 1 teaspoon of dark rum to mirror the deep caramel notes of the butterscotch.

With a dollop of lightly sweetened whipped cream on top, my butterscotch pudding was the ultimate version—simple to make yet with a flavor so complex and sophisticated that I wouldn't hesitate to serve it to company.

BEST BUTTERSCOTCH PUDDING
SERVES 8

When taking the temperature of the caramel in step 1, tilt the pan and move the thermometer back and forth to equalize hot and cool spots. Work quickly when pouring the caramel mixture over the egg mixture in step 4 to ensure proper thickening. Serve the pudding with lightly sweetened whipped cream.

- 12 tablespoons unsalted butter, cut into ½-inch pieces
- ½ cup (3½ ounces) granulated sugar
- ½ cup packed (3½ ounces) dark brown sugar
- ¼ cup water
- 2 tablespoons light corn syrup
- 1 teaspoon lemon juice
- ¾ teaspoon salt
- 1 cup heavy cream
- 2¼ cups whole milk
- 4 large egg yolks
- ¼ cup cornstarch
- 2 teaspoons vanilla extract
- 1 teaspoon dark rum

1. Bring butter, granulated sugar, brown sugar, water, corn syrup, lemon juice, and salt to boil in large saucepan over medium heat, stirring occasionally to dissolve sugar and melt butter. Once mixture is at full rolling boil, cook, stirring occasionally, for 5 minutes (caramel will register about 240 degrees). Immediately reduce heat to medium-low and gently simmer (caramel should maintain steady stream of lazy bubbles—if not, adjust heat accordingly), stirring frequently, until mixture is color of dark peanut butter, 12 to 16 minutes longer (caramel will register about 300 degrees and should have slight burnt smell).

2. Remove pan from heat; carefully pour ¼ cup cream into caramel mixture and swirl to incorporate (mixture will bubble and steam); let bubbling subside. Whisk vigorously and scrape corners of pan until mixture is completely smooth, at least 30 seconds. Return pan to medium heat and gradually whisk in remaining ¾ cup cream until smooth. Whisk in 2 cups milk until mixture is smooth, making sure to scrape corners and edges of pan to remove any remaining bits of caramel.

3. Meanwhile, microwave remaining ¼ cup milk until simmering, 30 to 45 seconds. Whisk egg yolks and cornstarch together in large bowl until smooth. Gradually whisk in hot milk until smooth; set aside (do not refrigerate).

4. Return saucepan to medium-high heat and bring mixture to full rolling boil, whisking frequently. Once mixture is boiling rapidly and beginning to climb toward top of pan, immediately pour into bowl with yolk mixture in 1 motion (do not add gradually). Whisk thoroughly for 10 to 15 seconds (mixture will thicken after a few seconds). Whisk in vanilla and rum. Spray piece of parchment paper with vegetable oil spray and press on surface of pudding. Refrigerate until cold and set, at least 3 hours. Whisk pudding until smooth before serving.

Really Good Oatmeal Muffins

What should be a satisfying breakfast treat is often a dry, chewy regret. The key to a moist, tender crumb turned out to be choosing the proper oats and treating them right.

≥ BY DAN SOUZA ≤

I've always been interested in the idea of a breakfast that boasts the best qualities of a great bowl of oatmeal—lightly sweet, oaty flavor and satisfying heartiness—in the convenient, portable form of a muffin. But I've yet to find a decent example of the confection. I suppose it isn't all that surprising: Oats are dry and tough, making them difficult to incorporate into a tender crumb. And what chance does their mild, nutty flavor have of shining through when it is clouded by loads of spices and sugar? Determined to bake my way to a richly flavored, moist, and tender oatmeal muffin, I headed into the kitchen and got to work.

Separating the Oats from the Chaff

Aside from a barrage of sugar and spice, the real problem with most of the initial recipes I tested was the oats themselves. The most common approach was to toss a few handfuls of the old-fashioned rolled type (our usual choice for baking) into a quick bread–style muffin batter. This calls for separately combining the wet ingredients (melted butter, milk, light brown sugar, and eggs) and dry ingredients (all-purpose flour, baking powder, baking soda, and salt) and then blending the two mixtures together. The result of this dead-simple style? Muffins speckled with dry, chewy oats featuring raw white centers.

It was clear that simply stirring raw oats into the batter wasn't enough to sufficiently hydrate and cook them. A few recipes sought to avoid the problem by calling for quick oats, which are precooked and

A crunchy cinnamon sugar–laced topping crowns a moist, tender muffin that is jam-packed with oats.

rolled into thin flakes before packaging, but these muffins presented their own issues. Gone were the dry, uncooked bits flecking the crumb, but with them went any trace of oat taste.

Sticking with the more robust old-fashioned rolled oats, I set about trying to find the best way to ensure that they would cook through. When a soak in cold milk (the primary liquid for my muffin

batter) failed to soften the sturdy flakes, I tried heating the milk first. I poured 2 cups of boiling milk over an equal amount of oats and after allowing the mixture to cool to room temperature, I incorporated the oatmeal mush into my batter. Still no luck: The muffins were now riddled with gummy pockets. I produced similar results—a crumb dotted with gummy spots—in a batch in which I simmered the oats and milk on the stovetop as I would for a bowl of oatmeal. What had gone wrong?

Well, it turns out that when oats are hydrated and heated, they release gobs of starch. This is good news if you're trying to make a creamy bowl of porridge, but it spells disaster when it comes to baking muffins. The oat starch ends up trapping some of the moisture in the batter, thus preventing the flour from evenly hydrating. The result: those ruinous thick, gummy patches.

Frustrated, I scratched soaking the oats from my list and took a step back to reflect. When I used quick oats, the texture of the muffins had been perfect. Because they are broken down and precooked, quick oats absorb liquid more readily than do thicker rolled oats and thus fully soften during baking. What if I processed my rolled oats so that they would drink up liquid more easily?

I broke out my food processor and whizzed 2 cups of chunky rolled oats into a pile of fine oat flour—just 30 seconds did the trick. Exactly as I'd hoped, the finely ground meal readily absorbed milk (heating it was now unnecessary) and fully softened once incorporated into the batter and baked. There was just one caveat: My home-ground oat flour absorbed liquid much more slowly than wheat flour did. I found that if I mixed up the batter and immediately portioned it into a muffin tin, its consistency was too thin and my muffins spread and ran into one another during baking. This was an easy problem to fix: After mixing the batter, I gave it a 20-minute rest to fully hydrate, thereby ensuring that the batter would be thick enough to scoop.

Oat Cuisine

I was finally making progress on the texture, so I switched my attention to flavor. With a ratio of 2 cups oats to 1¾ cups flour, my muffins boasted a prominent oat flavor. Still, I wanted their nutty

Muffin Mishaps

Developing a great oatmeal muffin required a lot of trial and error, particularly when it came to deciding which type of oats to use and how to incorporate them. Here are a few of our not-so-successful attempts.

PRETTY BUT BLAND
Highly processed quick oats produced an attractive muffin—with dull flavor.

DRY AND CRUMBLY
Raw rolled oats never fully hydrated, leading to a dry, chewy crumb.

SQUAT AND GUMMY
Cooked rolled oats were too wet, yielding a muffin with gummy patches.

taste to be even more noticeable, so I turned to a technique that we've used to intensify oat flavor when making granola: toasting. I evaluated two options: tossing the whole oats in a dry skillet over medium heat until they turned golden versus sautéing them in a couple tablespoons of butter. It was no contest: The muffins made with butter-toasted oats won hands down for their richer, more complex taste and aroma. While I was focused on flavor, I experimented with adding spices and seasonings. I incorporated varying amounts of ground nutmeg, ground ginger, cinnamon, and vanilla extract, yet time and again tasters singled out the muffins without any extras. With great buttery, toasted-oat flavor in the mix, spices seemed to only muddy the waters.

With clean, rich oat flavor nailed down, I was close to wrapping things up, but there was one issue that I had yet to address: When mixed with the wet ingredients, the oat flour occasionally developed a few large clumps that stubbornly refused to hydrate and dissolve into the batter during baking, leaving dry, floury pockets in the finished muffins. To find a route to a consistently hydrated batter, I tried vigorously folding with a spatula, whisking energetically, and even processing the mixture in a blender. But manhandling the batter to smooth it out only resulted in a crumb with a tough texture—a repercussion of overworking the oat starch and gluten.

Seeing my predicament, a colleague suggested that I try a lesser-known technique called whisk folding. In this method, a whisk is gently drawn down and then up through the batter before being tapped lightly against the side of the bowl to knock any clumps back into the mixture. The wires of the whisk exert very little drag and thus develop minimal gluten, while the tapping action helps rupture pockets of dry ingredients. Sure enough, whisk folding made all the difference, ridding the batter of large clumps and preserving a tender, moist texture.

Muffin Top

Happy with my tender, jam-packed-with-oats muffins, it was time to come up with a topping. Just as one might garnish a bowl of oatmeal with crunchy nuts or chewy, sweet raisins, I wanted a contrasting adornment on my muffin that featured crunch and a bit of sweetness. I played around with toasted nuts, a cinnamon sugar mixture, and even an unconventional broiled icing, but nothing tasted quite right. While pondering my next move, I watched a colleague pull a bubbling hot apple crisp from the oven and it hit me: A crisplike topping would be just right.

I excitedly stirred together more oats, finely chopped pecans, brown sugar, flour, melted butter, salt, and a hint of cinnamon in a medium bowl, and then I crumbled my crisp-inspired topping evenly over the muffin batter before baking. Twenty minutes later, my muffins emerged with a proud crown of crunchy, chewy, sweet, and salty oats and nuts—the perfect accent to the rich crumb. Finally, I'd succeeded in turning the best traits of a humble bowl of oatmeal into a satisfying breakfast on the go.

GETTING ROLLED OATS TO BAKE INTO MOIST, FLAVORFUL MUFFINS

Old-fashioned rolled oats have a subtle taste and don't easily absorb the liquid in a batter. Here are the steps we took to transform their flavor and texture.

TOAST IN BUTTER
Browning the oats in butter develops rich, complex flavor and aroma.

GRIND INTO FLOUR
Processing the oats into a fine meal ensures that they will absorb liquid.

MIX INTO BATTER; LET SIT
A 20-minute rest gives the oat flour time to hydrate in the batter.

OATMEAL MUFFINS
MAKES 12 MUFFINS

Do not use quick or instant oats in this recipe. Walnuts may be substituted for the pecans. The easiest way to grease and flour the muffin tin is with a baking spray with flour.

Topping
- ½ cup (1½ ounces) old-fashioned rolled oats
- ⅓ cup (1⅔ ounces) all-purpose flour
- ⅓ cup pecans, chopped fine
- ⅓ cup packed (2⅓ ounces) light brown sugar
- 1¼ teaspoons ground cinnamon
- ⅛ teaspoon salt
- 4 tablespoons unsalted butter, melted

Muffins
- 2 tablespoons unsalted butter, plus 6 tablespoons melted
- 2 cups (6 ounces) old-fashioned rolled oats
- 1¾ cups (8¾ ounces) all-purpose flour
- 1½ teaspoons salt
- ¾ teaspoon baking powder
- ¼ teaspoon baking soda
- 1⅓ cups packed (9⅓ ounces) light brown sugar
- 1¾ cups milk
- 2 large eggs, beaten

1. FOR THE TOPPING: Combine oats, flour, pecans, sugar, cinnamon, and salt in medium bowl. Drizzle melted butter over mixture and stir to thoroughly combine; set aside.

2. FOR THE MUFFINS: Grease and flour 12-cup muffin tin. Melt 2 tablespoons butter in 10-inch skillet over medium heat. Add oats and cook, stirring frequently, until oats turn golden brown and smell of cooking popcorn, 6 to 8 minutes. Transfer oats to food processor and process into fine meal, about 30 seconds. Add flour, salt, baking powder, and baking soda to oats and pulse until combined, about 3 pulses.

3. Stir 6 tablespoons melted butter and sugar together in large bowl until smooth. Add milk and eggs and whisk until smooth. Using whisk, gently fold half of oat mixture into wet ingredients, tapping whisk against side of bowl to release clumps. Add remaining oat mixture and continue to fold with whisk until no streaks of flour remain. Set aside batter for 20 minutes to thicken. Meanwhile, adjust oven rack to middle position and heat oven to 375 degrees.

4. Using ice cream scoop or large spoon, divide batter equally among prepared muffin cups (about ½ cup batter per cup; cups will be filled to rim). Evenly sprinkle topping over muffins (about 2 tablespoons per muffin). Bake until toothpick inserted in center comes out clean, 18 to 25 minutes, rotating muffin tin halfway through baking.

5. Let muffins cool in muffin tin on wire rack for 10 minutes. Remove muffins from muffin tin and serve or let cool completely before serving.

TECHNIQUE | A GENTLE WAY TO CUT DOWN ON LUMPS

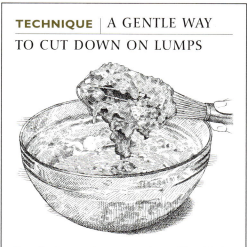

Even finely ground oats create lumps. To minimize lump size without overworking the oat starch and gluten—and thus toughening the crumb—draw a whisk gently down and then up through the batter. Tap the whisk against the bowl to release clumps.

Wild Rice and Mushroom Soup

For a rich, earthy, nutty-tasting soup, we had to figure out how to make its signature ingredients do more than just add bulk.

> ≥ BY CELESTE ROGERS ≤

Wild rice has made numerous appearances at my dinner table over the years, but it's almost always been in the form of a salad or stuffing for the Thanksgiving bird. The long smooth grains, which were first harvested from lake grasses by several Great Lakes–area Native American tribes and are now largely cultivated in artificial paddies, have remarkably nutty, savory depth, not to mention a distinct chew that makes them an ideal base for hearty side dishes.

That profile also lends itself to another popular wild rice application—soups—and I've come across quite a few recipes that pair the grain with mushrooms. The combination makes sense: Together, the two should produce a soup that's substantial, but not heavy, and full of earthy depth. Just the kind of food I want to tuck into in the dead of winter.

Having said that, I've never had a wild rice and mushroom soup fitting this description—including the handful I tried when I set out to make my own version. Whether they were minimalist broths or stewlike concoctions, all the soups I made shared a common flaw: The namesake ingredients didn't play a starring role.

I knew I could do better, so I decided to develop this soup with a clear objective in mind: Namely, keep the focus on the nutty wild rice and meaty mushrooms, and limit any additions to ingredients that could amplify their earthy, *umami*-rich flavor.

Hunting for Flavor

For the sake of establishing a working recipe, I tabled all testing of wild rice cooking methods and simply boiled the grains separately until they were firm-tender, which took a good hour. In the meantime, I built my soup base from an entire pound of sliced cremini mushrooms (a test kitchen favorite for their meaty flavor and texture and wide availability) sautéed in a Dutch oven with aromatic foundations like onion, garlic, and tomato paste. By the time the mushrooms had taken on color, I was left with a dark fond at the bottom of the pot that I easily liberated with a generous pour of sherry. A few minutes of reduction left me with a fortified mushroom concentrate to which I added chicken stock (for savory

A combination of sliced cremini mushrooms and finely ground shiitake mushrooms packs in earthy flavor without turning our soup into stew.

depth) and water before stirring in the cooked rice.

This early iteration was several steps in the right direction, but I still had a ways to go. The most glaring issue was the mushroom flavor, which was subtler than I'd hoped. Replacing some of the salt with soy sauce boosted savoriness, but the earthy quality I was after hadn't come through yet.

The thing was, the soup was already brimming with mushrooms. I considered trading inexpensive cremini for more costly portobellos, oysters, or shiitakes, but when I did, none of the other varieties provided significant flavor improvement. Instead, I opted to supplement the cremini with an alternative that packed the intense mushroom flavor I wanted without the bulk: dried shiitakes. We stock these umami-loaded pantry staples for just such applications, but rather than tease out their flavor using the usual steeping and chopping method, we prefer to grind the pieces into a powder that we stir into the broth. Just ¼ ounce, pulverized in a spice grinder (or in a blender), infused the soup with full-bodied mushroom flavor.

Flavorwise, I was making strides, but so far my versions didn't have enough body. Without it, the liquid was not only unsatisfying but also too thin to support the heftier mushrooms and rice. I hoped that a flour-based roux might be an easy way to thicken the pot—and it was, but I needed a full ½ cup to get the consistency I wanted, which dulled the flavor I'd worked so hard to build. Thankfully, there was an easy substitute: cornstarch. Unlike flour, cornstarch is a pure starch and a more powerful thickener, which meant I could get away with just ¼ cup.

Robust mushroom flavor? Check. Hearty body? Check. Now my soup just needed to earn the other half of its title.

Simmer Down

I suppose I could have just dumped the boiled rice into the soup and called it a day, but marrying the liquid and rice at the last minute wouldn't allow much time for a flavor transfer. As it was, the rice needed an hour of cooking time on its own, so waiting to simmer it in the soup base would really drag out the overall cooking time. Thinking there had to be a better way, I read up on wild rice cookery and ran some tests. Turns out I was right.

Each grain of wild rice is enveloped in a thick pectin-rich coat that hardens further when the rice is dried during processing. Wild rice is properly cooked when this black seed coat splits and the grains are tender yet still chewy. But stovetop simmering—I was using the pasta method, cooking the rice in an excess of water and then draining it—was not only a long process but an inconsistent one as well, unless I constantly fiddled with the heat to make sure the pot wasn't bubbling too slowly or too quickly. The other problem: Using the pasta method meant that I was discarding the cooking liquid—literally pouring some of the flavor from the wild rice down the drain. Thinking I'd keep all that flavorful liquid in the pot, I tried the absorption method—cooking the rice in a measured amount of water that the grains completely soak up—but that method required even more babysitting to prevent the liquid from evaporating too quickly. No thanks.

Instead, I abandoned stovetop simmering altogether and turned to a more even heat source: the oven. After setting the dial to 375, I switched back

SCIENCE Making Wild Rice Act like Steak

We brown meat, baked goods, and many other foods as a matter of course, since the deeper color is an indication of the Maillard reaction, the process triggered by heat that causes a food's proteins and sugars to recombine into hundreds of new flavor compounds that boost complexity. To achieve richer browned flavor in ordinary rice, we often toast the raw grains in the pan before adding liquid. But toasting doesn't work as well with wild rice, since it is technically a grass with a hard pectin-rich coating that must break down before the proteins and sugars on the inside can brown. However, we stumbled upon another way to achieve browning: adding baking soda to the cooking water. Baking soda not only breaks down the pectin seed coat to speed cooking (our original goal) but also lowers the temperature necessary for browning to occur—from at least 300 degrees to below water's boiling point of 212. Another factor in our favor: Wild rice is high in the amino acids lysine and glycine, proteins that are particularly sensitive to browning. Baking soda added to the pot led to nuttier-tasting wild rice and a savory, deep-brown stock that enriched the soup. –C.R.

RICH COLOR, RICH FLAVOR
This stock boasts some of the same "browned" flavors as seared meat.

White mushrooms can be substituted for the cremini mushrooms. We use a spice grinder to process the dried shiitake mushrooms, but a blender also works.

¼	ounce dried shiitake mushrooms, rinsed
4¼	cups water
1	sprig fresh thyme
1	bay leaf
1	garlic clove, peeled, plus 4 cloves, minced
	Salt and pepper
¼	teaspoon baking soda
1	cup wild rice
4	tablespoons unsalted butter
1	pound cremini mushrooms, trimmed and sliced ¼ inch thick
1	onion, chopped fine
1	teaspoon tomato paste
⅔	cup dry sherry
4	cups low-sodium chicken broth
1	tablespoon soy sauce
¼	cup cornstarch
½	cup heavy cream
¼	cup minced fresh chives
¼	teaspoon finely grated lemon zest

to the pasta method and brought the water to a boil on the burner, added the rice, covered the pot, and transferred the vessel to the oven. Just as I'd hoped, the rice cooked—babysitter-free—at an even simmer and emerged firm yet tender with pleasant chew.

I was about to reluctantly pitch the leftover cooking liquid when an obvious thought occurred to me: Why not strain the flavorful liquid and substitute it for some of the water in the soup? One test proved that it was an easy way to ensure that the flavor of the wild rice permeated the broth.

Going Wild with pH

The good news: I finally had a foolproof cooking method and rich wild rice flavor throughout my soup. The bad: It was still costing me an hour. I wasn't sure how I could speed things along until a colleague reminded me that we had solved a similar dilemma in our recipe for polenta by adding a pinch of baking soda to the pot. The more basic environment facilitated the breakdown of the pectin and shaved 15 minutes off the cooking time, and this approach worked beautifully with the rice, too. When I added just ¼ teaspoon, the seed coat broke down faster, cutting down the rice's cooking time to about 45 minutes.

There was also a side benefit to my baking soda trick that I didn't realize until I took a closer look at the strained cooking liquid. Unlike prior batches, which were straw-colored, this wild rice stock was deep brown. A spoonful surprised me with its savory nuttiness—it was far richer and more complex than the prior baking soda–free batches.

Our science editor explained that baking soda not only helps break down the pectin in the seed coat but also lowers the temperature necessary for Maillard reaction–induced browning to occur. Though most commonly associated with the browning of meat or baked goods, Maillard reactions occur when heated proteins and sugars undergo chemical changes, resulting in entirely new flavors. Typically these reactions require much higher temperatures (at least 300 degrees) than a simmering pot can achieve, but alkaline baking soda effectively lowers this temperature barrier and allows the reactions to occur below the

boiling point of water (212 degrees). Also working in my favor: Wild rice is especially well suited for the Maillard reaction, as it contains high concentrations of amino acids (lysine and glycine) that are particularly reactive.

Deeper, more complex flavor as a result of a faster cooking method? I'd take it. In fact, this soup was so full of earthy depth that my tasters suggested I balance it out with some fresher flavors. Chives and lemon zest brightened things up nicely. I also stirred in ½ cup of cream, which enriched the earthy broth.

Robustly flavored with its namesake ingredients, this soup had finally earned its title, not to mention a permanent spot in my collection of staple soups.

TASTING Wild Rice

Wild rice is not rice at all, but an aquatic grass that grows naturally in lakes and is cultivated in man-made paddies. When we tasted five brands both plain and in our Wild Rice and Mushroom Soup, textural differences stood out the most. The top three, including our winner, from Goose Valley,

WE'RE WILD ABOUT THIS RICE
"Plump" Goose Valley Wild Rice boasts "great chew" and "woodsy" flavor.

cooked up springy and firm, while the other two blew out. The difference was processing. To create a shelf-stable product, manufacturers heat the grains, which gelatinizes their starches and drives out moisture by parching (the traditional approach) or parboiling. To parch, manufacturers load the rice into cylinders that spin over a fire—an inexact process that produces "crumbly" results. Parboiling, a newer method, steams the grains in a controlled pressurized environment for more uniform and complete gelatinization, which translates into rice that cooks more evenly. For complete testing results, go to CooksIllustrated.com/feb13. –Hannah Crowley

1. Adjust oven rack to middle position and heat oven to 375 degrees. Grind shiitake mushrooms in spice grinder until finely ground (you should have about 3 tablespoons).

2. Bring 4 cups water, thyme, bay leaf, garlic clove, ¾ teaspoon salt, and baking soda to boil in medium saucepan over high heat. Add rice and return to boil. Cover saucepan, transfer to oven, and bake until rice is tender, 35 to 50 minutes. Strain rice through fine-mesh strainer set in 4-cup liquid measuring cup; discard thyme, bay leaf, and garlic. Add enough water to reserved cooking liquid to measure 3 cups.

3. Melt butter in Dutch oven over high heat. Add cremini mushrooms, onion, minced garlic, tomato paste, ¾ teaspoon salt, and 1 teaspoon pepper. Cook, stirring occasionally, until vegetables are browned and dark fond develops on bottom of pot, 15 minutes. Add sherry, scraping up any browned bits, and cook until reduced and pot is almost dry, about 2 minutes. Add ground shiitake mushrooms, reserved rice cooking liquid, broth, and soy sauce and bring to boil. Reduce heat to low and simmer, covered, until onion and mushrooms are tender, about 20 minutes.

4. Whisk cornstarch and remaining ¼ cup water in small bowl. Stir cornstarch slurry into soup, return to simmer, and cook until thickened, about 2 minutes. Remove pot from heat and stir in cooked rice, cream, chives, and lemon zest. Cover and let stand for 20 minutes. Season with salt and pepper to taste, and serve.

See the Browning Happen
Video available FREE for 4 months at CooksIllustrated.com/feb13

Bringing Home Pasta all'Amatriciana

To perfect this controversial Italian dish, we looked to a staple of the American larder.

> BY DAN SOUZA

If there's one thing that Italians love more than eating it's arguing about cooking. Case in point: *pasta all'amatriciana*. Residents of Amatrice (a mountain town northeast of Rome) claim to have originated the dish and outline an official recipe calling for spaghetti, *guanciale* (salt-cured pork jowl), fresh or canned tomatoes, hot red peppers, freshly grated pecorino, and sometimes white wine. Romans, on the other hand, insist on bucatini (long, thin, hollow pasta) for this recipe and incorporate onions but don't usually add wine. On a recent excursion through the region, I sampled both versions and sided with the Amatricians, whose take elegantly balances the bold flavors of the dish, with no alliums to distract. Leaving the cacophony of disagreement in the Italian countryside, I headed home to reproduce the Amatrician recipe.

Guanciale, the star of the dish, can be difficult to find in the United States. Made by salting and drying hog jowls, it boasts unmatched pure-pork flavor. My first idea for a substitute was pancetta, which is essentially spiced, unsmoked Italian bacon. I prepared two sauces: one with guanciale that I had splurged on for testing purposes and one with pancetta. For each sauce, I sautéed pork pieces, bloomed red pepper flakes in the rendered fat, stirred in and cooked down wine and tomatoes, tossed the sauce with spaghetti, and finished the dish with grated Pecorino Romano. My colleagues' frowns said it all: Pancetta produced an oddly sour-tasting dish that lacked the heady porkiness of the guanciale version.

American bacon was another option, but I knew that its smoky taste would be out of place. How about bacon's cousin, salt pork? It may have a humble American pedigree, but, like guanciale, it is simply salt-cured. The difference is that the meat for salt pork comes from the belly of the pig, not the jowl. And sure enough, tasters found that the clean, meaty flavor of salt pork closely mimicked that of guanciale. Now I just needed to weed through conflicting advice to figure out how best to cook it.

Some recipes recommend lightly browning the pork before simmering it in the sauce, and others warn against doing so. In a side-by-side test, sauces made with lightly browned pork boasted a richer flavor. This method also rendered more fat from the pork, which boosted meaty flavor and led to a more voluptuous sauce. One problem remained: The pork pieces had turned tough during browning.

I looked to a recent test kitchen discovery: We found that simmering bacon in water until the moisture evaporates and the strips brown and sizzle holds the temperature low enough to keep the bacon tender. I gave it a shot with the salt pork and was extremely pleased. It remained supple even after browning and simmering.

When it came to white versus red wine, it made sense to depart from tradition: The heartier red wine provided a deeper, richer background flavor. And while the official recipe from Amatrice allows for fresh or canned tomatoes, we decisively preferred canned diced, which offered satisfying, sweet bites throughout. To help the sauce cling to the pasta, I also added a couple of spoonfuls of tomato paste.

I turned my attention to the cheese. Pecorino Romano is a sheep's-milk cheese with real funk and bite that pairs extremely well with the rich pork, tomato, and red pepper flakes. But I kept running into the perennial problem with stirring grated aged cheese into a hot pot of pasta: It clumps into unattractive globs. With most pastas, I work around the problem by simply passing the cheese at the table. But all'amatriciana relies on the tang and saltiness of the Pecorino Romano throughout the dish. Another solution is to mix the grated cheese with cream and starch to provide stability while the cheese melts into the pasta. But this only resulted in muted flavors. What if instead of cream I mixed the cheese with some cooled pork fat? Success: I now had a clump-free dish and extra pork flavor to boot. The fat acted as a barrier to prevent the proteins in the cheese from bonding together as the cheese melted.

By questioning each ingredient, I had finally developed an authentic-tasting version of this classic dish. Let the dining—and the disagreement—begin.

PASTA ALL'AMATRICIANA
SERVES 4 TO 6

Look for salt pork that is roughly 70 percent fat and 30 percent lean meat; leaner salt pork may not render enough fat. If it is difficult to slice, put the salt pork in the freezer for 15 minutes to firm up. Use high-quality imported Pecorino Romano—not the bland domestic cheese labeled "Romano."

- 8 ounces salt pork, rind removed, rinsed thoroughly, and patted dry
- ½ cup water
- ½ teaspoon red pepper flakes
- 2 tablespoons tomato paste
- ¼ cup red wine
- 1 (28-ounce) can diced tomatoes
- 2 ounces Pecorino Romano cheese, finely grated (1 cup)
- 1 pound spaghetti
- 1 tablespoon salt

1. Slice pork into ¼-inch-thick strips, then cut each strip crosswise into ¼-inch pieces. Bring pork and water to simmer in 10-inch nonstick skillet over medium heat; cook until water evaporates and pork begins to sizzle, 5 to 8 minutes. Reduce heat to medium-low and continue to cook, stirring frequently, until fat renders and pork turns golden, 5 to 8 minutes longer. Using slotted spoon, transfer pork to bowl. Pour off all but 1 tablespoon fat from skillet. Reserve remaining fat.

2. Return skillet to medium heat and add pepper flakes and tomato paste; cook, stirring constantly, for 20 seconds. Stir in wine and cook for 30 seconds. Stir in tomatoes and their juice and rendered pork and bring to simmer. Cook, stirring frequently, until thickened, 12 to 16 minutes. While sauce simmers, smear 2 tablespoons reserved fat and ½ cup Pecorino Romano together in bowl to form paste.

3. Meanwhile, bring 4 quarts water to boil in large Dutch oven. Add spaghetti and salt and cook, stirring often, until al dente. Reserve 1 cup cooking water, then drain spaghetti and return it to pot.

4. Add sauce, ⅓ cup cooking water, and Pecorino Romano–fat mixture to pasta and toss well to coat, adjusting consistency with remaining cooking water as needed. Serve, passing remaining ½ cup Pecorino Romano separately.

Pork versus Pork

Guanciale, which is made by salting and drying hog jowls, is the traditional choice for this dish due to its intense pure-pork flavor. Looking for something equally porky but more readily available, we turn to salt pork, which is also salt-cured but is made from the belly.

GUANCIALE
Salted jowl.

SALT PORK
Salted belly.

Why You Should Buy a Pressure Cooker

The convenience, ease, and (yes!) safety of the modern pressure cooker will put dinner on the table fast—and make it taste as if you spent the whole day at the stove.

> BY LISA McMANUS ≥

Pressure cookers can be intimidating. Before I began testing them, I had heard countless stories about exploding cookers—usually ones belonging to someone's grandmother. This made the whole enterprise seem mysterious and dangerous, or at least very messy. But after spending weeks testing 12 models of pressure cookers, I can report that they are as safe as any other cookware—and definitely worth getting to know. Pressure cookers are surprisingly simple to use and in less than an hour can produce food that tastes as if you spent all day over the stove. You don't have to tell a soul that your savory, fork-tender pot roast, pulled pork, short ribs, or stew cooked in record time—and most of that time was hands-off. Dried beans are creamy and tender after just 10 minutes under pressure. Risotto needs just 6 minutes under pressure to reach the perfect consistency. Recipes once saved for weekends, or the slow cooker, can be started when you get home from work.

Pressure cookers function based on a very simple principle: In a tightly sealed pot, the boiling point of liquid is higher. As the pot heats up, pressure begins to build. This pressure makes it more difficult for water molecules to turn to vapor—therefore raising the boiling point from 212 to 250 degrees. Why does this matter? The superheated steam generated in the cooker makes food cook faster. And because the pot stays closed, cooking requires much less liquid than usual, and flavors concentrate. As a bonus, this method also uses less energy: Once pressure is reached, you cook with the heat turned down as low as possible, and cooking times are short.

Pressure cookers have been around for a long time. In 1679, French mathematician and physicist Denis Papin invented the "steam digester," the earliest-known pressure cooker; still, it wasn't until the beginning of the 20th century that smaller pressure cookers were introduced for home cooks. After World War II, demand boomed for pressure cookers, and some accounts note that unscrupulous manufacturers made shoddy cookers that were prone to explosions. Older cookers had "jiggle tops" that rattled and puffed while they cooked. Today's models use spring-loaded valves, which are silent and vent mere wisps of steam when pressurized. In other words, today's pressure cookers are quieter and simpler and have many more safety features than your grandmother's cooker did.

Across-the-board improvements over the years didn't necessarily mean that all models would work equally well, and we wondered what characteristics to look for in a good pressure cooker. They certainly look similar, resembling large metal saucepans or stockpots, but with heavy lids that have removable silicone rings, called sealing gaskets, around their inner rims. We selected sturdy, nonreactive stainless steel over aluminum cookers and came up with eight stovetop cookers—most with an 8-quart capacity—from a wallet-friendly $65 or so to a whopping $280. (We tested four electric pressure cookers separately. Ultimately, we preferred the stovetop models. See "Electric Pressure Cookers.") We used each of the models to prepare risotto; chicken stock; beef stew; Boston baked beans; and thick, meaty tomato sauce with pork ribs. Since plenty of recipes call for sautéing food in the bottom of the pot before sealing the lid for pressure cooking, we checked evenness of browning by cooking crêpes in the pan bottoms.

Sizing Them Up

While 6-quart cookers are popular, we soon realized the value of more capacity. First, you must never fill a pressure cooker more than two-thirds of the way (lines indicate the maximum level), which limits the available space. Some recipes don't fit in 6-quart cookers, including ours for chicken stock (for our test, we had to cut down the recipe). And if you can make 3 quarts of stock in the same time it takes to make 2 quarts, why not buy a pot that allows you to produce a bigger quantity?

The shape of the pot was equally important. Low, wide cookers provided a generous cooking surface, helping food brown thoroughly and efficiently before the cook closes the pot. Wide pots also let us brown meat in fewer batches. And testers found this shape easier to see and reach into while working. The narrowest among our cookers was a mere 6⅛ inches across; most were around 7½ inches, but the best performers had interior cooking surfaces of 9 inches in diameter—almost as much space as you get across the bottom of a 12-inch skillet.

But shape plays another role: Stovetop pressure cookers are made with a thick metal disk base (an aluminum disk covered by stainless steel, attached to the pan bottom) to retain and regulate heat. Every manufacturer warns that you must keep the heat source directly under that disk, since flames licking up the sides of the pot will damage the locking mechanisms in the handles and the sealing gasket around the rim. Trouble is, because that disk base is expensive to make, manufacturers keep it as small as

possible: In many of our models, the disks were even smaller than the bases of the pots, which ballooned out over the burner. In these models food routinely scorched wherever the base did not shield it from direct heat, and later we spent more time scrubbing those pots clean. Using a smaller flame under a smaller disk also means the pot heats up more slowly, taking minutes longer to reach pressure—minutes that you'll need to wait by the stove. Straight-sided pots with broad disks performed best in our cooking tests, and cleanup was easier with them.

This leads us to the next point: steady heating. With stovetop cookers, you bring the contents up to a boil, wait for the pressure indicator to show that it's at high pressure, and then turn down the heat as low

How Pressure Cookers Work

UNDER PRESSURE
In a tightly sealed cooker, water molecules are trapped, creating a dramatic increase in pressure. With more pressure, the temperature rises, and food cooks much more quickly.

ORDINARY POT
Even with a lid on, steam escapes, preventing an increase in pressure—and temperature.

The way pressure cookers work may rely on physics, but don't let that scare you. The science is pretty simple, really. In an open pan at sea level, the temperature of boiling water can't exceed 212 degrees. If you add a fitted lid to the pan, this loosely traps steam, which also stays at 212 degrees. But everything changes when you boil water in a sealed environment like a pressure cooker. When water is brought to a boil in the cooker, the water molecules can't escape, increasing the pressure within. More energy is needed for the water to boil and steam, which in turn increases the temperature in the chamber. In some pressure cookers, the pressure can reach up to 15 pounds per square inch (psi) above standard atmospheric pressure. Fifteen psi elevates the boiling point to about 250 degrees. At this temperature, water contains about 27 percent more energy than water at 212 degrees, helping to cook food much more quickly.

Electric Pressure Cookers

Electric pressure cookers offer one big advantage over stovetop models: You can set them and walk away. And many will produce great food in your absence. But electric models have several disadvantages. First, they are small, usually holding only 6 quarts rather than the 8 quarts we prefer. Inside electric pressure cookers, food cooks in a small liner pot with a nonstick coating, which is far less durable than stainless steel stovetop models. These lightweight pots spun around as we stirred food and, lacking handles, felt dangerous when we needed to pour off hot liquid. Their heating elements are weaker than those of a stove, so browning can be challenging. Electric pressure cookers are designed to switch to "keep warm" mode after cooking. We also discovered that

IT'S ELECTRIC
EMERIL 1000-Watt 6-Quart Electric Pressure Cooker by T-fal
Price: $119
Comments:
This efficient (though small, with only a 6-quart capacity) winner did a good job browning and stewing meats—not to mention cooking beans.

they can switch to "keep warm" mode during cooking when there's not enough liquid in the pot—a problem when cooking a whole chicken or meatloaf. Given these factors, we prefer stovetop models. But if you want an electric cooker, there are two we recommend, albeit with caveats. For complete testing results, go to CooksIllustrated.com/feb13. –L.M.

as possible while maintaining pressure. This operation was dead easy with some pots but tricky with other models, in which the pressure tended to drop after we turned down the heat, forcing us to hover, adjusting it up and down like a yo-yo. Cookers whose pressure dropped too readily produced meat, beans, and rice that were not sufficiently tender by the end of the cooking time; after tasting these, we had to close the pot and bring it back to pressure for several minutes to finish the job, introducing guesswork. What made the difference? The bottom thickness of the cookers ranged from 4.64 millimeters to 7.24 millimeters. The top two performers were the thickest, both more than 7 millimeters thick. These cookers' wide, thick bottoms retained heat well, resulting in quickly reaching pressure, followed by steady, hands-off cooking.

In pressure-cooker recipes, cooking times begin only after you reach the desired pressure, which is indicated with a pop-up stick or button on the cooker. Maddeningly, some manufacturers set these indicators deep in a hole, making us lean over the cooker to see them, while others were confusing to interpret. The best models had pressure indicators that were brightly colored, prominently raised, and easy to read at a glance from several feet away.

Getting Steamed
Pressure cookers always require a minimal amount of liquid in order to generate the steam that cooks the food. As the cookers heat up, valves in their lids generally release a trickle of steam right until the moment they come to pressure, but a few continued venting lightly throughout cooking. Cookers that allow less evaporation are less prone to scorch during cooking from loss of liquid. Though evaporation loss didn't affect the final quality of the particular dishes we tested, it can be an issue in recipes that call for only a small amount of liquid. Therefore, we gave points to

models with little evaporative loss. When we heated 32 ounces of water for an hour at high pressure, the average loss was just more than 2 ounces. But one model lost 5.6 ounces—more than ½ cup of water, or 17.5 percent of the total. Many of our preferred models, on the other hand, evaporated only 0.8 ounce.

Finally, we measured the temperature reached by each cooker at high pressure—after all, temperature correlates directly with pressure. "High pressure" for a pressure cooker is considered to be 15 pounds per square inch (psi) above atmospheric pressure, which is reached when the liquid in the cooker is boiling at 250 degrees. The majority of pressure-cooker recipes call for this standard. But most of these cookers never achieved that temperature. We boiled water for 30 minutes at high pressure with each model and measured the internal temperature. We found that our three top-performing cookers reached or came closest to 250 degrees, but as we went down the lineup, cookers' top temperatures steadily declined: The lowest reached only 230 degrees, which is 6 psi. (The bottom-ranked cooker was the exception—it failed on other factors.) It was no great mystery, then, why we'd found the cooking results less satisfying in our bottom-ranking models. Food wasn't fully cooked at the designated time in these pots, forcing us to close

PRESSURE-COOKER RECIPES
These recipes from our forthcoming book, *Pressure Cooker Magic* (available in February) are FREE for 4 months at CooksIllustrated.com/feb13.
Asian-Style Boneless Beef Short Ribs
Chicken Broth
Easy Chicken and Rice
Easy Ziti with Sausage and Peppers
Parmesan Risotto

the lid and repressurize, unsure how much longer to cook. (One took 10 extra minutes, adding almost 50 percent to the original cooking time.)

After testing was complete, we had a clear winner: the Fissler Vitaquick 8½-Quart Pressure Cooker ($279.95). Sturdily built, with a low and wide profile, steady heating, an easily monitored pressure indicator, a convenient automatically locking lid, and low evaporation, this cooker was a pleasure to use and produced perfect finished dishes. It was also the only cooker in our testing to reach 250 degrees, or 15 psi, at high pressure, so it should perform accurately in all standard pressure-cooker recipes. But at that price, it's an investment. Our Best Buy is the Fagor Duo 8-Quart Stainless Steel Pressure Cooker ($109.95), which performed nearly as well at a fraction of the price. It is similar in shape and size to our winner, and while it's not as expensively constructed (it is lighter and feels more "economy" than the Fissler) and its peak temperature under pressure fell slightly short of the 250-degree target, its cooking results were very good. Above all, it's easy to operate, even if you're new to pressure cooking.

TESTING PRESSURE COOKERS

We tested eight stovetop pressure cookers. They are listed in order of preference. All were purchased online. Sources for the top models appear on page 32.

WEIGHT We measured the total weight of each cooker with its lid.

BOTTOM THICKNESS We measured the thickness of the bottoms of the cooking pots. Thicker bottoms generally held more heat for steadier cooking under pressure.

COOKING SURFACE DIAMETER We measured inside across the bottom, indicating actual space for cooking.

HIGHEST TEMPERATURE We measured the temperature inside the cooker under high pressure for 30 minutes and noted the peak temperature reached. Because temperature is directly related to pressure, this indicates the pounds per square inch (psi) of pressure generated by each cooker. Since recipes calling for "high pressure" are designed to cook at 15 psi, which is achieved at 250 degrees, pots that could reach 250 degrees were rated higher.

COOKING We prepared our pressure-cooker recipes for risotto, Boston baked beans, chicken stock, a meaty tomato sauce with pork, and beef stew, rating the dishes' tastes and textures and the cookers' steadiness of heating and evenness of browning (which we also checked by making crêpes).

EASE OF USE We evaluated shape, size, weight, and handle comfort; the design of locking mechanisms, pressure indicators, and steam-release mechanisms; cleanup; and other features that enhance user-friendliness.

EVAPORATION LOSS We added 2 pounds of water to each cooker, weighed the whole cooker with water inside, and boiled it at high pressure for 1 hour, checking the weight at 20, 40, and 60 minutes to determine the amount of water that had evaporated. Cookers with lower evaporation levels rated higher.

	CRITERIA		TESTERS' COMMENTS
HIGHLY RECOMMENDED			
FISSLER Vitaquick 8½-Quart Pressure Cooker Model: 600 700 08 079 Price: $279.95 **Weight:** 8.95 lb Bottom Thickness: 7.24 mm Cooking Surface Diameter: 9 in Highest Temperature: 253 degrees	Cooking Ease of Use Evaporation Loss	★★★ ★★★ ★★★ (0.8 oz)	Solidly constructed, with a low, wide profile that made browning food easy, this well-engineered cooker has an automatic lock and an easy-to-monitor pressure valve. The only cooker to reach 250 degrees at high pressure, it cooked food to perfection in the time range suggested by the recipes.
FAGOR Duo 8-Quart Stainless Steel Pressure Cooker Model: 918060787 Price: $109.95 **Weight:** 6.85 lb Bottom Thickness: 7.15 mm Cooking Surface Diameter: 9 in Highest Temperature: 246 degrees *BEST BUY*	Cooking Ease of Use Evaporation Loss	★★★ ★★★ ★★★ (0.8 oz)	Performing much like our winner at a fraction of the price (though lighter and less smooth to latch), this cooker has low sides and a broad cooking surface; its pressure indicator and dial are easy to monitor. Falling just short of the 250-degree target, it performs well nonetheless.
RECOMMENDED			
PRESTO 8-Quart Stainless Steel Pressure Cooker Model: 01370 Price: $64.54 **Weight:** 6.2 lb Bottom Thickness: 4.76 mm Cooking Surface Diameter: 8½ in Highest Temperature: 249 degrees	Cooking Ease of Use Evaporation Loss	★★½ ★★ ★★★ (0.8 oz)	The lowest-priced cooker in our lineup, this flimsier model has a hard-to-monitor recessed pressure indicator and bulging sides that encourage scorching. Still, its low, wide profile was good for browning and stirring; it cooked meats and beans well. This model has no low-pressure setting, the usual temperature for cooking grains.
TRAMONTINA 8-Quart Heavy-Duty Pressure Cooker Model: 80130500 Price: $99.95 **Weight:** 6.7 lb Bottom Thickness: 5.19 mm Cooking Surface Diameter: 7¾ in Highest Temperature: 243 degrees	Cooking Ease of Use Evaporation Loss	★★½ ★★ ★★ (2.4 oz)	A narrower cooking surface forced us to brown meat in more batches, but the red pressure indicator was simple to monitor and its controls are straightforward. The cooker didn't reach 250 degrees, so we wound up with slightly too-firm beans, beef, and risotto at the end of the cooking time.
RECOMMENDED WITH RESERVATIONS			
KUHN RIKON Duromatic 8½-Quart Stockpot Pressure Cooker Model: KU3044 Price: $179.99 **Weight:** 6.25 lb Bottom Thickness: 7.09 mm Cooking Surface Diameter: 8¼ in Highest Temperature: 240 degrees	Cooking Ease of Use Evaporation Loss	★★ ★★ ★ (5.6 oz)	This cooker's small disk bottom caused scorching and forced us to keep flames low, delaying reaching pressure. It is deeper and narrower than we prefer. The pressure indicator was easy to monitor, though the pressure often dipped, forcing us to hover to adjust the temperature. That said, this model produced tender beans and stew.
FAGOR Futuro 6-Quart Pressure Cooker Model: 918013142 Price: $95.73 **Weight:** 6.1 lb Bottom Thickness: 4.64 mm Cooking Surface Diameter: 6⅛ in Highest Temperature: 238 degrees	Cooking Ease of Use Evaporation Loss	★½ ★ ★★½ (1.6 oz)	While this pot's design was light and maneuverable, with a low, wide shape, its 6-quart capacity (the biggest size available) was a drawback. Bulging sides hang over the disk bottom, leading to scorching. Beans and beef weren't properly tender at the end of the cooking time.
NOT RECOMMENDED			
MAGEFESA Practika Plus Stainless Steel 8-Quart Super Fast Pressure Cooker Model: 01OPPRAPL75 Price: $77.84 **Weight:** 6.55 lb Bottom Thickness: 6.19 mm Cooking Surface Diameter: 7½ in Highest Temperature: 230 degrees	Cooking Ease of Use Evaporation Loss	★½ ★ ★★ (2.4 oz)	With a tall, moderately narrow pot that overhangs its even narrower disk bottom and a hard-to-interpret, recessed pressure indicator, this model created extra work. Its valves made odd noises; it sometimes struggled to retain pressure and took longer than other cookers to make tender beef stew and beans.
WMF Perfect Plus 8½-Quart Pressure Cooker Model: 0793149300 Price: $246.99 **Weight:** 7.95 lb Bottom Thickness: 5.38 mm Cooking Surface Diameter: 7½ in Highest Temperature: 247 degrees	Cooking Ease of Use Evaporation Loss	★½ ½ ★★½ (1.6 oz)	While solidly built, this cooker had a tall, narrow shape that made more work, as did its fussy extra valve. One sample stopped working properly halfway through testing. While the food wasn't bad, it was not worth the effort. For the price, this cooker should be perfect.

The Best Supermarket Hummus

This creamy chickpea spread has gone from health food obscurity to the No. 1 refrigerated dip. But some brands definitely aren't worth a swipe.

⇒ BY AMY GRAVES ⇐

With just five ingredients—chickpeas, tahini, garlic, olive oil, and lemon juice—plus a smattering of spices, hummus couldn't be easier to make at home. But that doesn't mean we can resist the convenience of the store-bought stuff, especially now that it's sold everywhere. Fifteen years ago, a handful of companies shared the $5 million U.S. market for hummus. Today hummus dominates the category known as refrigerated spreads, which raked in more than $430 million in retail sales last year. Brands can be found coast to coast, even at the 7-Eleven—a trend no doubt fueled by the fact that hummus is something you can feel good about eating. It's a protein-rich food far lower in fat than the typical cream-based dip.

As for supermarket shelves, they are jammed with an ever-expanding menu of "hummus and" riffs: sun-dried tomatoes, jalapeños and cilantro, roasted garlic and chives—there's even guacamole hummus. Flavor options aside, the explosion in brands alone makes it harder to know which one to buy. The ideal spread is appealingly smooth and creamy, with the fresh, clean flavor of buttery chickpeas in balance with the earthy toasted-sesame taste of tahini, set off by a lemon-garlic bite. But some store-bought hummus doesn't even come close, with funky off-flavors and stodgy, grainy consistency.

To find the best supermarket version, we rounded up eight nationally available samples of plain hummus (no flavor variations). Along with the usual refrigerated concoctions in party-size plastic tubs, we found a shelf-stable hummus that uses no oil, a soy-chickpea-blend hummus, and a box mix that has you stirring in hot water and olive oil. We included them all, setting them before 21 staff members who sampled them with warm pita in two blind tastings.

Our findings confirmed that many spreads simply aren't worth buying—in fact, five of the eight products we tasted didn't earn our recommendation at all. But the good news is that a few hit the mark with nutty, earthy flavor and a wonderfully thick, creamy texture.

Ancient Origins

All hummus starts with the chickpea, the creamy yellow seed of a legume pod first cultivated thousands of years ago. The ancient Romans bought roasted chickpeas from street stalls. One of the earliest recipes for *hummus bi tahina* (chickpeas with tahini) appeared in a 13th-century Egyptian cookbook. Today chickpeas are the most consumed legume in the world, and hummus is a staple in the Middle East, where hummus shops are as common as pizza parlors in this country. Heated debate can erupt over whose hummus is best, and exact recipes are carefully guarded secrets.

As we scooped our way through the hummus brands in our lineup, our first realization was that some of them didn't taste much like hummus. The outliers were easiest to dismiss. One, which relies on soybeans in addition to chickpeas, was clearly not what we had in mind for superior store-bought hummus: It had "odd soy sauce" flavors that lingered. A shelf-stable product that uses no oil had a "runny" texture "reminiscent of baby food" and tasted more of mustard than of sesame. As for the box mix, prepared with olive oil and hot water per the package instructions, it had "an odd wheaty flavor" and a "sandy," "dry" texture.

But nothing seemed to account for our disappointment in products that, on their labels, listed the same ingredients as the ones that won us over. One sample was undermined by "random grains of chunky chickpeas." Another tasted "like a sandwich spread" instead of like hummus. Most of the losers tasted lean in comparison with the products that passed muster, in which tasters found the "earthy," "rich" flavors they were looking for, along with "smooth" textures that ranged agreeably from "super-soft and silky" to "hearty but not dense." What was the top of our lineup doing that the bottom wasn't?

Hummus Humongous

According to industry experts, the process for making hummus is pretty much the same from brand to brand. It starts with opening and inspecting enormous 2,000-pound bags of the legumes, which are emptied onto long conveyor belts that shake twigs and dirt off the beans. Then the beans soak in huge vats before cooking, which softens them before they are ground and mixed with tahini and oil. Next, the mixture flows into huge mixer-like bowls fitted with paddles, and the salt, garlic, and spices go in. This blending/pureeing step varies depending on whether the hummus maker wants the texture to be chunky with unpulverized bits of chickpea or completely smooth. Hummus makers can dispense with whole-chickpea processing by using preground chickpeas or chickpea flour—the obvious downfall of the product we faulted for having a gritty texture.

Brands can also prolong product shelf life by using preservatives or by pasteurizing the finished hummus to 180 degrees before packaging. Was this a flavor factor? Not that we could see, since our two top products did one or the other, and the preservative used, potassium sorbate, imparted no off-flavors. In fact, the product that uses this preservative rated highest with tasters for its "very nutty and fresh" flavor. So what, exactly, was the key to this brand's success? We were stumped, since none of the hummus companies were willing to tell us what proportion of tahini, chickpeas, or other ingredients they use. So we sent all of our samples to an independent laboratory for an analysis of the fat, sodium, protein, and moisture levels of each product. (Labels include some of these percentages, but they aren't exact.) Finally we had our answer: It turned out that our favorite hummus contains the least moisture and the highest combined level of fat and protein—including almost twice the fat of bottom-ranking products. These least-favorite products also tended to have the highest sodium content—presumably to make up for their lack of flavorful fat.

The source of all that richness? Tahini, the second

What We Want in Hummus

With its simple ingredient list, you'd think that producing great hummus would be a snap. Apparently not: The majority of the brands we tasted were plagued with off-flavors, subpar textures, or both. Here are the hard-to-find qualities we were after:

FRESH, CLEAN FLAVOR
Our favorites kept things simple, showcasing a perfect balance of the primary ingredients: ripe, buttery chickpeas, nutty sesame tahini, fruity olive oil, spicy garlic, and tart lemon juice.

SMOOTH, CREAMY CONSISTENCY
The best brands of hummus boasted a thick, creamy, scoopable texture—not a watery or grainy one.

TASTING HUMMUS

In two blind tastings, 21 *Cook's Illustrated* staff members tasted eight plain hummus samples from a list of top-selling national brands compiled by the Chicago-based market research firm SymphonyIRI Group. We sampled the hummus on wedges of plain, warm pita and rated it on flavor, texture, and the presence of off-flavors. We also sent the hummus to an independent laboratory to determine fat, sodium, protein, and moisture levels. Results were averaged, and the hummus products appear below in order of preference. All hummus was purchased at Boston-area supermarkets.

RECOMMENDED

SABRA Classic Hummus

Price: $4.49 for 10 oz (45 cents per oz)
Fat: 18.8%
Sodium: 420 mg in 100 g
Protein: 7.4%
Water/Moisture: 55.4%
Comments: This "hearty but not dense" hummus had a "very clean flavor of tahini" that was also "earthy," and had tasters praising it as "tahini heaven." Its richness made it taste "like good homemade: real, buttery, almost sweet." One taster confessed, "I'd eat this with a spoon."

CEDAR'S All Natural Hommus, Classic Original

Price: $3.49 for 8 oz (44 cents per oz)
Fat: 12.1%
Sodium: 370 mg in 100 g
Protein: 6.8%
Water/Moisture: 67.2%
Comments: This less tahini-forward, "lemony" hummus had a "super-soft and silky," "smooth" texture. With its high degree of moisture, it struck some tasters as "watered down" and "lacking substance." But most found it "good all around." "Now this is a hummus I can get with," one taster raved.

TRIBE Classic Hummus

Price: $3.49 for 8 oz (44 cents per oz)
Fat: 15.4%
Sodium: 430 mg in 100 g
Protein: 7%
Water/Moisture: 59.9%
Comments: "Creamy," with a "thick and smooth," "very likable texture," this "clean-tasting" hummus had "deep savory notes." A few tasters acknowledged its "strong tahini flavor," which was "almost like peanut butter." For some, it was overload: "Not to be Goldi-hummus, but this has too much tahini."

NOT RECOMMENDED

ATHENOS Original Hummus

Price: $3.75 for 7 oz (54 cents per oz)
Fat: 8.9%
Sodium: 580 mg in 100 g
Protein: 6.3%
Water/Moisture: 65.2%
Comments: "Tastes like taco night," and not in a good way, with "too much cumin." Tasters also complained that it was "too tangy." Its "creamy" texture was undermined by "random grains of chunky chickpeas." For others it was "a touch bitter."

NOT RECOMMENDED CONTINUED

WILD GARDEN Traditional Hummus Dip

Price: $1.90 for 1.76-oz Tetra Pack ($1.08 per oz)
Fat: 7.4%
Sodium: 580 mg in 100 g
Protein: 5.4%
Water/Moisture: 71.3%
Comments: With the highest amount of water and the lowest amount of protein and fat among the products in our lineup, this shelf-stable hummus was "like mustard," with a "runny" texture "reminiscent of baby food." Some tasters found its "citrusy," "garlicky" flavors "almost abrasive."

FANTASTIC WORLD FOODS Original Hummus

Price: $3.65 for 12 oz prepared from 6-oz box (30 cents per oz)
Fat: 10.4%
Sodium: 410 mg in 100 g
Protein: 6.6%
Water/Moisture: 64.1%
Comments: Reconstituted from chickpea flour and dried tahini and seasonings, this box mix hummus failed mainly on the basis of its "dry" and "sandy" texture. It was also "bland" and "stale," with "lots of raw spice in there," and most of us "could barely taste any tahini."

ATHENOS Greek-Style Hummus

Price: $3.75 for 7 oz (54 cents per oz)
Fat: 10.2%
Sodium: 490 mg in 100 g
Protein: 5.7%
Water/Moisture: 67.1%
Comments: If this was hummus, some tasters didn't believe it. With "very little chickpea except in the finish," it "tastes like sandwich spread" or "like an Italian seasoning packet." Several tasters found it "sour," and a few faulted it for being "quite salty."

NASOYA Classic Original Super Hummus

Price: $2.99 for 10 oz (30 cents per oz)
Fat: 10.1%
Sodium: 350 mg in 100 g
Protein: 12.9%
Water/Moisture: 65.7%
Comments: With a "very creamy," "mousselike" texture, this soybean-chickpea hummus had "maple-like undertones." No wonder: It was the only product in our lineup that lists sugar in its ingredients. Though it was high in protein, the soybeans made this hybrid hummus taste strange; some tasters speculated that it was "fermented."

---

key ingredient in hummus. Made from hulled, roasted sesame seeds crushed into a thick paste, its flavor can range from milky and mild to overroasted and bitter. Tahini has 20 percent protein by weight (compared with 23 percent for chickpeas) as well as most of the fat found in hummus. Both translate into fuller, richer flavor and less taste-diluting moisture. No wonder tasters called their favorite product "tahini heaven."

Reviewing tasters' responses again, we began to see that our winning hummus had another quality beyond all that tahini-delivered protein and richness. Tasters raved about a "very clean" and "earthy"

flavor that was also "well-rounded." Was chickpea quality a deciding factor? Although he declined to name the companies, George Vandemark, a research geneticist at Washington State University and a chickpea expert, told us that large-scale hummus makers sometimes include green, unripened beans to keep down costs. "It is a very price-sensitive business," Vandemark said.

The maker of our winning product, Sabra Classic Hummus, buys all of its chickpeas from a cooperative of U.S. farmers that supplies the company with only fully mature beans, according to Sabra's head chef, MaryDawn Wright. "Harvest time is very

critical," she said. "You have to have all the sugars and starches developed." Immature chickpeas, she added, "have less of a rich, sweet, earthy note and more of a green bean note. That's what makes [mature] chickpeas so wonderful. They are the one bean with a real *umami* characteristic."

Whether from just the right amount of tahini or the ripest chickpeas available, Sabra Classic Hummus brought the most flavor to the table, winning both of our tastings easily. Its texture was "hearty but not dense," and its "earthy" and "very clean flavor" was the closest we came to a stand-in for a homemade spread.

Foolproof Pie Dough, Revisited

In our Foolproof Pie Dough (September/October 2010), we swap some of the water with vodka to produce dough that bakes up tender and flaky. Because alcohol doesn't contribute to the development of gluten (the protein network that makes dough tough), we can add enough of it to create dough that's unusually soft and malleable and that can be rolled out without the risk of overworking it. (The vodka then burns off in the oven, leaving no trace of alcohol flavor.) This super-malleable dough requires more flour than usual on your work surface; in the past, we suggested using up to ¼ cup. But we wish to revise our language. Not only can you use that much flour, but indeed you should—the full ¼ cup of flour is key to preventing the moist, soft dough from sticking to the counter as well as to providing structure in the final baked crust. –D.S.

DON'T SKIMP ON FLOUR
When rolling out our soft Foolproof Pie Dough, a full
¼ cup of flour is necessary to prevent sticking.

Got Ghee?

The clarified butter known as ghee is indispensable in Indian cooking, but it's also a handy ingredient to have around for other uses. Ghee is made by slowly simmering butter until all of its moisture has evaporated and its milk solids begin to brown. These solids are then strained out, and the remaining pure butterfat has a nutty flavor and aroma and an ultrahigh smoke point (485 degrees). It can be used as a slightly richer, more buttery substitute in any recipe that calls for clarified butter (such as baklava) and can even be used for high-heat applications—such as frying and making popcorn—in which regular butter (with a smoke point of 250 to 300 degrees) would burn. Another benefit: Its pure state means that unlike regular butter or simple clarified butter (which contains water that contributes to rancidity), it doesn't have to be refrigerated, and it will keep for at least three months. Traditionally ghee is made on the stovetop, but we like this hands-off oven method. –A.J.

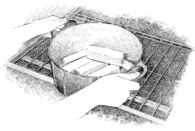 

Place 1 to 2 pounds unsalted butter in Dutch oven and cook, uncovered, on lower-middle rack of 250-degree oven for 2 to 3 hours, or until all water evaporates and solids are golden brown.

Let cool slightly and strain ghee through fine-mesh sieve lined with cheesecloth. Pour into clean glass jar, let cool completely, and seal. Ghee can be kept, sealed, in cool, dark place for up to 3 months or refrigerated for up to 1 year.

For Creamy Custards, Go Stir Crazy

While developing our recipe for Best Butterscotch Pudding (page 19), we noticed that some batches turned out slightly grainy, while others were silky smooth. The problem, we were surprised to learn, wasn't undissolved cornstarch: It was the butter. Once the pudding cooled and the fat solidified, any bits that hadn't been thoroughly broken down came across as grainy on the tongue. Vigorously whisking the pudding—or any custard with a generous amount of butter—breaks down the fat into tiny droplets that are too small to detect once the mixture cools. (It's the same principle as emulsifying a vinaigrette: Thoroughly whisking in the oil ensures that the fat breaks down into tiny droplets that don't "break" the dressing.) –D.S.

SCIENCE Blooming in Oil for Flavor

We've long advocated "blooming" spices and certain herbs in oil or fat before adding liquid to the pot, which our tastebuds tell us extracts more of their flavors. But we wondered if we could get at a more objective assessment of blooming's impact.

EXPERIMENT We steeped 50 grams of crushed red pepper flakes in 100 grams of canola oil and another batch in 100 grams of water, holding both liquids at a constant 200 degrees and steeping for 20 minutes. We then strained out the pepper flakes and sent the oil and water to a lab to test for capsaicin (the compound responsible for a chile pepper's heat). We repeated the experiment with thyme and sent the oil and water samples to the lab to test for its main flavor compound, thymol.

FULLY BLOOMED
Spices and herbs bloomed in oil can
have 10 times more flavor.

RESULTS The pepper-infused oil had a stronger flavor, with more than double the amount of heat-producing capsaicin, than the pepper-infused water. The results for thyme were even more dramatic: The herb-infused oil contained 10 times the amount of thymol as the herb-infused water.

EXPLANATION The main flavor compounds in many spices and some herbs (including thyme, rosemary, lavender, sage, savory, and bay leaves) are largely fat-soluble. So by briefly heating spices (or herbs) in fat before the liquid goes into the pot, you can extract far more flavor than you could by simply simmering these ingredients in water. –D.S.

Sweet Solution to Brown Fruit

Most people toss cut apples and other fruits prone to browning in lemon juice. But here's another way: Toss them in honey water. We diluted 2 tablespoons of honey with 1 cup of water, added one apple cut into slices, and left it to soak. Compared with untreated apple slices, which began to brown after a few minutes, the apples in honey water were kept bright for more than 24 hours. This is because browning is caused by the action of an enzyme known as polyphenol oxidase, and a peptide compound found in honey deactivates this enzyme just as the acid in lemon juice does. Even better: We found that the fruit needed only a 30-second dunk in the same solution to inhibit browning for a solid 8 hours. (Incidentally, honey seems to work just as well at stopping browning in vegetables such as potatoes.) –A.J.

Taking the Bite out of Garlic

Many cooks like to temper the harsh bite of raw garlic before adding it to foods like pesto, hummus, and salad dressing—but there's no end to the suggestions for how to do that. We tested four methods: blanching whole cloves in milk for 5 minutes, blanching them in water for 5 minutes, microwaving the cloves until warmed through, and toasting them in their skins in a dry skillet until lightly browned.

Both forms of blanching worked equally well, as did microwaving. Toasting was the least effective in mellowing out garlic's taste. Here's why: Garlic's sharpness is caused by a sulfur-containing molecule called allicin. Allicin is produced through an enzymatic reaction by the enzyme alliinase, only after the cell walls of the garlic are damaged during cutting or chopping. To deactivate alliinase, you must raise the clove's temperature to 140 degrees or above—which both microwaving and blanching accomplished (the type of liquid used is irrelevant). With light toasting, only the outer layers of the cloves got sufficiently hot to turn alliinase inert.

For simplicity's sake, we prefer heating garlic cloves in the microwave to blanching them. Microwave the cloves in a small bowl for 2 to 3 minutes, or until warm to the touch but not cooked. –A.J.

Turning Bread into *Boules*

French bakers achieve the symmetrical round loaves of bread known as *boules* by transferring the dough to shallow, linen-lined woven baskets known as *bannetons* or *brotforms* for the last rising step before baking. The cloth-lined basket serves two functions: It retains the round shape of the loaf as it proofs, and its breathable construction wicks away moisture from the dough's surface, for a crisper, browner crust. While an ordinary bowl isn't a suitable substitute, you can still create an improvised banneton at home: Line a metal or plastic colander with a linen dish towel (linen is preferable to cotton, since cotton has microscopic fibers that can stick to dough) and dust it liberally with flour. Place the formed loaf upside down in the colander, fold the cloth loosely over it, and place the colander (which allows in more air than a true banneton) in a loose plastic bag to protect the dough from drafts. The method will produce a beautifully shaped boule that would be impossible to replicate if you simply left the dough to proof on its own. –A.J.

AUTHENTIC BANNETON
This French basket retains the round shape of a loaf during proofing.

OUR FACSIMILE
A dish towel and a colander work just fine as a stand-in for the real thing.

Taking Stock: Pot versus Pressure Cooker

Obviously, cooking stock in a pressure cooker is faster than cooking it in a regular pot, but we wondered if this method would change the flavor, too. To find out, we made a simple chicken stock by simmering 3 pounds of chicken wings (which are both flavorful and loaded with collagen) in 3 quarts of water in a large Dutch oven on the stovetop for 2 hours. We made an identical batch of stock in a pressure cooker, cooking it for 1½ hours.

To our surprise, both the color and the flavor of the stocks were noticeably different from each other. The pressure-cooked broth was darker, with a more complex,

PRESSURE POINT
Pressure-cooked stocks taste more complex than those made in a pot.

meaty flavor, while the broth prepared in a Dutch oven had a cleaner, purer chicken taste. What gives? It turns out that the high temperature inside a pressure cooker does more than just speed up the cooking time. It also promotes more extraction of flavor compounds from the skin and bones while encouraging the breakdown of proteins into peptides, which produce rich meatiness. Without these additional flavors, the broth cooked in a Dutch oven tasted more like chicken but was less meaty-tasting overall.

Do we have a favorite? Not exactly. When clean chicken flavor is the goal—as in a simple chicken soup—we might prefer the stock cooked in the Dutch oven. But for adding meaty richness to stews and braises, pressure-cooked chicken stock is an asset. –D.S.

When to Salt Burgers

For the ideal tender, open texture in beef or turkey burgers, minimal handling of the ground meat and loosely packing it into patties are key. But when—and where—you salt the meat before cooking is equally important.

We seasoned ground beef three ways: In the first batch, we salted the meat before shaping the patties so that some of the salt got worked into the interior. In the second batch, we formed the patties and salted them on the outside 30 minutes before cooking. In the third batch, we salted the patties just before cooking. We found that the burgers salted before being formed into patties had a firm, almost snappy texture that was closer to sausage than any of us would have liked. (The salt works quickly; it makes a difference even if a burger sits for only a minute or two before cooking.) The patties that rested for 30 minutes after being salted on the outside had a tender interior but a dry and springy exterior, where the salt came into contact with the meat. Only the burgers that were seasoned on the outside and at the very last minute had the texture we liked.

What's going on? Salt removes water from and dissolves some of the meat proteins, causing them to bind the insoluble proteins together—something good for the springy bite to sausages, not for a tender burger. So wait to salt your burgers until just before they hit the pan or grill. –A.J.

Immersion Course

Creating a perfectly emulsified salad dressing by slowly whisking the oil into the vinegar isn't difficult, but it is tedious. Here's a way to shortcut the process: Use your immersion blender and a tall narrow container; these allow you to add all the oil at once and still create a stable emulsification. Thanks to the tight confines of the container, as you pull up the blender, the vortex created by the spinning blades will pull down the oil a little at a time, creating a creamy emulsification in seconds. This method works equally well for emulsifying mayonnaise. –A.J.

1. Add solids and vinegar to cup; stir. Pour in all of oil.

2. Place blender at bottom of cup. Blend on lowest speed.

3. Gradually increase speed to medium, slowly pulling blender to top until dressing is emulsified.

≋ BY AMY GRAVES & LISA McMANUS ≋

NEW Cheese Storage Wraps

Keeping cheese fresh in the refrigerator is tricky. As cheese releases moisture, tight wrappings encourage mold; loose ones let it dry out and harden. But Formaticum uses a two-ply material—wax-coated paper lined with thin, porous polyethylene plastic—in both its Cheese Paper ($9 for 15 sheets with stickers) and Cheese Bags ($9 for 15 bags). This combination (often used by professional cheesemongers) has a salutary effect, allowing moisture to wick off the cheese but not escape entirely. We wrapped cheddar, Brie, and goat cheese in both the paper and the bags, put them in the refrigerator, and checked on them every other day for a month. Both products kept all cheese types pristine for two weeks longer than identical samples that we double-wrapped with parchment and aluminum foil. Slightly more convenient to use than the cheese paper, the bags didn't need to be sealed with stickers: Just fold over the ends a few times to close. –A.G.

IT'S A WRAP
Formaticum Cheese Bags and Cheese Paper keep cheese fresher longer.

UPDATE Food Processors

Recently, we evaluated two new food processors: the Breville Sous Chef Food Processor, 16-Cup ($399.99), and the KitchenAid 13-Cup Food Processor with ExactSlice System ($299.95)—which

KITCHEN HELPER
The Cuisinart food processor does a great job—at a reasonable price.

has been updated since we reviewed (and disliked) it previously. We compared them with our current top-rated Cuisinart Custom 14-Cup Food Processor ($199). After running 12 tests (everything from making a double batch of pizza dough to slicing tomatoes), we believe the Cuisinart is still the best choice. It lacks the dazzling attachments and secondary abilities, such as variable slicing thickness, offered by the other two processors, but it performs basic chopping and slicing tasks extremely well, and

you can change slicing thickness by buying extra disks. The Breville performed solidly and efficiently, but we're not convinced that its extra features are worth an additional $200. Also, the Breville chopped so fast that it was hard not to make a puree when we wanted diced vegetables. As for the KitchenAid, the newest version has improved. The jar lid no longer sticks, the pulse button starts faster (but is still hard to engage), and the chopping is better. But in almost every task, it lagged behind the Cuisinart and the Breville. –L.M.

NEW Wine Chilling Devices

An ice bucket keeps wine cool for the duration of a meal and can even chill a room-temperature bottle. But we found three innovative wine chillers priced from $25 to $50. Could they beat the bucket? The Corkcicle, a cork-capped prefrozen plastic tube inserted in the bottle, kept Chablis that we prechilled in the refrigerator below 50 degrees for only 20 minutes. The Ravi Instant Wine Refresher, a freezer-gel cartridge that fits on the mouth of the bottle, made pouring slow and awkward and lost its cooling ability after only 25 minutes. That left us with the Rabbit Wine Chilling Carafe by Metrokane ($49.95), a glass carafe with a stainless steel insert that holds ice, which kept the wine below 50 degrees for 90 minutes. It was also the only device able to chill a room-temperature bottle, dropping it to 50 degrees in 15 minutes. –A.G.

CHILLING EFFECT
The Rabbit Wine Chilling Carafe keeps white wine properly chilled for 90 minutes.

NEW Eggies

Eggies ($4.99 for six) are plastic, egg-shaped containers for hard-cooking eggs without the shell so you don't have to peel a thing. We cooked eggs according to the manufacturer's instructions, first spritzing all of each Eggie's five parts with vegetable oil spray before partly assembling the tool, breaking in an egg, screwing on the top, and placing it in boiling water. Despite the oil, the eggs stuck after cooking, which had us prying them out with a spoon. We were left with flat-topped eggs pitted by droplets of oil and a boatload of tiny plastic pieces to wash. We'd rather peel a dozen hard-cooked eggs than wrestle with another Eggie. –L.M.

A BAD EGG
The Eggies Hard Boiled Egg System is not worth shelling out for.

For complete testing results for each item, go to CooksIllustrated.com/feb13.

Sources

Prices were current at press time and do not include shipping. Contact companies to confirm information or visit CooksIllustrated.com for updates.

PAGE 13: EGG TOPPER
- Rösle Egg Topper: $22, item #12827, Rösle USA (302-326-4801, rosleusa.com).

PAGE 27: PRESSURE COOKERS
- Fissler Vitaquick 8½-Quart Pressure Cooker: $279.95, item #07-2129, Chef Tools (206-933-0700, cheftools.com).
- Fagor Duo 8-Quart Stainless Steel Pressure Cooker: $109.95, item #300474, Cooking.com (800-663-8810, cooking.com).

PAGE 32: CHEESE STORAGE WRAPS
- Formaticum Cheese Bags: $9, Formaticum (800-830-0317, formaticum.com).
- Formaticum Cheese Paper: $9, Formaticum.

PAGE 32: FOOD PROCESSOR
- Cuisinart Custom 14-Cup Food Processor: $199, item #DFP-14BCN, Cuisinart (800-211-9604, cuisinart.com).

PAGE 32: WINE CHILLING DEVICE
- Metrokane Rabbit Wine Chilling Carafe: $49.95, item #76222, Wine Enthusiast Catalog (800-356-8466, wineenthusiast.com).

U.S. POSTAL SERVICE STATEMENT OF OWNERSHIP, MANAGEMENT AND CIRCULATION

1. Publication Title: *Cook's Illustrated*; 2. Publication No. 1068-2821; 3. Filing Date: 9/15/12; 4. Issue Frequency: Jan/Feb, Mar/Apr, May/Jun, Jul/Aug, Sep/Oct, Nov/Dec; 5. No. of Issues Published Annually: 6; 6. Annual Subscription Price: $35.70; 7. Complete Mailing Address of Known Office of Publication: 17 Station Street, Brookline, MA 02445; 8. Complete Mailing Address of Headquarters or General Business Office of Publisher: 17 Station Street, Brookline, MA 02445; 9. Full Names and Complete Mailing Address of Publisher, Editor and Managing Editor: Publisher: Christopher Kimball, 17 Station Street, Brookline, MA 02445; Editor: Jack Bishop, 17 Station Street, Brookline, MA 02445; Managing Editor: Rebecca Hays, 17 Station Street, Brookline, MA 02445; 10. Owner: Boston Common Press Limited Partnership, Christopher Kimball, 17 Station Street, Brookline, MA 02445; 11. Known Bondholders, Mortgagees, and Other Securities: None; 12. Tax Status: Has Not Changed During Preceding 12 Months; 13. Publication Title: *Cook's Illustrated*; 14. Issue Date for Circulation Data Below: September/October 2012; 15a. Total Number of Copies: 1,027,026 (Sep/Oct 2012: 995,137); b. Paid Circulation: (1) Mailed Outside-County Paid Subscriptions Stated on PS Form 3541: 765,775 (Sep/Oct 2012: 756,057); (2) Mailed In-County Paid Subscriptions Stated on PS Form 3541: 0 (Sep/Oct 2012: 0); (3) Paid Distribution Outside the Mail Including Sales Through Dealers and Carriers, Street Vendors, Counter Sales, and Other Paid Distribution Outside the USPS: 71,723 (Sep/Oct 2012: 64,236); (4) Paid Distribution by Other Classes of Mail Through the USPS: 0 (Sep/Oct 2012: 0); c. Total Paid Distribution: 837,498 (Sep/Oct 2012: 820,293); d. Free or Nominal Rate Distribution: (1) Free or Nominal Rate Outside-County Copies Included on PS Form 3541: 4,043 (Sep/Oct 2012: 3,556 (2) Free or Nominal Rate In-County Copies Included on Form PS 3541: 0 (Sep/Oct 2012: 0); (3) Free or Nominal Rate Copies Mailed at Other Classes Through the USPS: 0 (Sep/Oct 2012: 0); (4) Free or Nominal Rate Distribution Outside the Mail: 515 (Sep/Oct 2012: 515); e. Total Free or Nominal Rate Distribution: 4,558 (Sep/Oct 2012: 4,071); f. Total Distribution: 842,056 (Sep/Oct 2012: 824,364); g. Copies Not Distributed: 184,970 (Sep/Oct 2012: 170,773); h. Total: 1,027,026 (Sep/Oct 2012: 995,137); i. Percent Paid: 99.46% (Sep/Oct 2012: 99.51%).

INDEX
January & February 2013

COOK'S LIVE VIDEOS
Available free for 4 months at
CooksIllustrated.com/feb13

AMERICA'S TEST KITCHEN
Public television's most popular cooking show

Join the millions of home cooks who watch our show, *America's Test Kitchen*, on public television every week. For more information, including recipes and program times, visit AmericasTestKitchenTV.com.

AMERICA'S TEST KITCHEN RADIO

Tune in to our new radio program featuring answers to listener call-in questions, ingredient taste test and equipment review segments, and in-depth reporting on a variety of topics. To listen to episodes, visit AmericasTestKitchen.com/Radio.

NEW! ONLINE COOKING SCHOOL

Learn how to think—and cook—like a pro from real test cooks who work here at America's Test Kitchen. We combine personalized instruction with leading-edge technology to offer an unparalleled learning experience. Try it free at OnlineCookingSchool.com.

COOK'S ILLUSTRATED IS NOW AVAILABLE ON iPAD AND iPHONE!

Download the new *Cook's Illustrated* app for iPad and start a free trial subscription or purchase a single issue. Issues are enhanced with recipe videos, full-color step-by-step slide shows, and expanded reviews and ratings. Go to CooksIllustrated.com/iPad to download our app through iTunes.

Download our free *Cook's Illustrated* app for iPhone featuring a collection of our top recipes, tastings, videos, and useful timer and shopping list features. CooksIllustrated.com members can access all 20 years of recipes, videos, and tastings. Go to CooksIllustrated.com/iPhone.

Follow us on Twitter: twitter.com/TestKitchen
Find us on Facebook: facebook.com/CooksIllustrated

Crispy Orange Beef, 15

Soft-Cooked Eggs, 13

Citrus Salad with Watercress, 10

Best Butterscotch Pudding, 19

Garlicky Roasted Shrimp with Parsley and Anise, 9

Wild Rice and Mushroom Soup, 23

French-Style Chicken and Stuffing in a Pot, 7

Oatmeal Muffins, 21

Pasta all'Amatriciana, 24

PHOTOGRAPHY: CARL TREMBLAY; STYLING: MARIE PIRAINO

Leberwurst

Holsteiner

Gelbwurst

Frankfurters

Landjäger

Weisswurst

Knackwurst

Blutwurst

Debrecziner

GERMAN SAUSAGES

COOK'S
ILLUSTRATED

Better Beef Burgundy
French Classic Streamlined

Fluffy Omelets
Easy and Impressive

Essential Guide
to Knife Care
8 Common Myths Debunked

Spaghetti Carbonara
Dump the Fat; Keep the Flavor

Lemon Chiffon Pie
Ultra Lemon Flavor

Best Everyday Coffee
Are Lighter Roasts Better?

Chicken Parmesan
Crisp Crust, Tender Chicken

Simpler Roast Leg of Lamb
Foolproof Brioche
Testing Drip Coffee Makers

CooksIllustrated.com
$5.95 U.S./$6.95 CANADA

CONTENTS
March & April 2013

Founder and Editor Christopher Kimball
Editorial Director Jack Bishop
Editorial Director, Magazines John Willoughby
Executive Editor Amanda Agee
Test Kitchen Director Erin McMurrer
Managing Editor Rebecca Hays
Senior Editors Keith Dresser
Lisa McManus
Senior Editor, Features Elizabeth Bomze
Associate Editor, Features Molly Birnbaum
Copy Editors Nell Beram
Megan Chromik
Associate Editors Andrea Geary
Amy Graves
Andrew Janjigian
Chris O'Connor
Dan Souza
Test Cook Lan Lam
Assistant Editors Hannah Crowley
Shannon Friedmann Hatch
Taizeth Sierra
Assistant Test Cooks Dan Cellucci
Sara Mayer
Celeste Rogers
Executive Assistant Christine Gordon
Assistant Test Kitchen Director Leah Rovner
Senior Kitchen Assistant Meryl MacCormack
Kitchen Assistants Maria Elena Delgado
Ena Gudiel
Andrew Straaberg Finfrock
Executive Producer Melissa Baldino
Associate Producer Stephanie Stender
Production Assistant Kaitlin Hammond
Contributing Editor Dawn Yanagihara
Consulting Editor Scott Brueggeman
Science Editor Guy Crosby, Ph.D.
Managing Editor, Web Christine Liu
Associate Editors, Web Eric Grzymkowski
Mari Levine
Roger Metcalf
Assistant Editor, Web Jill Fisher
Senior Video Editor Nick Dakoulas

Design Director Amy Klee
Art Director Julie Cote
Deputy Art Director Susan Levin
Associate Art Director Lindsey Timko
Deputy Art Director, Marketing/Web Jennifer Cox
Designer, Marketing/Web Mariah Tarvainen
Production Designer, Marketing/Web Judy Blomquist
Staff Photographer Daniel J. van Ackere
Photo Editor Steve Klise

Vice President, Marketing David Mack
Circulation Director Doug Wicinski
Circulation & Fulfillment Manager Carrie Fethe
Partnership Marketing Manager Pamela Putprush
Marketing Assistant Joyce Liao
Customer Service Manager Jacqueline Valerio
Customer Service Representatives Megan Hamner
Jessica Haskin

Chief Operations Officer David Dinnage
Production Director Guy Rochford
Senior Project Manager Alice Carpenter
Production & Traffic Coordinator Brittany Allen
Workflow & Digital Asset Manager Andrew Mannone
Production & Imaging Specialists Heather Dube
Lauren Pettapiece
Lauren Robbins
Systems Administrators Scott Norwood
Marcus Walser
Business Analyst Wendy Tseng
Web Developers Chris Candelora
Cameron MacKensie
Human Resources Director Adele Shapiro

VP New Media Product Development Barry Kelly

Chief Financial Officer Sharyn Chabot
Director of Sponsorship Sales Anne Traficante
Retail Sales & Marketing Director Emily Logan
Client Services Associate Kate May
Sponsorship Sales Representative Morgan Ryan
Publicity Deborah Broide

PRINTED IN THE USA

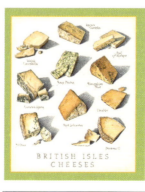

BRITISH ISLES CHEESES STILTON is protected by legislation: It can be made in only three English counties. Similar in flavor to Stilton (a pungent blue cheese), assertive SHROPSHIRE BLUE is made with milk tinted orange with annatto seeds. Nutty-flavored RED LEICESTER and crumbly CHESHIRE are also dyed with the tropical seeds. Produced by mixing sage leaves with the curd, SAGE DERBY has a subtle herbal taste. Rich and complex, KEEN'S is a fine example of British cheddar. Cheddaring refers to a step in cheese making in which the curds are salted and repeatedly cut, stacked, and pressed. MULL OF KINTYRE is a Scottish cheddar that's nutty and sharp. Made with sheep's milk, BERKSWELL is aged in a colander, which gives it a disk shape. CORNISH YARG is wrapped in nettle leaves before being aged, which lends it a faint mushroom flavor. WELSH CAERPHILLY has a fresh taste and crumbly texture.

COVER (Avocados): Robert Papp; BACK COVER (British Isles Cheeses): John Burgoyne

America's Test Kitchen is a very real 2,500-square-foot kitchen located just outside Boston. It is the home of *Cook's Illustrated* and *Cook's Country* magazines and is the workday destination of more than three dozen test cooks, editors, and cookware specialists. Our mission is to test recipes over and over again until we understand how and why they work and until we arrive at the best version. We also test kitchen equipment and supermarket ingredients in search of brands that offer the best value and performance. You can watch us work by tuning in to *America's Test Kitchen* (AmericasTestKitchenTV.com) on public television.

RECIPES THAT WORK®

OUT OF THE ORDINARY

Three days after Christmas, the first winter storm softly blanketed our small Vermont town with 10 inches of fresh powder. Suffering from an early case of cabin fever, Tom and I decided to head out for a day of rabbit hunting, up behind Mike Lourie's dairy farm. We parked Tom's Ford pickup by the snowmobile trail on the abandoned railroad bed; opened the crate to let out Bernadette, Tom's plump 7-year-old beagle; and set out over a small bridge up onto the side hills that we have hunted for a dozen years.

Expectation is the first thing that comes to mind as one starts off on a hunt. I remembered the time that we chased the legendary "ghost rabbit" up and down the mountains and how he outfoxed us at every turn. And the warm, wet day in late fall when we ran more than half a dozen rabbits, Bernadette circling down a side hill, through the swamp, and back up to the hilltop while we watched both her and the rabbit with the satisfaction of a proud parent. And the day that a large "brownie" kept crossing a narrow field, always just out of range, making me feel like Elmer Fudd trying to outsmart Bugs Bunny.

But on this day, there would be no rabbits. Bernadette was having a hard time breasting the windswept snowfall, following my footsteps instead. The rabbits were holed up, well concealed under brambly thickets or in old woodchuck holes. Bernadette was game enough, heading into hedgerows with enthusiasm but emerging with snow-filled snout, sheepish and hangdog. I saw snow-sketched tracks of squirrel and chipmunk but hardly a sign of rabbits, as if they had all headed south for the winter with the geese. Rabbit populations rise and fall in cycles, or so the locals say: something to do with disease or an influx of coyotes or, more likely, simply the ebb and flow of nature.

After a couple of hours of hard going, my expectations dwindled and it became clear that today was not going to offer much excitement, and then disappointment set in. I stopped, wolfed down half of a roast beef sandwich with a gulp of water, and then decided to take the long route around a large two-acre patch of brambles and up to the top of the hill.

It had been cloudy and sharply cold all morning but then a royal-blue pennant of sky emerged above the treetops and floated out triumphantly across the broader horizon. The sun made a shy appearance, snow sparkled, ice crystals glistened, and the distant frosted mountains, still in dark relief, set off the bright white-clapboard village below: a winter diorama. I watched the sky, a quick-change actor of great experience: a gunmetal weight of clouds, a hazy sun spotlighting open fields, a pop of sunlight, and, finally, a wisp of snowflakes and the swift return of a winter countenance. I heard Tom and Bernadette below, so I shadowed their movements, but higher up, to catch a rabbit running uphill if one should appear.

The afternoon lengthened and disappointment faded. I saw frozen, icy milkweed and thistle; a weight of snow on a canopy of thornbush; a small encampment of scalloped deer beds in the snow; and drunken deer track, weaving in and out of the tree line, hunting something good to eat overnight

Christopher Kimball

in the storm. The walk reminded me of a Sunday cocktail hour the prior week in Boston, in the living room of a friend who had suddenly turned ill. We chatted up the little things—the muted football game on TV, a speech on the occasion of a 75th birthday, a child's portrait, the lack of skating ice last winter, and the subtleties of soup making. The room was comfortable and steam-heated, decorated with a child's ladder-back chair; a defiantly joyful Christmas tree; a dimpled, late-middle-aged sofa; the hollow chunk of ice against glass; a lifetime of helter-skelter knickknacks; and a whiff of incense, myrrh perhaps (a hint of ritual purification).

When you step out your back door to hunt, expectation preempts the ordinary nature of most outings. One sits in a tree, in nature's living room, and listens to the conversation or walks through a snowy field, in vain pursuit of quarry. There, in a cozy parlor, or on a cold, wintry landscape in brambled pastures, we harbor hope for the future.

On occasion, however, whether from fate or snowfall, we must set hope adrift and turn back toward familiar shores. We return to the pickup, legs rubbery and worn, faces ruddy from pale winter sun. Or we end our visit with friends, twist mufflers against the cold, and don heavy peacoats in familiar ritual for the December walk home. We will say later that, all in all, it has been a good day, a day for the little things, a day when we took full measure of the ordinary and did not find it wanting.

FOR INQUIRIES, ORDERS, OR MORE INFORMATION

CooksIllustrated.com
At CooksIllustrated.com, you can order books and subscriptions, sign up for our free e-newsletter, or renew your magazine subscription. Join the website and gain access to 20 years of *Cook's Illustrated* recipes, equipment tests, and ingredient tastings, as well as companion videos for every recipe in this issue.

COOKBOOKS
We sell more than 50 cookbooks by the editors of *Cook's Illustrated*, including *The Cook's Illustrated Cookbook* and *The Science of Good Cooking*. To order, visit our bookstore at CooksIllustrated.com.

COOK'S ILLUSTRATED MAGAZINE
Cook's Illustrated magazine (ISSN 1068-2821), number 121, is published bimonthly by Boston Common Press Limited Partnership, 17 Station St., Brookline, MA 02445. Copyright 2013 Boston Common Press Limited Partnership. Periodicals postage paid at Boston, Mass., and additional mailing offices, USPS #012487. Publications Mail Agreement No. 40020778. Return undeliverable Canadian addresses to P.O. Box 875, Station A, Windsor, ON N9A 6P2. POSTMASTER: Send address changes to *Cook's Illustrated*, P.O. Box 6018, Harlan, IA 51593-1518. For subscription and gift subscription orders, subscription inquiries, or change-of-address notices, visit us at AmericasTestKitchen.com/customerservice, call us at 800-526-8442, or write us at *Cook's Illustrated*, P.O. 6018, Harlan, IA 51593-1518.

FOR LIST RENTAL INFORMATION Contact Specialists Marketing Services, Inc., 777 Terrace Ave., 4th Floor, Hasbrouck Heights, NJ 07604; 201-865-5800.
EDITORIAL OFFICE 17 Station St., Brookline, MA 02445; 617-232-1000; fax 617-232-1572. Subscription inquiries, visit AmericasTestKitchen.com/customerservice or call 800-526-8442.
POSTMASTER Send all new orders, subscription inquiries, and change-of-address notices to *Cook's Illustrated*, P.O. Box 6018, Harlan, IA 51593-1518.

NOTES FROM READERS

⇒ BY ANDREA GEARY, ANDREW JANJIGIAN, LAN LAM & CELESTE ROGERS ⇐

Are Vanilla Pods Worth Saving?

I love baking with vanilla beans, but it feels like such a waste to just throw out the spent pods. Is there anything I can do with them?

LUCY TRIFIRO
MADBURY, N.H.

➤Vanilla beans bring a complex flavor to many of our desserts, but good beans are definitely expensive. Since the pod itself contains a significant amount of vanillin—the primary molecule that gives vanilla its distinctive aroma—we wondered if we could use it as a substitute for beans or extract.

We saved our spent pods, dried them on a rack in a very low oven, and then finely ground them in a spice grinder. We tested the "pod powder" in our recipes for sugar cookies and vanilla ice cream, comparing them with the same recipes made with vanilla extract (cookies) or beans (ice cream), using a 1:1 substitution. The dried ground pods definitely had a different flavor profile, with "malty" or "floral" notes not found in the extract or beans—and not especially welcome flavors either. One taster likened the taste to a "vanilla-scented candle." The powder also lent the cookies and the ice cream a tan color the other forms of vanilla did not. Our conclusion? Though we hate discarding the pods, their flavor isn't close enough to extract or to beans to warrant the time and effort it takes to turn them into powder. –A.J.

BAG THE (SPENT) BEANS
Vanilla pods aren't a good substitute for beans or extract.

Toning Down Tomato Sauce

My grandmother used to finish tomato sauce with a pinch of baking soda. Is this trick worth continuing?

ALLISON NEILL
SAN ANTONIO, TEXAS

➤An important factor in achieving great tomato flavor is balancing acidity and sweetness. Too much of either can leave you with a sauce that tastes one-dimensional. Your grandmother likely thought her tomato sauce tasted too tart. Adding baking soda changed the pH of her sauce, making it less acidic. Generally, we balance tomato sauce acidity by adding a bit of sugar. While sugar can't neutralize acidity in the same way that baking soda can, it does change our perception of other tastes.

We made a giant batch of tomato sauce, divided

it into 3-cup samples, and spiked some with either sugar or baking soda. The sample enhanced with just ¼ teaspoon of sugar tasted bright, balanced, and more intense in tomato flavor, while the sample with an equal amount of baking soda was deemed flat and solely sweet. When we scaled back the baking soda to ⅛ teaspoon, tasters found it closer to the sugar-adjusted sauce but still not as complex. We will continue to reach for sugar (add ¼ teaspoon at a time until the desired flavor is reached) to balance our sauces and enhance their complexity. –C.R.

Low-Sugar Pectin Substitute

Your recipes for Fresh Strawberry Pie (May/June 2011) and Raspberry Sorbet (July/August 2012) call for Sure-Jell low-sugar pectin. Will other brands work?

JUDY HOOVER
HAVERHILL, MASS.

➤We use low-sugar pectin in these recipes because it is capable of providing a subtle gel without the large amount of sugar required by regular pectin, and we recommend Sure-Jell for Less or No Sugar Needed Recipes simply because it is the most available brand. But we were curious to see if other brands would measure up.

We found two brands: Ball RealFruit Low or No-Sugar Needed Pectin and Pomona's Universal Pectin. Both are carried at the hardware store with the canning supplies. Like Sure-Jell, the Ball product is a mixture of powdered pectin and dextrose (a filler), along with additives. When we tested it against Sure-Jell using a one-for-one substitution in both the strawberry pie and the sorbet, we found it completely acceptable.

Pomona's couldn't be directly swapped into our recipes. This powder is pure pectin with no dextrose added, so using the amount called for in our recipe would add more pectin than we intended. What's more, its jelling power is activated by a calcium powder that must be added separately in a prescribed amount depending on the type of fruit and the amount of sugar in your recipe. If you want an easy one-for-one substitute for low-sugar Sure-Jell, low-sugar Ball RealFruit is the one to pick. –A.G.

SURE-JELL   BALL   POMONA'S
Sure-Jell and Ball can be used interchangeably,
but Pomona's is tricky to substitute.

Cookie Swap for Crumb Crusts

The last time I made a crumb crust for a pie, I ran out of graham crackers and substituted gingersnaps. The crust looked sturdy as I patted it in the pie plate but slumped during baking. What happened?

LESLIE STARR
HADDAM, CONN.

➤Crumb crusts slump when there is too much fat or sugar in the mixture, either from the cookies or from the added butter and sugar in the recipe. Therefore, we figured the key to finding a graham cracker substitute would be identifying cookies that contain a similar combined weight of fat and sugar relative to the total weight of the cookies—around 35 percent. Still, we rounded up options with varying levels just to be sure. Our lineup included gingersnaps, Lorna Doone shortbread, Nilla Wafers, and animal crackers, all of which we used in our standard graham cracker crust recipe (see page 23).

The numbers didn't lie. Animal crackers, which contain about 39 percent fat and sugar, produced sturdy, even crusts. Meanwhile, crusts made with gingersnaps, Lorna Doones, and Nilla Wafers slid down the sides of the pie plate—no surprise, since the combined fat and sugar content of these cookies is considerably higher: between 45 and 57 percent.

Bottom line: Animal crackers make a fine substitute in graham cracker crust recipes, but for any other option, be sure to use a recipe that's engineered to work with that particular cookie. –L.L.

Oatmeal Overboard

Whenever I make oatmeal in the microwave, it boils over. I've read that putting a pat of butter on the oats will prevent this from happening. Does it work?

JEFFREY ZIEGER
ARLINGTON, MASS.

➤Here's why oatmeal boils over: As the oatmeal cooks, the water boils and bubbles appear. At the same time, the starches in the cereal swell and uncoil to form a mesh. As this mesh thickens, it becomes more difficult for the escaping bubbles from the boiling water to burst through it. Eventually, so many bubbles form that the oatmeal rises up and spills over the sides of the bowl. This problem can also occur when oatmeal is cooked in a pot.

Hypothetically, fat works to prevent boilovers by coating some of the oatmeal starches, weakening the mesh so that air bubbles can escape. That said, we found that we needed a hefty 2½ tablespoons of butter to prevent a boilover in a single serving of oatmeal cooked in the microwave—and 10 tablespoons of butter when we cooked four servings in a pot. Not much of a remedy, in our opinion. Another recommended solution—laying a chopstick across the bowl in the microwave or a wooden spoon across the pot on the stove—didn't work at all.

The best prevention when cooking oatmeal in a pot is what we recommend in our recipes: Stir the oatmeal a few times as it cooks, which breaks up the bubbles. The solution to boilovers in a microwave is even simpler—just use a larger, wider bowl. –L.L.

Coring Parsnips

I've heard that the cores of large parsnips should always be removed and discarded before cooking. Is this step really necessary?

HUAN-HUA CHYE
MADISON, WIS.

➤The core of a parsnip is leathery, but we found a way to lessen its impact in our Roasted Root Vegetables (November/December 2012): cutting the parsnips on the bias into oblong disks before roasting, which shortens their tough center fibers and makes them less noticeable. To find out if the cores should be removed when the parsnips are pureed, we compared cored versus uncored samples in a simple pureed soup. Tasters found the flavor of the cored sample only marginally preferable to the flavor of the uncored batch; some found that the cores contributed a slightly bitter flavor. When it came to texture, however, there was no difference: The cores weren't noticeable in the soup.

The takeaway? For pureed applications, don't bother coring parsnips. If you plan to serve parsnips whole and don't want to cut them on the bias, they're much more pleasant to eat if you remove the tough, chewy cores before cooking. –A.G.

HARD CORE
Tough parsnip cores should be removed before roasting but aren't noticeable in pureed applications.

Fish Sauce, Hold the Fish

Is there a homemade vegetarian substitute for fish sauce?

KATHERINE HIGHSMITH
BELMONT, MASS.

➤Fish sauce is rich in glutamates, tastebud stimulators that give food the meaty, savory flavor known as *umami*. Glutamates are often found in animal proteins, and in the case of fish sauce, they come from fermented fish.

Knowing that seaweed is a potent (and vegetarian) source of glutamates, we optimistically tried subbing a strong salted kelp broth for fish sauce in a Thai dipping sauce. When it failed to contribute

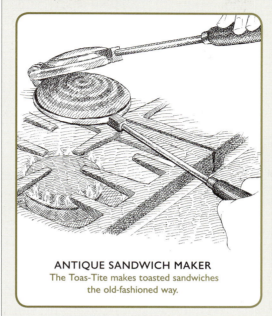
sufficient depth, we turned to another source of savory flavor: nucleotides.

When flavor-boosting nucleotides are paired with glutamates, the perception of umami is significantly increased. Sure enough, a salty broth made with dried shiitake mushrooms (rich in nucleotides) and soy sauce (glutamates) provided just the right meaty punch as a 1:1 substitute for fish sauce. Here's how to make it: In a saucepan, simmer 3 cups of water, ¼ ounce of dried sliced shiitake mushrooms, 3 tablespoons of salt, and 2 tablespoons of soy sauce over medium heat until reduced by half. Strain, cool, and store in the fridge for up to three weeks. –A.G.

Getting the Most out of Saffron

I heard a Spanish chef say that you can intensify saffron's flavor by toasting it in a foil packet. Does that really work?

CAROL WILSON
PORTLAND, ORE.

➤We've found that many spices benefit from toasting before use because heat intensifies their flavor, so we thought it would also work for saffron, although we questioned whether the foil was necessary.

We tried toasting ¼-teaspoon samples of saffron in a hot skillet for 30 seconds, both dry and tightly wrapped in foil. We then made risotto and *aïoli* with both and compared them with samples made with untreated saffron. The outcome? The foil-wrapped saffron had the most flavor, while the dry-toasted saffron had the least.

Our science editor explained how saffron is different from other spices: The molecule primarily responsible for its aroma, safranal, is highly volatile in the presence of both oxygen and heat. But heat doesn't just cause safranal to evaporate; at the same time (and at a slightly faster rate), it converts another compound called picrocrocin into safranal. When saffron is heated in a closed foil packet, where it's protected from exposure to air, its flavor is enhanced—and preserved. Bottom line: Toasting does intensify saffron's flavor—as long as it's kept tightly wrapped during the process. –A.G.

Erratum

In our March/April 2012 issue, we recommended soaking brown rice in room-temperature water for 6 to 24 hours to speed up the cooking. It is important to refrigerate grains during soaking to avoid the potential formation of a toxin that can cause low-level gastrointestinal distress.

SEND US YOUR QUESTIONS We will provide a complimentary one-year subscription for each letter we print. Send your inquiry, name, address, and daytime telephone number to Notes from Readers, *Cook's Illustrated*, P.O. Box 470589, Brookline, MA 02447, or to NotesFromReaders@AmericasTestKitchen.com.

Quick Tips

≥ BY SHANNON FRIEDMANN HATCH ≤

A Cleaner Break

Rather than crack eggs on the edge of a bowl or countertop and risk dripping the raw contents on the work surface, Judy Spanyers of San Antonio, Texas, breaks each egg on a flat rimmed surface, such as a large plate or plastic container lid. It not only offers easy cleanup but also prevents any uncracked eggs from rolling away and holds broken shells before they're discarded.

A Homemade Pasta Dryer

Joan Burns Brown of Emeryville, Calif., frequently makes fresh spaghetti and fettuccine, but finding a spot for drying the long strands can be a challenge. Her solution: Attach a swing-arm dish towel rack to a kitchen wall. The arms don't use up any counter space and fold flat against the wall when not in use.

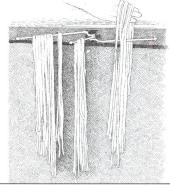

Sog-Free Salad On the Go

Bringing a salad for lunch usually means packing a separate container of dressing, as even the hardiest predressed greens quickly turn soggy. Joanne Kramer of Cleveland, Ill., takes a multilayered approach to fitting everything in one container: She adds the dressing to the bottom of the container; covers it with chopped vegetables, fruit, beans, and cheese; and places the greens on top. To dress the salad, she simply shakes the container.

Apple Armor, Peach Protector

A piece of fruit is a great snack to bring to work, but if it's bruised and mushy by the time it arrives, it loses its appeal. Manda Lo of Albuquerque, N.M., uses a foam drink cozy to shield apples, peaches, and other round, easily damaged fruit from bumps and jostles in her bag during her commute.

Covering Up Leeks

Long vegetables such as leeks and celery often don't fit in produce bags. To remedy this, Emily Hunter of Belmont, Calif., saves empty sandwich bread bags that are long enough to completely contain the stalks.

A Slick Solution for Sticky Dough

Working with high-hydration bread doughs that are extremely wet can be messy, especially when it comes to prying the sticky mass from the mixing bowl or food processor. Brenda Rodman of Springfield, Mass., has found that spraying both sides of a spatula with vegetable oil spray allows her to effortlessly scrape the dough from the container.

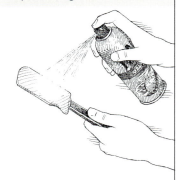

SEND US YOUR TIPS We will provide a complimentary one-year subscription for each tip we print. Send your tip, name, address, and daytime telephone number to Quick Tips, *Cook's Illustrated*, P.O. Box 470589, Brookline, MA 02447, or to QuickTips@AmericasTestKitchen.com.

Keeping Oven Mitts Within Reach

Shaneitra Johnson of Columbus, Ohio, could never find her oven mitt or dish towel when she needed it, so she devised a simple way to keep it in sight: Hang the mitt or towel from a shower curtain hook placed on the oven door's handle.

Digital Shopping List

Instead of writing down the ingredients he needs for a particular magazine or cookbook recipe, Justin Keith of Boston, Mass., has a high-tech solution: He snaps a picture of the ingredient list with his smartphone. He can easily reference it at the market and is sure to grab exactly what he needs.

A Tip for Tenting Plastic Wrap

Covering potluck-bound dishes with plastic wrap protects the food, but it can also pull away the top layer when removed. To preserve the presentation, Tess Bosher of Richmond, Va., uses several pastry tips to prop up the plastic when transporting her dish and removes them prior to serving.

Tidy Breakfast Sandwiches

Metal egg rings confine fried eggs to a circular shape—perfect for breakfast sandwiches served on an English muffin or a bagel. Looking for a no-gadget solution that delivered the same neat results, Elizabeth Fallon of Coventry, R.I., turned to her crisper drawer.

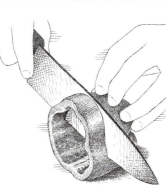 

1. Slice a ring from a cored, seeded bell pepper. (Alternatively, an onion also works well.)

2. Melt a pat of butter in a nonstick skillet and then place a pepper ring in the pan. Crack an egg inside the ring and cook to the desired doneness.

A Better Way to Organize Your Fridge

When a refrigerator is packed with food, it's easy to forget about items that are lingering in the back until they're long past their expiration dates. Megha Satyanarayana of Detroit, Mich., avoids that by placing a rotating lazy Susan on one of her fridge shelves. Now everything is visible (and accessible) with a quick spin.

Putting a Lid on Proofing Dough

Many bread recipes call for the rising dough to be covered with plastic wrap to prevent it from drying out and to protect it from drafts. Greg Lozano-Buhl of Altadena, Calif., found a more economical alternative: a glass pot lid (tight-fitting is best, but any lid that covers the surface is fine). Just as with plastic wrap, he can gauge the dough's progress through the glass.

Cooling Melted Butter More Quickly

When Jen Chandler-Ward of Somerville, Mass., is preparing a recipe that calls for melted butter cooled to room temperature, she speeds up the process with this method: Melt three-quarters of the desired amount of butter on the stovetop or in the microwave. Off heat, whisk the remaining one-quarter cold butter into the melted butter. The unmelted portion will help lower the warm butter's temperature in less time than it takes to heat and then cool the full amount.

The Best Chicken Parmesan

What good does it do to create a crisp crust on this Italian American standard if it turns soggy as soon as it's sauced? We wanted a juicy cutlet that kept its crunch.

⇒ BY ANDREA GEARY ⇐

It's surprising that chicken Parmesan ever became so popular. True, at its best it's a wonderful combination of juicy chicken, crisp crust, and rich cheesy flavor offset by zippy tomato sauce, but the classic cooking method makes it difficult for the home cook to achieve such results with any degree of regularity.

In the traditional recipe, boneless, skinless chicken breasts are pounded until thin and then coated in breading and fried until crispy and golden—so far so good. But then those fully cooked cutlets are blanketed with tomato sauce, mozzarella, and a token dusting of Parmesan and baked in the oven. During baking, the sauce saturates and softens the crust, the chicken overcooks, and the cheeses meld into a thick mass that turns tarpaulin-tough soon after being removed from the oven. After all that work, what should be a delicious indulgence is all too often a soupy, soggy, chewy disappointment.

Contrary to popular belief, chicken Parmesan is a fairly recent American invention, not a sacred recipe with a noble and distinguished old-world provenance. That was good news for me; not beholden to any tradition, I was free to create a version that delivered the best features every time. Only then would it earn a place in my collection of classic recipes.

Fry Away

First, I wondered if I could avoid the usual frying step by coating the chicken with precrisped crumbs and a bit of fat and then baking it—an approach that could potentially simplify the dish and make it a bit lighter at the same time. No such luck. The coating wasn't as crunchy or cohesive as I would have liked, and it sogged out the second it came in contact with the sauce. Shallow frying it would have to be.

Following the usual method, I pounded four boneless, skinless chicken breasts with a rubber mallet until they were ¼ inch thick. Their surface area increased almost threefold, so maneuvering the wide

Spooning just a little sauce on the cutlets before serving (and passing the rest at the table) preserves the crust's crispness.

pieces through the breading treatment (flour, then beaten egg, and then seasoned bread crumbs) was unwieldy, but I consoled myself with the thought that more surface area would mean more crunch.

I shallow-fried the cutlets in batches in several tablespoons of oil until they were crispy, drained them on paper towels, shingled them in a baking dish covered with a simple tomato sauce, and then topped it all with a layer of mozzarella and Parmesan. After 20 minutes in a 375-degree oven, the cheese was bubbly and starting to brown in spots.

This test turned out to be a successful demonstration of everything that can possibly go wrong. The cutlets were overcooked and tough, while the delicate crust that frying had wrought was soft and soggy. And the cheese? It quickly coagulated into a sheet so unyielding that I had difficulty getting my knife through it.

Cutting-Edge Cutlets

I flirted with the idea of subbing chicken thighs for the usual breasts, thinking that they would stay

moister, but I tried it and the flavor was all wrong. Chicken Parmesan relies on the clean, neutral flavor of white meat to balance the fried coating, zesty sauce, and creamy cheese—the slight gaminess of dark meat just didn't work. Breasts it would be, but I'd have to find a way to keep them moist and tender.

I realized that pounding the chicken very thin increased the likelihood of overcooking, but taking the breasts straight from the packaging to the breading didn't work either. The thick breasts didn't cook through in the quick skillet fry, so they had to spend more time in the oven, which gave the crust even more time to get soggy.

Eventually, I settled on slicing two large breasts horizontally and pounding only the thick end of each piece to achieve a consistent ½-inch thickness from end to end. I salted the cutlets for 20 minutes, knowing that the salt would penetrate the surface of the meat and alter the proteins in such a way as to help them hold on to more of their moisture. These two changes gave me the moistest, most tender, most well-seasoned cutlets yet—but the crust still had no chance against the sauce.

Pork to Parm

There are three parts to the crust problem. The first and biggest issue is that bread crumbs are starch, and starch readily absorbs liquid and turns soft. Second, completely covering the crusted cutlets in a very wet sauce exposes the most crust to the most liquid. And third, waiting around for the cheese to melt in the oven gives the sauce plenty of time to saturate and soften the crust.

I turned my attention to the sauce and began by cooking the combination of canned tomatoes, garlic, and seasonings longer so that it thickened—and then brightened it with red pepper flakes and fresh basil. Rather than cover the entire surface of the chicken, I put just a small amount on top of each cutlet, figuring I could pass more at the table. And I radically limited the time the two components spent together. Because the dish was going into the oven only to melt the cheese, I swapped the moderate oven for the fiercer heat of the broiler and took the 20 minutes of "together time" down to 2.

A more reduced sauce and less oven time helped

the situation, but they didn't fix it completely. The breading would still need to be reengineered. And how do you get around the problem that breading is, well, bread? It occurred to me that there was one recipe I'd come across in my research that actually didn't have a breaded coating. Instead, it featured a coating so outlandish that I'd rejected it outright: crushed pork rinds. (Confession: The recipe was from a low-carb cookbook.) But why not give it a shot? After all, since pork rinds are simply rendered pig skin and composed of nothing more than proteins and fat, in theory they wouldn't be prone to the sogginess of a starch-based breading. However, my hopes were quickly dashed. Pulverized pork rinds had a light, fluffy texture, and when used in place of breading, they gave the cutlets an oddly puffy, delicate exterior, nothing like the crunch I sought. And the flavor was noticeably porcine.

But this got me thinking about what else is mostly protein and fat and contains no starch . . . perhaps the most obvious choice of all: Parmesan cheese. Replacing more than half of the bread crumbs with grated Parmesan not only made the crust on my cutlets more moisture-proof but also meant that my chicken Parmesan was starting to earn its surname.

Unfortunately, my cheese problems were not completely solved. The mozzarella continued to mar the dish by forming a leathery layer on top. Recalling a test kitchen recipe for macaroni and cheese in which the solution to a texture problem was using a combination of cheeses, I considered possible creamy, tenderizing companions for the rubbery mozzarella. Cream cheese and heavy cream were too liquid, and cheddar and Monterey Jack (the solution to the mac and cheese) had the wrong flavors. Mozzarella's ideal accomplice turned out to be creamy, nutty fontina. Used in equal parts, the two cheeses provided the perfect combination of authentic Italian flavor and tender, soft texture.

My Chicken Parmesan required a few final adjustments, the first of which concerned the tedious and messy three-step breading procedure. For some recipes each step of the process is vital: The initial coat of flour helps the egg stick, and the egg helps the crumbs stick. Not in this case. I found that I could simply mix a bit of flour into the egg; coat the cutlets with the mixture; and proceed straight to crumbs with cleaner fingers, one less dish to wash, and no decrease in crumb adherence.

The soggy crust problem had lessened, but it was not completely solved—not until I began to play with the order in which the components of the dish were assembled. Instead of putting the cheese combo on top of the sauce, I placed it between the crust and the sauce so it melted to form a cheesy raincoat that protected the cutlet. Sogginess? Gone.

Every bite of my revamped Chicken Parmesan offered crispy, juicy chicken; wispy strands of creamy mozzarella and fontina cheeses; fresh, bright tomato sauce; and nutty Parmesan flavor. Finally it was worth the indulgence.

BEST CHICKEN PARMESAN
SERVES 4

Our preferred brands of crushed tomatoes are Tuttorosso and Muir Glen. This recipe makes enough sauce to top the cutlets as well as four servings of pasta. Serve with pasta and a simple green salad.

Sauce

- 2 tablespoons extra-virgin olive oil
- 2 garlic cloves, minced
  Kosher salt and pepper
- ¼ teaspoon dried oregano
  Pinch red pepper flakes
- 1 (28-ounce) can crushed tomatoes
- ¼ teaspoon sugar
- 2 tablespoons coarsely chopped fresh basil

Chicken

- 2 (6- to 8-ounce) boneless, skinless chicken breasts, trimmed, halved horizontally, and pounded ½ inch thick
- 1 teaspoon kosher salt
- 2 ounces whole-milk mozzarella cheese, shredded (½ cup)
- 2 ounces fontina cheese, shredded (½ cup)
- 1 large egg
- 1 tablespoon all-purpose flour
- 1½ ounces Parmesan cheese, grated (¾ cup)
- ½ cup panko bread crumbs
- ½ teaspoon garlic powder
- ¼ teaspoon dried oregano
- ¼ teaspoon pepper
- ⅓ cup vegetable oil
- ¼ cup torn fresh basil

1. FOR THE SAUCE: Heat 1 tablespoon oil in medium saucepan over medium heat until just shimmering. Add garlic, ¾ teaspoon salt, oregano, and pepper flakes; cook, stirring occasionally, until fragrant, about 30 seconds. Stir in tomatoes and sugar; increase heat to high and bring to simmer. Reduce heat to medium-low and simmer until thickened, about 20 minutes. Off heat, stir in basil and remaining 1 tablespoon oil; season with salt and pepper to taste. Cover and keep warm.

2. FOR THE CHICKEN: Sprinkle each side

CREATING THIN, EVEN CUTLETS

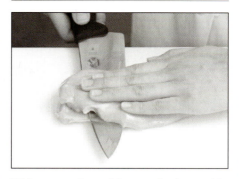

While most recipes call for pounding breasts thin, we prefer to slice them horizontally (freeze them first for 15 minutes to help with slicing), pounding only the fat ends to achieve an even thickness.

of each cutlet with ⅛ teaspoon salt and let stand at room temperature for 20 minutes. Combine mozzarella and fontina in bowl; set aside.

3. Adjust oven rack 4 inches from broiler element and heat broiler. Whisk egg and flour together in shallow dish or pie plate until smooth. Combine Parmesan, panko, garlic powder, oregano, and pepper in second shallow dish or pie plate. Pat chicken dry with paper towels. Working with 1 cutlet at a time, dredge cutlet in egg mixture, allowing excess to drip off. Coat all sides in Parmesan mixture, pressing gently so crumbs adhere. Transfer cutlet to large plate and repeat with remaining cutlets.

4. Heat oil in 10-inch nonstick skillet over medium-high heat until shimmering. Carefully place 2 cutlets in skillet and cook without moving them until bottoms are crispy and deep golden brown, 1½ to 2 minutes. Using tongs, carefully flip cutlets and cook on second side until deep golden brown, 1½ to 2 minutes. Transfer cutlets to paper towel–lined plate and repeat with remaining cutlets.

5. Place cutlets on rimmed baking sheet and sprinkle cheese mixture evenly over cutlets, covering as much surface area as possible. Broil until cheese is melted and beginning to brown, 2 to 4 minutes. Transfer chicken to serving platter and top each cutlet with 2 tablespoons sauce. Sprinkle with basil and serve immediately, passing remaining sauce separately.

When Parm Goes Wrong

Look familiar? Just about every chicken Parmesan recipe we tried suffered from at least one of these common flaws.

PROBLEM Soggy crust
SOLUTION Reduce the sauce to make it less watery and replace some of the moisture-absorbing bread crumbs in the crust with grated Parmesan.

PROBLEM Chewy cheese
SOLUTION Supplement chewy mozzarella (a must for flavor) with creamy, tender fontina.

PROBLEM Dry, chewy chicken
SOLUTION Turn thick breasts into tender cutlets and briefly salt them, which seasons them and helps them retain moisture.

Beef Burgundy Makeover

Most recipes for this French classic require you to stand at the stove tediously batch-searing beef and sautéing vegetables. But what if the whole operation could move to the oven?

≽ BY ANDREW JANJIGIAN ≼

Julia Child once wrote that *boeuf bourguignon* "is the best beef stew known to man," and I'm inclined to agree. This hearty braise, arguably one of the most defining dishes in French cuisine, is the ultimate example of how rich, savory, and satisfying a beef stew can be: By gently simmering large chunks of well-marbled meat in beef stock and a good amount of red wine, you end up with fork-tender beef and a braising liquid that's transformed into a silky, full-bodied sauce. The result is equally suitable for a Sunday-night supper or an elegant dinner party.

Problem is, boeuf bourguignon is a pain to make. Most recipes, Child's included, come with a serious time commitment: roughly 40 minutes of browning bacon lardons and batch-searing beef, in addition to the lengthy braising time. Then there's the "garnish"—in this case not a quick embellishment but an integral serving of pearl onions and button mushrooms that get cooked in separate pans and added to the stew toward the end of cooking. The combination of all three is enough to deter most of us busy home cooks from attempting the dish even on weekends, which is a shame. But what if there was a way to revise the old-school technique, eliminating some of the fuss while staying true to this stew's bold, sumptuous profile? I couldn't resist trying.

An Unlikely Vessel

The classic bourguignon formula goes something like this: Crisp strips of salt pork in a Dutch oven, sear the beef in batches, sprinkle it with flour, and toss it over the heat to create a sauce-thickening roux. Then add a few cups of beef stock, a bottle of wine, and some tomato paste and aromatics (onions, garlic, herbs, and peppercorns); bring the pot to a boil; cover it; and set it in a low (325-degree) oven to simmer until the meat is tender and the sauce is full-bodied and lush. That takes a good 3 hours, during

Our stew tastes just as beefy as classic French versions but boasts bolder wine flavor because we add part of the bottle after the long simmer.

which time you make the garnish by browning and braising the onions in one pan and lightly sautéing the mushrooms in another. When the meat is done, the sauce gets strained and reduced, and vegetables join the pot just before serving.

I decided to start with the original and see where I could pare down. On my first attempts, I also incorporated a couple of tweaks from other test kitchen beef stew recipes: salting the meat (well-marbled chuck-eye roast is our go-to for stews) for 30 minutes, which seasons it and helps it retain moisture during cooking, and beefing up the lackluster commercial broth I was using with *umami* enhancers like anchovy paste and porcini mushrooms. (However, the latter wouldn't replace the mushrooms in the garnish.) To build body, I added a couple of packets of powdered gelatin; when stirred into the braising liquid, it mimics the rich, glossy consistency of stock made from gelatin-rich beef bones.

I'd be lying if I said the stew didn't taste beefy and sumptuous, with wine flavor that was full if a bit flat-tasting after cooking. But, as predicted, I'd hovered

at the stove for well over 30 minutes, and all that searing had produced a greasy mess. My knee-jerk reaction was to try something drastic, so I started another batch, this time ditching the browning step altogether. Unsurprisingly, it was a flop; sure, it radically cut back on the active work time, but without all those new complex flavors that develop in meat during browning (known as the Maillard reaction), the sauce was downright dull.

Fortunately, I had a better approach to try thanks to a braised meat discovery that we made a few years back: Given enough time, and provided the pieces are not fully submerged in liquid, braising meat can develop color because its exposed surface will eventually reach 300 degrees—the temperature at which meat begins to brown. Figuring that the same logic would apply here, I proceeded with another test, placing the raw meat chunks on top of the aromatics so that they broke the liquid line. Indeed, after 3 hours in the oven, the bare surfaces looked almost seared, and my tasters attested to the meat's savoriness. But they wanted even more flavorful browning. The only problem was that the liquid covered too much of the meat to generate sufficient browning. If only I had a wider vessel to use in the oven.

But it occurred to me that I did have one: a roasting pan. It would be plenty deep to contain the stew, and its generous surface area would ensure that the braising liquid pooled less deep, exposing more of the beef chunks for better browning. When I tried it, the result was better than I'd expected: The tops of the meat chunks took on lots of color, and that rich browning flavor seeped into the sauce. (Defatting and reducing the sauce on the stove were still necessary, but with the searing step gone it didn't seem too much to ask.)

I was so pleased with my roasting pan technique that I wondered if I could streamline my recipe even further and brown the salt pork in the roasting pan before I added the beef. This, too, turned out to be easy. By initially cranking the oven to 500 degrees, I mimicked the stove's searing heat and got the pork pieces good and crispy. I also realized that the salt pork could serve as a platform for the beef chunks to sit on as they cooked, raising them even higher out of the liquid and encouraging more browning. And since I was going for the meatiest flavor I could get, I tossed in the trimmed beef scraps and browned them with the salt pork.

Browned (But Not Braised)

Now that the oven was doing most of the flavor-development work for me, I wanted to pare down the time-consuming garnish steps, too. Cooking the mushrooms and pearl onions separate from the stew was already asking a lot, to say nothing of the good hour that I spent browning and braising just the onions. I tried simply tossing the vegetables into the stew, but the spongy, bland result was a nonstarter. Instead, I spread the onions and mushrooms on a baking sheet with a pat of butter and slid the sheet onto the lower of the two oven racks while the salt pork and beef scraps cooked above in the roasting pan. Stirred once or twice, the vegetables were nicely glazed by the time the pork and beef scraps were rendered. Tossing the vegetables with a touch of sugar before roasting deepened their caramelized color and flavor.

The only matter left unattended? Punching up the wine flavor. Adding part of another bottle to the braising liquid seemed extravagant, and the flavor wasn't much better. A more successful—and economical—solution was to hold back part of the wine until the final reduction of the sauce, which left the flavor noticeably brighter.

I had no doubt that my mostly hands-off method was considerably less fussy than classic recipes, but I was curious to see just how much time I'd trimmed. I went back to my notes about how long it had taken me to make Julia Child's boeuf bourguignon recipe. Turns out that I'd saved a very respectable 45 minutes. What's more, the flavors of the stews were remarkably similar.

An almost entirely hands-off boeuf bourguignon that tasted just as rich and complex as the classic version? The thought was almost as satisfying as the stew itself.

MODERN BEEF BURGUNDY
SERVES 6 TO 8

If the pearl onions have a papery outer coating, remove it by rinsing them in warm water and gently squeezing individual onions between your fingertips. Two minced anchovy fillets can be used in place of the anchovy paste. To save time, salt the meat and let it stand while you prep the remaining ingredients. Serve with mashed potatoes or buttered noodles.

- 1 (4-pound) boneless beef chuck-eye roast, trimmed and cut into 1½- to 2-inch pieces, scraps reserved
  Salt and pepper
- 6 ounces salt pork, cut into ¼-inch pieces
- 3 tablespoons unsalted butter
- 1 pound cremini mushrooms, trimmed, halved if medium or quartered if large
- 1½ cups frozen pearl onions, thawed
- 1 tablespoon sugar
- ⅓ cup all-purpose flour
- 4 cups beef broth
- 1 (750-ml) bottle red Burgundy or Pinot Noir
- 5 teaspoons unflavored gelatin
- 1 tablespoon tomato paste
- 1 teaspoon anchovy paste
- 2 onions, chopped coarse
- 2 carrots, peeled and cut into 2-inch lengths
- 1 garlic head, cloves separated, unpeeled, and crushed
- 2 bay leaves
- ½ teaspoon black peppercorns
- ½ ounce dried porcini mushrooms, rinsed
- 10 sprigs fresh parsley, plus 3 tablespoons minced
- 6 sprigs fresh thyme

1. Toss beef and 1½ teaspoons salt together in bowl and let stand at room temperature for 30 minutes.

2. Adjust oven racks to lower-middle and lowest positions and heat oven to 500 degrees. Place salt pork, beef scraps, and 2 tablespoons butter in large roasting pan. Roast on lower-middle rack until well browned and fat has rendered, 15 to 20 minutes.

3. While salt pork and beef scraps roast, toss cremini mushrooms, pearl onions, remaining 1 tablespoon butter, and sugar together on rimmed baking sheet. Roast on lowest rack, stirring occasionally, until moisture released by mushrooms evaporates and vegetables are lightly glazed, 15 to 20 minutes. Transfer vegetables to large bowl, cover, and refrigerate.

4. Remove roasting pan from oven and reduce temperature to 325 degrees. Sprinkle flour over rendered fat and whisk until no dry flour remains. Whisk in broth, 2 cups wine, gelatin, tomato paste, and anchovy paste until combined. Add onions, carrots, garlic, bay leaves, peppercorns, porcini mushrooms, parsley sprigs, and thyme to pan. Arrange beef in single layer on top of vegetables. Add water as needed to come three-quarters up side of beef (beef should not be submerged). Return roasting pan to oven and cook until meat is tender, 3 to 3½ hours, stirring after 90 minutes and adding water to keep meat at least half-submerged.

5. Using slotted spoon, transfer beef to bowl with cremini mushrooms and pearl onions; cover and set aside. Strain braising liquid through fine-mesh strainer set over large bowl, pressing on solids to extract as much liquid as possible; discard solids. Stir in remaining wine and let cooking liquid settle, 10 minutes. Using wide shallow spoon, skim fat off surface and discard.

6. Transfer liquid to Dutch oven and bring mixture to boil over medium-high heat. Simmer briskly, stirring occasionally, until sauce is thickened to consistency of heavy cream, 15 to 20 minutes. Reduce heat to medium-low, stir in beef and mushroom-onion garnish, cover, and cook until just heated through, 5 to 8 minutes. Season with salt and pepper to taste. Stir in minced parsley and serve. (Stew can be made up to 3 days in advance.)

RECIPE SHORTHAND ## Mostly Walk-Away Beef Burgundy

Doing most of the cooking in the oven in a roasting pan and on a baking sheet makes our Modern Beef Burgundy more user-friendly than classic recipes.

1. BUILD FLAVOR IN OVEN
Roast salt pork and beef trimmings in roasting pan until deeply browned. At same time, roast mushroom and onion garnish on baking sheet until lightly glazed; set aside.

2. ADD EVERYTHING BUT BEEF
Sprinkle flour over rendered fat, whisking until combined. Add broth, 2 cups wine, gelatin (to boost body in sauce), tomato and anchovy pastes, and aromatics.

3. SKIP SEAR; PROP UP BEEF
Instead of batch-searing beef, place salted pieces on top of roasted meat scraps and aromatics. They will poke above liquid and brown.

4. BRAISE
Return roasting pan to oven and cook 3 to 3½ hours, stirring once halfway through cooking. Keep meat at least halfway submerged by adding water.

5. STRAIN; FINISH SAUCE
Transfer beef to bowl with vegetable garnish, strain liquid, and add remaining wine to brighten flavor. Pour liquid into Dutch oven and simmer on stove.

6. PUT IT ALL TOGETHER
Add beef and vegetable garnish to Dutch oven and briefly heat through. Season with salt and pepper to taste and finish with chopped parsley.

Better, Lighter Spaghetti Carbonara

An overload of fat makes a smooth, stable sauce for this classic Roman pasta. But could we dial back the fat and still have a velvety consistency?

⇒ BY CELESTE ROGERS ⇐

There's a reason that *spaghetti alla carbonara* is wildly popular not just in Rome but here in the United States, too. It's one of those minimalist Roman pastas made from a handful of pantry staples—pasta, eggs, some form of cured pork, Pecorino Romano, garlic, and black pepper—that add up to something incredibly satisfying and delicious. But don't be fooled by its short ingredient list: The dish is devilishly hard to get right. The finicky egg-based sauce (made from either whole eggs or just yolks, plus finely grated cheese) relies on the heat of the warm pasta to become lush and glossy, but that rarely happens. Instead, the egg either scrambles from too much heat or, as the pasta cools, the sauce thickens and turns gluey. Often the cheese clumps, too. The few recipes that do produce a creamy, velvety sauce succeed by adding tons of fat. Case in point: The silky-smooth carbonara recipe from British chef Jamie Oliver that's built on five egg yolks, nearly ½ cup of heavy cream, and a goodly amount of rendered bacon fat. Delicious as it was, I couldn't handle more than a couple of forkfuls.

That, I realized, was precisely the problem I had to solve as I set out to perfect my own version: how to make a classic carbonara that was foolproof but not so rich that eating a full serving was impossible.

Egg-speriments

The ingredient list for carbonara is already short, but to isolate what makes or (literally) breaks the sauce, I started my testing with an even more pared-down recipe: two whole eggs, a couple ounces of finely grated Pecorino Romano, and 8 ounces of cooked bacon pieces drained of all their rendered fat. (In Italy, *guanciale*, or cured pork jowl, is a more typical choice than bacon in this dish, but I wanted to stick with an ingredient that's a pantry staple here.) I boiled 1 pound of spaghetti, set it aside briefly, and

A sleeper ingredient turned out to be the key to our carbonara's glossy, stable sauce.

created the sauce by thoroughly whisking the eggs and finely grated cheese in a serving bowl before tossing the mixture with the hot pasta and crisp bacon pieces. The final product? Dry, thin, and, thanks to the cheese, a little gritty. Things went even further downhill after just a few minutes. The longer the sauced pasta sat the pastier it became. Also, my tasters complained that it lacked the eggy richness they were expecting and that the pork flavor was a little faint.

I figured that adding a third egg would help with the dryness and the thinness. (I'd circle back to boosting porkiness later.) And it did—at least for a couple of minutes. But just as with my first batch of carbonara, the light, glossy sauce I started with quickly dried up and left the pasta coated with a thin, pasty residue; those who caught the tail end of the tasting were left with a bowl of dry, stuck-together spaghetti strands.

Since a sauce made with whole eggs didn't seem to have much staying power (or rich flavor), I decided to try changing course. I'd ditch the whites and revisit the idea of an entirely yolk-based sauce,

minus all the extra fat in the Oliver recipe. I cooked another pound of spaghetti, mixed up a new batch of sauce with six yolks and the same amount of cheese, and for a few moments things looked better: The fat and emulsifiers in the yolks made for a sauce with velvety body, not to mention superbly eggy flavor. But once again my success was short-lived, as that same combination of fat and emulsifiers—and the fact that the sauce was drier without the moisture contributed by the whites (which are about 90 percent water)—quickly caused the sauce to tighten up into a tacky glue.

Lessons learned: Yolks—plenty of them—were a must for flavor and richness, but without enough water in the mix, there was no hope for producing a fluid sauce. The challenge would be making a sauce that was loose enough to gloss the pasta strands but creamy and viscous enough to cling nicely—and would stay that way through most of a meal.

Heavier on the Starch, Please

I was about to go back to testing whole eggs when I realized that I had another liquid source I could use: the pasta cooking water. Reserving some of the starchy liquid after draining spaghetti and adding it to dressed spaghetti is a common trick that Italians use to loosen over-thickened sauces. Taking this approach, I thinned out my all-yolk mixture with ¾ cup of cooking water and once again met with initial success: The sauce was rich and creamy and, as expected, looser than the all-yolk sauce made without the added water. But maddeningly, the dressed noodles turned gluey moments later and continued to tighten up no matter how much extra cooking liquid I added.

The only scenario left was to make a sauce with whole eggs and try using the cooking water to moisten that. I circled back to the one I'd made with three whole eggs, to which I added the cheese and a little less of the starchy cooking liquid to account for the extra water introduced by the whites. This time something had changed: The sauce wasn't as velvety as I wanted, but it was surprisingly stable, holding creamy and fluid for a good 10 minutes without need for further water adjustment. The gritty bits of cheese were gone, too.

Pleased as I was with my success, I was also

PHOTOGRAPHY: CARL TREMBLAY

Less Fat, More Stable Sauce

The hardest part about making carbonara isn't coming up with the right ratio of egg whites to yolks to make a creamy, rich sauce; it's figuring out how to make a sauce that doesn't curdle, turn gritty, or tighten up into a glue—the usual problems as the pasta cools down. Some recipes get around the issues by adding lots of fat, which boosts the viscosity of the sauce and makes it more stable. We came up with a better, less cloying alternative: starchy pasta cooking water. Starch performs two functions. First, it coats the proteins in the eggs and the cheese, preventing them from curdling in the heat and clumping, respectively. Second, it combines with ovomucin, a protein in the egg whites, to form a network that is relatively resistant to temperature change, which means the sauce does not tighten up as it cools.

To take full advantage of the starch's effect, we concentrate it by cooking the pasta in half the usual amount of water and then add up to 1 cup of the starchy water to the sauce. The dressed pasta stays silky for a good 15 minutes. –C.R.

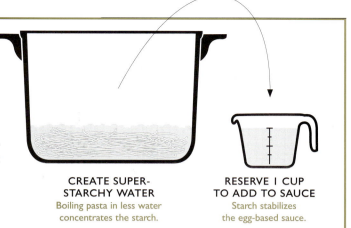

CREATE SUPER-STARCHY WATER
Boiling pasta in less water concentrates the starch.

RESERVE 1 CUP TO ADD TO SAUCE
Starch stabilizes the egg-based sauce.

baffled. Why would a combination of whole eggs and pasta water create a smoother, more stable sauce than yolks and pasta water? The key turned out to be the relationship between the starch and ovomucin, one of 148 different proteins in egg whites. When ovomucin and the starch from the cooking water interact, they form a network that not only contributes viscosity but is also fairly stable and less responsive to temperature decline than a sauce made with just egg yolks. The starch was also coating both the egg and the cheese proteins, preventing the eggs from curdling and the cheese from clumping.

This information was encouraging and also gave me an idea about how to further boost the viscosity of the sauce—add more starch. I decided to try a trick we discovered when developing our recipe for Cacio e Pepe (January/February 2010), another of those minimalist Roman pasta dishes: cooking pasta in less water (just 2 quarts per pound of pasta rather than the typical 4) to produce a starchier liquid that in turn leads to a "creamier" sauce when tossed with the spaghetti. I did the same here, halving the amount of water that I used to cook the spaghetti

and then whisking ½ cup of this super-starchy liquid into the eggs and cheese before combining the sauce with the pasta. It was a huge success. The sauce was rich and glossy and, what's more, held that consistency for a record 15 minutes. To ensure that the egg mixture thickened properly, I also made two small (but critical) tweaks to my technique. First, I warmed the empty serving bowl with the drained cooking water—another classic Italian pasta trick—to be sure that there was enough heat to "cook" the sauce. Second, I let the sauced pasta rest briefly and tossed it several times before serving; as the pasta cooled, the sauce reached just the right consistency.

Flavor Finessing

This carbonara sauce was already the best I'd had to date: stable and creamy but not cloyingly rich. What it lacked was the true egg flavor of the all-yolk sauce, so I made that my next goal. And while I was at it, my tasters reminded me, could I please amp up and even out the meaty pork flavor?

Since yolks were the key to eggy richness, I tried adding an extra one to my three-whole-egg formula, not knowing if the flavor of just one would suffice or how it would affect the holding time of the sauce. Fifteen minutes later, I was pleasantly surprised to see that the sauce was just as glossy and loose as the batch without the extra yolk. And the flavor? Custardy rich but not heavy.

As for the bacon, I was sure the ½ pound I was using was plenty, but my tasters were right: Tossing bacon bits into the pasta didn't make for well-rounded pork flavor. The carbonara traditionalists among us also wished that the texture of the bacon could more closely mimic the satisfying chew of guanciale. I had ideas for addressing both issues. First, I cooked the bacon with a little water, which we recently discovered produces tender-chewy—not crumbly—pieces. Second, I caved on my resolution not to add extra fat—but just a little. Whisking a mere tablespoon of bacon fat into the sauce before tossing it with the pasta brought bacon flavor to every bite.

Finally, I'd nailed it: carbonara that was lush and rich with egg, bacon, and cheese but still light enough that my tasters didn't just eat a full bowl: They went back for seconds.

FOOLPROOF SPAGHETTI CARBONARA
SERVES 4

It's important to work quickly in steps 2 and 3. The heat from the cooking water and the hot spaghetti will "cook" the sauce only if used immediately. Warming the mixing and serving bowls helps the sauce stay creamy. Use a high-quality bacon for this dish; our favorites are Farmland Hickory Smoked Bacon and Vande Rose Farms Artisan Dry Cured Bacon, Applewood Smoked.

- 8   slices bacon, cut into ½-inch pieces
- ½   cup water
- 3   garlic cloves, minced
- 2½   ounces Pecorino Romano, grated (1¼ cups)
- 3   large eggs plus 1 large yolk
- 1   teaspoon pepper
- 1   pound spaghetti
- 1   teaspoon salt

1. Bring bacon and water to simmer in 10-inch nonstick skillet over medium heat; cook until water evaporates and bacon begins to sizzle, about 8 minutes. Reduce heat to medium-low and continue to cook until fat renders and bacon browns, 5 to 8 minutes longer. Add garlic and cook, stirring constantly, until fragrant, about 30 seconds. Strain bacon mixture through fine-mesh strainer set in bowl. Set aside bacon mixture. Measure out 1 tablespoon fat and place in medium bowl. Whisk Pecorino, eggs and yolk, and pepper into fat until combined.

2. Meanwhile, bring 2 quarts water to boil in Dutch oven. Set colander in large bowl. Add spaghetti and salt to pot; cook, stirring frequently, until al dente. Drain spaghetti in colander set in bowl, reserving cooking water. Pour 1 cup cooking water into liquid measuring cup and discard remainder. Return spaghetti to now-empty bowl.

3. Slowly whisk ½ cup reserved cooking water into Pecorino mixture. Gradually pour Pecorino mixture over spaghetti, tossing to coat. Add bacon mixture and toss to combine. Let spaghetti rest, tossing frequently, until sauce has thickened slightly and coats spaghetti, 2 to 4 minutes, adjusting consistency with remaining reserved cooking water if needed. Serve immediately.

Rethinking Leg of Lamb

Roast leg of lamb can be difficult—it cooks unevenly and is hard to both flavor and carve.
We take another approach: Leave out the bone and bring on the bloom (of spices, that is).

≥ BY DAN SOUZA ≤

Who cooks lamb? Not many people. Not often. Not in America, anyway. I know. Not even I cook it, and it's not because I don't enjoy eating it. Lamb has a richness of flavor unmatched by beef or pork, with a meaty texture that can be as supple as that of tenderloin. It pairs well with a wide range of robust spices, and my favorite cut, the leg, can single-handedly elevate a holiday meal from ordinary to refined. The real reason I avoid leg of lamb is that my past experiences cooking it were undermined by the many challenges it can pose.

Roasting a bone-in leg of lamb invariably delivers meat of different degrees of doneness; the super-thin sections of muscle near the shank go beyond well-done while you wait for the meat closest to the bone to come up to temperature. And even when I've successfully roasted this cut, carving it off the bone into presentable pieces proved humbling. Opting for a boneless, tied leg of lamb partly alleviates these issues—the meat cooks more evenly and carving is simplified. But this approach presents problems of its own, the biggest being the poor ratio of well-browned crust to tender meat and the unavoidable pockets of sinew and fat that hide between the mosaic of muscles.

Maybe it would be easiest to just pick up a user-friendly rack of lamb next time I'm in the ovine mood, but that smacks of defeat, and I love a challenge. I wanted a roast leg of lamb with a good ratio of crispy crust to evenly cooked meat and one that was dead simple to carve and serve, all the while providing me with a ready-made sauce. I guess you could say I was after a lazy man's roast leg of lamb.

A Cut Above

I immediately decided to forgo bone-in and tied boneless roasts in favor of a different preparation: a butterflied leg of lamb. Essentially a boneless leg in which the thicker portions have been sliced and

Without the bone, carving lamb can be as easy as slicing steak.

opened up to yield a relatively even slab of meat, this cut is most often chopped up for kebabs or tossed onto a hot grill. But its uniformity and large expanse of exterior made me think it might do well as a roast, too. My first move was to ensure an even thickness by pounding any thicker areas to roughly 1 inch. Examining this large slab of lamb on my cutting board, I realized an unexpected benefit of this preparation: access to big pockets of intermuscular fat and connective tissue. These chewy bits, which aren't accessible even in boneless roasts, don't render or soften enough during cooking. Now I was able to carve out and remove them easily. Another benefit was the ability to season this roast far more efficiently than either a bone-in or a boneless leg.

Though many people brine lamb, I noticed that the profile of this butterflied leg resembled that of a very large, thick-cut steak. I decided to treat it like one: I seasoned both sides with kosher salt and let it sit for an hour. Treating the lamb this way provided many of the benefits of a brine: It was better seasoned, juicier, and more tender than untreated samples. Unlike brining, however,

salting left my lamb with a relatively dry surface—one that could brown and crisp far better during roasting. To ensure that the salt would cover more of the meat, I crosshatched the fat cap on the top surface of the leg by scoring just down to the meat in ½-inch intervals. Roasted to 130 degrees on a baking sheet in a moderate oven, the lamb was well seasoned and featured a decent crust, but still the exterior portions were overcooked by the time the center came up to temperature. I knew I could do better.

Twice-Cooked Leg of Lamb

Years of roasting meat have helped us figure out how to do it well. One thing we know is that roasting low and slow ensures good moisture retention and even cooking. The exterior and interior temperatures will be much closer in a roast cooked at 300 degrees than in one blasted at 500 degrees. With this in mind, I tried roasting my salted lamb at a range of relatively low oven temperatures, from 225 degrees on up to 325 degrees. Sure enough, going lower resulted in juicier, more evenly cooked meat. I struck a balance between time and temperature at 250 degrees. So far so good: I was turning out tender, juicy leg of lamb in only 40 minutes of roasting.

But now I ran up against a second tenet of good roasting: High heat develops the rich, meaty flavors associated with the Maillard reaction. It's a paradox we commonly address by cooking at two different heat levels—sear in a skillet over high heat and then gently roast. But my roast was too large for stovetop searing. It was clear that I'd need to sear it in the oven, where my options for high heat were 500 degrees or the broiler. I tested both options and found that beginning in a 500-degree oven was too slow for my thin roast. By the time I rendered and crisped the exterior, I'd overcooked the meat below the surface. Broiling was markedly better. I achieved the best results by slow-roasting the lamb first and then finishing it under the broiler, which allowed me to further dry the meat's surface and promote faster browning. Just 5 minutes under the broiler produced a burnished, crisped crust but left the meat below the surface largely unaffected. Now it was time to address the spices.

Spice World

Lamb's bold flavor is complemented, rather than overpowered, by a liberal use of spices. I wanted to find the ideal way to incorporate a blend of them, and my first thought was to include them from the outset. I toasted equal parts cumin, coriander, and mustard seeds and rubbed the mixture over both sides of the lamb along with the salt. Things looked (and smelled) quite good while the lamb gently cooked at 250 degrees, but they took a turn for the worse once I transitioned to broiling. The broiler's intense heat turned the top layer of spices into a blackened, bitter landscape in a matter of minutes.

Luckily it wasn't all bad news—the spices under the lamb had started to bloom and soften during their stay in the oven, adding texture and bursts of flavor where they clung to the meat. What if I ditched the top layer of spices and focused on getting the most out of what was underneath? After salting my next lamb, I placed whole coriander, cumin, and mustard seeds, as well as smashed garlic and sliced ginger, on a baking sheet along with a glug of vegetable oil and popped it in the oven. This would take full advantage of the concept of blooming—a process by which, through the application of heat, fat-soluble flavor compounds in a spice (or other aromatic ingredient) are released from a solid state into a solution, where they mix together and physically interact with one another, therefore gaining even more complexity. When the lamb was ready to be cooked, I simply removed the baking sheet, placed the lamb (fat side up) on top of the spice-oil mixture, and returned it to the oven to roast.

I had hit the roast-lamb jackpot. Without a layer of spices to absorb the heat, the top of the roast once again turned a handsome golden brown under the broiler, while the aromatics and infused oil clung to the bottom and provided rich flavor. Tasters were pleased but wanted more complexity, so I added shallots, strips of lemon zest, and bay leaves (which I removed before adding the lamb) to the pan oil. This lamb was close to my ideal: a browned crust encasing medium-rare meat, perfumed with pockets of spice and caramelized alliums. The last step was to put all of that infused oil to good use.

While the lamb rested, I strained the infused oil and pan juices into a bowl and whisked in some lemon juice, shallot, and cilantro and mint. This

Configured for Easy Carving

First position the meat so that a long side is facing you. Then slice the lamb with the grain into three equal pieces. Turn each piece so that you can now cut across the grain, and cut into ¼-inch-thick slices.

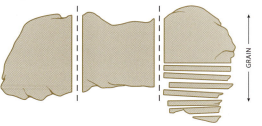

GRAIN

ILLUSTRATION: JAY LAYMAN, JOHN BURGOYNE

TECHNIQUE | A BETTER WAY TO SPICE UP LAMB

Rather than rub spices and aromatics on the lamb's surface, where they can burn, we bloom them on a baking sheet and then roast the meat on top. The lamb protects the spices and picks up flavor.

1. Bloom spices and aromatics. 2. Place lamb on top to roast. 3. Use flavored oil to make sauce.

vinaigrette was meaty, aromatic, and fresh-tasting. The time had come to carve (a term I now used quite loosely), and it proved as simple as slicing up a steak. I transferred the meat to a platter, dressed it with some of the sauce, and—in less than 2 hours—was ready to eat. Lazy man's leg of lamb, indeed.

ROAST BUTTERFLIED LEG OF LAMB WITH CORIANDER, CUMIN, AND MUSTARD SEEDS
SERVES 8 TO 10

We prefer the subtler flavor and larger size of lamb labeled "domestic" or "American" for this recipe. The amount of salt (2 tablespoons) in step 1 is for a 6-pound leg. If using a larger leg (7 to 8 pounds), add an additional teaspoon of salt for every pound. For our free recipe for Roast Butterflied Leg of Lamb with Coriander, Fennel, and Black Pepper, go to CooksIllustrated.com/apr13.

Lamb

1	(6- to 8-pound) butterflied leg of lamb
	Kosher salt
⅓	cup vegetable oil
3	shallots, sliced thin
4	garlic cloves, peeled and smashed
1	(1-inch) piece ginger, sliced into ½-inch-thick rounds and smashed
1	tablespoon coriander seeds
1	tablespoon cumin seeds
1	tablespoon mustard seeds
3	bay leaves
2	(2-inch) strips lemon zest

Sauce

⅓	cup chopped fresh mint
⅓	cup chopped fresh cilantro
1	shallot, minced
2	tablespoons lemon juice
	Salt and pepper

1. FOR THE LAMB: Place lamb on cutting board with fat cap facing down. Using sharp knife, trim any pockets of fat and connective tissue from underside of lamb. Flip lamb over, trim fat cap so it's between ⅛ and ¼ inch thick, and pound roast to

even 1-inch thickness. Cut slits, spaced ½ inch apart, in fat cap in crosshatch pattern, being careful to cut down to but not into meat. Rub 2 tablespoons salt over entire roast and into slits. Let stand, uncovered, at room temperature for 1 hour.

2. Meanwhile, adjust oven racks 4 to 5 inches from broiler element and to lower-middle position and heat oven to 250 degrees. Stir together oil, shallots, garlic, ginger, coriander seeds, cumin seeds, mustard seeds, bay leaves, and lemon zest on rimmed baking sheet and bake on lower-middle rack until spices are softened and fragrant and shallots and garlic turn golden, about 1 hour. Remove sheet from oven and discard bay leaves.

3. Thoroughly pat lamb dry with paper towels and transfer, fat side up, to sheet (directly on top of spices). Roast on lower-middle rack until lamb registers 120 degrees, 30 to 40 minutes. Remove sheet from oven and heat broiler. Broil lamb on upper rack until surface is well browned and charred in spots and lamb registers 125 degrees, 3 to 8 minutes for medium-rare.

4. Remove sheet from oven and, using 2 pairs of tongs, transfer lamb to carving board (some spices will cling to bottom of roast); tent loosely with aluminum foil and let rest for 20 minutes.

5. FOR THE SAUCE: Meanwhile, carefully pour pan juices through fine-mesh strainer into medium bowl, pressing on solids to extract as much liquid as possible; discard solids. Stir in mint, cilantro, shallot, and lemon juice. Add any accumulated lamb juices to sauce and season with salt and pepper to taste.

6. With long side facing you, slice lamb with grain into 3 equal pieces. Turn each piece and slice across grain into ¼-inch-thick slices. Serve with sauce. (Briefly warm sauce in microwave if it has cooled and thickened.)

ROAST BUTTERFLIED LEG OF LAMB WITH CORIANDER, ROSEMARY, AND RED PEPPER
SERVES 8 TO 10

Omit cumin and mustard seeds. Toss 6 sprigs fresh rosemary and ½ teaspoon red pepper flakes with oil mixture in step 2. Substitute parsley for cilantro in sauce.

Introducing Fluffy Omelets

It's like a soufflé in a skillet—or would be if we could figure out how to keep it from collapsing before it got to the plate.

⇒ BY LAN LAM ⇐

I've worked a lot of restaurant brunch shifts over the years, so I've made my fair share of omelets. Most of those have been either the refined French roll with its pure yellow surface and creamy, sparingly filled center or the hearty diner version that's browned spottily, generously stuffed with cheese and other fillings, and folded into a half-moon. But there's a third, less familiar style that's nothing like these other two. Often referred to as a fluffy omelet, this version dwarfs the diner type by at least a couple of inches. Some specimens are so puffed up that they look like folded-over soufflés—which, in a sense, they are. Most call for whipping air into the eggs and baking the omelet in the oven, where it rises above the lip of the skillet. Beyond the appeal of this omelet's lofty height and its promise of delicate, airy texture, I've always been attracted to the idea of cooking an omelet in the oven, since this would eliminate the usual fiddling with the burner flame to prevent overcooking. Using the oven's ambient heat also seemed like a more forgiving approach.

With high expectations, I tried several recipes, figuring I'd pull pan after pan of tall, gently set omelets from the oven. I did not. With few exceptions, I got a motley crew of oozing soufflés and dry, bouncy Styrofoam rounds, as well as some omelets that barely puffed up at all. Where had these recipes taken a wrong turn? I stocked up on eggs and headed into the kitchen to find out.

Whipped into Shape

Texturewise, the most promising recipe I tried began with whipping four whole eggs in a stand mixer until the mixture was foamy (aerating the eggs helps them rise), then pouring the whipped eggs into a buttered nonstick skillet, and baking them in a 375-degree oven for 7 minutes. The omelet's inside had set nicely, but not before its sides and bottom had toughened up. Adjusting the cooking times and

The beauty of this omelet (other than impressive height)? It's forgiving. Simply spread the whipped eggs in the pan and let the oven do the rest.

oven temperature didn't substantially improve the results. I even introduced a lid to the pan, hoping that trapping steam would prevent the omelet from drying out, but this kept only the top tender and moist; the bottom still formed a tough, scaly crust. Flavorwise, it was also pretty lean.

Leaving the oven alone, I moved on to examine the other core variable: the eggs. The omelets were cooking up tough, so my job was to tenderize them, which meant figuring out a way to weaken the structure of the egg foam—the cluster of air bubbles made by whipping them. Adding dairy seemed logical, since it contains the dual tenderizers water and fat (we add it to scrambled eggs for these very reasons). When the proteins in eggs are heated, they bond to form a latticed gel in a process known as coagulation. Fat from the dairy coats the proteins and prevents the bonds from becoming so strong that the eggs toughen, while the dairy's water dilutes the proteins and makes it more difficult for them to come into contact with each other in the first place.

Working through the options, I tried 1 table-

spoon each of milk, heavy cream, and—mindful of my omelet's lean taste—melted butter. But I didn't get very far, as each one weakened the egg foam so dramatically that it couldn't hold enough air to increase in volume. The only upside was that the melted butter added a particularly nice richness, and I decided to stick with it. For a second attempt, I whipped the eggs before adding the butter, thinking that building structure before introducing a tenderizer might help. But that method flopped, too. The egg foam simply wasn't strong enough to support the extra fat, so it collapsed before cooking—hardly the more tender structure I had in mind.

I was several dozen tests (and many dozens of eggs) in at this point, but these experiments had clarified a valuable point: While I needed to tenderize the eggs, I also needed to start with the strongest possible egg foam. That wasn't going to happen by whipping whole eggs, since the fat in the yolks was already tenderizing the mixture a little. Instead, I separated the eggs, whipping just the whites to form stiff peaks (think meringues) and whisking 1 tablespoon of melted butter with the yolks before folding them into the whites. This test was the turning point. Now that the whites were stiff and stable, they were able to support the additional fat of the yolks and butter.

Tartar Control

Well, at least they held on for a couple of minutes. Then the mixture separated and finally deflated again. I felt defeated, until I thought more about that meringue analogy. Whipping the egg whites to stiff peaks is part of what ensures stable meringues; the other is adding a stabilizer such as cream of tartar. The acidic ingredient preserves that stability by slowing the formation of sulfur bonds in egg whites; if too many bonds form, the white's protein structure becomes too rigid, and the network that holds the whipped air and water in place begins to collapse. I saw no reason why it wouldn't have the same effect in my omelet. Before beating the whites, I sprinkled ¼ teaspoon of cream of tartar evenly over their surface. This batch of whites didn't look any different as they whipped, but the results were convincing after I folded in the yolk mixture and waited. Seven minutes later, they were still standing tall.

I proceeded with my method, melting a pat of butter in the skillet, pouring in the airy eggs, smoothing the top with a spatula, and sliding the pan into a preheated oven. About 4 minutes later, I pulled a gorgeously puffed omelet out of the oven. It not only looked beautiful and held its shape but was also perfectly tender, with the requisite richness.

Getting My Fill

My only remaining task was to come up with fillings. The delicate nature of this omelet meant that I couldn't throw just anything in there—and certainly not in large quantities. Instead, I would need to use small amounts of bold ingredients. A light sprinkle of Parmesan made for a nice minimalist option, but I also worked up a few more substantial variations: one with asparagus and smoked salmon, one with mushrooms, and another with artichokes and bacon.

The trick was figuring out when, exactly, to add the fillings. Sprinkling them on after the omelet had baked meant that the filling rested on—but did not mesh with—the puffy bed of eggs. Filling the omelets before they went into the oven was a better solution. To make sure that the eggs set but didn't brown too thoroughly, I poured them into the hot buttered skillet and then immediately removed the skillet from the heat to sprinkle on the fillings. Then into the oven it went. When I pulled the baked omelet from the oven, the eggs were beautifully puffed up and, what's more, gently surrounded the fillings, ensuring that each bite contained a flavor and texture contrast: rich but delicate eggs, a hit of salty Parmesan, and savory vegetables or meat.

It was safe to say that my puffy omelet was the most impressive-looking omelet I'd ever made—and now it was the most forgiving to pull off, too.

SCIENCE Going Their Separate Ways

To create an omelet that was fluffy but didn't taste like Styrofoam, we first needed to separate the whites from the yolks and treat them as separate entities. This is because each component contributes a different—and competing—quality to the results: Whites build structure, while the rich-tasting fat in yolks weakens it. Next steps: We whipped the whites with cream of tartar to add stability and stirred a little melted butter into the yolks to enhance their rich taste. We then gently recombined the two components. The extra fat kept the omelet from tasting too lean, while the cream of tartar allowed the omelet to stand tall and sturdy, despite the weakening effects of butter and yolks. –L.L.

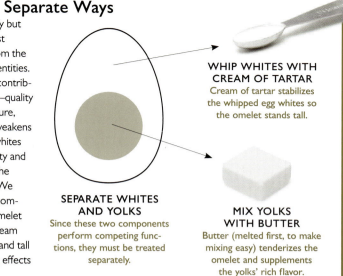

WHIP WHITES WITH CREAM OF TARTAR
Cream of tartar stabilizes the whipped egg whites so the omelet stands tall.

SEPARATE WHITES AND YOLKS
Since these two components perform competing functions, they must be treated separately.

MIX YOLKS WITH BUTTER
Butter (melted first, to make mixing easy) tenderizes the omelet and supplements the yolks' rich flavor.

FLUFFY OMELET
SERVES 2

A teaspoon of white vinegar or lemon juice can be used in place of the cream of tartar, and a handheld mixer or a whisk can be used in place of a stand mixer. We recommend using the fillings that accompany this recipe; they are designed not to interfere with the cooking of the omelet. For our free recipe for Artichoke and Bacon Filling, go to CooksIllustrated.com/apr13.

- 4 large eggs, separated
- 1 tablespoon unsalted butter, melted, plus 1 tablespoon unsalted butter
- ¼ teaspoon salt
- ¼ teaspoon cream of tartar
- 1 recipe filling (recipes follow)
- 1 ounce Parmesan cheese, grated (½ cup)

1. Adjust oven rack to middle position and heat oven to 375 degrees. Whisk egg yolks, melted butter, and salt together in bowl. Place egg whites in bowl of stand mixer and sprinkle cream of tartar over surface. Fit stand mixer with whisk and whip egg whites on medium-low speed until foamy, 2 to 2½ minutes. Increase speed to medium-high and whip until stiff peaks just start to form, 2 to 3 minutes. Fold egg yolk mixture into egg whites until no white streaks remain.

2. Heat remaining 1 tablespoon butter in 12-inch ovensafe nonstick skillet over medium-high heat, swirling to coat bottom of pan. When butter foams, quickly add egg mixture, spreading into even layer with spatula. Remove pan from heat and gently sprinkle filling and Parmesan evenly over top of omelet. Transfer to oven and cook until center of omelet springs back when lightly pressed, 4½ minutes for slightly wet omelet and 5 minutes for dry omelet.

3. Run spatula around edges of omelet to loosen, shaking gently to release. Slide omelet onto cutting board and let stand for 30 seconds. Using spatula, fold omelet in half. Cut omelet in half crosswise and serve immediately.

ASPARAGUS AND SMOKED SALMON FILLING
MAKES ¾ CUP

- 1 teaspoon olive oil
- 1 shallot, sliced thin
- 5 ounces asparagus, trimmed and cut on bias into ¼-inch lengths
  Salt and pepper
- 1 ounce smoked salmon, chopped
- ½ teaspoon lemon juice

Heat oil in 12-inch nonstick skillet over medium-high heat until shimmering. Add shallot and cook until softened and starting to brown, about 2 minutes. Add asparagus, pinch salt, and pepper to taste, and cook, stirring frequently, until crisp-tender, 5 to 7 minutes. Transfer asparagus mixture to bowl and stir in salmon and lemon juice.

MUSHROOM FILLING
MAKES ¾ CUP

- 1 teaspoon olive oil
- 1 shallot, sliced thin
- 4 ounces white or cremini mushrooms, trimmed and chopped
  Salt and pepper
- 1 teaspoon balsamic vinegar

Heat oil in 12-inch nonstick skillet over medium-high heat until shimmering. Add shallot and cook until softened and starting to brown, about 2 minutes. Add mushrooms and ⅛ teaspoon salt and season with pepper to taste. Cook until liquid has evaporated and mushrooms begin to brown, 6 to 8 minutes. Transfer mixture to bowl and stir in vinegar.

The Essential Guide to Knife Care

Knives are vital kitchen workhorses, and it's important to keep them sharp. But what does that mean? How do you accomplish it? What should you *not* believe? BY MOLLY BIRNBAUM

OUR FAVORITE KNIVES

Victorinox Fibrox 8-Inch Chef's Knife ($24.95)
This lightweight knife can outperform heavier, more expensive blades. Its pronounced curve gives it great maneuverability.

Wüsthof Classic 10-Inch Bread Knife ($109.95)
The uniformly spaced, moderately sized pointed serrations on this knife excelled at slicing through food quickly and easily.

Wüsthof Classic with PEtec 3½-Inch Paring Knife ($39.95)
This knife is nimble and precise with its thin, slightly curved blade, pointed tip, and comfortable grip.

Victorinox Fibrox 12-Inch Granton Edge Slicing Knife ($39.95)
This knife has a tapered 12-inch blade with scallops that help prevent sticking. It's perfect for slicing large cuts of meat.

Masamoto VG-10 Gyutou ($180)
This hybrid knife has a slim, sharp tip and an acutely tapered blade, which makes it feel especially light as well as slightly flexible.

Keeping Knives Clean

We recommend cleaning knives with a sponge, hot water, and soap. Scrub pads do a fine job of removing gunk from blades but can eventually damage the finish. Avoid a dishwasher: The knocking around can damage the edges, as can the corrosive nature of dishwasher detergent. If you have a carbon steel knife, we likewise recommend a sponge, hot water, and soap—just be sure to dry it or it will rust and blacken.

Understanding Degrees of Dullness

It doesn't take months or weeks for a knife to lose its sharpness. Even a few minutes of cutting can cause the blade to feel slightly dull. That said, a knife that feels only a little dull probably does not need to be sharpened. The edge of a slightly dull knife is usually just misaligned and merely needs to be repositioned with a honing steel. A truly dull knife has an edge that is rounded and worn down and needs a sharpener to restore the standard Western 20- to 22-degree angle of each side of the edge.

SHARP
A sharp knife holds a 20-degree angle on each side of the edge.

SLIGHTLY DULL
The misaligned edge of a slightly dull knife is easily fixed with a steel.

VERY DULL
A very dull, worn-down knife needs a sharpener to restore the edge.

How to Tell If Your Knife Is Sharp

In the test kitchen, we use a very simple test to see if knives need to be honed or sharpened: the paper test. Hold a sheet of paper by one end and drag your knife, from heel to tip, across it. If the knife snags or fails to cut the paper, it needs to be honed or sharpened. Try honing first. If the knife still fails the test, run it through a sharpener.

GOOD OPTIONS FOR KNIFE STORAGE

If you store your knives loose in a drawer, you're putting the sharp edge of your blades—not to mention your fingers—in danger.

Knife Guard
The **Victorinox 8- to 10-Inch BladeSafe Knife Guard** ($5.95) is a wide polypropylene case that securely covers a variety of chef's, slicing, and paring knives.

Magnetic Knife Strip
The **Messermeister Bamboo Knife Magnet** ($69.99) is a wall-mounted magnetic knife strip that offers ample room to store knives without demanding drawer or counter space. It can accommodate even the longest knives.

Universal Knife Block
The **Bodum Bistro Universal Knife Block** ($49.95) boasts a "slotless" frame filled with a nest of plastic rods to accommodate any arsenal of cutlery and holds knives in a compact footprint.

DON'T BELIEVE THESE COMMON SHARPENING MYTHS

MYTH Honing steels sharpen your knives.

TRUTH: These rods merely straighten the cutting edge. As a knife is used, the cutting edge tends to bend and fold over slightly, giving the perception of a less sharp knife. Running the edge of a knife across a steel straightens the edge, making the knife perform better. A knife sharpener, on the other hand, actually removes metal from the blade's edge, creating a new surface for cutting.

MYTH For a truly sharp knife, you need to use a whetstone.

TRUTH: A whetstone is just one way to return a factory edge to a knife. A sharpening stone, or whetstone, is an abrasive block that removes metal from a knife's blade to re-create its sharp edge. If you know how to use it, a whetstone can be a very effective tool. However, using one is a specialized skill that takes a good deal of time and practice to do properly. And so if you don't know how to use a whetstone, it can do more harm than good.

MYTH Electric sharpeners take off too much metal.

TRUTH: With the right brand of electric sharpener, there's no need to worry about excessive metal loss. Electric sharpeners do take off a small amount of metal each time you grind your knife—especially if you are using a coarse-grind setting to sharpen an especially dull knife. But our favorite electric sharpener has three options for sharpening: coarse, fine, and a nonmotorized steel. The fine slot is the one you will use most often just to polish up a barely dull knife. Because you will be maintaining the sharpness of your knife with the lightest of the sharpening options rather than giving it an intense regrinding with the coarse slot, you shouldn't worry about metal loss.

MYTH For that matter, honing steels can take off too much metal.

TRUTH: Again, with the right tool, metal loss is nothing to worry about. The three types of steels on the market—regular, fine, and polished cut—all accomplish the same task to a lesser or greater degree. The rough, filed lines of the regular-cut steel are best for home cooks who only occasionally steel the edge of a knife. For professional chefs and meat cutters who use their knives for hours on end (and steel them multiple times per day), the fine and polished cuts are a better choice, as constant contact with the rougher surface of a regular-cut steel could wear away their knives' edges.

MYTH Electric sharpeners are better than manual ones.

TRUTH: A good manual sharpener can be as effective as an electric model. When we pitted our favorite electric sharpener against our top manual model, we found that the manual sharpener was every bit as good as the electric one when it came to restoring a worn blade. Nicked or badly damaged knives were another story. Manual sharpeners take off less metal than electric ones and simply can't remove enough, in a reasonable amount of time, to restore a proper edge to really damaged blades. In such cases, an electric sharpener is the better choice.

MYTH You can't sharpen a serrated knife at home.

TRUTH: You can—but only with a manual sharpener. Though serrated-specific sharpeners do exist, we've found them to be disappointing. And electric sharpeners don't do enough: Their spinning wheels sharpen merely the edges and tips of the serrations, not the valleys between these tips. But that doesn't mean you need to send out your serrated knives to a professional. Our favorite manual sharpener uses a V-shaped tungsten carbide blade that can ride up and down the serrations, sharpening not only the edges and tips but also the deep valleys. (Serrated edges don't need to be sharpened nearly as often as smooth blades: Their pointed teeth do most of the work while the edges endure less friction.)

MYTH You can't sharpen an Asian knife in a Western sharpener.

TRUTH: It's not ideal, but you can sharpen an Asian knife in a Western sharpener. Asian knives have a 15-degree cutting angle on one or both sides of the blade, while European knives use a 20-degree angle. But this doesn't mean that you can't use your regular sharpener on them. We dulled one of our favorite Japanese chef's knives and then sharpened it in our favorite electric sharpener, which creates a 20-degree angle, and compared it with the same type of knife dulled and then sharpened in an Asian sharpener. The good news: Both the 15- and 20-degree edges were sharp enough to slice a tomato effortlessly. Only a few testers noticed some drag with the 20-degree angle that wasn't there with the 15-degree blade. So in a pinch, you could just use a good Western knife sharpener—it's always better than a dull knife. Your best bet is to use our recommended Asian sharpener.

MYTH And you can't sharpen a Western knife in an Asian sharpener.

TRUTH: You can—but we don't recommend it. The metal and geometry of a 20-degree Western knife are not designed to be at 15 degrees. When our favorite Western chef's knife was sharpened to an Asian edge, most testers enjoyed more precision with the blade. That said, sharpening a 20-degree angle to 15 degrees will likely require frequent resharpening, which will rapidly wear down your blade. If your knife didn't cost a lot, replacing it might be OK. But with expensive knives, it's best to maintain the original edge.

OUR RECOMMENDED SHARPENERS

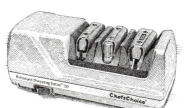

Electric

The **Chef's Choice Model 130** ($139.99) creates a sharp, polished edge on knives. Its spring-loaded blade guides allow no ambiguous wiggle room as they hold the blade against the sharpening wheels at the proper angle. One slot acts like a honing steel but removes all the guesswork.

Bolster Blues

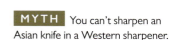

If you have a knife with a full bolster, we don't recommend using an electric sharpener: The thick end of the blade can't be run all the way through. Instead, use a manual sharpener.

Manual

The **AccuSharp Knife and Tool Sharpener** ($7.99) makes admirably quick and thorough work of basic sharpening tasks at a fraction of the price of an electric sharpener.

Asian

The **Chef's Choice Diamond Hone Asian Knife Sharpener Model 463** ($39.99) is an economical manual sharpener that uses diamond abrasives in two stages: coarse and fine. It efficiently restored a crisp, smooth, 15-degree angle on a completely dull knife. Note: This model can handle only double-beveled knives, such as hybrid *gyutous*, which are sharpened on both sides of the blade (traditional Japanese knives are single-beveled).

ILLUSTRATION: JOHN BURGOYNE

Spanish Lentil and Chorizo Soup

To achieve authentically deep, complex flavor in this hearty soup, we had to turn down the flame.

⊰ BY DAVID PAZMIÑO ⊱

Spaniards have a long tradition of taking *la comida*, their largest meal of the day, in the early afternoon. Hearty, sustaining soups and stews, many of which economically pair dried beans with some form of flavor-packed pork such as ham, bacon, or sausage, are typically on the table. A particularly intriguing example is *sopa de lentejas con chorizo* (lentil and chorizo soup). It's a standout not just for its robust taste—provided by rich, garlicky chorizo, heady smoked paprika (*pimentón*), and the bright depth of sherry vinegar—but also for its unique texture: Neither entirely brothy nor creamy, the soup features whole lentils suspended in a thick broth.

To come up with my own recipe, I started by evaluating different types of lentils. Spaniards are fond of *lentejas pardinas* (*pardo* means brownish or darkish) from *Castilla y León*. I mail-ordered a bag and found that they cooked up with a nutty, buttery flavor. But since pardinas are difficult to locate, I also simmered a few more common varieties, finding that they were all similar though not without unique subtleties. French green *lentilles du Puy* were earthy; black beluga lentils, meaty; and standard brown lentils, vegetal. The du Puy type had the best tender-firm texture, so I would use them for my remaining tests.

There was just one problem: keeping them intact. The "meat" of a lentil swells as it cooks, all too easily slipping out of its shell (which is called a blowout) and creating a mushy, split pea soup–like texture. Over the years, we have found two ways to address this issue. Both methods make use of salt and/or acid to weaken the pectin and soften the

A specialized technique ensures that the lentils cook up intact but creamy.

shell, leading to fewer blowouts. The first approach involves cooking the lentils with salt and vinegar before adding liquid and fully cooking them; the second requires soaking the beans in a warm saltwater brine for an hour prior to cooking. I tried the salt and acid method first, sautéing some chopped onion in olive oil and then adding the lentils along with a bit of salt and sherry vinegar. I covered the pot and let the lentils cook for a few minutes before adding water, bay leaves, smoked paprika, and cloves and simmering until the beans were fully cooked. While

the shape of these lentils was somewhat retained, many did still slip out of their skins and form mush. I got much better results when I combined the approaches by brining the lentils (using boiling water cut the soaking time to 30 minutes) before sweating them with the salt and vinegar. Now each and every bean emerged fully intact and beautifully creamy.

Hitting the Links

With the lentils up to par, I focused on the chorizo. The word chorizo covers many versions of pork sausage made in Spain. The kind typically available in the United States is a cured sausage with a strong garlicky flavor, colored a distinctive red by pimentón. It is important not to confuse it with Mexican chorizo, which combines fresh ground pork or beef with chili powder and vinegar. To keep the links as moist as possible, I left them whole and browned them in olive oil, transferred them to a plate while I sweated the lentils, and then plopped them back into the pot along with the water to simmer (I would cut them into bite-size pieces toward the end of cooking). Prepared this way, the chorizo cooked up with a dense, juicy texture. But as good as the sausage was, the flavor of the soup itself wasn't nearly as complex as I wanted it to be. (Its consistency was also too thin, but I'd deal with that later.)

Low and Slow

My first idea for creating depth was to swap chicken broth for some of the water, but that only seemed to cloud the soup's overall flavor. Next, I tried caramelizing the aromatics, but the profound sweetness that developed only obscured the smoky chorizo and tart vinegar. But all was not lost. The failed caramelized vegetable test got me thinking about an entirely different technique for enhancing the flavor of aromatics: sweating. This approach, used by cooks around the world, involves slowly cooking aromatics in a small amount of fat in a covered pot. The vegetables are kept just this side of browning, and during the process they develop a distinctive yet subtle flavor that is said to improve almost any dish.

It was certainly worth a try. I prepared another batch of soup, first browning the chorizo and removing it from the pot and then slowly cooking the

What Makes It Spanish?

Three quintessential ingredients provide our soup with authentic Spanish flavor.

SMOKED PAPRIKA
Pimentón, made by drying red peppers over an oak fire, offers a distinctive rich and smoky taste.

SHERRY VINEGAR
Lightly sweet sherry vinegar boasts assertive yet balanced acidity.

SPANISH CHORIZO
This heady sausage combines coarsely ground, dry-cured pork with a hit of pimentón.

PHOTOGRAPHY: CARL TREMBLAY

onion (plus carrots and parsley for a vegetal boost) in the rendered fat on low heat, all while the lentils brined. After 30 minutes, I dipped my spoon in for a sample and discovered that a real transformation had occurred: The unbrowned vegetables boasted a clean, pure, sweet flavor that was altogether different from the sweet, roasted taste produced via caramelization. In the finished soup, the effect was equally impressive: The slow-cooked aromatics turned out to be an extremely well-balanced base that highlighted the main flavors of the dish.

I was really getting somewhere, but the soup still didn't have that elusive "wow factor." As I mulled over ideas, a rather unorthodox thought came to mind: Since lentils are not only a staple of Mediterranean cooking but also of Indian cuisine, why not consult Indian cookbooks? Thumbing through classic sources, I found a technique that Indian cooks use to bolster flavor in all sorts of dishes: stirring in a so-called *tarka*, a mixture of spices and finely minced aromatics quickly bloomed in oil. Since the test kitchen recently discovered that a brief exposure to hot oil can boost the flavor of spices tenfold, I knew that the technique held a lot of promise.

Inspired, I whipped up a Spanish tarka for my next batch of soup: Instead of adding the smoked paprika to the simmering lentils, I sizzled it in olive oil along with black pepper, minced garlic, and finely grated onion (the small pieces ensured that it would soften quickly). This is potent stuff. Thinking that it might overwhelm the soup as a garnish, I decided to drizzle it into the broth for a few more minutes of simmering. While I was at it, I addressed the thickness of my soup (or, more accurately, the lack thereof) by adding flour. I stirred some into the oil in the tarka to make a sort of roux, finding that just 1 tablespoon was enough to develop the signature spoon-coating consistency. With my first taste, I knew I'd hit the jackpot with my multicultural approach. The soup had a lush consistency, not to mention tons of flavor: sweet, savory, and smoky, with a hint of acidity.

HEARTY SPANISH-STYLE LENTIL AND CHORIZO SOUP
SERVES 6 TO 8

We prefer French green lentils, or *lentilles du Puy*, for this recipe, but it will work with any type of lentil except red or yellow. Grate the onion on the large holes of a box grater. If Spanish-style chorizo is not available, kielbasa sausage can be substituted. Red wine vinegar can be substituted for the sherry vinegar. Smoked paprika comes in three varieties: sweet (*dulce*), bittersweet or medium hot (*agridulce*), and hot (*picante*). For this recipe, we prefer the sweet kind.

- 1 pound (2¼ cups) lentils, picked over and rinsed
  Salt and pepper
- 1 large onion
- 5 tablespoons extra-virgin olive oil
- 1½ pounds Spanish-style chorizo sausage, pricked with fork several times
- 3 carrots, peeled and cut into ¼-inch pieces
- 3 tablespoons minced fresh parsley
- 7 cups water, plus extra as needed
- 3 tablespoons sherry vinegar, plus extra for seasoning
- 2 bay leaves
- ⅛ teaspoon ground cloves
- 2 tablespoons sweet smoked paprika
- 3 garlic cloves, minced
- 1 tablespoon all-purpose flour

1. Place lentils and 2 teaspoons salt in heatproof container. Cover with 4 cups boiling water and let soak for 30 minutes. Drain well.

2. Meanwhile, finely chop three-quarters of onion (you should have about 1 cup) and grate remaining quarter (you should have about 3 tablespoons). Heat 2 tablespoons oil in Dutch oven over medium heat until shimmering. Add chorizo and cook until browned on all sides, 6 to 8 minutes. Transfer chorizo to large plate. Reduce heat to low and add chopped onion, carrots, 1 tablespoon parsley, and 1 teaspoon salt. Cover and cook, stirring occasionally, until vegetables are very soft but not brown, 25 to 30 minutes. If vegetables begin to brown, add 1 tablespoon water to pot.

3. Add lentils and sherry vinegar to vegetables; increase heat to medium-high; and cook, stirring frequently, until vinegar starts to evaporate, 3 to 4 minutes. Add 7 cups water, chorizo, bay leaves, and cloves; bring to simmer. Reduce heat to low; cover; and cook until lentils are tender, about 30 minutes.

4. Heat remaining 3 tablespoons oil in small saucepan over medium heat until shimmering. Add paprika, grated onion, garlic, and ½ teaspoon pepper; cook, stirring constantly, until fragrant, 2 minutes. Add flour and cook, stirring constantly, 1 minute longer. Remove chorizo and bay leaves from lentils. Stir paprika mixture into lentils and continue to cook until flavors have blended and soup has thickened, 10 to 15 minutes. When chorizo is cool enough to handle, cut in half lengthwise, then cut each half into ¼-inch-thick slices. Return chorizo to soup along with remaining 2 tablespoons parsley and heat through, about 1 minute. Season with salt, pepper, and up to 2 teaspoons sherry vinegar to taste, and serve. (Soup can be made up to 3 days in advance.)

HEARTY SPANISH-STYLE LENTIL AND CHORIZO SOUP WITH KALE

Add 12 ounces kale, stemmed and cut into ½-inch pieces, to simmering soup after 15 minutes in step 3. Continue to simmer until lentils and kale are tender, about 15 minutes.

See the Low and Slow
Video available FREE for 4 months at CooksIllustrated.com/apr13

SWEATING IT OUT FOR A SWEET, VEGETAL TASTE

Caramelized vegetables are prized for a sweet, deeply roasted flavor—and the darker they get the richer they taste. But what about the opposite approach, called sweating, which keeps vegetables entirely pale by cooking them ever so slowly in a covered pot? I knew that long cooking would develop a certain amount of sweetness in the chopped onion, carrot, and parsley I was using, as well as remove any trace of unpleasant sulfuric compounds in the onion. What I didn't know was that their flavor would be a revelation: The sweated aromatics offered a pure, sweet background taste that not only allowed my soup's primary ingredients (smoked paprika, chorizo, lentils, and sherry vinegar) to come to the fore but also seemed to fortify their individual flavors. –D.P.

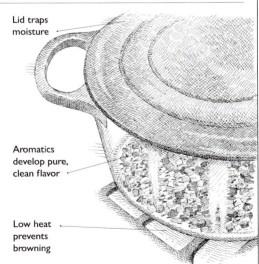

Lid traps moisture

Aromatics develop pure, clean flavor

Low heat prevents browning

Foolproof Brioche

We'd make this rich, incredibly tender bread a lot more often if we didn't have to spend 20 minutes kneading in perfectly room-temperature butter.

≥ BY ANDREW JANJIGIAN ≤

Well-made brioche is something of a miracle: Despite being laden with butter and eggs, it manages to avoid the density of a pound cake and turn out incredibly light and airy. Yet this gossamer-wing texture still provides brioche with enough structure to serve as a base for a sandwich, a slice of toast slathered with jam, or even the foundation for bread pudding. But achieving these results is a balancing act—and a tricky one at that.

Most butter-enriched doughs, like those for sandwich bread or dinner rolls, contain between 10 and 20 percent butter. The average brioche recipe brings the ratio up to 50 percent (or 5 parts butter to 10 parts flour). Because fat lubricates the wheat proteins in the flour, any amount at all will inhibit their ability to form gluten, the network of cross-linked proteins that gives bread its structure. The more fat the greater the interference. This can make brioche incredibly tender—or it can cause the dough to separate into a greasy mess.

The typical brioche method goes as follows: After a sponge of flour, yeast, and water sits overnight in order to ferment and build flavor, additional flour, yeast, and water, as well as salt, sugar, and several eggs, are added, and the mixture is kneaded in a stand mixer until a strong gluten network has begun to form. The next step is to add butter, softened to just the right temperature, a few tablespoons at a time. Only after one portion is fully incorporated into the dough is the next added. This painstaking process, which can take more than 20 minutes, is necessary to ensure that the butter is completely and evenly combined without causing the dough to separate. Next, the dough is left to rise at room temperature for a few hours and then chilled in the refrigerator for anywhere from an hour to overnight to firm up the butter—an essential step when shaping a sticky, wet dough. Once cold, the dough is shaped into loaves, left to rise yet again, and—at long last—baked. Phew.

My goal: to make tender, plush brioche with butter-rich flavor but no butter-induced headache.

Butter Up

Though tempting, I knew that dumping everything (butter included) together at the start and letting the

The double mounds of these loaves may look appealing—but more important, they help give the bread structure during shaping.

stand mixer knead it all into submission wouldn't work. All that softened butter would coat the wheat proteins (which normally come together to form gluten as soon as water is added to the mix) so thoroughly that no amount of kneading would develop sufficient structure.

But what about cold butter? Cut into the flour before adding other ingredients, the solid little chunks surely wouldn't coat the proteins as readily as softened fat, making it possible to develop at least some gluten—or so I hoped.

Using a respectable 45 percent fat-to-flour ratio and simplifying things by leaving out the sponge, I began by cutting cold butter into flour in a food processor. After transferring the mixture to the bowl of a stand mixer, I threw in the yeast, sugar, and salt. With the dough hook turning, I gradually added some water and a few beaten eggs. The dough was quite wet but still had a surprising amount of structure. After putting the dough through the usual steps—proof, chill, proof—I baked it, fingers crossed.

The results? Not great, but not half bad either. The interior crumb was far too open, with large, irregular holes, and the bread had a cottony, crumbly texture, both of which suggested that it needed more gluten development. But its having any structure at all meant that I was onto something.

Kneadlessly Complicated

A familiar approach popped to mind: the "no-knead" bread technique first popularized by Mark Bittman and Jim Lahey in *The New York Times*, which we adapted for our Almost No-Knead Bread (January/February 2008). Basically, you combine all your ingredients and let the mixture sit for hours. During this long rest, enzymes naturally present in wheat help untangle the wheat proteins that eventually come together to form an organized gluten network. This allows the dough to stitch itself together into a loaf containing plenty of structure with only a bit of stirring and a couple of folds—no actual kneading required. The key to this technique is a very wet dough (the more water the more efficient the enzymes). And happily, brioche dough is highly hydrated.

I gave the no-knead approach a whirl, cutting

---

the butter into the flour in the food processor like before but then simply mixing the liquid ingredients into the dry ones and stirring with a wooden spoon. This produced a dough that was soupy—exactly what I wanted. I covered it and let it sit at room temperature while it proofed, giving it a series of folds at 30-minute intervals to encourage the gluten to form. As I'd hoped, after several hours, the dough had just as much strength as the previous machine-kneaded one. Even better: After being chilled, shaped, and proofed a second time, it baked up just as nicely. Feeling emboldened, I wondered if I could eliminate the food processor step as well. So this time, I simply melted the butter, let it cool, and then whisked it into the egg and milk mixture before adding the liquid to the dry ingredients. To my gratification, this simplification produced a loaf that was indistinguishable from the one in which I'd cut the butter into the flour first.

Structural Engineering

Still, my loaves remained cottony and open-crumbed—a sure sign that they needed more gluten than my hand-mixed method could provide on its own. But I had a few tricks up my sleeve.

First, the flour: Since its protein content is directly related to its ability to form gluten (the more protein it has the more structure it can provide to the dough), it was no shock that brioche made with flour containing the highest amount of protein—bread flour—was the clear winner.

Next, I'd let the dough sit even longer, a process that would not only increase gluten development but also add more flavor, since it would give the starches in the dough more time to ferment (a role

---

Brioche for Brunch

DAY BEFORE:
- Make dough; let rest for 10 minutes
- Fold every 30 minutes for 2 hours
- Refrigerate overnight

MORNING OF, 7 A.M.:
- Shape; let rise for 1½ to 2 hours
- Bake for 35 to 45 minutes
- Let cool for 2 hours

---

normally played by a sponge). Gluten development and fermentation are slowed but not halted by cold temperatures, so I'd also extend the dough's second rest in the fridge (where it wouldn't run the risk of overproofing and collapsing), giving it even more strength. Sure enough, brioche made from dough that was allowed to rest overnight in the fridge was much improved: It had a more finely textured and resilient crumb than any previous versions, as well as a more complex flavor.

Lastly, I gave some consideration to my shaping method. Until now, I'd been forming the dough into a single long loaf. I realized that I could add even more strength and structure to the dough by dividing it in two and shaping each half into a tight, round ball instead. Placed side by side in the pan, the two balls merged during rising and baking to form a single loaf. Even this little bit of extra manipulation made the crumb a bit finer and more uniform. And if shaping them once was good, I figured that twice might be even better. After letting the dough rounds rest, I patted them flat once more and then reshaped them into tight balls. As expected, the interior crumb was fine-textured, uniform, and resilient but still delicate.

Finally, I had a reliable and relatively hands-off brioche recipe that could hold its own against those from the best bakeries in town.

NO-KNEAD BRIOCHE
MAKES 2 LOAVES

High-protein King Arthur Bread Flour works best with this recipe, though other bread flours will suffice. If you don't have a baking stone, bake the bread on a preheated rimmed baking sheet. For our free recipes for No-Knead Brioche Buns and No-Knead Brioche à Tête, go to CooksIllustrated.com/apr13.

3¼	cups (17¾ ounces) bread flour
2¼	teaspoons instant or rapid-rise yeast
1½	teaspoons salt
7	large eggs (1 lightly beaten with pinch salt)
½	cup water, room temperature
⅓	cup (2⅓ ounces) sugar
16	tablespoons unsalted butter, melted and cooled slightly

1. Whisk flour, yeast, and salt together in large bowl. Whisk 6 eggs, water, and sugar together in medium bowl until sugar has dissolved. Whisk in butter until smooth. Add egg mixture to flour mixture and stir with wooden spoon until uniform mass forms and no dry flour remains, about 1 minute. Cover bowl with plastic wrap and let stand for 10 minutes.

2. Holding edge of dough with your fingertips, fold dough over itself by gently lifting and folding edge of dough toward middle. Turn bowl 45

degrees; fold again. Turn bowl and fold dough 6 more times (total of 8 folds). Cover with plastic and let rise for 30 minutes. Repeat folding and rising every 30 minutes, 3 more times. After fourth set of folds, cover bowl tightly with plastic and refrigerate for at least 16 hours or up to 48 hours.

3. Transfer dough to well-floured counter and divide into 4 pieces. Working with 1 piece of dough at a time, pat dough into 4-inch disk. Working around circumference of dough, fold edges of dough toward center until ball forms. Flip dough over and, without applying pressure, move your hands in small circular motions to form dough into smooth, taut round. (If dough sticks to your hands, lightly dust top of dough with flour.) Repeat with remaining dough. Cover dough rounds loosely with plastic and let rest for 5 minutes.

4. Grease two 8½ by 4½-inch loaf pans. After 5 minutes, flip each dough ball so seam side is facing up, pat into 4-inch disk, and repeat rounding step. Place 2 rounds, seam side down, side by side into prepared pans and press gently into corners. Cover loaves loosely with plastic and let rise at room temperature until almost doubled in size (dough should rise to about ½ inch below top edge of pan), 1½ to 2 hours. Thirty minutes before baking, adjust oven rack to middle position, place baking stone on rack, and heat oven to 350 degrees.

5. Remove plastic and brush loaves gently with remaining 1 egg beaten with salt. Set loaf pans on stone and bake until golden brown and internal temperature registers 190 degrees, 35 to 45 minutes, rotating pans halfway through baking. Transfer pans to wire rack and let cool for 5 minutes. Remove loaves from pans, return to wire rack, and let cool completely before slicing and serving, about 2 hours.

Melted Butter Eases the Way

Traditionally, making a rich dough like brioche means kneading all of the ingredients to develop gluten—except butter. Butter (softened to 68 degrees) is added tablespoon by tablespoon only after the mixture begins to develop into dough. This is a long and painstaking process. It's an important one, too: If the butter isn't added slowly, the dough can break into a greasy mess. When we decided to ditch tradition and use a "no-knead" technique, we realized that this would also solve our tricky butter problem. In a no-knead approach, the dough (which must be very wet) sits for a long time, stitching itself together to form gluten—all without any help from a mixer. With kneading out of the equation, we were able to melt the butter and add it all at once—a faster and far less demanding approach. –A.J.

Perfecting Lemon Chiffon Pie

While elegant and easy to make, this classic dessert is often marred by a texture that's either too soupy or overly dense, along with lemon flavor that's just so-so.

≥ BY LAN LAM ≤

When it hit the dessert scene in the early 20th century, chiffon pie was a breakthrough idea. Not only was the filling particularly light and silky, but it came together in no time—with nothing more than egg yolks, sugar, fruit juice or puree, and a little cream cooked into a curd and folded with sweetened whipped egg whites. Many versions didn't even require baking; instead, they were set with gelatin and chilled in the refrigerator. Even the crust was a snap to make: Around the same time that chiffon pies became popular, crumb crusts did, too. They were easier to make than pastry, and their crisp, delicate texture became a common base for the billowy curd. It's no wonder the concept made its way into dozens of American cookbooks and magazines over the years and spawned dozens of flavor variations—strawberry, pumpkin, and my favorite, lemon, among them.

The dessert's popularity has waned somewhat, but to me its combination of ease and elegance is as appealing as ever. And yet I've never managed to produce a version that I'd consider perfect. Some attempts have even been complete failures, either because the filling failed to set properly and gushed like soup when I attempted to remove a slice or, conversely, because it set up too much and turned out springy and chewy like a marshmallow. And the citrus flavor? With all those egg whites and the sugar, it was usually a little flat. In other words, this retro classic was due for a makeover. I moved ahead with my own ideal in mind: a filling that's creamy, rich, and set but not stiff—and that packs plenty of bright lemon punch.

Getting Set Up

A classically crisp, buttery graham cracker crust seemed just fine here, so I skipped straight to the filling and sized up a handful of different recipes. For

For an extra jolt of citrus flavor, we line the pie shell with a layer of straight lemon curd before covering it with the chiffon.

the most part, the formulas were about the same, and all were quite simple: After cooking the lemon curd until it thickens, stir in a couple of teaspoons of unflavored gelatin (dissolved in a little water) and let the mixture cool. Then whip egg whites with sugar until they hold stiff peaks, gently but thoroughly combine the curd and whites, pour the pale yellow filling into a prebaked crumb crust, and chill until set. Given the uniformity of the methods, I wasn't surprised when most of the finished pies shared the same core flaw: a filling so bouncy that the most glaring example drew comparisons to marshmallow Peeps.

I knew that too much gelatin was responsible for the springiness, but I also knew that I couldn't do without at least a small amount of this particular thickener. The outlier recipe I'd tried, an approach from mid-20th-century pie baker Angie Earl, relied on cornstarch (¼ cup dissolved in ½ cup of water), not gelatin, to thicken the filling, and the results had been disastrously soupy. I tried upping the amount of cornstarch that I was adding to the lemon curd and couldn't deny that the sturdiness of the filling

improved with every extra tablespoon. But the more cornstarch I added the duller the lemon flavor became—not surprising, since starch granules are known to absorb flavor molecules. I tried going back to gelatin and made several more pies with varying amounts but had no consistent luck. The problem, I discovered, was that gelatin is finicky. Even when I used the right amount, if I allowed the gelatin-thickened curd to firm up a bit too long, it wouldn't incorporate evenly and left streaks of curd in the chiffon. I even tried adding more eggs (both whole and just yolks) to the cornstarch curd, hoping that their proteins, fat, and emulsifiers would help the filling gel better. Including two egg whites helped a little; when heated, their proteins form a gel that traps water. But any more egg and the chiffon tasted more like an omelet than a dessert.

I'd exhausted my options when it came to trying each of the thickeners alone, but what about using them together in moderation? Assuming that I could nail the right ratio, the gelatin would supply the chiffon with just enough structure to make it sliceable, while the cornstarch would give it a bit more body. (For more information, see "For Flawless Chiffon, Two Thickeners Are Better than One.") A few days' worth of tests (and several pie breaks for my colleagues) later, I almost had it: 1 tablespoon of cornstarch plus a mere teaspoon of gelatin—about half as much as most recipes call for—produced a filling that wasn't soupy. However, it still seemed too airy and flimsy. Not wanting to risk dulling the flavor with more cornstarch, I wondered if I could make the filling a little denser with something other than a thickener. That's when I thought of whipping: Most chiffon pie recipes call for gently folding the curd into the whipped whites to preserve the filling's cloudlike consistency. I wanted to pull back on that approach, so I switched to a much more aggressive incorporation method: whipping the two components together in a stand mixer. Just as I'd hoped, this vigorous approach produced a filling that was less foamy and a bit thicker and more dense.

Now that I'd straightened out the structural issues, I could work on brightening up the lemon flavor and hopefully make the filling a bit richer, too.

Watch the Layering Happen
Video available FREE for 4 months at CooksIllustrated.com/apr13

PHOTOGRAPHY: CARL TREMBLAY

COOK'S ILLUSTRATED
22

One-Two (Layer) Punch

Some of the most lemony pies I'd made early on got their citrus flavor not only from fresh-squeezed juice but also from zest and even lemon extract. Extract gave the filling an unappealing "cooked" lemon flavor, but grating some of the fruit's fragrant skin and adding it to the filling rounded out the acidity of the juice with a fresher, more complex perfume. And yet the big lemon kick that my tasters clamored for still hadn't fully come through. What the pie needed, they said, was another layer of lemon flavor.

Another layer—that wasn't a bad idea, actually. What if, instead of mixing all of the potent lemon curd with the whipped egg white mixture, I reserved a portion of it to line the pie shell? I took 1¼ cups of the curd base (a little more than half of the total), spread it in the bottom of the pie shell, and froze it briefly to help it set. It delivered precisely the extreme tanginess we'd been craving, not to mention an eye-catching pop of color. The only hitch was that now the ratio of curd to whipped egg whites had changed, so the texture of the filling was off. Since I was losing some of the gelatin to the curd liner, the chiffon layer now squished a bit under the knife when I sliced. It also tasted a bit lean, since the curd took some of the yolks and cream with it, too. Fortunately, there was an obvious way to solve the consistency problem: Divide the teaspoon of gelatin between the two layers. This way, both components contained just enough to be creamy yet stable.

Dairy was the obvious go-to for richness, but I could add only so much before the gelatin lost its grip on the chiffon. That ruled out liquids like heavy cream and half-and-half. But what about something more solid, like cream cheese? Four ounces, stirred into the remaining portion of the curd, enriched the chiffon nicely and also thickened it up a bit.

Creamy but sturdy, rich but still lightweight, and full of bright citrus tang, this pie was a showstopper.

CREATING A SMOOTH LEMON LAYER

After spreading the lemon curd over the crust, we briefly pop the curd-lined crust in the freezer to firm it up; that way, it won't squish when topped with the chiffon.

RECIPE TESTING

For Flawless Chiffon, Two Thickeners Are Better than One

Most chiffon pies call for adding only one thickener—usually gelatin or cornstarch—to the curd before combining it with the whipped egg whites. We made dozens of pies with both thickeners and produced dozens of failures (some stiff, some soupy) before we realized that the solution was to use a little of both.

JUST GELATIN: RUBBERY

Gelatin, a pure protein, works by forming a gel network that traps the liquid in the filling. But too much can lead to a bouncy texture—and even the ideal amount produces inconsistent results. If the gelatin-thickened curd is allowed to firm up a tad too long before being combined with the egg whites, it leaves streaks.

JUST CORNSTARCH: SOUPY

Cornstarch thickens when its starch molecules bond together and trap water, creating a solid, jellylike structure. It's more forgiving to work with than gelatin, but unless you add a glut of it, the filling will be loose. And too much cornstarch will mute the flavor of the filling.

GELATIN + CORNSTARCH: PERFECT

Using both gelatin and cornstarch in moderation produces chiffon that sets up reliably but isn't rubbery. The proteins in just 1 teaspoon of gelatin are enough to form a gel network, while a mere tablespoon of cornstarch acts as a filler that makes the network more stable without dulling the filling's lemony punch.

LEMON CHIFFON PIE
SERVES 8 TO 10

For tips on shaping the crust, see page 31. Before cooking the curd mixture, be sure to whisk thoroughly so that no clumps of cornstarch or streaks of egg white remain. Pasteurized egg whites can be substituted for the 3 raw egg whites. Serve with lightly sweetened whipped cream.

Crust

- 9   whole graham crackers
- 3   tablespoons sugar
- ⅛   teaspoon salt
- 5   tablespoons unsalted butter, melted

Filling

- 1   teaspoon unflavored gelatin
- 4   tablespoons water
- 5   large eggs (2 whole, 3 separated)
- 1¼ cups (8¾ ounces) sugar
- 1   tablespoon cornstarch
- ⅛   teaspoon salt
- 1   tablespoon grated lemon zest plus ¾ cup juice (4 lemons)
- ¼   cup heavy cream
- 4   ounces cream cheese, cut into ½-inch pieces, softened

1. FOR THE CRUST: Adjust oven rack to lower-middle position and heat oven to 325 degrees. Process graham crackers in food processor until finely ground, about 30 seconds (you should have about 1¼ cups crumbs). Add sugar and salt and pulse to combine. Add melted butter and pulse until mixture resembles wet sand.

2. Transfer crumbs to 9-inch pie plate. Press crumbs evenly into bottom and up sides of plate. Bake until crust is lightly browned, 15 to 18 minutes. Allow crust to cool completely.

3. FOR THE FILLING: Sprinkle ½ teaspoon gelatin over 2 tablespoons water in small bowl and let sit until gelatin softens, about 5 minutes. Repeat with second small bowl, remaining ½ teaspoon gelatin, and remaining 2 tablespoons water.

4. Whisk 2 eggs and 3 yolks together in medium saucepan until thoroughly combined. Whisk in 1 cup sugar, cornstarch, and salt until well combined. Whisk in lemon zest and juice and heavy cream. Cook over medium-low heat, stirring constantly, until thickened and slightly translucent, 4 to 5 minutes (mixture should register 170 degrees). Stir in 1 water-gelatin mixture until dissolved. Remove pan from heat and let stand for 2 minutes.

5. Remove 1¼ cups curd from pan and pour through fine-mesh strainer set in bowl. Transfer strained curd to prepared pie shell (do not wash out strainer or bowl). Place filled pie shell in freezer. Add remaining water-gelatin mixture and cream cheese to remaining curd in pan and whisk to combine. (If cream cheese does not melt, briefly return pan to low heat.) Pour through strainer into now-empty bowl.

6. Using stand mixer, whip 3 egg whites on medium-low speed until foamy, about 2 minutes. Increase speed to medium-high and slowly add remaining ¼ cup sugar. Continue whipping until whites are stiff and glossy, about 4 minutes. Add curd–cream cheese mixture and whip on medium speed until few streaks remain, about 30 seconds. Remove bowl from mixer and, using spatula, scrape sides of bowl and stir mixture until no streaks remain. Remove pie shell from freezer and carefully pour chiffon over curd, allowing chiffon to mound slightly in center. Refrigerate for at least 4 hours or up to 2 days before serving.

A New Way of Cooking Beets

Our simple method saves time, intensifies flavor, and even yields a beet-enriched sauce.

> BY CELESTE ROGERS

Beets are packed with complex earthy sweetness, but preparing them is no small feat. Roasting them concentrates their flavor but can take more than 90 minutes—way too long for a weeknight side dish. Boiling might shave off time, but one taste of the earthy, sweet crimson cooking liquid proves that this convenience exacts its own toll. Not wanting to pour flavor down the drain or wait longer than an hour, I went in search of a more streamlined approach to bringing out the best in beets.

Most quick-cooking beet recipes begin by cutting the beets down to bite size. While this reduces the roasting time to less than a half-hour, peeling and cutting the rock-hard raw beets is a tedious and messy task. Part of the satisfaction of cooking beets whole (either roasting or boiling) is slipping their skins off post-cooking with the simple rub of a paper towel and easily slicing their softened flesh with a knife. I wanted the same easy technique—but faster.

I decided to turn to the epitome of speed and convenience: the microwave. But as it turns out, this is the wrong appliance for beets. When I pulled a tender batch from the microwave after 12 minutes, I found that their skins were impossible to remove without some arm strength and a vegetable peeler. This is because the microwave heats the outermost inch of food so fast that moisture in the beet flesh doesn't have time to evaporate and cause the flesh to shrink and separate slightly from the skin—the key to easy removal. And easy removal of the skins was a must.

I knew I would have to use a more traditional method, and boiling had the most potential for speed. I tried halving the raw beets before placing them in a large saucepan with about a quart of water to cover (turning a blind eye to any consequential flavor loss for now). This small investment in prep work cost less than a minute but shaved 10 to 15 minutes off the hour of cooking time typically required for whole beets. As an added benefit, the cooked beet halves cooled to handling temperature more quickly than whole beets and shed their peels just as easily under the pressure of my thumb and the gentle friction of a paper towel. Done.

My next step? I had to face the flavor lost to all that cooking water. Instead of sheepishly pouring the vibrant "beet broth" down the drain after cooking

Braising the beets in a small amount of liquid creates the base for a flavorful sauce to finish the dish.

up my next batch, I decided that I would reduce it to about a tablespoon and use it to build a dressing for the beets—nothing wasted and no flavor lost. Unfortunately, reducing a quart of water took upwards of 25 minutes.

Not wanting to devote this much time to reduction, I tried cooking the beets in less liquid to begin with. A mere 1¼ cups was enough to submerge a small portion of each beet and provide ample steam. By reducing the amount of liquid, I effectively switched from boiling to braising, relying on a small amount of water to gently simmer and steam my beets in a tightly covered pot. For even braising, I needed to make certain that the beets were in a single layer, so I switched from a large saucepan to a broader covered straight-sided skillet. (A Dutch oven worked, too.) The beets finished cooking in the same time period and were just as tender, but now the leftover braising liquid reduced in just 5 minutes flat.

To play up the earthy sweetness of the beets and introduce a complementary acidity, I added a tablespoon of light brown sugar and 3 tablespoons of vinegar to the beet reduction. Just 1 more minute of cooking gave the resultant sweet-and-sour sauce enough body to coat the peeled wedges. Thin slices of shallot underscored the savory depth, while toasted nuts, aromatic citrus zest, and fresh herbs added just enough contrast without overshadowing the robust beet flavor I had worked so hard to preserve. As the self-proclaimed roasted beet lovers went back for seconds, I considered my work done. Armed with a simple method that cost me less than an hour, I was ready to add beets to my midweek vegetable roster.

See Our Every Step

Video available FREE for 4 months at CooksIllustrated.com/apr13

BEETS WITH LEMON AND ALMONDS
SERVES 4 TO 6

To ensure even cooking, we recommend using beets that are of similar size—roughly 2 to 3 inches in diameter. The beets can be served warm or at room temperature. If serving at room temperature, wait to sprinkle with almonds and herbs until right before serving. For our free recipe for Beets with Ginger and Cashews, go to CooksIllustrated.com/apr13.

1½	pounds beets, trimmed and halved horizontally
1¼	cups water
	Salt and pepper
3	tablespoons white vinegar
1	tablespoon packed light brown sugar
1	shallot, sliced thin
1	teaspoon grated lemon zest
½	cup whole almonds, toasted and chopped
2	tablespoons chopped fresh mint
1	teaspoon chopped fresh thyme

1. Place beets, cut side down, in single layer in 11-inch straight-sided sauté pan or Dutch oven. Add water and ¼ teaspoon salt; bring to simmer over high heat. Reduce heat to low, cover, and simmer until beets are tender and tip of paring knife inserted into beets meets no resistance, 45 to 50 minutes.

2. Transfer beets to cutting board. Increase heat to medium-high and reduce cooking liquid, stirring occasionally, until pan is almost dry, 5 to 6 minutes. Add vinegar and sugar; return to boil; and cook, stirring constantly with heat-resistant spatula, until spatula leaves wide trail when dragged through glaze, 1 to 2 minutes. Remove pan from heat.

3. When beets are cool enough to handle, rub off skins with paper towel or dish towel and cut into ½-inch wedges. Add beets, shallot, lemon zest, ½ teaspoon salt, and ¼ teaspoon pepper to glaze and toss to coat. Transfer beets to serving dish; sprinkle with almonds, mint, and thyme; and serve.

BEETS WITH LIME AND PEPITAS

Omit thyme. Substitute lime zest for lemon zest, toasted pepitas for almonds, and cilantro for mint.

BEETS WITH ORANGE AND WALNUTS

Substitute orange zest for lemon zest; walnuts, toasted and chopped, for almonds; and parsley for mint.

A Great Coffee Maker for Less?

The success of our favorite—but very pricey—Dutch automatic drip model spurred the launch of new rivals. Could any brew a great cup with less pain to our wallets?

> BY LISA McMANUS ⋲

In 2008, we tested automatic drip coffee makers and got disappointing results. Only one gave us great coffee—rich and smooth. We discovered that it was the lone product to achieve research-based standards for brew cycle time and water temperature, two factors necessary for bringing out the fullest flavor in coffee without bitter notes. That machine, the Technivorm Moccamaster KBT 741, uses a powerful heating element of highly conductive copper that quickly brings water to the proper range of 195 to 205 degrees and sends it over the coffee grounds in no less than 2 minutes and no more than 8—the point beyond which undesirable flavor compounds are extracted, according to coffee experts.

Five years ago, that hand-built Dutch machine was known only to coffee aficionados, but it was easy to use and brewed a great cup. Only problem: It cost $240. Nevertheless, coffee drinkers, perhaps tired of drinking subpar brew at home or shelling out $4 per cup at coffeehouses, still snapped it up.

Since then, other manufacturers took notice and launched their own high-end coffee makers. While a couple of models cost almost as much as the Technivorm, many are cheaper. All claim to reach the optimal time and temperature standards for great coffee flavor; a few have even won certification from the Specialty Coffee Association of America (SCAA), which five years ago endorsed only the Technivorm. The most important question to us: Would these newcomers produce coffee just as reliably good, and with as little fuss, as the Technivorm? To find out, we bought seven coffee makers with thermal carafes (the hot plates beneath most glass carafes scorch coffee in minutes). Among those were three models that won SCAA certification, one of which was an updated Technivorm Moccamaster, now priced at an even more staggering $299. Thirsty for a bargain, we ordered pounds of coffee and set to work.

Time and Temperature

Following manufacturers' instructions for how much coffee to use in each model, we brewed coffee in all of the machines using the same freshly roasted batch of high-quality light-medium-roast beans. (This style of roast would make it easier to detect flaws in coffee flavor.) The brews' surprisingly broad range of flavors and body reminded us that the machine you use can bring out the best in beans—or totally ruin them. But compared with the last time we rated coffee makers, things were looking up: Three models produced great coffee (one of them was the Technivorm). The remaining four, however, still missed the mark.

We already knew that the amount of time the grounds are exposed to water (the brew cycle) influences the quality of the extraction and which of the more than 1,000 volatile flavor and aroma compounds identified in roasted coffee beans make it into your cup. For the most desirable flavor compounds to be drawn out, that exposure can be no more than 8 minutes long, the SCAA says. If the water spends more time than that in contact with the grounds, it begins to extract undesirable compounds, leading to bitter-tasting coffee. No surprise, then, that "bitter" was exactly the word tasters used to describe the brews from the two machines that averaged more than 10 minutes to run a cycle. It also wasn't surprising that the coffee we liked best came from the machines that stayed within the optimal range. (How coarsely or finely the coffee is ground also affects the quality of the extraction, but since there's no way to know what grinder and what setting consumers might use, we didn't consider this.)

Once again, we also discovered that brew temperature—that is, the temperature of the water when it's in contact with the coffee grounds—factors into the quality of the extraction. According to the SCAA, optimal extraction happens when the water temperature spends most (ideally, about 90 percent) of the brew cycle between 195 and 205 degrees, and manufacturers are anxious to market their commitment to this standard. One even broadcast "Optimal Brew" on its label—but in that case, and a few others, the reality didn't live up to the claims. When we ran two rounds of temperature checks on all of the machines by taping thermocouple probe wires to the center of each brew basket atop the coffee grounds (where the heated water would drip directly on them) and averaged the amount of time the water spent in the optimal zone, the so-called Optimal Brew machine barely broke 60 percent. Two others spent roughly 35 percent of the cycle in the zone; one strayed above the 205-degree ceiling for most of the cycle and made "scorched" coffee. The worst averaged a feeble 16 percent. Meanwhile, two of the three SCAA-certified models, the Technivorm and the Bunn, clocked in at 87 percent, while the third SCAA-certified model, the Bonavita, trailed slightly. The numbers lined up with our tasting results: Those that hovered in the zone the longest brewed "complex," "velvety-smooth" coffee, while more erratic models produced "weak" coffee that "lacked depth."

The Right Ratio for a Good Brew

You can start with the best beans and the best coffee maker, but those choices won't matter if you don't also use the right ratio of coffee to water (several of the models we tested call for insufficient coffee). For the ideal cup, the Specialty Coffee Association of America recommends 9 to 11 grams (about 2 tablespoons of medium-grind coffee) per 6 ounces of water.

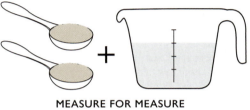

MEASURE FOR MEASURE
Use 2 tablespoons of coffee for every 6 ounces of water.

Weak Links

Time and temperature numbers didn't tell the whole story, though. Our least favorite model, as well as others, brewed coffee within the ideal time range and spent more of the brew cycle in the optimal temperature zone than many machines, yet most tasters agreed that its coffee tasted weak—or, as one taster put it, like "dishwater."

The problem came down to the simplest consideration of all: the ratio of coffee to water. "The Gold Cup ratio is 9 to 11 grams of freshly ground coffee per 6 ounces of water," said Emma Bladkya, the SCAA's coffee science manager and head of its certification program. (The definition of a "cup" is not standardized throughout the coffee industry; depending on the manufacturer, it can equal anywhere from 4 to 6 ounces.) That formula breaks down to between 1.5 and 1.83 grams of coffee per ounce of water. Some models suggested less and their brews tasted predictably weak, but the biggest offender was that lowest-ranked model, Mr. Coffee, which recommended using just 0.75 grams per ounce—hence the "dishwater" comment.

A few manufacturers recommended using an adequate amount of coffee for a partial pot—and then warned that the ratio of coffee to water should be decreased when brewing a full pot. The 10-cup Bodum, for example, recommended one scoop of coffee for every cup but no more than eight scoops in total—leaving you two scoops short if you make a whole pot. The problem, Bladkya says, is small brew

Why Would a Coffee Maker Skimp on Coffee?

Several of the coffee makers we tested contain warnings in their manuals that limit the total amount of ground coffee you should use when brewing a full pot. The reason for the cap is simple: to avoid overflows. (As hot water infuses the coffee grounds, they expand.) In some cases, these limits restrict the user to just a fraction of the SCAA's recommended ratio of 2 tablespoons of ground coffee for every 6 ounces of water.

Not surprisingly, when we tried brewing the SCAA-recommended ratio of coffee to water in our three lowest-ranked machines—all of which call for too little coffee in their manuals—the results left us with messes on our hands. In the Breville, that meant adding 20 tablespoons of coffee (the manufacturer's limit is 16 tablespoons); the machine's filter basket was heaped to the brim with no room for expansion and no way to close its swing door without pushing ground coffee into the machinery. Brewed coffee grounds puffed up over the rim of the Bodum coffee maker, coated its showerhead, and sent coffee pouring down the sides of the machine. In the Mr. Coffee, grounds overflowed the 8- to 12-cup filter (the largest size we could find in the supermarket) and gunked up the brew basket.

WHAT THE MR. COFFEE MANUAL RECOMMENDS **WHAT YOU REALLY NEED**

Like other bottom-ranked machines, Mr. Coffee calls for far less than the SCAA-recommended amount of ground coffee when you brew a full pot. The ideal amount caused overflows.

---

baskets. "In order to fit [9 to 11 grams of coffee per cup] in, say, a 10-cup brewer, you'd need to allow room for that coffee to expand once wetted, and a lot of brewers don't have enough room in their brew basket."

That's putting it mildly. When we added the SCAA-recommended amount of coffee for a full pot to machines that called for too little coffee, the results were disastrous. The Breville's basket was so heaped with grounds that we couldn't even close its swing door. The requisite quantity of coffee caused grounds to puff up over the rim of the Bodum basket during brewing, spilling down the side and onto the carafe (a problem we noticed even with a lesser amount of coffee). Coffee grounds flooded over Mr. Coffee's filter, creating a lavalike mess in its basket. Any other issues these machines might have aside, we weren't about to recommend them if they couldn't brew a full pot with the ideal amount of ground beans.

(Design) Detail-Oriented

Other design defects were merely bothersome. Adding water or coffee to some models meant moving them away from any obstructions: The Capresso maker requires 2 feet of vertical space; Mr. Coffee needs more than half a foot of clearance on the side—annoyances if your coffee maker must live under a countertop cabinet or wedged between other appliances. Thoughtfully designed models, like the Bunn, load coffee from the front, without requiring you to move the appliance. All the carafes kept coffee hot for at least a couple of hours, but some were hard to open and dribbled. We preferred brew-through lids; otherwise, you must remove the brew basket to pour a cup and then screw on a separate lid to keep coffee hot. One machine, the Breville, was just fussy to operate: While it features an attached burr grinder and is endlessly customizable, it is also endlessly time-consuming in terms of setup and features an upward-tilting display that's hard to read. And the machine is

riddled with annoying (and worrisome) reminders to clean and dry various parts or risk failure.

Top Pots

After brewing gallons of coffee, we still think the Technivorm Moccamaster is the best auto drip machine on the market. It's utterly consistent: During every cycle, it hit the ideal temperature zone for the optimal length of time, which explains why its coffee was always smooth and full-flavored. It was also intuitive to use—a perk we don't take for granted when we're dialing up our first cup of coffee in the morning. On this updated model, the KBGT 741, Technivorm removed the manual "hold-back" switch on the brew basket that let users choose to slow or temporarily stop the flow of coffee into the carafe (which you might do to steep the grounds longer or to pour a quick cup before brewing finishes). The new model does this

automatically, holding back the outflow of coffee for about 30 seconds before letting it drip into the carafe, to ensure that water fully saturates the grounds; it also cuts off flow if you pull out the carafe to pour a cup. Whether you like this change depends on how much you enjoy (and would miss) coffee-geek-like tinkering; for example, some precisionists might prefer to vary the hold-back time. (The old model, the KBT 741, is still available and we still highly recommend it.)

That said, we also identified an excellent alternative for half the money. The Bonavita 8-Cup Coffee Maker ($149) achieves nearly the same high standards for brew time and temperature as the Technivorm, but because it heats the water to a slightly higher temperature, its coffee is brighter and slightly more acidic—a plus or not, depending on your taste preference. Either way, it's our highly recommended Best Buy.

See How They Drip

Video available FREE for 4 months at CooksIllustrated.com/apr13

Which Winner Is Right for You?

Many coffee drinkers will be pleased with the excellent performance of the Bonavita, but if you want to invest in the best machine money can buy, the Technivorm might be for you. Here's how they differ.

BREWING PERFORMANCE

The **Technivorm** is robotic, reaching the same optimal time and temperature numbers every single time you brew a pot. The **Bonavita** wavers in and out of the ideal temperature zone a bit more.

HEATING ELEMENT

Though its exterior parts are made from inexpensive lightweight plastic (meant to be replaceable), the **Technivorm**'s nervous system is built to last. Specifically, its heating element is made of expensive, highly conductive copper—a metal that can reach a higher temperature more quickly than can aluminum, which is what **Bonavita** (and most other coffee maker manufacturers) uses.

SATURATION OF GROUNDS

The new **Technivorm** KBGT and the older **Technivorm** KBT each have a hold-back function that slows or stops the flow of coffee into the

carafe, steeping the grounds longer. (On the old model, this function is manually controlled; on the new model, it automatically waits about 30 seconds.) The **Bonavita** does not have this function, though it's equipped with a showerhead that helps saturate the grounds evenly.

CARAFE LID

The **Technivorm**'s carafe features a convenient brew-through lid; the **Bonavita** requires you to remove the brew basket and screw on a separate lid to keep coffee hot.

CONSTRUCTION

The **Technivorm** is hand-built in the Netherlands. The **Bonavita** is machine-built in China from a German design.

LENGTH OF WARRANTY

Technivorm: five years; **Bonavita**: two years.

TESTING AUTOMATIC DRIP COFFEE MAKERS

We tested seven automatic drip coffee makers with thermal carafes. All were purchased online; sources for highly recommended models are on page 32.

BREW FLAVOR: We used the same batch of freshly roasted, freshly ground beans; brewed the beans with spring water; and followed manufacturer directions for a full pot. We held a blind taste test, assessing flavor, acidity, body, and overall appeal.

BREW TIME AND TEMPERATURE: We brewed full pots, measuring brew cycle time, water temperature, and the percentage of brew time that the water temperature was in the ideal range. Models that brewed coffee in no more than 8 minutes and kept water between 195 and 205 degrees for nearly 90 percent of the cycle—industry standards for optimal flavor—rated best.

DESIGN: We assessed the coffee maker's and the carafe's construction and user-friendliness, including how difficult it was to fill the water reservoir and load the coffee and filter; to set up and start the machine and monitor its progress; and to open, close, and pour from the carafe, as well as to remove the used grounds and clean up.

CARAFE TEMPERATURE: All carafes kept the coffee at or above 165 degrees for 1 hour and 150 degrees for 2 hours. Carafes that kept the most heat got more stars, but the score didn't affect a machine's ranking.

WATER CAPACITY: We listed the water capacity of each machine in ounces because the definition of a "cup" is not standardized throughout the coffee industry. Coffee maker "cups" range from 4 to 6 ounces.

	CRITERIA		TESTERS' COMMENTS

HIGHLY RECOMMENDED

TECHNIVORM Moccamaster 10-Cup Coffee Maker with Thermal Carafe
Model: KBGT 741 Price: $299
Average Brew Time: 6 min, 11 sec
Brew Temperature in Ideal Range: 87%
Water Capacity: 40 oz

Brew Flavor ★★★
Design ★★★
Carafe ★

Certified by the SCAA, the updated version of our old favorite (the KBT 741, now also $299) meets time and temperature guidelines with utter consistency. As a result, it produces a "smooth," "velvety" brew. It's also intuitive to use. The carafe lost some heat after 2 hours but still kept the coffee above 150 degrees.

BONAVITA 8-Cup Coffee Maker with Thermal Carafe *BEST BUY*
Model: BV 1800 TH Price: $149
Average Brew Time: 6 min, 43 sec
Brew Temperature in Ideal Range: 78%
Water Capacity: 40 oz

Brew Flavor ★★★
Design ★★½
Carafe ★

Simple to use and SCAA-certified, this brewer spends most of the cycle in the ideal temperature range. Its coffee had "bright," "full" flavor that was a bit more "acidic" than the Technivorm's. The widemouthed carafe is easy to clean, but there's no brew-through lid; you must remove the brew basket and screw on a separate lid to keep coffee hot.

RECOMMENDED

BUNN HT Phase Brew 8-Cup Thermal Carafe Coffee Maker
Model: HT Price: $139.99
Average Brew Time: 4 min, 49 sec
Brew Temperature in Ideal Range: 87%
Water Capacity: 40 oz

Brew Flavor ★★½
Design ★★★
Carafe ★★

This SCAA-certified pot heats the water completely before releasing it over the grounds. That explained its impressive temperature accuracy, though the coffee was somewhat "acidic." (Note: Early versions of this model shorted out when home voltage fluctuated; Bunn states that it has solved this problem, and our machine worked fine.)

NOT RECOMMENDED

CAPRESSO MT600 PLUS 10-Cup Programmable Coffee Maker with Thermal Carafe
Model: 485 Price: $129.99
Average Brew Time: 10 min, 26 sec
Brew Temperature in Ideal Range: 35%
Water Capacity: 40 oz

Brew Flavor ★½
Design ★½
Carafe ★★

This model's water temperature climbed above the ideal zone for most of the cycle—hence the "burnt" complaints. Its cycle also ran too long. The design wasn't great: Controls were confusing, loading the reservoir was awkward (you must peer around the side to see the water level), and the carafe dribbles.

BODUM BISTRO b. over Coffee Machine
Model: 11001-565US Price: $250
Average Brew Time: 5 min, 54 sec
Brew Temperature in Ideal Range: 35%
Water Capacity: 40 oz

Brew Flavor ★½
Design ★
Carafe ★★★

This machine's brew cycle was erratic (running first cool and then hot); its design was flimsy; and, most damning, its small brew basket overflowed, pouring coffee and grounds onto its power button, which stuck "on." The carafe was the best heat retainer of the lineup and was easy to pour from.

BREVILLE YouBrew Drip Coffee Maker with Built-In Grinder
Model: BDC600XL Price: $279.95
Average Brew Time: 10 min, 57 sec
Brew Temperature in Ideal Range: 16%
Water Capacity: 60 oz

Brew Flavor ★½
Design ★
Carafe ★★

This is a pricey grind-and-brew machine that does the thinking for you—after you fuss with the endless customizable options. It spent a measly 16 percent of its long brew cycle in the ideal temperature zone—no wonder the coffee tasted "weak" and "bitter." Most important, the brew basket is too small to hold the SCAA-recommended amount of coffee when brewing a full pot.

MR. COFFEE Optimal Brew Thermal Coffeemaker, 10 Cup
Model: BVMC-PSTX91 Price: $69.99
Average Brew Time: 7 min, 41 sec
Brew Temperature in Ideal Range: 63%
Water Capacity: 50 oz

Brew Flavor ½
Design ★
Carafe ★★★

By prescribing far less than the SCAA-recommended amount of grounds, this machine brewed "dishwater." Adding the right amount of coffee for a full pot caused the grounds to overflow the filter and gunk up the brew basket. Other design flaws: The basket's side drawer must be pulled out completely to fill—annoying if your counter is crowded—and its reservoir acquired a musty smell we couldn't eradicate.

What Makes a Good Medium Roast?

Decades after they convinced Americans to drink ultradark French and Italian roasts, the producers of blackened beans are coming out with lighter options. So how's the coffee?

≥ BY AMY GRAVES ≤

Well into the late 1990s, most of the coffee consumed in this country was a medium roast. This was the classic American cup: lighter and more acidic than today's espresso-dark brew. Lighter coffees prevailed in part because they maximized yield: The less coffee companies roasted the beans the more weight they retained and turned into profit. It took West Coast coffee-house roasters like Peet's and Starbucks to show us another side of coffee flavor. They began roasting coffee dark—so dark that practically all you taste is the smoky depth of the roast versus the beans' individual flavors. That profile appealed to many coffee drinkers; when they jumped on board, sales of dark beans shot up in supermarkets.

But all along, fans of medium-roast coffee resisted, insisting that überdark French and Italian roasts tasted charred. These holdouts helped ensure that lighter coffee continued to do a brisk business in stores. And lately, it's not just ordinary coffee drinkers who think these roasts have merit. An increasing number of mail-order roasters are now specializing in lighter roasts, extolling their broader spectrum of flavors. "The objective is to protect the volatile aromas and fleeting flavors that dissipate with darker roasting," explained Ric Rhinehart, executive director of the Specialty Coffee Association of America. These attributes can include floral, fruity notes and bright, lively acidity.

Perhaps in response to this mini-movement, some of the big-name dark-roast pioneers have also thrown their hats into the lighter-roast ring. A year ago in January, Starbucks came out with its "blonde" roasts, two blends of lighter-roasted beans now sold in all of its outlets and in grocery stores. Peet's Coffee & Tea answered with two blends roasted more lightly than its other offerings. We decided it was time to give medium roasts a closer look. We selected a new lighter roast from Peet's and one from Starbucks, along with the medium roasts of five other top-selling supermarket brands. Which would do a better job? And, most important, would we even like the coffee?

Not-So-Dark Arts

Despite the fact that these coffees were the lightest roasts available at the supermarket, the colors of the beans told another story. To find out exactly what we were dealing with, we gave samples to a lab to measure their Agtron scores. The Agtron is an instrument that analyzes how much light the beans reflect; the more light reflected the lighter the roast and the higher the Agtron number. Our samples ranged from 57 (a solid medium roast according to industry standards) to 39 (a dark roast by a hair), demonstrating that "medium roast" is a pretty vague term.

As we sampled all seven coffees without milk or sweeteners in a blind tasting, it appeared that most of us weren't ready to switch our allegiance to the lighter side of flavor. Our favorite brew was the one with the significantly lower Agtron score, making it the darkest roast of the bunch by far. Tasters lauded this coffee's "toasty" earthiness and hints of "chocolate." By and large, super-bright, acidic flavors—hallmarks of lighter roasts—didn't rate well. The lightest roast in our lineup was panned for having the most markedly acidic taste and fell to second-to-last place. In fact, only one brew with the recognizably bright notes of a medium-roast flavor profile made it into the "recommended" category.

But as we analyzed taster comments more closely, we realized that when tasters didn't love a brew, it often had nothing to do with light- or dark-roast preferences. In our least favorite sample, tasters ferreted out "sour," "fermented" flavors that were simply out of place in coffee. The most acidic brand hinted of "cherry/almond" notes that were also jarring. And some brands simply lacked oomph, tasting "flat." Although the coffees we brewed were well within the expiration dates printed on the bags, a few samples tasted stale—even old. Given this, could it be that some of these brews were just mediocre coffee?

A Good Bean for a Good Brew

Countless variables can influence coffee flavor, from varietal; to origin; to growing conditions; to how the beans are fermented, dried, and stored; to the age of the beans when they arrive at a roaster; to how many of the wrinkled, underripened beans known as "quakers" slip through in a shipment. Quakers can have a surprisingly significant impact on coffee flavor. While almost all coffee contains a few of these bad beans, more than three per pound can impart unpleasant nut- and cereal-like tastes to the brewed cup. And sure enough, when we sent samples of our coffees to the lab to weed out the underripened beans (which don't darken during roasting), we found a direct correlation between number of quakers and our tasters' preferences: Our least favorite coffee had 14 bad beans; our next least favorite had 7; our top finisher, 1.

All of the above factors affect coffee before it reaches the roaster, and the best brands are very selective in how they source beans. But another critical factor influencing quality happens during roasting: regulating moisture level. Green beans typically contain about 10 percent moisture; after roasting, that level should remain between 0.5 percent and 3 percent. Some specialty roasters are even more precise. George Howell, of George Howell Coffee Company, in Acton, Massachusetts, aims for a moisture level of 1.7 to 2.5 percent. Why is the amount of moisture in beans so important? The best coffee, regardless of roast color, should taste full-bodied with a flavor that lingers pleasantly. But if the beans are too dry, they

Medium Roast by the Numbers

Like all types of roasts, medium-roast coffee means different things to different roasters, as evidenced by the color of the beans in our lineup, which ranged from a medium tan, to milk chocolate, to dark brown. A more objective assessment is an Agtron analysis, which measures how much light is reflected from the beans and classifies them according to industry standards. By this scale, only one coffee in our lineup was a true medium roast (Dunkin' Donuts), while our winner (Peet's) was technically a dark roast. The other coffees (including runner-up Millstone) were on the dark side of medium.

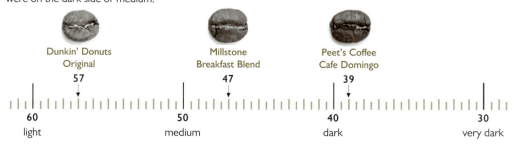

Dunkin' Donuts Original — 57
Millstone Breakfast Blend — 47
Peet's Coffee Cafe Domingo — 39

60 light — 50 medium — 40 dark — 30 very dark

won't extract properly when brewed, which in turn affects the coffee's body and richness.

Curious how the beans in our lineup would rate when it came to moisture, we sent samples back to the lab. This measurement also strongly correlated with how tasters experienced a coffee. The two brands we recommend were the only coffees to be solidly within the optimal moisture range. Three brands tested well below the ideal target—unsurprisingly, they were the same ones that tasters downgraded for having "flat" or "cardboard" tastes. And there is also such a thing as coffee that is too moist: The bottom-ranking sample, with a moisture level almost a full percentage point above the ideal cutoff, was the one marred by "sour," "fermented" flavors.

Roast to Taste

If the beans' moisture level is so important, why didn't more brands in our lineup fall within the ideal range? Sourcing cheaper, lower-quality beans is one way for a roaster to control costs—but so is streamlining the roasting process. Roasters typically evaluate bean moisture at the start of roasting and then set time and temperature monitors that will help determine when a batch is done. But for the most discriminating roasters, sensory cues are even more crucial: the first crack of the beans popping as they roast; their aroma as they develop; the way they look, feel, and taste. These roasters taste, or "cup," the batches continually to determine precisely when the beans have hit their sweet spot. Though this step slows the overall process, it's critical, the experts we talked to told us, since every batch of beans behaves differently. Limiting how often beans are cupped can help a roaster economize. And so can "quenching," whereby the roaster douses the beans with water to cool them before bagging. Specialty roasters favor slower air drying, which also doesn't introduce unwanted moisture.

The roasters of our winning coffee, Café Domingo from Peet's Coffee & Tea (named for Peet's third café on Domingo Avenue in Berkeley, California), go to particularly great lengths to achieve optimal results, tasting batches about 50 times in a typical shift—an unusually high amount. Tasters praised Café Domingo not only for its "bold," "burnt caramel" flavors that were not so far from those of dark roasts but also for its "smooth, full-bodied taste"—a quality that belongs to any good cup of coffee.

Our other winner, Millstone Breakfast Blend, was closer to a true medium roast. Though its producer wouldn't reveal details of its sourcing or roasting processes to us, the company is also clearly doing many things right. Tasters lauded this brew for a "satiny," "lemony" taste that was "a good compromise between acidity and earthiness." The numbers lined up, too: These beans were in the ideal moisture range and just two were defective. For those seeking the brighter flavors of medium-roast coffee, Millstone Breakfast Blend is a good choice.

TASTING: SUPERMARKET MEDIUM-ROAST COFFEE

In a blind tasting, 21 *Cook's Illustrated* staff members tasted seven whole-bean medium-roast coffees from a list of top-selling national brands compiled by the Chicago-based market research firm SymphonyIRI Group. We sampled the coffees without milk or sweeteners. Coffee Analysts, an independent laboratory in Burlington, Vermont, analyzed each coffee to obtain its Agtron rating (a measure of roast darkness), the number of defective green "quaker" beans, pH level, and moisture content (the ideal target is between 0.5 percent and 3 percent). Prices were paid in Boston-area supermarkets, and the brands appear below in order of preference.

RECOMMENDED

PEET'S COFFEE
Café Domingo
Price: $13.95 for 1-pound bag
($0.87 per oz)
Agtron: 39 Quakers: 1
pH: 5.33 Moisture: 1.28 percent

TASTERS' COMMENTS

By far the darkest roast in the lineup, this sample came across as "extremely smooth" and "bold-tasting," with a "stronger finish" than other samples. It tied for the smallest number of defective beans and had low acidity and optimal moisture. Its "rich," "chocolate," and "toast" flavors make it the perfect brew for those who want a break—but not too much of one—from ultradark French roasts.

MILLSTONE
Breakfast Blend
Price: $9.17 for 12-ounce bag
($0.76 per oz)
Agtron: 47 Quakers: 2
pH: 5.22 Moisture: 1.6 percent

This "satiny" coffee was "lemony" and "very enjoyable," with a "slightly nutty aftertaste." It "hit the middle of the road" for "acidity, earthiness, and complexity." As with our winner, lab results showed low acidity, few defective beans, and ideal moisture. It's a good choice for those who enjoy brighter, livelier medium-roast flavors.

RECOMMENDED WITH RESERVATIONS

CARIBOU COFFEE
Daybreak
Price: $12.54 for 12-ounce bag
($1.05 per oz)
Agtron: 46 Quakers: 1
pH: 5.19 Moisture: 0.06 percent

Some tasters were able to detect a "slight berry taste" with "black tea–like" undertones in this coffee. For others, it was "flat," "bland," and "not very distinctive." "Smells nutty but no taste," is how one taster put it. The lab results indicated extremely low moisture in the beans, which almost certainly weakened the brew.

STARBUCKS BLONDE
Veranda Blend
Price: $11.95 for 1-pound bag
($0.75 per oz)
Agtron: 46 Quakers: 5
pH: 5.25 Moisture: 0.14 percent

The "approachable" taste of this offering from the dark-roast giant of coffee companies "goes down pretty smooth," though some thought it "one-dimensional," like "cardboard." Said one taster: "It doesn't have that weight-on-your-tongue feeling that I like in coffee." Lab tests confirmed the problems, finding low moisture and some defective beans.

GREEN MOUNTAIN COFFEE
Our Blend
Price: $9.36 for 12-ounce bag
($0.78 per oz)
Agtron: 46 Quakers: 3
pH: 5.09 Moisture: 0.14 percent

This sample had "a little dried fruit toward the finish but that's it," as one taster put it. Though "robust upfront," it finished with an overly "flat, lemony" taste. Lab results supported these impressions, showing relatively high acidity and not much moisture, which limited its extraction.

NOT RECOMMENDED

DUNKIN' DONUTS
Original
Price: $11.99 for 12-ounce bag
($1 per oz)
Agtron: 57 Quakers: 7
pH: 4.94 Moisture: 0.68 percent

This medium-roast stalwart, the lightest roast in our tasting, was so "sharp and bright and very acidic" that it had one taster pleading, "I need milk!" Another deemed it an "acid bomb"; lab tests confirmed that this was the most acidic coffee we tasted. A high number of defective beans gave it weird "cherry/almond" off-tastes.

EIGHT O'CLOCK COFFEE
Original
Price: $6.95 for 12-ounce bag
($0.58 per oz)
Agtron: 47 Quakers: 14
pH: 5.06 Moisture: 3.85 percent

Our least favorite coffee was "sour" and "dirty-tasting—like socks," with a "fermented taste." This brew was also "slightly metallic," "like coffee you'd get at a diner." With the highest number of defective beans of all the coffees we sampled, it tasted "sweetly acidic"; the fermented flavor likely came from its high level of moisture.

How to Make a Stovetop Smoker

Just because the weather isn't cooperating doesn't mean that you can't smoke food. Indoor smoking delivers some of the same complexity and aromas that you'd produce on a grill. Here's our method.

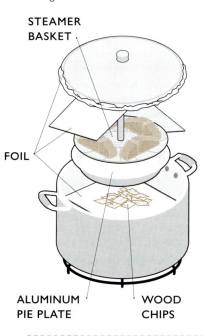

STEAMER BASKET

FOIL

ALUMINUM PIE PLATE

WOOD CHIPS

1. Place 7-inch square of heavy-duty aluminum foil on bottom of large Dutch oven (not nonstick) with tight-fitting lid. Sprinkle ¼ cup unsoaked wood chips on foil.
2. Place disposable aluminum pie plate (to catch fat) on chips, followed by steamer basket.
3. Brush 4 (6-ounce) skinless fish fillets or 4 chicken pieces (bone-in or boneless) with oil and season with salt and pepper. Arrange food in steamer basket and tent with foil.
4. Place pot over high heat until chips begin to smoke, 5 to 8 minutes.
5. Cover pot and seal rim with foil. Reduce heat to medium and cook 15 minutes.
6. Off heat (and in well-ventilated area), transfer food to serving platter (for fish) or wire rack set in rimmed baking sheet (for chicken). Broil or bake chicken until dark meat reaches 175 degrees and white meat reaches 165 degrees. –D.S.

SCIENCE Does Fattier Meat Need More Salt?

Throughout years of cooking in the test kitchen, we've noticed that we tend to season fatty meat more generously than lean meat. To bolster our anecdotal evidence with real data, we set up the following experiment.

EXPERIMENT

We rounded up five meats ranging in fat content: turkey breast, pork loin, strip steak, and both 80 percent and 90 percent lean ground beef. We cooked the meat and chopped it into pieces. We then tossed 10-gram portions of each meat with increasing amounts of salt (0.1 percent, 0.25 percent, 0.5 percent, 0.75 percent, 1 percent, and 1.5 percent by weight of each sample). We had tasters try the samples in order, starting with an unsalted control, and had them record at what percentage the meat tasted properly seasoned. We also sent cooked samples of each type of meat to a lab to determine fat content.

RESULTS

Sure enough, the fattier the meat the more salt it needed to taste properly seasoned. Tasters preferred the lean turkey breast (0.7 percent fat) and pork loin (2.6 percent fat) seasoned with 0.5 percent salt by weight. The strip steak (6 percent fat) and 90 percent lean ground beef (10 percent fat) required about 0.75 percent salt by weight to taste seasoned. And finally, the 80 percent lean ground beef (20 percent fat) tasted seasoned to a majority of tasters only when it reached 1 percent salt by weight.

TAKEAWAY

Our experiment adds credence to the conclusion of several recent published studies that fat has a dulling effect on taste. So when you season meat, remember to use a heavier hand on fatty burgers than you would on moderately fatty meats like strip steak and 90 percent ground beef. Use a lighter hand on lean meats like turkey breast and pork loin. –D.S.

Roasting Coffee in a Popcorn Popper

We've always been intrigued by the idea that roasting coffee beans at home could be as simple as calling for an air popcorn popper, a method embraced by DIY diehards. Air poppers use a fast-spinning vortex of very hot air (just under 500 degrees) to agitate the popcorn kernels so that they heat evenly and don't burn—conditions that in theory should make these gadgets ideal for quickly roasting green coffee beans. (Green coffee can be purchased online, or even from your local barista.) We dug out one of our air poppers to give it a try and were amazed by how easy it was—and how much we liked the results—once we learned to follow these guidelines.

PROPER VENTILATION IS ESSENTIAL Roasting coffee emits smoke, so if you don't have a vent, consider roasting next to a window fan or on a porch (but not on a cold day, which can prevent proper heating of the beans).

THINK SMALL The amount of coffee that you can roast in an air popper is small—usually about ½ cup.

CATCH THE CHAFF As the beans roast, a thin, papery outer membrane (chaff) will slough off. Place a bowl beneath the popper chute to catch it or orient the popper chute next to the sink.

WATCH THE TIME Roasting will take anywhere from 3 to 7 minutes, depending on how dark you like your coffee. Since beans will continue to darken even after you remove them from the popper, stop roasting just before they reach the desired color.

POP YOUR BEANS
The vortex of very hot air in a popcorn popper is also surprisingly good for roasting coffee beans.

LISTEN FOR "CRACKS" After about 3 minutes, the coffee beans will emit a loud "first crack," an indication that they're at the "light roast" stage. A minute or two later they'll be at "medium roast." At about the 6-minute mark, the beans will emit fainter, more tinny "second crack" sounds (the "dark roast" stage). If you haven't already done so, take them out immediately, before they burn and turn bitter.

COOL RAPIDLY Dump the beans into a metal colander that's been chilled in the freezer and then agitate them quickly until they are just warm to the touch.

LET THEM REST The beans will taste better the next day as the flavor develops. Freshly roasted beans also emit a lot of carbon dioxide, so wait at least 12 hours before transferring them to a sealed container. –A.J.

Easiest Way to Skin Hazelnuts

The most common method for removing hazelnut skins—toasting them and then rubbing them in a towel—can still leave some skin stubbornly hanging on. Here's a better approach: Boil 1 cup of untoasted hazelnuts in 2 cups of water and 3 tablespoons of baking soda for 3 minutes. Transfer the nuts to a bowl of ice water with a slotted spoon, drain, and slip the skins off with a towel. The hot alkaline water quickly breaks down the pectin, the primary component in the skins, allowing them to peel off not only more easily but also more completely. –D.S.

Making a crumb crust is a cinch compared with working with pie pastry, but unless you pack the crust properly, you risk crumbling edges during baking and slicing. Our method ensures a tight, clean edge and works for all types of crumbs: graham cracker, animal cracker, Oreo, etc.

Using the bottom and sides of a measuring cup, press the crumb mixture firmly and evenly across the bottom of the pie plate. Then pack the crumbs against the side of the pie plate, using your thumb and the measuring cup simultaneously. –L.L.

For Meatier Flavor, Season with Sherry

To enhance meaty, *umami* flavors in food, we typically turn to ingredients like soy sauce and anchovies, which are rich in the glutamates and nucleotides that create this savory taste. But when we read that British chef Heston Blumenthal uses sherry—an ingredient not known to contain these compounds—for the same purpose, it piqued our interest. The fortified wine supposedly increases savoriness through a different mechanism—the synergistic relationship between compounds called diketopiperazines, or DKPs (which likely result from the yeastlike growth that sherry develops as it ages), and umami-boosting elements in food.

To test his theory, we added ¼ teaspoon of dry sherry to 1 cup of beef broth and ¾ teaspoon to an equal amount of tomato sauce, both of which contain high levels of umami-enhancing glutamic acid. (We added more sherry to the tomato sauce because it's more concentrated and complex.) Tasters compared these with samples of broth and tomato sauce treated with the same amounts of ruby port and Madeira—fortified wines that don't develop a yeastlike growth—as well as with an untreated control sample. Though we couldn't confirm Blumenthal's research on DKPs, he may be onto something. Tasters found that even these scant amounts of sherry boosted complexity and savoriness in both the broth and the tomato sauce, while the port and Madeira had little to no effect. In the future when our soups, stocks, and sauces need an umami boost, we'll consider adding a splash of sherry—¼ to ¾ teaspoon per cup, depending on the complexity of the liquid. –D.S.

Don't Be Afraid to Rotate Cakes

In the test kitchen, we often recommend rotating cakes, pastries, and breads in the oven halfway through baking to promote even browning. (This is especially important because most ovens do not heat evenly.) But we don't generally recommended rotating delicate, airy cakes for fear that they will collapse. Without any conclusive evidence that this was the case, however, we decided to put it to the test.

We made two pairs of the most delicate cakes we could think of: fluffy yellow layer cake and angel food cake, both containing whipped egg whites, which we figured would make them prone to collapse if disturbed during baking. One set of cakes we rotated at the halfway point, jostling them clumsily in order to drive the point home. The other we left alone.

The result? Neither of the rotated cakes was worse for wear, and both were more evenly browned than the undisturbed cakes. It seems that even delicate cakes are fully set early on during baking, so there's little risk of collapse halfway through. From now on, we will call for rotating all baked goods—even delicate cakes—halfway through baking. If you are baking on upper and lower racks, we recommend switching rack positions and rotating the cakes at the same time. It will only improve your results. –A.J.

GIVE IT A SPIN
Rotating any cake—even a delicate one—during baking won't cause it to collapse.

Getting the Most from Your Microwave

Microwave cooking is unlike any other cooking method in the kitchen. It can seem at once to be the fastest method and the most uneven. To illustrate the difference between microwave cooking and simmering, we ran the following experiment.

EXPERIMENT
We microwaved a potato on a plate for 3 minutes, sliced it in half, and compared it with a potato that we simmered in water for 3 minutes.

RESULTS
The microwave cooked a large portion of the potato in just 3 minutes, but the heat penetration was very uneven. In contrast, the simmered potato featured a thin, consistent line of cooked potato around the perimeter.

TAKEAWAY
The electromagnetic waves produced by a microwave oven create an electric field that reverses direction 4.9 billion times per second. Water molecules are polar, meaning that they contain a partial positive and a partial negative electrical charge. In the presence of the oscillating electric field, the water molecules in the potato (or any food) change direction at the same incredibly fast rate. This rapid reversal causes the water molecules to bump into one another, effectively increasing their temperature. The problem is that microwaves can't penetrate more than an inch into food (the heat continues to move toward the center via conduction, just as it does in food cooked in an oven). What's more, microwaves hit foods in an unpredictable pattern, so some parts will cook faster than others. Microwave ovens use turntables to help even out cooking to some degree, but only on one axis. To ensure even cooking:
1. Stir or flip food often.
2. Add a cover to trap steam that can provide another form of cooking.
3. Rest foods for a few minutes after cooking to allow hot and cool spots to even out (especially important for foods that can't be stirred). –D.S.

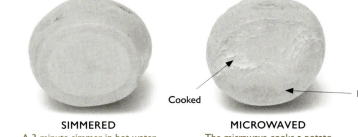

Cooked   Raw

SIMMERED
A 3-minute simmer in hot water begins to evenly cook a potato from the outside in.

MICROWAVED
The microwave cooks a potato unevenly, making covering, flipping, and stirring during cooking crucial.

Fast Route to Parlor-Worthy Crust

The best restaurant pizzas are baked in ultrahot ovens (some reaching temperatures as high as 1,000 degrees), guaranteeing a beautifully browned crust before the toppings overcook. However, even the best home ovens max out at about 550 degrees, meaning that getting a crisp, bronzed edge before the interior of the crust overcooks is difficult. We've devised techniques to maximize the heat output in the oven for our own pizza recipes—preheating the baking stone and positioning it close to the top of the oven to capture reflected heat—but we wondered if we might modify our dough recipes, too.

Since the browning temperatures of sugars are as much as 75 degrees lower than those of the starches and proteins in flours, we tried adding increasing amounts of sugar to the dough for our Thin-Crust Pizza (January/February 2011). As expected, the more sugar we added the faster and more evenly the crust browned. In the end, we found that 4 percent sugar, or 2 teaspoons per cup of flour, was an ideal amount: It guaranteed quick browning in the time it took the crust to cook through without adding any noticeable sweetness or affecting the rising time. It's an easy addition and one that we'll be keeping in our pizza repertoire from now on. –A.J.

EQUIPMENT CORNER

≥ BY HANNAH CROWLEY, LISA McMANUS & TAIZETH SIERRA ≤

NEW | Large-Capacity Food Scale

A good kitchen scale makes measurements super-accurate, but our longtime favorite OXO Good Grips Food Scale ($49.99) tops out at 11 pounds. Now the company has introduced the OXO Good Grips 22-Lb Food Scale with Pull-Out Display ($69.99), which can weigh ingredients up to 22 pounds—handy for large-batch canning or baking. (It's fine for small-scale jobs, too, as it measures in 1/8-ounce and 1-gram increments.) Like its smaller sibling, this scale is very easy to use: Its clever pullout display means you don't have to peer under overhanging bowls,

ON A GRAND SCALE
The OXO Good Grips 22-Lb Food Scale is handy for big-batch cooking.

and a "zero" (tare) function lets you subtract the weight of the vessel or additional ingredients. We weighed 30-, 200-, and 500-gram calibration weights and found it to be accurate. It also measures in cups and milliliters for "water-based" ingredients, but we don't recommend using those features; they can be inaccurate if employed for liquids other than water. (A conversion chart for liquids with different densities is included.) Despite this quibble, we found this scale useful and worth buying if you regularly cook big batches. –L.M.

NEW | Mushroom Growing Kit

You can't get any more local than food you grow yourself on spent coffee grounds. That's the idea behind Back to the Roots' Grow-Your-Own Mushroom Garden, which claims to grow oyster mushrooms in as few as 10 days: Just cut into the cardboard box and spritz the coffee grounds, which are injected with mushroom spawn, with water twice a day. After harvest you can turn over the box and grow a second batch. We placed two kits in the test kitchen away from direct sunlight as advised. After

ONE TO GROW ON
Gardeners might enjoy the Grow-Your-Own Mushroom Garden, but it didn't quite deliver on its promises.

10 days, the mushrooms had sprouted but remained too small to bother cooking—that is, until one weekend when we left them in a room with a humidifier. By the following Tuesday, the boxes had exploded into big, beautiful mushrooms, though by this point it had been a month since we started. So is it worth it? Only if you enjoy the gardening process, since the kit won't save you any money: Oyster mushrooms sell for about $12 per pound and our $19.95 kits each yielded two 1/2-pound batches. –T.S.

NEW | Pour-Over Coffee Brewer

Coffee enthusiasts love manual pour-over brewing devices because they let you control water temperature and steeping time—both key to a good cup. The Incred 'a Brew by Zevro ($24.99) has a brewing chamber that you fill with ground coffee; you add 195- to 205-degree water and then let it steep. It uses a built-in wire mesh filter (similar to a French press) instead of paper filters. After steeping, place the Incred 'a Brew carafe atop a mug to open the valve that releases the coffee (and closes when lifted from the mug's rim). The tool produced 2½ cups of flavorful, full-bodied coffee with some sediment, just like from a French press. Using this product means that we'll never have to worry about run-

POUR IT ON
The Incred 'a Brew uses a built-in wire mesh basket instead of filters.

ning out of filters—a big plus. One caveat: It won't work with mugs wider than 3½ inches in diameter, since they won't engage the valve to dispense the coffee. –H.C.

NEW | Coffee Temperature Regulator

Coffee Joulies ("JOO-lees"), small stainless steel capsules meant to be dropped into your mug, promise to cool your coffee quickly to the ideal drinking temperature (140 degrees) and keep it there. How do they work? The "phase change" material encapsulated within each Joulie has a melting temperature of 140 degrees. Surrounded by hotter liquid, this material absorbs heat (cooling the surrounding liquid) until it's completely melted inside the Joulie. Then it slowly releases this heat back out into the coffee, keeping the temperature stable. With a set of five Joulies ($49.95) and instructions to use one "bean" for every 4 ounces of coffee, we tested Joulies in our favorite 16-ounce travel mug and in a 12-ounce ceramic mug. In the open mug, Joulies worked halfway: They quickly cooled coffee to 140 degrees but didn't maintain the temperature any better than

THAT'S USING THE OLD BEAN
Coffee Joulies regulate the temperature of hot beverages, provided that you use them in a travel mug.

coffee without Joulies. In the travel mug, the coffee quickly cooled to 140 degrees and held steady for 2 hours. (Coffee in the travel mug without Joulies took just over 2 hours to cool to 140 degrees.) Joulies work as advertised, but only in a travel mug. –T.S.

Tortilla Presses

Making corn tortillas is easy if you use a tortilla press to flatten the balls of dough into disks. We tested four, priced from roughly $14 to $65. Heavy cast-iron and wood models practically flattened the dough for us, while the lighter cast-aluminum and plastic models required more muscle. We preferred models with large plates; on smaller presses dough sometimes squeezed out the sides. La Mexicana Tortilladora de Madera Barnizada/Mesquite Tortilla Press ($64.95), a wooden press, was weighty enough (almost 12 pounds) to make pressing effortless; had an ample 8-inch pressing surface; and produced even tortillas. If $65 is too steep, we recommend the Imusa Victoria Cast Iron Tortilla Press ($23.99). –T.S.

BEST PRESS
With the La Mexicana Tortilladora de Madera Barnizada/Mesquite Tortilla Press, homemade tortillas are a cinch.

For complete testing results for each item, go to CooksIllustrated.com/apr13.

Sources

Prices were current at press time and do not include shipping. Contact companies to confirm information or visit CooksIllustrated.com for updates.

PAGE 15: BUTTER KEEPER
- Lock & Lock Rectangular Food Container with Tray: $4.99, item #16183709, Bed Bath & Beyond (800-462-3966, bedbathandbeyond.com).

PAGE 20: BRIOCHE PAN
- Gobel 8-Inch Tinned Steel Brioche Mold, 6-Cup: $10, item #611004, Sur La Table (800-243-0852, surlatable.com).

PAGE 27: AUTOMATIC DRIP COFFEE MAKERS
- Technivorm Moccamaster KBGT-741 10-Cup Coffee Maker with Thermal Carafe: $299, item #KBGT-741, Boyd Coffee Company (800-545-4077, boyds.com).
- Bonavita 8-Cup Coffee Maker with Thermal Carafe: $149, George Howell Coffee Company (866-444-5282, terroircoffee.com).

PAGE 32: LARGE-CAPACITY FOOD SCALE
- OXO Good Grips 22-Lb Food Scale with Pull-Out Display: $69.99, item #1128380, OXO (800-545-4411, oxo.com).

PAGE 32: MUSHROOM GROWING KIT
- Back to the Roots Grow-Your-Own Mushroom Garden: $19.95, Back to the Roots (510-922-9758, backtotheroots.com).

PAGE 32: POUR-OVER COFFEE BREWER
- Incred 'a Brew by Zevro: $24.99, item #IAB109, Zevro (847-676-0123, zevro.com).

PAGE 32: COFFEE TEMPERATURE REGULATOR
- Coffee Joulies 5-Pack: $49.95, Coffee Joulies (joulies.com).

PAGE 32: TORTILLA PRESSES
- La Mexicana Tortilladora de Madera Barnizada/Mesquite Tortilla Press: $64.95, item #50409-87289, MexGrocer.com (877-463-9476, MexGrocer.com).
- Imusa Victoria Cast Iron Tortilla Press: $23.99, item #10827940, Target (800-440-0680 target.com).

INDEX
March & April 2013

Fluffy Omelet, 15

Best Chicken Parmesan, 7

Modern Beef Burgundy, 9

Foolproof Spaghetti Carbonara, 11

No-Knead Brioche, 21

Hearty Spanish-Style Lentil and Chorizo Soup, 19

Beets with Lemon and Almonds, 24

Roast Butterflied Leg of Lamb, 13

Lemon Chiffon Pie, 23

AMERICA'S TEST KITCHEN COOKING SCHOOL

Let us help you become a better cook. Offering more than 100 courses for cooks at every level, our school combines personalized instruction from real *America's Test Kitchen* test cooks with leading-edge technology to offer a unique and effective learning experience. Start a 14-day free trial at OnlineCookingSchool.com.

COOK'S ILLUSTRATED IS NOW AVAILABLE ON iPAD!

Download the new *Cook's Illustrated* app for iPad and start a free trial subscription or purchase a single issue. Issues are enhanced with recipe videos, full-color step-by-step slide shows, and expanded reviews and ratings. Go to CooksIllustrated.com/iPad to download our app through iTunes.

Follow us on Twitter: twitter.com/TestKitchen
Find us on Facebook: facebook.com/CooksIllustrated

PHOTOGRAPHY: CARL TREMBLAY; STYLING: MARIE PIRAINO

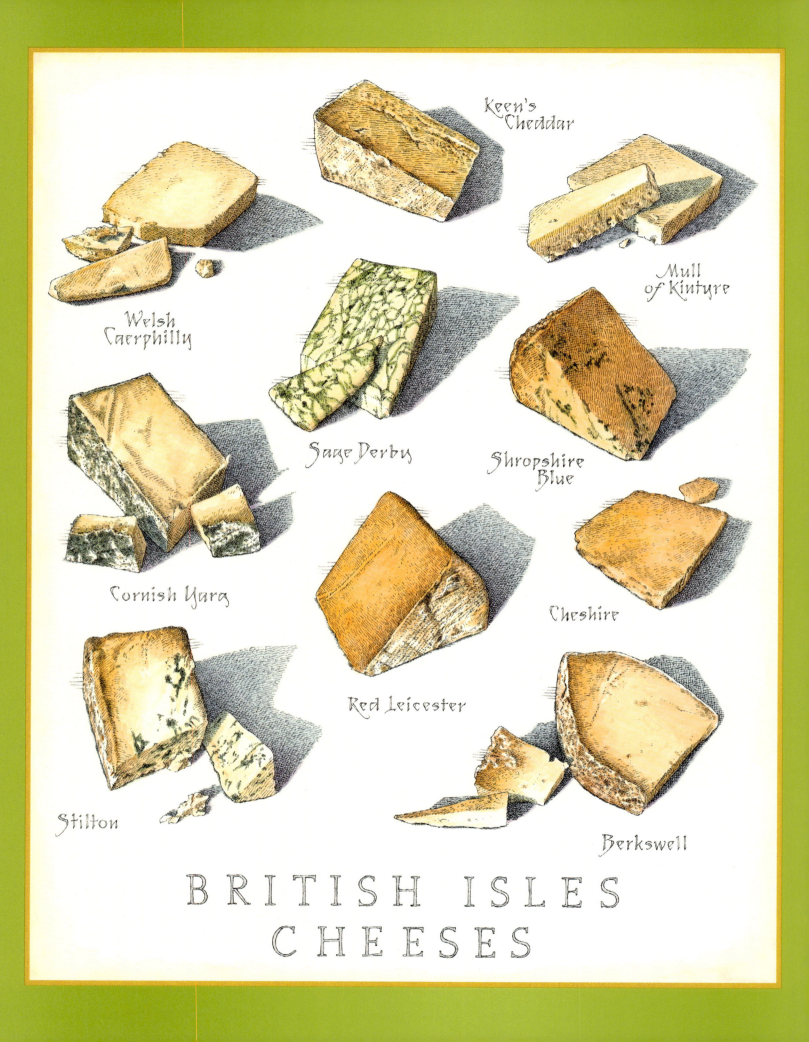

Keen's
Cheddar

Mull
of Kintyre

Welsh
Caerphilly

Sage Derby

Shropshire
Blue

Cornish Yarg

Cheshire

Red Leicester

Stilton

Berkswell

BRITISH ISLES
CHEESES

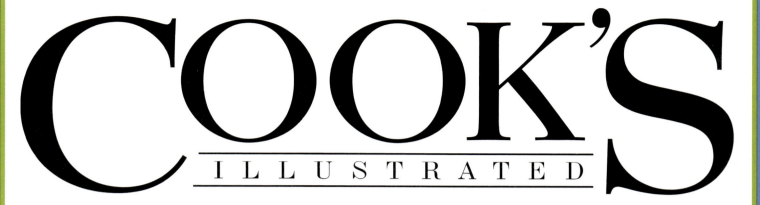

COOK'S
ILLUSTRATED

Naked Grilled Chicken
Strip Away Problems

Herb-Crusted Salmon
Crunchy Crust Stays On

Blueberry Bundt Cake
The Secret's in the Swirl

Best Charcoal Grill
Longtime Champ Dethroned

Stir-Fried Asparagus
Steam Power to the Rescue

Quick Grilled Ribs
Fast Enough for Weeknights

The Frugal Kitchen
28 Money-Saving Tips

New Way to Cook Potatoes
Best Whole-Wheat Pizza
Italian Chicken Soup
Tasting Goat Cheeses

CooksIllustrated.com
$5.95 U.S./$6.95 CANADA

0 74470 62805 7

0 6>

CONTENTS

May & June 2013

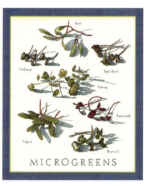

MICROGREENS

MICROGREENS The young seedlings of vegetables, herbs, and other plants, microgreens are harvested even earlier than baby greens. Magenta-colored AMARANTH microgreens have a mineral-like flavor and grassy texture. Bright pink BEET microgreens are rich and earthy with a hint of citrus. Delicate OPAL BASIL microgreens taste similar to the full-grown herb and boast an intriguing purple color. BROCCOLI microgreens, with dark green leaves, are peppery without the sulfurous flavor of mature broccoli. With purple-tinted leaves, CABBAGE microgreens have a rich, spicy flavor. CELERY microgreens have feathery foliage that tastes like the mature plant without the stringiness. CHARD microgreens can be identified by their slender, delicate green leaves, bright ruby red stems, and slightly bitter bite.

COVER (Rhubarb): Robert Papp; BACK COVER (Microgreens): John Burgoyne

America's TEST KITCHEN

RECIPES THAT WORK®

America's Test Kitchen is a very real 2,500-square-foot kitchen located just outside Boston. It is the home of Cook's Illustrated and Cook's Country magazines and is the workday destination of more than three dozen test cooks, editors, and cookware specialists. Our mission is to test recipes over and over again until we understand how and why they work and until we arrive at the best version. We also test kitchen equipment and supermarket ingredients in search of brands that offer the best value and performance. You can watch us work by tuning in to America's Test Kitchen (AmericasTestKitchenTV.com) on public television.

COOK'S ILLUSTRATED

Founder and Editor	Christopher Kimball
Editorial Director	Jack Bishop
Editorial Director, Magazines	John Willoughby
Executive Editor	Amanda Agee
Test Kitchen Director	Erin McMurrer
Managing Editor	Rebecca Hays
Executive Food Editor	Keith Dresser
Senior Editors	Lisa McManus
	Dan Souza
Senior Editors, Features	Molly Birnbaum
	Elizabeth Bomze
Copy Editors	Nell Beram
	Megan Ginsberg
Associate Editors	Hannah Crowley
	Andrea Geary
	Amy Graves
	Andrew Janjigian
	Chris O'Connor
Test Cooks	Dan Cellucci
	Lan Lam
Assistant Editors	Shannon Friedmann Hatch
	Taizeth Sierra
Assistant Test Cook	Cecelia Jenkins
Executive Assistant	Christine Gordon
Assistant Test Kitchen Director	Leah Rovner
Senior Kitchen Assistants	Michelle Blodget
	Meryl MacCormack
Kitchen Assistants	Maria Elena Delgado
	Ena Gudiel
	Andrew Straaberg Finfrock
Executive Producer	Melissa Baldino
Co-Executive Producer	Stephanie Stender
Production Assistant	Kaitlin Hammond
Contributing Editor	Dawn Yanagihara
Consulting Editor	Scott Brueggeman
Science Editor	Guy Crosby, Ph.D.
Managing Editor, Web	Christine Liu
Senior Editor, Cooking School	Mari Levine
Associate Editors, Web	Eric Grzymkowski
	Roger Metcalf
Assistant Editors, Web	Jill Fisher
	Charlotte Wilder
Senior Video Editor	Nick Dakoulas
Design Director	Amy Klee
Art Director	Julie Cote
Deputy Art Director	Susan Levin
Associate Art Director	Lindsey Timko
Deputy Art Director, Marketing/Web	Jennifer Cox
Designer, Marketing/Web	Mariah Tarvainen
Production Designer, Marketing/Web	Judy Blomquist
Staff Photographer	Daniel J. van Ackere
Photo Editor	Steve Klise
Vice President, Marketing	David Mack
Circulation Director	Doug Wicinski
Circulation & Fulfillment Manager	Carrie Fethe
Partnership Marketing Manager	Pamela Putprush
Marketing Assistant	Joyce Liao
Customer Service Manager	Jacqueline Valerio
Customer Service Representatives	Megan Hamner
	Jessica Haskin
Production Director	Guy Rochford
Senior Project Manager	Alice Carpenter
Production & Traffic Coordinator	Brittany Allen
Workflow & Digital Asset Manager	Andrew Mannone
Senior Color & Imaging Specialist	Lauren Pettapiece
Production & Imaging Specialists	Heather Dube
	Lauren Robbins
Systems Administrator	Scott Norwood
Business Analyst	Wendy Tseng
Web Developer	Cameron MacKensie
Human Resources Director	Adele Shapiro
VP New Media Product Development	Barry Kelly
Chief Financial Officer	Sharyn Chabot
Director of Sponsorship Sales	Anne Traficante
Retail Sales & Marketing Director	Emily Logan
Client Services Associate	Kate May
Sponsorship Sales Representative	Morgan Ryan
Publicity	Deborah Broide

PRINTED IN THE USA

THE GROUND BENEATH OUR FEET

Mr. President, titular head of the Old Rabbit Hunter's Association, is not one to jump headlong into a campaign. The pickup must be parked properly beside the railroad bed, the dogs removed from their cages and leashed, the tattered hunting vest donned along with his vintage Mossy Oak camouflage cap, and then, and only then, can we parade across the bridge that brings us to our hunting ground. The casual reader could not know that this bit of protocol—crossing the bridge with beagles in hand, gear and sandwiches properly stowed, and our hearts light with anticipation—has its share of pomp and circumstance. This particular bit of ground that we see before us, part of Mark Lourie's dairy farm, is hallowed. It is an endless expanse of scrub-filled sidehill—dense, thorny undergrowth punctuated by hay fields, brooks, and access roads, the perfect habitat for cottontails, *Sylvilagus floridanus*. Mr. President has hunted the larger snowshoe hare, *Lepus americanus*, and I have had the pleasure of photographing him with a particularly large example of this species in hand after a successful hunt, but it is the more commonplace brownie, the cottontail, that is the object of our passionate quest on winter weekends, as we once again enter this heralded preserve.

This has been a poor season for rabbit hunters, an admittedly small association of those of us who are at the very bottom of the hunting hierarchy. Not for us the majestic elk or the 12-point South Dakota mule deer. Not for us makeshift blinds, bird dogs, and the incoming whoosh of a flock of canvasbacks or goldeneyes. And although we approach deer season with eager anticipation, we miss the bark of the dogs, the gentle walks through wintry landscapes, and the hour-long runs as the rabbits double back and take unexpected turns, the chase often ending with the triumph of rabbit cunning and experience. For those unfamiliar with this commoner's sport, thinking that the hunter and hunted are terribly mismatched, I can only recount the following story. One day 30 years ago, Mr. President found his dog running hard in a circle with the rabbit watching contentedly, seated on a tree stump, smack in the middle of the action.

Despite a low population of rabbits and a prior hunt that unearthed not one encounter, the dogs were hot on the trail of the first rabbit in just minutes. Mr. President and I waited for the cottontail to make the turn, and we were soon heartened by the sound of incoming, full-throated beagles. We waited but the rabbit was clever: It ducked down below us into the scrub before it came in range and then holed up; the dogs lost the scent.

It is curious that many of us go through life living in a place that is quite the opposite of our natural territory. Rabbits are well adapted to their environment, with large ears for sensing predators, eyes located on the sides of their head for wide vision, and camouflage: Some species, such as snowshoe hares, even turn white in the winter and brown in the summer. And, like Briar Rabbit, they choose a landscape well suited to survival: dense, thorny scrub with easy access to food and water.

Mr. President, who often remarks that he was born to hunt rabbits, is similar in nature. He needs to live in a place where he can step out the back door to hunt, sit down after dinner and watch his potatoes grow in the summer, or tap trees in February to get ready for the first run of sap and the first boil. It is a life of engine oil and welding equipment, of 16-gauge shells and pig feed, of rabbit dogs and sand spreaders, of pellet stoves and binoculars. But so many of us—my father, for example—never found their spot, the place where you stand and feel life coursing up through your legs, animating one's spirit and fueling optimism for the future. For some, it is the streets of Paris, while others ache for the soft impression of a mossy bog.

The trail of the next rabbit was picked up down by the stream that trickles through a reedy marsh and then runs behind the farm. Bernadette, the more experienced dog, sniffed out the track, and Nellie, the 2-year-old with her first scent of rabbit, opened up as well, with high-pitched yips of childish enthusiasm. Off they went, barking and bugling, through

Christopher Kimball

a hedgerow, into the next field, and then up the sidehill and into 2 acres of dense undergrowth. The rabbit went for a long, straight run and then turned; we could hear the dogs getting louder, and then the chase paused, the dogs sniffing in circles to pick up the scent. I waited in the next field, watching the hedgerow. Finally, I thought I saw young Nellie through the brush, paused. Then, with two hops, a buck rabbit emerged and sat quietly on the edge of the field, just 15 yards away. Any hunter who has come face-to-face with one's quarry knows the truth of this encounter. The rabbit is perfectly at home in a world that is beyond human understanding. As a hazy sun emerged and I saw the upshot ears, the overstuffed face, and the motionless outline, I did not lift my gun. Then, with an explosion of speed, he wheeled and ran up the hill through the undergrowth; I picked a clear patch about 40 yards out in front, amid the brush, and waited until the very last moment, when he was almost out of range.

It is 8 degrees today, the day after the hunt. The ground is frozen, the sky is gray, and we await the running of the sap, the white smoke billowing forth from the sap house, and the coming of another season. But even walking through a frozen, snow-crusted field, I know what lies beneath my feet: a thin layer of mountain soil, clay, schist, slate, perhaps marble, and then a porridge of glacial moraine. I have walked these woods for more than a half century, and they offer hard-earned intimacy: a bear and her cub sashaying through a forest clearing, a great horned owl eating a field mouse in a tree at dawn, and a great vortex of honeybees moving like a cloud over a pasture, floating up into the woods. All that is required is to know where to stand, to choose the right floor for naked feet at morning's first light. With the ground solidly beneath us, we can stand up for what we believe and remain standing no matter what life has to offer.

Thanks and apologies to Gordon MacQuarrie, author of *Stories of the Old Duck Hunters*.

FOR INQUIRIES, ORDERS, AND MORE INFORMATION

CooksIllustrated.com

At CooksIllustrated.com, you can order books and subscriptions, sign up for our free e-newsletter, or renew your magazine subscription. Join the website and gain access to 20 years of *Cook's Illustrated* recipes, equipment tests, and ingredient tastings, as well as companion videos for every recipe in this issue.

COOKBOOKS

We sell more than 50 cookbooks by the editors of *Cook's Illustrated*, including *The Cook's Illustrated Cookbook* and *The Science of Good Cooking*. To order, visit our bookstore at CooksIllustrated.com/bookstore.

COOK'S ILLUSTRATED MAGAZINE

Cook's Illustrated magazine (ISSN 1068-2821), number 122, is published bimonthly by Boston Common Press Limited Partnership, 17 Station St., Brookline, MA 02445. Copyright 2013 Boston Common Press Limited Partnership. Periodicals postage paid at Boston, Mass., and additional mailing offices, USPS #012487. Publications Mail Agreement No. 40020778. Return undeliverable Canadian addresses to P.O. Box 875, Station A, Windsor, ON N9A 6P2. POSTMASTER: Send address changes to *Cook's Illustrated*, P.O. Box 6018, Harlan, IA 51593-1518. For subscription and gift subscription orders, subscription inquiries, or change-of-address notices, visit us at AmericasTestKitchen.com/customerservice, call us at 800-526-8442, or write us at *Cook's Illustrated*, P.O. 6018, Harlan, IA 51593-1518.

FOR LIST RENTAL INFORMATION Contact Specialists Marketing Services, Inc., 777 Terrace Ave., 4th Floor, Hasbrouck Heights, NJ 07604; 201-865-5800.
EDITORIAL OFFICE 17 Station St., Brookline, MA 02445; 617-232-1000; fax 617-232-1572. Subscription inquiries, visit AmericasTestKitchen.com/customerservice or call 800-526-8442.
POSTMASTER Send all new orders, subscription inquiries, and change-of-address notices to *Cook's Illustrated*, P.O. Box 6018, Harlan, IA 51593-1518.

NOTES FROM READERS

≫ BY MOLLY BIRNBAUM, KEITH DRESSER, ANDREA GEARY, ANDREW JANJIGIAN & LAN LAM ≪

Grinding Cardamom

You often recommend grinding whole spices for more complex flavor. Is it also worth grinding cardamom, which already seems pretty potent when it comes preground?

EMILIE ROGERS
SAN ANTONIO, TEXAS

➤Cardamom adds a fruity flavor to both savory and sweet recipes that is simultaneously warming and cooling. You can purchase the spice preground or as pods—fibrous husks surrounding tiny dark seeds. To see if grinding the whole spice offered a significant flavor advantage, we compared the taste of the preground spice with that of freshly ground pods in cardamom-spiced cookies and cardamom-infused oil. Because we have also heard that some cooks insist on ditching the husk of the pod and grinding just the interior seeds (which make up almost 70 percent of the pod), we made these recipes with just the ground seeds as well.

USE THE WHOLE POD
Grinding whole cardamom pods creates a full-flavored spice.

Tasters agreed that home-ground cardamom (both whole pod and seeds only) boasted much stronger flavor than did preground. They also found that there was very little difference in flavor whether the spice was ground from the seeds alone or with the husks included. Given these results, we'll grind the pods instead of buying preground cardamom—but take the easy road and leave the husks on. –C.R.

Different Stoves, Different Heat

In recipes, you often recommend using medium, medium-high, or high heat. What do those terms mean? How can I make sure my recipe turns out right?

RAY RICKS
SPRINGFIELD, ILL.

➤One thing we've learned through years of cooking on different stoves in the test kitchen is that it's difficult to universalize the settings of a burner. Every stove is different. Even every burner is different. In fact, in the test kitchen we tested burners on seven different gas stoves set to high heat to see how long it would take a 10-inch disposable pie plate filled with 16 ounces of room-temperature water to come to a boil. For each test we started the timer when the gas was lit. The results? Wild variation. The shortest amount of time it took for the water to boil was 2 minutes and 43 seconds. The longest was 3 minutes and 50 seconds. It seems safe to assume that different stoves would vary on other settings as well.

The vagaries of heat output from stove to stove are the reason we include a time range in our recipes and give visual cues for determining when food has reached the desired stage. It's much easier to see the changes in your ingredients as they cook than to guess the exact heat output of your burner. –M.B.

Mixing a More Flavorful Martini

When I mix a martini, I stir it with ice until well chilled, about 30 seconds. A bartender friend insists that the cocktail tastes better stirred a lot longer: around 2 minutes. Is he right?

CAROL GOLDBERG
SILVER SPRING, MD.

➤Most recipes for a classic martini advise stirring with ice for about 30 seconds. To see if extra stirring was worth it, we made four martinis, adding 1¼ cups of ice, 3 ounces of gin, and 1 ounce of vermouth to each of four cocktail shakers. We then stirred the martinis for 15 seconds, 30 seconds, 1 minute, and 2 minutes, respectively. When we took the temperature of each drink, we weren't surprised to discover that the longer we stirred the colder the cocktail: The temperature of the drinks ranged from 40 degrees to 35 degrees. Since longer stirring causes more ice to melt, we also weren't surprised that their volumes differed, ranging from 5 ounces in the drink stirred for 15 seconds to 6 ounces in the 2-minute cocktail.

What did startle us was just how different each martini tasted. Tasters found the martini that was stirred for 15 seconds to have not only a stronger alcohol flavor but also less noticeable aromatic herbal notes. The longer the drink was stirred the more pronounced these other flavors became.

Why does a colder, more dilute cocktail exhibit a broader spectrum of flavors and aromas? First, chilling makes the harsh-tasting ethanol less volatile and assertive, allowing more pleasant, subtle flavors to come through. Second, the ethanol in gin (and other spirits like scotch and whiskey) dissolves some of the water-insoluble aroma compounds. Diluting with water (from the ice) drives these molecules (and their aromas) out of the solution and into the air.

In conclusion? Your friend is onto something. Cocktails like martinis require stirring with ice not just for lowering the temperature of the drink but also for the added water that the ice throws off as the drink cools. If you're a fan of stiffer drinks that taste more of ethanol, by all means, stir for only 30 seconds. If you'd like a martini that's more aromatic in flavor, be patient and keep stirring for a minute or two. –L.L.

Cupcake Conversion

Can I make cupcakes/muffins with my favorite cake batter?

REBECCA ANZALONE
SAN FRANCISCO, CALIF.

➤To answer this question, we chose a handful of quick bread and cake recipes with different mixing techniques and varying ratios of ingredients: angel food cake, chiffon cake, banana bread, cornbread, carrot cake, devil's food cake, and a yellow layer cake. After preparing the batters as directed in each recipe, we simply portioned them into greased, standard 12-cup muffin tins and baked them on the middle rack at the oven temperature specified and at about half the time called for.

The results were a mixed bag. The cupcakes made from angel food and chiffon cakes, batters that receive lift from whipped egg whites, failed miserably. They came out of the oven looking perfect but quickly collapsed as they cooled. The devil's food and yellow cakes fared better. They baked up with flat tops (ideal for a layer cake but not so much for a cupcake) and several stuck to the pan because of their high sugar content, but overall they were acceptable. All the quick breads turned out very nicely.

So with the exception of angel food and chiffon cakes, the next time you want to transform your favorite batter into muffins or cupcakes, go ahead. Divide your batter into a greased 12-cup muffin tin (use paper liners for tender layer cake batters) and bake the batter until a toothpick inserted in the center comes out with just a few crumbs attached, about (or a little less than) half the time called for in the original recipe. Rotate the muffin tin halfway through baking. –K.D.

GO FOR IT
Quick bread and (most) cake batters work well as cupcakes.

THINK AGAIN
Delicate cakes like angel food or chiffon don't translate well as cupcakes.

SEND US YOUR QUESTIONS We will provide a complimentary one-year subscription for each letter we print. Send your inquiry, name, address, and daytime telephone number to Notes from Readers, *Cook's Illustrated*, P.O. Box 470589, Brookline, MA 02447, or to NotesFromReaders@ AmericasTestKitchen.com.

Tasting Raw Honey

How is raw honey different from regular honey?

MARLENE STANGER
NASHVILLE, TENN.

➤When we compared six samples of raw honey with conventional supermarket honey, we noticed that, first and foremost, the texture of raw honey ranged widely—from smooth and creamy to rough and almost crunchy—while the supermarket specimens were uniformly clear and free-flowing. The opaque appearance of raw honey is due to crystallization, which is the natural state for most kinds of honey, with the size and shape of the crystals dependent on the balance of sugars in the honey.

As the name suggests, raw honey is never heated, but conventional supermarket honey is heated to about 155 degrees for three reasons: to kill any yeasts that might initiate fermentation and cause undesirable flavors; to make it easier to pass the honey through a very fine filter, removing all particles of wax, pollen, and even air bubbles (these particles are considered desirable features in many raw honeys); and to dissolve every last crystal, rendering the honey fluid and transparent. That clarity is not permanent, though, and even supermarket honey is eventually vulnerable to crystallization.

RAW STATE
Unpasteurized honey is often thick with lots of crystallization.

Raw honey differs in flavor as well. Supermarket honey is often blended for a characteristic (if generic) "honey" flavor, but raw honey is a hyper-local product that varies greatly and reflects its region of origin. Some of the raw honeys we tasted were minty, some were as floral as hand soap, and some had a tart citrus edge. Supermarket honey is reliable and familiar, and we like it for cooking and everyday applications, but the terroirlike properties of raw honey were a revelation. –A.G.

Mustards in Vinaigrette

Why do recipes for mustard vinaigrette always seem to call for Dijon mustard? Can other styles be used instead?

FRANCIS PENNMAN
CINCINNATI, OHIO

➤We typically add Dijon mustard to our vinaigrettes, but we decided to see how three other common varieties—whole-grain, yellow, and dry mustard powder—would compare. We made four batches of dressing using ½ cup of olive oil, 2 tablespoons of vinegar, and 1 tablespoon of each type of mustard, whisking each batch by hand for 1 minute.

Flavorwise, the dressing made with Dijon had a mellow, well-balanced bite that tasters unanimously preferred. Whole-grain mustard was a close second, with flavors that were more muted; its tamer taste was not surprising when we learned that mustard's potent flavor is contained within these seeds, which must be ground to fully release flavor. Tasters weren't wild about the tart, tangy flavors of yellow mustard in vinaigrette, but only the harsh, sharp taste of dry mustard powder didn't pass muster.

But mustard is also added to dressing as an emulsifying agent that encourages oil and vinegar to stay together. The Dijon dressing held for 2 hours with no sign of separating, the batch made with the mustard powder never came together at all, and the vinaigrette made with the yellow mustard began to separate soon after we stopped whisking. The strongest emulsifier was the whole-grain mustard, which held the oil and vinegar together for a full week in the fridge. The reason for these differences? It all comes down to mucilage, a mix of proteins and polysaccharides that surrounds the mustard seed hull and is highly effective at stabilizing emulsions. Because whole-grain mustard has the most seed hulls, it contains the most mucilage and therefore builds a thicker, longer-lasting vinaigrette. Dijon mustard is made with finely ground whole seeds, which is why it works well, too.

Our advice? Save the yellow mustard for hot dogs and the powdered stuff for baked beans. If you'd like a more subtle mustard flavor and a longer-lasting emulsion, go with the whole-grain stuff. –A.G.

Capers 101

I occasionally see salt-cured capers at the store. Can I use them interchangeably with brined capers?

ALEX VORCE
DENVER, COLO.

➤Capers are the unopened flower buds of the spiny shrub *Capparis spinosa*. They get their sharp pungency from a sulfurous, mustardlike compound called glucocapparin and are ubiquitous in dishes like veal piccata, tartar sauce, and *spaghetti alla puttanesca*. Capers of all sizes may be cured in salt or brined in salt and vinegar. To see how the preservation method affects a recipe, we compared brined and salt-cured nonpareil capers plain and in caper-mustard sauce.

The brine-cured capers had a firm texture and "floral," "grassy" flavors. The salt-cured capers (which must be rinsed several times in water to remove salt) were more tender, with hints of "meaty," "fermented" flavors. Because these differences were subtle, tasters agreed that both styles can be used interchangeably in recipes in which the capers are pureed. But when whole capers are called for, we have a slight preference for the firmer brined kind. (Caper berries, by the way, are not interchangeable with capers. The ripe seedpods of the caper plant, these berries have a crunchy skin, a soft interior, and a mild "fruity" taste. Try them as a garnish on fish platters or as a substitute for olives in martinis.) –A.J.

BRINE-CURED	SALT-CURED	BERRIES
Our favorite for using whole.	Rinse before using in purees.	Good as a garnish.

DID YOU KNOW? All products reviewed by America's Test Kitchen, home of *Cook's Illustrated* and *Cook's Country* magazines, are independently chosen, researched, and reviewed by our editors. We buy products for testing at retail locations and do not accept unsolicited samples for testing. We do not accept or receive payment or consideration from product manufacturers or retailers. Manufacturers and retailers are not told in advance of publication which products we have recommended. We list suggested sources for recommended products as a convenience to our readers but do not endorse specific retailers.

WHAT IS IT?

My uncle, who collects antique kitchen tools, just bought this ice shave. Can you tell us anything about it?
ANDREW HUMMEL, CHICAGO, ILL.

As the embossed label suggests, the manufacturers of this ice shave, North Bros Mfg. Co., were based in Philadelphia, Pennsylvania. Between 1880 and 1946, the company produced a large inventory of kitchen and household tools, including ice cream freezers, egg beaters, and ice shaves like yours. The heavy cast-iron tool, which is shaped like a parallelogram with a blade running across the width of the bottom, measures roughly 6 inches long and 2 inches tall and works like a wood plane: Simply run it back and forth over a smooth block of ice and the snowy shavings will collect in the hollow interior. The top of the shave is hinged and lifts up, allowing you to dump the ice into another vessel before topping it with flavored syrups, condensed milk, and other sweets to make frozen desserts like shave ice or snow cones.

We gave it a try and found that it works adequately: The shavings weren't as uniform or fine as we'd have liked, but the tool is easy to use and serviceable if you want to make ice-based desserts at home. –Elizabeth Bomze

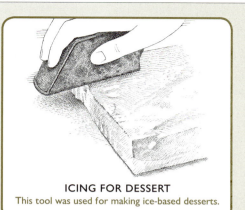

ICING FOR DESSERT
This tool was used for making ice-based desserts.

Quick Tips

⇒ COMPILED BY DANETTE ST. ONGE ⇐

Shaken—Not Scrambled

Chris Braiotta of Somerville, Mass., uses his cocktail mixer every morning—but not for a liquid breakfast.

1. Fill the shaker with eggs, milk, and seasonings and give it a few good shakes.

2. Pour out a perfectly mixed base for fluffy scrambled eggs or omelets.

An Eggs-cellent Charcoal Lighter

To light charcoal briquettes quickly and efficiently, Dorothy Quade of Akron, Ohio, uses a standard-size cardboard egg carton. She places the empty carton in the kettle, stacks up to 3 quarts of briquettes on top of the open carton, and then lights the cardboard to start the flame, adding more briquettes once the first batch is lit. This way, the coals light quickly and evenly, without needing to be stacked in a chimney. Rearrange the hot coals in the kettle as needed.

In-a-Pinch Dish Drying

Jenny Villagrán of San Francisco, Calif., doesn't own a dishwasher and often runs out of space in her dish-drying rack. Her fix: Repurpose a colander with extending arms as an extra, over-the-sink drainer for small dishes, utensils, or cutlery when the countertop rack is full.

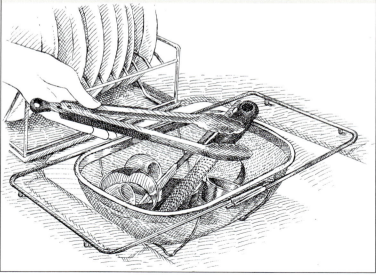

Instant Wine Bucket

When he needed a way to quickly chill a bottle of white wine at a picnic, Tim Farrell of Bayside, N.Y., improvised by cutting the top off an empty plastic 2-liter soda bottle, filling it about one-third of the way with ice and water, and placing the wine bottle inside. The wine was crisp and cool in minutes.

Premarked Butter Measurements

It's a pain when the butter wrapper or box with measurement markings gets discarded before a stick of butter is used up, leaving you guessing just how to measure a tablespoon of solid butter. Erica Wilson of Mount Holly, N.J., avoids this quandary by lightly marking all 8 tablespoons with a knife before unwrapping each stick of butter, so she's always able to easily measure out the amount that she needs.

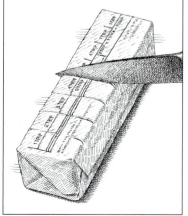

Efficient Shrimp Battering

It's tedious to individually dip shrimp in batter before deep-frying, and the cooked shellfish are also hard to pick up and eat when their tails are covered in batter. Helen Rosner of Hoboken, N.J., came up with an ingenious technique that keeps the tails clean and gets the job done quickly: She tucks the ends of three shrimp (shelled and deveined but with the tails left on) between the fingers of one hand, forms a loose fist around the tails, and dips all three shrimp at once into a bowl of batter.

Bagel Bunker

Rodrigo Piwonka of Santiago, Chile, often brings bagel sandwiches to work. The only problem? Fitting them into sandwich-size zipper-lock bags. (In larger bags, they shifted around, spilling their contents everywhere.) His fix: an empty CD spindle. The sandwich fits perfectly into the crush-proof case, and its filling stays in place.

Smarter Strawberry Hulling

Natalie Burks of Elkhart, Texas, found that the serrated tip of a grapefruit spoon is a better tool than a paring knife for removing the green crown from strawberries. It's faster, easier to maneuver, and wastes less fruit.

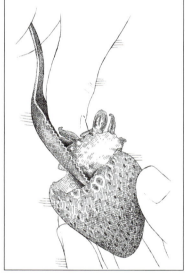

Using Your Noodle

Rather than purchase the special scalloped-edge square cookie cutter called for in a recipe, Stephanie Keller of Glen Rock, N.J., used the curved edge of a dry lasagna noodle to cut her rolled-out cookie dough. In fact, it was better than a cookie cutter because the long noodle could cut more dough at once, and without the wasted in-between scraps left by a stamp-style cutter.

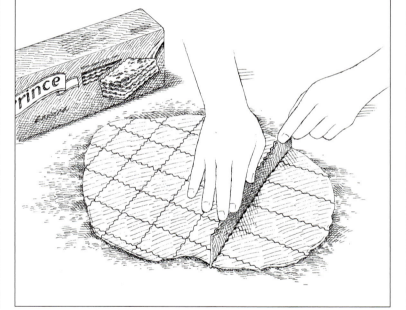

Less Pain, Better Strain

Laurel Damashek of Belmont, Mass., has learned that pushing any type of food through a fine-mesh strainer goes much faster—and requires less elbow grease—when the round bottom of a ladle is used instead of a spatula or wooden spoon. Simply press the bowl of the ladle, which follows the curve of the strainer, against the solids in a circular motion.

A Stovetop Kettle Grill

A grill pan is a good alternative when outdoor grilling is not an option, but it tends to create messy grease splatters and imparts minimal smoke to the food. Casey Grant of Covington, Ky., inverts a disposable aluminum roasting pan over the top of his grill pan to catch splatters. The technique also concentrates smoky flavor in whatever food he is grilling, much like the closed lid of a kettle grill.

Naked Grilled Chicken

Throw a whole chicken on the grill and you're bound to end up with unevenly cooked meat and skin that's charred from flare-ups. So why not strip away those problems?

⇒ BY ANDREA GEARY ⇐

The embarrassing truth is that I'm not the most confident of grill cooks. For most of my career I've worked with sophisticated restaurant stoves and ovens, so the primitive unresponsiveness of a backyard charcoal grill feels daunting. I can handle low-and-slow projects like barbecued ribs, and quickly searing a steak is no big deal. But grilling a whole chicken brings out my insecurities.

The problem is that you can't treat a chicken like a steak and simply throw it over a blazing fire. The fat in the skin will melt and rain onto the coals, sending up flames that carbonize the exterior before the interior is cooked. For this reason, most grilled chicken recipes call for variable heat: low and slow first—to gently render fat and initiate cooking—and then high heat to finish cooking, crisp the skin, and get that enticing char.

Determined to vanquish my combustible nemesis once and for all, I headed for the grill. I would start with a half fire, made by pouring all the lit coals over one side of the grill for intense heat and leaving the other side empty for indirect cooking—in other words, a prime whole-chicken-cooking environment. I would keep grilling until I could consistently produce moist, well-flavored, pleasantly charred birds—and without the intervention of the local fire department.

The Need for Speed

I started simply: one whole chicken and a grill. I knew that cooking a 3½-pounder would take a while, but this was tedious even by my tolerant standards: I placed the chicken breast side down over low heat to cook off some of the fat and then flipped it. By the time I got to the hotter side, the coals no longer had enough oomph to brown the skin. Yes, it was simple, and there were no flare-ups; but with no high-temperature char, the meat looked and tasted more roasted than grilled, and the white meat was as dry as one might expect after 90 minutes on the grill.

Skewers help keep this skinless whole chicken together as it cooks in about 30 minutes on the grill.

Brining the next chicken in a saltwater solution helped keep it more moist, but it still required a solid chunk of time on the grill. In an attempt to shorten the cooking time of the next bird, I employed a technique I've used when roasting chickens: butterflying. That is, I removed the backbone with a pair of kitchen shears and pressed on the breastbone to flatten the bird to a more-or-less uniform thickness. Butterflying the bird would speed up cooking by increasing the meat's exposure to heat. I rubbed some lemon zest, mustard, rosemary, and seasoning on the skin of the chicken for added flavor.

I placed the wide, flat chicken breast side down over the cooler side of the grill, and then I flipped it to finish the rendering job before moving it over to the hotter side (after 30 minutes it was still plenty hot) to get grill marks on each side. This chicken had promise—evenly cooked meat, a bit of char, and no scary fire—but it still took almost an hour, and tasters observed that the meat was a bit dry. The good news was that they liked the lemon-herb rub; the bad news was that its flavor was only skin-deep.

The Skinny on Skin

Thinking about dishes that combine poultry and high heat, I remembered tandoori chicken, which is traditionally cooked in a 900-degree clay oven without bursting into flames. Why does it work? Because the skin has been removed before cooking.

The three separate problems I was trying to fix—flare-ups, long cooking time, and lack of flavor penetration—were all caused by the same thing: the skin. Yes, the skin protects the meat during cooking—but remove it and you remove most of the fat, so you can put the chicken directly over high heat without fear of flare-ups, not to mention that the chicken cooks so quickly that it has less time to dry out.

A whole chicken with no skin seemed odd at first. I mean, I like chicken skin. But I also know that not everyone does; I've witnessed many a guest discreetly set it aside before eating. Maybe a naked chicken was worth a try.

Turns out that taking the skin off a butterflied chicken is pretty easy; using just my hands, a paper towel to improve my grip, and the kitchen shears, I got the job done in just a couple of minutes, and I was even able to remove the small pockets of fat that lay on the surface of the meat. However, I had underestimated the structural service provided by the skin, and the legs dangled precariously. I strategically threaded a couple of skewers through the thighs and breast to fix that. After drying off the bird, I applied the rub directly to the meat and then placed the chicken breast side down over the hotter side of the grill (7 quarts of coals strong) and closed the lid to modify the flow of oxygen and discourage flare-ups.

There was smoke, the smell of charring, and a lot of sizzling noises, too. When I peeked, I did see some flames, but they were weak. After a mere 10 minutes, I flipped the chicken, and after another 10 minutes, I moved it over to the cooler side of the grill to finish cooking. When it reached the target temperature (160 in the breast, 175 in the thigh) in just 8 more minutes, I knew I was onto something. This chicken was the juiciest yet, and who can find fault with a whole chicken that cooks in just 28 minutes?

I can, of course. It was good, but it wasn't perfect. The brief time over intense heat (necessary to prevent overcooking) meant that the surface of the meat

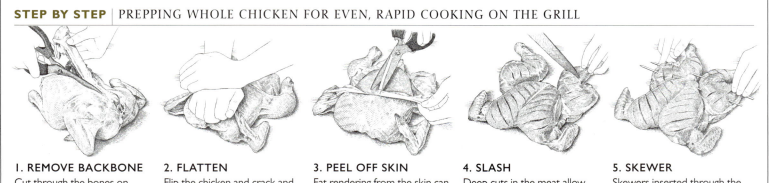

I. REMOVE BACKBONE
Cut through the bones on either side of the backbone; discard.

2. FLATTEN
Flip the chicken and crack and flatten its breastbone for fast, even grilling.

3. PEEL OFF SKIN
Fat rendering from the skin can cause flare-ups. We take it off.

4. SLASH
Deep cuts in the meat allow seasonings to penetrate to the bone.

5. SKEWER
Skewers inserted through the thighs and legs provide stability.

was a bit pale and, while not exactly dry, had a tight, cauterized feel to it. And the flavor of the rub was still a bit superficial.

To address the paleness problem, I spiked my brine with sugar, which I hoped would be absorbed into the bird and aid browning. To solve the flavor penetration issue, I turned once again to tandoori chicken for inspiration. Tandoori cooks cut deep slits in meat before it goes into the oven, so I did the same before brining my bird. When it came out of the brine, I massaged the rub deep into the knife cuts. I reserved a bit of the flavoring agents from the rub—lemon juice, rosemary, mustard, and pepper—and mixed them into a small amount of melted butter to use as a basting sauce. Thinking ahead, I cut an additional lemon into quarters and brought it out to the grill with my chicken and sauce.

Once again, I laid the chicken skinned side down over the hotter side, and this time I also placed the lemon quarters onto the grate to char. The sugar in the brine caused this bird to achieve a beautiful brown color after just 8 minutes. When I flipped it, I brushed the cooked surface with the flavored butter to prevent it from tightening up, and I tented it

No Skin—Really?

Trust us: This "naked" chicken is good. Really good. While skin can provide protection against the high heat of grilling, we make up for its absence with two measures: After the bird is flipped and the risk of flare-ups is receding, we brush a melted butter mixture on the exposed flesh to prevent the meat from becoming leathery, and we also tent the chicken with foil. The result? Juicy, tender chicken.

COVER UP
We use melted butter and foil to protect the bird.

with foil as extra insurance. The lemons went into a bowl to cool. After another 8 minutes, I moved the chicken to the cooler side and basted it again, and in 8 more minutes it was done. I took it off the grill and basted it with the last of the butter.

The moist brown exterior of this chicken was accented with hints of tasty black char, and carving it revealed a juiciness that went all the way to the bone and took the flavorful rub along for the ride. A spritz of charred lemon over the top completed the dish. I had met the enemy and emerged victorious. No fire department necessary.

GRILLED LEMON CHICKEN WITH ROSEMARY
SERVES 4

For a better grip, use a paper towel to grasp the skin when removing it from the chicken.

I	(3½- to 4-pound) whole chicken, giblets discarded
¾	cup sugar
	Salt and pepper
2	lemons
I	tablespoon vegetable oil
2	teaspoons minced fresh rosemary
1½	teaspoons Dijon mustard
2	tablespoons unsalted butter

1. With chicken breast side down, using kitchen shears, cut through bones on either side of backbone; discard backbone. Flip chicken over and press on breastbone to flatten. Using fingers and shears, peel skin off chicken, leaving skin on wings.

2. Tuck wings behind back. Turn legs so drumsticks face inward toward breasts. Using chef's knife, cut ½-inch-deep slits, spaced ½ inch apart, in breasts and legs. Insert skewer through thigh of 1 leg, into bottom of breast, and through thigh of second leg. Insert second skewer, about 1 inch lower, through thigh and drumstick of 1 leg and then through thigh and drumstick of second leg.

3. Dissolve sugar and ¾ cup salt in 3 quarts cold water in large, wide container. Submerge chicken in brine, cover, and refrigerate for at least 30 minutes or up to 1 hour.

4. Zest lemons (you should have 2 tablespoons grated zest). Juice 1 lemon (you should have 3 tablespoons juice) and quarter remaining lemon lengthwise. Combine zest, oil, 1½ teaspoons rosemary, 1 teaspoon mustard, and ½ teaspoon pepper in small bowl; set aside. Heat butter, remaining ½ teaspoon rosemary, remaining ½ teaspoon mustard, and ½ teaspoon pepper in small saucepan over low heat, stirring occasionally, until butter is melted and ingredients are combined. Remove pan from heat and stir in lemon juice; leave mixture in saucepan.

5. Remove chicken from brine and pat dry with paper towels. With chicken skinned side down, rub ½ teaspoon zest mixture over surface of legs. Flip chicken over and rub remaining zest mixture evenly over entire surface, making sure to work mixture into slits.

6A. FOR A CHARCOAL GRILL: Open bottom vent completely. Light large chimney starter mounded with charcoal briquettes (7 quarts). When top coals are partially covered with ash, pour evenly over half of grill. Set cooking grate in place, cover, and open lid vent completely. Heat grill until hot, about 5 minutes.

6B. FOR A GAS GRILL: Turn all burners to high, cover, and heat grill until hot, about 15 minutes. Leave primary burner on high and turn off other burner(s).

7. Clean and oil cooking grate. Place chicken, skinned side down, and lemon quarters over hotter part of grill. Cover and cook until chicken and lemon quarters are well browned, 8 to 10 minutes. Transfer lemon quarters to bowl and set aside. Flip chicken over and brush with one-third of butter mixture (place saucepan over cooler side of grill if mixture has solidified). Cover chicken loosely with aluminum foil. Continue to cook, covered, until chicken is well browned on second side, 8 to 10 minutes.

8. Remove foil and slide chicken to cooler side of grill. Brush with half of remaining butter mixture, and re-cover with foil. Continue to cook, covered, until breasts register 160 degrees and thighs/drumsticks register 175 degrees, 8 to 10 minutes longer.

9. Transfer chicken to carving board, brush with remaining butter mixture, tent loosely with foil, and let rest for 5 to 10 minutes. Carve into pieces and serve with reserved lemon quarters.

Herb-Crusted Salmon

For a crust both herby and crunchy, we had to take it apart in order to keep it together.

≥ BY LAN LAM ≤

Herb-crusted salmon always sounds like a good idea. Its very name suggests so much: fresh herb flavor and a crunchy coating that contrasts nicely with the silky salmon. It also sounds simple: Just sprinkle bread crumbs mixed with chopped herbs on a fish fillet and stick the whole thing under the broiler. An easy weeknight meal, served. But as soon as I began my testing, I knew I was in for a challenge. My first attempts were neither herby nor well crusted. The fresh herb flavor vanished under the intense heat of the broiler, and the oily, overcharred smattering of bread crumbs fell off with the touch of a feather. I set out to make a quick herb-crusted salmon that not only was herby but also had a crust that both stayed in place and delivered a substantial crunch.

A Crust Divided

I decided to focus first on the crust and worry about incorporating herb flavor later. My earlier tests proved that coarse, Japanese-style panko bread crumbs were a must. I seasoned them with salt and pepper; then, to moisten the mix and increase its cohesion, I tried adding small amounts of mayonnaise, mustard, melted butter, and olive oil, respectively, to four different batches. I applied the mixture to the fish and then cooked the fillets on a rack in a 325-degree oven. (I dismissed the char-inducing broiler from the get-go.) Though the added fats helped the crumbs brown evenly and the mustard increased the crust's flavor, none of these additions did much to help it all hold together.

I would need something stickier. I tried 2 tablespoons of beaten egg along with some mayo and mustard. This simple combination yielded a crust that held together but wasn't at all tough and could easily be cut with a fork. On to the crust's flavor.

One of my favorite herbs to pair with salmon is tarragon, so I started with that. The tarragon certainly smelled delicious as it baked on the fish, but by the time the crust was browned and the salmon had cooked, its delicate leaves had lost all their fragrance and flavor. It turns out that herbs can be divided into two categories: The major aromatic compounds in hardy herbs like thyme and rosemary are chemically stable and so do not dissipate when heated. Delicate herbs like tarragon, basil, and dill, however, contain

We protect delicate tarragon by placing it under the crust; hardy thyme gets mixed in with the crumbs.

unstable aromatic compounds that do not fare well at high temperatures. To protect the tarragon from the heat of the oven, I would need a shield.

What about a bread-crumb shield? I combined tarragon, mayo, and mustard, which I then spread over the top of each salmon fillet. I mixed the egg and panko separately before pressing them on top of the herb spread and baking my fish. The first time I opened the oven door, I smelled success. Instead of the familiar waft of tarragon, I smelled cooked salmon, which implied that the herb flavor was still contained beneath its crusty shield. Happily, the tarragon flavor was clear and fresh.

But since it didn't contain fat, the crust itself was pale blond in color and a bit bland. I didn't want to lose fresh tarragon flavor by upping the oven temperature. Instead, I browned the panko in a pan with some butter and then added just a bit of thyme to the mix. I knew that this hardy herb's flavor compounds could handle the heat.

A Salty Solution

The last issue was that the salmon occasionally sported a splotchy white layer of albumin, a protein in fish and other foods that congeals when heated. We've previously found that brining helps prevent some of the albumin formation: The salt in the brine keeps the surface proteins from contracting as they cook and therefore prevents the albumin from being squeezed out of the fish. A quick 15-minute brine worked wonders. This batch had very little of the unsightly white film; plus, it was perfectly seasoned and far moister. It turns out that brining fish works

in a similar fashion to brining proteins like chicken and pork. The salt is drawn into the flesh, followed by water, leading to juicier fish. And because muscles in fish are shorter and looser than in meat, the salt penetrates more rapidly, leading to shorter brining times. (See "Why You Should Brine Fish," page 31, for more details on this process.) Now I could celebrate success: My redesigned herb-crusted salmon was silky, well seasoned, and both herby and crusty.

HERB-CRUSTED SALMON
SERVES 4

For the fillets to cook at the same rate, they must be the same size and shape. To ensure uniformity, we prefer to purchase a 1½- to 2-pound center-cut salmon fillet and cut it into four pieces. Dill or basil can be substituted for tarragon.

	Salt and pepper
4	(6- to 8-ounce) skin-on salmon fillets
2	tablespoons unsalted butter
½	cup panko bread crumbs
2	tablespoons beaten egg
2	teaspoons minced fresh thyme
¼	cup chopped fresh tarragon
I	tablespoon whole-grain mustard
1½	teaspoons mayonnaise
	Lemon wedges

1. Adjust oven rack to middle position and heat oven to 325 degrees. Dissolve 5 tablespoons salt in 2 quarts water in large container. Submerge salmon in brine and let stand at room temperature for 15 minutes. Remove salmon from brine, pat dry, and set aside.

2. Meanwhile, melt butter in 10-inch skillet over medium heat. Add panko and ⅛ teaspoon salt and season with pepper; cook, stirring frequently, until panko is golden brown, 4 to 5 minutes. Transfer to bowl and let cool completely. Stir in egg and thyme until thoroughly combined. Stir tarragon, mustard, and mayonnaise together in second bowl.

3. Set wire rack in rimmed baking sheet. Place 12 by 8-inch piece of aluminum foil on wire rack and lightly coat with vegetable oil spray. Evenly space fillets, skin side down, on foil. Using spoon, spread tarragon mixture evenly over top of each fillet. Sprinkle panko mixture evenly over top of each fillet, pressing with your fingers to adhere. Bake until center of thickest part of fillets reaches 125 degrees and is still translucent when cut into with paring knife, 18 to 25 minutes. Transfer salmon to serving platter and let rest for 5 minutes before serving with lemon wedges.

How to Stir-Fry Asparagus

The key to perfectly cooked, deeply flavorful spears? Steam power.

⇒ BY KEITH DRESSER ⇐

It's no secret that stir-frying brings a lot to the table: Intense heat has the potential to beautifully caramelize ingredients, creating a natural sweetness that pairs perfectly with a potent, Asian-inspired sauce. I particularly like to stir-fry vegetables; since they cook in a flash, their crisp-tender bite is preserved. But things can go awry when a delicate, quick-cooking choice like asparagus hits the pan. Many recipes produce both overdone and underdone spears in a single batch, and the pieces often lack sufficient browning or flavor from the sauce.

Gorgeously browned, deeply flavorful, evenly cooked spears were my goal, so I got my bearings by following a basic stir-fry technique. I snapped the tough ends from a bunch of asparagus, cut them on the bias into bite-size lengths, and tossed them into an oil-slicked nonstick skillet (our choice over a wok since its flat-bottomed design allows more of its surface area to come in direct contact with the flat burner of a Western stove). I stirred the pieces almost constantly for a couple of minutes, until they were nearly crisp-tender, and then sprinkled in some grated fresh ginger. As soon as its pungent aroma was released (this took about 30 seconds), I poured in a sauce of dry sherry, sesame oil, soy sauce, and brown sugar and let the asparagus cook for a minute longer before scattering some sliced scallions on top for a fresh finish.

Sure enough, the browning in my dish was spotty. So was the cooking: Mushy and crunchy pieces converged in the same bite. The problem of pale spears was easy to fix. I simply used the takeaway from our Thai-Style Stir-Fried Noodles with Chicken and Broccolini recipe (September/October 2012): Stir less—much less. Indeed, when I only occasionally stirred as the asparagus cooked, the longer periods of contact with the hot pan caramelized the spears nicely, boosting their inherent sweetness. But this step did nothing to even out the inconsistent cooking—in fact, it seemed to only exacerbate it.

For that problem I turned to a method we've used for hardy vegetable stir-fries: adding ¼ cup of water to the hot skillet and then covering it to trap

Shiitake mushrooms add meatiness to asparagus.

the steam. The moist environment evenly cooked the asparagus, but by the time I added the aromatics and sauce, the frail spears were all but mush. Plus, all that water had diluted the taste of the flavorful browning I had worked so hard to achieve.

Just Add Water

For spears that are well browned and crisp-tender, stir-fry them first and then steam them in a sauce diluted with water.

I tinkered with the steaming time, the amount of water, and whether to leave the cover on. Ditching the lid and using very little water—just 1 or 2 tablespoons, depending on the other liquids in my sauces—created a burst of steam that evenly cooked the spears without ruining their texture or browning. I also found that when I combined the water with the sauce, the mixture reduced quickly, glazing the asparagus and infusing it with the flavors of the sauce.

Next, I addressed the serving size. I wanted to serve four, but a single bunch of asparagus weighs about a pound—enough to serve only two or three. Instead of using 1½ bunches, I wondered about increasing the yield with a second, complementary vegetable. As it turned out, this was a very good idea. Shiitake mushrooms, red bell pepper, red onion, and carrot added contrasting flavor and color and cooked up nicely, provided that I cut each vegetable so that its stir-fry time aligned with that of the asparagus. Finally, to complete my mastery of asparagus stir-fries, I used a few common Asian pantry ingredients to create intense sauces to match up with each variation.

STIR-FRIED ASPARAGUS
WITH SHIITAKE MUSHROOMS
SERVES 4

To allow it to brown, stir the asparagus only occasionally. Look for spears that are no thicker than ½ inch. For our free recipe for Stir-Fried Asparagus with Carrot, go to CooksIllustrated.com/june13.

- 2 tablespoons water
- 1 tablespoon soy sauce
- 1 tablespoon dry sherry
- 2 teaspoons packed brown sugar
- 2 teaspoons grated fresh ginger
- 1 teaspoon toasted sesame oil
- 1 tablespoon vegetable oil
- 1 pound asparagus, trimmed and cut on bias into 2-inch lengths
- 4 ounces shiitake mushrooms, stemmed and sliced thin
- 2 scallions, green parts only, sliced thin on bias

1. Combine water, soy sauce, sherry, sugar, ginger, and sesame oil in bowl.

2. Heat vegetable oil in 12-inch nonstick skillet over high heat until smoking. Add asparagus and mushrooms and cook, stirring occasionally, until asparagus is spotty brown, 3 to 4 minutes. Add soy sauce mixture and cook, stirring once or twice, until pan is almost dry and asparagus is crisp-tender, 1 to 2 minutes. Transfer to serving platter, sprinkle with scallion greens, and serve.

STIR-FRIED ASPARAGUS
WITH RED BELL PEPPER

Omit soy sauce, sherry, brown sugar, ginger, and sesame oil. Reduce water to 1 tablespoon. Whisk 1 tablespoon orange juice, 1 tablespoon rice vinegar, 1 tablespoon granulated sugar, 1 teaspoon ketchup, and ½ teaspoon salt into water. Substitute 1 stemmed and seeded red bell pepper cut into 2-inch-long matchsticks for shiitakes.

STIR-FRIED ASPARAGUS WITH RED ONION

Omit soy sauce, sherry, ginger, and sesame oil. Whisk 4 teaspoons fish sauce, 1 tablespoon lime juice, 2 teaspoons minced fresh lemon grass, and ⅛ teaspoon red pepper flakes into water, along with sugar. Substitute ½ red onion sliced through root end into ¼-inch-thick pieces for shiitakes and 2 tablespoons chopped fresh mint for scallion greens.

PHOTOGRAPHY: CARL TREMBLAY; ILLUSTRATION: JAY LAYMAN

Quick Weeknight Ribs

Boiling ribs before putting them on the grill is a surefire way to quickly tenderize their tough meat. If only that method didn't also leach away flavor.

> BY LAN LAM

It's a widely known truth among rib aficionados that boiling a rack in water before grilling it is the most effective rib-cooking shortcut you can take. Precooked this way, the meat's tough collagen breaks down exponentially faster than it does when ribs are cooked according to the traditional barbecue method: from start to finish over a low, steady fire for several hours. That's because unlike air, water conducts heat extremely efficiently—about 25 times faster than air, according to research. It's also well-known that, unfortunately, this shortcut comes at a considerable cost, as boiling ribs is guaranteed to wash out rich porky flavor.

Such was the predicament I faced as I set out to develop a method for "weeknight" ribs—a recipe that I was pursuing because, as much as I love the smoky, super-tender results produced by hours of barbecuing, I simply don't have that kind of time (or patience) most nights of the week. All the same, I wasn't willing to completely forgo flavor for the sake of speed. But I was willing to compromise some on tenderness—and even on barbecue smokiness—if it meant that I could have ribs any night of the week. Besides, who says ribs have to be fall-off-the-bone tender? I, for one, like the meat to have a little resistance. Ignoring the skepticism of my barbecue-devoted colleagues, I set my sights on grilled ribs that were reasonably tender but still boasted some satisfying chew. My ideal cooking time: about an hour.

Rib Rules

Even though I wasn't aiming for barbecue-tender results, I still needed to come up with a cooking method that tenderized the tough meat, so I started with a review of why barbecuing works so effectively. Like other tough cuts, ribs are full of collagen, the protein that holds meat fibers together and also holds muscle tissue to bone. As collagen heats up during cooking, it not only unravels, making the

Using small, relatively tender baby back ribs is just one of our keys to cooking ribs in a hurry.

meat more tender, but also slowly turns into gelatin. Since gelatin holds up to 10 times its weight in water, it helps keep some of the moisture in meat that would otherwise be lost during cooking. Slow, steady barbecuing maximizes the conversion of collagen into gelatin, since the meat lingers between 160 and 190 degrees—the so-called sweet spot for collagen breakdown. The longer the meat hovers in this zone (particularly around the 190-degree mark) the more of its collagen converts into gelatin.

I kept those tenets in mind as I surveyed my rib options and looked for the quickest-cooking cut I could get. Though meaty, spareribs, which are cut from near the pig's belly, are also gristly and tough and really best left for slow cooking. That also eliminated St. Louis–style ribs, which are just spareribs that have been trimmed of some meat and excess cartilage. Instead, I stocked up on baby back ribs—a slab that cooks faster because the ribs are smaller and come from the more tender loin area of the pig.

Shopping questions addressed, I looked into alternative moist heat methods that would speed along the

rib-cooking process but wouldn't wash away the pork's flavor. I thought that I might have some luck with the oven, as most of the "quick" rib recipes I came across called for wrapping the racks in aluminum foil and baking them before transferring them to the grill. The idea is that the ribs "steam" in their own exuded moisture—a method that should save time while saving flavor, too. It sounded promising, so I wrapped a pair of 2-pound racks (enough to feed at least four rib enthusiasts) in aluminum foil and baked them in a 325-degree oven until they reached 165 degrees, at which point it seemed reasonable to move them out to the grill to finish cooking. There, I unwrapped them, basted them with bottled barbecue sauce (I'd develop my own sauces later), and grilled them over a moderately hot fire until they hit the target doneness temperature—195 degrees at the thickest part—and had developed a nice lacquered crust.

Baking the foil-wrapped racks did hasten the cooking process as promised, and the results were pretty good: firm but not leathery, with decent charring. But the method hadn't been nearly the timesaver I was hoping for. Forty-five minutes of oven steaming had passed by the time the ribs reached 165 degrees, and they needed another solid hour of grilling time before they hit 195 degrees—not a feasible plan for a weeknight. Pressed for time (and out of other ideas), I reluctantly moved my operation to the stove. After all, I thought to myself, I hadn't actually tried boiling a rack of ribs. Maybe I'd discover a way to make cooking them in water work.

Testing the Waters

This time, I cut the two rib racks in half, which allowed them to fit snugly in a large Dutch oven. Then I poured in just enough water to cover them (2½ quarts), cranked the dial to high, and set the lid in place. The cooking time difference was even more dramatic than I'd expected: Barely 10 minutes had ticked by before the thick end of the rack reached 165 degrees. Trouble was, the thin end was also cooking at a much faster rate and now registered 20 degrees more than the meaty section, and a discrepancy remained when I moved the racks out to the grill to finish cooking. By the time the thick portion reached 195 degrees, the slimmer

PHOTOGRAPHY: CARL TREMBLAY

end had blown by that target and hit 210 degrees, and its meat tasted predictably dry and stringy. And of course boiling the ribs had dulled their flavor.

Putting aside the flavor issue for a moment, I wondered if simmering the ribs would help prevent the thin sections of meat from overcooking since simmering occurs at around 200 degrees—much closer to the meat's target doneness temperature than boiling, which happens at 212 degrees. I brought another pot of water and ribs to a simmer, turned the dial to low, and let the pot bubble gently until the meaty portions reached 165 degrees, about 15 minutes. These ribs were considerably more tender from end to end than the boiled batch, and I quickly realized how significant that 12-degree temperature drop had been: Now the temperature difference between the two ends was about 10 degrees, and lowering the temperature cost me only another 5 minutes. Even better, starting the ribs in cold water and then simmering them made for more tender ribs: As the ribs heated gradually with the water, the meat had more time to break down the tough collagen, and because the meat simmered (rather than boiled), it spent longer in that ideal collagen-breakdown temperature range.

Now that the ribs were cooking quickly indoors, I moved out to the grill to see if I could speed up that leg of the process, too. The challenge was that the 165-degree ribs lost a good 20 degrees in their travels from the Dutch oven to the grill—and then cooled further every time I brushed on a coat of sauce during cooking. It occurred to me that the best approach would be to take full advantage of simmering and bring the racks to 195 degrees in the water, and then use the grill just to char them. Since I wasn't going for barbecue, I didn't need lots of grilling time to infuse the meat with smoke, and briefly grilling the ribs probably wouldn't overcook the meat. My expectations panned out: About 20 minutes of simmering plus roughly 20 minutes of searing produced ribs that were reasonably tender but pleasantly chewy and beautifully lacquered. I even managed to squeeze in a 10-minute rest after the ribs came off the grill and still keep the overall cooking time to about an hour.

Coming into Season
Of course, cooking the ribs quickly wasn't much of a success if their flavor was subpar. I tried to use the cooking water to my advantage, "infusing" it with every addition I could think of: garlic, paprika, chiles, soy sauce, chicken broth, onion powder, bacon, kombu (a seaweed known for its high glutamate content), and lots of salt. While none of those flavors penetrated beyond the ribs' exterior, the salt was surprisingly effective at offsetting the small loss of porky taste. I settled on 2 tablespoons for the 2½ quarts of cooking water, essentially cooking the ribs in a "brine."

That left just the sauce. The bottled stuff was out. In fact, since these ribs weren't barbecued, I saw no reason to limit myself to the usual tomato-based condiment. Instead, I paired no-cook ingredients that would color quickly over the fire: hoisin sauce and

Speeding Up the Process with Water—Without Watering Down Flavor

For their tough collagen to break down and the meat to turn tender, ribs must reach about 195 degrees—a process that takes several hours on the grill. The most effective shortcut is to boil the ribs before they go on the fire. Boiling brings the meat up to 195 degrees in a matter of minutes, at which point the ribs need only a quick stint over the coals to char. But boiling also dulls flavor (and risks overcooking the thinner end of the rib). Here's how we got water to speed up the process—without washing away meaty taste.

SIMMER IN A BRINE
Cooking the ribs in a concentrated saltwater solution allows the salt to penetrate the meat, seasoning it throughout and making up for the loss of pork flavor. Because food can never rise above the temperature of its environment, simmering the meat (at about 200 degrees) instead of boiling it (at 212 degrees) means that the thinner end of the rib won't overcook as the thicker end more slowly comes up to 195 degrees. The upshot: moister meat from end to end.

FINISH ON THE GRILL
After simmering, the now-tender ribs need only 15 to 20 minutes over the fire (and a few coats of glaze) to develop a nice lacquer and char flavor.

coconut milk, lime juice and ketchup, and orange marmalade and cider vinegar. I brushed these glazes over the racks before, during, and after grilling and made sure to rotate and flip the ribs as needed to ensure that they colored evenly.

As my tasters and I tore into these final batches of ribs, I couldn't decide which was more satisfying: the racks' meaty chew and nicely glazed char or the fact that I could easily pull off this recipe any night of the week.

GRILLED GLAZED BABY BACK RIBS
SERVES 4 TO 6

Try one of the glaze recipes that follow, or use 1 cup of your favorite glaze or barbecue sauce.

- 2 tablespoons salt
- 2 (2-pound) racks baby back or loin back ribs, trimmed, membrane removed, and each rack cut in half
- 1 recipe glaze (recipes follow)

1. Dissolve salt in 2½ quarts water in Dutch oven; place ribs in pot so they are fully submerged. Bring to simmer over high heat. Reduce heat to low, cover, and cook at bare simmer until thickest part of ribs registers 195 degrees, 15 to 25 minutes. While ribs are simmering, set up grill. (If ribs come to temperature before grill is ready, leave in pot, covered, until ready to use.)

2A. FOR A CHARCOAL GRILL: Open bottom vent halfway. Light large chimney starter filled with charcoal briquettes (6 quarts). When top coals are partially covered with ash, pour evenly over grill. Set cooking grate in place, cover, and open lid vent halfway. Heat grill until hot, about 5 minutes.

2B. FOR A GAS GRILL: Turn all burners to high, cover, and heat grill until hot, about 15 minutes. Turn all burners to medium-high.

3. Clean and oil cooking grate. Remove ribs from pot and pat dry with paper towels. Brush both sides of ribs with ⅓ cup glaze. Grill ribs, uncovered, flipping and rotating as needed, until glaze is caramelized and charred in spots, 15 to 20 minutes, brushing with another ⅓ cup glaze halfway through cooking. Transfer ribs to cutting board, brush both sides with remaining glaze, tent loosely with aluminum foil, and let rest for 10 minutes. Cut ribs between bones to separate, and serve.

HOISIN-COCONUT GLAZE
MAKES ABOUT 1 CUP

- ⅔ cup hoisin sauce
- ⅓ cup canned coconut milk
- 3 tablespoons rice vinegar
- ¾ teaspoon pepper

Whisk all ingredients together in bowl.

LIME GLAZE
MAKES ABOUT 1 CUP

- ⅔ cup lime juice (6 limes)
- ⅓ cup ketchup
- ¼ cup packed brown sugar
- 1 teaspoon salt

Whisk all ingredients together in bowl.

SPICY MARMALADE GLAZE
MAKES ABOUT 1 CUP

- ⅔ cup orange marmalade
- ⅓ cup cider vinegar
- 2 tablespoons hot sauce
- ¾ teaspoon salt

Whisk all ingredients together in bowl.

A New Way to Cook Potatoes

What if you could get the creamy interiors produced by steaming red potatoes
and the browned exteriors produced by roasting—without doing either of those things?

> BY DAN SOUZA <

I love the versatility of waxy potatoes like Red Bliss. Steamed whole, they turn tender and creamy—perfect canvases for tossing with butter and fresh herbs. They also take well to halving and roasting, which browns their cut surfaces. So when I came across recipes for braised new potatoes, I wondered if this approach, which pairs dry heat for browning with moist heat for simmering, would yield the best of both worlds. In fact, I thought there might be a third benefit to braising: Since many recipes call for simmering the spuds in chicken broth, I reasoned that the potatoes would soak up all that flavorful liquid like little savory sponges. All in all, it sounded like a promising—and super-simple—alternative method for cooking waxy potatoes.

Charting a New Course

Except it wasn't that simple. To my surprise, the recipes I made were failures. Any flavor that the potatoes might have picked up from the chicken broth was barely discernible—even after I'd halved or thin-sliced the spuds to expose their flesh to the cooking liquid. Worse, the typical brown-and-then-simmer approach to braising had been a bust, as all the flavorful brown color that the potatoes developed during searing washed off by the time they had cooked through in the liquid.

But by this point, I was fixated on braised potatoes and convinced that if I could revise the technique, the results would surely be ideal. Enter my first change: ditching the chicken broth, since there was no point in using broth if it wasn't considerably improving the potatoes' flavor. Instead, I would use heavily salted water. (While most of the aromatic flavor molecules in chicken are fat-soluble and won't penetrate water-filled potatoes, salt is water-soluble and will seep into the spuds' flesh.) I halved 1½ pounds of small red potatoes—enough to feed at

Our unlikely source of inspiration for this new approach to cooking potatoes: Chinese potstickers.

least four—placed them cut side down in an oiled 12-inch skillet, and turned the dial to medium-high. Once they'd browned, I reexamined the steaming step by adding 2 cups of seasoned water (to evenly cover the surface of the pan), covering the pan, and leaving the potatoes to braise until tender. Removing the lid revealed potatoes with smooth and creamy interiors. But as expected, their cut sides were wan in appearance—and flavor.

That's when I realized I should reverse the order of operations and brown the potatoes after simmering them to guarantee good browning. I moved ahead with this plan and, once the potatoes were tender, carefully drained off the water, added some oil to the dry pan, and let the pieces brown over high heat. This time, my colleagues assured me that I was getting somewhere, as the salt had thoroughly seasoned the spuds and searing after simmering had produced the rich, deeply flavorful browning that I'd had in mind.

The downside was that straining off simmering water from a large skillet was cumbersome, and

rearranging each of the hot potato halves cut side down to ensure that they browned properly was fussy—too fussy for a simple side dish. When a colleague suggested that I simply simmer the potatoes uncovered so that the water would evaporate, I was skeptical: The time it would take to simmer off a full 2 cups of liquid would certainly mean overcooking the spuds. But at that point, I didn't have any better ideas, so I decided to give it a shot.

It did, in fact, take about 35 minutes for the water to cook off, at which point I expected to find a mushy, overcooked mess. Imagine my surprise, then, when I stuck a fork into a few of the potatoes and found that they were holding together just fine. More than that, these potatoes were remarkably silky and smooth—by far the best texture I'd produced to date. Pleased by the results, I researched an explanation and learned that if low-starch potatoes like Red Bliss are cooked long enough, they exude a fluid gel that keeps the potato "glued" together and also gives the impression of extreme creaminess. (For more information, see "The Benefits of Overcooking Waxy Potatoes.")

Still, my newfound cooking method for waxy potatoes wasn't entirely without fault: In my excitement over these ultracreamy spuds, I'd ignored that their undersides, now in contact with a dry, hot skillet, were stuck fast to the pan and scorched.

Eastern Inspiration

The more I thought about it the more I realized that my recipe shared the basic framework of a classic Chinese dish: potstickers. After browning these flat-sided dumplings in an oil-coated skillet, you add water and simmer them until the water evaporates and the dumplings once again make contact with the skillet and crisp in the oil. The main difference was that with potstickers, the oil goes in at the beginning. I wondered if adding the fat earlier in the potato-cooking process might gloss the potatoes and prevent them from sticking after the water evaporated.

So I combined everything—water, salt, potatoes, and a few tablespoons of oil—in the skillet and brought it to a simmer. After a few minutes of

PHOTOGRAPHY: CARL TREMBLAY

covered cooking (which ensured that any sections of unsubmerged potato would steam), I removed the lid and cranked the burner to medium-high. My hope was that, just as with potstickers, the water would evaporate and leave the oil and potatoes alone in the pan to brown. About 15 minutes later, I got my wish: As the last few wisps of steam escaped, the oil sizzled and the potatoes developed rich color—but I knew that I could do even better if I switched from oil to butter. Indeed, the protein in the butter's milk solids magnified the effects of browning (known as the Maillard reaction) and left the potatoes significantly richer and more complex-tasting.

Even better, as I poked a fork into the velvety pieces, every bit of their deeply browned surface pulled away cleanly from the pan's surface. I was thrilled with this unlikely approach to potato cookery. All I had left to do was jazz up the potatoes' earthy flavor.

Buttery Finish

Tossing a few sprigs of thyme into the pan during the covered simmering step was an easy way to add some herbal depth (thyme is soluble in both water and fat), but garlic was trickier. Though a natural partner with potatoes, garlic burned when added while the spuds browned, and stirring in raw minced garlic at the end led to a flavor that was unpalatably sharp. Instead, I simmered whole cloves with the potatoes to mellow their bite before mincing them into a paste, which I stirred into the finished potatoes. Tasters loved the now-mellow garlic's flavor, not to mention the body that it lent to the sauce. After a few grinds of black pepper, a squeeze of fresh lemon juice, and a sprinkling of minced chives, these spuds had it all: creamy, well-seasoned interiors; flavorful browned exteriors; and a heady sauce. (I also worked up a variation with Dijon mustard and tarragon and a super-savory version with miso and scallions.) Best of all, I'd done little hands-on cooking and dirtied just one pan.

BRAISED RED POTATOES WITH LEMON AND CHIVES
SERVES 4 TO 6

Use small red potatoes measuring about 1½ inches in diameter. For our free recipe for Braised Red Potatoes with Miso and Scallions, go to CooksIllustrated.com/june13.

1½	pounds small red potatoes, unpeeled, halved
2	cups water
3	tablespoons unsalted butter
3	garlic cloves, peeled
3	sprigs fresh thyme
¾	teaspoon salt
1	teaspoon lemon juice
¼	teaspoon pepper
2	tablespoons minced fresh chives

1. Arrange potatoes in single layer, cut side down, in 12-inch nonstick skillet. Add water, butter, garlic, thyme, and salt and bring to simmer over medium-high heat. Reduce heat to medium, cover, and simmer until potatoes are just tender, about 15 minutes.

2. Remove lid and use slotted spoon to transfer garlic to cutting board; discard thyme. Increase heat to medium-high and vigorously simmer, swirling pan occasionally, until water evaporates and butter starts to sizzle, 15 to 20 minutes. When cool enough to handle, mince garlic to paste. Transfer paste to bowl and stir in lemon juice and pepper.

3. Continue to cook potatoes, swirling pan frequently, until butter browns and cut sides of potatoes turn spotty brown, 4 to 6 minutes longer. Off heat, add garlic mixture and chives and toss to thoroughly coat. Serve immediately.

BRAISED RED POTATOES WITH DIJON AND TARRAGON

Substitute 2 teaspoons Dijon mustard for lemon juice and 1 tablespoon minced fresh tarragon for chives.

Simmered 'n' Seared—in One Pan

Our new approach to cooking waxy potatoes produces spuds with super-creamy interiors and nicely browned patinas.

COOK COVERED FOR SILKY INTERIORS
Braise the potatoes with water, butter, garlic, thyme, and salt in a covered skillet until the spuds soften.

COOK UNCOVERED FOR CRISPY CRUSTS
Remove the lid to evaporate the liquid. The butter eventually browns, coloring (and enriching the flavor of) the potatoes.

Italian Chicken and Dumpling Soup

Light, tender dumplings deeply flavored with Parmesan? Sounded like a winner. But while we were at it, we also wanted to turn this traditional Italian first course into a full meal.

> BY CELESTE ROGERS

Anyone who's ever sat down to a steaming bowl of matzo ball soup knows that the matzo balls are the main event—the chicken broth is merely the vehicle for cooking and serving them. So it goes with the rustic Northern Italian specialty *passatelli in brodo*. Passatelli are tender dumplings formed by pressing dough made from bread crumbs, eggs, and Parmesan cheese—and in the best versions, beef marrow—through the holes of a specialized tool. The resulting skinny, noodle-shaped dumplings are so deeply flavorful that as a first course they need nothing more than to be poached in a light chicken broth.

A fan of most anything that pairs cheese with bread, I was smitten with this dish from my very first taste at the home of an Italian friend. But making it in my own kitchen would require some significant adjustments. For one thing, if I'm going to make dumplings from scratch, I don't want the soup to be simply a first course: I want it to be a satisfying meal. This meant that the broth would need some bulking up. Then there was the matter of the dumpling-making tool. Surely there was a way to shape dough that would cook up light and chewy without my having to buy a whole new gadget. And since leftover beef bones aren't something that I always have in the back of my fridge, that secret weapon for savory flavor would also need a substitute.

Sticky Wicket

I started with a basic chicken broth as a placeholder and focused my attention on piecing together a recipe for the dumplings. When I gathered a stack of cookbooks and started reviewing recipes, I was relieved to see that many of them called for shaping dough with something other than the traditional tool. But I also noticed that there was no consensus as to what, exactly, went into this simple dough.

Watch: Lightness Created

Video available FREE for 4 months at CooksIllustrated.com/june13

In Italy, *passatelli* are poached in a light broth. We make a meal by cooking the dumplings in a rich stock with chunks of chicken and vegetables.

Some recipes called for dried, store-bought bread crumbs, others fresh. And while whole eggs seemed most common, a few outlier recipes specified adding richness with extra yolks. In addition, the ratios of eggs to bread crumbs and grated cheese were all over the map, so I wasn't surprised that the consistency of the resulting doughs varied greatly. I found myself forcing stiff, claylike doughs through slotted spoons, hand-rolling more delicate ones into bite-size balls, and even dripping some batterlike versions through ricers or colanders. What's more, each dough cooked up in the simmering broth quite differently. They ranged from gummy to overly dense and tough.

This sorry lot convinced me that I should build my own recipe from scratch, examining each variable independently. Whatever dough I came up with, I wanted it to lend itself to hand rolling—the easiest method by far. I would shape nice, plump dumplings big enough to support my goal of a main-dish soup. I just needed to figure out how to keep them light.

A New Grating Equation

I started with the bread crumbs. I'd already discovered that dried store-bought crumbs were too finely ground and led to dense dumplings, but what if I substituted panko? I rolled a batch of round dumplings made from these coarse, crisp Japanese-style crumbs, whole eggs, and finely grated Parmesan, and simmered them in broth. Unfortunately, tasters found these dumplings rather dull—a criticism that propelled me to switch to homemade crumbs. But fresh or toasted? I tried both and found that toasted crumbs (made by pulsing fresh bread in the food processor and then browning the crumbs in the oven) nicely underscored the nuttiness of the Parmesan. So far so good—but these dumplings still lacked the rich flavor of my friend's passatelli, and I wondered if it was the absence of bone marrow.

Perhaps, I thought, I could boost flavor by increasing the Parmesan, which at the moment was a paltry 1½ ounces. I went out on a limb and increased it to 3 ounces. This jump gave my dumplings a far more robust flavor. But when cooked, all that melting cheese turned the dough into gluey balls.

It occurred to me that the problem I'd had with the store-bought fine bread crumbs—they packed together too tightly—was similar to the trouble I was having with the Parmesan: The finely grated wisps created by my rasp-style grater were gluing too tightly to one another upon heating. Since I already had my food processor out to make the bread crumbs, I wondered if using it to process the cheese would help. I first shredded the Parmesan on the large holes of a box grater (starting with even shreds of cheese reduced the risk of over- or underprocessing it) and then pulsed the shreds in the food processor until they resembled bread crumbs. After tasting the dumplings made with these ground bits, I knew that I was onto something. Now that the cheese was roughly the same shape and texture as the bread crumbs, the bits clung to the crumbs and were less likely to melt into one another when cooked, resulting in dumplings that were tender, not gummy.

But I wanted to lighten my dumplings even more, so I mixed a batch of dumpling ingredients with whipped egg whites (instead of the whole eggs I'd been using). But as soon as I mixed the whipped whites into the dough, I could see all the aeration collapse under the weight of the bread crumbs and cheese. Still, upon cooking, I was surprised by the dumplings' noticeably lighter texture. I wondered if the aeration was even needed. For my next batch, I added just plain egg whites—no whipping at all. The results? Exactly the same. The success was in omitting the dense yolks rather than in incorporating more air.

One final problem remained: When first mixed, the dough was still a bit too sticky to handle. I solved that by giving the dough a 15-minute rest in the refrigerator, which allowed the bread crumbs to hydrate more evenly and chilled the dough so that it was firm enough to hold its shape.

Making a Meal of It

But there was still the matter of the rest of the soup. Instead of using a light and delicate broth, I wanted to create a richer, more satisfying broth, but without spending all day on it. I turned to our trick of enriching store-bought broth with chicken thighs and aromatic vegetables, including onion, carrots, and celery. Browning only the skin side of the thighs produced flavorful fond on the bottom of the pot, and to avoid any need for skimming fat off the finished broth, I poured off the rendered fat and removed the skin before simmering the thighs with the sweated vegetables and broth. In just 30 minutes, I had a rich and savory broth as well as enough cooked meat to shred into my soup to make this into a meal.

And I realized that I had something else: extra fat. Rendered chicken fat is what gives matzo balls their rich flavor—why couldn't they do the same for my *passatelli*? Just a tablespoon stirred into the dough played up the savory flavor beautifully. Circling back to traditional recipes, I also added a pinch of nutmeg—enough to bring out the peppery bite of the Parmesan.

I was almost done, but the nutty Parmesan-enriched dumplings needed more complex accompaniments.

Swapping fennel for celery, deglazing with white wine, and stirring in some bitter escarole just before serving went far to improve things.

Traditional at heart yet modern in execution, my finished soup was filled with tender, Parmesan-spiked dumplings along with complex chicken broth and hearty shredded meat, earthy vegetables, and a hint of spice. Here was a soup that could both comfort and fill.

ITALIAN CHICKEN SOUP WITH PARMESAN DUMPLINGS
SERVES 4 TO 6

Use the large holes of a box grater to shred the Parmesan. To ensure that the dumplings remain intact during cooking, roll them until the surfaces are smooth and no cracks remain.

4	(5- to 7-ounce) bone-in chicken thighs, trimmed
	Salt and pepper
1	teaspoon vegetable oil
1	fennel bulb, 1 tablespoon fronds minced, stalks discarded, bulb halved, cored, and cut into ½-inch pieces
1	onion, chopped fine
2	carrots, peeled and cut into ¾-inch pieces
½	cup dry white wine
8	cups low-sodium chicken broth
1	Parmesan cheese rind, plus 3 ounces Parmesan, shredded (1 cup)
2	slices hearty white sandwich bread, torn into 1-inch pieces
2	large egg whites
¼	teaspoon grated lemon zest
	Pinch ground nutmeg
½	small head escarole (6 ounces), trimmed and cut into ½-inch pieces

1. Pat chicken dry with paper towels and season with salt and pepper. Heat oil in Dutch oven over medium-high heat until just smoking. Add chicken, skin side down, and cook until well browned, 6 to 8 minutes. Transfer chicken to plate. Discard skin.

2. Drain off all but 1 teaspoon fat from pot and reserve 1 tablespoon fat for dumplings. Return pot to medium heat. Add fennel bulb, onion, carrots, and ½ teaspoon salt and cook, stirring occasionally, until vegetables soften and begin to brown, about 5 minutes. Add wine and cook, scraping up any browned bits, until almost dry, about 2 minutes. Return chicken to pot; add broth and Parmesan rind and bring to boil. Reduce heat to low, cover, and simmer until chicken is tender and registers 175 degrees, about 30 minutes. Transfer chicken to plate. Discard Parmesan rind. Cover broth and remove from heat. When cool enough to handle, use 2 forks to shred chicken into bite-size pieces. Discard bones.

3. While broth is simmering, adjust oven rack to middle position and heat oven to 350 degrees. Pulse bread in food processor until finely ground, 10 to 15 pulses. Measure out 1 cup bread crumbs and transfer to parchment paper–lined rimmed baking sheet (set aside remainder for another use). Toast until light brown, about 5 minutes. Transfer to medium bowl, reserving sheet and parchment, and let bread crumbs cool completely.

4. Pulse shredded Parmesan in now-empty food processor until finely ground, 10 to 15 pulses. Transfer Parmesan to bowl with cooled bread crumbs and add reserved 1 tablespoon fat, egg whites, lemon zest, ⅛ teaspoon pepper, and nutmeg. Mix until thoroughly combined. Refrigerate dough for 15 minutes.

5. Working with 1 teaspoon dough at a time, roll into smooth balls and place on parchment-lined sheet (you should have about 28 dumplings).

6. Return broth to simmer over medium-high heat. Add escarole and chicken and return to simmer. Add dumplings and cook, adjusting heat to maintain gentle simmer, until dumplings float to surface and are cooked through, 3 to 5 minutes. Stir in fennel fronds. Season with salt and pepper to taste, and serve.

TO MAKE AHEAD: Prepare recipe through step 5. Refrigerate broth, shredded chicken, and dumplings separately for up to 24 hours. To serve, proceed with step 6 as directed.

Adjusting the Dumpling

Our Italian-style dumplings combine the nutty Parmesan taste of traditional *passatelli* with the shape of matzo balls and their secret weapon for savory flavor.

PASSATELLI
In Italy, a dough made of bread crumbs, Parmesan, egg, and beef marrow is extruded through a special tool.

MATZO BALLS
Matzo balls are formed by hand out of matzo meal, egg, and chicken fat.

OUR HYBRID
Instead of hard-to-get beef marrow, we add extra cheese and chicken fat to boost savory flavor and hand-roll the dough into plump balls.

The Frugal Kitchen

No cook likes needless waste in the kitchen. And why spend money on expensive equipment if you don't have to? BY MOLLY BIRNBAUM

BE SCRAPPY WITH YOUR INGREDIENTS

Here are some of our favorite ways to repurpose scraps and leftovers.

Refresh and Renew

These tricks give stale, limp, or hardened ingredients and leftovers a new lease on life.

Celery

Place limp stalks of celery cut side down in a tall, narrow container with at least 2 inches of water. Refrigerate until the stalks are crisp and sprightly, 6 to 12 hours. Trim and discard the bottom end of each stalk before using.

Cookies

Place hardened, stale cookies on a plate and microwave for 10 seconds. It is important to eat the cookies while they are warm before they lose their softness.

Polenta

Using quick pulses, process cold polenta in a food processor, adding a few tablespoons of warm water for every cup of cooked polenta, until the mixture is creamy. Transfer the polenta to a bowl, cover, and microwave until warm.

Potato Chips

To restore crispiness, spread 2 cups of stale potato or tortilla chips on a Pyrex pie plate and microwave for 1 minute. Place the hot chips on a double layer of paper towels and allow them to cool completely.

Marshmallows

To soften dry, stale marshmallows, place them in an airtight container with a slice of bread for 24 hours. Once the marshmallows are soft, discard the bread and reseal the container.

Vanilla Beans

Return moisture to hardened vanilla beans by placing them in an airtight container overnight (or better yet, for two nights) with a slice of bread. The moisture from the bread should soften the bean enough to let you split it and scrape out the seeds.

Cheese Rinds

Save your Parmesan rinds and do as the Italians do: Toss one into a soup or stew. It's an age-old trick for adding savory depth. Stored in a zipper-lock freezer bag in the freezer, the rinds will keep indefinitely (no need to thaw them before using).

Fry Oil

Unless you have used it to fry fish, don't throw away your leftover fry oil—you can use it three or four more times. Once the oil has cooled, we filter it through a strainer lined with two or three layers of cheesecloth or paper coffee filters. For short-term storage, store oils (leftover or new) in a cool, dark spot, since exposure to air and light makes oil turn rancid faster. But for long-term storage (beyond one month), the cooler the storage temperature the better— we recommend the freezer.

Cured Meat Scraps

Instead of tossing out scraps of cured meat such as dry sausage and prosciutto, place leftovers in a zipper-lock freezer bag and store them in the freezer. When making tomato sauce, soups, or stews, add the meat to the simmering pot for extra flavor.

Stale Bread

Bread that is two to three days old is ideal for making bread crumbs: It has become quite firm but still retains some moisture. Pulse leftover slices in a food processor until crumbs are formed and then use them right away or freeze them in a zipper-lock freezer bag. (In recipes, 2/3 cup of finely processed frozen crumbs or 1 cup of coarsely processed frozen crumbs equals one large 1.5-ounce slice of sandwich bread.) Stale bread can also be a great thickener for soups and stews.

Cilantro Stems

While some herb stems (like parsley) can taste bitter, cilantro is different. Sure, the leaves are tasty, but the great flavor found in the stems caught us off guard. Sweet, fresh, and potent, the flavor intensified as we traveled down the stem but never became bitter. If a recipe calls for cilantro and a slightly crunchy texture isn't an issue, use the stems as well as the leaves—you'll get more for your money.

Pickle Juice

Instead of tossing out a jar of pickle juice after finishing the last spear, use the tangy liquid to make a new condiment. Add thinly sliced onions to the juice and let them marinate in the refrigerator for a few days. The drained pickled onions can be used as a topping for hot dogs and hamburgers or in salads. This method also works well with the spicy packing juice from pickled peppers.

ILLUSTRATION: JOHN BURGOYNE

FREEZE FOR LATER USE

When it's not possible to use leftover ingredients immediately, we turn to the freezer for longer-term storage. You'll be surprised at what keeps.

FOOD	PREP FOR FREEZER	STORAGE AND USE
Bacon	Roll up bacon in tight cylinders, with two to four slices of bacon in each; place in zipper-lock freezer bag and freeze.	When ready to use, simply pull out desired number of slices.
Bananas	Peel bananas and freeze in zipper-lock freezer bag.	Use to make banana bread or muffins, or drop into blender while still frozen for fruit smoothies.
Buttermilk	Place some small paper cups on tray and fill each with ½ cup buttermilk; place tray in freezer.	Once buttermilk is frozen, wrap each cup in plastic wrap and store in large zipper-lock freezer bag. Defrost amount needed in refrigerator before use.
Canned chipotle chiles in adobo	Spoon out chiles, each with a couple teaspoons of adobo sauce, onto different areas of baking sheet lined with parchment paper and freeze.	Transfer frozen chiles to zipper-lock freezer bag for long-term storage.
Citrus zest	Remove zest from entire fruit. Deposit grated zest in ½-teaspoon increments on plate and transfer plate to freezer.	Once piles are frozen, place them in zipper-lock freezer bag and return them to freezer.
Herbs	Chop leftover fresh parsley, sage, rosemary, or thyme by hand or in food processor; transfer by spoonful into ice cube trays; and top with water to cover. For standard ice cube tray, place 2 tablespoons chopped herbs and 1 tablespoon water in each cube. Freeze tray.	Once cubes are frozen, transfer to zipper-lock freezer bag. Store until you want to add herbs to sauces, soups, or stews.
Nuts	Freeze nuts in zipper-lock freezer bag.	Frozen nuts stay fresh for months. No need to defrost before using; frozen nuts can be chopped just as easily as fresh.
Stock	Pour stock into coffee mug lined with quart-size zipper-lock freezer bag. Place bag on baking sheet and freeze.	Once stock is frozen, remove bag from sheet and return to freezer.
Tomato paste	Open both ends of tomato paste can. Remove lid from one end and use lid at other end to push out paste onto sheet of plastic wrap. Wrap paste in plastic and place in freezer.	When paste has frozen, cut off only as much as needed for particular recipe and return frozen log to freezer.
Wine	Measure 1 tablespoon wine into each well of ice cube tray and freeze.	Use paring knife or small spatula to remove each frozen wine cube and add as desired to pan sauces.

Don't Throw Away
Expired doesn't always mean retired.

Canned Goods
The "best by" date printed on some canned foods is not an "expiration" date: It refers strictly to the manufacturer's recommendation for peak quality, not safety concerns. As long as cans look good and have been stored well (in a dry place between 40 and 70 degrees), their contents should remain safe to use indefinitely. Be sure to discard cans with a compromised seal or cans that are bulging or that spurt liquid when opened.

"Expired" PAM
Nonstick vegetable oil spray likewise lasts past its "best by" date. We tested this by making two sheet cakes. For one, we sprayed the pan with a can of PAM that was a year past its "best by" date, and for the other, we used a new can of the same product. The results? Both cakes tasted exactly the same.

Fats are most likely to spoil by exposure to oxygen, which makes them turn rancid. But the fats in cans of vegetable oil spray are contained under pressure with a gas, preventing oxygen from coming in contact with the fat. As long as the can is still functional, the product should be in good shape. (The makers of PAM do not advise using products past their "best by" dates—but we feel comfortable using our slightly "vintage" spray.)

QUALITY ON THE CHEAP

You don't always have to pay top dollar to get high-performing pots, pans, and knives. Here are some of our favorite best buys.

Tramontina 6.5-Qt. Cast Iron Dutch Oven, $49.97
Crafted from enameled cast iron, this pot produced glossy, deeply flavored beef stew; fluffy white rice; and crispy French fries in the test kitchen—in other words, it works as well as pots costing more than five times as much.

Victorinox (formerly Victorinox Forschner) Fibrox 8-Inch Chef's Knife, $24.95
This chef's knife is one of the cheapest we've ever tested. Nonetheless, it is also a longtime favorite among test cooks who fancy lighter knives. The grippy material, shape, and overall comfort of the handle drew testers' praise.

Cuisinart MultiClad Unlimited 4-Quart Saucepan, $69.99
At about a third of the price of the top saucepan we tested, this lightweight saucepan performed virtually identically. It boasts a well-balanced handle and a rolled lip, ensuring a spill-free pour.

T-fal Professional Non-Stick Fry Pan, 12.5 inches, $34.99
Outperforming competing models at a fraction of the price, this pan had the slickest, most durable nonstick coating; it released perfectly. It is well proportioned, with a comfy handle and a generous cooking surface.

Cuban-Style Picadillo

There's lots to recommend this tangy, sweet, judiciously spiced Latin beef hash—but only if we could trade a painstakingly hand-chopped roast for the convenience of ground meat.

⇒ BY BRIDGET LANCASTER ⇐

Back in college, when I was living on gloppy dining hall food, I loved when my Cuban American roommate's mother ("Mama Estelle" to us) would visit and make a batch of *picadillo*. This Latin staple varies widely depending on the region, the country, and indeed the very household (picadillo is more of a home-cooked dish than restaurant fare). Mama Estelle's take involved chopping a beef roast into tiny pieces and then stewing the meat with tomatoes and her homemade *sofrito*—a flavor base of cooked onion, green bell pepper, and garlic. Along the way, she stirred in spices like cumin and cinnamon, and for the dish's trademark sweet-sour balance, she finished it with raisins and chopped pimento-stuffed olives. The result was tangy, sweet, and satisfying, and it came together in about an hour. The spread of traditional accompaniments that she made—rice, black beans, and sometimes fried plantains or potatoes—turned it into a complete meal.

I wish I'd paid more attention while Mama Estelle was cooking, but coming up with my own picadillo recipe couldn't be too hard, I figured. The ingredients are easily accessible and the whole dish comes together in one pot. I just had some experimenting to do.

Ground Meat TLC

Per tradition, I started by sautéing chopped aromatic vegetables for the aforementioned sofrito in a Dutch oven. But I had to forgo tradition when it came to the meat. Many of the oldest and most authentic picadillo recipes call for hand-chopping or grinding beef (the Spanish verb *picar* means "to mince" or "to grind") as Mama Estelle did, but I wanted my picadillo to be a quick weeknight option, which meant switching to the convenience of preground beef. I swapped in a couple of pounds for the roast and browned it. Then I chopped up a can's worth of tomatoes, added it to the pot with

Pinching the ground beef into large chunks (rather than breaking it up into fine bits) helps the meat stay juicy as it cooks.

spices, and let it simmer down. When the mixture had thickened a little, I added handfuls of chopped green olives and raisins for punchy, briny, and sweet flavors.

This first attempt was . . . OK. While the savory-sweet profile was appealing, it tasted off-balance, more like beef chili with olives and raisins tossed in at the last minute. Worse, I'd paid dearly for the convenience of switching to ground beef, which was chalky, dry, and dull rather than tender and juicy.

Going back to chopping up a roast wasn't an option, but I had another idea. While doing research, I'd come across a number of recipes that supplemented the beef with ground pork or chorizo. When I tried it, there was no question that the sausage was a mistake. Its heat overwhelmed the other flavors—even when I added just a small amount. The ground pork was a good move, though: With a full pound of it, the meat mixture was juicier and more supple. It also tasted a touch sweeter than beef alone—something I've noticed in other dishes when I've added pork. I did some investigating and learned

that as it cooks, pork develops a relatively high concentration of glycine, an amino acid formed by the breakdown of proteins. It's the glycine that lends a subtle sweetness that helps boost complexity whenever pork makes its way into a recipe. With that mystery solved, I turned my attention to texture: Neither the beef nor the pork was as tender as I wanted it to be.

Fortunately, I had a couple of ground-meat-tenderizing tricks to fall back on. In other recipes, we've briefly treated the raw meat with baking soda. Just a pinch (mixed with a little water to dissolve it, plus salt and pepper for seasoning) raises the beef's pH, which prevents it from toughening during cooking. Second, since browning and simmering the ground beef was causing it to dry out, I skipped the sear, pinched the meat into 2-inch chunks (the larger the pieces the moister the meat would stay), and added them directly to the simmering sauce. Sure enough, these changes rendered the meat tender and juicy. The problem was that since meat develops its deepest, most savory flavor when it browns (during a process called the Maillard reaction), doing away with that step was a blow to the dish's meaty depth. Still, I wasn't about to undo the textural progress I'd made, so I moved on to tinkering with the flavors, hoping that the right combination of spices, acidity, and sweetness would boost the dish's complexity.

See the *Picadillo* Process

Video available FREE for 4 months at CooksIllustrated.com/june13

Making Ground Beef Better

Using ground beef (rather than chopping up a roast) turned this dish into a quick weeknight supper, but the convenience came with a couple of drawbacks—namely, the beef's one-note flavor and dry, chalky texture. Here's our two-part fix.

➤ **Add ground pork for sweetness**
Cooked pork contains relatively high levels of an amino acid called glycine, which lends the meat a faint sweetness.

➤ **Treat with baking soda for tenderness**
Tossing the ground meats with baking soda (dissolved in a little water) tenderizes their texture by raising their pH.

Balancing Act

While onion, grassy green bell pepper, and lots of garlic were picadillo mainstays, I had some play in the choice of spices. Ground cumin was a given, but many recipes use various combinations of thyme, oregano, bay leaf, clove, allspice, and cinnamon—and several call for all of the above. I tried various combinations and amounts of spices until my tasters and I pared down the list to a judicious tablespoon each of oregano and cumin, three bay leaves, and ½ teaspoon of ground cinnamon. I also switched up my order of operations and sautéed the spices along with the onion and bell pepper (the bay was left for adding later) in a little oil—standard practice for drawing out their fat-soluble flavor compounds.

Next I turned to the acid sources, which were twofold, since most recipes call for both tomatoes and a dry wine called *vino seco*. But tomatoes must walk a fine line in picadillo: While they are almost always included, the finished dish should not taste tomato-based. I reached for a small can of whole tomatoes (fresh ones are inevitably bad at this time of year). After a few rough chops, into the pan they went. As for the vino seco, I wasn't impressed with either the red or the white versions that I tried, and I wasn't surprised. The product, which is treated with salt as a preservative, is salty and acidic—more akin to the seasoning liquid known as cooking wine than to drinking wine. Switching to a dry white (such as Sauvignon Blanc) balanced out the picadillo's spices and provided the punch that it needed. And yet neither the tomatoes nor the wine had compensated enough for the missing meatiness, so I reached for a more direct source: beef broth. Just ½ cup gave the meat the rich, savory boost it needed.

Finally, I went back to the traditional last-minute additions. Raisins and coarsely chopped green olives were givens, but I was also intrigued by other possibilities I'd read about—namely, capers, vinegar, and chopped almonds. A couple of spoonfuls of the capers plus a last-minute splash of red wine vinegar cut the spiced meat. But the pleasant crunch of the almonds quickly softened when I stirred them into the meat mixture. They were much better sprinkled on each dish at the table.

The sauce was now perfect—at least the bites with the raisins were perfect. But since I'd been stirring them into the pot in the last minutes of cooking, they remained sporadically scattered throughout the mixture. I wanted each bite to have some of that jammy grape flavor, so I added the raisins earlier, along with the broth and bay leaves. Allowed to simmer, the fruit's sweet flavor diffused through the dish and evened out the recipe's other strong flavors.

Savory, sweet, and briny, the ground beef mixture was now a showpiece, but it was a truly impressive spread when partnered with all the trimmings: rice and beans on the side and fresh parsley, toasted almonds, and chopped hard-cooked egg sprinkled over the top. The dish was a snap to throw together, too. Who knows? Maybe one day it will be me bringing this satisfying meal to my kids when they're in college.

Putting the Punch in *Picadillo*

Picadillo may be humble fare, but thanks to its mix of warm spices and sweet and tart elements, the flavors of this dish are anything but ho-hum.

SWEET
Adding jammy raisins early in the cooking process allows their sweetness to diffuse evenly.

BRINY AND BRIGHT
Chopped green olives, capers, and a last-minute splash of red wine vinegar add piquant flavors.

SPICED
Warm spices like cinnamon and cumin bring out the meats' rounder, more complex flavors.

CUBAN-STYLE PICADILLO
SERVES 6

We prefer this dish prepared with raisins, but they can be replaced with 2 tablespoons of brown sugar added with the broth in step 2. *Picadillo* is traditionally served with rice and black beans. It can also be topped with chopped parsley, toasted almonds, and/or chopped hard-cooked egg. For our free recipe for Cuban-Style Picadillo with Fried Potatoes, go to CooksIllustrated.com/june13.

- 1 pound 85 percent lean ground beef
- 1 pound ground pork
- 2 tablespoons water
- ½ teaspoon baking soda
  Salt and pepper
- 1 green bell pepper, stemmed, seeded, and cut into 2-inch pieces
- 1 onion, halved and cut into 2-inch pieces
- 2 tablespoons vegetable oil
- 1 tablespoon dried oregano
- 1 tablespoon ground cumin
- ½ teaspoon ground cinnamon
- 6 garlic cloves, minced
- 1 (14.5-ounce) can whole tomatoes, drained and chopped coarse
- ¾ cup dry white wine
- ½ cup beef broth
- ½ cup raisins
- 3 bay leaves
- ½ cup pimento-stuffed green olives, chopped coarse
- 2 tablespoons capers, rinsed
- 1 tablespoon red wine vinegar, plus extra for seasoning

1. Toss beef and pork with water, baking soda, ½ teaspoon salt, and ¼ teaspoon pepper in bowl until thoroughly combined. Set aside for 20 minutes. Meanwhile, pulse bell pepper and onion in food processor until chopped into ¼-inch pieces, about 12 pulses.

2. Heat oil in large Dutch oven over medium-high heat until shimmering. Add chopped vegetables, oregano, cumin, cinnamon, and ¼ teaspoon salt; cook, stirring frequently, until vegetables are softened and beginning to brown, 6 to 8 minutes. Add garlic and cook, stirring constantly, until fragrant, about 30 seconds. Add tomatoes and wine and cook, scraping up any browned bits, until pot is almost dry, 3 to 5 minutes. Stir in broth, raisins, and bay leaves and bring to simmer.

3. Reduce heat to medium-low, add meat mixture in 2-inch chunks to pot, and bring to gentle simmer. Cover and cook, stirring occasionally with 2 forks to break meat chunks into ¼- to ½-inch pieces, until meat is cooked through, about 10 minutes.

4. Discard bay leaves. Stir in olives and capers. Increase heat to medium-high and cook, stirring occasionally, until sauce is thickened and coats meat, about 5 minutes. Stir in vinegar and season with salt, pepper, and extra vinegar to taste. Serve.

TASTING
Pimento-Stuffed Green Olives

Pimento-stuffed green olives add a briny jolt of flavor to food as well as to martinis. But after tasting the best-selling olive varietals from four nationally available brands, both straight from the jar and chopped up in *picadillo*, we discovered that a good olive is mostly about the other ingredients in the jar. Brines spiked with vermouth and vinegar make olives taste "mouth-puckering" (though cooking mellows the sharpness). Meanwhile, calcium chloride is a good thing, as it strengthens the flesh-firming pectin in the olives. As for varietals, larger Spanish Queen and Sevillano, such as our favorites from Mezzetta and Santa Barbara Olive Co., respectively, were "meaty" and "juicy"—pluses when snacking. For complete tasting results, go to CooksIllustrated.com/june13. –Amy Graves

THE QUEEN OF THE CROP
Mezzetta Super Colossal Spanish Queen Pimiento Stuffed Olives are great for snacking and cooking.

Blueberry Bundt Cake

Tossing large, cultivated blueberries into a Bundt cake gave us big blue blowouts and little fresh flavor. We looked for a way to make the star of the show less of a problem.

⋟ BY DAN SOUZA ⋞

Somewhere along the line, blueberries got the reputation of being a casual fruit, best fit for tossing into pancakes or folding into hearty snack cakes. My grandmother, a lifetime Mainer and baker, was never one to so pigeonhole them. Sure, she'd whip up a batch of rustic blueberry scones at the drop of a hat, but she'd just as often reserve her handpicked berries for more occasion-worthy desserts. My favorite? A delicate yellow Bundt cake speckled with intensely flavored wild Maine blueberries.

I no longer have my grandmother or easy access to fresh, wild Maine blueberries, but that does little to suppress my craving for the cake. I decided that it was time to take on the challenge of baking just such a cake—one that was truly packed with fresh blueberry flavor. I'd use widely available (and more affordable) cultivated blueberries and our years of baking experience to pay tribute to this memorable dessert.

Berry Trouble

While my intentions were good, my early tests were total failures. In every one of the recipes I tried, the large cultivated blueberries, rather than remaining evenly dispersed throughout like their compact wild forebears, drifted defiantly to the bottom of the pan. Those few berries that did manage to stay in place burst into big, soggy pockets when subjected to the heat of the oven. To make matters worse, tasters found that these watery cultivated blueberries tasted incredibly bland.

Undeterred by these early setbacks, I regrouped. I restarted my testing using one of the test kitchen's tried-and-true Bundt cake recipes (which uses a base of creamed butter and sugar for a light texture) and focused my efforts on wrangling the berries.

Meaning to address both flavor and texture issues in one fell swoop, I tried tossing the blueberries in various combinations of flour, cornstarch, and cornmeal, along with some sugar and lemon zest. My

A blueberry puree marbled throughout our Bundt cake guarantees bright, fresh fruit flavor in every bite.

hope was that the dry starches would not only absorb and trap the liquid as the berries burst but also provide some added texture to their smooth exteriors, and therefore enough drag that the fruit would stay put in the cake. No dice on either front. Most of the dry mixture simply sloughed off the berries as I incorporated them into the batter, leaving gummy streaks throughout. And the fruit still plummeted to the bottom of the pan like little stones.

Next I tried macerating 10 ounces of berries in sugar in a colander set over a bowl, hoping to draw

out excess liquid before they reached the cake. But after a full hour, the fruit hadn't exuded even a drop of juice. It turns out that in addition to their generous size, commercial blueberry breeds are selected for the durability of their skins—a boon for transport but a barrier against the hygroscopic pull of sugar. I attempted a second batch in which I first lightly squished the blueberries with a potato masher, but alas, the juice yield barely budged. But this got me thinking: If the berries insisted on bursting inside the cake, why not beat them to the punch and burst them myself before adding them to the batter?

Liquid Assets

Of course, adding plain crushed berries directly to the batter would be neither tasty nor attractive. But I could puree them and then swirl the thick mix through the batter to produce an elegant marbled cake. Pureeing was simple enough with a quick buzz in the blender. But the puree was too thin and liquidy to swirl into the cake batter on its own. I had to find a way to thicken it up.

My first thought was the simplest: Just fold a bit of the cake batter into the puree. This would add heft to the puree—no additional ingredients needed. But this method delivered nothing more than soggy, purple-blue cake that tasted weakly of blueberries. Next I tried cooking down the raw puree to thicken it, but tasters lamented the loss of fresh berry flavor. Beginning to get a bit worried, I rounded up the usual thickening suspects: flour, cornstarch, and tapioca. I tried cooking a small portion of the puree with various amounts of all three and then stirring that into the remaining raw puree in order to retain fresh flavor. Unfortunately, in

Overcoming Blueberry Bummers

Cultivated blueberries can be problematic in baking, often blowing out and clumping at the bottom of the pan. Plus, these watery berries taste disappointingly bland. Our solution? Puree the berries with sugar, salt, and lemon zest to improve flavor and then thicken the mixture with pectin and swirl it evenly through the batter.

CLUMPY BLOWOUTS   EVEN SUSPENSION

order to produce a mixture that was thick enough to be successfully swirled into the batter and didn't just bleed out into a leaky blue mess, I needed to use a significant amount of each starch. The fallout? Dulled flavor, an artificial texture, or, most often, both. I was at a loss.

While none of my thickening techniques had provided the texture that I was after, one positive had emerged from this barrage of testing. With the switch to pureed blueberries, I was able to bump up the flavor by adding sugar, lemon juice and zest, and a pinch of salt directly to the fruit. This stuff tasted bright and balanced. Still, if I couldn't get the puree to lace through the batter—and stay put—then this small victory would be for naught. After processing yet another batch of puree, I left my station in order to brainstorm with a few fellow test cooks. Following a healthy dose of suggestions and encouragement I returned to my blueberries. To my astonishment, the puree had slightly gelled and thickened—on its own. The reason? With some research, I learned that blueberries contain a small amount of natural pectin (it's stored in their cell walls and particularly in their skins), which had been released in the blender. My next move felt obvious: Boost the naturally present pectin with additional store-bought pectin.

I opted for pectin for low-sugar recipes, as my filling didn't have the requisite sweetness for the regular version. I tried dissolving varying amounts of pectin—along with sugar, lemon zest, and salt—in just ¼ cup of the puree on the stovetop. While it was still warm, I stirred this sticky mixture into the remaining blueberry puree and let it sit until slightly cooled. Just as I'd hoped, the extra pectin (3 tablespoons proved ideal) gelled my blueberry mixture just enough. I could now fold and swirl it into the cake batter, where it maintained a distinct identity and baked into a satisfying texture. And this swirl tasted like fresh fruit—something that couldn't be said for my starch-thickened trials. Finally satisfied with this filling, I focused on putting it all together.

Assembly

The reengineered filling was so good at staying in place that I couldn't simply swirl it into the top of the cake and let it flow into the rest of the batter during baking—it would remain stuck in place. Instead, I added it in two phases. After spraying my 12-cup nonstick Bundt pan with baking spray, I spooned in half of the batter and formed a shallow channel in the middle of it. I then added half of the filling to this depression and thoroughly swirled and folded it in with a butter knife, ensuring that no large pockets of filling remained. I repeated these steps for the second layer before baking my cake at 325 degrees for about an hour. The cake emerged from the oven lightly bronzed and smooth, with spotty hints of the lacy marbling that lay beneath. Tasters tucked into this cake and were pleased with its hits of blueberry in every bite. I think my grandmother would have been proud.

STEP BY STEP | LET IT SWIRL

Properly swirling the thickened blueberry puree is key to producing an elegantly marbled cake.

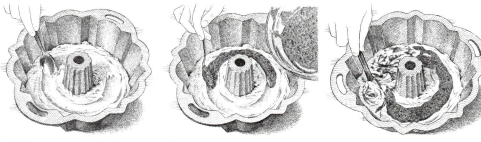

1. After spooning half of batter into Bundt pan, make channel with back of spoon.

2. Using spoon, fill channel with half of blueberry filling in even layer.

3. Using butter knife, swirl filling through batter. Repeat these steps with remaining batter and filling.

MARBLED BLUEBERRY BUNDT CAKE
SERVES 12

Spray the pan well in step 1 to prevent sticking. If you don't have nonstick baking spray with flour, mix 1 tablespoon melted butter and 1 tablespoon flour into a paste and brush inside the pan (see "A Truly Nonstick Bundt Pan," page 31). For fruit pectin we recommend both Sure-Jell for Less or No Sugar Needed Recipes and Ball RealFruit Low or No-Sugar Needed Pectin. If using frozen berries, thaw them before blending in step 3. This cake can be served plain or with Lemon Glaze or Cinnamon Whipped Cream (for our free recipes, go to CooksIllustrated.com/june13).

Cake
3	cups (15 ounces) all-purpose flour
1½	teaspoons baking powder
¾	teaspoon baking soda
1	teaspoon salt
½	teaspoon ground cinnamon
¾	cup buttermilk
2	teaspoons grated lemon zest plus 3 tablespoons juice
2	teaspoons vanilla extract
3	large eggs plus 1 large yolk, room temperature
18	tablespoons (2¼ sticks) unsalted butter, softened
2	cups (14 ounces) sugar

Filling
¾	cup (5¼ ounces) sugar
3	tablespoons low- or no-sugar-needed fruit pectin
	Pinch salt
10	ounces (2 cups) fresh or thawed frozen blueberries
1	teaspoon grated lemon zest plus 1 tablespoon juice

1. FOR THE CAKE: Adjust oven rack to lower-middle position and heat oven to 325 degrees. Heavily spray 12-cup nonstick Bundt pan with baking spray with flour. Whisk flour, baking powder, baking soda, salt, and cinnamon together in large bowl. Whisk buttermilk, lemon zest and juice, and vanilla together in medium bowl. Gently whisk eggs and yolk to combine in third bowl.

2. Using stand mixer fitted with paddle, beat butter and sugar on medium-high speed until pale and fluffy, about 3 minutes, scraping down bowl as needed. Reduce speed to medium and beat in half of eggs until incorporated, about 15 seconds. Repeat with remaining eggs, scraping down bowl after incorporating. Reduce speed to low and add one-third of flour mixture, followed by half of buttermilk mixture, mixing until just incorporated after each addition, about 5 seconds. Repeat using half of remaining flour mixture and all of remaining buttermilk mixture. Scrape down bowl, add remaining flour mixture, and mix at medium-low speed until batter is thoroughly combined, about 15 seconds. Remove bowl from mixer and fold batter once or twice with rubber spatula to incorporate any remaining flour. Cover bowl with plastic wrap and set aside while preparing filling (batter will inflate a bit).

3. FOR THE FILLING: Whisk sugar, pectin, and salt together in small saucepan. Process blueberries in blender until mostly smooth, about 1 minute. Transfer ¼ cup puree and lemon zest to saucepan with sugar mixture and stir to thoroughly combine. Heat sugar-blueberry mixture over medium heat until just simmering, about 3 minutes, stirring frequently to dissolve sugar and pectin. Transfer mixture to medium bowl and let cool for 5 minutes. Add remaining puree and lemon juice to cooled mixture and whisk to combine. Let sit until slightly set, about 8 minutes.

4. Spoon half of batter into prepared pan and smooth top. Using back of spoon, create ½-inch-deep channel in center of batter. Spoon half of filling into channel. Using butter knife or small offset spatula, thoroughly swirl filling into batter (there should be no large pockets of filling remaining). Repeat swirling step with remaining batter and filling.

5. Bake until top is golden brown and skewer inserted in center comes out with no crumbs attached, 60 to 70 minutes. Let cake cool in pan on wire rack for 10 minutes, then invert cake directly onto wire rack. Let cake cool for at least 3 hours before serving.

Whole-Wheat Pizza

Most whole-wheat pizza is as dry and dense as cardboard. But what if there was a way to make it as crisp and chewy as traditional pizza—and highlight its nutty, wheaty flavor?

⇒ BY DAN SOUZA ⇐

A quick survey of pizza parlor menus suggests that pies are going the way of rustic bread: They're no longer a white flour–only affair. Even most supermarkets offer a partial whole-wheat-flour dough alongside their standard white. In theory, this is good news, since whole wheat can lend rich, nutty flavor and satisfying depth to almost any kind of baked good. But in practice, I often find the marriage of whole wheat and pizza crust to be strained at best.

Most recipes seem to fear commitment to the style, casually throwing a scant amount of whole-wheat flour into a white flour formula. The resulting pies may have decent texture, but if they have zilch when it comes to nuttiness or flavor complexity, what's the point? At the other end of the spectrum, I've tried following pizza dough recipes with a high ratio of whole-wheat flour (some with as much as 100 percent), and I've found that for the most part they produce dense pies devoid of satisfying chew or crisp crust. Not to mention that these crusts have an overly wheaty flavor that competes for attention with even the most potent toppings. I decided to rethink whole-wheat pizza, examining it through the lens of a bread baker in order to formulate a dough (and a cooking technique) that would give me a crust with it all: good—but not overwhelming—wheat flavor; a crisp bottom; and a moist, chewy interior.

The Whole Problem

I started my journey by deciding exactly what style of crust I wanted. After all, whole-wheat pizza crusts run the same gamut as white flour ones: from thin and crispy to thick, deep-dish-style pies. I wanted a crust that could withstand some full-flavored toppings, but not one that would overwhelm with its wheaty heft. A thin-crust pizza like the one we developed in January/February 2011 seemed a good model: Its crust is thin and crisp with perfect spots of char alongside a tender, chewy interior. I would start there, tailoring the ingredient ratio and baking techniques to withstand the challenges of whole wheat.

This pizza uses high-protein bread flour and the food processor for fast kneading. The use of bread

A ratio of 60 percent whole-wheat flour to 40 percent white flour ensures that the nutty taste of our crust doesn't fade into the background.

flour, I knew before I even began baking, would be particularly important. Why? Bread flour contains more of the proteins (glutenin and gliadin) that form gluten—the network of proteins that gives dough structure and chew—than all-purpose flour. I would use King Arthur brand bread flour, which features a particularly high protein content of 12.7 percent. And while high in protein, whole-wheat flour has less gluten potential than does white flour for two reasons. One is the type of proteins in the mix (see "Why Whole Wheat Can Sabotage Texture"). The second is that whole-wheat flour, ground from the wheat berry, includes both the germ and the bran. These constituents provide great flavor, but the bran physically inhibits gluten development by cutting gluten strands with its sharp edges. I would therefore need to punch up the gluten potential in other ways; bread flour would be a great start.

But the thin-crust pizza recipe also used an overnight rise in the refrigerator to allow for better flavor development and an easier-to-stretch dough. I wondered if I could skip that step, therefore skipping

the need for so much forethought. The nutty flavor of the whole wheat, I figured, would make up for any other flavor benefits of letting the dough sit overnight.

Glutenous Maximus

I started my testing by swapping in varying proportions of whole-wheat flour in our thin-crust pizza dough recipe. My goal for this initial round of testing was to determine the ideal amount of whole-wheat flour from a flavor perspective and then deal with textural issues as they arose. For each test dough, I pulsed the flours, water, yeast, and a sweetener to promote browning (I opted for honey to complement the wheat flavor) until they were just combined, and then I allowed the doughs to sit for 10 minutes. During this brief respite, called an autolyse, gluten formation gets a jump start. I then added salt and oil and processed the doughs for a minute, until they were smooth and satiny. After a final rise, I shaped, topped, and baked the pizzas on a preheated 500-degree pizza stone. These test batches quickly confirmed that tasters preferred a dough with 60 percent whole-wheat (and the remainder white) flour. This ratio provided a distinct, pleasant wheatiness that was recognizable but not too strong. I was pleased with the flavor of my pizza, but the texture was still lacking. The flour choice was important, but now I looked to the second key ingredient: water.

I knew that dough with more water produces chewier breads, as the added hydration allows for a stronger, more stretchable gluten network. You can see water's impact by comparing tender, fine-crumb sandwich bread with chewy rustic bread. The former is often in the range of 55 to 60 percent hydrated (this number represents the weight of the water compared with that of the flour), whereas rustic bread's hydration starts in the low 60s and can creep up to nearly 100 percent. This was of relevance to my dough because whole-wheat flour, thanks to its mix of starch, bran, and germ, absorbs more water than does white flour. At about 64 percent hydration, my initial formula sat in the midrange of white flour doughs. With this in mind, I started increasing the water in batches and tracking the results.

Sure enough, more water led to a pizza with better chew and larger, slightly more irregular holes—something that bakers refer to as a more open crumb structure. It also made the dough easier to work with and stretch thin—at least to a point. I found that dough with a hydration of 80 percent and up was too soft and sticky to reliably form into a 13-inch disk, and the resulting pies had a tendency to stick to the pizza peel when I attempted to slide them into the oven. In the end, I found my sweet spot with 10 ounces of water for 13¾ ounces of flour, or roughly 73 percent hydration. But even this ratio could cause trouble when it came to stretching my dough out nice and thin with ease. I found myself doubling back to the overnight rise: I may not need it for flavor development, but it was undeniable that the long rest in the fridge did greatly improve the extensibility of our white flour thin-crust pizza. Would it do the same here? One try and I knew: Yes. This dough was a pleasure to handle and stretch, and it baked into a pizza with satisfying chew and a thin but airy interior.

But while the increased hydration helped gluten development and chew, it wasn't all roses. If I let my pizzas bake long enough for them to really crisp on the bottom, they overbaked and dried out. It turns out that browning and crisping the bottom of a pizza is much like trying to get a good sear on a steak. We all know that a wet steak takes much longer to sear than a dry one and that by the time you achieve a good crust on the former, much of the interior is overcooked. This holds true for pizza as well: A wetter dough will take longer to brown and crisp because more of the oven's energy is going into driving off the extra moisture, leaving less available for crisping. Feeling as though I'd just shot myself in the proverbial foot, I scrambled for a solution.

Better Baking

Up to this point, I'd been following our established pizza baking protocol, cooking my pies in a 500-degree oven on a preheated pizza stone set on the oven rack's second-highest position. By keeping the stone near the top of the oven (as opposed to the traditional method of setting it as low as possible), we create a smaller oven space where reflected heat is trapped around the pizza. This means the top and bottom of the pizza bake at a more even rate. This was good, but how could I speed up that rate?

Again, if I were dealing with a steak in a skillet, I'd simply turn up the heat. My oven was already set to 500 degrees, but I did have a super-hot broiler. Yet given that I was trying to get the bottom of the pizza to cook faster, I wasn't quite sure how to put it to use. After some failed experiments resulting in seriously burnt toppings, I hit on a winning solution. After preheating the stone in a 500-degree oven to ensure that it was fully saturated with heat, I turned on the broiler for 10 minutes. Then, when I slid in the pizza, I switched the oven back to bake. The brief blast from the broiler served two purposes: It increased the stone's exterior temperature by about 10 to 15 degrees, leading to better oven spring and faster evaporation of moisture from the bottom of the crust, and also boosted the air temperature above the stone. The upshot? I was pulling a finished pizza out of the oven after just 8 minutes—an almost 50 percent reduction in baking time. And you could taste it: This pizza featured a crisp bottom and a super-moist interior.

One problem remained. I had great crust, but it didn't quite fit with the flavor of the topping: an uncooked tomato sauce and some shredded mozzarella cheese. The sweetly acidic tomato sauce wasn't a perfect match with the slightly sweet whole-wheat flavor of the crust. My job was not yet done.

Topping It Off

I began experimenting with a range of ingredients. I made some interesting discoveries, such as that garlicky oil, rich and nutty cheeses, and punchy ingredients like pesto and anchovies are a better match for the earthy flavor of the crust than tomato sauce is. For one variation, I briefly heated garlic, anchovies, oregano, and red pepper flakes in extra-virgin olive oil, which I then brushed on the dough as a primer coat. Next, I added a layer of fresh basil leaves, grated Pecorino Romano, and shredded mozzarella. After the pie emerged from the oven, I dotted it with small dollops of fresh ricotta. This combination added richness and complexity without overpowering the flavorful crust. Another crowd-pleaser was an even simpler rendition: I spread a garlicky basil pesto over the pie and sprinkled it with a generous handful of crumbled goat cheese.

As taster after taster gave my pizza rave reviews, I realized why the pies were such a success: They didn't represent mere tweaks to traditional pizza. I'd invented an entirely new concept: truly good whole-wheat pizza meant to be enjoyed on its own terms.

SECRETS TO WHOLE-WHEAT PIZZA WORTH MAKING

Our approach transforms whole-wheat flour into a crust that's wonderfully chewy and crisp, with an earthy complexity that distinguishes it from a traditional pizza crust.

ADD BREAD FLOUR
Using both whole-wheat flour and white bread flour (which has more structure-building proteins than all-purpose flour does) increases chewiness.

USE LOTS OF (ICE) WATER Our highly hydrated dough helps strengthen the gluten network; ice water keeps the dough from overheating as it kneads in the food processor.

REST IT OVERNIGHT
This gives enzymes in the dough time to slightly weaken gluten strands, increasing extensibility; it also allows more flavor-boosting fermentation.

USE THE BROILER
Because our dough is so wet, preheating the pizza stone under the broiler's high heat (after an hour at 500 degrees) is key to a nicely browned crust.

NO TOMATOES!
The sweet-tart flavors of tomato sauce clash with earthy whole wheat. Instead, we top our pizza with three cheeses, garlicky oil, and basil.

THIN-CRUST WHOLE-WHEAT PIZZA WITH GARLIC OIL, THREE CHEESES, AND BASIL
MAKES TWO 13-INCH PIZZAS

We recommend King Arthur brand bread flour for this recipe. Some baking stones, especially thinner ones, can crack under the intense heat of the broiler. Our recommended stone, by Old Stone Oven, is fine if you're using this technique. If you use another stone, you might want to check the manufacturer's website. For our free recipes for Thin-Crust Whole-Wheat Pizza with Mushrooms and Fontina and Thin-Crust Whole-Wheat Pizza with Wine-Braised Onion and Blue Cheese, go to CooksIllustrated.com/june13.

Dough

1½	cups (8¼ ounces) whole-wheat flour
1	cup (5½ ounces) bread flour
2	teaspoons honey
¾	teaspoon instant or rapid-rise yeast
1¼	cups ice water
2	tablespoons extra-virgin olive oil
1¾	teaspoons salt

Garlic Oil

¼	cup extra-virgin olive oil
2	garlic cloves, minced
2	anchovy fillets, rinsed, patted dry, and minced (optional)
½	teaspoon pepper
½	teaspoon dried oregano
⅛	teaspoon red pepper flakes
⅛	teaspoon salt
1	cup fresh basil leaves
1	ounce Pecorino Romano cheese, grated (½ cup)
8	ounces whole-milk mozzarella cheese, shredded (2 cups)
6	ounces (¾ cup) whole-milk ricotta cheese

1. FOR THE DOUGH: Process whole-wheat flour, bread flour, honey, and yeast in food processor until combined, about 2 seconds. With processor running, add water and process until dough is just combined and no dry flour remains, about 10 seconds. Let dough stand for 10 minutes.

2. Add oil and salt to dough and process until it forms satiny, sticky ball that clears sides of workbowl, 45 to 60 seconds. Remove from bowl and knead on oiled countertop until smooth, about 1 minute. Shape dough into tight ball and place in large, lightly oiled bowl. Cover tightly with plastic wrap and refrigerate for at least 18 hours or up to 2 days.

3. FOR THE GARLIC OIL: Heat oil in 8-inch skillet over medium-low heat until shimmering. Add garlic; anchovies, if using; pepper; oregano; pepper flakes; and salt. Cook, stirring constantly, until fragrant, about 30 seconds. Transfer to bowl and let cool completely before using.

4. One hour before baking pizza, adjust oven rack 4½ inches from broiler element, set pizza stone on rack, and heat oven to 500 degrees. Remove dough from refrigerator and divide in half. Shape each half

Ensuring a Crispy Crust

It's always important to preheat your baking stone when making pizza—especially when using our whole-wheat pizza's extra wet dough. We ensure a well-browned and crispy crust by placing the stone near the top of the oven to trap reflective heat. And to get the stone as hot as possible, we heat it at 500 degrees for 1 hour and then broil it for 10 minutes.

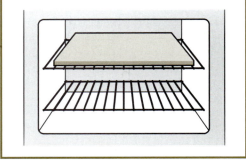

into smooth, tight ball. Place balls on lightly oiled baking sheet, spacing them at least 3 inches apart. Cover loosely with plastic coated with vegetable oil spray; let stand for 1 hour.

5. Heat broiler for 10 minutes. Meanwhile, coat 1 ball of dough generously with flour and place on well-floured countertop. Using your fingertips, gently flatten into 8-inch disk, leaving 1 inch of outer edge slightly thicker than center. Lift edge of dough and, using back of your hands and knuckles, gently stretch disk into 12-inch round, working along edges and giving disk quarter turns as you stretch. Transfer dough to well-floured peel and stretch into 13-inch round. Using back of spoon, spread half of garlic oil over surface of dough, leaving ¼-inch border. Layer ½ cup basil leaves over pizza. Sprinkle with ¼ cup Pecorino, followed by 1 cup mozzarella. Slide pizza carefully onto stone and return oven to 500 degrees. Bake until crust is well browned and cheese is bubbly and partially browned, 8 to 10 minutes, rotating pizza halfway through baking. Remove pizza and place on wire rack. Dollop half of ricotta over surface of pizza. Let pizza rest for 5 minutes, slice, and serve.

6. Heat broiler for 10 minutes. Repeat process of stretching, topping, and baking with remaining dough and toppings, returning oven to 500 degrees when pizza is placed on stone.

THIN-CRUST WHOLE-WHEAT PIZZA WITH PESTO AND GOAT CHEESE

Process 2 cups basil leaves, 7 tablespoons extra-virgin olive oil, ¼ cup pine nuts, 3 minced garlic cloves, and ½ teaspoon salt in food processor until smooth, scraping down sides of bowl as needed, about 1 minute. Stir in ¼ cup finely grated Parmesan or Pecorino Romano and season with salt and pepper to taste. Substitute pesto for garlic oil. In step 5, omit basil leaves, Pecorino Romano, mozzarella, and ricotta. Top each pizza with ½ cup crumbled goat cheese before baking.

Choosing a Great Charcoal Grill

We've happily made do with Weber's basic kettle for years.
But would newer, more tricked-out charcoal cookers be worth the upgrade?

⇒ BY LISA McMANUS ⇐

There's a lot to be said for the basic Weber kettle. The company's 22.5-inch One-Touch Gold model, the test kitchen's house charcoal grill for years, accommodates a full 6-quart chimney's worth of charcoal and features a large enough cooking surface to grill burgers for a crowd. It also has a domed lid tall enough to house a whole turkey, and its well-designed venting system allows barbecue buffs to jury-rig the unit into a competent smoker. The sturdy ash catcher keeps cleanup to a minimum. Moving and storing the kettle's small frame is easy, and the price tag—$149—is nice.

And yet it's never been a perfect package. This model's tripod base is notoriously wobbly and prone to lose a limb, and when we're adding food to or removing it from the fire, we wish there was a place to set down a platter. Drawbacks like these led our eyes to wander back over the charcoal grill marketplace, where we discovered a vast array of competitors across an even more vast price scale—everything from simple, comparably priced designs to beefed up, luxe models fetching significantly more than $2,000. The Rolls-Royce of charcoal grills wasn't our target, though. We wanted a well-engineered, user-friendly model that's up to any outdoor cooking task—ribs, pork loin, fish, burgers, chicken—without having to take out a second mortgage. So we set an upper price limit of $400 and lined up seven promising grills, including our trusty Weber kettle. Our battery of cooking tests included both grilling and low, slow tasks: big batches of burgers, skewers of sticky glazed beef satay, and thick salmon fillets, as well as barbecued ribs. We ran a height check by shutting—or, in some cases, cramming—each grill's lid over a whole turkey; we threaded thermocouple wires under the lids to monitor temperature retention; and we kept track of how easy the grills were to set up when new and to clean up after cooking.

Multitasking

The good news was that most of the grills did a decent job grilling, and several models also fared well with barbecued ribs. The problem was that even when a grill was capable of both grilling and

slow-cooking food, some models had design flaws that limited how easy they were to use.

Grilling requires, for example, regularly flipping and rearranging multiple pieces of food, so it's crucial that the food be within easy reach—a glaring issue with the Brinkmann Trailmaster. This long, horizontal tube, which is billed as both an all-purpose grill and a smoker, features a lid that only partially uncovers its generous cooking surface. As a result, the cook must reach underneath the covered area to access food—not a big deal when you're infrequently reaching for a smoked pork shoulder but a pain when checking several burgers or fish fillets every few minutes. Worse, since pulling up the lid doesn't uncover the grill completely and the opening is angled toward the cook, smoke blows directly in your face. This flaw made grilling with the lid open particularly unpleasant.

Grill roasting, meanwhile, was a challenge for the Portable Kitchen (PK) and STOK Tower units, both of which skimp on the space beneath their cooking grates. When we dumped a standard 6-quart chimney of coals into these cookers, the hot briquettes piled up to the grates, wall-to-wall, creating a fierce fire with no cooler zones for indirect cooking. Even a single-level fire was tricky to control: If we didn't watch carefully, food scorched in minutes. Only the Char-Broil has a crank that let us raise and lower the bed of charcoal to adjust the heat—a useful function that we wish other models offered. On the flip side, the PK, STOK, and Brinkmann grills lacked ample space between their grates and lids. A good 3 inches or more of headroom above food is ideal for proper air circulation (and, therefore, even cooking), but on these units we could just barely pull the lids over a 14-pound turkey.

Nobody Wants a Grill That …

IS A PAIN TO CLEAN
Without an ash catcher, you'll be shoveling out soot and spent coals scoop by scoop.
Worst offender: Portable Kitchen

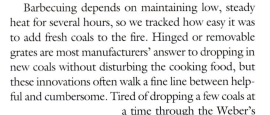

CAN'T HOLD THE HEAT
Shoddily constructed grills don't hold heat and, therefore, don't cook efficiently.
Worst offender: Char-Broil

LETS FOOD FALL
If a grate sits flush with the grill's edges, food can slip off the sides.
Worst offender: Portable Kitchen

IS HARD TO MOVE
Ever try moving a heavy, awkwardly shaped grill? It's like dragging a tank around your yard.
Worst offender: Brinkmann

TAKES HOURS TO ASSEMBLE
This onetime job can be maddening if directions are unclear or there are a million pieces.
Worst offender: Char-Broil

Barbecuing depends on maintaining low, steady heat for several hours, so we tracked how easy it was to add fresh coals to the fire. Hinged or removable grates are most manufacturers' answer to dropping in new coals without disturbing the cooking food, but these innovations often walk a fine line between helpful and cumbersome. Tired of dropping a few coals at a time through the Weber's too-narrow grate openings along both sides of the grill, we were pleased to see that the folks behind the Rösle vessel improved on this idea with grate openings that are a bit wider. We thought PK had done the same until we discovered that only one half of this vessel's rectangular grate opens—and it wasn't the side where we'd piled the coals. Still, we found hinged grates more user-friendly than the removable grates that come with the STOK, Char-Broil, and Brinkmann grills; lifting a section of the cooking surface often forced us to relocate food and, more annoyingly, the searing-hot grate to the ground.

As for the grates themselves, we preferred thick cast-iron bars for the vivid grill marks and crisp crusts they produced but cared even more about how deep the grate sat in the grill. Because the PK and Char-Broil grates were flush with the cooker's top edge, a few burgers slipped off.

Barbecuing also depends on how well the grill retains heat, so we added 7 quarts of hot coals to each grill, wired them up with thermocouples, and tracked temperatures just above the grates for 2 hours without opening lids. Predictably, the bigger Brinkmann, Char-Broil, and Rösle cookers had more trouble retaining heat. After 2 hours, their temperatures had dropped most steeply; the worst drop was almost twice that of the far more stable Weber, STOK, and PK cookers. Flimsy construction was also to blame for the Char-Broil: Its thin metal walls and gaps around the lid let heat escape, and ribs weren't fully cooked after 4 hours.

The Air in There

Digging deeper into heat control, we also evaluated each model's venting system: the openings on the vessel's base and lid that draw in (or shut out) and direct air inside the grill, making it possible to cook a larger variety of foods with greater precision. Smartly designed lids wear their top vents off-center, which encourages heat and smoke to be pulled from the coals across the cooking surface and around the indirectly cooking food. If this seems like a fussy point, consider the kettle grill by Rösle: Its upper vent is cut dead center into its lid, and as a result, heat and smoke get sucked straight up and out of the vessel instead of over to the cooking meat.

Bottom vents, meanwhile, draw air into the coals. Fully open, they make the fire burn hotter and faster; partially closed, they cool the temperature and slow coal consumption; fully closed, they put out the fire. You'd think a feature this critical would demand careful design attention, but we struggled to adjust the vents on the STOK cooker, which never fully aligned to shut off airflow, and that was minor compared with the PK cooker. This model's

Perks Worth Paying For

oversize vents slide open directly under hot coals and ash, inviting burns and dropping soot on the shelf below—unfortunate if you're storing food there. Making matters even more difficult, the PK cooker sits very low on its cart, which means you'll be fumbling blindly with tongs to adjust the bottom apertures. Char-Broil and Brinkmann fared better with dial-shaped side vents that were easier to see and adjust, as did the Rösle and Weber kettles, whose long exterior levers kept our hands far from the coals.

Why Grills Need to Vent

Grill vents are like the dials on your stovetop: They allow you to manipulate how hot the fire gets and how the food cooks—both especially important functions when cooking food indirectly (that is, opposite, not over, the coals). They do this by controlling airflow.

The bottom vent raises or lowers the temperature of the fire by drawing in or shutting out air, which fuels or stifles the fire, respectively. (Closing the vent entirely extinguishes the coals.) The top vent directs air inside the grill, pulling heat and smoke from the coals to the opening. The location of the lid vent affects how much heat and smoke reaches the food.

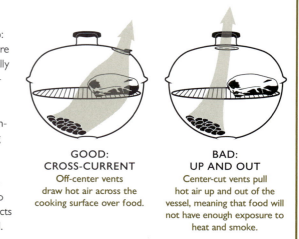

GOOD: CROSS-CURRENT
Off-center vents draw hot air across the cooking surface over food.

BAD: UP AND OUT
Center-cut vents pull hot air up and out of the vessel, meaning that food will not have enough exposure to heat and smoke.

At Ease

While we're sticklers for flawless cooking performance, we're also the first to acknowledge that convenience can make or break your charcoal grilling experience. For example, a sturdy ash-catcher bucket is a must for cleanup, but we didn't fully appreciate this feature on the Weber and Rösle kettles until we found ourselves shoveling spent coals and soot out of the PK and Brinkmann grills, which lack them. (The STOK kettle also comes with an ash bucket, but it was flimsy and regularly threatened to fall off; the Char-Broil's unwieldy ash drawer was better than nothing.)

Simple assembly is another powerful plus, so we timed a pair of testers to see how long it took them to take each grill from box to upright. The Weber snapped together in 21 minutes—a breeze compared with the near-2-hour job they put into piecing together the Char-Broil. Moving and storage are also factors: The Char-Broil rolled smoothly but rattled as if it might fall apart. The tanklike Brinkmann was more cumbersome, and many of us wondered where we'd store its 6-foot frame.

Good built-in accessories like roomy carts and shelves are also more than just frivolous perks; they held serving platters and tools while we cooked. Lids that were hinged or sat in holders spared us from grasping the hot covers or setting them on the ground. Tool hooks, built-in thermometers, and charcoal-holding baskets also eased the way. Best of all was the gas ignition button on the Weber Performer, a major convenience that makes a chimney starter unnecessary.

In fact, this more tricked-out Weber came with all the aforementioned bells and whistles, essentially combining all the conveniences of gas grilling with the flavor advantage of charcoal. Once we'd been so pampered, we couldn't resist its conveniences and declared this model our new winner—even though, at $349, it'll cost you more than twice the price of our old favorite Weber. That said, the more basic, budget-minded Weber One-Touch (which is the same grill that sits in the Weber Performer's frame) still offers all the cooking functions we want, plus the simplest assembly and cleanup, so it stands just behind the Performer as our Best Buy.

The souped-up Weber Performer, our new favorite charcoal model, comes with all the features we liked in the basic Weber kettle, along with a host of new accessories that make outdoor cooking much more enjoyable.

1. ROLLING CART: This sturdy, easy-to-roll cart boasts a heavy-duty plastic surface with plenty of room for setting down platters. There is also a wire shelf underneath.

2. TUCK-AWAY LID HOLDER: Instead of holding the hot lid (or setting it on the ground), slide it into this metal ring that loops around part of the kettle's circumference.

3. PUSH-BUTTON GAS IGNITION: A small, inexpensive propane bottle lights the coals—no chimney starter, matches, newspaper, or lighter fluid necessary.

4. CHARCOAL STORAGE BIN: This durable plastic tub not only holds about 20 pounds of coals but also keeps them dry when it rains.

5. HINGED GRATE: Flip up these hinged flaps to add charcoal to the fire without removing the whole grate.

6. ASH CATCHER: Sturdy and deep, this steel bucket keeps ashes contained and detaches easily for cleanup.

7. THERMOMETER: A built-in thermometer allows you to monitor the grill's temperature without removing the lid.

8. TOOL HOOKS: Keep your grill brush, tongs, and mitts within easy reach.

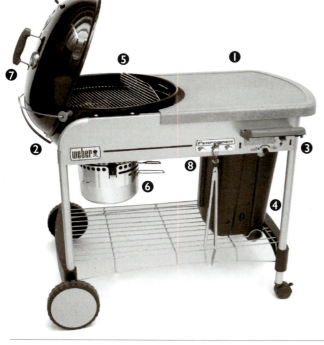

TESTING CHARCOAL GRILLS

We tested seven charcoal grills priced at $400 or less. Grills were purchased online for the prices cited. They are listed in order of preference. Sources for winners are on page 32.

GRILLING: We grilled hamburgers, fish fillets, and beef satay skewers, rating grills on their performance during quick, hot cooking. Grills that provided a thick sear rated highest.

BBQ/HEAT RETENTION: We barbecued baby back ribs for 4 hours, turning them every 30 minutes and adding coals after 2 hours. We also monitored the temperatures of the grills for 2 hours with identical volumes of hot coals and half-open vents, without opening lids. The best grills maintained steady heat with the least temperature drop.

DESIGN: We considered how easy it was to add coals, as well as grill layout, air vent position and control, lid, wheels, handles, and other features that contributed to the grills' performance, ease of use, and versatility.

ASSEMBLY: We timed a pair of testers with no special training as they assembled each grill, noting the quality of the instructions. Faster assembly times earned high marks.

CLEANUP: Grills that made it easier to remove ashes rated higher.

CAPACITY: We tested the fit of 14-pound turkeys under the lid of each grill and whether eight 4-inch hamburgers could be grilled at once.

CONSTRUCTION QUALITY: We observed the sturdiness of each grill and its condition by the end of testing.

GRATE: We preferred cast-iron bars and roomy cooking surfaces.

FAVORITE FEATURES: We noted parts of the grill that helped it perform better or made it easier to use.

HIGHLY RECOMMENDED

	CRITERIA		TESTERS' COMMENTS
WEBER Performer Platinum 22.5-Inch Charcoal Grill with Touch-n-Go Gas Ignition **Model:** 1481001 **Price:** $349 **Grate:** Steel, 363 square in **Favorite Features:** Push-button gas ignition, rolling cart, charcoal storage bin, Tuck-Away lid holder, ash catcher, thermometer	Grilling BBQ/Heat Retention Design Assembly Cleanup Capacity Construction Quality	★★★ ★★★ ★★★ ★★★ ★★★ ★★★ ★★★	The convenience of gas plus the flavor of charcoal make this grill a worthwhile (albeit pricey) upgrade from the basic model. Built around our favorite 22.5-inch Weber kettle is a roomy, easy-to-roll cart (much sturdier than the kettle's legs) with a pullout charcoal storage bin; a lid holder; and, most significant, a gas ignition system that lights coals with the push of a button—no chimney starter needed.
WEBER One-Touch Gold 22.5-Inch Charcoal Grill **Model:** 1351001 **Price:** $149 **Grate:** Steel, 363 square in **Favorite Features:** Ash catcher, thermometer (on newest model), hinged grate *BEST BUY*	Grilling BBQ/Heat Retention Design Assembly Cleanup Capacity Construction Quality	★★★ ★★★ ★★½ ★★★ ★★★ ★★★ ★★½	Weber's versatile, well-designed classic kettle was an expert griller and maintained heat well, and its well-positioned vents allowed for excellent air control. The sturdy ash catcher makes cleanup a breeze, and it was the fastest and easiest model to assemble and move. We wish its tripod legs were sturdier and that the hinged portions of its grate were slightly larger.

RECOMMENDED

	CRITERIA		TESTERS' COMMENTS
RÖSLE 24-Inch Charcoal Grill **Model:** 25004 **Price:** $400 **Grate:** Steel, 416 square in **Favorite Features:** Ash catcher, lever that marks vent position, hinged lid, thermometer	Grilling BBQ/Heat Retention Design Assembly Cleanup Capacity Construction Quality	★★★ ★★ ★★½ ★★★ ★★★ ★★★ ★★★	This pricey kettle is sturdier than the Weber One-Touch and offers more cooking space, plus a few perks: a lever that marks vent positions and a hinged lid. But while it grilled well, its roomy interior lost heat relatively quickly. Its top vent sits in the center of the lid—a disadvantage for indirect cooking.
STOK Tower Charcoal Grill **Model:** SCC0140 **Price:** $122 **Grate:** Cast iron, 363 square in **Favorite Features:** Cast-iron grate, built-in chimney starter, thermometer	Grilling BBQ/Heat Retention Design Assembly Cleanup Capacity Construction Quality	★★★ ★★½ ★★ ★★ ★★ ★★ ★★	Its cast-iron grate is just as big as the Weber's (and seared beautifully), but everything else about this inexpensive kettle is small—from its footprint to the space above and below the grates. Consequently, it holds heat well but struggles with indirect cooking since there is little room for a cooler zone. We appreciated its built-in chimney starter.

RECOMMENDED WITH RESERVATIONS

	CRITERIA		TESTERS' COMMENTS
PORTABLE KITCHEN Cast Aluminum Grill and Smoker **Model:** 99740 **Price:** $300 **Grate:** Steel, 301 square in **Favorite Feature:** Rolling cart	Grilling BBQ/Heat Retention Design Assembly Cleanup Capacity Construction Quality	★★ ★★★ ★★ ★★ ★ ★½ ★★½	Heat retention was great on this cast-aluminum cooker, but space was tight. We crammed 6 quarts of coals below the grate (and a turkey above it), so scorching was a risk. The bars sat level with the rim, so food slipped off. Bottom vents released soot onto the shelf beneath; there was no ash catcher.
BRINKMANN Trailmaster Limited Edition Grill and Smoker **Model:** 855-6305-S **Price:** $299 **Grate:** Steel, 938 square in **Favorite Feature:** Small firebox for smoking, thermometer	Grilling BBQ/Heat Retention Design Assembly Cleanup Capacity Construction Quality	★★ ★★ ★½ ★ ★ ★★★ ★★★	This grill-smoker combo boasts plenty of cooking surface (including a separate firebox for smoking), but since opening the lid uncovered only part of that space, visibility was limited and smoke blew into our eyes. Without an ash catcher, shoveling is the only option. Also, it's a big, heavy beast: Moving it was a chore, and storing it was a challenge.

NOT RECOMMENDED

	CRITERIA		TESTERS' COMMENTS
CHAR-BROIL 30-Inch Charcoal Grill **Model:** 12301672 **Price:** $199 **Grate:** Cast iron, 504 square in **Favorite Features:** Crank for adjusting coal height, rolling cart, cast-iron grate, flip-up side shelves, thermometer, warming shelf	Grilling BBQ/Heat Retention Design Assembly Cleanup Capacity Construction Quality	★★½ ½ ★★ ½ ★★ ★★★ ★	This grill was a heartbreaker. Though outfitted with great features—a crank that adjusts coal height, a high lid, cast-iron cooking grates, a "keep-warm" shelf, and flip-up side tables—its cheap construction defeated it at every turn. Paper-thin walls and an ill-fitting lid leaked heat (barbecued ribs were not quite finished after 4 hours). Assembly took hours. When it rolled, it rattled horribly.

The Best Fresh Goat Cheese

Why do some goat cheeses boast creamy texture and a bright and lemony taste, while others are chalky, gamy, or—worse—utterly flavorless?

⇒ BY AMY GRAVES ⇐

In 1981, Alice Waters topped a simple green salad with a round of baked goat cheese at her Berkeley restaurant, Chez Panisse. The tangy creaminess of this supple cheese was a revelation to most Americans. For centuries, France was the primary producer of goat cheese—*chèvre* in French means goat—and at that point, it was scarcely produced (or even found) domestically. In fact, Waters's cheese came from a neighbor who kept goats and had learned to make it in France. But Waters was onto something. With that salad, a trend was born. Americans quickly developed a taste for this tangy fresh cheese.

Since then, the United States has seen a boom in goat-cheese making. Production has increased every year since 2002, according to U.S. Department of Agriculture figures, and dairy goat operations can now be found in 43 of the 50 states. The number of goat cheese entries in annual competitions sponsored by the American Cheese Society has doubled since 2005, and the sales of both domestic and imported goat cheese in supermarkets have experienced a huge surge—a whopping 10 percent increase in 2010 alone.

It's not hard to see why fresh goat cheese is so popular: With its unmistakable tang, it can be eaten straight on crackers, enliven the simplest salad or pasta dish, enhance pizza toppings, and add creamy richness to sautéed greens. With so many new domestic choices now available, which one comes out on top? We gathered nine widely available samples (seven of them stateside products), ranging from $0.82 to $1.63 per ounce, and set to work finding out.

The Whole Schmear

We first tasted the cheese straight out of the package on plain crackers. Then, to see if heat changed its character, we rolled it in bread crumbs and baked it. The good news: Sampled straight from the fridge, the majority of our nine selections were smooth and creamy, with a distinctly tangy, grassy taste—just what we want in goat cheese. Only a few had issues, including a chalky, Spackle-like texture; a too-neutral flavor that seemed more like cream cheese than like goat cheese; or an overly gamy taste, reminiscent of a "barnyard" or even "lamb fat."

When we baked them, the gamiest samples mellowed to a gentler but still present tang, inspiring descriptions like "savory" and "goaty in a good way." That made sense when we learned that the

compounds that set up gamy flavors in goat cheese are volatile and flash off in the oven's heat. Heat's impact on texture, though, was another story. Products that were chalky straight out of the package didn't improve with baking—and several that were creamy sampled plain surprised us by baking into crumbly, grainy blobs.

Since baking goat cheese isn't something that we do every day, we tried another recipe, warming our favorite and least favorite goat cheese samples in pasta. Same problem, new variation: Tossed with hot pasta, the lowest-ranked cheese, which had turned crumbly when baked, transformed into a grainy paste, with bits of cheese visible in the mix. The top product, which had stayed creamy and intact when baked, melted nicely into a cohesive sauce with the pasta.

Despite the samples' different responses to heat, at the end of our taste trials, we liked six of the nine products. With just three ingredients on the label—pasteurized goat's milk, enzymes, and salt—what made these products stand out?

Milk and Make

Perhaps unsurprisingly, the flavors in goat cheese begin with the animal's diet. Unlike cows, goats are browsers, not grazers. Their strong stomachs can tolerate many bitter plants that cows avoid, and if left to feed in an open pasture, they gravitate toward shrublike plants that are close to the ground and that can have a pungent taste. Their milk picks up these acrid flavors, so cheesemakers aiming for a tangy but still grassy-sweet profile make sure to source the goats' milk from animals on a restricted diet of mild-tasting grains, grasses, and hay. These nanny goats must also be kept separate from male bucks, or billies, during milking: The powerful scent of the billies raises the nannies' hormone levels, charging up the flavor of their milk and giving it a barnyard taste.

The freshness of the milk is also essential to an optimal flavor profile in the cheese: Producers either milk their own goats or source the milk from nearby farms and use it within a few days of milking. Freezing the milk is not a desirable option. The sharp drop and then spike in temperature when the milk is defrosted damages the membrane protecting the milk fat from the lipase enzyme, which in turn releases three fatty acids: capric, caproic, and caprylic. While a moderate amount of these fatty acids is desirable—they give goat cheese its

Good Flavor Starts on the Farm

The ideal light, lemony taste of goat cheese begins with what the nanny goats eat—and the company they keep.

RESTRICTED DIET
If left to roam, goats eat pungent plants, whose flavors wind up in their milk. A bland diet of grains, soybeans, and grasses ensures milder milk.

BAN THE BILLIES
The presence of male goats when female goats are being milked increases their hormone levels and gives the milk a strong gamy taste.

characteristic tangy flavor—too much is a bad thing. Rough handling can also lead to the release of too many fatty acids.

Though all of the makers of the products in our lineup assured us that they paid close attention to each of these considerations—setting strict specifications for the milk they use, handling it carefully, and never freezing it—there must have been more variation than producers would admit to, given the range of flavors that we detected. Still seeking concrete answers regarding the differences in flavor and texture, we looked next at the cheese-making process itself. After it's pasteurized (a measure taken by all of the companies in our lineup), the milk goes into closed fermentation tanks, where bacterial cultures are traditionally added. Over the next several hours, the bacteria produce enzymes that cause the pH of the milk to drop, separating the mixture into curds and whey. After hanging the curds in cheesecloth bags or in bundles to drain, the cheesemaker adds salt and then presses the cheese into the familiar log or medallion shape.

Most of the samples in our lineup used the traditional approach to curdling the cheese: adding bacterial cultures in the form of ripened curds from an earlier cheese making. But one product used the so-called quick-set method, adding citric or lactic acid directly to the milk to trigger faster curdling. Cheese experts told us that this shortcut can turn the cheese slightly grainy or chalky, a problem that we noticed in this cheese and that only worsened when it was baked.

Beyond this one particular variable, however, we were still at a loss as to why some cheeses had a different taste and texture than others. So we sent them to an independent lab for some closer scrutiny, having each sample tested for fat, salt, and pH levels. These tests showed that fat didn't matter, since one of the leanest products fared well with tasters on both flavor and texture in each trial. Ditto for pH: With one exception, the levels were all very close. That left salt.

The Power of Salt

If goat-cheese makers disagree about anything, it's the amount of salt that should go into the finished product. The salt content in these samples ranged from 1,200 milligrams in 100 grams down to considerably less than half of that, or 441 milligrams per 100 grams. Though some cheesemakers deliberately keep the salt to a minimum because they maintain that it can cancel out the clean, citrusy taste of goat cheese, we preferred the samples with the most sodium, while those with the least amounts tasted "neutral," or even "flat." We weren't that surprised, since salt can enhance many flavors already present in food. What did surprise us was that salt's benefits didn't stop with flavor. Products with more salt also stayed smooth and cohesive when baked, whereas those with less salt were described as "mealy" or "crumbly."

Cheese scientists at the University of Wisconsin explained that the ions in salt help the proteins in cheese bind and retain water, which in turn means that more moisture is retained during cooking and that the cheese melts more smoothly. "That is why you have a creamy, smooth texture after baking with the higher-salt goat cheeses," noted Bénédicte Coude, assistant coordinator of the Cheese Industry and Applications Program at the Wisconsin Center for Dairy Research. Adding salt helps only up to a point, however. "Cheese that is very salty will readily lose its water during baking," said senior scientist Mark Johnson. That's why cheeses like cheddar and Parmesan, which typically have significantly more salt, can separate when baked.

With a taste-enhancing 1,053 milligrams of salt in 100 grams, our favorite product, Laura Chenel's Chèvre, was "mildly goaty" and "rich-tasting," with a "grassy" and "tangy" finish straight out of the package. Either baked or tossed with hot pasta, it stayed "lemony" and "bright," with a "creamy, buttery texture." It is the same goat cheese that Alice Waters used at Chez Panisse some 30 years ago. In 2006, Waters's neighbor, Laura Chenel, sold her business to the Rians Group, a French company, but kept her goats. These animals continued to supply milk for the brand until 2010, when Chenel retired completely—but according to the Rians Group, the recipe remains the same. In every taste trial, this cheese landed at the top of the heap.

TASTING GOAT CHEESE

Choosing from a list of top-selling supermarket brands compiled by the Chicago-based market research firm SymphonyIRI Group and recent winners of American Cheese Society awards, we rounded up nine fresh goat cheeses. We sampled all nine cheeses first unheated and then baked, rating them on flavor, texture, tanginess, and overall appeal. We also tasted the top- and bottom-ranked cheeses tossed with hot pasta. An independent laboratory determined amounts of fat and sodium and pH levels. Scores were averaged and the products appear in order of preference.

RECOMMENDED

LAURA CHENEL'S CHÈVRE Fresh Chèvre Log
Price: $6.99 for 8 oz ($0.87 per oz)
Made In: California
Salt: 1,053 mg in 100 g pH: 4.05
Fat: 21.20 g in 100 g
(6 g in 1-oz serving)

"Rich-tasting," "grassy," and "tangy," our favorite goat cheese was "smooth" and "creamy" both unheated and baked, and it kept its "lemony, bright flavor" in both iterations. A high salt content helped: Salt not only enhances flavor but also contributes to keeping the cheese creamy when heated.

VERMONT CREAMERY Fresh Goat Cheese, Classic Chèvre
Price: $4.99 for 4 oz ($1.25 per oz)
Made In: Vermont
Salt: 784 mg in 100 g pH: 3.95
Fat: 20.96 g in 100 g (5.9 g in 1-oz serving)

"Smooth and creamy" and with a "slightly citrusy," "clean, lactic" taste, this was one of our favorite goat cheeses for sampling straight from the package. Its moderate salt content allowed it to turn slightly "mealy" when baked, but its "grassy," "citruslike" flavors continued to earn raves from tasters.

CHEVRION Plain Goat Cheese
Price: $4.29 for 4 oz ($1.07 per oz)
Made In: France
Salt: 1,200 mg in 100 g pH: 3.91
Fat: 16.89 g in 100 g (4.8 g in 1-oz serving)

This "tangy," "creamy" sample was "very strong" and "goaty" eaten unheated, but it mellowed to "bright, tangy, and sweet" when baked, when it also retained a "luscious" texture, thanks to its high salt content.

CYPRESS GROVE CHÈVRE Ms. Natural Goat Milk Cheese
Price: $6.50 for 4 oz ($1.63 per oz)
Made In: California
Salt: 955 mg in 100 g pH: 4.04
Fat: 21.55 g in 100 g (6.1 g in 1-oz serving)

Unheated, this cheese wowed us with "lemony," "grassy" flavors and a "smooth," "melts-in-your-mouth" texture. Though baking dried out its texture a bit, tasters still gave it an enthusiastic thumbs-up.

SIERRA NEVADA CHEESE CO. Bella Capra Chèvre
Price: $7.99 for 8 oz ($1.00 per oz)
Made In: California
Salt: 882 mg in 100 g pH: 3.86
Fat: 25.56 g in 100 g (7.2 g in 1-oz serving)

"Fresh" and "tangy" and with a "creamy" texture when sampled unheated, this cheese with a moderate salt content turned a little "crumbly" when baked but still offered "tang" and "good goat flavor."

CHAVRIE Fresh Goat Cheese
Price: $8.99 for 11 oz ($0.82 per oz)
Made In: Pennsylvania
Salt: 1,078 mg in 100 g pH: 4.66
Fat: 22.86 g in 100 g
(6.5 g in 1-oz serving)

Though it had some fans, the "barnyard" and "gamy" flavor of this cheese reminded some tasters of "lamb fat." These flavors dissipated in baking, when this sample shone with a "tasty tang and milky flavor" and a "nice creamy texture."

RECOMMENDED WITH RESERVATIONS

MONTCHÈVRE Fresh Goat Cheese
Price: $3.99 for 4 oz ($1.00 per oz)
Made In: Wisconsin
Salt: 686 mg in 100 g pH: 4.27
Fat: 24.49 g in 100 g (6.9 g in 1-oz serving)

Though "very creamy" and with a "nice smooth consistency" when unheated, without much salt, it was "neutral" to many and just "mildly tangy." Too little salt also left it "watery and crumbly" when baked.

ILE DE FRANCE Chèvre Fresh Goat Cheese
Price: $10.99 for 10.5 oz ($1.05 per oz)
Made In: France
Salt: 637 mg in 100 g pH: 3.96
Fat: 22.95 g in 100 g (6.5 g in 1-oz serving)

Also low in salt, this sample had a pleasant but "mild-mannered" taste and "slightly chalky" texture when eaten from the package. Baking turned it "crumbly," a flaw that was offset by its "subtle herb" flavor notes.

NOT RECOMMENDED

COACH FARM Natural Goat's Milk Cheese
Price: $4.50 for 4 oz ($1.13 per oz)
Made In: New York
Salt: 441 mg in 100 g pH: 3.93
Fat: 23.59 g in 100 g (6.7 g in 1-oz serving)

Its very low salt content didn't do this cheese any favors. Unheated, it had a "chalky," "puttylike" texture and "weak" taste. Baking didn't redeem it: Most tasters found it "chalky" again, with "not enough goat" flavor.

Three Keys to Better Vacuum Sealing

Vacuum sealing food for storage can greatly improve shelf life and help maintain quality—but only when done properly. Poorly sealed bags allow oxygen to contact food, speeding spoilage and freezer burn. We do a lot of vacuum sealing here in the test kitchen and over the years have found a few tricks to make it more foolproof.

FREEZE LIQUIDS FIRST

We generally try to avoid liquids when vacuum sealing as they are notoriously problematic for all but the very best machines. If you have to do it, we recommend freezing the liquid before sealing the bag.

Place the bag in a loaf pan (to provide stability in the freezer) and pour in the soup or broth. Transfer the loaf pan and bag to the freezer and freeze until firm. Remove the bag from the loaf pan and vacuum-seal.

COVER BONES

We often vacuum-seal large roasts for freezing, but protruding bones can easily puncture the bag during vacuuming or storage. To prevent this, use plastic wrap to secure a layer of parchment paper to the bones, effectively blunting them.

FOLD BAGS

When loading food into vacuum bags, it can be difficult to keep the cut end of the bag free of grease and moisture, two enemies of a proper seal. To guarantee a clean sealing edge, fold back the last 2 to 3 inches of the bag into a cuff. Once the food is in the bag, simply unfold the cuff and seal. –D.S.

Wait for Your Coffee

We know the temptation: First thing in the morning, the coffee is brewing, and you can't help sticking your mug beneath the spigot on the coffee maker to steal a cup before the pot has finished. But how much does removing some coffee early influence the flavor of the final pot? Armed with an array of coffee mugs and a coffee refractometer, a tool that measures the amount of soluble flavor compounds, or total dissolved solids (TDS), extracted from the beans, we put that question to the test.

As a pot of coffee brewed in our favorite coffee maker, the Technivorm Moccamaster, we took samples from the brewing spout every 30 seconds and measured the TDS in each. As we had suspected, the coffee coming out of the spout at the beginning of the brew time was significantly stronger than the last few drops: 3.93 parts per million (ppm) versus 0.44 ppm, or more than eight times as concentrated. It was also more than twice as strong as coffee from a fully brewed pot (1.54 ppm). Only at the midway point of the brew cycle did the concentration of the sample come close to that of a fully brewed pot.

What does this mean? Hold on to your mug. Most of the flavor in a pot of coffee comes during the early stages of brewing. And if you sneak a cup early on, not only will it be far too strong but you'll be running off with most of the good stuff and spoiling the pot for others. –A.J.

Keeping Basil Green in Pesto

There's no getting around it: Pesto looks the best right after you make it. With time, it can oxidize into a drab army green. But there seem to be as many suggested techniques for keeping pesto bright green as there are cooks who make it. We tried four methods, including using vitamin C powder, which left our pesto with an odd sour taste, as well as parsley, which does contain the antioxidant ascorbic acid—just not enough to make a big difference. Here are two methods that work. –D.S.

Method	BLANCHING	ADDING LEMON JUICE

How It Works	Blanching deactivates the enzyme that causes browning when cut basil leaves interact with oxygen.	Lemon juice contains the antioxidants citric and ascorbic acids.
How to Use It	Blanch basil for 30 seconds in boiling water and then shock it in ice water before drying it and proceeding with the recipe. This brief dunk causes minimal flavor loss.	Add 4 teaspoons of lemon juice per 2 cups of packed basil. Lemon juice lends a pleasant acidity to pesto.

Two Cultured Creams, One Simple Method

Cultured creams like crème fraîche and Mexican *crema* have many uses. They both begin with heavy cream and a natural culturing agent and end up thick, creamy, and lush. The former is used to dress up fresh fruit, dollop on pureed soups, and even withstand boiling temperatures in a sauce without breaking, while the latter is spiked with lime to garnish countless Mexican and Latin dishes. But both products can be difficult to find, and crème fraîche in particular can be five times the price of ordinary sour cream. Luckily, both are easy to make at home.

For crème fraîche: Stir together 1 cup of pasteurized cream (avoid ultrapasteurized, which has been heated to higher temperatures, killing enzymes and bacteria and even altering the cream's protein structure, making it hard to achieve the right texture) and 2 tablespoons of buttermilk in a container. Cover and place in a warm location (75 to 80 degrees is ideal; lower temperatures will lengthen fermentation time) until the crème fraîche is thickened but still pourable, 12 to 24 hours. For crema, dissolve ⅛ teaspoon of salt in 2 teaspoons of lime juice and add to finished crème fraîche. Refrigerate for up to two months. –D.S.

1. For crème fraîche, combine 1 cup cream and 2 tablespoons buttermilk.

2. Cover container tightly.

3. Let sit in warm spot for 12 to 24 hours.

For crema, add ⅛ teaspoon salt and 2 teaspoons lime juice to crème fraîche.

The Importance of Preheating Your Pizza Stone

A hot pizza stone is key to producing pizza with a well-browned, crisp bottom crust. To ensure that your stone is hot, we recommend placing it in the oven, setting the oven dial to 500 degrees, and leaving it there for a full hour. And yet many folks (even a few here in the test kitchen) question whether this lengthy preheat is really necessary. So what happens if you try to shortcut the process and preheat for less time?

To find out, we preheated four baking stones in four separate 500-degree ovens for 15 minutes, 30 minutes, 45 minutes, and 1 hour, respectively. Once the stones were preheated, we baked pizzas for exactly 10 minutes on each stone and examined their undersides for browning and crisping.

To back up our browning observations, we also took infrared temperature readings of the stones' surfaces right before sliding on each pizza. The results? Dramatically different. The pizza baked on the 1-hour preheated stone (which clocked in at 509 degrees) was well browned and crisp after 10 minutes, while the 45-minute preheated stone (451 degrees) produced only moderate browning in the same period of time. The pizza baked on the stone preheated for just 30 minutes (415 degrees) was anemic in color, and the one on the 15-minute preheated stone (291 degrees) was downright pale.

The takeaway: While it may feel like overkill, it's important to preheat a pizza stone for a full hour to ensure proper browning and crisping. –D.S.

| 15 MINUTES | 30 MINUTES | 45 MINUTES | 1 HOUR |

For Creamier Hummus, Skin Your Chickpeas

When we were developing our recipe for Restaurant-Style Hummus (May/June 2008), we discovered that removing the tough skins from the garbanzo beans resulted in a far creamier end product. Because it was such a hassle, however, we opted not to do so. But when we saw a recipe for hummus in Yotam Ottolenghi and Sami Tamimi's cookbook *Jerusalem* that used baking soda to make the process easier, we decided to give it a try. Ottolenghi and Tamimi stir baking soda into dried chickpeas that have been soaked overnight and drained. They heat the mixture in a pot for a few minutes before adding water and cooking the chickpeas as usual. The alkaline environment created by the baking soda helps break down the pectin in the beans, softening the beans' skins so well that they disintegrate during cooking and are easily rinsed away.

We wondered if a similar approach might work for canned chickpeas as well. Sure enough, it did, with just a few modifications. For our method, toss the rinsed and drained chickpeas with baking soda (1½ teaspoons per 14-ounce can) and then heat them in the microwave or in a skillet over medium heat for 2 to 3 minutes until the beans are hot. Transfer the beans to a large bowl and wash with three or four changes of cold water, all the while agitating the beans vigorously between your hands to release the skins, which will float easily away. Easy, creamy hummus? Yes, please. –A.J.

Why You Should Brine Fish

In the test kitchen, we brine meats like turkey, chicken, pork, and lamb to improve both flavor and texture. But brining fish can be beneficial, too. We set up a series of tests using different brine concentrations (3, 6, and 9 percent salt-to-water solutions by weight) and types of fish (tuna, salmon, swordfish, and halibut). We found that, for up to six 1-inch-thick steaks or fillets, the optimum concentration was a 6 percent brine (5 tablespoons of salt dissolved in 2 quarts of water) and the ideal time was 15 minutes. It worked no matter the species, improving the texture of the fish without overseasoning.

As it does with meat, brining fish serves two purposes: One, it helps season the flesh, which improves flavor, and two, by partially dissolving muscle fibers to form a water-retaining gel, it helps prevent the protein from drying out. And brining works a lot faster on fish because the structure of muscle in fish is different than that in meat: Instead of long, thin fibers (as long as 10 centimeters in meat), fish is constructed of very short (up to 10 times shorter) bundles of fibers.

In addition, we seared each species of fish to see if using a wet brine would inhibit browning. Luckily, it did not, so long as the fish was dried well with paper towels just before cooking. Finally, we've found that brining helps reduce the presence of albumin, a protein that can congeal into an unappealing white mass on the surface of the fish when heated. –A.J.

TECHNIQUE | A TRULY NONSTICK BUNDT PAN

There's little more frustrating than trying to unmold a cake and having it stick and crumble into an unappetizing mess. When working with standard round and square cake pans, this unfortunate occurrence can be easily avoided by using parchment liners and vegetable oil spray. Bundt pans, however, with their plethora of crevices and curves, prove significantly more challenging. Our preferred method is to coat a nonstick Bundt pan thoroughly with baking spray, which contains both oil and flour. For those who don't have baking spray, we recommend applying a paste of melted butter and flour. Using melted butter instead of more common softened butter makes for a thinner paste that can be easily applied to every nook and cranny using a pastry brush. –D.S.

1. Make paste with 1 tablespoon flour and 1 tablespoon melted butter.

2. Use pastry brush to apply to pan.

Ancient Chinese Secret: Tofu That Soaks Up More Sauce

We've often wondered why some tofu in Chinese restaurants has a distinctive spongy texture that allows it to soak up more of the sauce in a dish. This texture is produced by freezing the tofu solid before thawing and cooking it—a method that was originally used in China (and Japan) to preserve tofu during the winter months. Tofu is about 86 percent water; as it freezes, the ice crystals expand, pushing apart the protein network. When thawed, the water drains away, leaving the tofu with a spongy consistency that is highly absorbent. We experimented with freezing tofu in the test kitchen and quite liked the results. When stir-fried, the slabs did absorb sauce readily and had a resilient, slightly chewy texture that was far more meatlike than fresh tofu. And because the thawed tofu contained so little water, it formed a nice crust when deep-fried. To freeze, slice extra-firm tofu into ½- to ¾-inch-thick slabs, spread them in a single layer on a baking sheet or plate, and place them in the freezer overnight. (At this point, the tofu can be placed in zipper-lock bags and stored in the freezer for up to a month.) To use, thaw to room temperature and press each slab gently over a colander to expel any remaining water before cooking. –A.J.

Heavy-Duty Handled Scrub Brushes

It takes a serious cleaning tool to tackle seriously dirty pots and pans. No scrub brush can scour like our favorite chain mail cleaner, the 4-inch square CM Scrubber by KnappMade ($19.95), but the metal is awfully tough on hands and requires that you keep them dunked in the hot water. For a tool that puts a premium on comfort, a handled brush is a better option. We gathered six heavy-duty models (priced from $5 to $7.99) made of plastic or wood with natural or synthetic bristles. After scraping away stuck-on scrambled eggs from cast-iron skillets, glazed salmon residue from the ridges of grill pans, and a burned-on mixture of tomato paste, mustard, and molasses from casserole dishes, we concluded that long, soft bristles are poor scrubbers. Some scrubbers also trapped food and odors as well as stained or bent after just a few uses. The shorter, stiff bristles of the OXO Grill Pan Brush ($7.99) worked much better, making quick work of even the toughest jobs. Its scraping ridge at the top took care of crusty burned-on bits, and the thick nonslip handle provided a sure, comfy grip (though we wish it were a bit longer). A bonus: It rinsed completely clean even without a trip through the dishwasher (though it is dishwasher-safe). We still like the chain mail scrubber, but it's nice to have an option that's not as hard on our hands. –L.M.

DOWN AND DIRTY
The short, sturdy bristles of the OXO Grill Pan Brush scrub skillets, grill pans, and more with ease.

NEW Citrus Spritzer

At first glance, the Stem Citrus Spritzer ($4.99) looked a little silly to us, but when you need just a squirt of lemon juice for finishing fish, shellfish, vegetables, or sauces, this tool is a surprisingly efficient alternative to a citrus juicer. About 3 inches long, it looks like the plastic pump from the top of a spray bottle. All you do is stick it into a lemon—no peeling or knife work needed. Within seconds after inserting it, we were releasing a fine, even mist of juice without the bother of fishing out seeds released in the process. It gave us 10 to 12 full sprays per insertion—and if that's all you want, the rest of the fruit can be stored in the fridge for later use. –A.G.

A FINE MIST
The Stem Citrus Spritzer sprays an even mist of juice directly from citrus fruits.

NEW Pie Drip Catchers

Baking pies (especially juicy, fruit-filled kinds) inevitably means drips burn onto the oven floor. We often put a baking sheet under the pie plate to catch the spills, but would pie drip catchers—nonstick-coated steel or aluminum rings that fit snugly under pie plates—be simpler to clean than the large, unwieldy sheets? We made blueberry pies in our favorite Pyrex pie plate and perched them atop four different models (ranging from $4.49 to $19.95). All were wide enough to contain the drips, which easily washed away from their slick surfaces. But only one solved the unforeseen problem of the pie plate sliding around atop the band. The raised silicone ring in the center of the Chicago Metallic No-Drip Pie Shield

CATCHER FOR THE PIE
The Chicago Metallic No-Drip Pie Shield captures pie filling drips—and keeps the pie in place.

($14.95) kept the pie plate anchored, allowing us to securely transfer it into and out of the oven. Plus, the wide rim on opposite sides of its oval shape was easiest of all to grasp through oven mitts. –A.G.

UPDATE
Cuisinart Perfec Temp Coffeemaker

After our March/April 2013 testing of coffee makers that aim to meet research-based standards for producing the best-tasting coffee, we found another candidate, the Cuisinart Perfec Temp 12-Cup Thermal Coffeemaker ($129), and put it through the paces. While we liked its clear, intuitive controls, this machine brewed too slowly, averaging 13 minutes versus the 8 minutes or less recommended by the Specialty Coffee Association of America. The ideal temperature for water to extract coffee's fullest flavor is 195 to 205 degrees; the

BITTER BREW
The Cuisinart Perfec Temp fell far short of its "perfect" claims.

Cuisinart spent barely half of its brew cycle in that zone. Finally, its brew basket is too small to accommodate the appropriate coffee-to-water ratio when brewing a full 60-ounce pot: The manual recommends a maximum of 15 tablespoons; 20 tablespoons are needed. When we compared its coffee with brews from our favorite coffee maker, tasters criticized its "watered-down," "bitter" flavor. For automatic drip coffee, we'll stick with the rich, smooth coffee from our winners, the Technivorm Moccamaster KBGT-741 ($299) and the Bonavita BV 1800 TH ($149). –L.M.

Innovative Ice Cube Trays

We've all done battle with rigid plastic ice cube trays. Transferring filled trays to the freezer without spilling is dicey, and dislodging frozen cubes is tricky. Worse, most trays aren't covered, so the ice readily absorbs smells. We tested three models (priced from $4.50 to $32.99) that attempt to solve these problems with silicone or plastic covers or other innovations. Unfortunately, most of the modifications backfired: Filling the Fox Run No Spill Ice Tray through a small opening in its lid—a feature meant to prevent spilling—was difficult because the lid was opaque; as a result, we added too much water and ended up with cubes covered by a sheet of ice. The

PUT A LID ON IT
OXO's No-Spill Ice Cube Tray keeps ice odor-free.

silicone tray of the Lekue Ice Box Ice Cube Tray and Bucket is too wobbly to transfer to the freezer once filled. The clear winner, the OXO No-Spill Ice Cube Tray ($9.99), sports a sturdy plastic base with rounded indents for easily dislodging cubes and a flexible lid that you press into place while pouring off excess water. It prevented spills and kept ice odor-free. –T.S.

For complete testing results for each item, go to CooksIllustrated.com/june13.

Sources

Prices were current at press time and do not include shipping. Contact companies to confirm information or visit CooksIllustrated.com for updates.

PAGE 24: BAKING STONES
- Old Stone Oven Pizza Baking Stone: $39.99, item #B0000E1FDA, Amazon (amazon.com).
- The Baking Steel: $72, item #3424321, Stoughton Steel Company (781-826-6496, stoughtonsteel.com).

PAGE 27: CHARCOAL GRILLS
- Weber Performer Platinum 22.5-Inch Charcoal Grill with Touch-n-Go Gas Ignition: $349, item #203597717, The Home Depot (800-430-3376, homedepot.com).
- Weber One-Touch Gold 22.5-Inch Charcoal Grill: $149, item #203597028, The Home Depot.

PAGE 32: HANDLED SCRUB BRUSH
- OXO Grill Pan Brush: $7.99, item #1312580, OXO (800-545-4411, oxo.com).

PAGE 32: CITRUS SPRITZER
- Stem Citrus Spritzer: $4.99, item #STEM, Quirky (866-578-4759, quirky.com).

PAGE 32: PIE DRIP CATCHER
- Chicago Metallic No-Drip Pie Shield: $14.95, item #1015668, Sur La Table (800-243-0852, surlatable.com).

PAGE 32: ICE CUBE TRAY
- OXO No-Spill Ice Cube Tray: $9.99, item #1132080, OXO.

INDEX
May & June 2013

Thin-Crust Whole-Wheat Pizza, 24

Marbled Blueberry Bundt Cake, 21

Italian Chicken Soup, 15

Braised Red Potatoes with Lemon and Chives, 13

Grilled Glazed Baby Back Ribs, 11

AMERICA'S TEST KITCHEN COOKING SCHOOL

Let us help you become a better cook. Offering more than 100 courses for cooks at every level, our school combines personalized instruction from real *America's Test Kitchen* test cooks with leading-edge technology to offer a unique and effective learning experience. Start a 14-day free trial at OnlineCookingSchool.com.

Herb-Crusted Salmon, 8

Stir-Fried Asparagus with Shiitake Mushrooms, 9

COOK'S ILLUSTRATED IS NOW AVAILABLE ON iPAD!

Download the new *Cook's Illustrated* app for iPad and start a free trial subscription or purchase a single issue. Issues are enhanced with recipe videos, full-color step-by-step slide shows, and expanded reviews and ratings. Go to CooksIllustrated.com/iPad to download our app through iTunes.

Grilled Lemon Chicken with Rosemary, 7

Cuban-Style Picadillo, 19

Follow us on Twitter: twitter.com/TestKitchen
Find us on Facebook: facebook.com/CooksIllustrated

PHOTOGRAPHY: CARL TREMBLAY; STYLING: MARIE PIRAINO

Beet

Cabbage

Opal Basil

Celery

Chard

Amaranth

Broccoli

MICROGREENS

NUMBER 123

JULY & AUGUST 2013

COOK'S
ILLUSTRATED

Best BBQ Chicken
Not Burnt, Dry, or Goopy

How to Fry an Egg
It's Harder than We Thought

Classic Lobster Roll
Treat the Lobster Right

Rating Store-Bought Chicken Broths

Grilled Glazed Pork Tenderloin
Double Up for Perfection

Summer Berry Trifle
Classic English Showstopper

Testing Innovative Kitchen Equipment

Guide to Stir-Frying
Original Pesto Pasta
Best-Ever Kebabs

CooksIllustrated.com
$6.95 U.S. & CANADA

CONTENTS

July & August 2013

Founder and Editor Christopher Kimball
Editorial Director Jack Bishop
Editorial Director, Magazines John Willoughby
Executive Editor Amanda Agee
Test Kitchen Director Erin McMurrer
Managing Editor Rebecca Hays
Executive Food Editor Keith Dresser
Senior Editors Lisa McManus
　　Dan Souza
Senior Editors, Features Molly Birnbaum
　　Elizabeth Bomze
Copy Editors Nell Beram
　　Megan Ginsberg
Associate Editors Hannah Crowley
　　Andrea Geary
　　Amy Graves
　　Andrew Janjigian
　　Chris O'Connor
Test Cooks Daniel Cellucci
　　Lan Lam
Assistant Editors Shannon Friedmann Hatch
　　Taizeth Sierra
Assistant Test Cook Cecelia Jenkins
Executive Assistant Christine Gordon
Assistant Test Kitchen Director Leah Rovner
Senior Kitchen Assistants Michelle Blodget
　　Meryl MacCormack
Kitchen Assistants Maria Elena Delgado
　　Ena Gudiel
Executive Producer Melissa Baldino
Co-Executive Producer Stephanie Stender
Production Assistant Kaitlin Hammond
Contributing Editor Dawn Yanagihara
Consulting Editor Scott Brueggeman
Science Editor Guy Crosby, Ph.D.
Managing Editor, Web Christine Liu
Senior Editor, Cooking School Mari Levine
Associate Editors, Web Eric Grzymkowski
　　Roger Metcalf
Assistant Editors, Web Jill Fisher
　　Charlotte Wilder
Senior Video Editor Nick Dakoulas

Design Director Amy Klee
Art Director Julie Cote
Deputy Art Director Susan Levin
Associate Art Director Lindsey Timko
Deputy Art Director, Marketing/Web Jennifer Cox
Associate Art Director, Marketing/Web Mariah Tarvainen
Production Designer, Marketing/Web Judy Blomquist
Staff Photographer Daniel J. van Ackere
Photo Editor Steve Klise

Vice President, Marketing David Mack
Circulation Director Doug Wicinski
Circulation & Fulfillment Manager Carrie Fethe
Partnership Marketing Manager Pamela Putprush
Marketing Assistant Joyce Liao

VP, Technology, Product Development Barry Kelly
Director, Project Management Alice Carpenter
Production & Traffic Coordinator Brittany Allen
Development Manager Mike Serio

Chief Operating Officer Rob Ristagno
Production Director Guy Rochford
Workflow & Digital Asset Manager Andrew Mannone
Senior Color & Imaging Specialist Lauren Pettapiece
Production & Imaging Specialists Heather Dube
　　Lauren Robbins
Director of Sponsorship Sales Anne Traficante
Client Services Associate Kate May
Sponsorship Sales Representative Morgan Ryan
Customer Service Manager Jacqueline Valerio
Customer Service Representatives Megan Hamner
　　Jessica Haskin
　　Andrew Straaberg Finfrock

Chief Financial Officer Sharyn Chabot
Retail Sales & Marketing Director Emily Logan
Human Resources Director Adele Shapiro
Publicity Deborah Broide

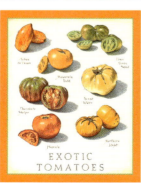

EXOTIC TOMATOES

EXOTIC TOMATOES The color of a tomato's skin and flesh can give clues about its flavor. Creamy-fleshed GREAT WHITES are wonderfully sweet. Yellow varieties, like MOUNTAIN GOLD, tend to be high in sugar but have a subtle acidity and are best sliced and served raw. The red PHOENIX offers a balance of brightness and sugar. Its firmness makes it a good pick for burgers. The fiery-colored TETON DE VENUS is earthy but mild. Often used to make tomato paste, it's best fit for cooking or canning. Green tomatoes plucked prematurely from the vine tend to be quite tart, but the LIME GREEN SALAD variety is chartreuse even when ripe and is juicy and pleasantly tangy. Variegated tomatoes often have a complex flavor. NORTHERN LIGHTS' end-to-stem blush encases a green-apple tang. Meaty CHOCOLATE STRIPES are full of rich-tasting jelly.

Cover (Corn): Robert Papp; BACK COVER (Exotic Tomatoes): John Burgoyne

America's TEST KITCHEN

RECIPES THAT WORK®

America's Test Kitchen is a very real 2,500-square-foot kitchen located just outside Boston. It is the home of *Cook's Illustrated* and *Cook's Country* magazines and is the workday destination of more than three dozen test cooks, editors, and cookware specialists. Our mission is to test recipes over and over again until we understand how and why they work and until we arrive at the best version. We also test kitchen equipment and supermarket ingredients in search of brands that offer the best value and performance. You can watch us work by tuning in to *America's Test Kitchen* (AmericasTestKitchenTV.com) on public television.

PRINTED IN THE USA

TOOLS OF THE TRADE

You may have never heard of a Hotsy, but Tom and Nate, my Vermont neighbors, certainly have. It is just one of hundreds of tools that are housed in their commercial garage just across the road from Floyd Skidmore's place, the one with a front yard that looks like Old MacDonald's farm, assuming that he lived in a used-car lot. It's a carnival of plows, campers, brush hogs, pickups, tires, trailers, beefers, and goats, the latter often making forays into Tom's garage, looking for a nice PVC pipe connector to gnaw on for lunch.

The Hotsy is a pressure washer with a twist. It is a large water heater powered by kerosene. Just press the trigger and you get instant hot water, great for cleaning trucks, pickups, bulldozers, and excavators. Tom picked it up for $200, refurbished it, and, with a twinkle in his eye, noted that a new one will run you $4,500. His garage has a well for changing oil that is kept dry by a sump pump. (The garage was built in a swamp years ago.) He has welders, grinders, sharpeners, drills, bits, wrenches, chop saws, air compressors, plumbing pipe, chain saws, washers, bolts, machine screws of every size, wire, gaskets, oil filters, a small office, and a STIHL calendar featuring a chain saw, a chopped motorcycle, and, of course, the girl. Outside, there are 200 tons of screened gravel, a sander, a small fortune in good topsoil, and a salt pit for storing the sand-salt combination that they use for doing driveways in winter. He plans on installing a septic system later this year and sprucing up the property with evergreens.

I've seen Tom fix a hundred different things over the years, including bad taillights, generators that wouldn't start, grumpy chain saws, and an old Jaguar that had stuck float valves in one of its carburetors. (He gently whacked the outside of the carburetor with a large wrench.) He's used a Sawzall to free a large woman trapped after she fell through rotten decking around a log cabin; he's winched his Ford pickup and mine out of countless mud holes and ditches; he's repaired the ancient oil furnace in the basement of his farmhouse on sub-zero nights in a snake-infested dirt cellar; he can change the oil on everything from an excavator to a rototiller; and he can pull a lead ball out of a black powder rifle that misfired without shooting himself. He can also field dress a deer, hill a row of potatoes, disk a field, and drain the water from a cabin before winter sets in. He doesn't like bats or spiders, although he once had to chase a colony of bats out of his living room with an old tennis racket, something that I remind him about at least once per year.

More than 20 years ago, I was having trouble with my International 404, a large mule of a tractor that was about as easy to turn as an oil tanker. It wouldn't start, so I called Salem Farm Supply for help. The repair guy showed up, cleaned the battery posts in 2 minutes flat using a battery post brush, started up the tractor, and charged me $65. Since then, that brush has been my favorite tool. I have saved the day numerous times when guests at the farm could not start their cars on Sunday afternoon or when an old jalopy sitting in my barn wouldn't start even after the spring battery charge. For less than $10, this tool makes me look like an expert.

The right tool, however, is mostly a modern

Christopher Kimball

invention. Even as a kid on the farm, I remember when a hammer, pliers, wire, baling twine, a screwdriver, and a crowbar took care of most in-the-field repairs, like when the baler was delivering broken bales or the plow on a pickup would not lower properly. Today, we depend on the right tool for the job; back then, we depended mostly on confidence. I have watched Tom's son Nate do the near impossible: replace hard-to-reach hydraulic hoses on a backhoe or loosen up a frozen bolt the width of a bread plate. Most of us would give up before we got started.

One August evening a dozen years ago my oldest daughter, Whitney, took off down the road on her pink and white bicycle, handlebar streamers afloat as she passed our neighbor's henhouse, and then disappeared down the narrow dirt road. I waited a bit, figuring that she needed to have a good head start, and then finally started up the red Ford 150 and headed out toward New York State. I found her a few miles away, down on the flats between hay fields. Twilight was coming, a dog was barking, and she was stopped by the side of the road, the bike hidden in the long grass. I drove by, turned around, and came back. I put her bike in the flatbed and she hopped in. We drove back home without a word spoken.

Sometimes one is not given the right tools to deal with what life has to offer. You just do your best, like the old farmer with nothing more than a hammer, pliers, and the confidence that things will turn out right.

FOR INQUIRIES, ORDERS, OR MORE INFORMATION

CooksIllustrated.com
At CooksIllustrated.com, you can order books and subscriptions, sign up for our free e-newsletter, or renew your magazine subscription. Join the website and gain access to 20 years of *Cook's Illustrated* recipes, equipment tests, and ingredient tastings, as well as companion videos for every recipe in this issue.

COOKBOOKS
We sell more than 50 cookbooks by the editors of *Cook's Illustrated*, including *The Cook's Illustrated Cookbook* and *The Science of Good Cooking*. To order, visit our bookstore at CooksIllustrated.com/bookstore.

COOK'S ILLUSTRATED MAGAZINE
Cook's Illustrated magazine (ISSN 1068-2821), number 123, is published bimonthly by Boston Common Press Limited partnership, 17 Station St., Brookline, MA 02445. Copyright 2013 Boston Common Press Limited Partnership. Periodicals postage paid at Boston, Mass., and additional mailing offices, USPS #012487. Publications Mail Agreement No. 40020778. Return undeliverable Canadian addresses to P.O. Box 875, Station A, Windsor, ON N9A 6P2. POSTMASTER: Send address changes to *Cook's Illustrated*, P.O. Box 6018, Harlan, IA 51593-1518. For subscription and gift subscription orders, subscription inquiries, or change-of-address notices, visit us at AmericasTestKitchen.com/customerservice, call us at 800-526-8442, or write us at *Cook's Illustrated*, P.O. 6018, Harlan, IA 51593-1518.

FOR LIST RENTAL INFORMATION Contact Specialists Marketing Services, Inc., 777 Terrace Ave., 4th Floor, Hasbrouck Heights, NJ 07604; 201-865-5800.

EDITORIAL OFFICE 17 Station St., Brookline, MA 02445; 617-232-1000; fax 617-232-1572. Subscription inquiries, visit AmericasTestKitchen.com/customerservice or call 800-526-8442.

POSTMASTER Send all new orders, subscription inquiries, and change-of-address notices to *Cook's Illustrated*, P.O. Box 6018, Harlan, IA 51593-1518.

⇒ BY MOLLY BIRNBAUM, ANDREA GEARY & LAN LAM ⇐

Brownulated Sugar

I recently spotted Domino's Brownulated sugar in the baking aisle of my supermarket. How does it compare with regular brown sugar?

MATT NECHIN
SILVER SPRING, MD.

➤With its loose, dry texture and larger grain size, Domino's easy-pour, nonclumping Brownulated Light Brown Sugar resembles active dry yeast. One cup of Brownulated sugar weighs 1 ounce less than 1 (packed) cup of regular light brown sugar, and the bag advises subbing it cup for cup rather than ounce for ounce.

Doesn't an ounce less sugar make baked goods that are less sweet? Not necessarily. When we used the volume measurement to substitute Brownulated sugar for conventional Domino brown sugar in brown sugar cookies, butterscotch cookies, and pecan bars, we found the samples to be just as sweet. Brownulated sugar is in fact sweeter than the regular stuff, but tasters noted that it lacked "molasses backbone." Brownulated sugar also had a drying effect: The brown sugar cookie dough was crumbly, and the cookies didn't spread well in the oven. And the butterscotch cookies looked freckled because the Brownulated sugar didn't disperse properly. Only the moist interiors of the pecan bars weren't compromised.

The only ingredient listed on the bag of Brownulated sugar is brown sugar, so why the big differences in flavor and baking properties? When we inquired, Domino didn't offer an explanation, but here's our theory: Brownulated sugar is most likely made from a concentrated sugar solution (which accounts for the extra sweetness) that is spray-dried—a process that typically produces lighter, larger, and more porous particles that absorb more moisture during cooking. The larger particles dissolve readily in high-moisture environments (like that of the pecan bars) but not very well in drier cookie doughs. Our overall take? The convenience of Brownulated sugar is overrated. We're sticking with the sticky stuff. –A.G.

BROWNULATED SUGAR
Not recommended for most recipes.

BROWN SUGAR
Our choice for baking.

Take Cover?

Does covering the pot really make water boil faster?

EMILY GIORGIO
LANCASTER, PA.

➤When you heat water in an open pot, some of the energy that could be raising the temperature of the liquid escapes with the vapor. But as long as more energy is being added to the water than is being lost with the vapor, the temperature will continue to rise until the water boils. Covering the pot prevents water vapor from escaping, enabling the temperature to rise more quickly. How much more quickly? In our experience, not a lot. When we brought 4 quarts of water to a boil in covered and uncovered stainless steel Dutch ovens, the covered pot boiled in just over 12 minutes and the uncovered pot boiled in 13 minutes and 15 seconds. But why waste even a small amount of heat when it's so easy not to? That said, since you're not losing time or energy until the water begins to steam, put the water on to heat first and then go hunting for the lid. –A.G.

Creaming Butter and Sugar

Most recipes that call for creaming butter and sugar ask for softened butter. Is it OK to start with cold butter and just cream it longer?

KIRSTIN HUFF
LOUISVILLE, KY.

➤When you cream softened butter and sugar, the grains of sugar are forced through the fat, leaving millions of microscopic air bubbles in their wake and giving the butter a fluffy appearance. In the heat of the oven these bubbles expand, contributing to the lightness of the finished product. Room-temperature butter is best for aeration (we've found that about 67 degrees, or when the butter gives slightly when pressed, is ideal). If the butter is too firm and cold, the fat won't hold air; if it's too soft and warm, the bubbles collapse.

We cut 8 ounces of fridge-cold butter into small pieces and beat them at medium speed in a stand mixer fitted with a paddle, stopping occasionally to scrape down the sides of the bowl. It took 15 minutes for the butter to become as malleable as room-temperature butter, but without the sugar in the mix to aerate it, we had a hard time visually gauging its texture. Instead, we had to take its temperature—a fussy extra step.

Here's what worked: We added the sugar (1 cup) to the cold butter from the start. Then all we needed to do was beat the mixture until it turned pale yellow and fluffy, the usual visual indication that butter has been nicely aerated. This took a total of about 15 minutes, compared with the 3 minutes that it takes following the conventional method of first beating softened butter and then creaming it with sugar.

In sum, as long as you're willing to put in the extra mixing time, go ahead and use cold butter when creaming—just add sugar from the start. –A.G.

Unwilting Lettuce

I've read that soaking wilted lettuce in ice water and vinegar will crisp it up quickly. True or false?

JACOBA CHARLES
BOLINAS, CALIF.

➤Lettuce wilts because it loses water, so the key to reviving it is to put the water back in. We've had success simply soaking the wilted leaves in ice water for 30 minutes. But since water enters the lettuce's cells through openings called stomata—and ions including hydrogen ions from acids can cause the stomata to open and take in more water—adding vinegar to the water could help crisp lettuce faster, at least in theory. As a test, we took three heads of green leaf lettuce that we'd allowed to wilt and then split each head in half and tore up the leaves (tearing created more avenues for water to enter). Half of each head went into a bowl of ice water with 2 tablespoons of cider vinegar; the others went into plain ice water.

A REFRESHING DIP
Soak lettuce in plain ice water to restore crispness.

This acid test didn't pan out: All the samples rehydrated in the same amount of time—about 30 minutes—but the vinegar left a slight unwanted tang on the lettuce. Hydrogen ions should help the lettuce take up water, but vinegar, a rather weak acid, doesn't have enough of them to make a difference. We'll stick with plain ice water to refresh our salad leaves and save vinegar for the dressing. –A.G.

Lobster Tomalley

What is the green stuff in my lobster? Is it safe to eat?

HANNAH RODGER
BOXBOROUGH, MASS.

➤That soft green mass in the body of a cooked lobster is a digestive gland, sort of like a liver and a pancreas combined. It's known to marine biologists as the hepatopancreas and to lobster fans as the tomalley. Many in the latter group prize the tomalley for its creamy texture and intense flavor; our tasters described it as akin to "lobster concentrate." Tomalley is eaten as is, whisked into sauces, or mixed into a compound butter and spread on toast.

In recent years there has been concern that eating tomalley can lead to the contraction of paralytic shellfish poisoning (PSP), the illness caused by red tide. Red tide refers to a naturally occurring population explosion of particular types of poison-producing plankton that are ingested by filter feeders like clams and scallops. People who eat infected shellfish may experience dizziness and nausea. Lobsters do not filter-feed, but they do consume clams and scallops. If a lobster eats infected bivalves, the PSP could accumulate in its tomalley though not in the meat. So it's fine to eat lobster meat during red tide occurrences, but it's a good idea to forgo the tomalley when there's a shellfish ban in place. –A.G.

The Importance of a Tube Pan

Why do recipes for angel food cake and chiffon cake always call for a tube pan?

SUSAN WHEELER
CLEVELAND, OHIO

➤There's a good reason angel food and chiffon cakes are always baked in tube pans, and it's not just aesthetics. These specialty vessels actually help delicate cakes rise. Because egg foam–based cakes like angel food and chiffon contain very little flour, and therefore very little of the structure-building network called gluten, the batter needs something to cling to as it bakes, or it will collapse. Enter the tube pan's tall sides: As the egg foam heats up, it will climb up the sides (and conical center) of the pan. But its lofty structure isn't sturdy until the cake cools—which is why angel food and chiffon cakes are often cooled upside down on the pan's tripod feet.

Bottom line: Don't try baking traditional angel food or chiffon cakes in conventional cake or jelly roll pans; they will fall. In fact, the only way we were able to ditch the tube pan for the quick chiffon cake in our Summer Berry Trifle (page 23) was to add more flour to the batter. –M.B.

WELL RISEN
A tube pan is essential for egg foam–based cakes.

COLLAPSED
Angel food or chiffon cake baked in a conventional pan falls flat.

WHAT IS IT?

My friend and I are trying to figure out what this is. We're guessing it's a lemon slicer used in a bar. We'd appreciate any help!

LINDA CUTSON
NEW YORK, N.Y.

You won't find this tool next to martini shakers and muddlers, although it is useful in a bar—a clam bar, that is. Known as a clam opener, the utensil aids in prying the mollusk's meat from its stubbornly locked shells. To use it, hold the opener in one hand and place a rinsed, scrubbed clam, lip side up, into the cup. Squeeze the handles together to lower the thin blade between the shells, jimmying them open. The bladed arm is pronged and can be removed from the cup to help pluck out the meat.

We brought the vintage gadget into the test kitchen but found that while the clam opener offered some protection, it barely lived up to its name: Its hinges lowered the blade only enough to create a slight gap between the shells of our raw cherrystone clams. We had to finish the job with a clam knife.

–Shannon Friedmann Hatch

CLAM JAM
This antique clam opener fails to get the job done.

Lessening a Chile's Burn

Do you have any good suggestions for getting rid of the irritating burn that can happen when you accidentally touch a fresh hot chile?

CHARLEY HINES
COLORADO SPRINGS, COLO.

➤Capsaicin is the chemical in chiles responsible for their heat. It binds to receptors on the tongue or skin, triggering a pain response. To find out if anything could be done to lessen this burn, we rounded up some brave testers to seed chiles without gloves, smear chile paste onto patches of their skin, and eat scrambled eggs doused in hot sauce. We then tested some home remedies. For the skin, we washed with soap and water and rubbed the affected area with oil, vinegar, tomato juice, a baking soda slurry, and hydrogen peroxide. For the mouth, we swished with (but did not swallow) water, milk, beer, and a mixture of hydrogen peroxide and water.

Soap and water helped lessen the burn on skin a bit, but oil, vinegar, tomato juice, and baking soda didn't help at all. As for the mouth, water and beer failed, too. Milk had only a slight impact. What worked on both the skin and the mouth? Hydrogen peroxide.

It turns out that peroxide reacts with capsaicin molecules, changing their structure and rendering them incapable of bonding with our receptors. Peroxide works even better in the presence of a base like baking soda: We found that a solution of $\frac{1}{8}$ teaspoon of baking soda, 1 tablespoon of water, and 1 tablespoon of hydrogen peroxide could be used to wash the affected area or as a mouthwash (swish vigorously for 30 seconds) to tone down a chile's stinging burn to a mild warmth. (Toothpaste containing peroxide and baking soda is a somewhat less effective remedy.) Always keep peroxide, baking soda, and toothpaste away from your eyes. –L.L.

Feta Storage

What's the best way to store feta cheese if it doesn't come packed in a brine?

ERIC ASNIS
BERLIN, VT.

➤To find out, we submerged feta in a homemade brine (the exact concentration was a guess—we used 2 teaspoons of salt per cup of water), stored another in a tub of tap water, covered a third with olive oil, tightly wrapped a fourth in plastic wrap, and left the last unwrapped but sealed in an airtight container. Ten days later we compared the stored samples with feta from a freshly opened package.

The feta stored in the homemade brine was a bit too salty and dry (which meant that our brine was too strong and pulled water from the cheese). The opposite happened in the tap water sample: The salt was drawn out of the cheese, causing it to taste bland. Some tasters picked up off-notes in the cheeses that were either tightly wrapped in plastic or stored in an airtight container. The winner? The sample stored in olive oil. It seemed to do the best job of protecting the cheese from air, both sealing in moisture and discouraging the proliferation of oxygen-dependent bacteria, which can cause off-flavors. To store feta using a minimal amount of oil: Put the cheese in the corner of a small zipper-lock bag and pour in just enough oil to come up the sides. Place the bag in a cup and press down on the cheese to force the excess oil over the top. Stored this way, feta keeps for up to four weeks. –A.G.

SEND US YOUR QUESTIONS We will provide a complimentary one-year subscription for each letter we print. Send your inquiry, name, address, and daytime telephone number to Notes from Readers, *Cook's Illustrated*, P.O. Box 470589, Brookline, MA 02447, or to NotesFromReaders@AmericasTestKitchen.com.

Quick Tips

≈ BY DANETTE ST. ONGE ≈

Aluminum Foil Scrubber

When she runs out of steel wool but needs to get tough, baked-on food off glass baking pans or her oven rack, Allison Brown of San Francisco, Calif., uses dishwashing liquid and a crumpled-up ball of aluminum foil. The craggy foil is more abrasive than a sponge and is a great way to recycle used—but still clean—sheets of foil.

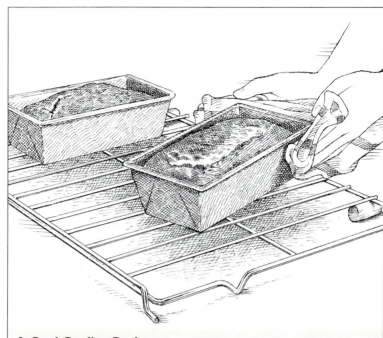

A Cool Cooling Rack

When baking in a kitchen that isn't equipped with a cooling rack, Jesse Gladin-Kramer of Durham, N.C., moves the extra oven rack to a countertop before heating the oven. She props up the rack with corks and then uses it as a cooling rack for her finished baked goods.

Hot (Tooth)Pick Dispenser

Sharon Potusky of Springfield, Ga., came up with a creative use for an empty hot sauce bottle: After washing it well, she filled it with toothpicks and replaced the plastic drip-dispenser top. The hole in the middle of the drip-dispenser top is the perfect size to dispense just one toothpick at a time when the bottle is shaken upside down.

Peeling Just One Tomato

Blanching tomatoes (or peaches) in a pot of boiling water is a great way to remove their peels, but when she needs to peel just a single piece of fruit, Monique Verrier of Healdsburg, Calif., takes a shortcut. She microwaves 1⅓ cups of water in a 2-cup liquid measuring cup for 1 to 2 minutes until simmering. Then she cuts a shallow X into the bottom of the fruit, drops it into the hot water for 30 seconds, and then transfers it to ice water for 30 seconds. The peel pulls right off.

Transporting Ice Cream

Faced with a long drive to a party on a hot summer day, Sara Fama of San Carlos, Calif., came up with a clever way to transport some of her homemade ice cream without it turning into soup: She used her ice cream maker's chilled freezer bowl as a mini cooler. It holds up to a quart of ice cream, sherbet, or sorbet, and when flexible ice packs are placed snugly against the sides and top of the container, the frozen treat stays solid for hours.

ILLUSTRATION: JOHN BURGOYNE

SEND US YOUR TIPS We will provide a complimentary one-year subscription for each tip we print. Send your tip, name, address, and daytime telephone number to Quick Tips, *Cook's Illustrated*, P.O. Box 470589, Brookline, MA 02447, or to QuickTips@AmericasTestKitchen.com.

Power Outage Indicator

When Cindy Klun of Minneapolis, Minn., travels, she worries about power outages occurring during her absence that can lead to spoilage in her fridge and freezer. Since it's hard to know exactly how long an outage has lasted, she came up with a homemade indicator: She takes an empty plastic soda bottle, fills it halfway with water, seals it, and places it on its side in the freezer. Once the water has frozen, she stands the bottle upright in the freezer so that the ice is now oriented vertically against one side of the bottle. When she returns from vacation, if the ice is still a vertical strip, she knows that the freezer wasn't off for an extended period of time. If ice has formed at the bottom of the bottle, however, it's time to clean out the fridge and freezer.

Clever Condiment Cups

When serving condiments at her backyard barbecues, Penny Senouci of Denver, Colo., uses a jumbo muffin tin to contain condiments like ketchup, mustard, relish, and chopped onion. The toppings stay together and she has only one container to clean at the end of the party. (A popover pan also works.)

Clean Fix for Containers

The dishwasher makes easy work of cleaning reusable containers—unless the lightweight plastic flips during the cycle and fills with dirty water. Genie Gunn of Asheville, N.C., keeps hers in place with a rubber spring clip. She slides the clip onto a rung of the rack for stability and then attaches it to a container. She's even found that one clip will keep an entire row in place.

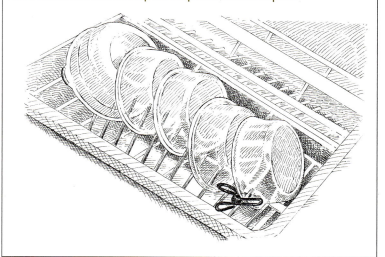

A Handy Rule of Thumb

After learning that for most people the length between the thumb's knuckle and its tip is almost exactly 1 inch, DeeDee Cooper of Los Angeles, Calif., no longer hunts for a ruler each time a recipe calls for a cut of a specific width or length. Instead, she uses her thumb as a guide for measuring and chopping the first few pieces and then uses those pieces as guides for the remaining cuts. (For some people, the distance between the second joint of the pointer finger and its tip is closer to 1 inch. Measure both your thumb and your pointer finger with a ruler to see which is more accurate.)

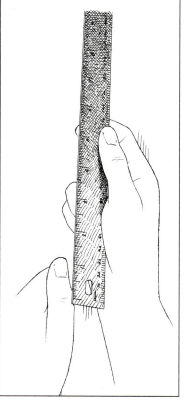

DIY Ice Pack

Instead of purchasing several individual ice packs to keep the food inside her cooler chilled, Lynn Carr of Lillian, Ala., has found a homemade solution in the empty liner of her boxed wine. The bag, which is made of thick, durable plastic, forms one large pack.

1. Squeeze out any residual air and wine from the bag and rinse out the bag.

2. Fill the bag halfway with water.

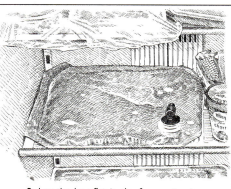

3. Lay the bag flat in the freezer to store. (Be sure the valve is closed when in use.)

Foolproof Barbecued Chicken

We've all had it: chicken with burnt skin, parched meat, and a coat of sweet, goopy sauce.
By applying some barbecue know-how, surely we could do better.

> BY LAN LAM

I have fond memories of eating barbecued chicken when I was growing up, but not because the chicken was any good. My family's version of this summertime staple, one of the few American dishes that my immigrant parents made, involved my father dousing chicken parts with bottled sauce and dumping the pieces over a ripping hot fire. He would then spend the next 45 minutes flipping and shuffling them around on the grate in a vain effort to get the pieces to cook evenly. Some of the pieces always cooked up dry, while others were raw at the bone. Worse, flare-ups caused by fat dripping onto the coals carbonized the skin well before its underbelly had a chance to fully render. But it was summer, it was fun to eat outside, and if we poured enough of the (inevitably) ultrasweet sauce on the chicken, we could mask its shortcomings.

Throughout the years I've eaten enough subpar barbecued chicken to realize that my dad is not the only one who doesn't know how to produce juicy, deeply seasoned, evenly cooked chicken parts on the grill—a lot of cooks don't either. With decades of test kitchen barbecuing experience on my side, I set out to foolproof this American classic.

Indirect heat and a water pan help ensure perfectly cooked chicken. A spice rub applied at least 6 hours before grilling boosts flavor.

Making Arrangements

There were a few basic barbecue tenets I put in place from the get-go. First, I ditched the single-level fire favored by my dad (and also recommended by a surprising number of recipes) and built an indirect one: I corralled all the coals on one side of the kettle, enabling me to sear the chicken over the hotter side and then pull it over to the cooler side, where the meat would cook gently and the skin could render slowly. Cooking the chicken opposite from (rather than on top of) the coals for most of the time would also cut back on flare-ups. Second, I salted the meat and let it sit for several hours before grilling it, since I assumed that this pretreatment would change the

meat's protein structure so that it would hold on to more moisture as it cooked—added insurance against overcooking. Finally, I would wait to apply barbecue sauce (which usually contains sugary ingredients) until after searing; this would prevent the sauce from burning and give the skin a chance to develop color first.

I proceeded to sear 6 pounds of breasts and leg quarters on the hotter part of the grill. Once both sides of the meat were brown, I dragged the pieces to the cooler part of the kettle, painted on some placeholder bottled sauce, and considered my core challenge: how to ensure that both the white and dark pieces cooked at an even pace.

Since food that sits closest to the fire cooks faster, I lined up the fattier, more heat-resistant leg quarters closest to the coals and the leaner, more delicate breasts farther away and covered the grill. About an hour later, the breast meat was just about done, the skin was nicely rendered and thin, and the sauce was concentrated and set. The problem was that several leg quarters were chewy and dry. Salting clearly wasn't enough to protect them from the heat, even

when positioned next to the coals instead of on top of them.

I thought that swapping the dark and white pieces midway through cooking to even out their exposure to the heat would help, but this just made things worse: Now both the white and dark pieces overcooked. Building a smaller fire wasn't an option either: When I used 25 percent less charcoal, the heat dwindled before the meat finished cooking.

Getting Even

Reducing the coals didn't work, but that didn't mean that I couldn't adjust the heat another way—by setting a disposable aluminum pan opposite the coals and partially filling it with water, a trick that we've used in other recipes that require low, even heat. Both the pan and the water absorb heat, lowering the overall temperature inside the kettle and eliminating hot spots. (For more information, see "Why Use a Water Pan in Your Grill?" on page 30.)

I cooked another batch using the water pan and finally made some headway. The ambient temperature inside the grill had dropped by about 50 degrees—a good sign. I checked the pieces midway through grilling and was pleased to see that the dark meat was cooking at a slower, steadier pace. By the end of the hour, both the white and dark pieces were hitting their target temperatures (160 and 175 degrees, respectively).

Flavor Makers

My cooking method had come a long way, but I could hardly call my results "barbecued." For one thing, I needed a homemade alternative for the characterless bottled sauce. My tasters also reminded me that, although the chicken was nicely seasoned after salting, the flavor of the meat itself was unremarkable once you got past the skin.

But salting the chicken reminded me that I could easily apply bolder flavor in the same way—with a rub. I kept the blend basic: In addition to the kosher salt, I mixed together equal amounts of onion and garlic powders and paprika; a touch of cayenne for subtle heat; and a generous 2 tablespoons of brown sugar, which would caramelize during cooking.

For the sauce, I fell back on the test kitchen's go-to

See the Proper Setup

Video available FREE for 4 months at
CooksIllustrated.com/aug13

recipe, which smartens the typical ketchup-based concoction. Molasses adds depth, while cider vinegar, Worcestershire sauce, and Dijon mustard keep sweetness in check. Grated onion, minced garlic, chili powder, cayenne, and pepper round out the flavors.

But there was a downside to applying the sauce just after searing: Namely, after cooking for an hour, it lost a measure of its bright tanginess. Instead, I applied the sauce in stages, brushing on the first coat just after searing and then applying a second midway through grilling. That minor adjustment made a surprisingly big difference. I also reserved some of the sauce for passing at the table.

This was perfectly cooked, seriously good chicken. Now all I have to do is convince my dad to let me handle the cooking at our next family barbecue.

SWEET AND TANGY BARBECUED CHICKEN

SERVES 6 TO 8

When browning the chicken over the hotter side of the grill, move it away from any flare-ups. For information on shopping for chicken parts, see page 31.

Chicken
- 2 tablespoons packed dark brown sugar
- 4½ teaspoons kosher salt
- 1½ teaspoons onion powder
- 1½ teaspoons garlic powder
- 1½ teaspoons paprika
- ¼ teaspoon cayenne pepper
- 6 pounds bone-in chicken pieces (split breasts and/or leg quarters), trimmed

Sauce
- 1 cup ketchup
- 5 tablespoons molasses
- 3 tablespoons cider vinegar
- 2 tablespoons Worcestershire sauce
- 2 tablespoons Dijon mustard
- ¼ teaspoon pepper
- 2 tablespoons vegetable oil
- ⅓ cup grated onion
- 1 garlic clove, minced
- 1 teaspoon chili powder
- ¼ teaspoon cayenne pepper

- 1 large disposable aluminum roasting pan (if using charcoal) or 2 disposable aluminum pie plates (if using gas)

1. FOR THE CHICKEN: Combine sugar, salt, onion powder, garlic powder, paprika, and cayenne in bowl. Arrange chicken on rimmed baking sheet and sprinkle both sides evenly with spice rub. Cover with plastic wrap and refrigerate for at least 6 hours or up to 24 hours.

2. FOR THE SAUCE: Whisk ketchup, molasses, vinegar, Worcestershire, mustard, and pepper together in bowl. Heat oil in medium saucepan over medium heat until shimmering. Add onion and garlic; cook until onion is softened, 2 to 4 minutes.

Add chili powder and cayenne and cook until fragrant, about 30 seconds. Whisk in ketchup mixture and bring to boil. Reduce heat to medium-low and simmer gently for 5 minutes. Set aside ⅔ cup sauce to baste chicken and reserve remaining sauce for serving. (Sauce can be refrigerated for up to 1 week.)

3A. FOR A CHARCOAL GRILL: Open bottom vent halfway and place disposable pan filled with 3 cups water on 1 side of grill. Light large chimney starter filled with charcoal briquettes (6 quarts). When top coals are partially covered with ash, pour evenly over other half of grill (opposite disposable pan). Set cooking grate in place, cover, and open lid vent halfway. Heat grill until hot, about 5 minutes.

3B. FOR A GAS GRILL: Place 2 disposable pie plates, each filled with 1½ cups water, directly on 1 burner of gas grill (opposite primary burner). Turn all burners to high, cover, and heat grill until hot, about 15 minutes. Turn primary burner to medium-high and turn off other burner(s). (Adjust primary burner as needed to maintain grill temperature of 325 to 350 degrees.)

4. Clean and oil cooking grate. Place chicken, skin side down, over hotter part of grill and cook until browned and blistered in spots, 2 to 5 minutes. Flip chicken and cook until second side is browned, 4 to 6 minutes. Move chicken to cooler part and brush both sides with ⅓ cup sauce. Arrange chicken, skin side up, with leg quarters closest to fire and breasts farthest away. Cover (positioning lid vent over chicken if using charcoal) and cook for 25 minutes.

5. Brush both sides of chicken with remaining ⅓ cup sauce and continue to cook, covered, until breasts register 160 degrees and leg quarters register 175 degrees, 25 to 35 minutes longer.

6. Transfer chicken to serving platter, tent loosely with aluminum foil, and let rest for 10 minutes. Serve, passing reserved sauce separately.

TECHNIQUE | DOES YOUR

LEG QUARTER NEED A TRIM?

Some leg quarters come with the backbone still attached. Here's an easy way to remove it.

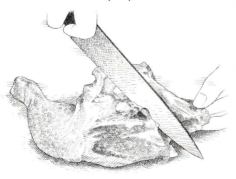

Holding the leg quarter skin side down, grasp the backbone and bend it back to pop the thigh bone out of its socket. Place the leg on a cutting board and cut through the joint and any attached skin.

ILLUSTRATION: JOHN BURGOYNE

Grilled Glazed Pork Tenderloin Roast

Overcoming pork tenderloin's challenges—lean, dry meat; mild flavor; and a tapered shape that cooks unevenly—required some rough treatment.

> BY DAN SOUZA <

Pork tenderloin is wonderfully tender and versatile, it doesn't require much prep, and it's relatively inexpensive. But alas, this cut also comes with a certain set of challenges. Because tenderloin is so incredibly lean, it's highly susceptible to drying out during cooking. Then there's its ungainly tapered shape: By the time the large end hits a perfect medium (140 degrees), the skinnier tail is guaranteed to be overdone. And while my favorite way to prepare mild meats like tenderloin is grilling (to develop a rich, meaty crust), extreme heat and natural fluctuations in temperature make this hard to do well. I wanted to find a way to make grilled pork tenderloin a bit more foolproof and at the same time elevate this cut above its "casual supper" status to something more special and elegant. Into the kitchen—and out to the grill—I went.

A Juicy Story

Keeping meat of any kind juicy on the grill is a perennial challenge. In the test kitchen, we have a couple of tricks for addressing the problem, namely salting or brining. Both techniques introduce salt into the flesh, where it tenderizes the meat and increases water retention. Using our preferred type of pork, unenhanced (or natural)—meaning that it has not been injected with a solution of water, salt, and sodium phosphate—I ran a side-by-side test in which I salted and brined a few tenderloins, slicked them with oil, and grilled them. Tasters reported that while both options proved juicier and more evenly seasoned than an untreated control, the brined samples were the most succulent. Settling on brining, I moved on to another variable that affects juiciness: grill setup.

Many pork tenderloin recipes call for grilling the meat directly over a hot fire the entire time. The result? A well-browned exterior with a thick band of dry, overcooked meat below its surface—no thanks. A better approach, we've found, is to employ a

We use an unusual technique to "glue" together two pork tenderloins to create a single roast.

combination high-low method: High heat provides great browning—which means great flavor—and low heat cooks meat evenly. And recently, we've favored cooking first over low heat followed by searing over high heat. During its initial stay on the cooler side of the grill, the meat's surface warms and dries, making for fast, efficient browning (and therefore precluding overcooking) when it hits the hotter part of the grate. Sure enough, when I gave this approach a try, I produced meat with rosy interiors surrounded by thin, flavorful crusts—at least at the thick ends. Unsurprisingly, the thin, tapered ends of the tenderloins (I was cooking two in order to serve six guests) were terribly overdone.

It Takes Two

There was nothing I could do to the grill setup to make the unevenly shaped meat cook evenly, so what about altering the tenderloins themselves? Assuming the role of mad butcher, I pounded and portioned untold samples in search of a more uniform shape. Flattening the thicker end of the roast certainly made

for more even cooking, but it also turned the cut into what looked like a gigantic, malformed pork chop. Slicing the tenderloin into medallions produced an awkward group of scallop-size pieces that were fussy to grill.

After a long, unsuccessful afternoon, I stood before the last two raw tenderloins on my cutting board. A light bulb went on: Why not tie them together? If I stacked the tenderloins the way that shoes come packed in a box—with the thick end of one nestled against the thin end of the other—I'd produce a single, evenly shaped roast. I gave it a shot, fastening together my brined double-wide roast with lengths of kitchen twine and brushing it with oil before heading out to the hot grill. About 35 minutes later, I had a piece of meat that was perfectly cooked from one end to the other. This larger roast took longer to come up to temperature, but the added grill time was a boon to taste: More time over the fire meant more smoky grill flavor.

These successes aside, there was still an obstacle in my way. When I carved my impressive-looking roast, each slice inevitably flopped apart into two pieces. While this wasn't a deal breaker, I was eager to see if I could establish a more permanent bond between the tenderloins.

The Glue That Binds

Trying to get meat to stick together might sound unorthodox, but it's something that happens naturally all the time, at least with ground meat. In sausages, burgers, meatballs, and meatloaf, tiny individual pieces of protein fuse together to form a cohesive whole. I wasn't working with ground meat, but maybe I could use it as inspiration.

It turns out that anytime meat is damaged (such as during grinding, slicing, or even pounding), sticky proteins are released. The proteins' gluey texture is what makes it possible to form a cohesive burger from nothing but ground beef. If salt is added—as it is to make sausage—the proteins become even tackier. When heated, the protein sets into a solid structure, effectively binding the meat together. To see if I could use this information for my tenderloins, I tried roughing up their surfaces in a variety of ways: lightly whacking them with a meat mallet, scraping them with a fork, and rubbing them vigorously with coarse salt. I tested these methods before brining, after brining, and both before *and* after brining. Yes, my oddball experiments garnered plenty of strange looks from my colleagues. But I'll keep those skeptical glances in my memory as a point of pride because, in the end, I found my solution.

The key to getting two tenderloins to bind together? A few simple scrapes of a fork along the length of each one before brining, followed by a very thorough drying after brining. The scrapes, acting much like grinding, released plenty of sticky proteins, which the salty brine made even stickier. Finally, thorough drying ensured that moisture wouldn't interfere with this bond during cooking (the sticky mixture continued to exude from the meat even after I blotted off moisture). The technique is simple and, while not perfect (some slices had better cling than others), it provided me with a platter of attractive, mostly intact slices. Hurdle cleared, I turned my attention to flavoring the roast.

Glazed and Infused

I wanted to dress up my beautifully browned pork tenderloin roast, and a bold, burnished glaze seemed like the ideal choice. Most glazes contain sugar, which caramelizes when exposed to heat, deepening flavor. But I wanted to add still more complexity—even meatiness. And I knew how to do it: by including glutamate-rich ingredients that enhance savory flavor. With this in mind, I combined glutamate-rich miso with sugar, mustard, mirin, and ginger. For my next version, I created a sweet and spicy glaze that benefited from the glutamates found in sweet and tangy hoisin sauce. And a satay-inspired version containing brown sugar, coconut milk, curry paste, and lime juice got its glutamate infusion from fish sauce. When I tried out these new glazes on the pork, I was surprised by how much more flavor—and yes, meatiness—they contributed. It turns out that pork has a high concentration of nucleotides. When glutamates and nucleotides are combined, these compounds have a synergistic effect

that magnifies meaty, savory flavor significantly more than glutamates alone do.

The only thing left was to refine how I applied the glaze. After slowly grilling my roast on the cooler side of the grill, I slid it to the hotter side to brown. I then glazed one side at a time, allowing the glaze to char before repeating the process with the other three sides. I also reserved some glaze to add an extra blast of flavor at the table. Time to get the party started.

GRILLED GLAZED PORK TENDERLOIN ROAST
SERVES 6

Since brining is a key step in having the two tenderloins stick together, we don't recommend using enhanced pork in this recipe. For our free recipe for Satay Glaze, go to CooksIllustrated.com/aug13.

2 (1-pound) pork tenderloins, trimmed
   Salt and pepper
   Vegetable oil
1 recipe glaze (recipes follow)

1. Lay tenderloins on cutting board, flat side (side opposite where silverskin was) up. Holding thick end of 1 tenderloin with paper towels and using dinner fork, scrape flat side lengthwise from end to end 5 times, until surface is completely covered with shallow grooves. Repeat with second tenderloin. Dissolve 3 tablespoons salt in 1½ quarts cold water in large container. Submerge tenderloins in brine and let stand at room temperature for 1 hour.

2. Remove tenderloins from brine and pat completely dry with paper towels. Lay 1 tenderloin, scraped side up, on cutting board and lay second tenderloin, scraped side down, on top so that thick end of 1 tenderloin matches up with thin end of other. Spray five 14-inch lengths of kitchen twine thoroughly with vegetable oil spray; evenly space twine underneath tenderloins and tie. Brush roast with vegetable oil and season with pepper. Transfer ⅓ cup glaze to bowl for

grilling; reserve remaining glaze for serving.

3A. FOR A CHARCOAL GRILL: Open bottom vent completely. Light large chimney starter filled with charcoal briquettes (6 quarts). When top coals are partially covered with ash, pour into steeply banked pile against side of grill. Set cooking grate in place, cover, and open lid vent completely. Heat grill until hot, about 5 minutes.

3B. FOR A GAS GRILL: Turn all burners to high, cover, and heat grill until hot, about 15 minutes. Leave primary burner on high and turn off other burner(s).

4. Clean and oil cooking grate. Place roast on cooler side of grill, cover, and cook until meat registers 115 degrees, 22 to 28 minutes, flipping and rotating halfway through cooking.

5. Slide roast to hotter part of grill and cook until lightly browned on all sides, 4 to 6 minutes. Brush top of roast with about 1 tablespoon glaze and grill, glaze side down, until glaze begins to char, 2 to 3 minutes; repeat glazing and grilling with remaining 3 sides of roast, until meat registers 140 degrees.

6. Transfer roast to carving board, tent loosely with aluminum foil, and let rest for 10 minutes. Carefully remove twine and slice roast into ½-inch-thick slices. Serve with remaining glaze.

MISO GLAZE
MAKES ABOUT ¾ CUP

3 tablespoons sake
3 tablespoons mirin
⅓ cup white miso paste
¼ cup sugar
2 teaspoons Dijon mustard
1 teaspoon rice vinegar
¼ teaspoon grated fresh ginger
¼ teaspoon toasted sesame oil

Bring sake and mirin to boil in small saucepan over medium heat. Whisk in miso and sugar until smooth, about 30 seconds. Remove pan from heat and continue to whisk until sugar is dissolved, about 1 minute. Whisk in mustard, vinegar, ginger, and sesame oil until smooth.

SWEET AND SPICY HOISIN GLAZE
MAKES ABOUT ¾ CUP

1 teaspoon vegetable oil
3 garlic cloves, minced
1 teaspoon grated fresh ginger
½ teaspoon red pepper flakes
½ cup hoisin sauce
2 tablespoons soy sauce
1 tablespoon rice vinegar

Heat oil in small saucepan over medium heat until shimmering. Add garlic, ginger, and pepper flakes; cook until fragrant, about 30 seconds. Whisk in hoisin and soy sauce until smooth. Remove pan from heat and stir in vinegar.

FUSION COOKING: TURNING TWO TENDERLOINS INTO ONE

To get around the usual problems with grilling pork tenderloin, we "fused" two together and cooked them as a single roast.

ROUGH UP Scrape the flat sides of each tenderloin with a fork until the surface is covered with shallow grooves. This releases sticky proteins that will act as "glue."

TIE TOGETHER Arrange the tenderloins with the scraped sides touching and the thick end of one nestled against the thin end of the other. Tie the tenderloins together.

The Best New England Lobster Roll

The sandwich is easy. The challenges are dealing with a live lobster and knowing when it's properly cooked.

⇒ BY ANDREA GEARY ⇐

Visitors to New England initially regard our beloved lobster roll with skepticism, and that's understandable. After all, we're talking about coating pricey lobster meat with mayonnaise, piling it into a supermarket hot dog bun, and serving it with pickles and potato chips. The usual venue for this meal—a weathered picnic table outside a roadside seafood stand—does little to dispel visitors' incredulity. It seems like a strangely cavalier treatment of a luxury foodstuff.

Such doubts vanish with the first bite. The simple mayo complements the richly flavored lobster without obscuring it, and the squishy bun molds like a custom-made cradle around the tender chunks of meat. The grilled sides of the top-loading bun provide a crisp, buttery frame for the cool salad within.

Because great seafood places are ubiquitous in these parts, New Englanders rarely make lobster rolls at home. But what if you live hundreds of miles from the Maine shore? Or what if it's January and all the lobster shacks are shut? Is it possible to re-create the New England lobster roll in your own kitchen? Sure. But first you have to figure out a safe and foolproof way to cook a live and kicking lobster.

Hard Boiled

Lobsters are cooked alive for two reasons: First, the instant a lobster dies, enzymes within its body begin to break down the flesh and cause it to turn mushy. Second, like other shellfish, deceased lobsters are vulnerable to bacterial contamination that can cause food poisoning. These days, many supermarkets cook live lobsters to order, but I wanted to control every part of my lobster roll, so I was determined to do the deed myself.

First decision: Would I be roasting, steaming, or boiling? Roasted lobster can be difficult to prepare because the slow heat of the oven causes proteins in the meat to adhere to the shell. I tried briefly boiling the lobster (which provides rapid heat transfer) to pull the meat away from the shell before roasting, but I found the two-step process awkward and with no apparent flavor or texture benefits. Steaming required a steamer or a rack, and it left the lobsters slightly underseasoned.

We pile lobster meat into the classic choice for this sandwich—a top-loading New England–style bun—instead of a regular side-loading hot dog bun.

Boiling in salt water was the way to go, but there was a problem: Every time I tried to maneuver a lobster into the pot, it spread its claws wide and thrashed its muscular tail in protest, often sending a wave of boiling water across the stovetop. Surely there was an easier way—at least for the cook.

The Big Chill

Many cooks advocate anesthetizing lobsters before cooking them. Some believe it is more humane, while others argue that gently handled lobsters are tastier and more tender. Mostly I hoped it would make the little guys more manageable. I tested several methods of desensitizing lobsters, and I tasted each supposedly desensitized lobster against one that was summarily tossed into the boiling water. The first few methods ranged from grisly to quirky, and—since they didn't sedate the lobster, didn't produce better flavor or texture, were too labor intensive, or all of the above—I quickly moved on (see "The Best Way to Get a Live Lobster into the Pot").

In Harold McGee's *On Food and Cooking*, I discovered the most successful technique for sedating a lobster yet: immersing the lobster in an ice bath for 30 minutes before cooking. The chilled lobster seemed comatose as I transferred it from ice bath to pot, and its meat was properly cooked. However, chilling a single lobster in this manner required a 6-quart container and 2 quarts of ice, and chilling additional lobsters would have required more space and more ice, making it impractical for preparing multiple lobsters simultaneously.

Wondering if a simpler method might work, I placed four wriggling lobsters in a large bowl, which I then placed in the freezer while I brought a stockpot of salted water to a boil. After 30 minutes, I nudged them gently: nary a twitch. When I transferred the chilled lobsters to the pot, they were limp and unresponsive, and they sank to the bottom with just a few reassuring flutters that indicated that they were still alive. I had found the safest, easiest way to get the lobsters into the pot. Now to make the cooking method foolproof.

Taking Temp

Most lobster recipes are accompanied by intimidating charts that tell you how long to boil based on your lobster's weight, whether it has a hard or soft shell, and how many are being cooked in the same pot. But what if your lobsters are different sizes? What if you're unsure about the comparative firmness of their shells? Why can't we simply take the temperature of a lobster the same way we do with other kinds of meat?

I discovered that we can do just that—but the target temperature turned out to be much higher than I expected. I usually cook fish to an internal temperature of 130 to 140 degrees, but when I pulled a lobster out at 135 (determined by a digital thermometer poked into the underside of the meaty tail), the meat was undercooked, translucent, and floppy. At 160 degrees it was still too soft. Eventually I landed at a tail temperature of 175 (after about 12 minutes of cooking), which guaranteed tender claws and knuckles and a pleasantly resilient tail.

Why the higher temperature? Because lobsters aren't just fish with snazzy red armor. Fish muscle is composed of very short muscle fibers that require only mild heat to shrink them so that they firm up and turn from translucent to opaque. The muscle fibers in lobsters are much longer, especially in the tail section, so they require a higher temperature to attain that desirably firm, snappy texture. Now I was ready to build my roll.

On a Roll

Want to watch a Yankee's cool, unemotional facade crumble? Lure him into a conversation about what constitutes the perfect lobster roll. A discussion of seemingly innocuous subjects, like the size of the lobster pieces and the inclusion of things like lettuce, herbs, and onions, quickly escalates into an impassioned debate. Luckily, I'm not afraid of a little controversy: My roll, my rules.

Traditionalists like to leave the lobster meat in generous hunks, and the effect is one of impressive opulence, but it's darn hard to eat. Chunks are fine for the claws and knuckles because they're tender and, being smaller, well seasoned by the salted cooking water. But the tail is so meaty and dense that large pieces can seem undersalted and tough. So I bucked tradition and cut the tail into smaller pieces, making it easier to eat and giving it more surface area for the seasoned dressing to cling to.

As for the contentious vegetable additions, I opted for a single soft lettuce leaf to line each roll

---

The Best Way to Get a Live Lobster into the Pot

To ensure food safety and firmer flesh, lobsters should be cooked alive. The most common method is to plunge them into boiling water, where they will continue to move about for approximately 2 minutes. Though there's no way to know the extent to which the lobster suffers during this time, most scientists agree that the lobster's primitive nervous system, more like that of an insect than a human, prevents it from processing pain the way we do. Still, most cooks find putting live lobsters into a pot unpleasant. If I could figure out how to sedate the lobster before cooking—and minimize the time it spent moving in the pot—these could be only positive developments.

First I tried the popular restaurant technique of slicing through the lobster's head. However, Win Watson of the University of New Hampshire's Department of Biological Sciences informed me that because a lobster's nervous system is distributed throughout its body, this method will not instantly kill the crustacean. Sure enough, lobsters dispatched this way continued to thrash vigorously before I put them in the pot—and I continued to see movement for another 2 minutes once they were in the water.

Next I "hypnotized" a lobster by rubbing its shell and standing it on its head, where it remained stock-still for a full hour. Unfortunately, it perked right up once in the pot. Then I tried soaking a lobster in a cold saltwater bath scented with clove oil, a technique recommended by the food science website cookingissues.com. This made the lobster's movements more languid—but those movements still continued for about 2 minutes. In the end, the simplest approach worked best: a 30-minute stay in the freezer, which rendered the lobster motionless before it went into the pot. After a few flutters, all motion stopped. –A.G.

---

and a couple of tablespoons of minced celery for unobtrusive crunch. Chopped onions and even milder shallots were nixed as too overwhelming, but a mere teaspoon of chives gave my salad a hint of bright herb flavor. A splash of lemon juice and a tiny pinch of cayenne pepper made a perfect counterpoint to the richly flavored meat and the buttery bun.

This was a New England lobster roll that would convince any skeptic. And now that I had a safe and foolproof way to cook lobster, I could enjoy it anytime.

BOILED LOBSTER
SERVES 4 OR YIELDS 1 POUND MEAT

To cook four lobsters at once, you will need a pot with a capacity of at least 3 gallons. If your pot is smaller, boil the lobsters in batches. Start timing the lobsters from the moment they go into the pot. See page 31 for how to extract lobster meat from the shell.

- 4 (1¼-pound) live lobsters
- ⅓ cup salt

1. Place lobsters in large bowl and freeze for 30 minutes. Meanwhile, bring 2 gallons water to boil in large pot over high heat.

2. Add lobsters and salt to pot, arranging with tongs so that all lobsters are submerged. Cover pot, leaving lid slightly ajar, and adjust heat to maintain gentle boil. Cook for 12 minutes, until thickest part of tail registers 175 degrees (insert thermometer into underside of tail to take temperature). If temperature registers lower than 175 degrees, return lobster to pot for 2 minutes longer, until tail registers 175 degrees, using tongs to transfer lobster in and out of pot.

3. Serve immediately or transfer lobsters to rimmed baking sheet and set aside until cool enough to remove meat, about 10 minutes. (Lobster meat can be refrigerated in airtight container for up to 24 hours.)

NEW ENGLAND LOBSTER ROLL
SERVES 6

This recipe is best when made with lobster you've cooked yourself. Use a very small pinch of cayenne pepper, as it should not make the dressing spicy. We prefer New England–style top-loading hot dog buns, as they provide maximum surface on the sides for toasting. If using other buns, butter, salt, and toast the interior of each bun instead of the exterior.

- 2 tablespoons mayonnaise
- 2 tablespoons minced celery
- 1½ teaspoons lemon juice
- 1 teaspoon minced fresh chives
  Salt
  Pinch cayenne pepper
- 1 pound lobster meat, tail meat cut into ½-inch pieces and claw meat cut into 1-inch pieces
- 6 New England–style hot dog buns
- 2 tablespoons unsalted butter, softened
- 6 leaves Boston lettuce

1. Whisk mayonnaise, celery, lemon juice, chives, ⅛ teaspoon salt, and cayenne together in large bowl. Add lobster and gently toss to combine.

2. Place 12-inch nonstick skillet over low heat. Butter both sides of hot dog buns and sprinkle lightly with salt. Place buns in skillet, with 1 buttered side down; increase heat to medium-low; and cook until crisp and brown, 2 to 3 minutes. Flip and cook second side until crisp and brown, 2 to 3 minutes longer. Transfer buns to large platter. Line each bun with lettuce leaf. Spoon lobster salad into buns and serve immediately.

Perfect Fried Eggs

A classic fried egg features a tender white with crisp, lacy, brown edges and a fluid but lightly thickened yolk. Could we crack the code to making a perfect one?

= BY ANDREW JANJIGIAN =

To me, a fried egg should be *fried*. I'm talking about the sort you find at the best diners: sunny-side up and crisp on its underside and edges, with a tender and opaque white and a perfectly runny yolk.

Ideally, I'd whip up this diner-style breakfast in my own kitchen, but the fried egg recipes I'd tried (and I'd run through my fair share) had failed to produce the results I wanted. Perhaps seasoned short-order cooks can consistently turn out great fried eggs because of their years of sheer practice. Or maybe a hot, slick commercial griddle is the key. All I knew for sure was that my home-cooked sunny-side up eggs always had one of two possible defects. The first was undercooked whites—specifically, a slippery, transparent ring of white surrounding the yolk. The second was an overcooked yolk—often it was fluid on top but cooked solid on the underside.

These faults are due to a predicament that plagues most types of egg cookery: Yolks and whites set at different temperatures. This means that yolks, which start to solidify at around 158 degrees, are inevitably over-cooked by the time the whites, which set up at 180 degrees, are opaque. My objective, then, was to get the whites to cook through before the yolks did. I also wanted whites with beautifully bronzed, crispy edges. I had my work cut out for me.

Getting Fried

There are two basic approaches for tackling an egg's disparate doneness temperatures: Cook low and slow or hot and fast. The former calls for breaking

For runny yolks, remove the eggs from the pan when the whites around the edge of the yolk are barely opaque.

the egg into a warm, greased nonstick skillet and letting it gradually come to temperature over low heat, which can take 5 or more minutes. If the flame is low enough, the heat will firm up the white before the yolk sets. The downside: This technique doesn't add browning or crispiness. Raising the heat toward the end of cooking only overcooks the entire egg.

The opposite method blasts the egg with fierce heat from the start in an attempt to cook the white so quickly that it is out of the pan before the yolk even considers setting up. The best example that I've tried comes from Spanish chef José Andrés, who calls for shallow-frying an egg in a tilted skillet containing an inch or so of very hot olive oil. Within seconds, the bottom of the white bubbles and browns, and as you continuously baste the egg with hot oil, the top of the white cooks through as well. The whole process happens so quickly (just 30 seconds or so) that the yolk can't possibly overcook, and the result—a filigree of browned, crispy egg surrounding a tender white and a runny yolk—is just what I wanted.

And yet, there were drawbacks. The flavor of the egg wasn't quite what I had in mind. Olive oil gave it a great savory taste, but it lacked the buttery richness of a diner-style egg. What's more, the sputtering oil made a mess of my stovetop and threatened to burn my forearms. The method also required cooking only one egg at a time. Sure, they cooked quickly, but I wanted to produce two or four eggs at one time. Could I use high heat and far less oil and be able to feed two people breakfast in one go?

Hatching a Plan

I reviewed what I had learned: First, it was difficult to get the eggs to cook evenly when I broke them one by one into the pan. Breaking the eggs into small bowls ahead of time so that all I had to do was slide them into the pan saved time—and went a long way in a recipe in which mere seconds make a difference. Plus, it worked equally well with two or four

Flawless Fried Eggs: It's All in the Details

PREHEAT THE PAN
Preheating your pan on low heat for 5 full minutes guarantees that there will be no hot spots in the skillet that could lead to unevenly cooked eggs.

USE TWO FATS
We use vegetable oil, with its high smoke point, while preheating the pan. Butter, added just before the eggs, imparts a diner-style richness.

ADD EGGS ALL AT ONCE Cracking the eggs into small bowls makes it possible to add them to the skillet simultaneously so they cook at the same rate.

COVER IT UP
Adding a lid to the skillet traps heat and steam so the egg cooks from above as well as below, firming up the white before the yolk overcooks.

FINISH OFF HEAT
Moving the pan off the heat after 1 minute of cooking allows the whites to finish cooking—gently—while keeping the yolks liquid.

PHOTOGRAPHY: CARL TREMBLAY; ILLUSTRATION: JAY LAYMAN

TASTING Gluten-Free Sandwich Bread

When you're avoiding gluten, it's tough to give up toast and sandwiches. Hoping to find a loaf that was a serviceable alternative to (not a sacrifice compared with) regular sandwich bread, we tasted eight national brands of gluten-free white sandwich bread both plain and toasted with butter.

Almost all of the breads tasted terrible straight out of the packaging. Toasting and buttering turned a few inedible samples palatable, but most were still far inferior to regular bread. The exception: a loaf from Udi's, whose "light wheatiness" and "yielding" chew were impressively close to that of ordinary white sandwich bread, even without toasting. So what was this manufacturer doing differently?

For one thing, Udi's contains far more protein than other breads—as much as 72 percent more. In regular bread made from grain flour, protein builds structure in dough by forming a network—gluten—that traps air during baking, allowing the loaf to expand and achieve a springy crumb and satisfying chew. Udi's, however, gets its protein from egg whites, which also build structure by trapping air in the baking bread. For more lift, Udi's also adds chemical leaveners, as well as yeast, and a goodly amount of salt, which boosts flavor.

We also looked into why gluten-free breads are often sold from the freezer case. It turns out that most products are high in moisture (as much as 55 percent compared with roughly 36 percent for regular sandwich bread) and starch—qualities that make them stale easily in a process known as retrogradation. The more water and starch in bread, the more susceptible its starch molecules are to moving around and crystallizing (trapping water inside the crystals), which renders the crumb dry. Freezing halts the staling process, since frozen starch molecules can't move around. (The lone product that wasn't frozen came vacuum-sealed with a sell-by date six months away.) What's more, gluten-free bread turnover in stores is slow, so freezing makes sense.

Bottom line: If you're looking for a gluten-free option, Udi's has clean, yeasty flavor and decent chew, making it the best—and only worthwhile—alternative to regular sandwich bread. For complete tasting results, go to CooksIllustrated.com/aug13. –Lisa McManus

BREADWINNER
UDI'S Gluten Free White Sandwich Bread
Price: $5 for 12-oz loaf
Comments: Thanks to its high protein and salt levels, our favorite gluten-free bread "looked good," "smelled nice," and boasted an "airy texture." Toasted, it was "crunchy yet yielding"—"close to 'real' bread," according to some tasters.

THINGS FALL APART
FOOD FOR LIFE Gluten Free White Rice Bread
Price: $6.79 for 24-oz loaf
Comments: A measly amount of protein left this second-to-last-place bread with "no structure at all." Its flavor also seemed "super-stale" and was marred by a "horrible aftertaste."

ON THE BORDER
CANYON BAKEHOUSE Mountain White Gluten Free Bread
Price: $5 for 18-oz loaf
Comments: This second-place bread tasted "boring but not actually bad." But its texture was "rubbery"—like "chewing gum."

DON'T BOTHER
ENER-G Gluten Free Tapioca Loaf, Regular Sliced
Price: $5.79 for 16-oz loaf
Comments: Tasters forced down bites of this losing loaf, which was "flat" and "dense," like a "coaster," and regretted its "scratchy" texture.

---

aluminum bowl on top of griddle-fried eggs to speed cooking. How about a lid? The reflected heat and steam trapped by a lid might just work.

For my next test, I covered the pan as soon as the eggs were in place. Ninety seconds later, I lifted the lid for a peek, fingers crossed, before using a spatula to quickly remove my specimens. The good news was that the vexing ring of jiggly, uncooked white around the yolk was gone, and the white was perfectly tender, with a nicely browned underside and edges. The bad news was that the lid had trapped too much heat: The yolk was now a bit overcooked.

Instead, I slid the covered skillet off the burner entirely, hoping the gentle residual heat of the pan would firm up the white but not the yolk. It took a few dozen more eggs to get the timing just right but—stopwatch in hand—I finally nailed down the proper intervals: One minute over medium-high heat followed by an additional 15 to 45 seconds off heat produced beautifully bronzed edges; just-set, opaque whites; and fluid yolks every time.

Mission accomplished: perfect diner-style fried eggs—no diner necessary.

PERFECT FRIED EGGS
SERVES 2

When checking the eggs for doneness, lift the lid just a crack to prevent loss of steam should they need further cooking. When cooked, the thin layer of white surrounding the yolk will turn opaque, but the yolk should remain runny. To cook two eggs, use an 8- or 9-inch nonstick skillet and halve the amounts of oil and butter. You can use this method with extra-large or jumbo eggs without altering the timing.

- 2 teaspoons vegetable oil
- 4 large eggs
  Salt and pepper
- 2 teaspoons unsalted butter, cut into 4 pieces and chilled

1. Heat oil in 12- or 14-inch nonstick skillet over low heat for 5 minutes. Meanwhile, crack 2 eggs into small bowl and season with salt and pepper. Repeat with remaining 2 eggs and second small bowl.

2. Increase heat to medium-high and heat until oil is shimmering. Add butter to skillet and quickly swirl to coat pan. Working quickly, pour 1 bowl of eggs in 1 side of pan and second bowl of eggs in other side. Cover and cook for 1 minute. Remove skillet from burner and let stand, covered, 15 to 45 seconds for runny yolks (white around edge of yolk will be barely opaque), 45 to 60 seconds for soft but set yolks, and about 2 minutes for medium-set yolks. Slide eggs onto plates and serve.

---

eggs. Second, it was important to let the pan fully preheat low and slow. A quick blast of high heat can cause hot spots to form and, thus, the eggs to cook at different rates. I got the best results by adding a teaspoon of vegetable oil to the skillet and setting it over low heat for a full 5 minutes. You also need a pan roomy enough for the eggs to spread out but not so much that large areas of the pan remain empty, which could cause the fat to burn. A 12- or 14-inch pan works best for four eggs, an 8- or 9-inch pan for two. Finally, adding a couple of pats of butter to the pan right before slipping in the eggs resulted in great flavor and browning due to the butter's milk proteins.

Going forward, I fried a few rounds of eggs on medium-high heat after preheating the skillet on low. The butter and oil sizzled nicely and the eggs started to brown almost immediately. But (perhaps predictably) things digressed from there, with the whites undercooking or the yolks overcooking, depending on when I reached for my spatula. Lowering the heat once the whites were browned at the edges did let them solidify before the yolks set up, but that process took so long that the whites, in effect, oversolidified, turning tough and rubbery.

For a moment I was stumped—until I thought back to the key to Andrés's shallow-fried eggs: basting. Basting the eggs with hot fat helped quickly cook the top and bottom of the white before the yolk could set up. I wasn't up for basting due to its accompanying splatter, but how else could I rapidly generate heat from above? I pictured myself in a diner, watching a line cook perch an overturned

Tunisian-Style Grilled Vegetables

The North African flavors lured us in; we just had to perfect the grilling method.

⇒ BY CELESTE ROGERS ⇐

Grilling brings out the best in summer vegetables, calling forth their sweetness and adding an accent of smoke. But by midsummer, I'm ready for something different from the same old tender-firm produce simply dressed with oil and vinegar. I knew that the Mediterranean region—particularly North Africa—has a rich tradition of grilling vegetables. Maybe I could learn from it. The particular recipe that caught my eye was *mechouia*, a Tunisian dish in which whole bell peppers or chiles, tomatoes, and sometimes onions or shallots are either buried in live embers or grilled until their skins blacken. After the carbonized exterior is peeled away, the soft, smoky flesh (the vegetables are cooked beyond a tender-firm state) is chopped or pounded into a coarse puree and mixed with a blend of warm spices called *tabil*, plus garlic, lemon juice, and olive oil. The dish can be served as a salad with pita bread, as a side dish to grilled meat, or even as a light lunch accompanied by canned tuna and hard-cooked eggs.

Lured by the promise of new flavors and textures, I oiled two bell peppers, eight plum tomatoes, and two shallots and grilled them over a medium-hot fire until they were entirely soft. When the vegetables were cool, I peeled them and mashed them with a fork and then drizzled on a garlic-lemon vinaigrette laced with tabil. (Recipes vary: My version included coriander, caraway, and cumin seeds; paprika; and cayenne.) The vegetables were wonderfully supple, with a smokier taste than that of most grilled vegetables, thanks to spending a longer time over the coals. The downsides were a somewhat soupy consistency and flavors that were a little too raw and pungent.

I'd deal with flavor issues later. To address consistency, for my next batch I chopped the vegetables into ½-inch pieces instead of mashing them, an approach preferred by some recipes I'd found. But the resulting salad was still watery. Thinking that my juicy, height-of-summer tomatoes were the culprit, I replaced half of them with sturdier eggplant and zucchini. (Since I wasn't intending to remove the zucchini's skin, I grilled it only until browned.)

Surprisingly, the mixture was still waterlogged. That's when I realized that grilling the vegetables whole trapped all of their moisture, which then flooded the salad. I would have to cut the vegetables before putting them over the coals, so they would release moisture during cooking and not after. I halved the zucchini and eggplant and cut deep cross-hatch marks in their flesh. I also halved the tomatoes and opened the peppers into long planks. It was a winning move: My salad was no longer soupy, and the whole operation took only about 15 minutes.

There was yet another benefit: I could now season the vegetable flesh before grilling. In addition to sprinkling the vegetables with salt, I also brushed on tabil-spiced oil. The spices bloomed on the grill and lost any trace of raw, dusty flavor. And to tame the harsh taste of the garlic, I sizzled it in some of the spiced oil before combining it with lemon juice to make the vinaigrette. The only thing missing was freshness. Lemon zest plus a trio of fresh herbs brought a tangy, lively taste. I now had grilled vegetables that enticed me as both cook and diner.

Most of the vegetables in this salad are peeled, giving them an ultravelvety texture once cooked.

TUNISIAN-STYLE GRILLED VEGETABLES (MECHOUIA)
SERVES 4 TO 6

Serve as a side dish to grilled meats and fish; with grilled pita as a salad course; or with hard-cooked eggs, olives, and premium canned tuna as a light lunch. Equal amounts of ground coriander and cumin can be substituted for the whole spices.

Vinaigrette
- 2 teaspoons coriander seeds
- 1½ teaspoons caraway seeds
- 1 teaspoon cumin seeds
- 5 tablespoons olive oil
- ½ teaspoon sweet paprika
- ⅛ teaspoon cayenne pepper
- 3 garlic cloves, minced
- ¼ cup chopped fresh parsley
- ¼ cup chopped fresh cilantro
- 2 tablespoons chopped fresh mint
- 1 teaspoon grated lemon zest plus 2 tablespoons juice
- Salt

Vegetables
- 2 bell peppers (1 red and 1 green)
- 1 small eggplant, halved lengthwise
- 1 zucchini (8 to 10 ounces), halved lengthwise
- 4 plum tomatoes, cored and halved lengthwise
- Salt and pepper
- 2 medium shallots, unpeeled

1. FOR THE VINAIGRETTE: Grind coriander seeds, caraway seeds, and cumin seeds in spice grinder until finely ground. Whisk ground spices, oil, paprika, and cayenne together in bowl. Reserve 3 tablespoons oil mixture. Heat remaining oil mixture and garlic in small skillet over low heat, stirring occasionally, until fragrant and small bubbles appear, 8 to 10 minutes. Transfer to large bowl and let cool, about 10 minutes. Whisk parsley, cilantro, mint, and lemon zest and juice into oil mixture; season with salt to taste.

2. FOR THE VEGETABLES: Slice ¼ inch off tops and bottoms of bell peppers and remove cores. Make slit down 1 side of each bell pepper and then press flat into 1 long strip, removing ribs and remaining seeds with knife as needed. Using sharp knife, cut slits in flesh of eggplant and zucchini, spaced ½ inch apart, in crosshatch pattern, being careful to cut down to but not through skin. Brush cut sides of bell peppers, eggplant, zucchini, and tomatoes with reserved oil mixture and season with salt to taste.

3. Grill vegetables, starting with cut sides down, over medium-hot fire, until tender and well browned and skins of bell peppers, eggplant, tomatoes, and shallots are charred, 8 to 16 minutes, turning and moving vegetables as necessary. Transfer vegetables to baking sheet as they are done. Place bell peppers in bowl, cover with plastic wrap, and let steam to loosen skins.

4. When cool enough to handle, peel bell peppers, eggplant, tomatoes, and shallots. Chop all vegetables into ½-inch pieces and transfer to bowl with vinaigrette; toss to coat. Season with salt and pepper to taste, and serve warm or at room temperature.

The Original Pasta with Pesto

This classic dish comes from the Liguria region of Italy, where pasta and pesto are paired with a surprising ingredient: potatoes.

> BY ANDREA GEARY

I'm oblivious when it comes to trends, but even I know that carbohydrates are out of fashion. That's why the notion of putting pasta and potatoes in the same dish initially struck me as just plain wrong. But I was intrigued to learn that the preferred way to serve pesto in Liguria, Italy—the birthplace of the basil sauce—involved just that combination. Wondering what the Italians knew that I didn't, I found a handful of recipes and gave them a whirl.

The Ligurian cook has two pasta options for this dish: trenette, a fettuccine-like strand, or trofie, a shorter, thicker twist. Neither was available at my supermarket, so I chose short, thick double helix–shaped gemelli. I ground one batch of basil leaves, garlic, and toasted pine nuts with a mortar and pestle as tradition dictated and buzzed another in a food processor before stirring in olive oil and grated Parmesan cheese. I then cooked batches of pasta, potatoes (peeled and cut into a variety of shapes), and green beans (cut into bite-size lengths) together in single pots of boiling salted water, staggering the addition of ingredients and hoping they would all finish cooking simultaneously. Finally, I tossed each dish's ingredients with pesto and some cooking water.

Some variations were dull and heavy, but I was surprised that many boasted a creamy lightness. Why? It all came down to how the potatoes were treated. The most successful recipes called for cutting the potatoes into chunks and then, once cooked, vigorously mixing them with the pesto, pasta, and green beans. The agitation sloughed off their corners, which dissolved into the dish, pulling the pesto and cooking water together to form a simple sauce.

But the recipe still needed work. The sauce was slightly grainy and the sharp, raw garlic dominated. Timing was another issue: The green beans could be jarringly crisp and the pasta way too soft—or vice versa. And that mortar and pestle? No thanks. I'd opt for the convenience of the food processor.

I knew that the potatoes were the key to the sauce, and I wondered if my choice of russets was the reason for the slightly rough texture. Sure enough, when I subbed waxy red potatoes for russets, the

Perfectly cooked potatoes keep the sauce creamy.

graininess disappeared. Why? Waxy red potatoes contain about 25 percent less starch than russet potatoes do. When waxy potatoes are boiled, they absorb less water and their cells swell less and do not separate and burst as those in russet potatoes do. As a result, waxy potatoes produce a smooth, creamy texture, while russets can be mealy and grainy.

Now to address the timing problem. The traditional method of staggering the addition of the ingredients to the pot doesn't allow for much variation in the size or quality of each, making it difficult to cook each element perfectly. But cooking each ingredient sequentially took too long, and boiling them simultaneously in separate pots dirtied too many dishes. By recycling my pine nut–toasting skillet to steam the beans and by fully cooking the potatoes in the water before the pasta went in, I was able to cook everything separately using only two pots. While the pasta bubbled, I made the pesto.

To mellow the garlic cloves, I toasted them skin on with the pine nuts before making the pesto. I drained the pasta and then returned everything to the pot, along with the pesto and 1¼ cups of cooking water. That sounds like a lot of cooking water (we usually call for about ⅓ cup), but the potato starch needs more water in which to disperse.

Finally, I stirred with a rubber spatula until the magic sauce formed. Two tablespoons of butter made it even silkier, and a splash of lemon juice brought all the flavors into focus. This simple classic taught me what the Ligurians have known all along: Fashion has its place, and the dinner plate isn't it.

PASTA WITH PESTO, POTATOES, AND GREEN BEANS
SERVES 6

If gemelli is unavailable, penne or rigatoni make good substitutes. Use large red potatoes measuring 3 inches or more in diameter.

- ¼ cup pine nuts
- 3 garlic cloves, unpeeled
- 1 pound large red potatoes, peeled and cut into ½-inch pieces
-   Salt and pepper
- 12 ounces green beans, trimmed and cut into 1½-inch lengths
- 2 cups fresh basil leaves
- 1 ounce Parmesan cheese, grated (½ cup)
- 7 tablespoons extra-virgin olive oil
- 1 pound gemelli
- 2 tablespoons unsalted butter, cut into ½-inch pieces and chilled
- 1 tablespoon lemon juice

1. Toast pine nuts and garlic in 10-inch skillet over medium heat, stirring frequently, until pine nuts are golden and fragrant and garlic darkens slightly, 3 to 5 minutes. Transfer to bowl and let cool. Peel garlic and chop coarsely.

2. Bring 3 quarts water to boil in large pot. Add potatoes and 1 tablespoon salt and cook until potatoes are tender but still hold their shape, 9 to 12 minutes. Using slotted spoon, transfer potatoes to rimmed baking sheet. (Do not discard water.)

3. Meanwhile, bring ½ cup water and ¼ teaspoon salt to boil in now-empty skillet over medium heat. Add green beans, cover, and cook until tender, 5 to 8 minutes. Drain green beans and transfer to sheet with potatoes.

4. Process basil, Parmesan, oil, pine nuts, garlic, and ½ teaspoon salt in food processor until smooth, about 1 minute.

5. Add gemelli to water in large pot and cook, stirring often, until al dente. Set colander in large bowl. Drain gemelli in colander, reserving cooking water in bowl. Return gemelli to pot. Add butter, lemon juice, potatoes and green beans, pesto, 1¼ cups reserved cooking water, and ½ teaspoon pepper and stir vigorously with rubber spatula until sauce takes on creamy appearance. Add additional cooking water as needed to adjust consistency and season with salt and pepper to taste. Serve immediately.

Check Out the Timing

Video available FREE for 4 months at CooksIllustrated.com/aug13

Everyday Stir-Frying

The beauty of stir-frying is that you can do it quickly with just about anything in your fridge—but it's not a free-for-all. Here's how to do it well. BY ELIZABETH BOMZE

CHOOSE YOUR INGREDIENTS

The best stir-fries feature a variety of textures and colors, which is largely determined by the vegetable choices. We recommend limiting yourself to two or three different types of produce; otherwise, the medley can become cluttered. Amounts mentioned yield four servings.

Protein

Use ¾ to 1 pound of one of the following tender cuts (best for stir-frying because they soften quickly). See page 30 for how to stir-fry tofu.

BEEF: Flank steaks, sirloin tip steaks, blade steaks
➤**Prep:** Cut the meat against the grain and on the bias into ¼-inch-thick slices.

CHICKEN: Boneless, skinless breasts
➤**Prep:** Remove the tenderloins if attached. Cut each breast across the grain into ¼-inch-thick slices.

PORK: Tenderloin
➤**Prep:** Cut crosswise into ¼-inch-thick slices and then cut each slice into ¼-inch-thick strips.

SHRIMP: Extra-large (21 to 25 shrimp per pound)
➤**Prep:** Thaw (if frozen), peel, devein, and remove the tails.

Vegetables

Mix and match your vegetables using a total of 1 to 1½ pounds.

LONG COOKING 3 to 7 minutes	MEDIUM COOKING 1 to 3 minutes	FAST COOKING 30 to 60 seconds
Broccoli	Asparagus	Bean sprouts
Carrots	Bell pepper	Bok choy greens
Cauliflower	Bok choy stalks	Celery
Green beans	Eggplant	Frozen peas
Green or red cabbage	Frozen shelled edamame	Napa cabbage
Snap peas	Mushrooms	Scallion greens
	Onions	Tender greens
	Scallion whites	Tomatoes
	Snow peas	Water chestnuts

Sauce

Prefab stir-fry sauces are usually too sweet or too salty, and making your own takes just minutes. For each recipe, whisk the ingredients in a medium bowl.

CLASSIC
Combine ½ cup chicken broth, ¼ cup dry sherry, 3 tablespoons hoisin sauce or oyster sauce, 1 tablespoon soy sauce, 2 teaspoons cornstarch, and 1 teaspoon toasted sesame oil.

COCONUT–RED CURRY
Combine 1 cup coconut milk, 1 tablespoon fish sauce, 2 teaspoons Thai red curry paste, 1 teaspoon packed brown sugar, and 1 teaspoon cornstarch.

SWEET-AND-SOUR
Combine 6 tablespoons red wine vinegar, 6 tablespoons orange juice, 6 tablespoons sugar, 3 tablespoons ketchup, 1 teaspoon cornstarch, and ½ teaspoon salt.

Chill Meat Before Slicing

Briefly freezing meat before cutting firms it up so that it is easier to slice. Freeze chicken breasts and steaks for 20 to 30 minutes, pork tenderloin for 30 to 45 minutes.

Cut Broccoli Down to Size

Trim the florets from the stalks and cut into ¾-inch pieces. Then trim and peel the stalks and cut them on a 45-degree bias into ¼-inch-thick slices. For techniques on cutting other vegetables, go to CooksIllustrated.com/aug13.

Try Our Favorite Combos

➤Beef, eggplant, and scallion greens with coconut–red curry sauce
➤Chicken, green beans, and shiitake mushrooms with classic stir-fry sauce
➤Shrimp, snow peas, and red bell pepper with sweet-and-sour sauce

PRETREAT YOUR PROTEIN

Don't skip these quick soaking steps. They help the meat cook up flavorful and tender.

BEFORE MARINATING, PROTECT CHICKEN AND PORK WITH BAKING SODA

Soaking lean meat slices in a baking soda solution before marinating softens them and helps them stay juicy during cooking. Don't soak meat longer than 15 minutes or it will break down too much. Be sure to rinse off the solution before marinating.
➤Soak meat for 15 minutes in 1 teaspoon baking soda dissolved in 2 tablespoons water.

MARINATE CHICKEN, PORK, AND BEEF IN A SALTY LIQUID

Salty liquids like soy sauce or fish sauce not only boost meat's savory flavor but also act as a brine, helping the meat retain moisture during cooking. Drain the meat well before cooking; removing excess moisture will ensure good browning.
➤Soak meat in 2 tablespoons soy or fish sauce for 15 minutes.

SOAK SHRIMP IN OIL

Salty marinades overwhelm the delicate flavor of shrimp, so we came up with a subtler soak: a mixture of vegetable oil, minced garlic, and salt. The salt seasons the shrimp and helps it retain moisture and draws out flavor from the garlic. Oil distributes those flavors evenly over the flesh.
➤Soak shrimp in 3 tablespoons oil, 6 cloves minced garlic, and ½ teaspoon salt for 30 minutes.

FOLLOW THIS SEQUENCE

It's easy to fail at stir-frying because the cooking happens so quickly. Being prepared—we even line up ingredients in the order in which they go into the pan—and sticking to this order of operations will guarantee success.

1. HEAT OIL

Measure 1½ teaspoons oil into 12-inch nonstick skillet set over high heat and heat until just smoking. Repeat every time you add food to pan.

➤ Peanut, vegetable, and canola oils are best for stir-frying because they're neutral and won't burn before the pan is hot enough for browning. However, any oil will burn if you don't start cooking as soon as it smokes. If the oil scorches, wipe out the pan and start over with fresh oil.

2. SEAR PROTEIN

Cook marinated protein in 2 batches, breaking up clumps, until browned. Transfer to bowl; cover to keep warm.

➤ Don't sear shrimp; their lean flesh overcooks quickly. Instead, add them to the pan after searing the vegetables and aromatics and stir-fry them over medium-low heat.

3. SEAR VEGETABLES

Cook vegetables sequentially according to chart, starting with longer-cooking items.

➤ Dry rinsed vegetables thoroughly to prevent them from steaming. To wick away trapped moisture, dry leafy vegetables in a salad spinner.

4. ADD AROMATICS

Clear center of pan and add 3 minced garlic cloves and 1 tablespoon grated ginger mixed with 1 teaspoon vegetable oil. Mash mixture until fragrant, 15 to 30 seconds, and stir into vegetables.

➤ Mixing aromatics with a little vegetable oil before adding them to the hot pan helps prevent them from burning.

5. COMBINE; ADD SAUCE

Return protein to pan. Whisk sauce to recombine, then add to skillet and toss constantly until liquid is thickened, about 30 seconds.

➤ If desired, garnish stir-fry with sliced scallions, toasted sesame seeds, chopped toasted nuts, or chopped cilantro; drizzle with toasted sesame and/or chile oil.

BREAK YOUR BAD HABITS

Some of the most common stir-fry practices are also the wrong ones.

DON'T

Use a Wok

The broad surface of a large (12-inch) nonstick skillet makes more contact with flat Western burners than a round-bottomed wok, making it a better choice for browning. Don't use a smaller pan.

DON'T

Crowd the Pan

Adding all the ingredients at once will cause the food to steam rather than sear. Cook in batches in even layers and leave space between pieces of meat so that they brown well.

DON'T

Add Aromatics Too Soon

Waiting to add ginger and garlic until after the protein and vegetables are cooked prevents them from scorching over the high heat.

DON'T

Stir Too Much

Nomenclature aside, it's best to stir your stir-fry infrequently. Western-style burners have a relatively low heat output, so stirring food infrequently during cooking allows for proper browning.

DON'T

Cook Fully When Searing

Remove meat and vegetables from the pan when they're just shy of being done. They will finish cooking when added back to the pan with the sauce.

A New Way with Kebabs

In the Middle East, kebabs called *kofte* feature ground meat, not chunks, mixed with lots of spices and fresh herbs. Our challenge: To get their sausagelike texture just right.

≥ BY ANDREW JANJIGIAN ≤

When I was growing up, my Armenian family had two basic meat-grilling modes for warm-weather events: skewered leg of lamb—shish kebab—or spiced ground lamb patties. Armenians call these *losh* kebabs, but they are known nearly everywhere else in the Middle East as *kofte*.

My family's version of kofte falls in line with some of the more common versions served in the Middle East, so when I set out to develop my own recipe, I used my father's as a baseline. He uses a mixture of hand-ground lamb, bread crumbs, grated onion, cumin, chiles, and whatever fresh herbs are available, kneading the ingredients together to disperse the fat and flavor and form an almost sausagelike springiness. His boldly spiced patties are quickly grilled over high heat on long metal skewers, making them tender and juicy on the inside and encased in a smoky, crunchy coating of char. To serve, he stuffs the kofte in pita and drizzles on a tangy yogurt-garlic sauce.

But it had always been my father who actually made this dish at our house, and when I began my testing I quickly learned that the problem with kofte is that it's finicky. Because the patties are small, the meat easily overcooks and becomes dry. And since kofte is kneaded by hand in order to get the meat proteins to cross-link and take on a resilient texture, I found that it's easy to make it too springy—or not springy enough. I rounded up a handful of existing kofte recipes using a range of binders, spices, and kneading times, but I found that most of the results turned out dry and crumbly or were simply tough. I wanted my kofte to be warm and flavorful, with a cooling sauce; tender yet intact; and easy to boot. And I wanted to achieve this without needing years of practice.

From the Ground (Meat) Up

Kofte is traditionally made by mincing meat—usually lamb—by hand with a cleaver. Unlike machine

Andrew Cooks the *Kofte*

Video available FREE for 4 months at CooksIllustrated.com/aug13

To mimic the concentrated heat of a traditional *kofte* grill, we pile charcoal into a disposable aluminum roasting pan and set it in the kettle.

grinding, which roughs up the meat fibers to the point that they can't easily hold on to moisture upon cooking, hand mincing is far gentler and leads to kofte that is juicy and tender. But hand mincing is a lot of work—and therefore, for me, a nonstarter. Even using the food processor to grind my own meat seemed like too much. I would stick with preground meat from the grocery store. And though I decided to go with lamb—its rich flavor pairs so well with earthy spices and smoky grill char—I wanted to develop a recipe that worked with ground beef, too.

After cobbling together a working recipe of ground lamb and grated onion, along with a little cumin, chile, and fresh parsley (knowing that I would return to deal with the spices later), I began trying to solve the moisture issue. In the test kitchen we usually turn to panades made from soaked bread or bread crumbs to keep ground meat patties moist when cooked through, since their starches help hold on to moisture released by the meat as it cooks. Many kofte recipes also use some form of binder, but when I tried bread crumbs, standard sandwich

bread, torn-up pita bread, and all-purpose flour, these add-ins introduced some other problems. While my tasters found that all helped retain a bit of moisture and kept the kofte together, when enough was used to prevent drying out on the grill, the starchy panades gave the kofte an unwelcome pastiness, and they muted the flavor of the lamb. But what other options did I have?

I thought about meatballs, and one recipe in particular: our Classic Spaghetti and Meatballs for a Crowd (November/December 2010). For this recipe, we used a panade along with powdered gelatin. Gelatin holds up to 10 times its weight in water, and the gel that forms when it hydrates is highly viscous (which is why sauces made from gelatin-rich reduced meat stocks are so silky smooth). And unlike starches, you need very tiny amounts of gelatin to see benefits, so it doesn't usually have negative effects on texture or flavor. Could gelatin work solo in my kofte? I tried adding a mere teaspoon per pound of lamb and then refrigerated the kofte to help the meat firm up and hold fast to the skewer, and I was pleased by the results: I now had nice, juicy kofte.

But I was still left with a problem. With the preground meat plus a solid 2 minutes of kneading, which was not only traditional but also necessary to help keep the kofte together on the grill, many of my finished products were so springy that they could practically bounce. I remembered a recipe I'd seen that had included bulgur. This coarse cracked wheat most likely wouldn't melt into the meat like bread crumbs but would instead keep the ground meat a bit separated and therefore less springy and more tender when cooked. I had high hopes. But when I tried bulgur, adding a couple of tablespoons to the mix, I found that it only made the kofte gritty. I tried it again in smaller quantities, but the unpleasant texture remained.

Going Nuts

The bulgur gave me an idea, though: What about incorporating something of a similar size but of a softer consistency? I'd seen a few kofte recipes containing ground pine nuts or pistachios, and I'd assumed that the nuts were used for flavor rather than texture. Coarsely ground nuts might be just the thing. So for my next test, I added

PHOTOGRAPHY: CARL TREMBLAY

a few tablespoons of ground pine nuts to the mixture. The results were even better than I'd hoped. The nuts helped prevent toughness in the kofte without adding their own texture. And best of all, thanks to the oil they contained, they gave the kofte a subtle but noticeable boost in richness.

Now all that remained was to sort out the flavorings and a sauce. Many kofte recipes contain *baharat*, a Middle Eastern spice blend that is a common seasoning for meat dishes. Recipes vary widely, but the common denominators are usually black pepper, cumin, coriander, and chile pepper. I came up with my own combination of these, with cumin as the dominant player and hot smoked paprika as the chile. To these I also added smaller amounts of ground cinnamon, nutmeg, and cloves. As for herbs, equal amounts of fresh parsley and mint did the trick. For the sauce, I borrowed an idea from a recipe I'd found in *Jerusalem*, the latest cookbook from British chefs Yotam Ottolenghi and Sami Tamimi: I added a small amount of tahini to the traditional mixture of crushed garlic, lemon juice, and yogurt usually served with kofte since this gave the sauce a depth to match that of the kofte itself.

With that, there was one last test to perform: Serve the kofte to my family. The result? My kofte was a big hit. Even my dad asked for the recipe.

Skip the Burger and Try This

These kebabs take only a little longer to throw together than burgers but boast far more complex flavors and textures. For sandwiches, serve in warm pita bread.

TANGY SAUCE
Ours features traditional garlicky yogurt, plus a little tahini for added complexity.

SPRINGY YET TENDER TEXTURE
Kneading the ground meat gives the *kofte* a sausagelike spring, while incorporating ground pine nuts ensures that it also stays tender.

WARM SPICES
Spices added to the meat, including hot smoked paprika, cumin, and cloves, contribute heat and depth.

FRESH HERBS
The bright, grassy flavors of two other mix-ins, parsley and mint, complement the kofte's richness.

GRILLED LAMB KOFTE
SERVES 4 TO 6

Serve with rice pilaf or make sandwiches with warm pita bread, sliced red onion, and chopped fresh mint.

Yogurt-Garlic Sauce
- 1 cup plain whole-milk yogurt
- 2 tablespoons lemon juice
- 2 tablespoons tahini
- 1 garlic clove, minced
- ½ teaspoon salt

Kofte
- ½ cup pine nuts
- 4 garlic cloves, peeled
- 1½ teaspoons hot smoked paprika
- 1 teaspoon salt
- 1 teaspoon ground cumin
- ½ teaspoon pepper
- ¼ teaspoon ground coriander
- ¼ teaspoon ground cloves
- ⅛ teaspoon ground nutmeg
- ⅛ teaspoon ground cinnamon
- 1½ pounds ground lamb
- ½ cup grated onion, drained
- ⅓ cup minced fresh parsley
- ⅓ cup minced fresh mint
- 1½ teaspoons unflavored gelatin
- 1 large disposable aluminum roasting pan (if using charcoal)

1. FOR THE YOGURT-GARLIC SAUCE: Whisk all ingredients together in bowl. Set aside.

2. FOR THE KOFTE: Process pine nuts, garlic, paprika, salt, cumin, pepper, coriander, cloves, nutmeg, and cinnamon in food processor until coarse paste forms, 30 to 45 seconds. Transfer mixture to large bowl. Add lamb, onion, parsley, mint, and gelatin; knead with your hands until thoroughly combined and mixture feels slightly sticky, about 2 minutes. Divide mixture into 8 equal portions. Shape each portion into 5-inch-long cylinder about 1 inch in diameter. Using 8 (12-inch) metal skewers, thread 1 cylinder onto each skewer, pressing gently to adhere. Transfer skewers to lightly greased baking sheet, cover with plastic wrap, and refrigerate for at least 1 hour or up to 24 hours.

3A. FOR A CHARCOAL GRILL: Using skewer, poke 12 holes in bottom of disposable pan. Open bottom vent completely and place pan in center of grill. Light large chimney starter filled two-thirds with charcoal briquettes (4 quarts). When top coals are partially covered with ash, pour into pan. Set cooking grate in place, cover, and open lid vent completely. Heat grill until hot, about 5 minutes.

3B. FOR A GAS GRILL: Turn all burners to high, cover, and heat grill until hot, about 15 minutes. Leave all burners on high.

4. Clean and oil cooking grate. Place skewers on grill (directly over coals if using charcoal) at 45-degree angle to grate. Cook (covered if using gas) until browned and meat easily releases from grill, 4 to 7 minutes. Flip skewers and continue to cook until browned on second side and meat registers 160 degrees, about 6 minutes longer. Transfer skewers to platter and serve, passing yogurt-garlic sauce separately.

GRILLED BEEF KOFTE

Substitute 80 percent lean ground beef for lamb. Increase garlic to 5 cloves, paprika to 2 teaspoons, and cumin to 2 teaspoons.

Really Good Brown Rice Salads

When we set out to create bold-tasting salads full of contrasting flavors and textures, we stumbled on a whole new—and better—way to cook brown rice.

⋟ BY ADAM RIED ⋞

Summertime invariably brings an endless stream of pasta salads. I don't have anything against a well-made pasta salad—but this year, I want to shake things up a bit. A rice salad would be a nice change of pace, except that the rice (which is typically white) usually offers little more personality than the pasta. Brown rice seems a lot more intriguing. It retains the bran and most of the germ that are removed to produce white rice—elements that give brown rice a nutty flavor and pleasantly chewy texture. Sounds perfect for a hearty, flavorful rice salad, yes?

Unfortunately, no. The recipes I tried demonstrated the usual problems with brown rice—it is gummy or tough (and sometimes both) and takes forever to cook. The dressings were also off the mark, often so dull or heavy that they weighed down rather than enlivened the salad. I set out to correct both problems.

The test kitchen actually has an oven method for cooking brown rice that consistently turns out perfectly separate grains. However, on hot summer days, I like to avoid turning on the oven. Furthermore, this method takes a full hour. I wanted to find a faster but equally reliable cooking method.

Which Rice Is Right?

First I needed to choose my rice. Temporarily using our tried-and-true oven method, I tested standard long-, medium-, and short-grain brown rice, preferring the longer variety since its grains were less starchy and sticky than the shorter types. I also tried two specialty long-grain rices—brown jasmine and brown basmati. Basmati took top honors for its mildly sweet, aromatic flavor.

I then cycled through my options for shortcutting the cooking time. I rejected the use of a rice cooker, as not everyone has this appliance. The microwave delivered, cooking 1½ cups of rice in a mere 25 minutes. Yet after testing countless combinations

Sprinkling vinegar or citrus juice on the warm cooked rice boosts its flavor.

of full and partial power, covered or not, stirring or not, different ratios of rice to liquid—you name it—I couldn't get the rice to cook evenly every time.

On to the stovetop. I already knew that the standard procedure of starting the rice in cold water (using twice as much water as rice) and simmering until the liquid was fully absorbed wouldn't lead to evenly cooked results, so I skipped this approach. Instead, I tried steaming the rice in a strainer perched over simmering water. As it turned out, this method required the same amount of time as a cold-water start (about 50 minutes), and the rice was still not uniformly tender—plus the tiny grains stuck to the strainer. I wondered if using the pilaf method of sautéing the rice in fat and aromatics before adding water would offer any benefits, but it didn't: The cooking time was the same, the rice texture was still uneven, and the flavor imparted by the aromatics wasn't noticeable in the finished salad.

I had seen a few recipes that called for boiling the rice in an abundance of water and then draining off the liquid as you would for pasta; these recipes claimed that this produced more evenly cooked rice.

If boiling had at least that advantage, I'd be making progress. I brought 10 cups of water to a rolling boil, added salt and 1½ cups of rice, and started testing for tenderness after 40 minutes. I was surprised to find the rice so tender that it was falling apart. I threw it out and started a new batch, this time checking at the 20-minute mark. To my delight, the rice was nearly done at that point and fully tender about 5 minutes later. But would it be evenly cooked? I drained the rice, spread it on a baking sheet to cool, and tried several samples. The grains were pleasantly chewy, separate, and uniformly cooked. I had hit the jackpot. But I wanted to know why.

One reason that the rice cooked faster in boiling water was simply that the water was hotter—212 degrees versus around 204 degrees when it simmers during the absorption method. But after a chat with our science editor, I realized the significant impact of the greater volume of water: Simply put, the more boiling water in the pot the more energy it has to transfer to the food. What's more, with an abundance of water, each grain of rice can absorb liquid from all sides, cooking faster and more evenly.

Salad Days

Next, I wanted to pair the nutty rice with bold flavors and contrasting textures. One winning combination featured asparagus, almonds, and goat cheese. Another incorporated the kick of jalapeño chiles with cherry tomatoes, velvety avocado, tender-crisp scallions, and lime juice. Yet another combined earthy mushrooms and walnuts with sweet fennel.

I also found that I had to enlist especially bright, lively vinaigrettes to balance the rice's earthiness. A standard vinaigrette contains just 1 part acid to 3 or 4—sometimes even 5—parts oil. I tinkered with this ratio, adding more acid until I reached a nearly 1:1 ratio, 2 tablespoons acid to 2½ tablespoons oil, which finally satisfied my tasters. I also learned to keep the quantity of dressing minimal: About ¼ cup for the entire salad allowed the nuttiness of the rice and the bold flavors of the mix-ins to shine through.

I also ran one final test in which I doubled back to the cooked rice itself. Borrowing an idea from several of the test kitchen's potato salad recipes, immediately after spreading the rice on a baking sheet to cool for about 15 minutes, I sprinkled it with 2 teaspoons of acid (vinegar or citrus juice). As it does with warm potatoes, the acid was absorbed into the rice, boosting the grain's flavor.

With hearty, lively flavors and substantial—but not heavy—textures, these quick salads may just steal the show at your next summer cookout.

BROWN RICE FOR SALAD
MAKES ABOUT 5 CUPS

We like the flavor of brown basmati rice, but any long-grain brown rice is acceptable. Use the same vinegar or citrus juice called for in the salad you plan to make. For our free recipe for Brown Rice Salad with Red Bell Peppers, Olives, and Manchego, go to CooksIllustrated.com/aug13.

1½	cups long-grain brown rice
2	teaspoons salt
2	teaspoons vinegar or citrus juice

Bring 3 quarts water to boil in large pot. Add rice and salt; cook, stirring occasionally, until rice is tender, 22 to 25 minutes. Drain rice, transfer to parchment paper–lined rimmed baking sheet, and spread into even layer. Drizzle rice with vinegar or citrus juice and let cool completely, about 15 minutes.

BROWN RICE SALAD WITH ASPARAGUS, GOAT CHEESE, AND LEMON
SERVES 6 TO 8

Look for asparagus that is bright green and firm.

1	tablespoon vegetable oil
1	pound asparagus, trimmed
	Salt and pepper
2½	tablespoons extra-virgin olive oil
1	shallot, minced
1	teaspoon grated lemon zest plus 2 tablespoons juice
1	recipe Brown Rice for Salad
4	ounces goat cheese, crumbled (1 cup)
½	cup slivered almonds, toasted
¼	cup chopped fresh parsley

1. Heat vegetable oil in 12-inch skillet over medium-high heat until shimmering. Add half of asparagus with tips pointed in 1 direction and remaining asparagus with tips pointed in opposite direction. Using tongs, arrange spears in even layer (they will not quite fit into single layer); cover and cook until bright green and still crisp, 2 to 5 minutes. Uncover, increase heat to high, season with salt and pepper to taste, and continue to cook until tender and well browned on 1 side, 5 to 7 minutes, using tongs to occasionally move spears from center to edge of pan to ensure all are browned. Transfer to plate and let cool completely. Cut into 1-inch pieces.

2. Whisk olive oil, shallot, lemon zest and juice, ½ teaspoon salt, and ½ teaspoon pepper together

ILLUSTRATION: JAY LAYMAN

SCIENCE
The Benefits of Boiling Brown Rice

When rice is cooked on the stovetop via the absorption method, the grains absorb almost all of the small amount of liquid that's in the pot early on in the cooking process. This can lead to uneven results, since only the grains that fully hydrate at the start will completely soften, while the grains that didn't initially absorb enough liquid will remain firm.

We found that boiling brown rice in an abundance of water not only cooked it more evenly but also shaved a good 25 minutes off the usual 50 minutes needed for the absorption method (i.e., simmering the rice in a set amount of liquid). With a large volume of boiling water in the pot (which is drained off when the rice is done), the liquid can penetrate the grains evenly from all sides, so their starches gelatinize more uniformly as well as more quickly. Boiling the rice (versus simmering it) also speeds up cooking because boiling water contains more energy than simmering water. All in all, boiling is an excellent way to cook brown rice. –A.R.

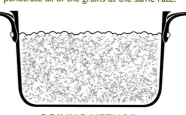

ABSORPTION APPROACH
Simmer rice, covered, in small amount of water.
Cook Time: 50 minutes
Results: Uneven. A small amount of water can't penetrate all of the grains at the same rate.

BOILING METHOD
Cook rice in lots of boiling water; drain.
Cook Time: 25 minutes
Results: Every grain absorbs the same amount of water, so the whole pot cooks evenly.

in bowl. Transfer cooled rice to large bowl. Add asparagus, all but 2 tablespoons goat cheese, and dressing; toss to combine. Let stand for 10 minutes.

3. Add ⅓ cup almonds and 3 tablespoons parsley; toss to combine. Season with salt and pepper to taste. Sprinkle with remaining almonds, reserved 2 tablespoons goat cheese, and remaining 1 tablespoon parsley; serve.

BROWN RICE SALAD WITH JALAPEÑOS, TOMATOES, AND AVOCADO
SERVES 6 TO 8

To make this salad spicier, add the reserved chile seeds.

2½	tablespoons extra-virgin olive oil
2	teaspoons honey
2	garlic cloves, minced
1	teaspoon grated lime zest plus 2 tablespoons juice
½	teaspoon ground cumin
	Salt and pepper
1	recipe Brown Rice for Salad
10	ounces cherry tomatoes, halved
1	avocado, halved, pitted, and cut into ½-inch pieces
1	jalapeño chile, stemmed, seeds reserved, and minced
5	scallions, sliced thin
¼	cup minced fresh cilantro

1. Whisk olive oil, honey, garlic, lime zest and juice, cumin, ½ teaspoon salt, and ½ teaspoon pepper together in bowl. Transfer cooled rice to large bowl. Add tomatoes, avocado, jalapeño, and dressing; toss to combine. Let stand for 10 minutes.

2. Add ¼ cup scallions and cilantro; toss to combine. Season with salt and pepper to taste. Sprinkle with remaining scallions and serve.

BROWN RICE SALAD WITH FENNEL, MUSHROOMS, AND WALNUTS
SERVES 6 TO 8

Cremini mushrooms can be substituted for the white mushrooms.

4	teaspoons vegetable oil
1	pound white mushrooms, trimmed and quartered
	Salt and pepper
1	large fennel bulb, stalks discarded, bulb halved, cored, and sliced thin
2½	tablespoons extra-virgin olive oil
2	tablespoons white wine vinegar
1	shallot, minced
1	recipe Brown Rice for Salad
⅔	cup walnuts, toasted and chopped coarse
2	tablespoons minced fresh tarragon
2	tablespoons minced fresh parsley

1. Heat 2 teaspoons vegetable oil in 12-inch skillet over medium-high heat until shimmering. Add mushrooms and ½ teaspoon salt; cook, stirring occasionally, until pan is dry and mushrooms are browned, 6 to 8 minutes. Transfer mushrooms to large plate and let cool completely. Heat remaining 2 teaspoons vegetable oil in now-empty skillet until shimmering. Add fennel and ¼ teaspoon salt; cook, stirring occasionally, until just browned and crisp-tender, 3 to 4 minutes. Transfer to plate with mushrooms.

2. Whisk olive oil, vinegar, shallot, ½ teaspoon salt, and ½ teaspoon pepper together in bowl. Transfer cooled rice to large bowl. Add vegetables and dressing; toss to combine. Let stand for 10 minutes.

3. Add ½ cup walnuts, tarragon, and 1 tablespoon parsley; toss to combine. Season with salt and pepper to taste. Sprinkle with remaining walnuts and remaining 1 tablespoon parsley; serve.

Summer Berry Trifle

To perfect this English classic, we'd need to ensure that the flavors and textures of each layer melded together—but without the whole thing turning to mush.

≥ BY ANDREA GEARY ≤

The elegant trifle had humble beginnings. It originated in 16th-century England as a soupy combination of sweetened cream, rose water, and spices, and by the 17th century the mixture was being called into service to soak stale bread and cake. Things got a bit more upscale with the introduction of wine and custard, but it wasn't until the Victorian era that trifle blossomed into its most awe-inspiring form, one involving ladyfingers, almond macaroons, jam, custard, whipped cream, brandy, sherry, candied fruits, and edible flowers.

Few people have the time or energy for that kind of trifle labor these days, but that hasn't diminished the celebratory appeal of this showstopper dessert. I wanted to make a luscious trifle completely from scratch—without going crazy in the process.

My goal was to combine four basic components—light cake, silky pastry cream, whipped cream, and lush summer berries (plus a generous dose of booze)—to make a simple but elegant trifle full of flavor from top to bottom. But as soon as I began testing recipes, I realized that there would be a few hurdles. First, many light cakes were also weak cakes, falling apart into a mushy mess as soon as they began to absorb moisture in the trifle. The pastry cream, which should be dense and silky, tended to break down as soon as I spread it in layers in the bowl. I also wanted the flavors of the sherry and fruit to permeate each bite. The sherry tended to mainly flavor the cake, while the berries seemed to remain too distinct from the rest of the dessert.

Foam Truths

With a simple pastry cream, fresh berries, and lightly sweetened whipped cream acting as placeholder components, I first focused on the cake.

A tender butter cake is my usual go-to for pairing with frosting, but it was a disaster in trifle. The sherry and creamy elements turned it to mush. Instead I

See the Trifle Constructed

Video available FREE for 4 months at CooksIllustrated.com/aug13

By slightly reengineering a classic chiffon cake, we created a fluffy crumb that holds up in the trifle—and bakes in only 15 minutes.

tried taking the historical route by using ladyfingers. Crisp and dry, they required so much booze to soften that the alcohol burn swamped the delicate cream and fruit. But they did hold their shape. This is because ladyfingers are simply small, dry angel food cakes based on a protein-rich whipped egg white foam. Because protein doesn't readily absorb water, ladyfingers hold up nicely against moisture.

An angel food cake wouldn't be dry like ladyfingers but it would require a tube pan—the center tube is essential in helping it rise. Plus, an angel food cake must thoroughly cool before being removed from the pan or it will collapse (see page 3 for more information). This would add fuss—and time—to a dessert I was trying to simplify. I needed a cake that would bake and cool quickly in a regular cake pan but with an angel food cake's ability to stand up to moisture.

A chiffon cake is similar to an angel food cake but contains more flour for structure. I wondered if adding more than the usual amount of flour to a chiffon cake would enable me to skip the tube pan and

perhaps even bake the batter in a rimmed baking sheet, which would allow it to bake and cool very rapidly. I mixed flour, sugar, baking powder, whole eggs, water, and oil and then folded in stiffly beaten egg whites. To my delight, by doubling the amount of flour I was able to bake a slim, fluffy modified chiffon cake in an 18 by 13-inch baking sheet in 15 minutes. It cooled in just 30 minutes.

Berries and Cream

Pastry cream is typically made with a mixture of heavy cream and milk, egg yolks, sugar, cornstarch, and a bit of butter and vanilla. Since my trifle was already going to be rich with whipped cream, I decided to make an all-milk pastry cream. This seemed to work well—until I spread the cream between layers of cake, an act that required a lot of manipulation, which caused the cream to turn runny. The lower fat content was partially to blame, but there was another factor at play: Cornstarch-thickened pastry cream is not what food scientists call "shear reversible," so it loses structure if you disturb the gel too much. The fix proved easy: Starting with a firmer gel by upping the cornstarch by 25 percent gave me a bit more leeway to stir and spread.

Next: berries. In my opinion, arranging whole berries in decorative layers misses the point: A trifle's components are supposed to coalesce. Whole berries don't release any juice, so they don't meld. But crushing all of my gorgeous berries seemed criminal. I settled on mashing one-third of the fruit and heating the mash with just a bit of cornstarch to thicken it and a bit of sugar to balance the flavor.

Then the fun part: construction. I spread a small amount of pastry cream in the bottom of my trifle bowl to anchor the first layer of cake. Then I sprinkled ¼ cup of sherry on top of the cake and piled on the juicy berries. Next came the silky pastry cream, topped by a thin layer of whipped cream (also spiked with a hint of sherry). I repeated the layers before refrigerating the trifle to set. Right before serving, I garnished the top with just a handful of berries.

Every component of my edible centerpiece had been made from scratch and fit together into a cohesive whole—without any headache.

SUMMER BERRY TRIFLE
SERVES 12 TO 16

For the best texture, this trifle should be assembled at least 6 hours before serving. Use a glass bowl with at least a 3½-quart capacity; straight sides are preferable. For a substitute for cream sherry, see "Turning Dry Sherry to Cream," page 31.

Pastry Cream
- 3½ cups whole milk
- 1 cup (7 ounces) sugar
- 6 tablespoons cornstarch
  - Pinch salt
- 5 large egg yolks (reserve whites for cake)
- 4 tablespoons unsalted butter, cut into ½-inch pieces and chilled
- 4 teaspoons vanilla extract

Cake
- 1⅓ cups (5⅓ ounces) cake flour
- ¾ cup (5¼ ounces) sugar
- 1½ teaspoons baking powder
- ¼ teaspoon salt
- ⅓ cup vegetable oil
- ¼ cup water
- 1 large egg
- 2 teaspoons vanilla extract
- 5 large egg whites (reserved from pastry cream)
- ¼ teaspoon cream of tartar

Fruit Filling
- 1½ pounds strawberries, hulled and cut into ½-inch pieces (4 cups), reserving 3 halved for garnish
- 12 ounces (2⅓ cups) blackberries, large berries halved crosswise, reserving 3 whole for garnish
- 12 ounces (2⅓ cups) raspberries, reserving 3 for garnish
- ¼ cup (1¾ ounces) sugar
- ½ teaspoon cornstarch
  - Pinch salt

Whipped Cream
- 1 cup heavy cream
- 1 tablespoon sugar
- 1 tablespoon plus ½ cup cream sherry

1. FOR THE PASTRY CREAM: Heat 3 cups milk in medium saucepan over medium heat until just simmering. Meanwhile, whisk sugar, cornstarch, and salt together in medium bowl. Whisk remaining ½ cup milk and egg yolks into sugar mixture until smooth. Remove milk from heat and, whisking constantly, slowly add 1 cup to sugar mixture to temper. Whisking constantly, return tempered sugar mixture to milk in saucepan.

2. Return saucepan to medium heat and cook, whisking constantly, until mixture is very thick and bubbles burst on surface, 4 to 7 minutes. Remove saucepan from heat; whisk in butter and vanilla until butter is melted and incorporated. Strain pastry

---

REFINING THE ELEMENTS

Here's how we tweaked three main components of our trifle so they all worked in tandem. The trifle is also prepared 6 to 36 hours in advance to give flavors and textures time to meld.

MAKE A STURDIER CAKE
An egg foam–based chiffon cake stands up better to a trifle's moisture than butter cake. By adding extra flour to it, we can bake it quickly in a rimmed baking sheet.

DEVELOP BERRY FLAVOR
We mash some of our berries. This allows the fruit juice—and therefore the flavor—to reach every bite of trifle.

STABILIZE THE CUSTARD
Adding extra cornstarch to the pastry cream keeps it from turning runny when spread between layers of cake.

---

cream through fine-mesh strainer set over medium bowl. Press lightly greased parchment paper directly on surface and refrigerate until set, at least 2 hours or up to 24 hours.

3. FOR THE CAKE: Adjust oven rack to middle position and heat oven to 350 degrees. Lightly grease 18 by 13-inch rimmed baking sheet, line with parchment, and lightly grease parchment. Whisk flour, sugar, baking powder, and salt together in medium bowl. Whisk oil, water, egg, and vanilla into flour mixture until smooth batter forms.

4. Using stand mixer fitted with whisk, whip reserved egg whites and cream of tartar on medium-low speed until foamy, about 1 minute. Increase speed to medium-high and whip until soft peaks form, 2 to 3 minutes. Transfer one-third of whipped egg whites to batter; whisk gently until mixture is lightened. Using rubber spatula, gently fold remaining egg whites into batter.

TECHNIQUE
LAYERING CAKE JUST RIGHT

Cutting and shingling the cake is the key to making it fit—and using every bit. First, slice the cake into 24 equal pieces and then shingle them (12 per layer), like fallen dominos, in the bowl.

---

5. Pour batter into prepared sheet; spread evenly. Bake until top is golden brown and cake springs back when pressed lightly in center, 13 to 16 minutes.

6. Transfer cake to wire rack; let cool for 5 minutes. Run knife around edge of sheet, then invert cake onto wire rack. Carefully remove parchment, then re-invert cake onto second wire rack. Let cool completely, at least 30 minutes.

7. FOR THE FRUIT FILLING: Place 1½ cups strawberries, 1 cup blackberries, 1 cup raspberries, sugar, cornstarch, and salt in medium saucepan. Place remaining berries in large bowl; set aside. Using potato masher, thoroughly mash berries in saucepan. Cook over medium heat until sugar is dissolved and mixture is thick and bubbling, 4 to 7 minutes. Pour over berries in bowl and stir to combine. Set aside.

8. FOR THE WHIPPED CREAM: Using stand mixer fitted with whisk, whip cream, sugar, and 1 tablespoon sherry on medium-low speed until foamy, about 1 minute. Increase speed to high and whip until soft peaks form, 1 to 2 minutes.

9. Trim ¼ inch off each side of cake; discard trimmings. Using serrated knife, cut cake into 24 equal pieces (each piece about 2½ inches square).

10. Briefly whisk pastry cream until smooth. Spoon ¾ cup pastry cream into trifle bowl; spread over bottom. Shingle 12 cake pieces, fallen domino–style, around bottom of trifle, placing 10 pieces against dish wall and 2 remaining pieces in center. Drizzle ¼ cup sherry evenly over cake. Spoon half of berry mixture evenly over cake, making sure to use half of liquid. Using back of spoon, spread half of remaining pastry cream over berries, then spread half of whipped cream over pastry cream (whipped cream layer will be thin). Repeat layering with remaining 12 cake pieces, sherry, berries, pastry cream, and whipped cream. Cover bowl with plastic wrap and refrigerate for at least 6 hours or up to 36 hours. Garnish top of trifle with reserved berries and serve.

Fresh Corn Cornbread

What about a cornbread that actually tastes like fresh, sweet corn instead of cornmeal?

≫ BY BRIDGET LANCASTER ≪

Cornbread falls into two main styles: the sweet, cakey Northern type and the crusty, savory kind more often found in Southern kitchens. Each has its die-hard fans, but—let's face the facts—neither tastes much like corn. This is because most cornbreads are made with cornmeal alone, and no fresh corn at all. Furthermore, the so-called "field" or "dent" corn used to make cornmeal is far starchier (read: less flavorful) than the sweet corn grown to eat off the cob.

So what would it take to get real corn flavor in cornbread? It wouldn't be as simple as just tossing some fresh-cut kernels into the batter. When I tried, I found that I needed to add at least 2 whole cups of kernels for the corn flavor to really shine, and that created a slew of problems. Since fresh kernels are full of moisture, the crumb of the cornbread was now riddled with unpleasant gummy pockets. What's more, the kernels turned chewy and tough as the bread baked. But there had to be a way to get true sweet corn flavor in cornbread, and I was determined to figure it out.

Corn Stalker

I decided to work on the cornbread base first. In my earlier tests, tasters found that the little bit of sweetener added to the Northern-style versions helped fresh corn flavor break through, so I settled on that cornbread archetype. For my working recipe, I used slightly more cornmeal than flour and decided to abandon fine-ground cornmeal in favor of the stone-ground type, which contains both the hull and the oil-rich germ of the corn kernel. The upshot: a more rustic texture and fuller flavor. For sweetness, honey, maple syrup, and brown sugar all masked the fresh corn taste, but 2 tablespoons of regular granulated sugar fell neatly in line. For the liquid component, I would stick with traditional tangy buttermilk. Three tablespoons of melted butter and two eggs provided richness, and baking the cornbread in a cast-iron skillet allowed it to develop a brown, crisp crust.

With the batter figured out, I turned back to the problems of the fresh corn. I wondered if I could get rid of the unpleasantly steamed, chewy texture of the kernels by soaking them in a solution of water and baking soda before adding them to the batter—a technique we recently used to tenderize kernels for a fresh corn salsa. The alkaline environment provided by the baking soda helps soften the hulls of the kernels. Sure enough, the kernels were tender . . . that is, until they were baked in the bread and the heat

We crammed three ears' worth of kernels into this bread but found a way around their distracting texture.

of the oven toughened them right back up. And I still had the issue of all those wet, gummy pockets.

With no new ideas to try, I was idly flipping through cookbooks when I came across a recipe for "corn butter" made by pureeing fresh kernels and then reducing the mixture on the stove until thick. I tried it using three large ears of corn and found that the puree thickened and turned deep yellow in minutes, transforming into a "butter" packed with concentrated corn flavor. While the recipes I found used the corn butter as a spread, I had another idea: I added the reduced puree to a batch of batter, baked it—and rejoiced. For the first time, my cornbread tasted like real corn—and without any distracting chewiness.

This method offered another benefit: Since cooking the corn puree drove off moisture, my bread no longer had gummy pockets surrounding the kernels. In fact, the bread was almost too dry and even a little crumbly—a result of the large amount of natural cornstarch (released by pureeing the kernels) that was now absorbing surrounding moisture in the batter. Happily, this problem was easy to solve by simply increasing the amount of fat in the batter: an extra egg yolk and 2 more tablespoons of butter did the trick. I had one more tweak: I melted a pat of butter in the skillet before adding the batter, which gave the bread a more crispy and buttery-tasting bottom crust.

Moist, tender, and bursting with corn flavor, my cornbread tasted like a bite of corn on the cob.

FRESH CORN CORNBREAD
SERVES 6 TO 8

We prefer to use a well-seasoned cast-iron skillet in this recipe, but an ovensafe 10-inch skillet can be used in its place. Alternatively, in step 4 you can add 1 tablespoon of butter to a 9-inch cake pan and place it in the oven until the butter melts, about 3 minutes.

- 1⅓ cups (6⅔ ounces) stone-ground cornmeal
- 1 cup (5 ounces) all-purpose flour
- 2 tablespoons sugar
- 1½ teaspoons baking powder
- ¼ teaspoon baking soda
- 1¼ teaspoons salt
- 3 ears corn, kernels cut from cobs (2¼ cups)
- 6 tablespoons unsalted butter, cut into 6 pieces
- 1 cup buttermilk
- 2 large eggs plus 1 large yolk

1. Adjust oven rack to middle position and heat oven to 400 degrees. Whisk cornmeal, flour, sugar, baking powder, baking soda, and salt together in large bowl.

2. Process corn kernels in blender until very smooth, about 2 minutes. Transfer puree to medium saucepan (you should have about 1½ cups). Cook puree over medium heat, stirring constantly, until very thick and deep yellow and it measures ¾ cup, 5 to 8 minutes.

3. Remove pan from heat. Add 5 tablespoons butter and whisk until melted and incorporated. Add buttermilk and whisk until incorporated. Add eggs and yolk and whisk until incorporated. Transfer corn mixture to bowl with cornmeal mixture and, using rubber spatula, fold together until just combined.

4. Melt remaining 1 tablespoon butter in 10-inch cast-iron skillet over medium heat. Scrape batter into skillet and spread into even layer. Bake until top is golden brown and toothpick inserted in center comes out clean, 23 to 28 minutes. Let cool on wire rack for 5 minutes. Remove cornbread from skillet and let cool for 20 minutes before cutting into wedges and serving.

PHOTOGRAPHY: CARL TREMBLAY

Engineering the Best Chicken Broth

Just about every broth in the supermarket amounts to a science project of flavor enhancers and salt. Does that have to be a bad thing?

⇒ BY HANNAH CROWLEY ⇐

Chicken broth isn't sexy like black truffles or trendy like pork belly, but in the test kitchen we rarely go a day without using it. As the backbone of much of our savory cooking, it appears in—at last count—586 of our recipes. That's more than 10 times the appearance of beef broth and 24 times that of vegetable broth. We use it as a base for soups and stews; for simmering pilafs and risottos; and to moisten braises, pan sauces, and gravies.

Of course, we use homemade stock when possible, but truth be told, it's not that often. Most of the time, we rely on our favorite commercial alternative, which for several years has been Swanson Certified Organic Free Range Chicken Broth. In our last tasting in 2005, its "chicken-y," "straightforward" qualities separated this product from more than a dozen others we tried, the worst of which reminded tasters of "chemicals" and "cardboard."

But like other processed foods, chicken broths are frequently revamped to keep in step with technology, so we decided it was time to take another look. When we surveyed supermarket shelves this go-round, we found them teeming with even more options than before—including more alternatives to canned or boxed liquid broths. Between the granulated powders, cubes, concentrates, and liquids—not to mention a headache-inducing array of sodium levels—we found more than 50 different chicken broth products.

To pare down this unwieldy number, we looked at salt levels. Our first move was to eliminate any broths with more than 700 milligrams of sodium per serving. Why? Because in previous taste tests we've found that broths containing more than this amount become too salty when reduced in a sauce or a gravy. We also avoided anything with less than 400 milligrams for two reasons: Since salt is a flavor enhancer, a judicious amount is required to bring out chicken taste. We also learned in our previous tasting that broths with less salt than this are entirely bland. Finally, we narrowed our focus to widely available national brands; nothing boutique or hard to find would do for such an everyday workhorse.

That left us with 10 broths: eight liquids (including our previous favorite) and two concentrates that are reconstituted with water. We set about tasting the finalists warmed plain, in a simple risotto, and reduced in an all-purpose gravy. Our goal: to find the richest, most chicken-y stand-in for homemade stock.

Stock Options

Given the results of our last tasting, we weren't surprised when several of the samples tasted awful. In fact, five flunked every test. Some of these had chicken flavor so wan that it was practically nonexistent; others were "beefy" or "vegetal" or had bizarre off-flavors recalling "Robitussin" or "dirty socks." Most of the remaining samples tasted promising out of the box but then exhibited flaws when cooked. A couple turned candy-sweet when reduced in gravy; the flavor of others disappeared entirely in the starchy risotto rice. Out of the 10 samples, there were only two that stood apart: One was a traditional boxed liquid, Swanson Chicken Stock (not our previous winner from Swanson; that broth has been reformulated and fell to the bottom of the pack). The other was one of the two concentrates in the lineup: Better Than Bouillon Chicken Base. While tasters praised Swanson's "rich," "meaty" flavor, they were even more impressed by the remarkably "clean," "savory" taste of the chicken base.

We have to admit that we weren't expecting Better Than Bouillon to perform so well. We went into the tasting thinking that a concentrate could never be quite as good as a liquid broth since it seemed more processed—and thus farther from homemade. Interestingly, we did a little digging and it turns out that nearly all supermarket chicken broths start out as concentrates; not only that, but most of them are made by the same company. According to Roger Dake, director of research and development for International Dehydrated Foods (IDF), most of the liquid broths in our lineup were made to order by IDF, which prepares them according to a brand's specifications. The broths are left concentrated because this makes them lighter and thus cheaper to ship. At the food production sites, the concentrates are reconstituted to their final liquid form, flavored with the other ingredients shown on the label, packaged for retail, and shipped out for sale.

Given this, our awarding highest marks to a concentrate wasn't all that remarkable. But there was something we weren't expecting: The difference in protein between Swanson Chicken Stock and Better Than Bouillon. While Swanson had a relatively high 4 grams of protein per cup, Better Than Bouillon got by with just 1. We weren't surprised that there was a wide range of protein among the products. The U.S. Department of Agriculture has a minimal standard that it requires for beef broth—at least

1 part meat to 135 parts water (roughly 1 ounce of meat to a gallon of water)—but there is no such standard for chicken broth or "stock" at all. What's more, we knew that more protein wasn't actually a guarantee of bigger chicken flavor because the broth with the highest amount of protein per cup, Kitchen Basics (5 grams), was panned for its "sour," "vegetal" flavor. What we couldn't figure out, though, was how Better Than Bouillon obtained its rich, chicken-y flavor with such a measly amount of protein.

Thinking Outside the Box

Savoriness is often associated with glutamates, forms of an amino acid that enhance a food's meaty, *umami* flavor. Glutamates are already found in chicken (and in particularly high concentration in many other foods including anchovies, Parmesan cheese, and tomato paste), but many companies add more in the form of yeast extract or hydrolyzed soy protein, so we made glutamates our next point of investigation. We packed up the broths and shipped them to an independent laboratory to be analyzed. The data helped confirm why Swanson Chicken Stock tasted good—it had the highest level of glutamates in the lineup. But it didn't shed any light on why we liked Better Than Bouillon, which ranked among the lowest by far.

How Much Sodium Is Best in Store-Bought Stock?

"Low sodium." "Very low sodium." "Reduced sodium." "Sodium-free." Suffice it to say that there are a dizzying number of sodium claims plastered on commercial chicken broths, and unless you're intimately familiar with their federally regulated definitions, the terms are more confusing than helpful.

We ignore these claims and turn the box around to look at the amount of sodium per serving printed on the nutrition label. The range can be dramatic—from no sodium at all to as much as 1,100 milligrams per 1-cup serving. We prefer broths with a moderate amount: between 400 and about 700 milligrams per serving. Any less than 400 milligrams and the food will be bland, while broths that contain much more than 700 milligrams can render a dish unpalatably salty. –H.C.

Even more puzzled, we looked closer at the products' ingredient lists and noticed that Better Than Bouillon adds nucleotides called disodium inosinate and disodium guanylate to its product. Like glutamates, these compounds are flavor enhancers that occur naturally in certain foods including meat, seafood, and dried mushrooms. Now things started to make sense. A while back, we learned that when nucleotides and glutamates are combined, they can dramatically increase savory flavors. By including both types of compounds, Better Than Bouillon was able to create the savory qualities we associate with good chicken flavor—even without much protein.

We were intrigued by the concentrate and decided to stretch its legs in the kitchen by incorporating it into more recipes. Then we hit a snag: Some dishes—particularly those that called for more than a quart of chicken broth, like soups, or those that were considerably reduced, like pan sauces—occasionally turned overly salty with Better Than Bouillon in the mix.

That saltiness was in part explained by Better Than Bouillon's adding more sodium than any of the other brands we sampled (680 milligrams per serving), just pushing at our upper limit. But we couldn't understand why the concentrate tasted nicely seasoned in some tests but too salty in others, until we took into account that the nutrition numbers for any product are allowed to vary by as much as 20 percent on either side of the stated value. Just to see what kind of range we might find, we rounded up 10 jars of Better Than Bouillon Chicken Base from 10 different batches (as determined by batch numbers on the labels) and sent them to the lab to analyze their sodium contents. Sure enough, the numbers were all over the map—from 380 to 770 milligrams per cup—which explained why our taste test results were, too. The greater than 20 percent swing made a considerable difference in a product that was already teetering on the edge of too salty.

The Perks of a Concentrate

Better Than Bouillon Chicken Base makes an appealing alternative to our winning Swanson broth for several reasons. First, you don't pay for the cost of packaging and transporting water, so it's cheap. Second, the opened jar keeps for years when stored in the fridge. Finally, reconstituting allows you to make only as much as you need, so you don't end up pouring expired broth (and money) down the drain.

But due to variation in sodium content from jar to jar that we discovered in a lab test, we don't advise following the company's prescribed concentrate-to-water ratio of 1 teaspoon per cup. We suggest dialing it back to ¾ teaspoon of concentrate per cup of water (which doesn't noticeably dilute the flavor of the broth), measuring very carefully, and tasting food before adding any salt during cooking. –H.C.

ONE JAR OF CONCENTRATE		ONE BOX OF LIQUID
38 cups of broth	YIELD	3 cups of broth
$0.16 per cup	PRICE	$1.06 per cup
Two years	SHELF LIFE*	14 days
Never	WASTE	Often

*Based on an open package that's stored in the fridge.

Home to Roost

Better Than Bouillon's tendency toward saltiness made us hesitate about stocking it in the test kitchen, but the concentrate did have other merits. At just 16 cents per cup, it was the cheapest by far—more than seven times cheaper than the priciest liquid broth ($1.15 per cup). Why the huge price gap? You aren't paying to transport all the water: Most cartons of liquid broth weigh 2 pounds and yield 4 cups, but an 8-ounce jar of Better Than Bouillon yields 38 cups. That much liquid broth would weigh nearly 20 pounds.

Another plus: Once opened, the concentrate will last for two years stored in the refrigerator. Liquid broths keep for no more than two weeks once opened. Even better, you can reconstitute only as much as you need—several cups for making soup or stew or just a few tablespoons for making a pan sauce. Having thrown away plenty of partially used cartons of broth, we really appreciate that option.

Reconstituting also allowed us to adjust the concentration of the broth. The package label prescribes 1 teaspoon of concentrate per cup of water. (The label also directs users to increase the ratio of concentrate to water when making more than 1 quart of broth, though at press time the company told us it was reviewing these instructions.) Scaling back to ¾ teaspoon per cup brought the saltiness in check without noticeably diluting the broth's flavor.

Those perks made Better Than Bouillon an appealing option, but we ultimately felt that we couldn't award it the top spot if it meant we had to ignore the package instructions. Instead, rich-tasting Swanson Chicken Stock will be our stand-in for homemade. But given its great flavor, long shelf life, and price, we're naming Better Than Bouillon Chicken Base our Best Buy. While we'd still like to see more actual meat in factory-made chicken broth, this product is proof positive that smart food science can go a long way toward engineering a better commercial broth.

SCIENCE Creating Chicken Flavor Without Much Chicken

In an ideal world, we'd buy a commercial chicken broth made with the same amount of chicken that we put into a homemade stock. But the government doesn't regulate how much chicken must go into broth, and we found that no manufacturer adds enough meat to make its product even remotely as chicken-y as good homemade stock. The best possible alternative: broths built on food science. Many producers add cocktails of flavor enhancers to their products to give them the illusion of true chicken flavor, but we found just one that does it well: Better Than Bouillon. This brand boosts meaty, *umami* taste in its broth by adding a pair of naturally occurring flavor-amplifying compounds: glutamates and nucleotides. (On the ingredient label, glutamates appear as "hydrolyzed soy protein" and nucleotides as "disodium inosinate" and "guanylate.") Glutamates are forms of an amino acid, the same molecules that build proteins. They exhibit some meaty flavor on their own, but pairing them with nucleotides—and especially inosinate and guanylate—greatly magnifies our ability to perceive their savory flavor. In fact, when glutamates and nucleotides are present at equal levels in food, the strength of meaty taste is as much as 20 to 30 times greater than it is for glutamates alone.

What makes that effect possible? Interestingly, it's not a chemical reaction between the two compounds when they're combined in cooking. Instead, it's how these compounds influence our tastebuds. We taste meaty, savory glutamates when they interact with the glutamate taste receptors in the mouth. Nucleotides change the shape of these receptors and allow them to send stronger signals to the brain. If tasting glutamates is like lifting a heavy box, then the addition of nucleotides would give us handles, making the box exponentially easier to pick up off the ground. –H.C.

TASTING: CHICKEN BROTH

After choosing from a list of top sellers compiled by IRi, a Chicago-based market research firm, and narrowing our results by sodium levels, our team had 21 *Cook's Illustrated* staff members taste 10 widely available chicken broths in three blind tastings: plain, in a simple risotto, and in gravy. The broths were rated on flavor, saltiness, and off-flavors, as well as on overall appeal. Nutrition information was taken from product labels and is expressed with a serving size of 1 cup. Scores were averaged and the products appear below in order of preference. (**Note:** We also tasted Better Than Bouillon's reduced-sodium version and determined that we didn't like this less-available product at all. Besides having less sodium, its formulation was markedly different.)

RECOMMENDED

SWANSON Chicken Stock
Price: $3.19 for 3 cups ($1.06 per cup)
Sodium: 510 mg
Protein: 4 g
Ingredients: Chicken stock; contains less than 2%: sea salt, dextrose, carrots, cabbage, onions, celery, celery leaves, salt, parsley
Comments: Unlike most of the other liquid broths in our lineup, this one achieved "rich," "meaty" flavor, and did so the old-fashioned way—with a relatively high percentage of meat-based protein. The only problem: Some tasters thought it came across as "beefy" or even "mushroomy," not chicken-y.

BETTER THAN BOUILLON Chicken Base
Price: $5.99 for 8-oz jar that makes 38 cups ($0.16 per cup)
Sodium: 680 mg
Protein: 1 g
Ingredients: Chicken meat including natural chicken juices, salt, sugar, corn syrup solids, chicken fat, hydrolyzed soy protein, dried whey (milk), flavoring, disodium inosinate, guanylate, turmeric
Comments: By adding nucleotides to its glutamate-rich base, this brand produced a remarkably "savory" broth, despite that it contains very little protein. It's also by far the cheapest broth we tasted, and once opened it lasts for two years in the fridge. However, this product's high sodium content pushed our upper limits for saltiness, so we had to dial back the company's prescribed ratio of concentrate to water.

(BEST BUY)

RECOMMENDED WITH RESERVATIONS

KNORR Homestyle Stock Reduced Sodium Chicken
Price: $3.99 for 4 tubs that make 3.5 cups each, 14 cups total ($0.29 per cup)
Sodium: 600 mg
Protein: 0 g
Ingredients: Water, maltodextrin (corn), salt, palm oil, autolyzed yeast extract, sea salt, sugar, carrots, lactic acid, chicken fat, leeks, potato starch, xanthan gum, garlic, chicken powder (with rosemary extract to protect quality), parsley, natural flavor, malic acid, locust bean gum, thiamin hydrochloride, disodium guanylate, disodium inosinate, disodium phosphate, glycerin, ascorbic acid, caramel color, succinic acid, spice, mustard oil, beta carotene (for color), coconut oil, sulfur dioxide (used to protect quality)
Comments: This concentrate's "meaty" depth is built on the same flavor-boosting combination of glutamates and nucleotides as Better Than Bouillon—and it fared quite well as straight broth. But 32 ingredients later, this concentrate fell short on actual chicken flavor. It was also sweet like "canned pumpkin" when reduced.

SWANSON Natural Goodness Chicken Broth
Price: $2.99 for 4 cups ($0.75 per cup)
Sodium: 570 mg
Protein: 2 g
Ingredients: Chicken stock; contains less than 2%: salt, flavoring, yeast extract, carrot juice concentrate, celery juice concentrate, onion juice concentrate
Comments: This broth was "not super-meaty"; it was like "sweet squash" when reduced in gravy. No surprise: It was average for salt and contains the most sugar per serving, carrot juice being the likely culprit.

PROGRESSO Reduced Sodium Chicken Broth
Price: $2.79 for 4 cups ($0.70 per cup)
Sodium: 560 mg
Protein: 3 g
Ingredients: Chicken broth, salt, sugar, natural flavor, carrot puree, yeast extract
Comments: Off-notes detracted from the otherwise "good chicken flavor" of this broth. Some of us called out a "sour" lemony taste, while others fingered "sweet," "floral," "gingery," and even "minty" flavors that were out of place in chicken broth.

NOT RECOMMENDED

IMAGINE Chicken Cooking Stock
Price: $4.29 for 4 cups ($1.07 per cup)
Sodium: 500 mg
Protein: Less than 1 g
Ingredients: Organic chicken stock (filtered water, organic chicken broth concentrate), sea salt, natural flavors, organic evaporated cane juice, organic chicken flavor, organic turmeric
Comments: Even though it contains only natural ingredients, this broth tasted artificial—like "ramen" or "powdered seasoning packets," tasters said. With less than 1 gram of protein, it's likely that this product contains very little actual chicken.

COLLEGE INN Light & Fat Free Chicken Broth, 50% Less Sodium
Price: $2.59 for 4 cups ($0.65 per cup)
Sodium: 450 mg
Protein: 1 g
Ingredients: Chicken broth, salt, dextrose, natural flavor, yeast extract, onion juice concentrate, carrot and carrot juice concentrate
Comments: This "weak" broth "could be dishwater," according to one taster. "Chicken of any kind is a stretch," wrote another. This makes sense considering that the broth has very little protein, which suggests that not much chicken was used in production. Instead, "vegetal" flavors came to the forefront. This product has the second lowest amount of sodium and low glutamate levels. At press time, we learned that the company was in the process of repackaging this product.

KITCHEN BASICS Original Chicken Cooking Stock
Price: $3.29 for 4 cups ($0.82 per cup)
Sodium: 430 mg
Protein: 5 g
Ingredients: Chicken stock, chicken flavor, sea salt, vegetable stocks (carrot, onion, mushroom, celery), honey, bay, thyme, pepper
Comments: Beyond tasting "bitter," "sour," and "burnt," this broth had strong "vegetal" flavors that spoke not of chicken but of mushrooms. We found that surprising given its high concentration of protein—until we noticed that it contained mushroom stock, which rendered the liquid "alarmingly" dark and tinted risotto the color of brown rice.

SWANSON Certified Organic Free Range Chicken Broth
Price: $3.29 for 4 cups ($0.82 per cup)
Sodium: 550 mg
Protein: 1 g
Ingredients: Chicken stock; contains less than 2%: sea salt, vegetables (carrots, onions, celery, spinach), chicken fat, yeast extract (wheat), cane juice, dehydrated onions, salt, canola oil, molasses, dehydrated carrots, flavoring (wheat), turmeric, potato flour, black pepper
Comments: The reformulated version of our previous favorite just didn't measure up. The manufacturer wouldn't specify the changes, but the ingredient label indicated that there was less sodium. The product was also low on protein. As a result, we found it "mild but genuine" as straight broth, but its flavor disappeared during cooking, leaving food "seriously bland," with "no meatiness whatsoever." As one taster put it, "Fess up: This is water, right?"

PACIFIC Organic Free Range Chicken Broth
Price: $4.59 for 4 cups ($1.15 per cup)
Sodium: 570 mg
Protein: 1 g
Ingredients: Organic chicken broth, organic chicken flavor, sea salt, organic cane sugar, organic onion powder, organic turmeric extract, organic rosemary extract
Comments: This was some seriously funky broth. For one thing, its taste was "not chicken-y . . . or meaty at all." Worse, "sour, vegetal" notes dominated, not to mention other "really odd" flavors reminiscent of "old Chinese buffet."

Testing Innovative Cookware

Can newfangled designs improve on—or even stand up to— the tried-and-true pots and pans we've used for years?

> BY AMY GRAVES AND LISA McMANUS

From heat-spreading fins on the bottoms of stockpots to ceramic nonstick coatings on skillets, innovations in cookware can make you wonder if you're looking at the future. Whether these innovations actually work is another story. To see if any new designs could do more—or better—than our long-standing favorite pots and pans, we rounded up three contenders in each of three major cookware categories: Dutch ovens (or stockpots), large (roughly 12-inch) nonstick skillets, and saucepans. (We also tested lightweight cast-iron skillets; to read about them, go to CooksIllustrated.com/aug13.) We took their newfangled features for a spin and then pitted them against our established winners. Could any of these tricked-out models unseat the champs?

TRIED AND TRUE

DUTCH OVEN
LE CREUSET 7¼-Quart Round French Oven
Model: LS2501-28 Price: $249.95
This gold standard of Dutch ovens puts a "gorgeous, golden crust" on meat and creates great fond. Stew, braises, and rice cook up perfectly (though cleanup requires long soaking for rice).

NONSTICK FRY PAN
T-FAL Professional Non-Stick Fry Pan, 12.5 Inches
Model: E9380864 Price: $25.27
This inexpensive pan has a slick, durable nonstick coating that released food perfectly throughout testing. It is lightweight and well proportioned, with a comfy handle and a generous cooking surface.

SAUCEPAN
ALL-CLAD Stainless 4-Quart Saucepan with Lid and Loop
Model: 4204 Price: $224.95
Our longtime champ heats slowly and evenly enough to prevent onions from scorching and pastry cream and rice from overcooking.

GOOD: ★★★	FAIR: ★★	POOR: ★

INNOVATIVE DUTCH OVENS

We love our favorite Le Creuset Dutch oven, but when we looked around at new options, we pondered the possibilities of even more. The Turbo Pot claims to speed up cooking with aluminum ridges on the outside of its base. The Never Burn Sauce Pot boasts a silicone oil chamber in its base that promises to build heat slowly, retain it evenly, and prevent scorching. And the Twiztt has a lid that locks in place for straining and a keep-warm bowl for nesting in the pot. To test these out, we browned meat and made it into stew, deep-fried a pound of frozen French fries, steamed 4 cups of rice, and timed boiling water.

The results? Mixed. The groove-bottom Turbopot excelled at deep frying, but browning meat or cooking rice forced us to drastically lower the flame—or get a burnt-on mess. The Twiztt was a disappointment, scorching any food that touched its thin walls near the base of the pot. And its built-in strainer? Large solids blocked the exit, rendering it useless. Only the Never Burn Sauce Pot delivered: That silicone oil chamber, which is sandwiched in the pot's base, retained heat brilliantly and never scorched even when we allowed chili to simmer in it unattended for an hour. Its unwieldy size was the only factor that kept it a notch below our winner.

RECOMMENDED

PAULI COOKWARE Never Burn Sauce Pot, 10 Quart
Model: 1001
Price: $229.99
Cooking Surface: 10.5 in
Weight: 11.9 lb
Innovation: Silicone oil chamber in base to provide slow, even heating and prevent scorching

CRITERIA	
Does innovation work?	Yes
Stew	★★★
Fries	★★
Rice	★★★

TESTERS' COMMENTS
This large, sturdy pot has a thick, multilayer base that encloses a silicone oil chamber designed to spread heat slowly and evenly. It browned meat uniformly and helped reduce stew to the ideal velvety thickness. It also retained heat well, producing fluffy rice. We let a big batch of chili bubble away for an hour without stirring, and it didn't scorch at all. The only drawback was its mammoth size. Heavy and broad, it needed well over 3 quarts of oil to get sufficient depth for cooking French fries; its tall sides got in the way when we scooped out fries, and its temperature recovery was a bit slow.

NOT RECOMMENDED

TURBO POT BY ENERON Stainless 7⅝-Quart SaucePot
Model: TPS4001
Price: $76.39
Cooking Surface: 8.75 in
Weight: 6.3 lb
Innovation: Aluminum ridges on bottom to channel heat and speed cooking (but only on gas stoves)

CRITERIA	
Does innovation work?	Partly
Stew	★
Fries	★★★
Rice	★

This steel stockpot features ½-inch-tall aluminum ridges across its base. They're designed to spread the heat of a gas flame more quickly across the base, and they do help: This pot was a brilliant French fry cooker, since the oil temperature recovered more quickly than it did with all the other innovators (and at about the same pace as the Le Creuset). Three quarts of water boiled in 10 minutes, shaving 2½ minutes off the time of the Le Creuset. But it was prone to overheat and scorch unless we lowered the flame substantially: Fond scorched and burned on when we browned meat for stew. The grooves don't work on electric or induction stoves.

TWIZTT BY JOAN LUNDEN 5-Quart Cook, Strain and Serve 3-Piece Set
Model: CW0004777
Price: $79.99
Cooking Surface: 7.5 in
Weight: 5.6 lb
Innovation: Integrated strainer, keep-warm bowl

CRITERIA	
Does innovation work?	Partly
Stew	★
Fries	★
Rice	★★

This flimsy pot scorched any food that touched its thin walls, which bulged out from its small 7.5-inch base. The small diameter of its cooking surface meant browning stew meat in five tedious batches. Rice came out mushy and unevenly cooked. As for the locking lid designed for safe straining, it worked adequately for straining pasta and egg noodles, but chunkier foods like butternut squash blocked the opening. The melamine keep-warm bowl worked, but it was hard to care about that when the pot itself was this poor.

NEWFANGLED NONSTICK SKILLETS

The biggest problem with nonstick skillets is that sooner or later they all quit being nonstick. Next on the list of gripes would be health concerns about the use of polytetrafluoroethylene (PTFE), a chemical that can release harmful fumes if heated to above 650 degrees. We wondered whether superior nonstick performance could be found without PTFE. Two of the pans we tested—Moneta and Berndes—use ceramic finishes, while the Gunter Wilhelm is a five-layer stainless steel and aluminum pan that promises to be nonstick without a coating. We tested them by making a series of single fried eggs without fat, not stopping until an egg stuck. Next we made crêpes to test for even browning and then moved on to beef stir-fry; frittata; and, lastly, scrambled eggs (which we also made without fat).

With fried eggs, the five-layer pan from Gunter Wilhelm failed: It couldn't release a single egg without sticking. The Berndes gave us 73 eggs before sticking firmly, while the Moneta only began to stick at 77 eggs. In all tests, the Gunter Wilhelm pan felt heavy and awkward. The two ceramic pans were easier to maneuver; the Moneta was lightest of all and more responsive to heat, but it had other flaws. While this testing gave us hope that a ceramic nonstick pan to rival our traditional favorite might come along someday, we're not quite there yet.

STATE-OF-THE-ART SAUCEPANS

Our favorite All-Clad saucepan is a kitchen workhorse—its hefty frame, deep bowl, long arm, and tight-fitting lid make it our go-to vessel for rice, soups, sauces, and even pastry cream. What could possibly be improved? Mainly space management, we discovered when we began to peruse cutting-edge options. We tested two saucepans with removable handles—the ABCT and the Cristel—which allow the cook to fit more pans on a small stovetop, in the dishwasher, or in a cupboard. The ABCT also boasts a lid that doubles as a trivet. And we were hopeful that the 2-quart Twiztt—which, like the same company's 5-quart pot, has an integrated strainer and a keep-warm bowl—would work better in saucepan form, so we also took it for a spin. We tested these new models by making pastry cream, sautéed onions, and rice pilaf.

The results? Disappointing. While they did save space, the two pans with removable handles either were out of balance or did not feel secure. The ABCT's wooden lid/trivet performed its heat-shield function well but prevented us from using the clamp-style handle, since the lid won't fit when the handle is attached. The Twiztt's innovative lid met the same fate as the one for its larger pot: Bulky solids tended to block the opening. The only innovation that held up was the same pan's nesting bowl: Placing the pan in the bowl let us take it to the table and kept the contents warm. None of the innovators came close to performing as well as our favorite.

RECOMMENDED WITH RESERVATIONS

	CRITERIA		TESTERS' COMMENTS

MONETA Padella Whitech Frypan, 28 Cm (11 inches)
Model: 3820128
Price: $110
Cooking Surface: 9 in
Oven-Safe Temperature: 350°
Innovation: Aluminum pan with ceramic interior, enamel exterior

Does innovation work? **Partly**
Cooking ★★★
Design ★
Coating Durability ★★½

This lightweight pan fried 77 eggs without fat before the coating began to wear off—almost as many as our favorite nonstick skillet. We liked its smooth interior and low flared sides; it nicely browned beef for stir-fry and wiped out easily throughout testing. But the handle loosened and was impossible to fix. The pan is also oven-safe to only 350 degrees (our winner is oven-safe to 450 degrees). A heat indicator spot on the handle stopped working. With these flaws, it's a hard sell.

NOT RECOMMENDED

BERNDES SignoCast Pearl Ceramic Coated Cast Aluminum 11½-Inch Open Fry Pan
Model: 697628
Price: $119.98
Cooking Surface: 9.75 in
Oven-Safe Temperature: 350°
Innovation: Cast aluminum pan with ceramic coating

Does innovation work? **Partly**
Cooking ★★
Design ★★
Coating Durability ★★

This gorgeous pan started out strong but eventually lost slickness: The 73rd fried egg stuck firmly. It seared meat for beef stir-fry well but was hard to clean after we made scrambled eggs without fat, revealing the loss of some nonstick capability. It developed stains on its surface. Its handle loosened, though we retightened it. Far more expensive than our favorite nonstick pan, with none of its durability, this pan is a no go.

GUNTER WILHELM 12-Inch Fry Pan with Standing Lid
Model: 305
Price: $179
Cooking Surface: 10 in
Oven-Safe Temperature: 450°
Innovation: Five-ply stainless steel and aluminum pan described as "nonstick" without special coating

Does innovation work? **No**
Cooking ★
Design ★
Coating Durability N/A

This pricey pan was supposed to be nonstick. But the first egg we fried in it stuck completely. A handsome traditional pan, it was also a heavy, unwieldy beast that was slow to heat up but then accumulated too much heat, scorching the meat for our stir-fry and the eggs in our frittata. Its surface was not very durable, becoming scratched when we sliced frittata.

RECOMMENDED WITH RESERVATIONS

	CRITERIA		TESTERS' COMMENTS

ABCT Low Casserole with Universal Handle and Mahogany Lid
Model: AB10324; handle AB200; lid AB10024
Price: $158 (pan $72; handle $40; lid $46)
Capacity: 2 qt
Cooking Surface: 9 in
Weight: 1.45 lb
Innovation: Removable handle, lid doubles as trivet

Does innovation work? **No**
Cooking ★★
Design ★

With its white ceramic coating and wooden lid that doubles as a trivet, this pan is designed to go elegantly from stovetop to table. But the removable tonglike handle, the clamp of which is wrapped in rubber to affix to the pan's walls, required near-constant squeezing to stay secure, which hurt our hands. The pan made great rice pilaf, but the very thin aluminum scorched onions and broke our pastry cream. With vigilance on the part of the cook, this pan does perform, but that makes extra work.

CRISTEL MultiPly Stainless 4.5 Quart Sauce Pan with Glass Lid
Model: F22QMPKP; handle PLSX
Price: $319.90 (pan $289.95; handle $29.95)
Capacity: 4.5 qt
Cooking Surface: 8.25 in
Weight: 5.15 lb (with handle)
Innovation: Removable handle

Does innovation work? **No**
Cooking ★★
Design ★

With five layers of metal—it's tri-ply throughout, with two additional layers on the bottom—this pan was heavy and out of balance when lifted by its stumpy, removable handle. The handle also got too hot to hold close to the pan, making it awkward for stirring pastry cream. Though it produced decent rice pilaf, it repeatedly scorched onions since its thick disk bottom heated slowly and then raced. For its price, this pan should have been perfect.

NOT RECOMMENDED

TWIZTT BY JOAN LUNDEN 2-Quart Cook, Strain and Serve 3-Piece Set
Model: CW0004775
Price: $49.99
Capacity: 2 qt
Cooking Surface: 5.75 in
Weight: 3.25 lb
Innovation: Strainer lid, keep-warm serving bowl

Does innovation work? **Partly**
Cooking ★½
Design ★

This thin, flimsy steel pan bulges out from its aluminum- and steel-clad disk-bottom base, which gave us scorched onions and rice that browned too much along the pan's sides. It uses a locking lid to allow safe straining, but solids pushed against the narrow opening when we poured, holding back the liquid. The pan fits into a keep-warm melamine bowl that let us bring it to the table, where it successfully kept the contents hot.

BY KEITH DRESSER, ANDREA GEARY, ANDREW JANJIGIAN, LAN LAM, DAVID PAZMIÑO & DAN SOUZA

Prepping Tofu for Stir-Frying

We've found that coating tofu with cornstarch and shallow-frying it prevents it from turning soggy when stir-fried. This treatment creates a crisp, craggy surface that holds sauce nicely and contrasts with the curd's soft, creamy interior. Cut a 14-ounce tofu block into 24 flat triangles for maximum surface area and lightly coat the pieces with ⅓ cup of cornstarch. Fry the tofu in 3 tablespoons of vegetable oil, turning once, until golden brown on both sides. Drain on a paper towel–lined plate. Add the tofu to the stir-fry toward the end of cooking, along with the sauce. –D.P.

SCIENCE Gluten, Up Close and Personal

Gluten—an elastic protein that has the ability to trap air, much like a balloon—is formed when two important proteins in wheat flour, glutenin and gliadin, bond together in the presence of water. Whether we are trying to create more of it in rustic bread or pizza dough or working to limit its development for tender baked goods like cakes and muffins, there's no denying gluten's importance. But beyond our conceptual understanding of it, is there a more tangible way to see and feel gluten? We ran a simple experiment to find out.

We made two basic doughs by mixing flour and water in a food processor until a smooth ball formed. For one dough we used cake flour, which contains between 6 and 8 percent protein, and for the other one we used bread flour, which usually runs from 12 to 14 percent protein. After making the doughs, we placed each in a mesh strainer and massaged them under running water to wash away all of the starch. Once the water ran clear (a sign that the starch was gone), we were left with two piles of essentially pure gluten. The differences in the appearance and texture of the two doughs were a dramatic confirmation of the profound impact of gluten. –D.S.

CAKE FLOUR

BREAD FLOUR

Low-protein cake flour formed a very small amount of sticky, weak gluten. This characteristic is a boon to cake and muffins, in which too much gluten can turn the crumb unappealingly tough.

High-protein bread flour formed a large ball of highly resilient, rubbery gluten that could be stretched very thin without tearing. This structure traps air in breads, providing high rise and good texture.

The Science of Cooking: Gluten
Video available FREE for 4 months at CooksIllustrated.com/aug13

SCIENCE Why Use a Water Pan in Your Grill?

Some grill experts put an empty aluminum pan in the grill in order to catch drips and prevent flare-ups. For recipes such as our Sweet and Tangy Barbecued Chicken (page 7), we not only put a pan on the grill but also fill it with water—for different reasons: Placing a pan of water opposite the coals lowers the heat inside a grill, allowing you to cook more slowly and gently; it also evens out the heat. But we weren't sure which component—the water or the pan—was more responsible for these benefits.

EXPERIMENT We gauged the heat disparities on three different grill setups by running a toast test. We built indirect fires in each grill and then placed a disposable aluminum pan opposite the coals in one, an aluminum pan filled with 3 cups of water in another, and nothing in the third grill. We let the coals burn for 15 minutes and then spread six slices of bread over each grill's cooler side and let them cook for 4 minutes.

NO PAN
Fierce, spotty heat chars bread in spots.

EMPTY PAN
Moderate, even heat lightly toasts bread.

WATER PAN
Slightly more moderate heat lightly toasts bread.

RESULTS Bread toasted on the grill without a pan turned dark brown and the pieces closest to the coals burned, while the slices cooked on the two grills with aluminum pans were lightly and evenly tanned. The bread toasted over the water-filled pan was slightly paler but not by much. The grill temperatures correlated with the toast results: The grill without the pan registered 415 to 425 degrees, the grill with the empty pan 385 to 395 degrees, and the grill with the water-filled pan 375 to 385 degrees.

EXPLANATION Even putting an empty aluminum pan in the grill will significantly drop its temperature. Aluminum is very efficient at absorbing heat, allowing it to lower the temperature inside the grill by about 30 degrees and to even out hot spots. Water added to the pan captures more heat, helping drop the temperature even further, but it's mainly the metal pan that's responsible for the change. So if you ever put an empty pan in the grill to catch drips, be aware that it will lower the temperature as well. –L.L.

Enhancing Flavor with Kombu

Kombu is a dried kelp rich in flavor-enhancing glutamic acid that's used extensively in Japanese cooking. One of its most popular applications is in dashi, Japan's multipurpose base for soups, stews, and sauces. Japanese cooks often add the seaweed to cold water, which is then brought to a simmer, at which point the kombu is removed (temperatures above a simmer can pull out off flavors). We found that the kelp can also be used to deepen flavor in nontraditional applications like vegetable soup and tomato sauce when small pieces of it are added to the pot with the soup's liquid ingredients and with the tomatoes in pasta sauce. For every quart of liquid (or liquid-like ingredients), add a 2 by 2-inch piece of kombu (which can be found in both Asian markets and many ordinary grocery stores), making sure to remove it just as the liquid begins to simmer. –D.S.

Mayo in the Microwave

Traditionally, mayonnaise is made with raw egg yolks—an ingredient many cooks prefer to avoid. Alternative approaches suggest making mayonnaise with hard-cooked eggs and even an eggless mayo with milk. But in his book *The Curious Cook*, Harold McGee has a novel method in which he heats the yolks to a food-safe 160 degrees, keeping them in liquid form. First the yolks are thinned out a bit with water and lemon juice (which helps stabilize them, as acids prevent curdling). Then they are microwaved briefly until slightly thickened, retaining nearly all their emulsifying power. We tested the technique and it worked well, giving us a billowy, creamy mayo.

Here's the method: Place one egg yolk in a bowl and whisk in 1 tablespoon of water and 1 tablespoon of lemon juice. Cover and microwave for 15 to 20 seconds, or until the egg starts to bubble. Uncover, whisk until smooth, and microwave for 5 seconds, or until the mixture comes to a boil again. Whisk again, cover, and let sit until cool. Add a pinch of salt and then whisk in 1 cup of oil in a thin stream. Note: Use only ⅓ cup or less of extra-virgin olive oil, since it contains trace impurities that can cause the emulsion, which is not quite as stable as a traditional mayo, to break within a few hours. Regular olive oil and other vegetable oils do not present this problem. –A.J.

Turning Dry Sherry to Cream

Cream sherry is a sweet, dark variety of barrel-aged sherry made in the oloroso style of fortified wines—by oxidative (or air) aging. We like the sweetness of cream sherry in our Summer Berry Trifle (page 23), but there's no need to run out to the liquor store if you have only dry sherry on hand. We've found that it's possible to create a reasonable facsimile of cream sherry by stirring 2 teaspoons of dark brown sugar into ½ cup of the dry kind. (But don't try serving the sweetened dry sherry to your great aunt Sadie as a sub for her favorite tipple; it's only suitable for recipes.) –A.G.

Packaged Parts Have a Weight Problem

Grabbing a package of chicken parts is usually a lot faster than standing in line at the meat counter to buy them individually. But that convenience may come at a cost. The same chicken parts aren't required to be the same weight and their size can vary dramatically. For example, the U.S. Department of Agriculture permits leg quarters sold together to weigh between 8.5 and 24 ounces; in other words, one leg quarter in a package can weigh almost three times as much as another. Breasts can come from chickens that weigh between 3 and 5.5 pounds—a difference that can't help but translate to the breasts themselves. Such a disparity can be a problem when you're trying to get food to cook at the same rate. This lack of standardization showed up in our own shopping. We bought 26 packages of split breasts and leg quarters (representing five brands) from five different Boston-area supermarkets. When we weighed each piece and calculated the maximum weight variation within each package, the differences were startling: The largest pieces were twice the size of the smallest. Worse, some leg quarters came with attached backbone pieces that had to be cut off and discarded (which means throwing away money). Lesson learned: Whenever possible, buy chicken parts individually from a butcher, who can select similar-size pieces. –K.D.

PASS ON PACKAGED PARTS
These leg quarters came in the same package, yet the one on the left weighs twice as much as the one on the right—a discrepancy that can lead to uneven cooking.

Technique: The Best Way to Extract Lobster Meat

There's a lot more meat in a lobster than just the tail and claws—if you know how to get it. Here's our tried-and-true approach to extracting every last bit, no special tools needed. The method works for both hard- and soft-shell lobsters. –A.G.

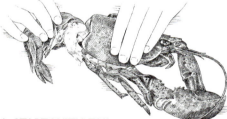

1. START WITH TAIL
Once cooked lobster is cool enough to handle, set it on a cutting board. Grasp tail with 1 hand and grab body with your other hand and twist to separate.

2. TAKE OUT TAIL MEAT
Many sources recommend using knife to cut down center of tail; we prefer to keep it in 1 piece. Lay tail on its side on counter and use both hands to press down on tail until shell cracks. Hold tail, flippers facing you and shell facing down, with your thumbs on opposite sides. Pull back on both sides to crack open shell and remove meat. Briefly rinse meat under running water to remove green tomalley if you wish (for more information, see "Lobster Tomalley" on page 2) and pat meat dry with paper towels. Remove dark vein from tail meat with paring knife.

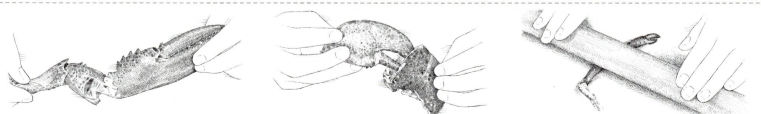

3. MOVE TO KNUCKLES
Twist "arms" to remove both claws and attached "knuckles" (2 small jointed sections) from body. Twist knuckles to remove them from claw. Break knuckles into 2 pieces at joint using back of chef's knife or lobster-cracking tool. Use handle of teaspoon or skewer to push meat out of shell.

4. NEXT UP: CLAWS
Wiggle smaller hinged portion of each claw to separate. If meat is stuck inside small part, remove it with skewer. Break open claws using back of chef's knife or lobster-cracking tool, cracking 1 side and then flipping them to crack other side, and remove meat.

5. FINISH WITH LEGS
Twist legs to remove them from body. Working with one at a time, lay legs flat on counter. Using rolling pin, start from claw end and roll toward open end, pushing out meat. Stop rolling before reaching end of legs; open tip of leg can crack and release pieces of shell.

EQUIPMENT CORNER

⇒ BY HANNAH CROWLEY, AMY GRAVES & TAIZETH SIERRA ⇐

NEW Planchas

Popular in Spanish cooking, a *plancha* is a flat griddle that fits on top of gas or charcoal grill grates. Its surface puts a good sear on meat, chicken, or fish and also prevents smaller foods from falling through the grates. We cooked steaks, scallops, vegetables, and bacon on three models priced from about $40 to $90. One model was cramped with four steaks; another was fussy, since its cast-iron surface needed frequent upkeep. When we challenged the planchas' ability to prevent grease-ignited flames by cooking a pound of bacon on each, the sloped surface of the winning Weber Style Porcelain-Enameled Cast Iron Plancha ($89.99) directed the fat away from the food, through a small hole in its lower end, and into the grill's grease drip pan, bypassing the heating element. Plus, this roomy cast-iron model boasts raised sides that prevented onions and peppers from spilling out. It is also enameled, which made cleanup a breeze. –T.S.

FLAT-OUT SUCCESS
The Weber Style Porcelain-Enameled Cast Iron Plancha has the goods for griddling on the grill.

NEW Basting Pots

Basting food while grilling can be messy; a pot that holds the sauce promises to make it easier. We tried out four, all sold in sets with silicone basting brushes and priced from $11.15 to $21.95, by holding the pots while slathering barbecue sauce on chicken and olive oil on vegetables. Two pots were made of cast iron and two of stainless steel. The material proved critical: Cast iron can sit right on the grill grates, whereas stainless steel models are not heatproof. A pot that can rest on the grate is closer to the food and heats the sauce so that it can be served tableside, while a stainless steel pot is no better than

SAUCING SIMPLIFIED
The Lodge Sauce Kit is comfortable to hold and keeps basting sauce on hand on a hot grill.

a bowl if you can't set it on the grates. One cast-iron pot had a sharp, short handle that was painful to hold. We much preferred the Lodge Sauce Kit ($21.95), with its comfy handle, stable shape that won't tip, and handy pouring spouts. While its brush was slightly shorter than we liked, it slathered sauce evenly and cleaned up quickly. (Plus, our favorite longer grill basting brush, $9.95 from Elizabeth Karmel's Grill Friends, also fit the pot just fine.) –H.C.

NEW Charcoal Storage Bag

When is a bag that holds a bag a handy thing? When it's holding 20 pounds of charcoal by way of a sturdy Velcro closure that seals out moisture so the coals are ready for the next grilling session. Late last year we left a bag of coals in the vinyl Charcoal Companion Charcoal Storage Bag ($19.99) outdoors for three months, during which it weathered two major storms, a few snow squalls, and countless rainy days. Our coals stayed dry throughout. On days when we grilled, we used the bag to pour out what we needed—the nylon strap along the length of the bag made it easy to hold it in place as we aimed the coals into the chimney starter. Resealing the bag was a simple matter of pressing together the Velcro strips across the top. For backyard grillers who don't have a shed or a garage, this bag stashes coals neatly and effectively. –A.G.

IT'S IN THE BAG
The Charcoal Storage Bag uses heavy vinyl and a tight Velcro closure to keep charcoal safe from the elements.

UPDATE
iGrill Wireless Cooking Thermometer

About a year ago, we tested the iGrill Wireless Cooking Thermometer, which allows you to monitor your food's temperature on the grill from your smartphone via a base unit with two meat probes that communicates readings wirelessly. We loved the concept but couldn't recommend the product wholeheartedly at $99.99 because of a few flaws. Now an updated version has arrived, for $79.99, minus earlier glitches and sporting a few new features. As we grill-roasted a pork shoulder, temperature readings from the iGrill's easier-to-read display matched what we got from our most reliable instant-read thermometer. We liked a new graph function that plots the meat's progress and downloads the readings to a laptop for reference. The device's signal is now stronger and didn't lose touch through the two walls between our grilling area and the test kitchen. Switching the connection between two users now requires fewer steps. It also comes with a new ambient temperature probe ($19.99), which monitors air temperature up to 400 degrees. –A.G.

i IS FOR IMPROVEMENT
Version 2.0 of the iGrill Wireless Cooking Thermometer boasts a brighter readout and a stronger connection to smartphones.

NEW Hot Dog Bun Pan

The classic New England split-top bun is a summertime staple, ideal for holding lobster salad or a hot dog. We usually buy buns, but this style can be hard to find outside this region. Now there's a way to bake them at home, with USA Pan's New England Hot Dog Bun Pan ($34.95). This sturdy steel pan makes 10 buns. We prepared the buns according to the instructions, which called for covering the pan with an inverted baking sheet weighted with a heavy cast-iron skillet. As the buns baked, the dough expanded and flattened against the baking sheet, and the pan released 10 evenly browned, flat-bottomed buns without a hitch. The buns resembled the store-bought versions but tasted even better. We won't always have time to bake homemade buns, but when we do, this pan will elevate our lobster rolls or any barbecue fare. –H.C.

HOME BUN
The New England Hot Dog Bun Pan bakes 10 classic split-top buns that look store-bought but taste homemade.

For complete testing results for each item, go to CooksIllustrated.com/aug13.

Sources

Prices were current at press time and do not include shipping. Contact companies to confirm information or visit CooksIllustrated.com for updates.

PAGE 7: HIGH-END BARBECUE SAUCE
• Pork Barrel Original BBQ Sauce: $5.49, BBQ Addicts (**bbqaddicts.com**).

PAGE 19: SKEWERS
• Norpro 12-Inch Stainless Steel Skewers: $6.85 for six, item #09-0513, ChefTools.com (206-933-0700, **cheftools.com**).

PAGE 28: NEVER BURN SAUCE POT
• Pauli Cookware Never Burn Sauce Pot: $229.99, item #24703, Chef's Catalog (800-338-3232, **chefscatalog.com**).

PAGE 32: PLANCHA
• Weber Style Porcelain-Enameled Cast Iron Plancha: $89.99, item #32405 0024, FireCraft (800-745-6109, **firecraft.com**).

PAGE 32: BASTING POT
• Lodge Sauce Kit: $21.95, item #LMPK, Lodge Manufacturing (423-837-7181, **lodgemfg.com**).

PAGE 32: CHARCOAL STORAGE BAG
• Charcoal Companion Charcoal Storage Bag: $19.99, item #CC4508, Grillstuff Grill Parts & Accessories (866-781-0997, **grillstuff.com**).

PAGE 32: IGRILL WIRELESS COOKING THERMOMETER
• iGrill Wireless Cooking Thermometer: $79.99, item #793573880987, iDevices (800-277-3381, **igrillinc.com**).

PAGE 32: HOT DOG BUN PAN
• USA Pan New England Hot Dog Bun Pan: $34.95, item #4666, King Arthur Flour Company (800-827-6836, **kingarthurflour.com**).

INDEX
July & August 2013

Sweet and Tangy Barbecued Chicken, 7

Perfect Fried Eggs, 13

Fresh Corn Cornbread, 24

New England Lobster Roll, 11

Grilled Glazed Pork Tenderloin Roast, 9

Pasta with Pesto, Potatoes, and Green Beans, 15

AMERICA'S TEST KITCHEN COOKING SCHOOL

Let us help you become a better cook. Offering more than 100 courses for cooks at every level, our school combines personalized instruction from real *America's Test Kitchen* test cooks with leading-edge technology to offer a unique and effective learning experience. Start a 14-day free trial at OnlineCookingSchool.com.

Brown Rice Salad, 21

Grilled Lamb Kofte, 19

COOK'S ILLUSTRATED IS NOW AVAILABLE ON iPAD!

Download the new *Cook's Illustrated* app for iPad and start a free trial subscription or purchase a single issue. Issues are enhanced with recipe videos, full-color step-by-step slide shows, and expanded reviews and ratings. Go to CooksIllustrated.com/iPad to download our app through iTunes.

Summer Berry Trifle, 23

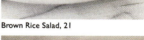

Tunisian-Style Grilled Vegetables, 14

PHOTOGRAPHY: CARL TREMBLAY; STYLING: MARIE PIRAINO

Teton de Venus

Lime Green Salad

Mountain Gold

Great White

Chocolate Stripe

Phoenix

Northern Light

EXOTIC TOMATOES

NUMBER 124

SEPTEMBER & OCTOBER 2013

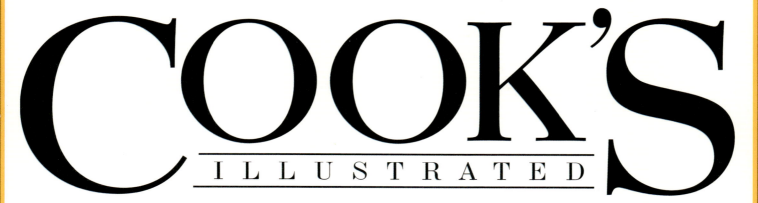

COOK'S
ILLUSTRATED

Grilled Glazed Chicken Breasts
Goodbye, Bland and Goopy

Grown-Up Grilled Cheese Sandwiches

Rating Bacons
Is Thicker Better?

Fresh Peach Pie
Juicy, Perfect Slices

Testing Inexpensive Chef's Knives
Can Any Beat the Champ?

French Pork Stew

Kitchen Myths
Water Boils Faster When Salted?

Best Grilled Corn
Cuban Shredded Beef
Summer Pasta Puttanesca

CooksIllustrated.com
$6.95 U.S. & CANADA

CONTENTS
September & October 2013

Founder and Editor Christopher Kimball
Editorial Director Jack Bishop
Editorial Director, Magazines John Willoughby
Executive Editor Amanda Agee
Test Kitchen Director Erin McMurrer
Managing Editor Rebecca Hays
Executive Food Editor Keith Dresser
Senior Editors Lisa McManus
Dan Souza
Senior Editors, Features Molly Birnbaum
Elizabeth Bomze
Copy Editors Nell Beram
Megan Ginsberg
Associate Editors Hannah Crowley
Andrea Geary
Amy Graves
Andrew Janjigian
Chris O'Connor
Test Cooks Daniel Cellucci
Lan Lam
Assistant Editors Shannon Friedmann Hatch
Taizeth Sierra
Assistant Test Cooks Cecelia Jenkins
Sarah Mullins
Executive Assistant Christine Gordon
Assistant Test Kitchen Director Leah Rovner
Senior Kitchen Assistants Michelle Blodget
Meryl MacCormack
Kitchen Assistants Maria Elena Delgado
Shane Drips
Ena Gudiel
Executive Producer Melissa Baldino
Co-Executive Producer Stephanie Stender
Production Assistant Kaitlin Hammond
Contributing Editor Dawn Yanagihara
Consulting Editor Scott Brueggeman
Science Editor Guy Crosby, Ph.D.
Managing Editor, Web Christine Liu
Senior Editor, Cooking School Mari Levine
Associate Editors, Web Eric Grzymkowski
Roger Metcalf
Assistant Editors, Web Jill Fisher
Charlotte Wilder
Senior Video Editor Nick Dakoulas

Design Director Amy Klee
Art Director Julie Cote
Deputy Art Director Susan Levin
Associate Art Director Lindsey Timko
Deputy Art Director, Marketing/Web Jennifer Cox
Associate Art Director, Marketing/Web Mariah Tarvainen
Designer, Marketing/Web Judy Blomquist
Staff Photographer Daniel J. van Ackere
Photo Editor Steve Klise

Vice President, Marketing David Mack
Circulation Director Doug Wicinski
Circulation & Fulfillment Manager Carrie Fethe
Partnership Marketing Manager Pamela Putprush
Marketing Assistant Joyce Liao

VP, Technology, Product Development Barry Kelly
Director, Project Management Alice Carpenter
Production & Traffic Coordinator Brittany Allen
Development Manager Mike Serio

Chief Operating Officer Rob Ristagno
Production Director Guy Rochford
Workflow & Digital Asset Manager Andrew Mannone
Senior Color & Imaging Specialist Lauren Pettapiece
Production & Imaging Specialists Heather Dube
Lauren Robbins
Director of Sponsorship Sales Anne Traficante
Client Services Associate Kate May
Sponsorship Sales Representative Morgan Ryan
Customer Service Manager Jacqueline Valerio
Customer Service Representatives Megan Hamner
Jessica Haskin
Andrew Straaberg Finfrock

Chief Financial Officer Sharyn Chabot
Retail Sales & Marketing Director Emily Logan
Human Resources Director Adele Shapiro
Publicity Deborah Broide

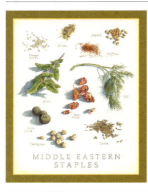

MIDDLE EASTERN STAPLES Fresh MINT brightens salads like tabbouleh. Feathery DILL, kept on hand in Turkish and Iranian kitchens, is added at the end of cooking. SESAME SEEDS are pulverized to make tahini. ROSE PETALS distilled into rose water flavor Turkish delight and desserts like rice pudding. MAHLEB, made from the pits of St. Lucie black cherries, spices desserts. BLACK LIMES, also known as Omani limes, are the result of drying the citrus for months in the sun. Punctured and added whole to stews, they impart a sharp flavor. A pinch of SAFFRON adds a golden hue and heady aroma to dishes like pilaf. ZA'ATAR is a spice blend that varies depending on region but often includes ground sumac, dried thyme, and sesame seeds. Mild-tasting CHICKPEAS are the basis of hummus. CUMIN boasts a complex, slightly smoky flavor.

COVER (Squash): Robert Papp; **BACK COVER** (Middle Eastern Staples): John Burgoyne

America's TEST KITCHEN
RECIPES THAT WORK®

America's Test Kitchen is a very real 2,500-square-foot kitchen located just outside Boston. It is the home of *Cook's Illustrated* and *Cook's Country* magazines and is the workday destination of more than three dozen test cooks, editors, and cookware specialists. Our mission is to test recipes over and over again until we understand how and why they work and until we arrive at the best version. We also test kitchen equipment and supermarket ingredients in search of brands that offer the best value and performance. You can watch us work by tuning in to *America's Test Kitchen* (AmericasTestKitchenTV.com) on public television.

PRINTED IN THE USA

THE FAMILY ALBUM

My winter project was to scan old family photos. I was reminded that my paternal grandfather (he also wore a bow tie) had more than a passing resemblance to Lurch from the Addams Family and that, yes, I actually did dress up in a cowboy hat, blue jean jacket, and the requisite boots during a vacation at a Wyoming dude ranch when I was 12. (The only redeeming feature was that my father, who was in the photo with me, looked even more out of place in a red plaid shirt and khakis.)

The gems from this collection are a sepia shot of my mother in fishing hat and sunglasses holding up a 20-inch trout while sitting in the bow of a canoe in Canada; a family portrait of my grandmother and her three sisters that included my great-grandmother, Caroline de Wolf, who was married to the portrait painter and Whistler contemporary Harper Pennington; and a color photo of yours truly at age 7 or 8 dressed in a baggy white baseball uniform with STARS sewn on the front. (I played Little League.) My other favorites were a shot of my mother, Mary Alice, standing at a small cookstove when she was just married (a rare shot indeed) and an old black and white of my sister, Kate, helping my mother collect sap for the local maple sugaring operation owned by Charlie Bentley.

It is tempting to offer homilies about the past. One might conclude that life was simpler, except that it wasn't. Lives were just as messy and complicated 50 years ago as they are today. If you say that we had a deeper sense of place, you might be right, since Americans were less nomadic, but I am reminded of a friend who grew up in the Midwest; he is now happily ensconced in New Orleans as a food writer and only returns to Minnesota once per year. Large extended families, three or more generations beaming out at the camera, tug at one's heartstrings but also remind us of the arguments (I remember a particularly bloody engagement one Thanksgiving regarding Spiro Agnew) and petty drawing room

back and forth that is part and parcel of family members packed tightly in a narrow social spiral.

Family albums can, however, bring back halcyon memories. The warm, sharp scent of wild sage on that Wyoming dude ranch. The feel of a soft, sun-warmed baseball mitt. Ribbons of light illuminating the dark interior of a steam-filled saphouse and the slow pooling and drip of thick syrup off the skimmer. My mother taking charge after a poor day of fishing in Maine, telling the guide where to position the canoe, and my first cast over a large pool and the almost immediate tug downward of a hungry trout. The nervous tail wagging of our overbred pointer, Kili, who shook her body so violently back and forth when you walked into a room that you thought she would die of happiness. One photo in particular brings back rich memories—a shot of our just-built Vermont cabin in 1955, taken from atop a nearby hill; it looks primitive and reminds me of pressed wildflowers, sweet corn dinners, frogs' legs, homemade beef and pork burgers, chopping kindling, Wilcox coffee ice cream, party line phones, gin and tonics on the porch, wildfires, snowbanks, Vermont cheddar, moonlit rides in our WWII jeep, creosote, summer saunas, and copperhead snakes slithering in the weeds by the lower pond.

Perhaps life can be judged by the number of family albums one has accumulated. Some lives are a straight line between birth and death; one album does the trick. Others live lives with many chapters, each one starting with a new photo placed on a crisp white page.

Dr. Seuss wrote, "Everyone is just waiting; waiting for the fish to bite or waiting for wind to fly a kite, or a pot to boil, or a Better Break, or a string of pearls, or a pair of pants, or a wig with curls, or Another Chance."

Christopher Kimball

And so, we sometimes find ourselves at the point when we need to begin a new album. Our "arms may get sore, and our sneakers may leak" but it's time to be off, "up many a creek." Photos are taken, pages are filled, and this becomes our legacy for the next generation.

Mary Alice, my mother, lived a life of many albums. The unlikely Washington, D.C., debutante. The gilt-edged bride at National Cathedral. Then WWII and working in an upstate New York wire factory, supporting the war effort. Posing by an apartment-size cookstove, the reluctant homemaker. Then fishing and hunting, in canoes, camping on lakeshores in Maine, and then caught off guard in an Elmer Fudd hunting cap during deer season in Vermont. The career professional, recorded in China at yet another academic conference. The later years in northwestern Connecticut, alone on her farm, ruddy-faced and a tad unsteady, watching grandchildren hunt for Easter eggs among the guinea hens and Rhode Island Reds. A parting snapshot, high in the Adirondacks in her mountaintop cabin, in splendid simplicity; a wood stove, binoculars, and a view across the top of the world. And then, just a sunset memory, not recorded, of an older woman with her hair down, veins still pumping vinegar, but having a quiet moment as if to say, from mother to son, all the things that are never said.

We don't choose how many albums we fill during a lifetime, but we can decide how to fill them. And it is worth remembering, as Dr. Seuss did, that today is always our day; we're off to great places, we're off and away!

Go to CooksIllustrated.com/cpkfamilyphotos to view selected photos from my family album (including me at the dude ranch). Apologies to Dr. Seuss.

FOR INQUIRIES, ORDERS, OR MORE INFORMATION

CooksIllustrated.com
At CooksIllustrated.com, you can order books and subscriptions, sign up for our free e-newsletter, or renew your magazine subscription. Join the website and gain access to 20 years of *Cook's Illustrated* recipes, equipment tests, and ingredient tastings, as well as companion videos for every recipe in this issue.

COOKBOOKS
We sell more than 50 cookbooks by the editors of *Cook's Illustrated*, including *The Cook's Illustrated Cookbook* and *The Science of Good Cooking*. To order, visit our bookstore at CooksIllustrated.com/bookstore.

COOK'S ILLUSTRATED MAGAZINE
Cook's Illustrated magazine (ISSN 1068-2821), number 124, is published bimonthly by Boston Common Press Limited Partnership, 17 Station St., Brookline, MA 02445. Copyright 2013 Boston Common Press Limited Partnership. Periodicals postage paid at Boston, MA, and additional mailing offices, USPS #012487. Publications Mail Agreement No. 40020778. Return undeliverable Canadian addresses to P.O. Box 875, Station A, Windsor, ON N9A 6P2. POSTMASTER: Send address changes to *Cook's Illustrated*, P.O. Box 6018, Harlan, IA 51593-1518. For subscription and gift subscription orders, subscription inquiries, or change of address notices, visit AmericasTestKitchen.com/customerservice, call 800-526-8442 in the U.S. (515-248-7684 from outside the U.S.), or write to us at *Cook's Illustrated*, P.O. 6018, Harlan, IA 51593-1518.

FOR LIST RENTAL INFORMATION Contact Specialists Marketing Services, Inc., 777 Terrace Ave., 4th Floor, Hasbrouck Heights, NJ 07604; 201-865-5800.
EDITORIAL OFFICE 17 Station St., Brookline, MA 02445; 617-232-1000; fax 617-232-1572. Subscription inquiries, visit AmericasTestKitchen.com/customerservice or call 800-526-8442.
POSTMASTER Send all new orders, subscription inquiries, and change-of-address notices to *Cook's Illustrated*, P.O. Box 6018, Harlan, IA 51593-1518.

⋟ BY ANDREA GEARY, ANDREW JANJIGIAN, LAN LAM & DAN SOUZA ⋞

Same Price, Less Bacon

I've been seeing "center-cut" bacon at the store. How is it different from regular bacon?

JONATHAN MILLER
HOUSTON, TEXAS

➤ Many brands now offer center-cut bacon, a product advertised to contain anywhere from 25 to 30 percent less fat than traditional bacon, uncooked. To see how it might compare with ordinary bacon, we rounded up samples of both kinds from the same brand and compared the cooked strips in a side-by-side tasting. We then sampled the same bacons in spaghetti carbonara. Our findings? Though the regular-cut bacon did have more fat on its ends, much of that fat melted off during cooking, and tasters across the board didn't experience the center-cut bacon, which is sold in shorter strips, as significantly less fatty. Tasters likewise found both products to be nearly identical in the carbonara. So what exactly does distinguish center-cut bacon from the ordinary kind?

As it turns out, not much. Center-cut bacon is nothing more than regular bacon with the fatty ends cut off. If you're looking for bacon with less fat, by all means go for center-cut strips. Just know that you'll be paying more for less: The 12-ounce center-cut packages we sampled were priced exactly the same as the 16-ounce regular packages from the same brand. –D.S.

REGULAR-CUT
Longer strips have more fat at the ends that mostly renders away.

CENTER-CUT
Shorter strips have less fat—but the same price.

Oatmeal Follow-Up

In your March/April 2013 issue, you suggest using a large bowl when microwaving oatmeal in order to prevent it from boiling over. Why not just cook the oatmeal at a lower power?

NELL JOSLIN
RALEIGH, N.C.

➤ You weren't the only one to question whether there were alternate ways to prevent boilovers. Oatmeal tends to overflow when the water boils and bubbles appear, while at the same time, the starches in the cereal swell and form a gel. This viscous gel makes it difficult for the bubbles to escape, causing the oatmeal to rise up and eventually spill over. Previously, we found that adding fat (we used butter) will coat the starches and prevent a strong gel from forming, but for the method to be successful, you have to use a lot of butter. We also tested laying chopsticks horizontally across the bowl, which didn't work at all.

Some readers suggested adding dried fruits or nuts to the oatmeal, but we found that the gel had no trouble forming around these add-ins, so spillovers still occurred. Your suggestion of lowering the power (and cooking longer) did actually work: The mixture boiled less vigorously, fewer bubbles formed, and the oatmeal never achieved the same height as the batch cooked at high power. But "low" power can vary significantly from microwave to microwave and might not be a guarantee that fewer bubbles will form. Therefore, we're sticking with our previous recommendation: Simply use a larger bowl, which gives the oatmeal more space to expand. –L.L.

Leftover Soft-Cooked Eggs

I often make soft-cooked eggs for my family, but sometimes we have leftovers. Can I reheat them?

AMBER BIDDLE
CHELMSFORD, MASS.

➤ As we discovered while developing our Soft-Cooked Eggs recipe (January/February 2013), attaining a warm, runny yolk and a set but tender white requires attention and precision. Our winning formula starts with fridge-cold eggs and ½ inch of boiling water in a medium saucepan. Once the eggs go into the pot, we cover it and cook them for exactly 6½ minutes before shocking them under cold running water. Given this delicate dance of time and temperature, we wondered if it was possible to reheat a soft-cooked egg without overcooking the perfectly runny yolk. We tested reheating dozens of eggs until we found a method that warms the yolk only to 110 to 140 degrees so it stays runny.

For up to six unshelled, refrigerated soft-cooked eggs, bring ½ inch of water to a boil in a medium saucepan over medium-high heat. Using tongs, gently place the eggs in the boiling water, cover, and cook for 3½ minutes. Remove the eggs with the tongs and serve; the yolks will remain warm and runny for up to 15 minutes. We don't shock the eggs when reheating because we're relying on the principle of carryover cooking to gently warm the yolk (which is already cooked perfectly) without cooking it further. (Note: We found that we couldn't give guidelines for reheating soft-cooked eggs that have simply cooled down versus chilled in the refrigerator. The exact temperature of the eggs—and therefore the reheating time—depends on how long they have been sitting at room temperature.) –D.S.

Leaves of (Lemon) Grass

Can I substitute dried lemon grass for fresh?

HEATHER ALEXANDER
BENNINGTON, VT.

➤ Woody stalks of lemon grass, a grassy herb native to India and tropical Asia, are used in many South Asian dishes, imparting citrusy and floral flavors to soups, curries, and stir-fries. Lemon grass is also sometimes dried and sold in jars.

To test the difference between fresh and dried, we used some of each to make a curry paste (which we tasted stirred into vegetable broth), a

Thai chicken soup, and a snow pea stir-fry. (Because dried herbs are more concentrated in flavor than fresh herbs, we followed our general rule by using half as much dried lemon grass as fresh in each recipe.) In all three cases, tasters found that the fresh lemon grass imparted a bright mix of citrus, floral, and minty notes, while the dried lemon grass contributed a less complex, woodsy flavor. That said,

DRIED
Avoid in applications without much liquid.

we still found the dried lemon grass to be an acceptable substitute for fresh in the paste and the soup, both of which also had a lot of other flavors contributing to the mix. But we don't recommend the dried herb at all in stir-fries. With this dry-heat cooking method, the parched pieces of lemon grass could not hydrate and retained the texture of hay. So if you're going to substitute dried lemon grass for fresh, make sure to use it only in recipes in which there is enough liquid for the herb to hydrate and soften. –L.L.

FRESH
More complex taste; works in everything.

The Color Purple in Bread

Why do my walnut breads sometimes turn purple? Is there anything I can do to prevent this?

GWYN BROWN
SEATTLE, WASH.

➤ Theories abound on why yeast breads that contain walnuts (or pecans) turn purple. After reading a paper in the *Journal of Agricultural and Food Chemistry*, we decided to pursue the one that seemed most plausible: that the iron in flour is reacting with gallic acid found in walnut skins to create a color change.

To confirm this theory, we combined walnuts, water, and (to minimize variables) crushed-up iron supplements from the vitamin aisle and watched the water immediately turn a deep purple. We repeated the experiment with pecans, which were equally reactive, and almonds and hazelnuts, both of which triggered a slightly less dramatic color change.

So why don't all baked goods containing these nuts turn purple? The answer has to do with acidity and time. The purple tint appears only in an acidic environment, and most baked goods aren't acidic enough to cause the reaction. But thanks to the acids produced by yeast as it ferments, bread dough does have what it takes. In addition, since gallic acid leaches out slowly, rising bread dough gives time for the effect to happen.

Only tiny amounts of gallic acid are needed to bring out the purple. The tint can't be prevented completely, but it can be minimized by blanching the walnuts in boiling water for 1 minute before using. –A.J.

Sprouted Onions

Is there anything wrong with using an onion that has sprouted a green shoot?

RON ALLEN
CINCINNATI, OHIO

➤ To answer your question, we tasted sprouted onions that we chopped and gently cooked in oil until softened, comparing them with onions with no sprouts prepared the same way. All tasters found the sprouted alliums less sweet and flavorful, and some also found them a bit more fibrous than their unsprouted counterparts. Though the sprouts themselves bore a physical resemblance to chives and scallions, tasters deemed them unpleasantly bitter rather than grassy and pungent.

Why the difference? Sprouts use the sugar stored in the parent onion as an energy source, so as the sprouts grow, the onion flesh loses sweetness. Sprouting also causes the onion to lose moisture, making it seem tougher and stringier.

Our advice: Cook sprouted onions as soon as possible after the sprouts appear, since the flavor and texture of the onion will only continue to deteriorate. And that green bit? Resist the temptation to use it in your food; garnish the compost pile with it instead. –A.G.

WHAT IS IT?

I love the look of retro kitchenware, so I picked up this gadget at an antiques market. What's its original use?

BARBARA O'CONNELL, WOODSTOCK, VT.

Promoted as a "kitchen marvel," the Foley Chopper, circa 1938, is essentially a primitive food processor: Its three blades are designed to chop fruits, vegetables, and nuts faster than a knife-wielding cook. The outer blades lower when downward pressure is applied to the handle. A center spring creates bouncing momentum from cut to cut. In theory, the Chopper would be like having two extra hands to help prep, and we were eager to give it a try. But it was immediately clear that we could not retire our chef's knife: The Chopper exclusively chops, so when we tried it on cabbage, the head first had to be quartered and cored. A center bar designed to prevent food from getting caught in the blades did its job but also stopped us from cutting through our stack of cabbage leaves. When we tried slicing a tomato, the tool just smashed the fruit. It also made a mess of a bunch of cilantro, bruising the leaves when we wanted clean cuts. Pecans fared the best, but each slap of the Chopper sent pieces flying. Sure, it was fun to use, but we'll continue to chop with a sharp chef's knife. –Shannon Friedmann Hatch

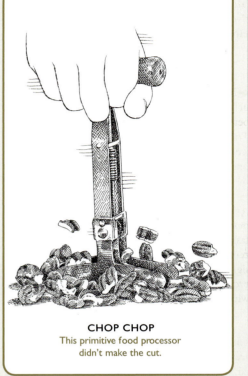

CHOP CHOP
This primitive food processor didn't make the cut.

Substituting Vegetarian Gelatins

I don't use gelatin to thicken desserts because it is an animal product. Can I use an unflavored gelatin substitute just like regular gelatin?

ETHEL GARRETT
SAN DIEGO, CALIF.

➤ While traditional gelatin is derived from animal collagen, unflavored vegetarian gelatin substitutes mainly come from vegetable gums and seaweed extracts. We found one vegetarian substitute—Natural Desserts Unflavored Jel Dessert—at a natural foods store.

Because the vegetable gum in this product is made up of polysaccharides versus the protein in gelatin, we weren't surprised when we found that it required different treatment than gelatin: The vegetarian substitute must be boiled to become activated, it must be added to the other ingredients immediately afterward, and it doesn't work in highly acidic environments.

There were two critical pieces of information the instructions didn't give us, however: what recipes the Natural Desserts product might work best in and how much we should use. Any dessert containing lemon was out, but we chose two recipes that—with tweaks—we thought could accommodate this vegetarian substitute's particularities: panna cotta and a strawberry gelatin mold. We began with a one-to-one swap for gelatin.

For the panna cotta, we boiled the vegetarian substitute in milk (rather than letting it hydrate cold and then gently heating), and it did eventually set—though a bit more loosely than the sample made with traditional gelatin. Increasing the amount of the Natural Desserts product to 1.5 times the traditional gelatin amount helped. The mold made with strawberries (which are mildly acidic) also set—loosely but adequately—with these same adjustments.

The bottom line: Substituting this thickening agent in existing recipes calling for gelatin isn't a simple swap—and may not even be possible if the item is highly acidic or doesn't lend itself to the adjustments required. As a starting point for adapting an existing recipe, increase the Natural Desserts product to 1.5 times the amount of gelatin called for. –L.L.

SEND US YOUR QUESTIONS We will provide a complimentary one-year subscription for each letter we print. Send your inquiry, name, address, and daytime telephone number to Notes from Readers, *Cook's Illustrated*, P.O. Box 470589, Brookline, MA 02447, or to NotesFromReaders@ AmericasTestKitchen.com.

Quick Tips

≥ BY SHANNON FRIEDMANN HATCH ≤

A Flexible Way to Weigh

Carol Vleck of Ames, Iowa, always weighs dry ingredients when baking, but pouring them from a standard bowl into her running stand mixer resulted in a messy countertop. Now she sets a silicone cake pan on her scale and measures her dry ingredients in it. The pan easily bends, so she can pour the ingredients without making a mess.

Better Oven-Fried Bacon

Many cooks line their baking sheets with aluminum foil when oven-frying bacon to simplify cleanup. Betty Pfeifer of Bay Village, Ohio, takes this idea a step further: She fashions a makeshift rack by crimping the foil at 1-inch intervals before placing the bacon horizontally across the crimps. This technique makes cleanup a snap and elevates the strips so that grease drips into the foil crevices during cooking, ensuring a crispier result.

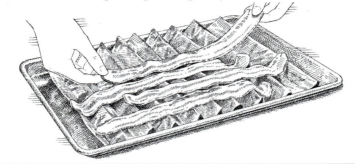

A Fine Kettle of Broth

Rather than ladling homemade chicken broth from one pot to another when making dishes such as risotto, Jodie Remick of Fort Lauderdale, Fla., pours it from her teakettle. The spout gives her better control than the ladle and thus prevents splatters and spills.

Homemade Specialty Coffee

Combining his love of flavored coffee and his stash of spent vanilla beans, Gregory Rubino of Lake Charles, La., makes his own vanilla-flavored brew. After air-drying empty vanilla bean pods for two to three days, he adds half of a pod to a coffee grinder full of enough coffee beans for a pot and processes it before brewing as usual.

Mobile Tasting Results

Shaun Breidbart of Pelham, N.Y., frequently tries new products at the grocery store but can't always recall his favorite brands. To help jog his memory, he uses his cell phone camera to snap a picture of the product with either a thumbs-up or a thumbs-down alongside it. Now he can quickly scroll through the images and know exactly what to buy.

Toaster Oven Trick

The small footprint of a toaster oven earns it a spot on many household counters, but the small rack leaves little room for a bulky oven mitt to grasp its edge. Rather than risk a burn, Eliana Weissman of New Orleans, La., grabs the rack using a smaller, more dexterous helper: a wooden clothespin.

SEND US YOUR TIPS We will provide a complimentary one-year subscription for each tip we print. Send your tip, name, address, and daytime telephone number to Quick Tips, *Cook's Illustrated*, P.O. Box 470589, Brookline, MA 02447, or to QuickTips@AmericasTestKitchen.com.

ILLUSTRATION: JOHN BURGOYNE

Shaker Maker

Rather than purchasing a specific shaker jar for dispensing ingredients like powdered sugar or cocoa, Eileen Jones of Lawrence, Kan., uses this resourceful solution.

1. Cut a 5-inch square of parchment or waxed paper. Place the sheet on top of a canning jar. Screw on the band to secure the paper.

2. Use a skewer to punch several holes in the center of the paper.

Mess-Free Muffin Making

Instead of portioning batter into a muffin tin using a spoon or a measuring cup—both of which tend to dribble batter on the counter—Diane Merkel of Fallbrook, Calif., employs an unusual tool: a canning funnel. The gadget neatly fits into each cup and allows her to deposit batter without any drips.

Custard's Last Stand

Individually portioned desserts such as custards are a great make-ahead solution when entertaining, but only if you have enough refrigerator space to accommodate multiple ramekins. Gilda Crisp of West Hills, Calif., maximizes space by placing a tiered cooling rack in the fridge. With multiple shelves, she can chill several servings at once.

Using Your Marbles to Save Wine

Air is wine's worst enemy, as it causes oxidation that dulls flavor. Transferring leftovers to a lidded Mason jar can create an airtight seal that prevents spoilage—but only if the wine completely fills the container. When Thor Simon of New York, N.Y., has only a small amount of wine left over, he adds clean marbles to the jar until the wine reaches the brim. No air; problem solved.

Extra Pastry Bag

Arielle Moyal of Los Angeles, Calif., fashions extra makeshift pastry bags when her canvas pastry bag is dirty or already filled.

1. Snip away one corner of a gallon-size zipper-lock bag. (A freezer bag is preferable, as it can withstand the pressure needed to pipe the bag's contents.) Make a small cut so just the end of the pastry tip is exposed.

2. Insert the pastry tip through the hole. Fill the bag and pipe as usual.

Brushing Off Beet Stains

No matter how hard you scrub your hands, simple soap and water do little to remove red beet stains. Lisa Morrison of West Tisbury, Mass., has discovered that rubbing a dab of whitening toothpaste with peroxide over the area helps erase the stains.

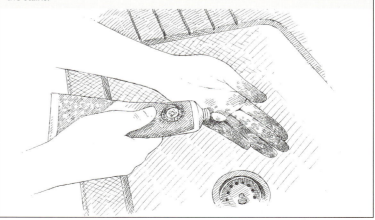

Grilled Glazed Chicken Breasts

Without skin or bone, this lean cut cooks so quickly that it's almost impossible to get it to taste both grilled *and* glazed. An unusual ingredient came to the rescue.

≥ BY KEITH DRESSER ≤

Throwing a few boneless, skinless chicken breasts on the grill and painting them with barbecue sauce always sounds like a good idea. This lean cut is available everywhere, it cooks fast, and it makes a light, simple meal. The trouble is that the results are usually flawed. Because these disrobed specimens cook in a flash over coals, it's hard to get chicken that not only tastes grilled but also has a good glaze without overcooking it. Here's the dilemma: If you wait to apply the glaze until the meat is browned well, it's usually dry and leathery by the time you've lacquered on a few layers. (And you need a few layers to build anything more than a superficial skim of sauce.) But if you apply the glaze too soon, you don't give the chicken a chance to brown, a flavor boost that this bland cut badly needs. Plus, the sugary glaze is prone to burning before the chicken cooks through.

But the ease of throwing boneless, skinless breasts on the grill is too enticing to pass up. I decided to fiddle with the approach until I got it right: tender, juicy chicken with the smoky taste of the grill, glistening with a thick coating of glaze. While I was at it, I wanted to create glazes specifically designed to accentuate, not overwhelm, this lean cut's delicate flavors.

Better Browning in a Hurry

My first step was to brine the meat. I knew that a 30-minute saltwater soak would help keep the chicken juicy and well seasoned and could be accomplished while the grill was heating. I also opted for a two-level fire, which means that I piled two-thirds of the coals on one side of the kettle and just one-third on the other side. This would allow me to sear the breasts over the coals and then move them to the cooler side to avoid burning when I applied the glaze.

My real challenge was to figure out how to speed up browning, also known as the Maillard reaction,

Flipping the chicken four times during grilling—and slathering it with glaze right after each flip—helps build a thick, lacquered coating.

and the consequent formation of all those new flavor compounds that help meat taste rich and complex. If the chicken browned faster, it would leave me more time to build a thick glaze that would add even more flavor. My first thought was to enlist the aid of starch in absorbing some of the moisture on the exterior of the meat that normally would need to burn off before much browning could occur. First I tried dredging the breasts in flour, but this made them bready. Next I tried cornstarch, but this approach turned the breasts gummy. A technique we have employed when pan-searing chicken breasts—creating an artificial "skin" using a paste of cornstarch, flour, and melted butter—gave us better results. The starches (which break down into sugars) and the butter proteins helped achieve a browned surface more quickly, and the porous surface readily held a glaze. Unfortunately, the chicken still tasted more breaded than grilled.

Switching gears, I tried rubbing the surface of the chicken with baking soda. Baking soda increases the pH of the chicken, making it more alkaline, which in

turn speeds up the Maillard reaction. Alas, while this did speed up browning, even small amounts left behind a mild soapy aftertaste.

I was unsure of what to do next. But then I remembered a really unlikely sounding test that one of my colleagues tried when attempting to expedite the browning of pork chops: dredging the meat in nonfat dry milk powder. While this strange coating did brown the meat more quickly, it made the chops taste too sweet. But might it be better suited for browning chicken? It was worth a try. After lightly dusting the breasts with milk powder (½ teaspoon per breast) and lightly spraying them with vegetable oil spray to help ensure that the powder stuck, I threw them on the grill. I was thrilled when the chicken was lightly browned and had nice grill marks in less than 2 minutes, or about half of the time of my most successful previous tests. Why was milk powder so effective? It turns out that dry milk contains about 36 percent protein. But it also contains about 50 percent lactose, a so-called reducing sugar. And the Maillard reaction takes place only after large proteins break down into amino acids and react with certain types of sugars—reducing sugars like glucose, fructose, and lactose. In sum, milk powder contained just the two components that I needed to speed things up.

But that wasn't the only reason milk powder was so successful in quickly triggering browning. Like starch, it's a dry substance that absorbs the excess moisture on the meat. This is helpful because moisture keeps the temperature too low for significant browning to take place until the wetness evaporates. There was yet one more benefit to using the milk powder: It created a thin, tacky surface that was perfect for holding on to the glaze. And now, with expedited browning in place, I had time to thoroughly lacquer my chicken with glaze by applying four solid coats before it finished cooking.

Great Glaze

Next it was time to focus on perfecting the glaze itself. I started with flavor. Since I knew that I wanted to limit the amount of sweetness so as not to overpower the mild flavor of the chicken, I began by testing a host of ingredients that would be thick enough to serve as a clingy base but weren't sugary.

Where Grilling and Glazing Go Wrong

Here's what usually happens when you try for a deep sear and a substantial glaze.

BURNT GLAZE, BLAND MEAT
Layer on glaze from the get-go and it tends to burn. The chicken may be moist, but it lacks flavorful browning.

NICE GLAZE, DRY MEAT
If you wait to apply the sauce, you'll get good browning and a substantial glaze but dry, overcooked chicken.

I settled on a diverse group that included coconut milk, mustard, and hoisin sauce. Then, in order to add balance and complexity, I introduced acidity in the form of citrus juice or vinegar, as well as a healthy dose of spices and aromatics, like red curry paste, fresh ginger, and spicy Sriracha sauce.

My next step was to add a sweet (but not too sweet) element, which would provide further balance, promote browning, and give even more of a sticky cling to the glaze. Sweeteners like maple syrup, brown sugar, and fruit jams made the glazes saccharine. Corn syrup, which is about half as sweet as the other sweeteners, worked far better, giving the glaze just a goodly amount of stickiness while keeping the sweetness level under control. Two to 3 tablespoons, depending on the other ingredients, was just the right amount.

But all was not perfect: The glazes still had a tendency to become too loose when applied to the hot chicken after it browned. Whisking in a teaspoon of cornstarch helped.

At this point I was feeling pretty good. But many tasters wanted an even thicker glaze. This time I looked to adjust my cooking technique. My fix? I switched up the point at which I applied the glaze. Instead of brushing it on right before flipping the chicken, I began to apply the glaze immediately after it was flipped. This meant that less glaze stuck to the grill—and the glaze applied to the top of the chicken had time to dry out and cling. The result? Chicken breasts robed in a thick, lacquered glaze. My dinner was ready.

The Power of Milk Powder

To make sure that our chicken breasts could be both browned *and* glazed in the time it took the chicken to cook, we had to accelerate browning. A surprising ingredient—milk powder—was the solution. Milk powder contains both protein and so-called reducing sugar (in this case, lactose), the keys to the Maillard reaction, the chemical process that causes browning. Faster browning gave us more time to layer on the glaze.

BROWNING BOOSTER

Flip chicken, brush with remaining glaze, and cook until chicken registers 160 degrees, 1 to 3 minutes. Transfer chicken to plate and let rest for 5 minutes before serving.

GRILLED GLAZED BONELESS, SKINLESS CHICKEN BREASTS

SERVES 4

For our free recipes for Miso Sesame Glaze and Molasses Coffee Glaze, go to CooksIllustrated.com/oct13.

- ¼ cup salt
- ¼ cup sugar
- 4 (6- to 8-ounce) boneless, skinless chicken breasts, trimmed
- 2 teaspoons nonfat dry milk powder
- ¼ teaspoon pepper
  Vegetable oil spray
- 1 recipe glaze (recipes follow)

1. Dissolve salt and sugar in 1½ quarts cold water. Submerge chicken in brine, cover, and refrigerate for at least 30 minutes or up to 1 hour. Remove chicken from brine and pat dry with paper towels. Combine milk powder and pepper in bowl.

2A. FOR A CHARCOAL GRILL: Open bottom vent completely. Light large chimney starter mounded with charcoal briquettes (7 quarts). When top coals are partially covered with ash, pour two-thirds evenly over half of grill, then pour remaining coals over other half of grill. Set cooking grate in place, cover, and open lid vent completely. Heat grill until hot, about 5 minutes.

2B. FOR A GAS GRILL: Turn all burners to high, cover, and heat grill until hot, about 15 minutes. Leave primary burner on high and turn other burner(s) to medium-high.

3. Clean and oil cooking grate. Sprinkle half of milk powder mixture over 1 side of chicken. Lightly spray coated side of chicken with oil spray until milk powder is moistened. Flip chicken and sprinkle remaining milk powder mixture over second side. Lightly spray with oil spray.

4. Place chicken, skinned side down, over hotter part of grill and cook until browned on first side, 2 to 2½ minutes. Flip chicken, brush with 2 tablespoons glaze, and cook until browned on second side, 2 to 2½ minutes. Flip chicken, move to cooler side of grill, brush with 2 tablespoons glaze, and cook for 2 minutes. Repeat flipping and brushing 2 more times, cooking for 2 minutes on each side.

COCONUT CURRY GLAZE

MAKES ABOUT ⅔ CUP

- 2 tablespoons lime juice
- 1½ teaspoons cornstarch
- ⅓ cup canned coconut milk
- 3 tablespoons corn syrup
- 1 tablespoon fish sauce
- 1 tablespoon red curry paste
- 1 teaspoon grated fresh ginger
- ¼ teaspoon ground coriander

Whisk lime juice and cornstarch together in small saucepan until cornstarch has dissolved. Whisk in coconut milk, corn syrup, fish sauce, curry paste, ginger, and coriander. Bring mixture to boil over high heat. Cook, stirring constantly, until thickened, about 1 minute. Transfer glaze to bowl.

HONEY MUSTARD GLAZE

MAKES ABOUT ⅔ CUP

- 2 tablespoons cider vinegar
- 1 teaspoon cornstarch
- 3 tablespoons Dijon mustard
- 3 tablespoons honey
- 2 tablespoons corn syrup
- 1 garlic clove, minced
- ¼ teaspoon ground fennel seeds

Whisk vinegar and cornstarch together in small saucepan until cornstarch has dissolved. Whisk in mustard, honey, corn syrup, garlic, and fennel seeds. Bring mixture to boil over high heat. Cook, stirring constantly, until thickened, about 1 minute. Transfer glaze to bowl.

SPICY HOISIN GLAZE

MAKES ABOUT ⅔ CUP

For a spicier glaze, use the larger amount of Sriracha sauce.

- 2 tablespoons rice vinegar
- 1 teaspoon cornstarch
- ⅓ cup hoisin sauce
- 2 tablespoons light corn syrup
- 1–2 tablespoons Sriracha sauce
- 1 teaspoon grated fresh ginger
- ¼ teaspoon five-spice powder

Whisk vinegar and cornstarch together in small saucepan until cornstarch has dissolved. Whisk in hoisin, corn syrup, Sriracha, ginger, and five-spice powder. Bring mixture to boil over high heat. Cook, stirring constantly, until thickened, about 1 minute. Transfer glaze to bowl.

Bringing Home Cuban Shredded Beef

We were sold on *vaca frita*'s crispy crust and garlicky flavor— but not on its dry, stringy interior.

> BY LAN LAM <

Citrusy, garlicky pork roasts are a hallmark of Cuban cuisine, but the country is also home to a lesser-known beef dish with similarly bold, bright flavors. *Vaca frita*, which literally translates as "fried cow," consists of an evenly grained flat cut such as flank or skirt steak that's cooked twice: first boiled to tenderize it and then pulled into meaty shreds and pan-fried until the exterior develops a deep golden-brown crust. Along the way, the meat is seasoned with liberal doses of garlic and fresh lime as well as a touch of ground cumin. Finally, an onion is sliced thin, fried in the same pan, and stirred together with the beef. Extra lime wedges are often passed at the table, and the mixture is usually accompanied by generous helpings of rice and beans.

I'm addicted to the combination of lime, garlic, and beef—especially when the beef comes with crispy edges—so vaca frita is almost always the first thing I order at Cuban restaurants. That said, sometimes the dish isn't perfect. The beef can be so much about crispiness that after a few bites it starts to seem a little dry and stringy. My ideal version would showcase the dish's tangy, garlicky aspect while offering shreds of beef that were crispy and richly flavored at the edges but moist and succulent inside.

This Cuban classic not only pairs well with rice and beans but also easily doubles as a filling for tacos, empanadas, or sandwiches.

Chuck It

I figured that cuts more marbled and collagen-rich than flank steak might not dry out as much. When heated, collagen breaks down into gelatin, which retains water, while fat bastes the cooked meat and increases its perceived juiciness. So I rounded up flap meat, boneless short ribs, and a chuck roast, all of which are streaked with fat and collagen, and prepared them according to a typical vaca frita recipe—but I made one notable change from the get-go. Instead of boiling the meats, I lowered the temperature of the cooking water to a simmer,

knowing that the amount of moisture that meat loses during cooking is directly related to the temperature at which it cooks. To the water in each Dutch oven I added a portion of one of the various cuts of beef, a halved onion, several garlic cloves, and a couple of bay leaves, all per tradition. I then let the pots bubble until the meats were tender. Once they'd cooled, I shredded the meats and tossed the strips with minced garlic, lime juice, ground cumin, salt, and pepper. While those flavors absorbed, I thinly sliced another onion for each batch, grabbed some large skillets, and fried the pieces in about 1 tablespoon of oil per batch until they'd softened but still retained a little crunch. I removed the onions from the pan, added more oil, and seared the various cuts of beef, letting them sizzle until their edges were crispy and deeply brown.

Compared with the flank steak vaca frita that I'd tasted, all three alternatives cooked up moister, and my colleagues and I favored chuck for its bigger beef flavor. But there were a number of problems left to solve. The most glaring was the amount of time that

it took to prepare the dish. Simmering the whole roast had taken almost 3 hours, so I cut it into 1½-inch cubes; that reduced the simmering time to less than 2 hours, making the extra knife work worth the time and effort. Cooking the beef in smaller chunks also allowed me to easily remove any large pockets of fat and connective tissue while I shredded the meat.

Hit It

My other substantial cooking issue was rather obvious: If you fry uniformly shredded meat, you're going to have uniformly dry (albeit crispy) strips because the moisture evaporates so easily. I certainly wanted those crispy, delicate filigrees of beef, but some of the beef also needed to stay fairly intact if it was going to hang on to any moisture. In other words, I needed to shred the beef into different-size pieces.

That thought reminded me of a time-saving technique that I'd come across in a recipe from a food blog called *Cuban in the Midwest*. Rather than pull apart the beef with two forks, the blogger placed the cooked meat on a rimmed baking sheet, covered it with plastic wrap, and pounded it with a mallet. Turns out that flattening, not shredding, the beef is a brilliant shortcut. (Since I didn't have a mallet, I used a meat pounder plus aluminum foil.) Not only was this method faster but it also generated irregular pieces—some fine threads and some broken but intact chunks. Once they hit the hot oil, these now-flattened chunks needed less than 5 minutes to form a crispy crust, and the abbreviated frying time ensured that their insides remained moist and tender. Meanwhile, the finer threads contributed more fine shards of pure crispiness.

Punch It Up

Having made progress with the meat's texture, I turned my focus to brightening the citrus flavor. Stripping zest off the lime and adding it to the juice didn't do enough, so I added more juice—which took the acidic bite too far and overwhelmed the beefy flavor. It wasn't until I thought about the flavors in Cuban roast pork that I realized I could supplement the lime juice with orange juice for bright (but not sharp) citrus flavor. Two tablespoons rounded out the fruity taste nicely and more subtly.

HOW CAN YOU MAKE BEEF BOTH TENDER AND CRISPY?

Unlike most versions of *vaca frita*, ours boasts a moist interior and a crispy crust—and comes together in just one pan.

SIMMER
Cook cubed beef at gentle simmer to help it retain moisture, then uncover and increase heat to burn off liquid.

POUND
Transfer beef to baking sheet (reserve fat) and flatten with meat pounder to produce mix of chunks and fine threads.

SAUTÉ ONION
Sauté onion slices in beef fat over high heat until golden, then deglaze with sherry and water. Transfer to bowl.

SEAR BEEF
Heat more reserved beef fat, then briefly sear meat until edges are dark brown and crispy.

BRIGHTEN
Clear center of pan; sauté minced garlic and cumin; then add orange juice, lime juice, and lime zest.

At the same time, the garlic element needed work, too. Three tablespoons of raw minced garlic wasn't just strong—it bit back. Instead, I treated it (and the cumin) as I would the aromatics in any sauté, pushing the browned meat to the sides of the skillet and quickly cooking the aromatics (with a little oil) in the center; after 30 seconds, the garlic's harshness had considerably softened and the cumin's flavor had bloomed. It was also time to test whether adding aromatics to the cooking water actually infused the meat with any noticeable flavor. I compared my working recipe with one in which I simmered the meat in plain salted water. It was impossible to tell which batch was which. Aromatics in the cooking water were out.

This change made me wonder whether I could make yet another one: Instead of simmering the meat in a big pot of water (which took a good 12 minutes to heat), what if I simply cooked it in a smaller amount of water in the skillet that I would then use to fry the beef? This way I could save time and reduce my dirty dish count. I threw a lid on the skillet while the beef simmered over low heat; when it was fully tender, I uncovered the pan and cranked the heat to medium so that any excess liquid would cook off. Once it had, only the beef fat was left—which gave me yet another idea. Rather than fry the onion and meat in vegetable oil, I'd reserve and reuse some of the rendered beef fat. One tablespoon turned out to be plenty. The trick ended up being more than thrifty; cooking in beef fat amped up the savory quality of the whole dish.

About the onion slices: I hadn't fiddled much with them, since my tasters and I liked how their faint crunch complemented the richer flavor and chew of the meat, but they were a tad on the sharp side. For due diligence, I tried bringing one batch to a caramelized stage, but their creamy, soft texture and deep sweetness just didn't mesh with the garlicky, tangy beef. Instead, I softened their sharp edge just a bit by deglazing the sautéed onion with a little dry sherry and water, knowing that the nutty fortified wine pairs naturally with onion.

The dish was finished when I added the onion slices back to the pan with the beef and tossed the whole mixture with the tangy citrus juices. Bright, garlicky, savory, and addictively crispy yet tender, vaca frita was well on its way to becoming one of my favorite beef preparations. And once I had scooped some beans and rice onto my plate, my vaca frita turned into one of the most satisfying meals I'd ever made.

CUBAN SHREDDED BEEF
SERVES 4 TO 6

Use a well-marbled chuck-eye roast in this recipe. When trimming the beef, don't remove all visible fat—some of it will be used in lieu of oil later in the recipe. If you don't have enough reserved fat in step 3, use vegetable oil.

- 2 pounds boneless beef chuck-eye roast, pulled apart at seams, trimmed, and cut into 1½-inch cubes
  Kosher salt and pepper
- 3 garlic cloves, minced
- 1 teaspoon vegetable oil
- ¼ teaspoon ground cumin
- 2 tablespoons orange juice
- 1½ teaspoons grated lime zest plus 1 tablespoon juice, plus lime wedges for serving
- 1 onion, halved and sliced thin
- 2 tablespoons dry sherry

1. Bring beef, 2 cups water, and 1¼ teaspoons salt to boil in 12-inch nonstick skillet over medium-high heat. Reduce heat to low, cover, and gently simmer until beef is very tender, about 1 hour 45 minutes. (Check beef every 30 minutes, adding water so that bottom third of beef is submerged.) While beef simmers, combine garlic, oil, and cumin in bowl. Combine orange juice and lime zest and juice in second bowl.

2. Remove lid from skillet, increase heat to medium, and simmer until water evaporates and beef starts to sizzle, 3 to 8 minutes. Using slotted spoon, transfer beef to rimmed baking sheet. Pour off and reserve fat from skillet. Rinse skillet clean and dry with paper towels. Place sheet of aluminum foil over beef and, using meat pounder or heavy sauté pan, pound to flatten beef into ⅛-inch-thick pieces, discarding any large pieces of fat or connective tissue. (Some of beef should separate into shreds. Larger pieces that do not separate can be torn in half.)

3. Heat 1½ teaspoons reserved fat in now-empty skillet over high heat. When fat begins to sizzle, add onion and ¼ teaspoon salt. Cook, stirring occasionally, until onion is golden brown and charred in spots, 5 to 8 minutes. Add sherry and ¼ cup water and cook until liquid evaporates, about 2 minutes. Transfer onion to bowl. Return skillet to high heat, add 1½ teaspoons reserved fat, and heat until it begins to sizzle. Add beef and cook, stirring frequently, until dark golden brown and crusty, 2 to 4 minutes.

4. Reduce heat to low and push beef to sides of skillet. Add garlic mixture to center and cook, stirring frequently, until fragrant and golden brown, about 30 seconds. Remove pan from heat, add orange juice mixture and onion, and toss to combine. Season with pepper to taste. Serve immediately with lime wedges.

Pick the Right Cut to Shred

Before we fine-tuned our *vaca frita* cooking method, we chose a cut of beef that would stay moist and tender during the two-part process. Flank steak is traditional, but we opted for chuck roast, which is streaked with fat and collagen—both of which increase the beef's perceived succulence.

CHOOSE CHUCK
For moist, tender meat, we ditch the traditional lean flank steak and use fattier, collagen-rich chuck roast instead.

Creamy Cauliflower Soup

The secret to the best-tasting cauliflower soup you've ever eaten?
Undercook some of the cauliflower—and overcook the rest.

≥ BY DAN SOUZA ≤

A drizzle of nutty browned butter and florets of cauliflower browned in the flavorful fat bring even more complexity to our soup.

If you judged cauliflower by typical cauliflower soups, you might think of it as a characterless white vegetable with no flavor of its own. This is because most classic cauliflower soups go overboard on the heavy cream; thicken with flour; or incorporate ingredients like bacon, tomatoes, or curry powder, whose potent flavors smother this vegetable's more delicate ones. But if you've ever experienced the full spectrum of cauliflower's flavors, which can range from bright and cabbagelike to nutty and even sweet, you know cauliflower to be imminently worthy of being the real focal point of the recipe. I set out to create a soup that was creamy without being stodgy and that highlighted, rather than covered up, the flavors of this often mistreated vegetable.

Moral Fiber

I started by stripping down the soup to just cauliflower and water. I cut a 2-pound head of cauliflower into ½-inch-thick slices (slices cook more evenly than florets, which are hard to cut into same-size pieces) and simmered the vegetable in salted water for 15 minutes before pureeing it in a blender. I was immediately struck by its texture. The soup was supremely silky and smooth. I couldn't detect any of the graininess that would be evident in a puree of, say, cooked peas, or any of the glueyness you'd get when pureeing potatoes. I called a few colleagues over to try it, and they were just as astonished. How could a soup with no cream be so creamy?

As I began to do research, I learned that how much a vegetable breaks down when it is cooked and pureed depends largely on one thing: fiber. Vegetables have two kinds: soluble and insoluble. When subjected to heat and liquid, soluble fiber readily breaks down and dissolves, providing viscosity, while insoluble fiber remains stable even when pureed. Cream's lubricating effect goes a long way toward mitigating the graininess of insoluble fiber, which is why cream is so often included in pureed vegetable soups. Cauliflower, however, is remarkably low in overall fiber—and especially in insoluble fiber, with just ½ gram per ½-cup serving. (This is about one-third as much insoluble fiber as found in green peas.) No wonder cauliflower could be blended to an ultrasmooth creamy consistency—no cream needed.

Bare Essentials

Next I looked for additions that would complement the cauliflower flavor rather than compete with or overwhelm it. I started by swapping in chicken and vegetable broth for the water. Each added more flavor, but I found that this wasn't necessarily a good thing. The chicken broth was too dominant, while the vegetable broth just muddied the flavor. I stuck with water alone and headed to the allium bin.

I tested onion, shallot, leek, and garlic, which I softened in the pot with some butter before I added the cauliflower. Garlic proved pungent and out of place, and the flavor of mild shallots simply disappeared. Onion, however, provided pleasant background sweetness, while leek lent a welcome grassiness, so I chose both.

I was wondering what to try next when I stumbled upon a cauliflower soup recipe from chef and restaurateur Thomas Keller that calls for cooking the vegetable for almost an hour. The recipe (from his book *Ad Hoc at Home*) also calls for a lot of cream, so when I tried the soup, it was hard to tell what impact longer cooking was having. But my curiosity was piqued, so I tried simmering the cauliflower in my working recipe for 30 minutes (twice as long as I had been simmering it up to this point). Even when I added back a little water to the pot to make up for the liquid that had evaporated over the longer cooking time, I was surprised by how much sweeter and nuttier-tasting this vegetable had become. Everything else being equal, was it possible that mere cooking time could so greatly affect flavor?

I ran a simple experiment: I simmered six batches of cauliflower, each in 2 cups of water, cooking the first batch for 10 minutes and each subsequent batch for 10 minutes more so that the last pot cooked for 60 minutes. I called over my colleagues to sample all the batches side by side. The cauliflower that had cooked for 10 minutes had a pronounced grassy, cabbagelike flavor that reminded some tasters of cooked broccoli. By 20 minutes, this sulfurous bite was starting to fade, and by 30 minutes, it had transformed

---

Creamy by Nature

Most soups made from pureed vegetables contain cream for a simple reason: to mitigate the effects of insoluble fiber. All vegetables have both soluble and insoluble fiber, but only the soluble kind fully breaks down during cooking, which contributes viscosity to the soup. Insoluble fiber remains intact, and the best that the blades of a blender can do is break it down into smaller bits. But cauliflower has a leg up on other vegetables. It's very low in overall fiber—and only half of it is insoluble. This means that cauliflower is easily pureed into a silky-smooth soup with no cream at all.

Vary Cooking Time to Coax Out Cauliflower's Different Flavors

While developing our recipe for cauliflower soup, we discovered that cauliflower's flavor changes dramatically depending on how long you cook it. Shorter cooking times bring out its cabbagelike flavors, while longer cooking times turn it nuttier and sweet. Too much cooking drives off all its flavor. To bring the full spectrum of possible flavors into our soup, we cooked some of the cauliflower for 15 minutes and the remainder for 30 minutes.

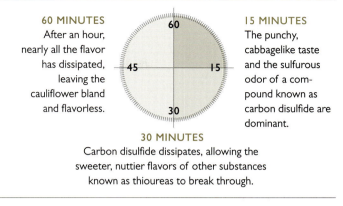

60 MINUTES
After an hour, nearly all the flavor has dissipated, leaving the cauliflower bland and flavorless.

15 MINUTES
The punchy, cabbagelike taste and the sulfurous odor of a compound known as carbon disulfide are dominant.

30 MINUTES
Carbon disulfide dissipates, allowing the sweeter, nuttier flavors of other substances known as thioureas to break through.

into a sweet nuttiness, which the cauliflower held on to through 40 minutes of cooking. Further cooking, however, led to a vegetable so tasteless that it was hard to identify it as cauliflower at all. Intrigued by this transformation, I contacted our science editor.

It turns out that cauliflower, like all cruciferous vegetables, contains a host of odorless compounds that convert into volatile aromatic ones, first during cutting and then during cooking. One such compound is carbon disulfide, which becomes a gas at cooking temperatures. Anyone who's walked into a kitchen where cauliflower is on the stove is familiar with its sulfurous, cabbagelike scent. For the first 15 minutes of cooking, the concentration of carbon disulfide is relatively high. Over time it dissipates, allowing the sweeter, nuttier flavors of other compounds known as thioureas to be formed and come to the fore. But by the hour mark, both types of compounds have disappeared so that the vegetable has almost no flavor at all.

So at what point in the cooking process does cauliflower taste best? Most tasters remarked that they liked the punchy, cabbagey flavor of the cauliflower cooked for 10 and 20 minutes as well as the nuttier, cleaner, sweeter flavor of 30-minute-cooked cauliflower. Could I get all these flavors in my soup? For my next batch, I sliced the head into ½-inch-thick slices as usual and simmered half (along with the tougher core, which is edible so long as it's cooked until tender) for 30 minutes, adding the remaining half of the cauliflower after

15 minutes. It was a simple adjustment to the recipe, but the results were dramatic. Not only did this soup taste more intrinsically of cauliflower than any of its predecessors but its flavors were also more complex. It was at once grassy, pleasantly sulfurous, sweet, and nutty. I turned my focus to a few final touches.

Buttery Finish

I've always been a big fan of the intense nuttiness of roasted cauliflower and wondered if there was a way to bring some of that intensity to the soup. I cut a cup of ½-inch florets from the cauliflower before slicing up the rest for the soup. I melted a few more tablespoons of butter in a small skillet and fried the florets to a golden-brown color. Tossed with a little sherry vinegar and sprinkled over the soup, they served as the ideal complement to my clean-tasting puree. But during frying, the cauliflower wasn't the only thing that was cooking—the butter also turned a rich golden brown. This gave me an idea. Why not cook the florets in extra butter and use a drizzle of it as a second garnish? Just a teaspoon or two of browned butter brought richness to each bowl of soup. A shower of minced chives and some fresh black pepper finished the job.

I like to think I'm the kind of cook whose recipes often get accolades from those who try them, but my tasters' raves went beyond anything I'd ever experienced for such a simple recipe—a soup by which cauliflower should be proud to be judged.

CREAMY CAULIFLOWER SOUP
SERVES 4 TO 6

White wine vinegar may be substituted for the sherry vinegar. Be sure to thoroughly trim the cauliflower's core of green leaves and leaf stems, which can be fibrous and contribute to a grainy texture in the soup.

- 1 head cauliflower (2 pounds)
- 8 tablespoons unsalted butter, cut into 8 pieces
- 1 leek, white and light green parts only, halved lengthwise, sliced thin, and washed thoroughly
- 1 small onion, halved and sliced thin
  Salt and pepper
- 4½–5 cups water
- ½ teaspoon sherry vinegar
- 3 tablespoons minced fresh chives

1. Pull off outer leaves of cauliflower and trim stem. Using paring knife, cut around core to remove; thinly slice core and reserve. Cut heaping 1 cup of ½-inch florets from head of cauliflower; set aside. Cut remaining cauliflower crosswise into ½-inch-thick slices.

2. Melt 3 tablespoons butter in large saucepan over medium-low heat. Add leek, onion, and 1½ teaspoons salt; cook, stirring frequently, until leek and onion are softened but not browned, about 7 minutes.

3. Increase heat to medium-high; add 4½ cups water, sliced core, and half of sliced cauliflower; and bring to simmer. Reduce heat to medium-low and simmer gently for 15 minutes. Add remaining sliced cauliflower, return to simmer, and continue to cook until cauliflower is tender and crumbles easily, 15 to 20 minutes longer.

4. While soup simmers, melt remaining 5 tablespoons butter in 8-inch skillet over medium heat. Add reserved florets and cook, stirring frequently, until florets are golden brown and butter is browned and imparts nutty aroma, 6 to 8 minutes. Remove skillet from heat and use slotted spoon to transfer florets to small bowl. Toss florets with vinegar and season with salt to taste. Pour browned butter in skillet into small bowl and reserve for garnishing.

5. Process soup in blender until smooth, about 45 seconds. Rinse out pan. Return pureed soup to pan and return to simmer over medium heat, adjusting consistency with remaining water as needed (soup should have thick, velvety texture but should be thin enough to settle with flat surface after being stirred) and seasoning with salt to taste. Serve, garnishing individual bowls with browned florets, drizzle of browned butter, and chives and seasoning with pepper to taste.

A New Spin on Grilled Corn

To infuse corn with summer flavors, some of the cooking needs to happen off the fire.

> BY BRIDGET LANCASTER

A whole year goes by while I wait for that perfect matchup: fresh summer corn and the lick of the grill flame. Fire does something magical to the kernels, toasting them and deepening their natural sweetness. When it's corn season, I toss ears on the grill a couple of times a week, so I wanted to find a way to incorporate herbs, spices, and other seasonings with the usual smear of butter.

Whipping up a flavored butter is easy, but getting it to penetrate the corn is a different story: Simply slathering grilled corn with compound butter fails to infuse flavor into the kernels. I'd have to apply the butter before or during cooking. I considered two methods of preparing the ears: entirely shucked or partially shucked (peeling away all but the inner layers of husk). I tried the latter first, mixing softened butter with fresh chopped basil, parsley, and grated lemon zest, and then smearing it onto the ears and reassembling the husks.

The result was one hot mess—literally. Once on the blazing fire, the butter leaked out of the husks and dripped—and dripped and dripped—into the grill until an inferno singed the entire setup.

As for the naked-ear method, I knew that to avoid flare-ups, I'd have to use a less aggressive fire. I smeared more basil butter onto a batch and set it on a moderate grill. No flare-ups—good. But the butter still trickled off before it could season the kernels, which picked up no char at all.

To char the corn as quickly as possible, I would have to at least start it over a hot fire. I also had to find a way to keep the butter on the corn. For my next try, I brushed the kernels with vegetable oil—to prevent them from drying out—and placed the corn on the hot grill. After it charred, I scooped basil butter onto several pieces of foil and topped each dollop with a hot ear of corn. Using my faux flameproof "husks," I was able to wrap up each ear tightly—that butter was going nowhere. I returned the shrouded corn to the grill until I could hear the butter sizzling. Once I unwrapped the corn, I got an instant whiff of aromatic basil and lemon and toasty corn. But opening the hobo packs was about as enjoyable as holding a hot potato—with a bonus of molten butter running down my arm.

I switched gears, ditching the foil packets for a

We char the corn and then sizzle it in flavored butter.

disposable pan. After searing the corn, I placed it in the pan along with the herb butter. I sealed the pan with foil, put it on the grill, and after a few minutes heard that sweet sizzling sound. To make sure that the corn was well coated, I shook the pan a few times—consider it my personal homage to Jiffy Pop.

For variations on the basil mixture, I stuck to "summery" flavors. One combo blended sweet honey and spicy red pepper flakes; another with smoky chipotles, cilantro, and tangy orange zest gave a nod to Latin flavors; and a third "barbecue" butter boasted bold Cajun flavors. As it turns out, you can improve on hot, buttered grilled corn.

GRILLED CORN WITH FLAVORED BUTTER
SERVES 4 TO 6

Use a disposable aluminum roasting pan that is at least 2¾ inches deep. For our free recipe for Spicy Old Bay Butter, go to CooksIllustrated.com/oct13.

- 1   recipe flavored butter (recipes follow)
- 1   (13 by 9-inch) disposable aluminum roasting pan
- 8   ears corn, husks and silk removed
- 2   tablespoons vegetable oil
    Salt and pepper

1. Place flavored butter in disposable pan. Brush corn evenly with oil and season with salt and pepper to taste.

2. Grill corn over hot fire, turning occasionally, until lightly charred on all sides, 5 to 9 minutes. Transfer corn to pan and cover tightly with aluminum foil.

3. Place pan on grill and cook, shaking pan frequently, until butter is sizzling, about 3 minutes. Remove pan from grill and carefully remove foil, allowing steam to escape away from you. Serve corn, spooning any butter in pan over individual ears.

BASIL AND LEMON BUTTER

Serve with lemon wedges, if desired.

- 6   tablespoons unsalted butter, softened
- 2   tablespoons minced fresh basil
- 1   tablespoon minced fresh parsley
- 1   teaspoon finely grated lemon zest
- ½   teaspoon salt
- ¼   teaspoon pepper

Combine all ingredients in small bowl.

HONEY BUTTER

- 6   tablespoons unsalted butter, softened
- 2   tablespoons honey
- ½   teaspoon salt
- ¼   teaspoon red pepper flakes

Combine all ingredients in small bowl.

LATIN-SPICED BUTTER

Serve with orange wedges, if desired.

- 6   tablespoons unsalted butter, softened
- 2   tablespoons minced fresh cilantro
- 1   tablespoon minced fresh parsley
- 1   teaspoon minced canned chipotle chile in adobo sauce
- ½   teaspoon finely grated orange zest
- ½   teaspoon salt

Combine all ingredients in small bowl.

NEW ORLEANS "BARBECUE" BUTTER

- 6   tablespoons unsalted butter, softened
- 1   garlic clove, minced
- 1   tablespoon Worcestershire sauce
- 1   teaspoon tomato paste
- ½   teaspoon minced fresh rosemary
- ½   teaspoon minced fresh thyme
- ½   teaspoon cayenne pepper

Combine all ingredients in small bowl.

Fresh Tomato Puttanesca

A bumper crop of sweet, ripe tomatoes can brighten the pungent flavors of this Italian classic—or leave the noodles drowning in a waterlogged sauce.

> BY ANDREW JANJIGIAN <

At the end of summer, I inevitably find myself with a glut of beautiful garden tomatoes, both small and large. As a result, I'm always searching for ways to use them beyond salads. Puttanesca, that most boisterous of classic Italian sauces (legend has it that it was invented by Neapolitan prostitutes on break between customers), is one of my favorite tomato-based sauces. I love the clash of flavors that it presents: Spicy pepper flakes, pungent garlic, and salty anchovies, olives, and capers meet up with clean-tasting fresh herbs and tangy-sweet tomatoes. Putting my harvest to use in this quick sauce appealed to both my pragmatic instincts and my stomach. Doing so would also address the generic "cooked" quality that stems from using canned tomatoes, the usual choice for this dish. I wasn't aiming for a no-cook sauce, but I did want a fresher puttanesca—one that retained the fruits' clean-tasting sweetness alongside the richer, more assertive flavors that are the essence of this dish.

A Fresh Start

My first step was trying several varieties of tomato in a basic puttanesca: minced garlic and anchovies (anchovy paste, for convenience), red pepper flakes, chopped black olives, and capers, all sautéed in olive oil. I quickly learned that this was not the place for larger tomatoes, which are typically full of juice. In order to keep that liquid from watering down my sauce, I had to reduce it—and when I did, its fresh flavor all but disappeared. Lesson learned: Use a low-moisture variety that wouldn't need much cooking. That decision pointed me to grape (or cherry) tomatoes; once halved, they need very little simmering time to reduce to a saucelike consistency. Availability was on my side, too: Not only is my garden full of these tomatoes by summer's end but they're also consistently decent in supermarkets year-round.

Of course there was a downside: The larger ratio of skin to flesh meant that my sauce was full of chewy skins. Peeling large tomatoes had been easy; after a quick dunk in boiling water, the skins slipped right off. But I wasn't about to fussily skin dozens of tiny tomatoes. Instead, I gave them a quick blitz in a blender, which pulverized the skins completely.

Unfortunately, doing so also caused them to shed more moisture—not as much as an equal quantity of big tomatoes but enough that it seemed I would have to revert to a longer simmering time. I had a better idea: What if I drained the pureed tomatoes in

Low-moisture grape tomatoes don't need to cook for long to shed liquid, so their bright flavor won't fade.

a strainer before adding them to the sauce? That way, I could use the pulp and discard the exuded liquid.

But just as I was about to discard the tomato juice, I realized my faulty thinking. The majority of tomato flavor resides in the juice, jelly, and seeds, so I'd essentially be throwing away the best part. The better approach was to briefly simmer the juice to concentrate its flavor. Once it had reduced to ⅓ cup, I added the uncooked pulp along with the olives and capers. When the sauce was heated through, the bulk of the tomatoes had softened but still tasted fresh.

Salty and Sour

Now I could concentrate on taming puttanesca's rowdier ingredients: the olives and the capers. I tested common varieties of high-quality black olives. Salt-cured were too salty, but brine-cured kalamata and Gaeta, both of which were fruity and pleasantly crisp-tender, were equally excellent choices. I chopped them coarsely—any finer and the sauce turned a muddy brown. I did finely chop the capers, however, so that their briny punch hit every bite. A smidgen of dried oregano introduced complexity; ½ cup of minced fresh parsley offered freshness.

I instituted one final adjustment: Finding myself out of the standard spaghetti or linguine, I reached for campanelle. Surprisingly, we all preferred the compact size and convoluted twists of this pasta, since it did a better job of trapping the coarse sauce. I also liked that aesthetically it hinted at a summertime pasta salad, giving the dish an overall fresher appeal.

SUMMER PASTA PUTTANESCA
SERVES 4

We prefer to make this dish with campanelle, but fusilli and orecchiette also work. Very finely mashed anchovy fillets (rinsed and dried before mashing) can be used instead of anchovy paste. Buy a good-quality black olive, such as kalamata, Gaeta, or Alfonso.

- 3 tablespoons extra-virgin olive oil
- 4 garlic cloves, minced
- 1 tablespoon anchovy paste
- ¼ teaspoon red pepper flakes
- ¼ teaspoon dried oregano
- 1½ pounds grape or cherry tomatoes
- 1 pound campanelle
  Salt
- ½ cup pitted kalamata olives, chopped coarse
- 3 tablespoons capers, rinsed and minced
- ½ cup minced fresh parsley

1. Combine oil, garlic, anchovy paste, pepper flakes, and oregano in bowl. Process tomatoes in blender until finely chopped but not pureed, 15 to 45 seconds. Transfer to fine-mesh strainer set in large bowl and let drain for 5 minutes, occasionally pressing gently on solids with rubber spatula to extract liquid (this should yield about ¾ cup). Reserve tomato liquid in bowl and tomato pulp in strainer.

2. Bring 4 quarts water to boil in large pot. Add campanelle and 1 tablespoon salt and cook, stirring often, until al dente. Reserve 1 cup cooking water, then drain campanelle and return it to pot.

3. While campanelle is cooking, cook garlic-anchovy mixture in 12-inch skillet over medium heat, stirring frequently, until garlic is fragrant but not brown, 2 to 3 minutes. Add tomato liquid and simmer until reduced to ⅓ cup, 2 to 3 minutes. Add tomato pulp, olives, and capers; cook until just heated through, 2 to 3 minutes. Stir in parsley.

4. Pour sauce over campanelle and toss to combine, adding reserved cooking water as needed to adjust consistency. Season with salt to taste. Serve immediately.

See the Sauce Happen
Video available FREE for 4 months at
CooksIllustrated.com/oct13

French-Style Pork Stew

We wanted a stew with lots of pork flavor but without a lot of heaviness. Could a traditional French recipe pave the way?

⇒ BY KEITH DRESSER ⇐

In the realm of stews, beef dominates. Pork stews are harder to come by, and when you do find them, the meat often gets lost in the shadows of more assertive ingredients. Consider Mexican *chili verde*, boldly flavored with tomatillos and spicy green chiles, or Hungarian pork stew, loaded with sweet paprika. As a pork lover I wanted to find a stew that put the spotlight on the headlining ingredient. But I also had another requirement: I wanted a stew that, while robust and satisfying, wouldn't be heavy.

I researched pork dishes and discovered a recipe that actually seemed pretty close to what I had in mind: *potée*. This French peasant recipe varies from region to region, but most versions take the form of an old-fashioned boiled dinner. They combine multiple cuts from almost any part of the pig (but always including one smoked cut); sausages; and a mix of cabbage, onions, and sturdy root vegetables. The ingredients are simmered together in liquid (usually water) until tender, and then the pork and sausages are sliced and served with the vegetables—the whole lot moistened with some of the cooking liquid. The dish is plenty porky, and because it's typically not thickened, the broth has the clean taste I was looking for.

That said, a couple of things didn't suit: With the meat and vegetables served in big pieces in only the barest suggestion of broth, potée is typically more of a knife-and-fork affair that requires plating. I wanted a true stew: in other words, bite-size chunks that could be scooped up with a spoon, swimming in lots of broth. And since I'd be using more of it, I wanted that broth to have as complex a flavor as possible.

Potée: Our Inspiration

The French boiled dinner known as *potée* inspired our rustic pork stew. Traditional recipes for potée are somewhat laissez-faire, calling for simmering any number of fresh and smoked cuts of pork in water with sausages and whatever sturdy vegetables are on hand. Once cooked, the meat is sliced and served on a platter with a small amount of broth. Our adaptation features a more thoughtful selection of bite-size chunks of pork, sausage, and vegetables in lots of flavorful broth.

With its abundance of vegetables and no added thickener, this meaty stew manages to boast a clean, light taste.

Mix 'n' Match Meats

Determining which cuts of pork to use was first on my agenda. Many potée recipes that I found called for large, tough whole roasts that required several hours of cooking to turn tender. Since I knew that I wanted to keep the stew somewhat light, I kicked off the testing process by simmering cubes of pork loin and tenderloin (which also had the benefit of cooking much faster) in separate pots of water. Both cuts are ultralean, so it was not much of a surprise that they cooked up dry and stringy, plus neither contributed much toward my goal of a broth that, while not overly rich, was still meaty. I moved on to try pork butt, which I first cut into 1½-inch chunks and browned before simmering. With its mix of lean and fat, the butt (which comes from the shoulder of the pig) contributed solid pork flavor to the broth, making the 2 hours it took to become succulent and fork-tender worth it. I settled on 3 pounds, which netted about 2 pounds of meat once the fat was trimmed.

Next up: choosing some kind of smoked pork; potée usually includes pork belly and/or ham hocks

or shanks. Since pork belly—the cut used to make bacon—can be tricky to find, I tried the latter instead, along with the hocks and shanks. But bacon, even when cut into bite-size pieces and browned before simmering, became limp and rubbery and left an oil slick on the surface of the broth. Smoked hocks weren't greasy, but this bony cut contributed very little meat that could be shredded and added back to the pot. A smoked shank was by far the best choice because of its size and meatiness—just one yielded well over a cup of shredded pork that was a nice supplement to the shoulder—and it infused the broth with a delicate smokiness. The shank, which is fully cooked but tough straight out of the package, was tender after about 1½ hours of simmering. I removed it at this point and allowed it to cool so that I could shred the meat.

Sausage (usually a regional variety) is the final meaty component. My options were limited by the offerings at the store, and the most widely available types, chorizo and Italian sausage, contained seasonings that seemed out of place in the stew. I opted for the firm bite and more straightforward smoked pork flavor of kielbasa. But unlike the butt and hock, the sausage did not take well to long cooking—it wound up bland and dry, having released its seasoning and fat into the simmering liquid. Adding the slices during the final 15 minutes or so of cooking heated them through and kept them moist.

I had one more tweak to investigate: Following typical stew-making protocol, I had been browning the pork butt before simmering it. Browning creates caramelized bits of fond in the pot and on the meat that contribute flavor compounds to the finished dish, but it's a step that takes time and makes a mess on the stovetop. With so much smoke flavor in the pot from the shank and the sausage, I wondered if browning was really necessary. When I made side-by-side batches, I was glad to find that any additional flavor benefit coming from browning was barely discernible. Browning was officially out.

I'd finally produced deeply meaty-tasting broth; now it was time to add more layers of flavor. Up to this point, I had been using water as the cooking liquid, as almost all potée recipes do, but I wanted to see if I could improve the stew with chicken broth.

Three Little Pigs: Less Work and More Flavor

Three types of pork give our stew contrasting textures and so much complex flavor that browning any of it (a typical step in stew) is unnecessary.

PORK BUTT
The fat-streaked shoulder of the pig turns succulent during cooking.

SMOKED SHANK
The collagen-rich front leg imparts a silky consistency and smoky flavor.

KIELBASA
Smoked sausage provides a snappy texture and mild garlic flavor.

Using all broth made the stew too reminiscent of chicken soup. Diluted with water, however, the chicken broth added a subtle flavor base that didn't compete with the pork. For even more depth, I added halved onions plus parsley, thyme, bay leaves, garlic, peppercorns, and a couple of whole cloves to the pot as the meat simmered—a step that many potées don't bother with.

The Vegetable Field

The last elements to consider were the vegetables. Literally anything goes in traditional potée, and six different vegetables is not uncommon. I wanted a nice mixture in the stew, but to simplify shopping and prep, I had to make careful selections.

One common addition, turnip, was eliminated when some tasters objected to its bitter taste. With onions flavoring the broth, leeks seemed redundant, so they were also shown the door. In the end, I settled on shredded cabbage (I used savoy for its delicate texture) and chunks of carrots and potatoes—a manageable lot that offered a balance of sweet, earthy flavor; nice texture; and appealing color. And I made sure to include enough of them to balance out the meat in the stew.

As for the best way to incorporate the vegetables, some potée recipes call for simply combining all the meat and vegetables in the pot, adding liquid, and simmering for hours, until the meat is done. Other recipes start with the meat and introduce the vegetables near the end of the cooking time. I knew that the latter method was superior, since vegetables cooked for too long would end up lifeless and limp. I ended up adding the carrots and potatoes to the pot for the last 40 minutes of cooking, and I found that the cabbage wilted nicely into the broth if cooked for just the final 15 minutes.

Next, I considered transferring the operation to the oven after bringing the stew to a simmer on the stovetop. Because the heat of the oven is steady, constant, and all-encompassing, we often prefer it for stews and braises. Indeed, 325 degrees was ideal for keeping the liquid at a gentle simmer and eliminated the need for frequent burner adjustments.

A sprinkle of chopped fresh parsley and my stew was done. Besides meeting my goal of a meaty yet light dish, I'd created a satisfying stew with little hands-on work.

FRENCH-STYLE PORK STEW
SERVES 8 TO 10

Pork butt roast, often labeled Boston butt in the supermarket, is a very fatty cut, so don't be surprised if you lose a pound or even a little more in the trimming process (the weight called for in the recipe takes this loss into account). Serve with crusty bread.

- 6 parsley sprigs, plus ¼ cup chopped fresh parsley
- 3 large sprigs fresh thyme
- 5 garlic cloves, unpeeled
- 2 bay leaves
- 1 tablespoon black peppercorns
- 2 whole cloves
- 5 cups water
- 4 cups chicken broth
- 3 pounds boneless pork butt roast, trimmed and cut into 1- to 1½-inch pieces
- 1 meaty smoked ham shank or 2 to 3 smoked ham hocks (1¼ pounds)
- 2 onions, halved through root end, root end left intact
- 4 carrots, peeled, narrow end cut crosswise into ½-inch pieces, wide end halved lengthwise and cut into ½-inch pieces
- 1 pound Yukon Gold potatoes, unpeeled, cut into ¾-inch pieces
- 12 ounces kielbasa sausage, halved lengthwise and then cut into ½-inch-thick slices
- ½ head savoy cabbage, shredded (8 cups)

1. Adjust oven rack to middle position and heat oven to 325 degrees. Cut 10-inch square of triple-thickness cheesecloth. Place parsley sprigs (fold or break to fit), thyme sprigs, garlic, bay leaves, peppercorns, and cloves in center of cheesecloth and tie into bundle with kitchen twine.

2. Bring water, broth, pork, ham, onions, and herb bundle to simmer in large Dutch oven over medium-high heat, skimming off scum that rises to surface. Cover pot and place in oven. Cook until pork chunks are tender and skewer inserted in meat meets little resistance, 1¼ to 1½ hours.

3. Using slotted spoon, discard onions and herb bundle. Transfer ham to plate. Add carrots and potatoes to pot and stir to combine. Cover pot and

return to oven. Cook until vegetables are almost tender, 20 to 25 minutes. When ham is cool enough to handle, using 2 forks, remove meat and shred into bite-size pieces; discard skin and bones.

4. Add shredded ham, kielbasa, and cabbage to pot. Stir to combine, cover, and return to oven. Cook until kielbasa is heated through and cabbage is wilted and tender, 15 to 20 minutes. Season with salt and pepper to taste, then stir in chopped parsley. Ladle into bowls and serve. (Stew can be made up to 3 days in advance.)

Watch Every Step
Video available FREE for 4 months at CooksIllustrated.com/oct13

Common Cooking Myths, Debunked

We believed some of them, too—until our testing proved us wrong. BY MOLLY BIRNBAUM

Seeds and Jelly

The best part of a tomato is the flesh.

FACT **The seeds and jelly contain the most flavor.**
Many believe it imperative to remove the seeds and jelly of tomatoes because they detract from the texture of your dish. That may be, but they affect flavor, too. We made two tomato gratins, one with intact tomatoes and the other with the seeds and jelly removed. We found that the gratin with the intact tomatoes had a richer, deeper flavor. This is because the seeds and jelly actually contain three times the amount of flavor-enhancing glutamic acid as the flesh. (Also called glutamate, this is the compound that supplies the savory quality known as *umami* in many foods.) Sometimes removing seeds may be necessary, but it should be a last resort.

A slammed door will ruin a soufflé or cake.

FACT **Slamming won't make a difference.**
Soufflés and cakes rise as tiny air bubbles in the batter expand in the heat of the oven. To find out if slamming the door shut would interrupt the process enough to spell disaster, we mixed batters for muffins, yellow cake, angel food cake, and cheese soufflé and loaded them into hot ovens. Just before each item reached its maximum height, we opened the oven door and gave it a hard slam. The muffins emerged unharmed, as did the yellow cake. Even the notoriously fragile angel food cake and the soufflé survived. A properly developed foam is pretty resilient.

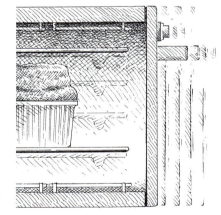

Bread stales because it loses moisture.

FACT **Bread stales because starch molecules absorb moisture.**
Once exposed to air, bread starch undergoes a process called retrogradation: The starch molecules begin to crystallize and absorb moisture, turning the bread hard and crumbly. This is why for certain recipes (like stuffing), you should dry bread in the oven (to drive out moisture) instead of letting it go stale.

Salt makes water boil faster.

FACT **Salt will increase the time it takes water to reach a boil—but only if you add a whole lot of it.** When we conducted an experiment (bringing 4 quarts of water to a boil with and without 1 tablespoon of salt, or the amount of salt we use to cook 1 pound of pasta), we found that salted and unsalted water came to a boil in the same amount of time: 17½ minutes. A whopping 1½ tablespoons of salt per quart of water is required to raise the boiling point by just 1 degree, thus slightly increasing the time it takes the water to reach a boil. Those proportions yield a super-salty solution, one that we wouldn't use to cook with anyway.

4 quarts water
1 TB SALT

= 17½ minutes to boil =

4 quarts water
NO SALT

Cooking wine removes all its alcohol.

FACT **Cooking reduces the alcohol content but rarely eliminates it.** When alcohol and water mix, they form an azeotrope—a mixture of two different liquids that behaves as if it were a single compound. This means that even though alcohol evaporates at a lower temperature than water, the vapors coming from an alcohol-water azeotrope will contain both alcohol and water until the entire mixture is gone. In sum, about 5 percent of the initial alcohol content will remain no matter how long you simmer the mixture.

Cold eggs will ruin baked goods.

FACT **In most cases you can use eggs of any temperature.**
We conducted a blind tasting of two yellow cakes: one made with room-temperature eggs, the other with eggs pulled from the refrigerator. The cake made with room-temperature eggs had a slightly finer, more even crumb. The cold-egg cake produced a thicker batter and took 5 minutes longer to bake than the room-temperature-egg cake but was entirely acceptable. So it's fine to use cold eggs in most basic cake recipes. But do be sure to use room-temperature eggs when making finicky cakes like angel food and chiffon, which rely on air incorporated into the beaten eggs as a primary means of leavening. In these cases, we found that cold eggs didn't whip nearly as well and the cakes didn't rise properly.

ROOM TEMPERATURE
Best for recipes in which whites are whipped.

FROM THE FRIDGE
Fine for everything else.

Cooking in liquid keeps meat moister.

FACT **Despite the wet conditions, braising adds no moisture.**
We simulated braising by placing samples of beef chuck, along with measured amounts of broth, in individual vacuum-sealed bags. We submerged the bags in water held at 190 degrees (the temperature of a typical braise) for 90 minutes. The weight of the meat decreased an average of 12.5 percent during cooking while the volume of liquid increased, demonstrating that moisture had been pulled from the meat into the surrounding liquid, not the other way around. Braised meat seems moist not because of the moisture surrounding the meat but because of the temperature at which the meat cooks. Gentle cooking is one way to help break down the meat's connective tissue and collagen, which lubricate and tenderize its fibers.

Oil and vinegar don't mix.

FACT **They can—and do—when properly emulsified.**
An emulsion is a combination of two liquids that don't ordinarily mix, whisked strenuously until one breaks down into droplets so tiny that they remain separated by the other liquid. The addition of an emulsifying agent (like mayonnaise or mustard) helps the two liquids stay together in a unified sauce. We made vinaigrettes with each emulsifier and found that the mayo sample lasted 1½ hours while the mustard dressing broke after 30 minutes. A sample with no emulsifier began to break immediately.

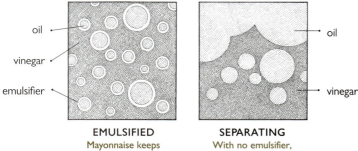

oil	oil
vinegar	
emulsifier	vinegar

EMULSIFIED
Mayonnaise keeps oil and vinegar suspended together in a sauce.

SEPARATING
With no emulsifier, vinegar and oil won't stay mixed.

Washing mushrooms makes them absorb water.

FACT **Soaking will, but a quick rinse won't.**
When we learned that mushrooms were more than 80 percent water, we began to question their ability to absorb yet more liquid. We weighed whole mushrooms before and after soaking them in water for 5 minutes and found that 6 ounces of mushrooms gained only 1½ teaspoons of water. But, to entirely prevent absorption, we wash mushrooms the same way we wash other vegetables: by rinsing them under cold water. However, if you will be using the mushrooms raw, rinse them just before serving or avoid rinsing altogether, since the surfaces of wet mushrooms turn slimy when exposed to air for more than 5 minutes.

Potatoes can make a dish less spicy.

FACT **You need fat or sugar to reduce the heat.**
We tried adding potatoes to foods to tame spiciness, but it simply doesn't work. There is another solution: Add ingredients from the opposite end of the flavor spectrum to balance things out. Depending on the recipe, you can add a fat (such as butter, cream, sour cream, cheese, or oil) or a sweetener (such as sugar, honey, or maple syrup) to counteract the offending ingredient. Obviously, it wouldn't make sense to add cheese to a too-spicy Thai beef stir-fry, so use your best judgment.

All parts of a chile are equally hot.

FACT **The pith contains the real spicy stuff.**
All chiles get their heat from a group of chemical compounds called capsaicinoids, the best known being capsaicin. It's often thought that the seeds have more heat than the flesh, but they are essentially guilty—or hot—by association. Most of the capsaicin is concentrated in the inner whitish pith, with progressively smaller amounts in the seeds and the flesh. We separated the outer green-colored flesh, the inner whitish pith, and the seeds from 40 jalapeños and then sent them to a food lab for analysis. We found that there were just 5 milligrams of capsaicin per kilogram of green jalapeño flesh, 73 milligrams per kilogram in the seeds, and 512 milligrams per kilogram in the pith.

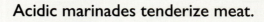

PITH: 512 mg
capsaicin/kg

SEEDS: 73 mg
capsaicin/kg

FLESH: 5 mg
capsaicin/kg

Acidic marinades tenderize meat.

FACT **In actuality, they can make meat mushy.**
To tenderize meat, you have to break down muscle fiber and collagen, the connective tissue that makes meat tough. While acidic ingredients do weaken collagen, their impact is confined to the meat's surface—and if left too long, acids turn the outermost layer of meat mushy, not tender. To minimize mushiness, we use acidic components sparingly and only for short marinating times. Truly tender meat comes down to the cut, cooking time, method, and temperature. Highly salted marinades can also act as brines, helping meat retain moisture and cook up more tender.

Pasta must be cooked in lots of water.

FACT **You don't actually need a full pot.**
If you don't have a pot large enough to handle the amount of water a pasta recipe calls for, don't panic. We've successfully cooked a pound of spaghetti in 2 quarts of water—about half of what a recipe usually suggests. As long as you stir the pasta frequently (we use tongs), it will be indistinguishable from pasta cooked in a larger quantity of water. (Just keep in mind that the pasta cooking water will be starchier than usual—which can be a good thing if you want your sauce to cling better to the pasta.)

Searing meat seals in juices.

FACT **Searing just creates a crusty layer of flavor.**
We cooked two batches of rib-eye steaks, searing the first batch in a skillet over high heat and then cooking the steaks in a 250-degree oven until they reached 125 degrees. For the second batch we reversed the order, first baking the steaks until they reached 110 degrees and then searing them until a crust developed and their interiors hit 125 degrees. We weighed the steaks before and after cooking

and found that both sets had lost around 22 percent of their weight. If searing truly seals in juices, the steaks seared first (while raw) would have had more moisture trapped inside them (and thus less weight loss) than the steaks seared after cooking in the oven.

The Best Way to Cook Mussels

Steamed mussels are quick and easy, with their own built-in, briny-sweet broth.
So what's the problem? Their stubborn refusal to cook at the same rate.

> BY ANDREW JANJIGIAN

I'm always amazed when I ask friends how often they make mussels—and their answer is "Never." I love cooking mussels. They're cheap and quick to prepare, with tender flesh and a briny-sweet, built-in broth created by the merging of the mussels and their steaming liquid. Their flavor is distinct but still tame enough to pair with a wide variety of aromatic ingredients.

So why don't more people make them? My friends all cite the same reasons: Mussels are hard to clean, and it seems a little dicey trying to figure out if they're safe to eat. Fortunately, these misconceptions are easy to dispel. Most mussels these days need very little cleaning. The vast majority are farmed, which leads to less sand and grit and fewer of the stringy beards that cling to the shell. As for figuring out whether a mussel is safe to cook, this couldn't be more straightforward. Your first clue is smell: A dead mussel smells very bad, whereas a live mussel should smell pleasantly briny, and its shell (if open) should close when tapped. That's it. If a mussel is alive before you cook it, it will be safe to eat when it's done.

The real problem with mussels, especially if you're a perfectionist like me, is that they come in all different sizes. They run from pinky-finger small to almost palm-size large, and buying them en masse—they're usually sold in multipound bags—makes it virtually impossible to select a group that's made up of mussels that are all the same size and, therefore, will all cook at the same rate. This means that when steamed, a solid number of mussels will turn out perfectly, with shells open and the meat within plump, juicy, and easy to extract. But inevitably some will remain closed (a sign that they're undercooked). If cooked until every last one has opened wide, however, an equal number of mussels will turn out overdone—shriveled, mealy, and tough. Could I figure out a way to get more of them to cook at the same rate?

First I needed a basic recipe. Most sources using

We steam mussels in a covered roasting pan rather than a Dutch oven to ensure even cooking; then we whisk butter into the broth for silky body.

the classic French method of steaming mussels, or *moules marinières*, follow this simple model: Sauté garlic and other aromatics in a Dutch oven, pour in wine and bring it to a boil, add the mussels, cover the pot, and cook for 10 minutes or so, until all the mussels have opened. Toss in a handful of herbs, stir, and serve with crusty bread to sop up the broth.

There were differences in the recipes I tried, of course. The more successful ones had you boil down the wine a bit before adding the mussels in order to take the edge off the alcohol and round out the flavors of the finished broth. Ditto for those recipes that added some sort of dairy as a thickener at the end of cooking to give the sauce body and help it cling to the mussels. Butter worked wonderfully, though cream and crème fraîche both served admirably as well (I saved these two ingredients to use in variations). Finally, although you don't want to overpower the mussels' own flavors, a little aromatic complexity is a plus. In the end, I decided that red pepper flakes, thyme sprigs, and bay leaves (along with a generous amount of parsley) were just the right combination.

Flex Mussels

With a good basic recipe in hand, I moved on to the major mussel-cooking conundrum. I wondered if a more gentle approach would prevent those mussels that opened first from drying out before their fellow bivalves caught up. I cooked two batches of mussels in big pots on the stove—one at a simmer and the other at a rolling boil. Not surprisingly, those cooked at a simmer took longer, and tasters found them a bit more moist and tender, but overall there wasn't a huge difference between the two approaches. If I waited for virtually every mussel to open, I was left with a fair number of tough, overcooked specimens.

But it was during this test that I realized another problem inherent in the traditional method of cooking mussels: the use of a big pot on the stove. With a relatively large number of mussels (at least a pound per person), my pot was nearly full to the brim, which made stirring once or twice to redistribute the mussels unwieldy. Shaking the pot, as other recipes have you do, was not at all effective at moving the mussels around. And if the mussels stay put, this only exacerbates the problem of uneven cooking, since the mussels at the bottom of the pot, whether small or large, are exposed to more heat. I tried cutting the amount of mussels in half so I could stir them more easily to see if that made more of them cook at the same rate. And sure enough, far

The Problem with the Pot

Because mussels steamed in a pot are crowded on top of one another, it's difficult to stir (or shake) them around—and cook them evenly. The mussels closest to the heat source cook faster than the ones on top.

CLOSE AND CROWDED
In a pot, mussels stuck on the bottom open more quickly.

PHOTOGRAPHY: CARL TREMBLAY; ILLUSTRATION: JAY LAYMAN

Six Good Things to Know About Mussels

1 They're safe to eat. Mussels are routinely tested by state and local agencies for the presence of algae-derived toxins. The Monterey Bay Aquarium's Seafood Watch program calls them a "Best Choice" for environmental sustainability.

2 They need almost no cleaning. Most mussels are cultivated on long ropes suspended from rafts, which leaves them free of sand and grit—and for the most part, beards. In general, all they need is a quick rinse under the tap.

3 It's easy to tell when they're fresh. A live mussel will smell pleasantly briny. If open, its shell should close up when lightly tapped (but give it a moment; some mussels take longer than others to clam up).

4 It's equally easy to tell when they're not. A dead mussel deteriorates rapidly and will smell almost immediately. Also discard any mussel with a cracked or broken shell or a shell that won't close.

5 You can store mussels for up to three days. As soon as you bring them home, place them in a bowl, cover it with a wet paper towel, and store it in the fridge.

6 Unopened cooked mussels needn't be discarded. A mussel that's closed after cooking isn't unfit to eat. It's a sign that the mussel needs more cooking. To open a reluctant mussel, microwave it briefly (30 seconds or so).

---

more mussels opened at the same time so that fewer were overcooked. But how could I mimic this result and still cook the quantity of mussels I wanted? A pot or pan with more surface area—or, better yet, a large roasting pan?

One way we've achieved more even cooking in recipes is by using the oven rather than the stove. In the oven, heat surrounds the food on all sides, leading to more even (and gentle) cooking than is possible on the stove, where the heat can't help but be more aggressive at the bottom of the pan. So for my next test, I preheated the oven to its highest setting. I placed 4 pounds of mussels in a large roasting pan, covered it tightly with foil, set it on the middle oven rack—and waited, fingers crossed. These mussels took a bit longer to cook (even at 500 degrees, the oven is more gentle than a direct flame), but when they were done, I breathed a sigh of relief: Only one or two hadn't opened and the others were moist and plump.

It was time to create a few variations. In one version, I paired the mussels with leeks and Pernod. In another, I substituted hard dry cider for the wine and added smoky bacon to temper its sweetness.

Now all that was left was convincing my friends to get past their objections to cooking mussels. Once they discovered how unfounded their fears were and tried my method for oven steaming, I knew they'd be as hooked as I am on cooking mussels at home.

OVEN-STEAMED MUSSELS
SERVES 2 TO 4

Discard any mussel with an unpleasant odor or with a cracked or broken shell or a shell that won't close. Serve with crusty bread. For our free recipe for Oven-Steamed Mussels with Tomato and Chorizo, go to CooksIllustrated.com/oct13.

1	tablespoon extra-virgin olive oil
3	garlic cloves, minced
	Pinch red pepper flakes
1	cup dry white wine
3	sprigs fresh thyme
2	bay leaves
4	pounds mussels, scrubbed and debearded
¼	teaspoon salt
2	tablespoons unsalted butter, cut into 4 pieces
2	tablespoons minced fresh parsley

1. Adjust oven rack to lowest position and heat oven to 500 degrees. Heat oil, garlic, and pepper flakes in large roasting pan over medium heat; cook, stirring constantly, until fragrant, about 30 seconds. Add wine, thyme sprigs, and bay leaves and bring to boil. Cook until wine is slightly reduced, about 1 minute. Add mussels and salt. Cover pan tightly with aluminum foil and transfer to oven. Cook until most mussels have opened (a few may remain closed), 15 to 18 minutes.

2. Remove pan from oven. Push mussels to sides of pan. Add butter to center and whisk until melted. Discard thyme sprigs and bay leaves, sprinkle parsley over mussels, and toss to combine. Serve immediately.

OVEN-STEAMED MUSSELS WITH HARD CIDER AND BACON

Omit garlic and red pepper flakes. Heat oil and 4 slices thick-cut bacon, cut into ½-inch pieces, in roasting pan until bacon has rendered and is starting to crisp, about 5 minutes. Proceed with recipe as directed, substituting dry hard cider for wine and ¼ cup heavy cream for butter.

OVEN-STEAMED MUSSELS WITH LEEKS AND PERNOD

Omit red pepper flakes and increase oil to 3 tablespoons. Heat oil; 1 pound leeks, white and light green parts only, halved lengthwise, sliced thin, and washed thoroughly; and garlic in roasting pan until leeks are wilted, about 3 minutes. Proceed with recipe as directed, omitting thyme sprigs and substituting ½ cup Pernod and ¼ cup water for wine, ¼ cup crème fraîche for butter, and chives for parsley.

Common Mussel Groups

The first mussels were farmed, as legend has it, in 1235 by a shipwrecked Irish sailor who planted two wooden poles affixed with a net into the seabed in hopes of catching birds. He caught no birds but did discover that mussels had colonized the bottoms of the poles. Today, nearly 90 percent of mussels eaten around the world are farmed. In the United States we import most of our farmed mussels from Canada and occasionally Europe.

BLUE MUSSEL
Cultivated mainly in Canada, the North Atlantic blue mussel (*Mytilus edulis*), with its distinctive blue-black shell and narrow wedge shape, is by far the most common variety sold in the United States. Its peak seasons are winter and spring. The blue mussel has a small body, with a "meaty," "dense" texture, and a pronounced sweetness.

MEDITERRANEAN MUSSEL
The so-called Mediterranean mussel (*Mytilus galloprovincialis*), which is grown on the West Coast or imported from Europe, has a slightly broader cross section than the blue mussel. Its peak seasons are summer and fall. These bivalves have plump bodies, with a softer texture than that of the blue mussel, and a "briny," "pleasantly fishy" flavor.

"BEARDED"? DON'T WORRY.

Because of the way they're cultivated, most mussels these days are free of the fibrous strands, or "beards," that wild mussels use to hold on to rocks and other surfaces. If your mussel has a beard, simply use a clean dish towel to grasp the beard and then pull it firmly to remove.

Fresh Peach Pie

The juiciness of a perfect peach is sublime—except when you want to bake it into a pie.

⇒ BY ANDREW JANJIGIAN ⇐

While the almost-impossible juiciness of a ripe peach is the source of the fruit's magnificence, it's also the reason that fresh peaches can be tricky to use in pies. The hallmark of any fresh fruit pie is fresh fruit flavor, but ripe peaches exude so much juice that they require an excess of flavor-dampening binders to create a filling that isn't soup. Fresh peaches can also differ dramatically in water content, so figuring out how much thickener to add can be a guessing game from one pie to the next. Finally, ripe peaches are delicate, easily disintegrating into mush when baked. In my book, a perfect slice of peach pie is a clean slice of pie, with fruit that's tender yet intact.

In the past, we've had some success in perfecting a filling by using potato starch, but this ingredient isn't always readily available. Furthermore, it still leaves the filling a little looser than I'd like. I wanted to make a peach pie with a filling that holds the slices in place without being the least bit gluey, grainy, or cloudy or preventing any of the fresh peach flavor from shining through.

Creating a Crust

But before I could nail down the filling, I'd need a reliable crust. Experimenting with a few recipes taught me one thing: The fillings in pies with lattice-top crusts had far better consistencies than those in pies with solid tops, since the crosshatch allows moisture to evaporate during cooking. Moreover, lattices served as windows into the pies' interiors, making it easy to know when the filling was bubbly at the center, a sure sign that it was fully cooked.

We use our Foolproof Pie Dough (November/December 2007) for most pie crusts, but in the case of a lattice-top pie, that recipe is not entirely appropriate. The vodka it contains allows us to add enough liquid to make the dough exceptionally easy to roll out without the risk of developing more gluten, which would lead to a tougher crust. (Unlike water, vodka doesn't interact with wheat proteins to form gluten.) But that same pliability makes it challenging to weave this dough into a lattice; when making a lattice, it's actually helpful to have a dough with a little more structure. Luckily, we have such a dough in our archives. It calls for a few more tablespoons of water than usual and a little less fat, both of which help create a sturdy dough that can withstand the

Cutting the peaches into large chunks rather than thin slices helps keep our pie tender and juicy—not soupy or mushy.

extra handling involved in making a lattice. Just as important, this dough still manages to bake up tender and taste rich and buttery.

With the choice of crust settled, I moved on to thinking about the mechanics of building the lattice itself. Whether you cut out strips and then weave them directly over the filling or do this handiwork on the side and then transfer the finished lattice to the pie, it takes practice to create neat, professional-looking results. I wanted a lattice that a novice baker could do perfectly. The best approach I found came from our Linzertorte (November/December 2005), which skips the weaving in favor of simply laying one strip over the previous one in a pattern that allows some of the strips to appear woven (see "Building a 'No-Weave' Lattice Top," page 30). Even with less handling, I still found it helpful to freeze the strips for 30 minutes before creating the lattice. Done.

Bound and Unbound

Now it was time to get down to the fruit. Most recipes I'd tested called for tossing thinly sliced peaches with sugar and spices before throwing them into the pie crust and then putting the pie into the oven.

But I'd noted that the peaches handled this way shed a lot of moisture before they even reached the oven, thanks to the sugar's osmotic action on the slices. Sugar is hygroscopic—meaning it easily attracts water to itself—making it superbly capable of pulling juice out of the peaches' cells. If I was going to gain control over the consistency of the filling, that's where I'd need to start. Since osmosis occurs on the surface, one obvious tweak would be to make the peach slices relatively large to minimize total surface area. So instead of slicing the peaches thin, I cut them into quarters and then cut each of these into thick—but still bite-size—1-inch chunks.

Another quick fix was to let the sugared peaches macerate for a bit and then drain off the juice before tossing the fruit into the pie, adding back only enough juice to moisten—not flood—the filling. This would allow me to control how much liquid the peaches contributed from batch to batch. I tossed 3 pounds of peaches with ½ cup of sugar, 1 tablespoon of lemon juice, and a pinch of salt. When I drained the peaches 30 minutes later, they yielded more than ½ cup of juice. I settled on using exactly ½ cup—the right amount to moisten the filling. To this I added just enough cinnamon and nutmeg to accent the flavor of the peaches without overshadowing it.

Now it was time to experiment with thickeners that would tighten up the fruit and juice while maintaining the illusion that nothing was in the pie but fresh peaches. Flour left the filling grainy and cloudy, while tapioca pearls never completely dispersed, leaving visible beads of gel behind. (Grinding the rock-hard tapioca pearls into finer grains helped but was a pain.) Potato starch and cornstarch each worked admirably up to a point, but after that they did not eliminate further runniness so much as turn the filling murky and gluey. More important, all these starches dulled the flavor of the peaches.

Maybe adding starch was not the best approach. I thought about apple pie, which barely needs any thickener to create a filling that slices cleanly. Apples are less juicy than peaches, but they also contain lots of pectin, which helps them hold on to their moisture and remain intact during baking. Peaches, on the other hand, contain much less pectin. For my next test I stirred some pectin (I used the low-sugar kind since I wanted to keep sweeteners to a minimum) into my reserved peach juice, heated the mixture briefly on the stove, and then folded it into the peach chunks. This filling turned out smooth and clear and tasted brightly of peaches. But it was still runnier than I wanted. Adding more pectin wasn't the solution; a hair too much and the filling turned bouncy. Then I thought back to our recipe for Fresh Strawberry Pie (May/June 2011), which used a combination of pectin and cornstarch. When we had added cornstarch alone, it left the pie gluey but still fluid. But could I find the sweet spot using both thickeners? Yes: Two tablespoons of pectin and 1 tablespoon of cornstarch left me with a filling that was smooth, clear, and moist from edge to center without being soupy.

One problem remained: a tendency for the peach chunks to fall out of the pie slices—because of the chunks' irregular shapes, they never fit together perfectly. I tried mashing a small amount of the macerated peaches to a coarse pulp with a fork and used it as a form of mortar to eliminate gaps and stabilize the filling. Happily, it worked.

At last, I had a fresh peach pie that looked perfect, tasted of fresh peaches, and sliced neatly.

FRESH PEACH PIE
SERVES 8

If your peaches are too soft to withstand the pressure of a peeler, cut a shallow X in the bottom of the fruit, blanch them in a pot of simmering water for 15 seconds, and then shock them in a bowl of ice water before peeling. For fruit pectin we recommend both Sure-Jell for Less or No Sugar Needed Recipes and Ball RealFruit Low or No-Sugar Needed Pectin. For illustrations of our no-weave lattice, see page 30.

- 3 pounds peaches, peeled, quartered, and pitted, each quarter cut into thirds
- ½ cup (3½ ounces) plus 3 tablespoons sugar
- 1 teaspoon grated lemon zest plus 1 tablespoon juice
- ⅛ teaspoon salt
- 2 tablespoons low- or no-sugar-needed fruit pectin
- ¼ teaspoon ground cinnamon
  Pinch ground nutmeg
- 1 recipe Pie Dough for Lattice-Top Pie
- 1 tablespoon cornstarch

1. Toss peaches, ½ cup sugar, lemon zest and juice, and salt in medium bowl. Let stand at room temperature for at least 30 minutes or up to 1 hour. Combine pectin, cinnamon, nutmeg, and 2 tablespoons sugar in small bowl and set aside.

2. Remove dough from refrigerator. Before rolling out dough, let it sit on counter to soften slightly, about 10 minutes. Roll 1 disk of dough into 12-inch circle on lightly floured counter. Transfer to parchment paper–lined baking sheet. With pizza wheel, fluted pastry wheel, or paring knife, cut round into ten 1¼-inch-wide strips. Freeze strips on sheet until firm, about 30 minutes.

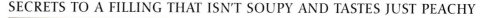

SECRETS TO A FILLING THAT ISN'T SOUPY AND TASTES JUST PEACHY

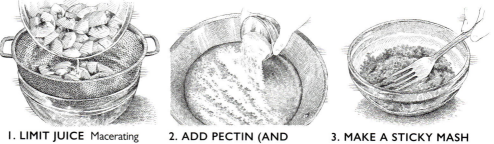

1. LIMIT JUICE Macerating large chunks of peaches and reserving the resulting juice allows us to add only as much liquid as the filling can handle—no more.

2. ADD PECTIN (AND CORNSTARCH) A combination of pectin and cornstarch keeps the filling smooth, clear, and moist without being soupy.

3. MAKE A STICKY MASH A bit of mashed-up peaches added to the filling acts like glue, preventing any peach chunks from falling out of a slice.

3. Adjust oven rack to lowest position, place rimmed baking sheet on rack, and heat oven to 425 degrees. Roll other disk of dough into 12-inch circle on lightly floured counter. Loosely roll dough around rolling pin and gently unroll it onto 9-inch pie plate, letting excess dough hang over edge. Ease dough into plate by gently lifting edge of dough with your hand while pressing into plate bottom with your other hand. Leave any dough that overhangs plate in place. Wrap dough-lined pie plate loosely in plastic wrap and refrigerate until dough is firm, about 30 minutes.

4. Meanwhile, transfer 1 cup peach mixture to small bowl and mash with fork until coarse paste forms. Drain remaining peach mixture through colander set in large bowl. Transfer peach juice to liquid measuring cup (you should have about ½ cup liquid; if liquid measures more than ½ cup, discard remainder). Return peach pieces to bowl and toss with cornstarch. Transfer peach juice to 12-inch skillet, add pectin mixture, and whisk until combined. Cook over medium heat, stirring occasionally, until slightly thickened and pectin is dissolved (liquid should become less cloudy), 3 to 5 minutes. Remove skillet from heat, add peach pieces and peach paste, and toss to combine.

5. Transfer peach mixture to dough-lined pie plate. Remove dough strips from freezer; if too stiff to be workable, let stand at room temperature until malleable and softened slightly but still very cold. Lay 2 longest strips across center of pie perpendicular to each other. Using 4 shortest strips, lay 2 strips across pie parallel to 1 center strip and 2 strips parallel to other center strip, near edges of pie; you should have 6 strips in place. Using remaining 4 strips, lay each one across pie parallel and equidistant from center and edge strips. If dough becomes too soft to work with, refrigerate pie and dough strips until dough firms up.

6. Trim overhang to ½ inch beyond lip of pie plate. Press edges of bottom crust and lattice strips together and fold under. Folded edge should be flush with edge of pie plate. Crimp dough evenly around edge of pie using your fingers. Using spray bottle, evenly mist lattice with water and sprinkle with remaining 1 tablespoon sugar.

7. Place pie on preheated sheet and bake until crust is set and begins to brown, about 25 minutes. Rotate pie and reduce oven temperature to 375 degrees; continue to bake until crust is deep golden brown and filling is bubbly at center, 25 to 30 minutes longer. Let cool on wire rack for 3 hours before serving.

PIE DOUGH FOR LATTICE-TOP PIE
FOR ONE 9-INCH LATTICE-TOP PIE

- 3 cups (15 ounces) all-purpose flour
- 2 tablespoons sugar
- 1 teaspoon salt
- 7 tablespoons vegetable shortening, cut into ½-inch pieces and chilled
- 10 tablespoons unsalted butter, cut into ¼-inch pieces and frozen for 30 minutes
- 10–12 tablespoons ice water

1. Process flour, sugar, and salt in food processor until combined, about 5 seconds. Scatter shortening over top and process until mixture resembles coarse cornmeal, about 10 seconds. Scatter butter over top and pulse until mixture resembles coarse crumbs, about 10 pulses. Transfer to bowl.

2. Sprinkle 5 tablespoons ice water over flour mixture. With rubber spatula, use folding motion to evenly combine water and flour mixture. Sprinkle 5 tablespoons ice water over mixture and continue using folding motion to combine until small portion of dough holds together when squeezed in palm of your hand, adding up to 2 tablespoons remaining ice water if necessary. (Dough should feel quite moist.) Turn out dough onto clean, dry counter and gently press together into cohesive ball. Divide dough into 2 even pieces and flatten each into 4-inch disk. Wrap disks tightly in plastic wrap and refrigerate for 1 hour or up to 2 days.

See the Perfect Slice
Video available FREE for 4 months at CooksIllustrated.com/oct13

Lemon Ricotta Pancakes

Ricotta cheese in pancakes? Sounds great. But how do you make them moist, tender, and fluffy instead of wet, heavy, and leaden?

⪼ BY ANDREA GEARY ⪻

I've always liked pancakes, but until recently I'd never been wowed by them. That all changed when I stole a forkful of ricotta pancakes from a friend's stack at brunch. I'd been seeing this style of pancake on upscale restaurant menus around town, but with a signature ingredient like ricotta, I'd always imagined them to be somewhat heavy and damp. These cakes were anything but. They had a remarkably light, tender, pillowy texture and a sweet, milky flavor that made them more intriguing than the usual griddle cakes. While I wouldn't consider making plain old pancakes and syrup for brunch guests, I could easily imagine dressing up the ricotta kind with confectioners' sugar or fresh fruit toppings and serving them to company.

Whipped into Shape

I gathered a handful of recipes, which by and large looked like variations on a typical pancake formula: flour, salt, a leavener, eggs, milk, sugar and vanilla extract for flavor, melted butter, and of course ricotta. Mostly it was the cheese content that varied; some batters were enriched with just a few spoonfuls of ricotta while others were loaded with it (more than a 2:1 ratio of cheese to flour). Presumably, the recipes that called for a conservative amount of cheese were trying to ensure that its moisture wouldn't weigh down the cakes, but with so little cheese in the mix, the results hardly earned their ricotta name. Meanwhile, the cheese-laden recipes confirmed that ricotta cakes could indeed be wet and heavy.

The obvious solution was to go down the middle, so I started with a moderate 1¼ cups of ricotta, which I stirred together with two eggs, a couple of tablespoons of melted butter, ⅓ of milk, and a little sugar and vanilla. Separately, I whisked ¾ cup of flour with ½ teaspoon each of baking powder and salt and then combined the wet and dry and ladled the batter onto a hot griddle, where the pancakes

Whipped egg whites folded into the batter help ensure that these pancakes are ultralight and tender but sturdy enough to flip without deflating.

cooked until golden on each side. It was a decent start, I thought, noticing the ricotta's rich, creamy presence when I took a bite. But texturewise, I had a ways to go: The pancakes had none of the billowy lightness of the ones I'd tasted at brunch.

Several recipes I'd found called for incorporating whipped egg whites into the batter like for a soufflé. I gave the technique a go, separating the two eggs in my working recipe and then beating the whites with the sugar and whisking just the yolks with the ricotta and milk before adding them to the dry ingredients. But it turns out that there's only so much heavy lifting two whipped whites and a little baking powder can do. The pancakes weren't exactly dense, but they'd maintained that somewhat starchy, conventional pancake texture.

I realized that if I wanted more soufflé-like pancakes, I'd have to cut back on the "bready" element: the flour. I took it down to ⅔ cup, and for a few minutes it seemed that my work was done. The cakes rose beautifully and collapsed only a bit when flipped, but then they completely deflated when they hit the

plate. It occurred to me that I might get better results if I added a second leavener, so ½ teaspoon of baking soda went into the mix. Of course, baking soda requires an acid in order to react, so I squeezed a few teaspoons of lemon juice into the batter as well and hoped that its brightness would complement the cheese. As it turned out, the lemon-ricotta flavor match was great—so I bolstered it with some lemon zest—and the hotcakes rose high on the griddle. Two leaveners seemed to be the answer—until the pancakes again fell flat on the plate.

Dropping Acid

At this point I either had to cut back on the cheese or call in reinforcements. Hedging my bets, I did a bit of both. I trimmed back the cheese to 1 cup and, invoking the "many hands make light work" principle, whipped two more whites. This, finally, was the combination I was looking for: The lift from the leavener combined with the four whipped egg whites made for the lightest pancakes ever. And yet the amateur scientist in me wondered if all three leavening sources—baking soda, baking powder, and a large amount of egg foam—were really necessary, so I made one more batch and ditched the baking powder (ditching the baking soda was out of the question since the lemon juice was a keeper). Happily, nobody missed it.

There was another bonus to switching to baking soda: The cakes were browning a little more deeply and evenly. While I was pleased by this effect, which boosted flavor, I was also a little surprised. Alkaline baking soda can enhance browning by raising the pH of a food, but I'd assumed that with a pure

See Our Pancakes Rise

Video available FREE for 4 months at CooksIllustrated.com/oct13

Roots of Ricotta Pancakes

Despite their Italian star ingredient, ricotta pancakes are not actually Italian. They have their roots in eastern Europe and Russia, where pancakes have traditionally been enriched with fresh cheeses like cottage cheese and farmer's cheese. The most well-known variety might be Russian *syrniki*: a dense, plump hotcake made from a soft, cheese-based dough that's often shaped by hand rather than poured onto a griddle.

Why So Light?

Here's how we keep the wet, milky ricotta from weighing down the pancakes.

LOTS OF WHIPPED WHITES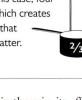
Just as when making soufflé, we whip the egg whites—in this case, four of them—which creates an egg foam that lightens the batter.

NOT TOO MUCH FLOUR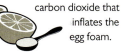
A moderate ⅔ cup of flour adds enough starch to shore up the egg foam's structure but not so much that the pancakes become bready.

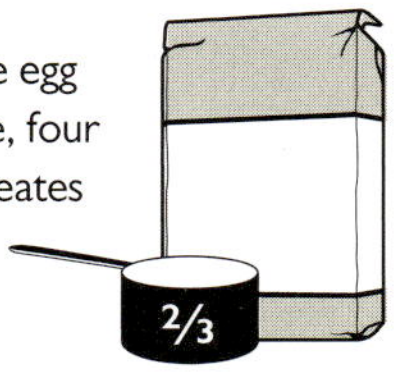

AN ACID PLUS A BASE 
Lemon juice not only contributes tangy flavor but also reacts with the alkaline baking soda to produce carbon dioxide that inflates the egg foam.

---

acid like lemon juice in the mix, its effect would be neutralized. But our science editor explained that there were two other acid neutralizers in the batter: egg whites, which contribute alkalinity, and cheese, which contains casein proteins that buffer the action of the acid. As a result, the batter's pH was more than high enough to allow for rapid browning.

These exquisitely light, tender, and golden-brown pancakes were so good that I found myself eating them straight from the pan without even a dusting of powdered sugar. But to dress them up for company, I threw together a few quick fruit toppings: one made with apples, cranberries, and nutmeg; another with pears, blackberries, and cardamom; and a third with plums and apricots. Conveniently, I was able to soften the fruits (with a little sugar) in the microwave while the pancakes cooked.

With pancakes this easy and this good, I might never go back to ordinary flapjacks.

LEMON RICOTTA PANCAKES
MAKES TWELVE 4-INCH PANCAKES; SERVES 3 TO 4

An electric griddle set at 325 degrees can also be used to cook the pancakes. We prefer the flavor of whole-milk ricotta, but part-skim will work, too; avoid nonfat ricotta. Serve with honey, confectioners' sugar, or one of our fruit toppings. For our free recipe for Plum-Apricot Pancake Topping, go to CooksIllustrated.com/oct13.

- ⅔ cup (3⅓ ounces) all-purpose flour
- ½ teaspoon baking soda
- ½ teaspoon salt
- 8 ounces (1 cup) whole-milk ricotta cheese
- 2 large eggs, separated, plus 2 large whites
- ⅓ cup whole milk
- 1 teaspoon grated lemon zest plus 4 teaspoons juice
- ½ teaspoon vanilla extract
- 2 tablespoons unsalted butter, melted
- ¼ cup (1¾ ounces) sugar
- 1–2 teaspoons vegetable oil

1. Adjust oven rack to middle position and heat oven to 200 degrees. Spray wire rack set in rimmed baking sheet with vegetable oil spray and place in oven. Whisk flour, baking soda, and salt together in medium bowl and make well in center. Add ricotta, egg yolks, milk, lemon zest and juice, and vanilla and whisk until just combined. Gently stir in melted butter.

2. Using stand mixer fitted with whisk, whip egg whites on medium-low speed until foamy, about 1 minute. Increase speed to medium-high and whip whites to soft, billowy mounds, about 1 minute. Gradually add sugar and whip until glossy, soft peaks form, 1 to 2 minutes. Transfer one-third of whipped egg whites to batter and whisk gently until mixture is lightened. Using rubber spatula, gently fold remaining egg whites into batter.

3. Heat 1 teaspoon oil in 12-inch nonstick skillet over medium heat until shimmering. Using paper towels, wipe out oil, leaving thin film on bottom and sides of pan. Using ¼-cup measure or 2-ounce ladle, portion batter into pan in 3 places, leaving 2 inches between portions. Gently spread each portion into 4-inch round. Cook until edges are set and first side is deep golden brown, 2 to 3 minutes. Using thin, wide spatula, flip pancakes and continue to cook until second side is golden brown, 2 to 3 minutes longer. Serve pancakes immediately or transfer to prepared wire rack in preheated oven. Repeat with remaining batter, using remaining oil as needed.

APPLE-CRANBERRY PANCAKE TOPPING
MAKES 2½ CUPS

Golden Delicious apples are a good year-round choice for this topping, but other seasonal varieties of apples can be used. Just make sure to choose an apple that will retain its shape when cooked.

- 3 Golden Delicious apples, peeled, cored, halved, and cut into ¼-inch pieces
- ¼ cup dried cranberries
- 1 tablespoon sugar
- 1 teaspoon cornstarch
  Pinch salt
  Pinch ground nutmeg

Combine all ingredients in bowl and microwave, covered, until apples are softened but not mushy and juices are slightly thickened, 4 to 6 minutes, stirring once halfway through microwaving. Stir before serving.

Want to Make Your Own Ricotta? It's Quick and Easy.

Our ricotta pancakes are exceptionally rich and tender if you use homemade ricotta.

HOMEMADE RICOTTA CHEESE
MAKES ABOUT 2 POUNDS (4 CUPS)

For best results, don't stir the milk too hard, and be very gentle with the curds once they form.

- ⅓ cup lemon juice (2 lemons)
- ¼ cup distilled white vinegar, plus extra as needed
- 1 gallon pasteurized (not ultrapasteurized or UHT) whole milk
- 2 teaspoons salt

1. Line colander with butter muslin or triple layer of cheesecloth and place in sink. Combine lemon juice and vinegar in liquid measuring cup; set aside. Heat milk and salt in Dutch oven over medium-high heat, stirring frequently with rubber spatula to prevent scorching, until milk registers 185 degrees.

2. Remove pot from heat, slowly stir in lemon juice mixture until fully incorporated and mixture curdles, about 15 seconds. Let sit undisturbed until mixture fully separates into solid curds and translucent whey, 5 to 10 minutes. If curds do not fully separate and there is still milky whey in pot, stir in extra vinegar, 1 tablespoon at a time, and let sit another 2 to 3 minutes, until curds separate.

3. Gently pour mixture into prepared colander. Let sit, undisturbed, until whey has drained from edges of cheese but center is still very moist, about 8 minutes. Working quickly, gently transfer cheese to large bowl, retaining as much whey in center of cheese as possible. Stir well to break up large curds and incorporate whey. Refrigerate ricotta until cold, about 2 hours. Stir cheese before using. Ricotta can be refrigerated for up to 5 days.

PEAR-BLACKBERRY PANCAKE TOPPING
MAKES 3 CUPS

- 3 ripe pears, peeled, halved, cored, and cut into ¼-inch pieces
- 1 tablespoon sugar
- 1 teaspoon cornstarch
  Pinch salt
  Pinch ground cardamom
- 5 ounces (1 cup) blackberries

Combine pears, sugar, cornstarch, salt, and cardamom in bowl and microwave, covered, until pears are softened but not mushy and juices are slightly thickened, 4 to 6 minutes, stirring once halfway through microwaving. Stir in blackberries before serving.

Grown-Up Grilled Cheese

The grilled cheese conundrum: Young cheeses have no taste but melt perfectly, while aged cheeses have sophisticated flavor but turn grainy. We wanted the best of both worlds.

⇒ BY LAN LAM ⇐

The first bite of a grilled cheese sandwich is always the best one. The aroma of toasted butter is a familiar prelude to the crunch of crispy bread, which gives way to warm, gooey cheese. But the mystique fades quickly, mainly because the American cheese that is typically used has no taste. I crave a grilled cheese with potent flavor, which means taking several steps up from American. But whenever I try to build a sandwich with, say, aged cheddar and a white sandwich loaf (its delicate crust and fine crumb make it ideal for grilled cheese), I end up disappointed, since upscale cheeses tend to become grainy and leak fat as they melt.

Before attempting a fix, I did some reading and learned that how well a cheese melts depends partly on its moisture level, which decreases with age. (It also depends on a process called proteolysis. For more on this, see page 31.) When a young, moist cheese is heated, its casein matrix—casein is the primary protein in cheese—remains intact and holds on to fat. But as a cheese ages and dries out, its casein binds more tightly together, making it more difficult to liquefy. When the clumpy bonded structure finally does break down, it is unable to contain the fat, so it leaks out.

I would have to restore moisture to coax my cheddar into melting smoothly. I decided to try wine. After all, wine is a key ingredient in fondue, which is basically just melted cheese. I cubed 9 ounces of cheddar, pulled out a food processor, and whizzed the pieces along with 2 tablespoons of white wine. After smearing the cheese mixture onto bread coated with softened butter, I heated a nonstick skillet and slowly toasted the sandwich until the cheese had melted and the bread had browned. The good news: The wine in the cheese tasted terrific (no surprise there) and the added liquid meant that the cheese was not nearly as broken as in my previous attempts. The bad news: It was still a little greasy.

I thought back to fondue, which also contains flour. Could starch absorb some of the fat in the cheddar? Yes, but at a cost: If I added enough flour, I could produce a nongreasy filling, but the starch muted the taste of the cheese. My next strategy: Instead of trying to soak up the cheddar's excess

oil, how about cutting back on the cheddar itself and replacing it with a moist, easy-melting cheese? I bought a block of Monterey Jack and a wedge of supermarket Brie and made batches of spread containing 7 ounces of cheddar and 2 ounces of one of these "melty" cheeses. Success: Using less cheddar and processing it with a smooth melter eliminated any trace of grease. I chose Brie over Jack since its buttery notes paired better with the sharp cheddar.

Now I just needed a little more depth of flavor. A few teaspoons of minced shallot did the trick, accenting the cheese with savory complexity.

To spice up the bread, I mixed a dollop of Dijon into the softened butter I had been slathering on the exterior of the sandwich. The result was a hit, smelling and tasting subtly of mustard. Emboldened by these results, I experimented and found that Asiago and dates on oatmeal bread, Comté and cornichon on rye, and Gruyère and chives on rye are fantastic combinations as well. Finally: I had a host of grilled cheese sandwiches engineered for adult tastes and good to the last bite.

GROWN-UP GRILLED CHEESE SANDWICHES WITH CHEDDAR AND SHALLOT
SERVES 4

Look for a cheddar aged for about one year (avoid cheddar aged for longer; it won't melt well). To quickly bring the cheddar to room temperature, microwave the pieces until warm, about 30 seconds. The first two sandwiches can be held in a 200-degree oven on a wire rack set in a baking sheet. For our free recipe for Grown-Up Grilled Cheese Sandwiches with Robiola and Chipotle, go to CooksIllustrated.com/oct13.

7	ounces aged cheddar cheese, cut into 24 equal pieces, room temperature
2	ounces Brie cheese, rind removed
2	tablespoons dry white wine or vermouth
4	teaspoons minced shallot
3	tablespoons unsalted butter, softened
1	teaspoon Dijon mustard
8	slices hearty white sandwich bread

1. Process cheddar, Brie, and wine in food processor until smooth paste is formed, 20 to 30 seconds. Add shallot and pulse to combine, 3 to 5 pulses. Combine butter and mustard in small bowl.

2. Working on parchment paper–lined counter, spread mustard butter evenly over 1 side of slices of

How do you make aged cheeses smooth and creamy when melted? Add youth and alcohol.

bread. Flip 4 slices of bread over and spread cheese mixture evenly over slices. Top with remaining 4 slices of bread, buttered sides up.

3. Preheat 12-inch nonstick skillet over medium heat for 2 minutes. (Droplets of water should just sizzle when flicked onto pan.) Place 2 sandwiches in skillet; reduce heat to medium-low; and cook until both sides are crispy and golden brown, 6 to 9 minutes per side, moving sandwiches to ensure even browning. Remove sandwiches from skillet and let stand for 2 minutes before serving. Repeat with remaining 2 sandwiches.

GROWN-UP GRILLED CHEESE SANDWICHES WITH ASIAGO AND DATES

Substitute Asiago for cheddar, finely chopped pitted dates for shallot, and oatmeal sandwich bread for white sandwich bread.

GROWN-UP GRILLED CHEESE SANDWICHES WITH COMTÉ AND CORNICHON

Substitute Comté for cheddar, minced cornichon for shallot, and rye sandwich bread for white sandwich bread.

GROWN-UP GRILLED CHEESE SANDWICHES WITH GRUYÈRE AND CHIVES

Substitute Gruyère for cheddar, chives for shallot, and rye sandwich bread for white sandwich bread.

What Makes a Great Cheap Knife?

One chef's knife has been a champ in our kitchen for nearly two decades.
Can any other blade come close to offering what it does—and at a bargain price?

≥ BY HANNAH CROWLEY ≤

During the past 20 years, we've conducted five chef's knife evaluations. Those tests have covered dozens of blades in styles ranging from traditional, to innovative, to hybrid knives combining Western and Asian features. And at the end of every test, we've told the same story: One bargain knife, the $27 Victorinox Fibrox, has typically trounced the competition—including knives costing 10 times its price tag.

While it's hard to imagine a factory-made knife that could surpass this one—either in price or quality—every so often we revisit the category to be sure. This time we sought out 8-inch chef's knives (the most all-purpose size) and capped our budget at $50. Ten models met our criteria—including a new Victorinox knife called the Swiss Classic that the company considers to be the "consumer" version of the Fibrox, a model that will eventually be available only commercially. We enlisted six testers, male and female and with varying hand sizes and kitchen abilities, and got each of them to spend weeks hacking, dicing, and chopping their way through 10 whole chickens, 10 butternut squashes, 10 onions, and 10 bunches of parsley. What we're always looking for: a strong yet agile blade that feels comfortable and secure in our hands.

By the time we wrapped up testing, we'd found one standout favorite and a couple of other knives that passed muster, but the rest of the models lagged behind, many of them by a considerable margin. While the top performers capably broke down whole birds and slid through dense squash, the bulk of the lot struggled—and at the end of testing, we had piles of ragged onion pieces and bruised parsley leaves to prove it.

The obvious question: What was it about our lone winner that made it a stellar performer? Its design wasn't radically different from that of other knives, and it was one of the least expensive knives in an already low-cost lineup. We decided to get to the bottom of what made this one knife so much better than all the others.

Degrees of Separation

The top priority for a good knife is razor sharpness. Right out of the box, some knives were sharper than others. Still others started out fairly sharp and quickly lost their edge. Either way, a dull knife turns a small pile of potatoes into a mountain and makes for sloppy food. ("I can hear the cells bursting," said

one tester as a dull blade sprayed onion juice across the cutting board. "Chicken, I feel sorry for you," said a second frustrated tester, vainly hacking away with another comparatively blunt edge.)

Sharpness is partly determined by the thinness of the blade's cutting edge. Any material can be sharp if its edge is thin enough—this is why an otherwise harmless piece of paper can deliver a paper cut. Traditionally, Western knives have been sharpened to 20 to 22 degrees on each side of the blade, while Asian knives are thinner—just 15 degrees on each side. However, those style markers appear to be blurring in favor of Asian knives: All the knives we tested are considered Western-style, yet when we asked the manufacturers, it turned out that half of the models sported 15-degree (or narrower) blades, including our top three favorites.

But a razor-thin cutting edge isn't everything: If the metal is too soft, it will easily develop microscopic chips, dings, and dents, and the edge will wear down quickly. So what makes one type of blade harder than another? It begins with the composition of the steel.

Steel is an alloy that always includes iron and carbon, but it may also contain other elements chosen to add particular characteristics to the metal. We were able to find out that the products in our lineup used one of three basic steel alloys: x50CrMoV15, x55CrMoV15, and 420. (To make the first two alloys easier to reference in this story, we'll refer to them simply as "x50" and "x55" steel, respectively.) When we checked the steel type of each blade against our ratings, we saw that knives made from the 420 steel were clearly inferior to blades made from the other two alloys, as they landed at the bottom of our rankings. These included the "dull," "flimsy" model from Dexter-Russell, which produced crushed, not diced, onions. Another blade made from 420 was the last-place OXO, which struggled to cleanly slice through sheets of copier paper (our standard sharpness test) and dulled rapidly as testing progressed. Meanwhile, the blades that started out sharp and stayed that way were crafted from x50 and x55 steel—and our top three models all used the x50 alloy.

These results suggested that the 420 alloy produced blades that weren't as hard as those made from the other two metals. When we consulted Bob Kramer, a master bladesmith, and Merrilea Mayo, a materials scientist and former president of the Materials Research Society, both experts confirmed

our hunch: 420 steel is indeed a softer metal than the other two alloys. This is because it usually contains less carbon and no vanadium, elements that act as hardening agents. So why would a manufacturer select for this quality? A softer steel is easier to cut into blades, lowering production costs. As for differences between x50 and x55 steel, their steel makeups are very similar, so we could only assume that something else was giving the x50 a literal edge over the others.

That something turned out to be how the metal is heated and cooled. Just as baking time and temperature affect the crumb of a cake, the "cooking" process determines the grain of a metal. For a harder product, small, close-knit grains are the goal. "Large grains," Mayo explained, "are functionally useless for knife blades because they are so soft." All manufacturers start the knife-making process the same way: by slowly cooling the molten metal. Next comes the proprietary part: a multistep tempering process of reheating and cooling the metal to help shrink the grains and/or encourage new, smaller ones to form. According to Mayo, tempering can have infinite variations, which in turn can lead to differences in grain size and pattern. We're betting that the specific way it was tempered helped give our front-runner superior hardness. (Heat treatment might also explain why some blades made from the same x50 steel didn't perform as well.)

Get a (Good) Grip

As for the other half of the knife—the handle—we figured that preferences would be a dividing point among testers. After all, the comfort of a grip is largely subjective and depends on variables from the size of your hand, to how you hold the blade, to your knife skills, to whether you prefer a brawnier or more svelte handle or one that's crafted from metal rather than nylon or wood.

Surprisingly, though, all six testers unanimously preferred one handle: that of the Victorinox Fibrox. This handle boasted no ergonomic grooves or bumps; compared with other models that we tested, it actually lacked design features. How could one grip—particularly one so basic-looking that it almost

The Handle: One Style Fits All

The knife with the most basic handle—no grooves or bumps—was also the most comfortable for all our testers. In fact, experts confirmed that the Victorinox Fibrox's lack of pronounced ergonomic features was precisely the reason that we favored it. Its neutral rectangular body, smooth edges, and rounded base made a variety of gripping positions comfortable, whereas other more contoured models with sharper angles forced our hands into unnatural positions or were too long and pointed and dug into our forearms when we choked up on the knife.

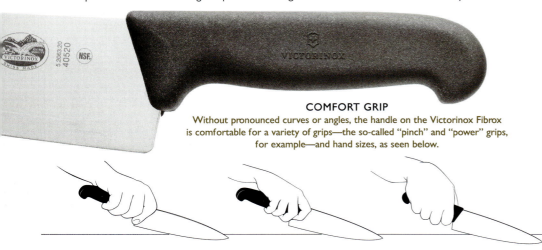

COMFORT GRIP
Without pronounced curves or angles, the handle on the Victorinox Fibrox is comfortable for a variety of grips—the so-called "pinch" and "power" grips, for example—and hand sizes, as seen below.

The Blade: What Makes It Sharp and Keeps It That Way

Creating the sharpest, most durable knives is a bit like baking a cake: Manufacturers have to start with the right ingredients and then treat the metal just so.

THE RIGHT MIX OF METALS

Because steel is an alloy, it can come in countless forms, depending on what metals it contains and in what proportion. Certain elements, such as carbon and vanadium, increase a steel's hardness so that it can hold its edge and resist chipping, denting, and folding over. The alloy used in our top-performing knives, x50CrMoV15, contained both elements in favorable proportions.

PRECISE TEMPERING

How the steel is heated and cooled helps determine the grain of the metal. Harder blades have a finer, tighter, more dense structure, softer blades a looser one. To achieve the target grain size, manufacturers put their steel through a proprietary multistep tempering process. The more exacting the process the smaller the grain and the harder the metal.

THIN CUTTING EDGE

The narrower the angle of the cutting edge the sharper the blade will be. Each of our top three knives was factory-sharpened to a slim 15-degree edge, an angle that once mainly defined Asian knives and is increasingly found on Western knives. (Our winner, the Victorinox Fibrox, has actually had this edge for decades.) Maintaining it requires an Asian sharpener; a Western sharpener will keep the knife sharp but not as thin.

seemed underdesigned—feel like a "natural extension" of so many different hands?

We showed the knives to Jack Dennerlein, professor of ergonomics and safety at Northeastern and Harvard Universities, who offered a one-word explanation: "affordance." This term, he explained, is what ergonomists use to describe the versatility that we ask of our chef's knives. Cutting is a complex task, and a well-designed handle affords multiple grips for the range of angles and forces required, allowing us to confidently drive the knife downward through a chicken bone just as easily as we make precise cuts in an onion. Dennerlein said that when knife makers add grooves and curves to a handle, like those on some of the less comfortable handles in our lineup, they are telling us how to hold the knife instead of allowing us to choose what's most comfortable. Sharp square angles on many of the knife handles and blade spines were a prime example of this (the Henckels International knife was a chief offender). They limited where our hands felt comfortable, as did pronounced bolsters, both of which dug into our palms when we used the so-called pinch grip, for which you choke up on the knife and grasp the back of the blade between your thumb and forefinger for control. Other handles (like Wüsthof's) were either too thin—"like holding a tube of lipstick with a sharp blade at the end"—or, like the Victorinox Swiss Classic's handle, too wide.

We also knocked points off the Swiss Classic for a "bellylike" curve to its grip and an indented ridge along the top. Victorinox claims that these features are tailored specifically for the home cook, but we're not sure why any cook would like them; we found that they made our fingers splay out as we grasped for a better hold, causing fatigue and decreasing control. Furthermore, the handle is made from a hard, slick plastic that didn't offer a lot of friction

between our hands and the handle. As a result, it felt slippery, especially during messy tasks like butchering a chicken.

But even when a handle was specifically designed to provide friction, it sometimes had other flaws. The plastic grip made of open ridges on the Dexter-Russell knife, for example, stayed put in our hands, but the deep grooves also dug into our palms. To some testers the wooden grips on the Schmidt and Cat Cora knives felt much better in hand, as the natural grain offered some traction, but to other testers these grips felt "rough."

Any Way You Slice It

After nearly two months of testing, we tallied our results—and we can't say that we were shocked to learn the winner. Once again, it was the Victorinox Fibrox that effortlessly ascended to the top spot for its exceptional cutting ability and a grip that all testers found particularly comfortable. Don't be misled by its unprepossessing design: The Fibrox embodies a number of subtle features that have helped propel it to the top of our rankings for the past two decades. For one, there's its plain-Jane handle. Made from a bumpy, grippy nylon material called polyamide, it has enough traction to stay put in your hand, and its basic design boasts the so-called affordance that makes it well suited for any kind of grip. Second, its blade is made of hard x50 steel—an alloy that Kramer agreed is likely put through a very fine-tuned heating and cooling process to develop the optimal hardness.

Third, the blade is sharpened to a thin 15 degrees. Given how easily the knife cuts through food, that discovery made sense, but it also raised another question: What's the best way to maintain that narrow edge? Victorinox originally designed the knife for chefs and food industry professionals with the

assumption that such users would be maintaining the edge on a sharpening stone. However, now that Asian-style sharpeners have become more widely available to consumers in Western countries, Victorinox also recommends these for keeping the Fibrox's edge at a factory-sharp 15 degrees. Going forward, we'll sharpen this knife on our winning product, the Chef's Choice Diamond Hone Asian Knife Sharpener, Model 463 ($39.99; for more information on Asian knife sharpeners, go to CooksIllustrated.com/asianknifesharpeners).

Also worth keeping in mind is Victorinox's plan to move the Fibrox out of retail stores in 3 years and make it available only to commercial outlets and restaurant supply shops, while its Swiss Classic product line will be available for retail sale. We hope that the company reevaluates that decision. Though the Swiss Classic shares the Fibrox's outstanding blade, we're not as enthusiastic about the former due to its less than perfect handle—and its $10-higher price tag. We will continue to monitor and report on the Fibrox's availability.

TESTING INEXPENSIVE CHEF'S KNIVES

Six test kitchen staffers subjected ten 8-inch chef's knives, priced at $50 or less, to a range of kitchen tasks and also assessed comfort and edge retention. Scores were averaged and knives are listed below in order of preference. Prices were paid online. A source for the winner appears on page 32.

BLADE DESIGN
We preferred slightly curved blades that rocked nicely and spines that didn't dig into our hands.

HANDLE
Handles that felt comfortable and secure for a range of tasks and a variety of grips rated highest.

KITCHEN TASKS
We butchered whole chickens; chopped unwieldy butternut squash; diced onions; and minced parsley, carrying out each task 60 times. We averaged scores from each test to get the overall rating.

EDGE RETENTION
We evaluated each blade fresh out of the box, during testing, and at the end of testing by slicing through sheets of copier paper—our standard sharpness test.

	CRITERIA		TESTERS' COMMENTS

HIGHLY RECOMMENDED

VICTORINOX 8" Swiss Army Fibrox Chef's Knife
Model: 47520 Price: $27.21
Blade Angle: 15 degrees
Steel Type: x50CrMoV15

Blade Design	★★★
Handle	★★★
Kitchen Tasks	★★★
Edge Retention	★★★

Still the best—and a bargain—after 20 years, this knife's "super-sharp" blade was "silent" and "smooth," even as it cut through tough squash, and it retained its edge after weeks of testing. Its textured grip felt secure for a wide range of hand sizes, and thanks to its gently rounded edges and the soft, hand-polished top spine, we could comfortably choke up on the knife for "precise," "effortless" cuts.

RECOMMENDED

VICTORINOX Swiss Army Swiss Classic 8" Chef's Knife
Model: 6.8063.20US1 Price: $37.62
Blade Angle: 15 degrees
Steel Type: x50CrMoV15

Blade Design	★★★
Handle	★★
Kitchen Tasks	★★★
Edge Retention	★★★

Marketed as the consumer version of the Fibrox with an identical blade (and a higher price tag), this sibling made equally sharp, agile cuts. The downside was the handle, which exchanges the textured grip for a "hard," "slippery" one with a "bigger belly" curve and an indented ridge. Testers complained that their hands were "pulled open wider" and that they were forced to grip "too far back," resulting in less comfort and control.

MERCER Renaissance Forged Riveted 8" Chef's Knife
Model: M23510 Price: $31.99
Blade Angle: 15 degrees Steel Type: x50CrMoV15

Blade Design	★★½
Handle	★★
Kitchen Tasks	★★½
Edge Retention	★★

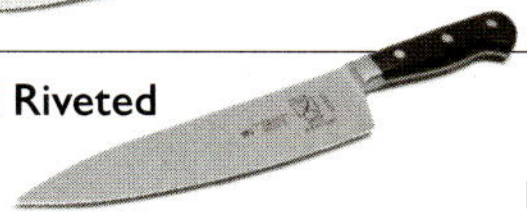

This knife's blade was "sturdy" and "plenty sharp"—splitting bone is "no problem," one tester said—and its curve "rocked well." However, we deducted minor points for a semisharp spine that dug into a few testers' hands. Some testers liked that the "heavier handle" felt "solid" and "nicely balanced"; others did not prefer the "heft."

RECOMMENDED WITH RESERVATIONS

MESSERMEISTER Four Seasons 8-Inch Chef's Knife
Model: 5025-8 Price: $42
Blade Angle: 20 degrees
Steel Type: x55CrMoV14

Blade Design	★½
Handle	★★
Kitchen Tasks	★★
Edge Retention	★★

"Chunky" and "fat" is how testers described this blade—the thickest and broadest that we tested. As a result, it "wedged" through squash instead of slicing it, but it made for a "solid butchering knife." Its "sharp" spine drew some complaints from testers using the pinch grip to choke up, but the handle was "comfortable."

NOT RECOMMENDED

SCHMIDT BROTHERS Cutlery Bonded Teak Series 8" Chef Knife
Model: SBOCH08 Price: $49.95
Blade Angle: 19 degrees
Steel Type: x50CrMoV15

Blade Design	★½
Handle	★½
Kitchen Tasks	★½
Edge Retention	★★

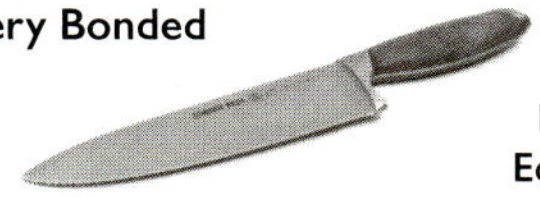

The "maneuverable" blade made "quick work" of a whole chicken, but its "dull" edge sprayed onion juice and got stuck, marooned halfway down a butternut squash. Testers wanted to choke up on the knife, but its sharp spine forced them to hold it farther back on the "rough wood" handle, decreasing leverage. Larger-handed testers struck their knuckles on the cutting board due to the lack of clearance underneath the handle.

HENCKELS INTERNATIONAL Classic 8-Inch Chef's Knife
Model: 31161-201 Price: $49.95
Blade Angle: 17.5 degrees Steel Type: x55CrMoV15

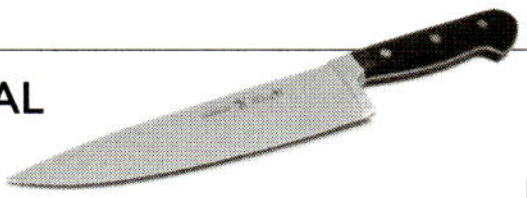

Blade Design	★½
Handle	★
Kitchen Tasks	★½
Edge Retention	★★½

This knife's squared-off, "uncomfortable" handle dug into testers' palms, the blade's spine into their fingers. Though the blade was "reasonably sharp," the last bit of edge near the handle was left unsharpened (the bolster blocks sharpening); as a result, we lost a centimeter of cutting real estate.

WÜSTHOF Silverpoint II 8-Inch Cook's Knife
Model: 4561/20 Price: $38.72
Blade Angle: 14 degrees
Steel Type: modified 420

Blade Design	★½
Handle	★
Kitchen Tasks	★½
Edge Retention	★★

This knife features a "thin," "lightweight" blade attached to a "skinny," "super-cheap" handle. Most testers found the knife "sharp" and "agile" but lamented that the blade felt "flimsy" and "wobbly" when cutting dense squash. Gripping the "pencil"-thin plastic handle was like holding a tube of lipstick—in other words, we "couldn't get a good purchase on it." Also, there wasn't enough clearance underneath the blade for our knuckles.

CAT CORA by Starfrit 8" Chef Knife
Model: 070301-006-0000 Price: $31.65
Blade Angle: 17.5 degrees
Steel Type: x50CrMoV15

Blade Design	★½
Handle	★½
Kitchen Tasks	★
Edge Retention	★½

Some testers appreciated this blade's upturned tip and pronounced curve for chicken butchering and rocking over herbs, respectively, but many found the angle uncomfortable, as it forced them to lift their elbows to direct the tip. The wooden handle was "secure" but "too narrow" and long—the end "hit my forearm," multiple testers complained, and it lacked sufficient clearance underneath for larger knuckles.

DEXTER-RUSSELL V-Lo 8-Inch Cook's Knife
Model: 29243 Price: $40.25
Blade Angle: 16 degrees
Steel Type: modified 420

Blade Design	★
Handle	★½
Kitchen Tasks	★
Edge Retention	★

"I can hear the cells bursting," one tester said as the knife crushed the onion she was chopping. This "dull," "flat" blade made from lower-quality steel "smushed" parsley rather than making precise cuts, while its spine dug into our hands as we choked up. The handle's rubber ridges were designed to be grippy, but they cut into our palms. There wasn't enough clearance underneath for our knuckles.

OXO Professional 8" Chef's Knife
Model: 1064648 Price: $19.99
Blade Angle: 15 degrees
Steel Type: 420

Blade Design	★
Handle	★
Kitchen Tasks	★
Edge Retention	★

Brand-new copies of this blade struggled to slice paper. It was "flimsy"; cutting chicken and squash felt "unsafe." It shared the same design issues as other models: a sharp spine and not enough knuckle clearance for larger hands. OXO's usual grippy handle was "comfortable" when dry but became super slick when held by wet hands.

The Best Supermarket Bacon

More and more thick slabs of "butcher cut" bacons are sharing the shelves
with thinner traditional strips. Does brawnier mean better?

≷ BY AMY GRAVES ≶

These days, buying bacon means choosing from a slew of options that range from center-cut to pepper-crusted, maple-flavored, specialty-wood-smoked, low-salt, or even reduced-fat. The latest style vying for market share? Thick-cut strips. Since we last compared major brands in 2004, a bevy of heftier bacons have shown up alongside the traditional thin, shingled slices. But does a thicker cut offer anything more than just a bigger bite of bacon? To find out, we rounded up six thick strips (based partly on actual thickness rather than labels, since some fatter slices weren't identified as such) and four traditional slices from nationally available supermarket brands (choosing both styles from the same brand when possible) and invited colleagues to a tasting.

From Belly to Bacon

Good bacon is meaty, smoky without tasting like an ashtray, salty without imitating a salt lick, and sweet without being cloying—what industry experts call "balanced bacon flavor." The five samples that consistently topped tasters' rankings had all these traits, and their "substantial," "crisp but not brittle" texture also won us over. Most of the rest didn't fare badly—they're still bacon, after all—but one failed to earn our unqualified recommendation, and one didn't pass muster at all, tasting "blah" and "not bacony enough." So what, exactly, did our highest-ranking products have that the others didn't?

To help answer this question, we reviewed how bacon is made. All bacon begins with curing a fatty, meaty cut from the underside of the pig, known as pork belly. Most of the products in our lineup use the modern wet-cure method, injecting the bellies with a brine composed of salt, sugar, sodium nitrite (to set color and act as a preservative), sodium phosphate (to retain moisture), and, in some cases, liquid smoke. The slabs are tumbled in rotating drums to work in the brine and then hung for a few hours to distribute the cure throughout the meat. Just one brand (Wellshire) used the more old-fashioned, artisanal method of dry-curing the bellies for several days with salt and sugar, but this turned out not to matter since tasters liked wet-cured bacons just as much or even more.

After curing comes thermal processing, a procedure in which the cured bellies are partially cooked to an internal temperature of up to 130 degrees. This is also when bacons that didn't get liquid smoke in their brine are smoked before being sliced and packaged. Most of the bacons in our lineup were dry-smoked (exactly how long is proprietary) with smoke derived from wood or sawdust, earning them the label "naturally smoked" or "old-fashioned smoked," according to U.S. Department of Agriculture standards. But one brand, Hormel, used the shortcut of spraying vaporized smoke onto its bellies. While some industry experts maintain that flavor differences between the two methods are hard to detect, our tasters disagreed. They panned Hormel's thick-cut strips in particular, demoting that style to ninth place (its thinner strips made it only to seventh place).

Differences in processing methods weren't the only factors that affected our opinions. Tasters also took off points for samples that veered into being too "fatty" and "flabby." Although bacon wouldn't be bacon without the fat, producers have known for years that shoppers habitually buy the leanest bacon, and most hogs destined for bacon have been bred to be leaner. When we sent samples of each bacon to an independent laboratory for analysis of their fat, protein, and salt levels, it turned out that, almost in exact rank order, the higher a bacon's protein-to-fat ratio the more we liked it. Tasters also judged meatier bacons (which have more moisture) to have more complex flavor. At first we thought that sounded odd; it's almost gospel that fat carries lots of flavor. But in bacon, experts told us, it's the moisture in the meat that carries the salty-sweet flavors of the cure, which also include the familiar "cured" taste created by water-soluble sodium nitrite.

The saltiest strips didn't necessarily taste the best, but neither did bacons with a combination of more fat and less salt. These were described by tasters as "bland" and "anemic." This made sense, since we've found in test kitchen experiments that fat masks salt flavor, meaning that fattier meats require more salting to taste fully seasoned.

In the Thick of It

Besides meatiness, the strongest predictor by far of which bacons would land at the top of our list did in fact turn out to be thickness. It wasn't simply that the brawnier strips, which ranged from ⅛ inch to ⅕ inch, boasted a more satisfying chew and cooked up to a just-firm crispiness that never shattered or crumbled. Heftier strips were also smokier strips.

But why would this be the case since, thick or thin, all but the Hormel products were smoked the same way—that is, with real smoke in a smokehouse? At first we surmised that some producers might simply smoke their bacon longer, which is one possibility. But when we talked to an expert on meat processing, Iowa State University Distinguished Professor Joe Sebranek, we discovered another possibility: that wider swath of edge on a slice of thick-cut bacon. "Smoke is applied to intact, unsliced bellies," Sebranek told us. "A thicker slice has more of the surface area where smoke is deposited included with the slice."

But could a few fractions of an inch more edge really account for a smokier taste? We froze our bacon samples and got out our digital calipers to measure them. Their thicknesses ranged from 1/15 inch all the way up to ⅕ inch—three times as thick. Sure enough, the thinnest strip of the lot, Plumrose Premium

---

Why Thicker Means Smokier

These two bacons by Plumrose—one thick and one thin—are processed exactly the same way, just cut to different widths. But they tasted so different that one went to the top of the lineup while the other was demoted to the very bottom. Thin Plumrose tasted "blah" overall and had a noticeable lack of smoke flavor, while its thicker cousin offered more of everything—more bacon per bite, of course, but also more meaty, salty-sweet flavor and lots of smokiness. Why the big difference in smoke flavor? Turns out that smoke—and therefore smoke flavor—is deposited on the exterior of whole slabs of bacon. When that slab is sliced, the thicker the strip the smokier the flavor.

BLAND BITE
Only 1/15 inch wide, less edge per slice meant less smoke for thin Plumrose—and less love from tasters.

SMOKY BITE
With an outer edge measuring ⅛ inch wide, the thick version of Plumrose boasted great smoke flavor.

TASTING THICK VS. THIN SUPERMARKET BACONS

In two blind tastings, 21 *Cook's Illustrated* staff members tasted six thick and four traditional bacon samples from a list of top-selling national brands compiled by the Chicago-based market research firm IRi. We sampled the bacons cooked according to our recipe for Oven-Fried Bacon and rated them on flavor, texture, and overall appeal. An independent laboratory analyzed salt, protein, and fat percentages for each product, and findings are shown per 100 grams of uncooked bacon. Tasting results were averaged; bacons appear below in order of preference. All bacon was purchased at Boston-area supermarkets.

HIGHLY RECOMMENDED — TWO WINNERS

FARMLAND Thick Sliced Bacon

Price: $7.99 for 1½ lb (33 cents per oz)
Thickness: ⅙ in
Salt: 2.17 g
Protein: 11.36 g **Fat:** 36.88 g
Comments: This thick strip was also one of the meatiest, with saltiness offset by sweetness, all combining to deliver bacon balance. Tasters described it as "a good meaty slice" that was "sweet," "smoky, porky, and salty."

PLUMROSE Premium Thick Sliced Bacon

Price: $5.99 for 1 lb (37 cents per oz)
Thickness: ⅛ in
Salt: 1.95 g
Protein: 13.96 g **Fat:** 30.48 g
Comments: With one of the highest amounts of protein, this "substantially meaty" bacon was "pleasantly smoky," "with very little fat." Plumrose is the only brand cured with brown sugar, which contributed to its "deeply browned, Maillard flavor."

RECOMMENDED

WRIGHT Naturally Hickory Smoked Bacon

Price: $7.48 for 1½ lb (31 cents per oz)
Thickness: ⅕ in
Salt: 1.28 g
Protein: 11.42 g **Fat:** 35.37 g
Comments: This thick-cut bacon was "good all around," delivering "great smoky flavor with enough salt and sweet." Other tasters rated it the smokiest in the lineup and also praised its "meaty" taste and "substantial" texture.

WELLSHIRE FARMS Black Forest Dry Rubbed Salt Cured Bacon
Price: $8.99 for 18 oz (50 cents per oz)
Thickness: ⅕ in
Salt: 1.2 g
Protein: 11.45 g **Fat:** 41.92 g
Comments: This "substantial" thick-cut slice, the only bacon we tasted that was dry cured, was "smoky, sweet, salty, meaty—the four basic bacon food groups!" Others compared its sweetness with "barbecued brisket" or "burnt ends," with its "porky, sweet-but-not-too-sweet" taste.

OSCAR MAYER Naturally Hardwood Smoked Thick Cut Bacon
Price: $7.49 for 1 lb (47 cents per oz)
Thickness: ⅙ in
Salt: 1.67 g
Protein: 12.86 g **Fat:** 38.28 g
Comments: The thick version of classic Oscar Mayer bacon ranked in the middle of the pack for smokiness, just ahead of its thinner companion product. It was "deeply porky" and "meaty"—"a very nice, satisfying slice."

RECOMMENDED CONTINUED

OSCAR MAYER Naturally Hardwood Smoked Bacon

Price: $7.49 for 1 lb (47 cents per oz)
Thickness: ⅒ in
Salt: 1.60 g
Protein: 13.24 g **Fat:** 37.86 g
Comments: With "a nice ratio of fat to lean meat," this regular-sliced strip cooked up "smoky" and "sweet," and tasted "not bad for thin bacon," as one taster deemed it. "Perfect in terms of crispness," summed up another.

HORMEL Black Label Bacon

Price: $6.99 for 1 lb (44 cents per oz)
Thickness: 1/11 in
Salt: 1.58 g
Protein: 10.85 g **Fat:** 43.39 g
Comments: Some found this bacon—one of two in our lineup that was sprayed with vaporized liquid smoke rather than dry smoked—"leathery" and "not very smoky." Others deemed it "good" and "decently meaty."

FARMLAND Hickory Smoked Bacon

Price: $5.99 for 1 lb (37 cents per oz)
Thickness: 1/11 in
Salt: 1.58 g
Protein: 10.37 g **Fat:** 48.65
Comments: While many tasters enjoyed our former favorite supermarket bacon's "woodsy smoke" and good "bacony flavor," perhaps due to unavoidable variation in agricultural products, it was far fattier than its thick-cut cousin. One taster described biting into it this way: "like eating a slab of fat."

RECOMMENDED WITH RESERVATIONS

HORMEL Black Label Thick Cut Bacon

Price: $6.99 for 1 lb (44 cents per oz)
Thickness: ⅛ in
Salt: 2.13 g
Protein: 10.49 g **Fat:** 47.43 g
Comments: Ranked low for smokiness (applied as vaporized liquid smoke) and sweetness, this "fatty" thick-cut bacon tasted "grilled rather than smoky." A few tasters praised its "good pork flavor," but most said that it lacked taste and was "chewy" rather than crispy.

NOT RECOMMENDED

PLUMROSE Premium Sliced Bacon

Price: $5.49 for 1 lb (34 cents per oz)
Thickness: 1/15 in
Salt: 2.07 g
Protein: 12.44 g **Fat:** 32.16 g
Comments: Sliced considerably thinner than most of the other regular-sliced strips, this "blah" bacon had so little smoke flavor that one taster likened its taste to that of "lunch meat." At best, its flavor was "middle-of-the-road."

Sliced Bacon, at 1/15 inch, had so little smoke flavor that tasters likened it to "lunch meat." They also decried it for tasting "blah," since its thinness meant that it had too little of any of the flavors that make bacon taste good. At ⅛ inch, on the other hand, the thick-sliced version of Plumrose drew raves for its smoke flavor—and for having plenty of "all the flavors that come to mind" for bacon. Meanwhile, the brand's spokeswoman assured us that both styles are produced exactly the same way except for the adjustment on the slicing mechanism.

In the end, we have two bacons to highly recommend, so evenly matched by tasters that we declared them co-winners. Both are thick-sliced and both have that perfect bacony balance of meatiness, salt, sweetness, and smoke. Farmland Thick Sliced Bacon boasted a "sweet," "smoky, porky, and salty" taste that added up to "a perfect mixture." Our co-winner, Plumrose Premium Thick Sliced Bacon, was "pleasantly smoky and substantially meaty." Tasters called it "*umami*-licious." It's worth noting that Plumrose is the only brand to use brown sugar in its cure, which accounts for this bacon's "deeply browned, Maillard flavor."

Does Cast Iron Work for Stir-Frying?

For stir-frying, our go-to pan is a 12-inch nonstick skillet. But given that a well-seasoned cast-iron pan also has excellent nonstick properties and that it could potentially do a better job at searing (thus more closely imitating restaurant-quality stir-fries cooked in a ripping hot wok), we wondered whether this style of pan could work for stir-frying. We compared results using two recipes: a stir-fried beef dish and a stir-fried noodle dish.

The beef cooked more or less similarly in both pans, though cast iron came with pros and cons. On the one hand, it gave the meat a deeper sear. On the other, the beef's marinade (which contained sugar) caused a good bit of fond to develop—and the meat to sometimes stick slightly, despite this vessel's seasoning. Stir-frying noodles in cast iron was a disaster: Both the noodles and the eggs in the dish stuck relentlessly to its surface. Frequently stirring those ingredients minimized sticking but also caused them to disintegrate. And where they did stick they burned, leaving behind black flecks and bitterness—a mess that stripped away the pan's seasoning when cleaned.

STICKY SITUATION

For stir-fries, not-so-nonstick cast iron turned delicate ingredients like noodles and eggs into a sticky mess.

Why the difference? Nonstick pan surfaces, whether cast iron or manufactured nonstick, rely on polymers for their slickness. When seasoning cast iron, we create the polymer ourselves by heating oil above its smoke point, at which time it forms a hard film on the pan surface. Most manufactured nonstick pans rely on polytetrafluoroethylene (PTFE), a polymer that creates a very slick surface. While both polymers repel water and fat, PTFE is more effective than is the homemade version on cast iron.

Furthermore, in both recipes, the added weight of the cast-iron pan was both an asset and a drawback. Thanks to the mass of the pan, once it got hot, it stayed hot, which meant that it needed less time to reheat between batches. But the heftiness also meant that it was hard work to both lift the pan and scrape out the food after each batch was cooked. The bottom line? We'll be sticking, so to speak, with nonstick skillets for stir-fries. –A.G.

Punching Up Potato Flavor

Our potato gnocchi recipe (September/October 2011) uses roasted potatoes in order to increase the gnocchi's earthy potato flavor. We wondered whether this same technique could be used to concentrate and enhance potato flavor in other dishes that usually call for boiled potatoes. Leek and potato soup and mashed potatoes seemed like good bets, as the moisture in the potatoes that would evaporate during roasting wouldn't affect the recipes.

We gave roasting a shot, cooking whole russets in a 400-degree oven for 45 minutes before peeling them and proceeding with the recipes. As with the gnocchi, tasters agreed that roasting the potatoes first did deepen the potato flavor in all the dishes. This is due to the Maillard reaction, which produces malty, caramel notes starting at 250 degrees in roasted potatoes—a temperature that won't be reached by boiling. Whether the additional flavor was an improvement wasn't as clear-cut. Some tasters, who felt that mashed potatoes shouldn't taste strongly of roasted flavors, found it an unwelcome change; others found it pleasing. But almost all tasters liked the deeper flavor that roasting lent to the potato soup, making roasting a technique that we'll consider using in the future for soup. –A.J.

Maximize Your Brine

When we brine meat, we generally call for a relatively large amount of saltwater solution for a small amount of meat. After all, we want to make sure that there's an adequate amount of brine to both season the meat and keep it tender and moist. Our standard brine for four boneless chicken breasts or four pork chops is 3 tablespoons of salt in 1½ quarts of water (or a 9 percent solution of salt to water by weight). We know that it's fine to add two more breasts or chops to the same brine, but since refrigerator space is always at a premium, we wondered if we could add a few more without having to increase the amount of brine. With more meat would there be enough salt present in the usual amount of brine to properly do its job?

To find out, we soaked four boneless chicken breasts and four pork chops in the standard brine for each quantity of meat. In addition, we soaked eight breasts and eight chops in the same amounts of brine. After 30 minutes, we grilled all the meat and tasted the results. For both chicken and pork, tasters couldn't tell which meats had had extra company in their respective pots.

Our conclusion? If you are short on space, it's fine to use up to eight breasts or chops in our recipes that call for four, while leaving the brine amount the same. But don't go any further than that. When we tripled or quadrupled the amount of chicken and pork, we ended up with underbrined meat. –A.J.

Building a "No-Weave" Lattice Top

Making a lattice top for a pie, such as for our Fresh Peach Pie (page 21) or for a Linzertorte, can be intimidating. But it need not be if you use our simple technique: Freeze strips of dough and then arrange them in a particular order over the filling. Done properly, our approach gives the illusion of a woven lattice, with less effort. –A.J.

1. Roll dough into 12-inch circle, transfer to parchment paper–lined baking sheet, and cut into ten 1¼-inch-wide strips with a fluted pastry wheel, pizza wheel, or paring knife. Freeze for 30 minutes.

2. Lay 2 longest strips perpendicular to each other across center of pie to form cross. Place 4 shorter strips along edges of pie, parallel to center strips.

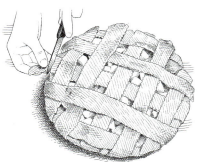

3. Lay 4 remaining strips between each edge strip and center strip. Trim off excess lattice ends, press edges of bottom crust and lattice strips together, and fold under.

A Better Way to Store (and Use) Vanilla Beans

Vanilla beans supply flavor that's superior to vanilla extract in ice cream and other custard-based desserts in which vanilla is the star, but beans have a few drawbacks. Besides being expensive, beans dry out in storage unless well wrapped, and they're more work, since you have to halve the bean lengthwise and scrape out the sticky seeds. So when we came across a technique on the website Chow that promised to solve both of these problems, we had to try it. The method calls for snipping off the end of a vanilla bean and standing it up in ½ inch of vodka (which is flavorless) or rum (which has flavors that complement that of vanilla) in a jar that is then sealed and stored in the fridge. After a month or so, the alcohol will have traveled up the inside of the bean, turning the seeds into a paste that is easily removed by pinching the bean between two fingers and squeezing. The alcohol also helps prevent the beans from drying out, which can make the seeds especially hard to remove. We found that the technique worked very well, especially after we added an improvement of our own: We cut the beans in the middle, rather than at the end, which left them half as long and able to absorb the vodka twice as fast: in only two weeks. (You can reuse the alcohol for another batch of beans; just top it off to a depth of ½ inch.) –A.J.

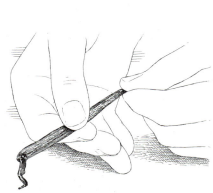

1. Snip vanilla bean in half, stand it up in ½ inch vodka, and refrigerate.

2. Pinch bean between fingers and squeeze out paste.

Cooking Steak? Try Whole Boneless Short Ribs

Typically, so-called boneless short ribs are not real ribs at all. They are cut from the meat above the ribs closest to the shoulder (i.e., the chuck). The bones near the shoulder are too narrow for it to make sense to keep them attached to the meat, so butchers simply remove them and cut the meat into short rectangular "ribs." (Why the practice of cutting the meat into rib facsimiles came about we can't say.) But there's a different way to enjoy this meat: Instead of cutting it into strips, the meat can be left whole and cooked just like a steak. Whole Foods began selling the whole cut as Jersey boneless short rib steak in 2012 (for about $9 a pound), and butchers we know rave about eating the meat this way. When we tried it, our tasters praised the cut's juiciness and beefy flavor—benefits of its deep marbling. While it's not a naturally tender cut, the steak doesn't have a lot of connective tissue, so it can be cooked quickly, either grilled or pan-seared. Cooked to medium-rare and sliced thin across the grain, it has a slight chew, similar to that of a flank steak. We like this cut when it is less than 1 inch thick. If your steak is more than 1 inch thick, slice it in half horizontally. To buy the steak, just tell your butcher that you want uncut boneless short ribs from the chuck. –A.J.

BONELESS SHORT RIB STEAK

If your steak is thicker than 1 inch, halve it horizontally.

Freezing Stew? Read This First

Freezing stew offers make-ahead convenience, but not all vegetables handle freezing and reheating well. To see which would make the cut, we gathered common stew vegetables (butternut squash; carrots; celery; celery root; parsnips; peas; sweet potatoes; turnips; and red, Yukon Gold, and russet potatoes) and simmered each separately until just tender. We let them cool, froze them in covered containers for one week, and then reheated them and examined them for structural integrity.

Most held their shape and texture well, but all the potatoes turned into a watery mash and the squash turned to mush with gentle pressure. Why? It all comes down to fiber. Fiber is resistant to breaking down, so the more a vegetable contains the more intact it will remain. Peas (which held together just fine) contain about 5.5 percent fiber, whereas weaker squash contains about 3.2 percent fiber, and potatoes just 1.5 percent. While squash and potatoes can handle normal cooking, freezing puts more strain on their structure as water in the vegetable expands and forms sharp ice crystals, which destroy cell walls that aren't reinforced with sufficient fiber.

So when making a stew that you plan to freeze, leave out potatoes and squash. Cook them on the side and add them to the reheated stew before serving. –D.S.

Why Young Cheese Melts Better than Aged Cheese

Anyone who's melted cheese for a sandwich knows that some types melt better than others, turning creamy without releasing fat. During our testing for Grown-Up Grilled Cheese Sandwiches (page 24), we found that younger cheeses almost always performed better than aged ones. This is partly because aged cheeses have less moisture, making them prone to clump. But our science editor told us that there are other more complicated factors at play as well, so we ran another test and controlled for moisture.

EXPERIMENT

We purchased Cabot Creamery cheddars aged for three, 16, and 24 months (all were sealed against evaporation during aging) and baked slices from each block on top of inverted metal cups that we preheated in a 175-degree oven until each slice had melted.

RESULTS

The three-month-old cheddar melted smoothly, evenly flowing down the cup's sides. Meanwhile, the 16-month-old cheddar showed signs of clumping as it slid down the metal, and the 24-month-old cheese actually broke into two large pieces and never melted.

THREE-MONTH-OLD | 16-MONTH-OLD | 24-MONTH-OLD

EXPLANATION

Moisture plays a part in how cheese melts, but the state of its protein—specifically, its network of casein protein—affects it most. In freshly made cheeses, casein proteins are in tightly wound clusters, allowing for little interaction with one another. As cheese ages, it goes through a process called proteolysis, in which bonds between individual casein molecules are "snipped," allowing the clusters to unwind and bind with other casein molecules, forming a matrix. Early in this process, the matrix is flexible, allowing young cheeses to melt smoothly. With time, the proteins bond together tighter, forming a stronger network that requires more heat to melt and is less flexible when melted. This can result in more separated fat and clumps, as with our older samples. –D.S.

The Science of Cooking: Cheese
Video available FREE for 4 months at CooksIllustrated.com/oct13

Innovative Pie Weight

Blind-baking with pie weights (metal or ceramic beads that hold down the pastry in the pie plate so that it bakes level) is easy—until you have to remove the ripping hot beads from the shell. Enter the Ventilated Pie Weight by Chicago Metallic ($12.95),

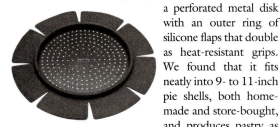

a perforated metal disk with an outer ring of silicone flaps that double as heat-resistant grips. We found that it fits neatly into 9- to 11-inch pie shells, both home-made and store-bought, and produces pastry as comparably flat and even as pie weights do. The only difference: It left a slight indentation on the crust bottom—a non-

EASY AS PIE
Skip the beads: Chicago Metallic's Ventilated Pie Weight is a simpler way to keep pie crust flat during blind baking.

issue once you add a filling. Overall, it's much easier to use than traditional weights, cleans up in the dishwasher (on the top rack), and stores easily. –T.S.

Rasp-Style Grater

For zesting citrus, finely grating chocolate and hard cheese, and turning ginger and garlic into fiber-free pulp, nothing beats the Microplane 8.5-Inch Classic Zester/Grater ($14.99). Its only flaw: Whatever you grate often clings to the back of the blade, especially sticky ginger and garlic.

The new Edgeware Better Zester (also $14.99) claims to fix that problem with a built-in squeegee that scrapes off the grated goods and deposits them in an attached container. We zested lemons, shaved chunks of chocolate, and grated ginger and Parmesan with both models, and sure enough the squeegee swiped all traces of grated food into the cup. But

BETTER—BUT NOT BEST
The Edgeware Better Zester's squeegee cleans the blade, but the Microplane Classic Zester/Grater is wider and dishwasher-safe.

while the Edgeware's surface worked just as well as the Microplane's, some testers preferred the latter's wider plane and simpler design—just a single piece of steel versus the Edgeware's steel blade set in a plastic frame. That made the Microplane easier to clean, since chocolate and cheese became trapped in the crevices where the plastic and metal met on the Edgeware. Plus, the Edgeware is not dishwasher-safe like the Microplane—a considerable disadvantage.

Bottom line: We liked the Edgeware enough to recommend it, but it isn't a trade-up on the classic Microplane. –T.S.

Portable Crock Pot

The Crock-Pot Lunch Crock Warmer ($19.99), a 20-ounce handled lunch tote that resembles a mini slow cooker, is designed to both transport and warm your food for hot lunches at your desk. Once plugged in, it sup-posedly warms food as a conventional slow cooker does—no office micro-wave necessary.

LEAKY LUNCH TOTE
The Crock-Pot Lunch Crock Warmer functioned fine as a food warmer but leaked after repeated heating, cooling, and cleaning.

We toted a crock filled with refrigerator-cold chicken soup and home-made chili to work and plugged it in as soon as we arrived. We also put the insert and lid through five dishwasher cycles. The good news was that the warm-ing element worked well: The Crock-Pot operated inside the temperature-safe zone by quickly heating food above 140 degrees. After about 2 hours, it reached a maximum of 175 degrees and held food at that temperature until the unit was unplugged, keeping our food safe and ready to eat. (Note: It does not insulate as a thermos does, meaning that food will not be kept cold before heating. Nor will it cook raw food like a slow cooker.)

The downside was durability. While the crock didn't leak when new, the lid lost its snug fit and began leaking a bit after repeated heating, cooling, and trips through the dishwasher. Given that, we'll con-tinue to use the microwave to reheat leftovers. –T.S.

UPDATE Dutch Oven

Our favorite Dutch oven, the Le Creuset 7¼-Quart Round French Oven, is a roomy, enameled, cast-iron pot that provides steady, even heating and makes great fond. But at more than $300, it's a big investment. Too bad our Best Buy, the Tramontina 6.5-Quart Dutch Oven ($49.99), has been discon-tinued: We recently discovered that Tramontina plans to redesign this model in the coming months. In the meantime, we recommend the Lodge Color Enamel 6-Quart Dutch Oven ($45), a sturdy

GOING DUTCH
The Lodge Color Enamel 6-Quart Dutch Oven is our new Best Buy.

vessel that gave us equally glossy, deeply flavored Belgian beef stew; fluffy white rice; and crispy, golden French fries, despite its slightly smaller capacity. We endorse it as our new Best Buy. –L.M.

NEW Mason Jar Drinking Lid

The Cuppow ($7.99) is a thick, BPA-free plastic lid that is designed to turn regular and widemouthed canning jars into spill-free drinking vessels. Simply secure the lid in place with a metal canning band and pop a straw into the raised diamond-shaped open-ing (which can also be used for sipping). However, we found that this hipster-y product wasn't especially practical. Tightening the band around the lid did create a leakproof seal, but unlike with many conven-tional water bottles, the Cuppow lid's opening cannot be closed to stop spills. What's more, it can't transform a jar into a hot

PUT A LID ON IT
The Cuppow turns your Mason jar into a trendy—but not spill-proof—beverage cup.

drink mug; the plastic lid is heat-resistant, but the glass isn't insulated and will burn your hand. We'll stick with turning canning jars into tumblers, not thermoses. –T.S.

For complete testing results for each item, go to CooksIllustrated.com/oct13.

Sources

Prices were current at press time and do not include shipping. Contact companies to confirm information or visit CooksIllustrated.com for updates.

PAGE 11: HERB KEEPER
- Norpro Herb Keeper: $15.74, item #811, Norpro (877-879-1360, **norprowebstore.com**).

PAGE 27: INEXPENSIVE CHEF'S KNIFE
- 8" Victorinox Swiss Army Fibrox Chef's Knife: $27.21, item #40520, Cutlery and More (800-650-9866, **cutleryandmore.com**).

PAGE 32: PIE WEIGHT
- Chicago Metallic Ventilated Pie Weight: $12.95, item #1183029, Sur La Table (800-243-0852, **surlatable.com**).

PAGE 32: RASP-STYLE GRATER
- Edgeware Better Zester: $14.99, Bed Bath & Beyond (800-462-3966, **bedbathandbeyond.com**).

PAGE 32: INEXPENSIVE DUTCH OVEN
- Lodge Color Enamel 6-Quart Dutch Oven: $45, item #EC6D43, Amazon (**amazon.com**).

DID YOU KNOW? All products reviewed by America's Test Kitchen, home of *Cook's Illustrated* and *Cook's Country* maga-zines, are independently chosen, researched, and reviewed by our editors. We buy products for testing at retail locations and do not accept unsolicited samples for testing. We do not accept or receive payment or consideration from product manufacturers or retailers. Manufacturers and retailers are not told in advance of publication which products we have recommended. We list suggested sources for recommended products as a convenience to our readers but do not endorse specific retailers.

INDEX
September & October 2013

AMERICA'S TEST KITCHEN COOKING SCHOOL

Let us help you become a better cook. Offering more than 100 courses for cooks at every level, our school combines personalized instruction from America's Test Kitchen test cooks with leading-edge technology to provide a unique and effective learning experience. Start a 14-day free trial at OnlineCookingSchool.com.

COOK'S ILLUSTRATED IS NOW AVAILABLE ON iPAD!

Download the *Cook's Illustrated* app for iPad and start a free trial subscription or purchase a single issue. Issues are enhanced with recipe videos, full-color step-by-step slide shows, and expanded reviews and ratings. Go to CooksIllustrated.com/iPad to download our app through iTunes.

Cuban Shredded Beef, 9

Fresh Peach Pie, 21

Grown-Up Grilled Cheese Sandwiches, 24

Oven-Steamed Mussels, 19

Grilled Glazed Chicken Breasts, 7

Lemon Ricotta Pancakes, 23

Creamy Cauliflower Soup, 11

French-Style Pork Stew, 15

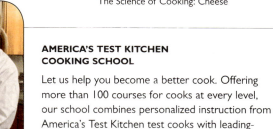
Grilled Corn with Flavored Butter, 12

Summer Pasta Puttanesca, 13

PHOTOGRAPHY: CARL TREMBLAY; STYLING: MARIE PIRAINO

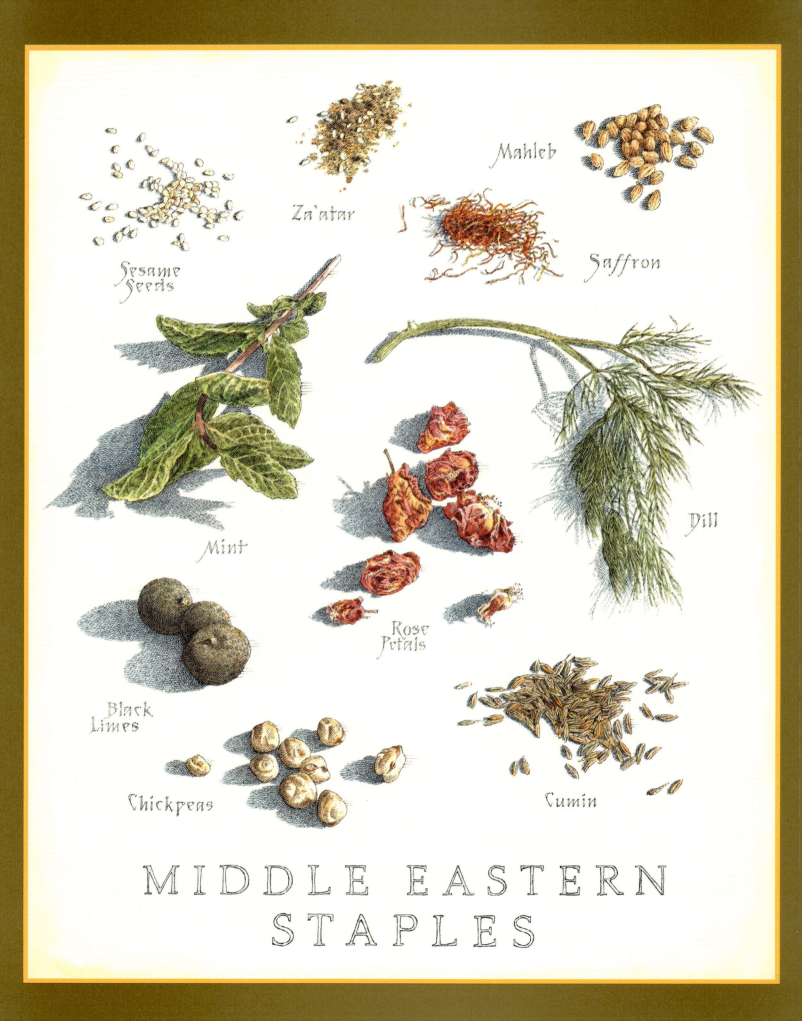

Sesame Seeds

Za`atar

Mahleb

Saffron

Mint

Rose Petals

Dill

Black Limes

Chickpeas

Cumin

MIDDLE EASTERN
STAPLES

NUMBER 125

NOVEMBER & DECEMBER 2013

COOK'S
ILLUSTRATED

Rich Chocolate Tart
New Low-Oven Method

Julia Child's Turkey
Easy Carving, More Stuffing

Hearty Chicken Stew

Testing Stand Mixers
$850 Model Places Sixth

Holiday Pork Roast
The New Prime Rib

Twice-Baked
Sweet Potatoes

How to Make Pizza
Step-by-Step Guide

Ragu Genovese
Tasting Dark Chocolate
Portuguese Kale Soup
Florentine Lace Cookies

CooksIllustrated.com
$6.95 U.S. & CANADA

7 25274 62805 6

CONTENTS
November & December 2013

COOK'S ILLUSTRATED

Founder and Editor — Christopher Kimball
Editorial Director — Jack Bishop
Editorial Director, Magazines — John Willoughby
Executive Editor — Amanda Agee
Test Kitchen Director — Erin McMurrer
Managing Editor — Rebecca Hays
Executive Food Editor — Keith Dresser
Senior Editors — Lisa McManus
Dan Souza
Senior Editor, Features — Elizabeth Bomze
Copy Editors — Nell Beram
Megan Ginsberg
Associate Editors — Hannah Crowley
Andrea Geary
Amy Graves
Andrew Janjigian
Chris O'Connor
Test Cooks — Daniel Cellucci
Lan Lam
Assistant Editors — Shannon Friedmann Hatch
Taizeth Sierra
Assistant Test Cooks — Cecelia Jenkins
Sarah Mullins
Executive Assistant — Christine Gordon
Assistant Test Kitchen Director — Leah Rovner
Senior Kitchen Assistants — Michelle Blodgett
Meryl MacCormack
Kitchen Assistants — Maria Elena Delgado
Shane Drips
Ena Gudiel
Executive Producer — Melissa Baldino
Co-Executive Producer — Stephanie Stender
Production Assistant — Kaitlin Hammond
Contributing Editor — Dawn Yanagihara
Consulting Editor — Scott Brueggeman
Science Editor — Guy Crosby, Ph.D.
Managing Editor, Web — Christine Liu
Senior Editor, Cooking School — Mari Levine
Associate Editors, Web — Eric Grzymkowski
Roger Metcalf
Assistant Editors, Web — Jill Fisher
Charlotte Wilder
Senior Video Editor — Nick Dakoulas

Design Director — Amy Klee
Art Director — Julie Cote
Deputy Art Director — Susan Levin
Associate Art Director — Lindsey Timko
Deputy Art Director, Marketing/Web — Jennifer Cox
Associate Art Director, Marketing/Web — Mariah Tarvainen
Designer, Marketing/Web — Judy Blomquist
Staff Photographer — Daniel J. van Ackere
Photo Editor — Steve Klise

Vice President, Marketing — David Mack
Circulation Director — Doug Wicinski
Circulation & Fulfillment Manager — Carrie Fethe
Partnership Marketing Manager — Pamela Putprush

VP, Technology, Product Development — Barry Kelly
Director, Project Management — Alice Carpenter
Production & Traffic Coordinator — Brittany Allen
Development Manager — Mike Serio

Chief Operating Officer — Rob Ristagno
Production Director — Guy Rochford
Workflow & Digital Asset Manager — Andrew Mannone
Senior Color & Imaging Specialist — Lauren Pettapiece
Production & Imaging Specialists — Heather Dube
Lauren Robbins
Director of Sponsorship Sales — Anne Traficante
Client Services Associate — Kate May
Sponsorship Sales Representative — Morgan Ryan
Customer Service Manager — Jacqueline Valerio
Customer Service Representatives — Megan Hamner
Jessica Haskin
Andrew Straaberg Finfrock

Chief Financial Officer — Sharyn Chabot
Retail Sales & Marketing Director — Emily Logan
Human Resources Director — Adele Shapiro
Publicity — Deborah Broide

PRINTED IN THE USA

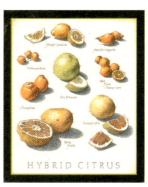

HYBRID CITRUS OJAI PIXIE TANGERINES are prized for their sweet juices. The aptly named HONEYBELL TANGELO, a cross between a tangerine and a pomelo, also delivers more sweet than sour. The edible sweet peel of MANDARINQUATS is a welcome foil to their tart flesh. Petite CALAMONDINS are bracingly acidic. Many cooks choose the lower-acid, floral-accented MEYER LEMON for desserts. To appreciate the homely UNIQ FRUIT, peel back its thick, mottled skin to reveal pink flesh with a delicate acidity. ORO BLANCOS owe their lack of tang and thick layer of cottony pith to their being part pomelo and part grapefruit. Although the sweet-tangy grapefruit, a cross between a pomelo and a sweet orange, is said to have originated in Barbados, the RUBY RED GRAPEFRUIT was first cultivated in Texas in 1929.

COVER (Walnuts): Robert Papp; BACK COVER (Hybrid Citrus): John Burgoyne

America's TEST KITCHEN
RECIPES THAT WORK®

America's Test Kitchen is a very real 2,500-square-foot kitchen located just outside Boston. It is the home of *Cook's Illustrated* and *Cook's Country* magazines and is the workday destination of more than three dozen test cooks, editors, and cookware specialists. Our mission is to test recipes over and over again until we understand how and why they work and until we arrive at the best version. We also test kitchen equipment and supermarket ingredients in search of brands that offer the best value and performance. You can watch us work by tuning in to *America's Test Kitchen* (AmericasTestKitchen.com) on public television.

WHAT I DIDN'T KNOW

When I was 10 years old, working for Charlie Bentley, I didn't know that if I shook his hand while he held fast to a strand of electric fence, I would be the one to get a shock. I didn't know that pulling a horse toward me was the best way to get it to move away. (This trick also works with people.) I was never told that trying to shoot crows with a 22 was pretty much a waste of time; I kept at it for years without even one confirmed kill. (Years later, a neighbor told me the secret: Build crow decoys out of Pabst Blue Ribbon cans.) And I never realized that eating bread baked in a Kalamazoo woodstove in a kitchen with no running water was a throwback. The world had moved on without me.

I also didn't realize, until years later, that parents aren't perfect and why my sister Kate cried during thunderstorms. I thought that everyone, on a hot July evening, got into the back of a jeep while their mother drove hell-for-leather up the mountain fueled by Jim Beam and the thrill of letting off steam. That's just what we did.

I didn't realize that death was a constant companion for adults, that it shadowed us out of the Methodist church after the open-coffin service. I never saw an adult cry or display a lack of conviction; they were steamships, plowing their course straight through heavy weather. And I didn't realize that my Vermont neighbors were poor; they appeared rich to me, lordly in companionship and sense of place, masters of their own mountain duchies. That is a view I still hold today, a half century later.

I didn't realize that one could read the woods like a good mystery, looking for scrapes and hookings to mark the midnight passage of bucks or to find a spot where a bear lay down in an overgrown pasture under a stand of overgrown apple trees. Scat can be read, too; it is a good storyteller of time, place, species, and location. So are silver leaf backs and the circling of red-tailed hawks.

I also didn't realize that most sayings are true but that truth is learned only through experience. I no longer look gift horses in the mouth or throw away small change; I keep my pennies in a large bowl by the back door for a rainy day. I also save string (except for the short pieces), mow hay while the sun shines, check my corn to see if it is "knee-high by the Fourth of July," and realize that most troubles will end up in a ditch before they ever get to me. But I know the difference between good advice and fiction. I still swim after eating, make silly faces (without worrying about permanent disfigurement), and go outside in winter with wet hair. I have stopped eating carrots for better eyesight and fretting about swallowed gum. And I still ignore much good advice for no good reason. I never stretch before or after running (that is why I can barely touch my knees) and I eat too quickly, eschewing the advice of the late 19th-century health nut Horace Fletcher, whose followers chewed each bite 100 times. Dinners must have been long affairs.

Of course, there are also big things that I didn't know. I didn't know that the Golden Rule is true. I didn't understand about smelling the roses; it just seemed like something that made it difficult for me to get from A to B. (For the record, I am still annoyed by anyone who does not decide what to order for takeout until they are first in line.) I also had to learn that kids do what you do, not what you

Christopher Kimball

say, and that even though we are just like our parents, we are not destined to live their lives; we really do have free will.

The big thing that I didn't know, however, was the importance of small kindnesses. When a neighbor is sick, bring soup. When a friend's son or daughter needs a summer job, give them one. Go to all the weddings, graduations, birthday parties, and funerals you can—don't make excuses. It matters. Write the thank-you note, pick up the phone, send an email, deliver flowers, and, for God's sake, remember the kids' names, even those belonging to the new employee in accounting. (My grandfather often called my mother by the dog's name—a source of much angst even in her later years.)

On one memorable occasion, I followed my own advice. A neighbor was taken ill with Lou Gehrig's disease. She held her memorial service on a bleak winter's afternoon while still alive because she did not want to miss her own party. Afterward, she gave away her jewelry like party favors. In early spring, I stopped by to chat and to say goodbye one last time. We sat on the deck overlooking a small apple orchard and the spot where her husband had been buried three decades before. She was happy and oddly radiant and talked about how they had found their farmhouse, surviving the first winters burning green wood and butchering whole deer on the dining room table.

She died two weeks later. Maybe that's what I didn't know. I didn't know how to pay my respects to others by showing up. It's a simple rule, an easy thing to remember, but one that is easy to forget.

FOR INQUIRIES, ORDERS, OR MORE INFORMATION

CooksIllustrated.com
At CooksIllustrated.com, you can order books and subscriptions, sign up for our free e-newsletter, or renew your magazine subscription. Join the website and gain access to more than 20 years of *Cook's Illustrated* recipes, equipment tests, and ingredient tastings, as well as companion videos for every recipe in this issue.

COOKBOOKS
We sell more than 50 cookbooks by the editors of *Cook's Illustrated*, including *The Cook's Illustrated Cookbook* and *The Science of Good Cooking*. To order, visit our bookstore at CooksIllustrated.com/bookstore.

COOK'S ILLUSTRATED MAGAZINE
Cook's Illustrated magazine (ISSN 1068-2821), number 125, is published bimonthly by Boston Common Press Limited Partnership, 17 Station St., Brookline, MA 02445. Copyright 2013 Boston Common Press Limited Partnership. Periodicals postage paid at Boston, MA, and additional mailing offices, USPS #012487. Publications Mail Agreement No. 40020778. Return undeliverable Canadian addresses to P.O. Box 875, Station A, Windsor, ON N9A 6P2. POSTMASTER: Send address changes to *Cook's Illustrated*, P.O. Box 6018, Harlan, IA 51593-1518. For subscription and gift subscription orders, subscription inquiries, or change of address notices, visit AmericasTestKitchen.com/customerservice, call 800-526-8442 in the U.S. (515-248-7684 from outside the U.S.), or write to us at *Cook's Illustrated*, P.O. 6018, Harlan, IA 51593-1518.

FOR LIST RENTAL INFORMATION Contact Specialists Marketing Services, Inc., 777 Terrace Ave., 4th Floor, Hasbrouck Heights, NJ 07604; 201-865-5800.
EDITORIAL OFFICE 17 Station St., Brookline, MA 02445; 617-232-1000; fax 617-232-1572. Subscription inquiries, visit AmericasTestKitchen.com/customerservice or call 800-526-8442.
POSTMASTER Send all new orders, subscription inquiries, and change of address notices to *Cook's Illustrated*, P.O. Box 6018, Harlan, IA 51593-1518.

NOTES FROM READERS

⋟ BY ANDREA GEARY & LAN LAM ⋞

Pearl Sugar

I recently came across a recipe for a sweet bread that calls for Swedish pearl sugar. What is it?

SALLY RIVAS
CAMBRIDGE, MASS.

⮞Swedish pearl sugar is made by compressing sugar crystals to form larger, round particles that won't dissolve in baked goods. (Another larger type of Belgian pearl sugar used almost exclusively in Belgian Liège waffles melts into the dough.) That quality makes it perfect as a finishing touch for cookies and sweet breads. When we mail-ordered a bag and used the crystals to top sugar cookies and sweet breads, we found that the "pearls" maintained their crunch and shape during baking in both applications. Use it as you would turbinado sugar: Sprinkle a few teaspoons onto muffins, biscuits, cookies, or breads (brushed first with beaten egg white) before baking. –A.G.

CRUNCHY CRYSTALS
Use Swedish pearl sugar to garnish baked goods.

Reboiling Water for Tea

Some tea drinkers claim that it's imperative to boil fresh water for tea. Why can't you just reboil leftover water?

JEFFREY RUSSELL
EL PASO, TEXAS

⮞The tea lover's argument is that water contains dissolved gases that contribute to flavor development as tea steeps. Reboiling water depletes the levels of dissolved gases, thus making a less flavorful brew.

To see if this theory held water, we compared a control batch of tea made with fresh-boiled water with tea made with water that was reboiled after we let it cool for 5 minutes. In a second test, we compared the control batch with tea brewed with water that was reboiled after returning to room temperature. We repeated each test three times. Our findings? All the teas tasted the same, whether they were made from water that was boiled once or twice, whether only briefly or completely cooled.

Our conclusion: The act of boiling water for the first time already removes so much of the water's dissolved gases that continued depletion from a subsequent boil won't be detectable. So if there's water left over in your kettle, there's no need to pour it out. –A.G.

Tenderizing and Time

In some of your recipes, meat is treated with baking soda dissolved in water to keep it tender. What happens if you leave the solution on the meat longer than the 15 to 20 minutes you call for?

RICHARD LEWIS
ASHLAND, OHIO

⮞Briefly soaking meat in a solution of baking soda and water raises the pH on the meat's surface, making it more difficult for the proteins to bond excessively, which keeps the meat tender and moist when it's cooked. Our recipes typically call for a 15- to 20-minute treatment, but what if your dinner prep is interrupted and that time is doubled or even tripled?

To find out if a soak longer than 15 to 20 minutes would do more harm than good, we treated 12 ounces each of ground beef, sliced chicken breast, and sliced pork with baking soda—¼ teaspoon for the beef and 1 teaspoon for the sliced meats—for different lengths of time before cooking them. We were surprised to find that samples that were treated for 45 minutes were identical to those treated for only 15 minutes.

Here's why: The acid/base reaction happens very quickly and does not build much over time. In fact, when we weighed the samples of treated ground beef before and after cooking, we found that the sample that had been treated for 45 minutes retained a mere 3 percent more moisture when cooked than meat that was treated for only 15 minutes. Our conclusion: Fifteen minutes is long enough to reap the benefits of a baking soda treatment, but don't worry if your dinner prep gets interrupted and you have to extend that time a bit. –A.G.

Preserving Puff Pastry

When I can't use an entire box of store-bought puff pastry, is it OK to refreeze dough that's already been thawed?

ERICA FREEMAN
GRAND RAPIDS, MICH.

⮞Whether store-bought or homemade, puff pastry is made by laminating fat between multiple layers of dough. When puff pastry is baked, the water in the dough turns to steam, creating flaky pockets.

To find out if we could reuse leftovers, we purchased two common brands: Dufour Pastry Kitchens, made with butter, and Pepperidge Farm, made with butter and shortening. We allowed a sheet from each brand to thaw overnight in the refrigerator (per the package directions). We then cut rounds of dough with a cookie cutter from half of each sheet and baked them until bronzed and cooked through. Meanwhile, we rewrapped the leftover doughs (being sure not to compress the layers) and put them back in the freezer. Two days later, we thawed the doughs and baked more rounds.

We couldn't tell the difference between the once- and twice-frozen Pepperidge Farm pastry, made with butter and shortening. But we did notice that the refrozen all-butter Dufour pastry didn't rise quite as high as the control sample when baked. Why? Butter has a lower melting point than shortening. This means that during the freeze-thaw-freeze-thaw cycle, butter melts more readily than shortening does. And when the butter melts, the pastry layers adhere, so refrozen dough is unable to rise quite as high.

That said, the effect is fairly minimal, and in the future we'll feel comfortable refreezing thawed pastry dough, even when it's made with just butter. –L.L.

Preventing Pasty Pasta

I just moved to a new house and noticed that although I cook the same pasta the same way that I always have, it now often emerges from the pot stuck together. What's going on?

PAIGE McDERMOTT
WOLFEBORO, N.H.

⮞Our hunch is that the problem is related to the pH of the tap water in your new home. While pure water has a pH of 7 (neither acidic nor basic), tap water is often alkaline. Water may be naturally alkaline if it contains lots of calcium or magnesium, or your local water authority may be adding alkali to reduce pipe corrosion.

ACIDIC SOLUTION
Add vinegar or lemon juice to prevent pasta from sticking in alkaline water.

When pasta is immersed in boiling water, its starches begin to absorb water and swell at the same time that the protein network surrounding them grows more elastic. Here's where pH comes into play: Alkaline water will weaken the protein network, which acts as a sort of protective mesh to contain the starches. This allows starches at the surface of the pasta to absorb water and burst, leaving a sticky residue that causes strands to stick together. Water that's even slightly acidic, however, can strengthen the protein mesh and prevent starch granules from swelling to the point that they burst.

If you think you have alkaline water, here's a quick fix: Add 2 teaspoons of lemon juice or white vinegar to 4 quarts of pasta water. This will help prevent your pasta from sticking without affecting its flavor. –L.L.

When to Wash Dried Mushrooms

When you call for grinding dried mushrooms in your recipes, should the mushrooms be washed first?

JENNIFER STOUT
SAN FRANCISCO, CALIF.

➤We often add dried mushroom powder to recipes that need a savory flavor boost. Because commercially produced shiitake mushrooms are grown in controlled conditions, they tend to emerge from packaging fairly clean and debris-free. Porcini mushrooms, on the other hand, are generally not farmed but foraged. Although they are harvested above the soil line, they vary in cleanliness. (Pieces with large pores tend to hold on to grit, so try to buy dried porcini that look smooth.)

Our advice for cleaning is the same as that of the chefs and mushroom foragers whom we consulted: Don't bother washing shiitakes, but swirl porcini in a large bowl of cold water, lift them out of the bowl, and shake off the excess water. Microwave them at high power for about a minute to remove any dampness. (The mushrooms should be steaming hot.) Let the mushrooms cool for about 2 minutes and then grind them to a fine powder in a spice grinder. –L.L.

An Orientation on Knife Storage

I know that wooden knife blocks are a traditional way to store knives, but can't the act of sliding a knife into a slot day after day eventually dull its edge?

TOM SLATE
AUGUSTA, MAINE

➤You raise an interesting question, since most people we know who own knife blocks slide in their knives blade side down when the slots run vertically on an angled face. To investigate whether this damages the knife, we first sharpened our favorite chef's knife, the Victorinox 8" Swiss Army Fibrox Chef's Knife, until it could smoothly slice a piece of paper (our standard method for gauging sharpness). We obtained a knife block with slanting vertical slots and then, to mimic daily activity, slid the knife in and out of the slots repeatedly, stopping every 10 strokes to check the blade's sharpness. After just 70 strokes, the knife was unable to cleanly cut through a piece of paper—a clear sign of dullness. We sharpened the knife and repeated the test again, this time storing the knife on its spine in the block rather than on its cutting edge. This time we found no discernible damage, even after 200 strokes.

Our recommendation? Magnetic knife strips, a universal knife block, or an upright

DON'T TAKE THE EDGE OFF
Storing knives on their spine prevents them from dulling.

wooden block are your best bets if you're concerned about damage from storage. If you own a wooden block with vertical slots, store knives on their spine rather than on their cutting edge, as this will help them keep a keener edge longer. –L.L.

Defending Home-Ground

Which is safer in terms of possible contamination: preground meat from the supermarket or meat that you grind at home?

JIM SCHEIP
SPRINGFIELD, VA., VIA WEB

➤Regardless of where the meat is processed, ground pork, poultry, and beef are safe to eat as long as they are cooked to temperatures at which potential pathogens are inactivated (145 degrees for pork and 160 degrees for poultry and beef). But since ground beef is frequently served at temperatures lower than 160 degrees, foodborne illness can be an issue. Meat-processing plants have stringent guidelines intended to prevent cross-contamination, but anyone who reads the news knows that outbreaks of salmonella and the harmful 0157:H7 strain of *E. coli* routinely occur.

However, only ground beef—not whole cuts—is considered risky. This is because contaminants do not penetrate the surface of a steak or a roast, and any that may be present on the surface will be killed during cooking, making the meat safe even if the interior is served rare. The risk occurs during grinding, when the exterior of the meat is distributed into the interior, taking any potential pathogens along with it.

As long as you follow safe-food-handling guidelines—including frequent and thorough hand washing, thorough cleaning of surfaces, and storing meat below 40 degrees—we believe that grinding beef at home is safer than buying ground beef at the store. Here's why: The chance of a single cut of beef (that you then grind at home) being contaminated is relatively slim. Conversely, a single portion of preground beef can be an amalgam of various grades of meat from different parts of many different cattle. In fact, when we consulted Robert V. Tauxe, deputy director of the Division of Foodborne, Waterborne and Environmental Diseases at the National Center for Emerging and Zoonotic Infectious Diseases, he estimated that a typical hamburger may contain meat from hundreds of different animals. And obviously, the more cattle that go into your burger the greater the odds of contamination.

Still, the only way to be absolutely certain that ground beef is free from harmful bacteria is to cook it to 160 degrees. –A.G.

SEND US YOUR QUESTIONS We will provide a complimentary one-year subscription for each letter we print. Send your inquiry, name, address, and daytime telephone number to Notes from Readers, *Cook's Illustrated*, P.O. Box 470589, Brookline, MA 02447, or to NotesFromReaders@AmericasTestKitchen.com.

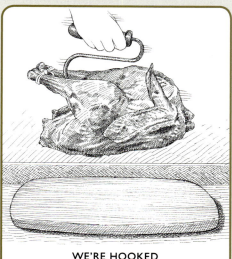

Quick Tips

≫ COMPILED BY SHANNON FRIEDMANN HATCH ≪

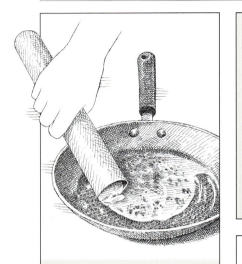

Down the Tube

Hot bacon grease can be poured into a container and thrown away, but bacon grease that has cooled in the pan and adhered to the sides is harder to remove. Geoff Gegwich of North Bend, Wash., offers this tip: Use the end of an empty paper towel roll to scoop out the leftover grease. The hollow tube offers a channel for the grease to collect in and allows you to remove every last bit without dirtying your hands.

Putting a Lid on Roasted Peppers

After roasting peppers, we usually place them in a bowl and cover them with plastic wrap, which loosens their charred skin and makes them easier to peel. Nick Swarr of Attleboro, Mass., suggests an alternative vessel: a tightly covered pot. The tight seal of the lid creates the same saunalike effect, with no wasted plastic.

Recipe Roundup

Neil Kushnir of Montreal, Quebec, offers this solution for keeping recipes at eye level while cooking: Using a magnet, he secures recipe cards to the metal hood above his stove. Not only are they near the stove but he can arrange several cards in a row for easy reference when he's preparing a complete meal.

Frozen Assets

Her favorite casseroles often produce too much food, but rather than scale down the recipes, Debbie Ide of Norton, Mass., makes the full yield and freezes the leftovers in individual portions for quick single-serving meals.

1. Let the casserole cool and then slice it into individual servings. Arrange the servings on a baking sheet and place the sheet in the freezer.

2. Move the frozen servings to a zipper-lock freezer bag. Reheat as needed.

Alternative Biscuit Cutter

Unable to find a biscuit cutter while in the midst of baking one day, Lindsay Westley of South Hero, Vt., reached for a canning jar ring. While its edge is slightly duller than that of the traditional tool, it easily stamps through dough and creates a perfect circle every time.

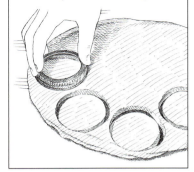

Perfecting the Proof

In the winter, the kitchen of Mark Carrara of Tucumcari, N.M., gets too chilly (less than 70 degrees) to proof bread dough. Expanding on a reader's idea for an improvised microwave proof box (March/April 2006), he uses his cooler and this method for larger batches.

1. Heat 1½ cups of water in a measuring cup in a microwave for 1 minute or until nearly simmering.

2. Place the cup of hot water and the dough in an insulated cooler. Close the lid and let the dough rise. (The hot water will keep the interior warm for up to 2 hours.) Remove the dough once it has doubled in size or reached the desired volume.

SEND US YOUR TIPS We will provide a complimentary one-year subscription for each tip we print. Send your tip, name, address, and daytime telephone number to Quick Tips, *Cook's Illustrated*, P.O. Box 470589, Brookline, MA 02447, or to QuickTips@AmericasTestKitchen.com.

The Spread on Spreaders

A butter knife is a serviceable utensil for spreading nut butters and preserves, but Naomi Lifejoy of Mendota Heights, Minn., takes a cue from cake decorating and reaches for her mini offset spatula. Just as it aids in frosting cupcakes, the tool's wider blade allows her to scoop more from the jar at once and spread with ease.

A Trick for Prepping Cake Pans

Greasing and flouring cake pans prevents baked goods from sticking, but Stacey McCullough of Arlington, Mass., often struggles with clumping flour and covering every nook and cranny. Instead of banging the pan on the counter to achieve an even coat, she uses her turkey baster like a bellows to spread the flour evenly. (Hold the pan upside down over the sink and tap once to remove any excess flour.)

A Solution on the Rise

Covering dough while it rises prevents it from drying out. Plastic wrap is a standard choice, but Emily Mullins of Southbury, Conn., prefers to reuse bags from the produce section of the supermarket. The long bags easily cover a loaf pan, and they are food-safe.

Rounding Out Pie Dough

Instead of trimming dough after she has placed it in the pie pan, Laurie Martin of Sweet Home, Ore., likes to create as perfect a circle as possible before it goes in the pan. Here's how she does it.

1. Roll the dough into an 11-inch round. Place a 10-inch-wide bowl on top and trim around the edge.

2. Finish rolling the circle into the desired size (the dough will be thin but sturdy enough to transfer to a pie plate).

(Splatter) Screen Test

When frying bacon, splatter screens prevent the hot grease from making a mess of the stovetop. But Carla Wheeler of Live Oak, Fla., also found that the perforated flat surfaces can double as platters to hold cooked slices. After removing the screen to retrieve cooked bacon from the pan, replace it and lay the strips on top while other slices finish cooking. The cooked bacon not only drains excess fat (blot it further before serving, if desired) but also stays warm.

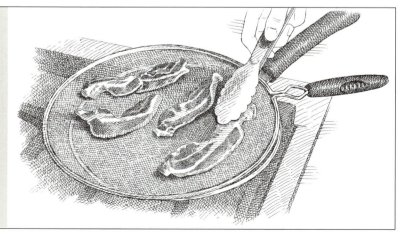

Securing Tipsy Wineglasses

While most dishwashers do a fine job of cleaning wineglasses, few have rack space engineered to prevent jostling (and breaking) during the cycle. Here's how Alan Marsh of Deer Park, Wash., locks his wineglasses into place.

1. Place the wineglass, bowl side down, on the upper rack. Loop a rubber band around one spoke and pull the opposite end over the stem of the glass.

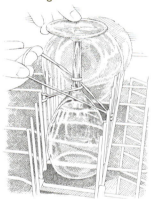

2. Loop the rubber band around a spoke on the other side of the rack and bring it up around the stem again. Repeat, if necessary, until the wineglass is secure.

Julia Child's Turkey, Updated

Julia broke apart turkeys in pursuit of quick and even cooking, effortless carving— and stuffing that tastes of the bird. We put our own spin on her approach.

⇒ BY ANDREA GEARY ⇐

Anyone who has roasted a turkey knows the method has problems. For one, cooking takes forever. What's more, the breast and leg quarters cook at different rates, which makes delivering both perfectly cooked white and dark meat challenging. In the past, one way we've tackled these issues is by buying and roasting separate turkey parts rather than the whole bird. After all, parts cook more quickly and evenly, mostly because we are able to control the exact placement and timing of each piece when roasting. But in the end, roasted turkey parts look like, well, roasted turkey parts—without the celebratory grandeur of a whole bird. Is it possible to have it both ways: a turkey that is perfectly cooked *and* a gorgeous centerpiece? I wasn't so sure—that is, until I picked up a copy of Julia Child's 1989 cookbook, *The Way to Cook*. In it, she offers an alternative.

Julia starts with a whole turkey that she turns into parts—first by using a cleaver and a rubber mallet to remove the turkey's backbone and then by lopping off the legs with a chef's knife. Next she bones the thighs and seasons their interiors with salt,

To achieve perfectly cooked meat and a table-worthy presentation, turkey parts are roasted in stages and then reassembled atop a mound of stuffing.

Julia's Way to Cook

In 1989 Julia Child published *The Way to Cook*, a cookbook that veered away from strictly traditional French recipes—something new for "the French chef." What did this mean? In addition to poultry recipes like coq au vin and fricassee, she included recipes for Thanksgiving turkey and stuffing. Deconstructing a turkey for faster cooking, easier carving, and the ability to make lots of traditional-tasting stuffing without the attendant food safety concerns was such a good idea that we couldn't resist borrowing it.

pepper, and chopped fresh sage. This way, the parts can be roasted separately, giving the breast a head start in a 325-degree oven before following with the leg quarters, which require less cooking time. Without the backbone (a poor conductor of heat) to slow things down, the bird cooked in about half of the time of a traditional whole turkey.

There are three major differences between Julia's deconstructed turkey and our recipes for roasted turkey parts. First, she roasts her turkey breast atop a pile of stuffing—which results in stuffing that is enriched with flavorful turkey juices and tastes as though it has been cooked right in the bird. (Because this stuffing has greater exposure to heat than traditional cooked-in-the-cavity stuffing does, it reaches a safe 165 degrees by the time the breast is done.) Second, her step of boning the thighs is a boon for carving: Some cooks remove the thighbones during carving in order to slice the meat against the grain for a more pleasing texture; with Julia's method the job is done upfront, before serving time. Third, and most important, is the assembly. Julia mounds the

stuffing on a platter, props the breast on top, and rests a leg quarter on each side, cleverly camouflaging any gaps with garnishes so the parts look like a whole, intact (and celebratory) bird.

Quick, even cooking; idiotproof carving; and rich stuffing, all endorsed by Julia Child? I was sold.

Easy Does It

I started by following Julia's recipe to a T. My first lesson? It turns out that dismantling a turkey with a cleaver and mallet isn't quite the carefree affair that Julia suggested, at least not for me. But with some experimenting, I figured out how to accomplish the task with just kitchen shears and a sharp knife: Happily, removing the legs and boning the thighs was a surprisingly simple operation that just involved cutting the meat away from the thighbone and then sliding a sharp knife under the bone to free the meat. With the shears I followed the vertical line of fat where the breast meets the back and then, using two hands, bent back the breast to pop out the shoulder joint and cut away the back. (For detailed butchering instructions, see "Carving the Turkey Before Cooking," page 8.)

With my turkey prep complete, I continued to follow Julia's lead by whipping up a mound of her sausage and bread stuffing, which contains eggs, celery, and onions in addition to the namesake ingredients. I placed the breast on top of the stuffing, roasted it at 325 degrees, and then put the seasoned leg quarters in the oven 45 minutes later. After 2½ hours, all the parts were done.

How did it taste? Well, the legs and thighs were fantastic. Seasoned from the inside out, they were tender and juicy. My colleagues were also suitably impressed when I sliced the boned thighs crosswise. The stuffing, however, was a little too wet and there certainly wasn't enough of it—though it did have that irresistible savory taste of stuffing that's been cooked in the bird, something that I've missed in the years since we all stopped stuffing turkeys out of concern for food safety.

But while the stuffing had its high points, the breast was another story: Somewhat dry, tough, and underseasoned, it needed some serious attention. I got to work.

The Wet/Dry Problem

To address the chalky, bland breast meat, I decided to employ our saltwater brining strategy. The meat would absorb some of the brine, and that would subtly alter the structure of the proteins, enabling them to retain more moisture during cooking: Turkey breast, salt, water, fridge, 6 hours—done.

But when I roasted this first brined breast, it released its saltwater juices onto the stuffing, rendering it wet and inedibly salty. To address this problem, I started by adding 50 percent more bread in order to absorb the liquid. But before adding the bread cubes to the mix, I dried them out in the oven. We've used this technique many times in the test kitchen for stuffing recipes, and even Julia calls for drying out the bread for her stuffing—just not for as long as we do. The key to a moist-but-not-too-moist stuffing cooked under a brined breast, I learned, was to dry the bread cubes for about 30 minutes at 300 degrees. The second tweak was to omit the sausage: Since all the turkey fat dripped into the stuffing, sausage was making the mixture overly rich and heavy, not to mention saltier. Third, I tossed in some dried cranberries along with the sautéed onions and celery that I'd retained from Julia's recipe, thinking that a sweet/tart note would be welcome. Finally, though stuffing recipes usually call for some added liquid, with all the turkey juices present, I introduced only eggs for a custardy richness.

When everything came out of the oven, this stuffing tasted great: It had just the right amount of moistness and was beautifully seasoned. But the breast, though now juicy, had pale, flabby skin. Plus the breast was taking too long to cook—about 2½ hours. I'd have to be more creative.

Some recipes call for jump-starting the turkey at a higher oven temperature to brown the skin and then finishing it at a lower temperature. I knew that would incinerate my stuffing. But who said the stuffing had to be part of the equation from the beginning?

For my next turkey, using the skillet in which I had softened the onions and celery for the stuffing, I arranged the breast skin side down to get a head start on browning. I blasted it in the oven at 425 degrees for 30 minutes while I set up my

For easy carving, we remove the thighbone and thoroughly season the meat's interior prior to cooking.

roasting pan with the stuffing and leg quarters. Then I arranged the breast, now skin side up, on top of the stuffing in the roasting pan and placed the whole assembly on the oven's upper-middle rack for even more browning. After another 30 minutes, I turned down the oven temperature to 350 degrees. Forty minutes later, my turkey was cooked through. I transferred the breast and legs to a cutting board to rest for 30 minutes and stirred the stuffing to redistribute the juices before returning it to the now-off but still-warm oven. I sneaked a taste before summoning my colleagues to give the dish a try and sighed with relief—this golden-brown, juicy bird was the best of them all, and it had cooked in just an hour and 40 minutes.

At serving time, I reassembled my turkey by mounding the stuffing in the center of a platter, placing the breast on top, and resting a leg quarter on each side. This reconstructed bird was a show-stopper indeed. And with that my turkey problems were solved, Julia-style.

JULIA CHILD'S STUFFED TURKEY, UPDATED
SERVES 10 TO 12

This recipe calls for a natural, unenhanced turkey and requires brining the turkey breast in the refrigerator for 6 to 12 hours before cooking. If using a self-basting turkey (such as a frozen Butterball) or a kosher turkey, do not brine in step 3 and omit the salt in step 2. Remove any large pockets of fat from the neck cavity of the bird to ensure that the stuffing doesn't become greasy. The bottom of your roasting pan should be 7 to 8 inches from the top of the oven. In this recipe, we leave the stuffing in a warm oven while the turkey rests. If you need your oven during this time, you may opt to leave the stirred stuffing in the uncovered roasting pan at room temperature while the turkey rests and then reheat it in a 400-degree oven for 10 minutes before reassembling your turkey.

1	(12- to 15-pound) turkey, neck and giblets removed and reserved for gravy
1	teaspoon plus 2 tablespoons minced fresh sage
	Salt and pepper
	Wooden skewers
1½	pounds hearty white sandwich bread, cut into ½-inch cubes
1	tablespoon vegetable oil
3	tablespoons unsalted butter
3	onions, chopped fine
6	celery ribs, minced
1	cup dried cranberries
4	large eggs, beaten

1. With turkey breast side up, using boning or paring knife, cut through skin around leg quarter where it attaches to breast. Bend leg back to pop leg bone out of socket. Cut through joint to separate leg quarter. Repeat to remove second leg quarter. Working with 1 leg quarter at a time and with skin side down, use tip of knife to cut along sides of thighbone to expose bone, then slide knife under bone to free meat. Without severing skin, cut joint between thigh and leg and remove thighbone. Reserve thighbones for gravy.

RECIPE SHORTHAND Perfectly Cooked Turkey with Stuffing

Breaking down the turkey before roasting allows every part to cook evenly in less than 2 hours.

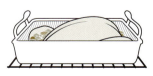

DECONSTRUCT BIRD
Prep the turkey by detaching the leg quarters, boning (and trussing) the thighs, and removing the backbone (see page 8 for instructions).

BRINE BREAST, SEASON THIGHS
Brine the breast for up to 12 hours to keep it juicy when roasting. Season the interiors of the thighs with sage, salt, and pepper.

MAKE STUFFING
Dry out the bread cubes in the oven (rather than simply using stale bread) to help ensure stuffing that becomes perfectly moist but not wet when roasted under the bird.

ROAST BREAST FIRST
Give the breast, placed skin side down in a skillet, a 30-minute head start in the oven to jump-start cooking and brown the skin—without incinerating the stuffing.

ROAST THE REST
Place the partially cooked breast and the leg quarters on the stuffing in a roasting pan and roast, reducing the heat after 30 minutes, until the turkey is done, about 40 minutes longer.

8. Reduce oven temperature to 350 degrees. Continue to roast until thickest part of breast registers 160 to 165 degrees and thickest part of thigh registers 175 to 180 degrees, 40 minutes to 1 hour 20 minutes longer. Transfer breast and leg quarters to cutting board and let rest for 30 minutes. While turkey rests, using metal spatula, stir stuffing well, scraping up any browned bits. Redistribute stuffing over bottom of roasting pan, return to oven, and turn off oven.

9. Before serving, season stuffing with salt and pepper to taste. Mound stuffing in center of platter. Place breast on top of stuffing with point of breast resting on highest part of mound. Remove skewers and twine from leg quarters and place on each side of breast. Carve and serve.

TURKEY GRAVY FOR JULIA CHILD'S STUFFED TURKEY, UPDATED
MAKES ABOUT 4 CUPS

If you do not have ¼ cup of reserved turkey fat in step 4, supplement with unsalted butter.

  Reserved turkey giblets, neck, backbone, and thighbones, hacked into 2-inch pieces
2 onions, chopped coarse
1 carrot, peeled and cut into 1-inch pieces
1 celery rib, cut into 1-inch pieces
6 garlic cloves, unpeeled
1 tablespoon vegetable oil
3½ cups chicken broth
3 cups water
2 cups dry white wine
6 sprigs fresh thyme
¼ cup all-purpose flour
  Salt and pepper

1. Adjust oven rack to middle position and heat oven to 450 degrees. Place turkey parts, onions, carrot, celery, and garlic in large roasting pan. Drizzle with oil and toss to combine. Roast, stirring occasionally, until well browned, 40 to 50 minutes.

2. Remove pan from oven and place over high heat. Add broth and bring to boil, scraping up any browned bits. Transfer contents of pan to Dutch oven. Add water, wine, and thyme; bring to boil over high heat. Reduce heat to low and simmer until reduced by half, about 1½ hours.

3. Strain contents of pot through fine-mesh strainer set in large bowl. Press solids with back of spatula to extract as much liquid as possible. Discard solids. Transfer liquid to fat separator and let settle, 5 minutes.

4. Transfer ¼ cup fat to medium saucepan and heat over medium-high heat until bubbling. Whisk in flour and cook, whisking constantly, until combined and honey-colored, about 2 minutes. Gradually whisk in hot liquid and bring to boil. Reduce heat to medium-low and simmer, stirring occasionally, until thickened, about 5 minutes. Season with salt and pepper to taste. (Gravy can be refrigerated for up to 2 days.)

2. Rub interior of each thigh with ½ teaspoon sage, ½ teaspoon salt, and ¼ teaspoon pepper. Truss each thigh closed using wooden skewers and kitchen twine. Place leg quarters on large plate, cover, and refrigerate for 6 to 12 hours.

3. Using kitchen shears, cut through ribs following vertical line of fat where breast meets back, from tapered end of breast to wing joint. Using your hands, bend back away from breast to pop shoulder joint out of socket. Cut through joint between bones to separate back from breast. Reserve back for gravy. Trim excess fat from breast. Dissolve ¾ cup salt in 6 quarts cold water in large container. Submerge breast in brine, cover, and refrigerate for 6 to 12 hours.

4. Adjust oven racks to upper-middle and lower-middle positions and heat oven to 300 degrees. Spread bread cubes in even layer on 2 rimmed baking sheets and bake until mostly dry and very lightly browned, 25 to 30 minutes, stirring occasionally during baking. Transfer dried bread to large bowl.

Increase oven temperature to 425 degrees.

5. While bread dries, remove breast from brine and pat dry with paper towels (leave leg quarters in refrigerator). Tuck wings behind back. Brush surface with 2 teaspoons oil. Melt butter in 12-inch nonstick ovensafe skillet over medium heat. Add onions and cook, stirring occasionally, until softened, 10 to 12 minutes. Add celery, remaining 2 tablespoons sage, and 1½ teaspoons pepper; continue to cook until celery is slightly softened, 3 to 5 minutes longer. Transfer vegetables to bowl with bread and wipe out skillet with paper towels. Place turkey breast skin side down in skillet and roast in oven for 30 minutes.

6. While breast roasts, add cranberries and eggs to bread mixture and toss to combine (mixture will be dry). Transfer stuffing to 16 by 13-inch roasting pan and, using rubber spatula, pat stuffing into level 12 by 10-inch rectangle.

7. Remove breast from oven and, using 2 wads of paper towels, flip breast and place over two-thirds of stuffing. Arrange leg quarters over remaining stuffing and brush with remaining 1 teaspoon oil. Lightly season breast and leg quarters with salt. Tuck any large sections of exposed stuffing under bird so most of stuffing is covered by turkey. Transfer pan to oven and cook for 30 minutes.

Twice-Baked Sweet Potatoes

Could a casserole trick turn watery sweet potatoes into a fluffy filling?

> BY CELESTE ROGERS

I love a good twice-baked potato. With their earthy skin, fluffy mash, and luxe toppings, these stuffed spuds—part baked potato, part casserole—are perfect for entertaining since they emerge from the oven in individual portions. But I've often wondered why sweet potatoes don't seem to get this royal treatment.

Making twice-baked potatoes is relatively simple: You roast russet potatoes in a hot oven and then halve them and scoop out their flesh, which is mashed with any combination of butter, dairy, and spice. After the skins are filled, you bake the spuds again, often with a creamy cheese topping. A quick search revealed that twice-baked sweet potato recipes do exist, and they follow basically the same procedure as russet recipes. Unfortunately, sampling a few of these recipes demonstrated why russets are the more common choice. The sweet potato flesh often baked into a loose, watery mess. What's more, the outermost portion of flesh tended to overcook and parch in the hot oven, causing it to shrink away from the delicate skins. The thin skins then tore, leaving nothing to stuff. These issues were really no surprise: Russets are floury and starchy; sweet potatoes are comparatively low in starch.

The first issue I tackled was the flesh retracting from the skin. The gentle heat of a very low oven might have mitigated overcooking and solved the problem, but I figured that this would take too long. (Already the first bake was taking an hour. Ideally, that would be the cooking time for the entire dish.) Instead, I turned to the microwave. This appliance works by jostling the water molecules in food; the motion generates heat that cooks the food. Since a raw sweet potato is about 70 percent water, the microwave seemed like a great candidate to produce even cooking. The first batch of tubers I zapped hit the mark—after just 12 minutes, the flesh was tender enough for scooping and mashing but still remained in contact with the skin. Just as we had done in our recipe for speedy twice-baked russets, I baked the empty shells on a wire rack set in a baking sheet for 10 minutes in a 425-degree oven. The skins were now dried out and stable enough to pack with filling.

Next up: dealing with the overly wet flesh. Mixing in loads of butter and cream (the usual richness enhancers) only exacerbated the problem. Dehydrating the mash by simmering it in a saucepan was time-consuming and relatively ineffective. Incorporating a roux (flour cooked with butter) only created gumminess and masked the potato flavor. Finally, remembering the pillowy texture of an egg-enhanced sweet potato casserole that my mother used to make, I cracked an egg into the mix before stuffing and baking the potatoes. When I peeked in the oven, I was excited to see that this mash had set and puffed slightly, transforming from watery to fluffy. Two tablespoons of butter, a bit of nutty Parmesan, and some salt lent savory qualities that accentuated the earthy side of the sweet potato.

I now had a deliciously savory, velvety filling. But it needed a textural counterpoint that a cheesy topping just couldn't provide. I thought of sweet potato casseroles covered with crunchy, streusel-like bits and decided to pursue something similar. Wanting to keep my options open for savory as well as sweet toppings, I cut fresh bread into small pieces and coated them with melted butter. Tossing the bread with sautéed shallots or bacon balanced the potato's sweetness and added complexity. For those who prefer a sweet variation, I developed a topping laced with browned butter and cinnamon sugar. Upon baking, all the toppings turned into crispy crowns well suited for the low-starch spud, which was now ready for its moment of glory.

Buttery bread bits top a fluffy mash enhanced by egg.

TWICE-BAKED SWEET POTATOES WITH SHALLOT AND PARMESAN TOPPING
SERVES 6

The skins of the sweet potato are edible and add an earthiness to the dish. When shopping, look for sweet potatoes that are uniform in size, with rounded ends. For our free recipes for Twice-Baked Sweet Potatoes with Bacon Topping and Twice-Baked Sweet Potatoes with Cinnamon Toast Topping, go to CooksIllustrated.com/dec13.

- 4 small sweet potatoes (8 ounces each), unpeeled, each lightly pricked with fork in 3 places
- 3 tablespoons unsalted butter, plus 2 tablespoons melted
- 2 shallots, sliced thin
- 2 slices hearty white sandwich bread, crusts removed, cut into 1/8- to 1/4-inch pieces
- 1 ounce Parmesan cheese, grated (1/2 cup)
- 1 teaspoon minced fresh thyme
  Salt and pepper
- 1 large egg, lightly beaten

1. Place potatoes in shallow baking dish. Microwave until skewer glides easily through flesh and potatoes yield to gentle pressure, 9 to 12 minutes, flipping potatoes every 3 minutes. Let potatoes cool for 10 minutes. Adjust oven rack to middle position and heat oven to 425 degrees.

2. Melt 3 tablespoons butter in 10-inch skillet over medium heat. Add shallots and cook, stirring occasionally, until softened, 2 to 5 minutes. Transfer shallots to bowl. Add bread pieces, 1/4 cup Parmesan, thyme, 1/4 teaspoon salt, and 1/4 teaspoon pepper to bowl with shallots. Toss to combine.

3. Halve each potato lengthwise. Using spoon, scoop flesh from each half into second bowl, leaving about 1/8- to 1/4-inch thickness of flesh. Place 6 shells cut side up on wire rack set in rimmed baking sheet (discard remaining 2 shells). Bake shells until dry and slightly crispy, about 10 minutes.

4. Meanwhile, mash potato flesh with ricer, food mill, or potato masher until smooth. Stir in egg, 2 tablespoons melted butter, 1/2 teaspoon salt, and remaining 1/4 cup Parmesan.

5. Remove shells from oven and reduce temperature to 375 degrees. Divide mashed potato mixture evenly among shells. Top each filled shell with bread mixture. Bake until bread mixture is spotty brown, about 20 minutes. Let cool for 5 minutes before serving.

TO MAKE AHEAD: Stuff potato shells as directed in step 5 but do not top. Store bread mixture at room temperature and refrigerate filled potatoes for up to 24 hours. To serve, top each shell and bake as directed, reducing oven temperature to 325 degrees and increasing baking time to 35 minutes.

The Best Chicken Stew

Everyone knows that when it comes to making stew, beef is king. Everyone is wrong.

⊰ BY DAN SOUZA ⊱

Living in a nation of chicken lovers, I'm always surprised at how rarely I find chicken stew on a menu or in a cookbook. We have great chicken pot pies, plenty of chicken casseroles, and some of the best chicken noodle soups going, but in the stew category we seem almost exclusively drawn to beef. The few chicken stews I have seen are either too fussy or too fancy, derivatives of French fricassee or coq au vin, or seem more soup than stew, with none of the complexity and depth I expect from the latter. It was time to make an adjustment to the American canon. I'd develop a chicken stew recipe that would satisfy like the beef kind—one with succulent bites of chicken, tender vegetables, and a truly robust gravy.

Where's the Beef?

Since my clear goal was to develop a beef stew–caliber chicken stew, that's exactly where I started. Beef is practically designed for stew. Chuck roast (cut from the shoulder) can be easily cubed into even pieces, seared hard to develop a rich-tasting crust, and simmered for hours until fall-apart tender, all the while remaining juicy. This treatment is made possible by the meat's tough network of connective tissue, which slowly converts into lubricating gelatin during cooking. This turns the beef tender while the gravy is infused with rich beefiness and body—a culinary win-win.

How could I make chicken behave like beef? Well, I couldn't—not really: Today's chicken is butchered very young so even its thighs and drumsticks have little time to develop much connective tissue. But obviously the fattier, richer-tasting dark meat was my best choice. I could start by subbing boneless, skinless thighs for the meat in a basic beef stew recipe, shortening the cooking time drastically for the quicker-cooking chicken. I didn't expect perfection, but perhaps I'd have a good jumping-off point from which I could tweak and adjust as needed.

I heated a couple of tablespoons of oil in a large Dutch oven and seared 2 pounds of halved thighs.

We use wings (later discarded) for a gravy that's rich and flavorful enough to rival that of beef stew. Thighs give us tender chunks of meat.

After they browned, I transferred them to a bowl. In the then-empty pot I softened some basic aromatics in butter and then sprinkled in flour to create a roux for thickening. Next I stirred in store-bought chicken broth, the browned chicken, and chunks of red potatoes and carrots. After an hour of gentle simmering, the vegetables were soft and the chicken was tender. The stew looked pretty good. But its appearance was deceiving: One bite revealed a weak-flavored gravy. Not to mention that the chicken, though not desiccated, showed a disappointing lack of juiciness. In fact, the vegetables were just about the only redeeming things in the pot.

I had a radical thought: What if, instead of trying to preserve some of its flavor and juiciness—which didn't work anyway—I cooked the life out of the chicken so that at least it would enrich the gravy? After the chicken had given it all up to the pot, I would discard it and cook more chicken in the stewing liquid just until tender. It didn't make sense to treat thighs or even drumsticks this way. But wings are another story. They actually have a decent amount of collagen, and because they're more

about skin and bones than about meat, discarding them after they'd enriched the gravy wouldn't seem wasteful. (Wings are fun to pick at during a football game, but shredding them individually after cooking and stirring the meat into a stew would be a hassle that most cooks would prefer to avoid.)

Winging It

I split a pound of wings at their joints to ensure that they'd lie flat and brown evenly, allowing me to maximize the flavorful Maillard reaction. After browning the wings on both sides, I removed them and built a gravy with aromatics, a roux, and chicken broth just as I had before. I then added the browned wings back to the pot along with potato and carrot pieces. I covered the pot and let everything simmer in a 325-degree oven for about 30 minutes.

Next I stirred in the halved boneless, skinless chicken thighs (I skipped searing this time to prevent them from drying out) and returned the pot to the oven until they were fork-tender, about 45 minutes longer. When I removed the wings from the pot, they literally fell apart in my tongs, a sure sign that much of their connective tissue had been converted into gelatin. I also tasted the meat to see what flavor it might have left to give. The answer: not very much, meaning that I'd effectively extracted it into the gravy. Indeed, the stew had improved dramatically. The thighs were tender and juicy and the gravy was more chicken-y and velvety. It wasn't beef-stew good, but I was making progress.

Flavor Savior

Next I focused on really ramping up flavor. While good chicken soup is all about attaining pure chicken flavor, stew requires more depth and complexity—the kind of richness that can stave off winter's harshest chill. Browning the wings was a step in the right direction, but I needed a lot more reinforcement. My first move was to the fridge, where I rounded up some big flavor boosters: bacon, soy sauce, and anchovy paste. A few strips of bacon, crisped in the pot before I browned the wings in the rendered fat, lent porky depth and just a hint of smoke. Soy sauce and anchovy paste may sound like strange additions to an all-American chicken stew, but their inclusion was strategically

This Is Fond, Too

We often use liquid to release the browned bits, or fond, that remain on the bottom of the pan after meat has been sautéed or pan-seared; this enables us to easily stir the fond into the dish. These bits are packed with the complex flavors that are created by the Maillard reaction and can greatly enhance the flavor of a braise or a sauce. We found that leaving the lid off our chicken stew as it cooked in the oven led to the development of fond on the sides of the Dutch oven as well. To take advantage of this flavor-packed substance, we deglazed the sides by wetting them with a bit of gravy and scraping it into the stew with a spatula. The result? A considerable flavor boost.

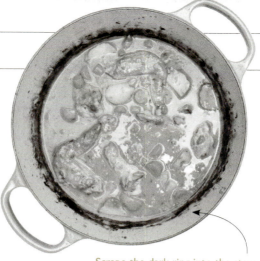

Scrape the dark ring into the stew.

sound. When ingredients rich in glutamates (such as soy sauce) are combined with those rich in free nucleotides (like anchovies), flavor-boosting synergy is achieved. The nucleotides affect our tastebuds so that our perception of meaty-tasting glutamates is amplified by up to 30 times.

I added 2 teaspoons of anchovy paste with the aromatics—minced onion, celery, garlic, and thyme—and a couple of tablespoons of soy sauce along with the broth. Just as I'd hoped, things took an immediate turn to the more savory—without tasting salty or fishy. My colleagues were finally going for seconds and admitting that they'd consider eating a bowl of my chicken stew over beef stew. I was feeling pretty good, but I knew that I could take things further.

When I used to work in restaurants, one of the most important tools in my repertoire was the technique of reduction. Whether I was dealing with a stock, broth, sauce, or stew, I could always count on reduction to evaporate water and concentrate flavors. In that vein, I tried cooking my stew uncovered to gain a bit more intensity. The flavors concentrated, plus I got an extra boost of browning on the surface

of the stew and around the rim of the pot. Deglazing the sides of the pot by wetting them with a bit of gravy and scraping it into the stew with a spatula produced a considerable flavor boost. Reduction was proving its value once again and I wondered if I could put it to even better use.

I started another batch. This time after the aromatics turned a fragrant golden brown, I stirred in a cup of the broth along with the soy sauce and a cup of white wine and brought everything to a boil. It took about 12 minutes for the liquid to fully evaporate, at which point the aromatics started to sizzle again and I proceeded to prepare the roux, add the rest of the broth, and continue with the recipe. A little over an hour later, I proudly presented my tasters with the results. The reduction had not only concentrated flavors but also mellowed everything for a rounder-tasting, soul-satisfying stew.

Having done essentially all the work upfront, all I had to do to finish the stew was remove the wings, add a splash of fresh white wine for some bright acidity, and sprinkle the pot with some chopped fresh parsley. This was truly a stew worthy of the name; the proof was in the pot, no beef necessary.

BEST CHICKEN STEW
SERVES 6 TO 8

Mashed anchovy fillets (rinsed and dried before mashing) can be used instead of anchovy paste. Use small red potatoes measuring 1½ inches in diameter.

- 2 pounds boneless, skinless chicken thighs, halved crosswise and trimmed
  Kosher salt and pepper
- 3 slices bacon, chopped
- 1 pound chicken wings, halved at joint
- 1 onion, chopped fine
- 1 celery rib, minced
- 2 garlic cloves, minced
- 2 teaspoons anchovy paste
- 1 teaspoon minced fresh thyme
- 5 cups chicken broth
- 1 cup dry white wine, plus extra for seasoning
- 1 tablespoon soy sauce
- 3 tablespoons unsalted butter, cut into 3 pieces
- ⅓ cup all-purpose flour
- 1 pound small red potatoes, unpeeled, quartered
- 4 carrots, peeled and cut into ½-inch pieces
- 2 tablespoons chopped fresh parsley

1. Adjust oven rack to lower-middle position and heat oven to 325 degrees. Arrange chicken thighs on baking sheet and lightly season both sides with salt and pepper; cover with plastic wrap and set aside.

2. Cook bacon in large Dutch oven over medium-low heat, stirring occasionally, until fat renders and bacon browns, 6 to 8 minutes. Using slotted spoon, transfer bacon to medium bowl. Add chicken wings to pot, increase heat to medium, and cook until well browned on both sides, 10 to 12 minutes; transfer wings to bowl with bacon.

3. Add onion, celery, garlic, anchovy paste, and thyme to fat in pot; cook, stirring occasionally, until dark fond forms on pan bottom, 2 to 4 minutes. Increase heat to high; stir in 1 cup broth, wine, and soy sauce, scraping up any browned bits; and bring to boil. Cook, stirring occasionally, until liquid evaporates and vegetables begin to sizzle again, 12 to 15 minutes. Add butter and stir to melt; sprinkle flour over vegetables and stir to combine. Gradually whisk in remaining 4 cups broth until smooth. Stir in wings and bacon, potatoes, and carrots; bring to simmer. Transfer to oven and cook, uncovered, for 30 minutes, stirring once halfway through cooking.

4. Remove pot from oven. Use wooden spoon to draw gravy up sides of pot and scrape browned fond into stew. Place over high heat, add thighs, and bring to simmer. Return pot to oven, uncovered, and continue to cook, stirring occasionally, until chicken offers no resistance when poked with fork and vegetables are tender, about 45 minutes longer. (Stew can be refrigerated for up to 2 days.)

5. Discard wings and season stew with up to 2 tablespoons extra wine. Season with salt and pepper to taste, sprinkle with parsley, and serve.

BUILDING A RICH, FLAVORFUL GRAVY

START WITH BACON AND WINGS
Brown chopped bacon, then sear halved wings in rendered fat to develop meaty depth. Set bacon and wings aside.

ENHANCE FLAVOR BASE
Sauté aromatics, thyme, and anchovy paste in fat to create rich fond. Add chicken broth, wine, and soy sauce, then boil until liquid evaporates.

COOK GRAVY
Cook reserved bacon and wings (with potatoes and carrots) in more broth. This extracts flavor from meats and body-enhancing collagen from wings (later discarded).

Holiday Roast Pork

A center-cut pork rib roast is as close to prime rib as you can get from the pig. So why not cook it the same way?

> BY ANDREW JANJIGIAN

I have never understood why, aside from the ubiquitous Easter ham, pork isn't served more often at big-deal occasions. A center-cut pork rib roast, in particular, has a lot of potential. Its cylindrical, uniform loin muscle and long bones make this cut so appealing for serving that I've known butchers to call it the "pork equivalent of prime rib." Treated in a way that makes up for its slight shortcomings in the flavor department, it can be truly impressive: moist, tender, and full of rich, meaty taste. All this—and for far less money than a prime rib costs. This year, I was intent on featuring the cut as the focal point of my holiday spread.

To get my bearings, I cooked an initial roast following a standard approach: I sprinkled the meat with salt and pepper and seared it on all sides in a hot skillet. Next I placed the roast on a wire rack set in a baking sheet (to prevent the meat from steaming in its juices) and transferred it to a 375-degree oven. After about 90 minutes, it reached 145 degrees (the ideal doneness temperature for pork). I let the roast rest for 30 minutes and then sliced it up for evaluation. Not too surprisingly, tasters found its flavor so-so.

Getting Prepped for Better Cooking

Pretreating the meat before cooking was definitely in order. Pork almost always benefits from the application of salt, whether the meat is soaked in a saltwater solution or rubbed with a coating of salt and left to sit in the refrigerator. Both techniques season the meat, which boosts flavor, and draw moisture into the flesh, helping keep it juicy.

Indeed, when I put the ideas into action, a simple salt brine produced a more flavorful roast that was very moist—but almost to a fault: It had a wet, almost spongy consistency, especially toward the exterior. The salt rub, which I left on for at least 6 hours, was far superior. It helped the meat hold on

Scoring the fat cap and coating the roast with a salt–brown sugar rub help it brown nicely in the oven—no presearing required.

to just the right amount of moisture.

For the next go-round, I added brown sugar to the salt rub, thinking that its mild molasses notes would pair nicely with the pork. (I also sprinkled black pepper onto the meat right before roasting.) With sugar in the mix, the meat took on not just deeper flavor but also a gorgeous mahogany color, thanks to the Maillard reaction. In fact, the method worked so beautifully that I made a bold decision: I would skip the tedious task of searing the meat before roasting. Happily, tasters didn't miss the searing since the meat browned nicely in the oven. The only problem was that the oven wasn't hot enough to render the dense fat cap. But I had an easy fix for that: I simply scored deep crosshatch marks into the fat with a sharp knife to help it melt and baste the meat during roasting.

And yet in spite of these efforts, my roast wasn't quite centerpiece-worthy. Salting had improved its texture considerably, but the meat still had a tendency to overcook and dry out toward the exterior. What's more, the meat closest to the bones

wasn't nearly as well seasoned as the rest of the roast.

It seemed likely that bones were preventing the salt and sugar from penetrating into the meat. For my next test, I gave a boneless rib roast the usual application of salt and sugar. As I had expected, this meat was far better seasoned than a bone-in roast treated the same way, but I could hardly call the result an improvement: Without the bones to insulate the meat, much of the roast ended up dry.

Treating the Pig like a Cow

I scrapped the boneless roast idea, racking my brain for other ways to improve a bone-in roast. Then it hit me: If this roast really was the pork equivalent of prime rib, why not cook it like prime rib? In the test kitchen's recent recipe for Best Prime Rib (November/December 2011), we removed the bones from the beef in order to salt the meat on all sides, and then we nestled the meat back up against the bones and secured it with kitchen twine before transferring the assembly to the oven for roasting. I applied this idea to my pork roast and it worked perfectly: The meat was now seasoned throughout, and since heat travels more slowly through bone than through flesh, the bones helped keep the center of the roast moist. Another plus was that the finished roast, free of bones, was even easier to carve.

Thinking of my pork roast as prime rib also gave me a potential solution to the problem of an overcooked exterior: I could use a low-and-slow approach (our prime rib cooks at 200 degrees). In general, the lower the oven temperature and the longer the cooking time the more evenly cooked the meat will be. Here's why: With traditional high-heat cooking, the final temperature of the center of the roast (145 degrees for pork) will be a few hundred degrees lower than the oven temperature. This means that by the time the core of the roast is properly cooked, the outermost layers are well past the ideal temperature. Bring the oven temperature closer to the desired internal temperature and this differential mostly goes away.

To put the theory into practice, I cooked a series of roasts at temperatures from 200 to 375 degrees. Sure enough, the roasts cooked at the low end of the range were the most evenly cooked. But because pork is cooked to a higher final temperature than beef (145 versus 125), the pork cooked in a 200-degree oven required a whopping 6 hours. I knew that no one would want to wait that long. Thankfully, the 250-degree-oven roast clocked in at a more reasonable 3½ hours and was nearly as evenly cooked. As a final measure, I crisped up the fat by blasting the roast under the broiler for a couple of minutes just prior to serving.

The Grand Finale

With juicy, well-seasoned meat ready for the table, all that remained was to create an elegant sauce. In my mind, nothing is more luxurious than a classic French beurre rouge, a reduction of red wine and wine vinegar emulsified with butter. Pork loin is relatively lean, so I knew that it would benefit from this rich, concentrated sauce. To give the mixture real character, I traded the red wine for tawny port and the wine vinegar for balsamic. I also incorporated cream (see "Why Add Cream to a Butter Sauce?"), minced shallots, fresh thyme, and a couple of handfuls of plump dried cherries.

This combination was a terrific match with my pork: The complex flavor with echoes of fruit and

---

SCIENCE | **Why Add Cream to a Butter Sauce?**

To dress up our pork, we turned to a classic French preparation: beurre rouge. The beauty of this sauce, which translates as "red butter," is that at its most basic it requires just two components: butter and an acidic liquid. (Red wine and red vinegar for beurre rouge and white for beurre blanc are traditional.) The preparation is equally simple: Just whisk cold butter into the reduced acidic liquid.

The problem is that butter sauces, like any mixture of fat and water, don't always stay emulsified. That's because the butter is highly temperature sensitive: If the sauce gets too hot (above 135 degrees), the butter—itself an emulsion of fat and water—will "break" and the butterfat will leak out. If it gets too cold (below 85 degrees), the butterfat solidifies and forms crystals that clump together and separate when the sauce is reheated.

The key to foolproofing a butter sauce is thus stabilizing the butterfat so that it doesn't separate. We do this by whisking in the butter a little bit at a time, which keeps the temperature of the sauce relatively stable. Even more important, we also add cream. Cream contains a relatively high proportion of casein proteins that surround and stabilize the butterfat droplets so that they don't separate from the emulsion. Cream is such an effective stabilizer that our sauce can be made ahead, chilled, and gently reheated before serving. –A.J.

TECHNIQUE | BUTCHERING PORK "PRIME RIB"

Remove the rib bones from the pork so that it can be seasoned on all sides, but don't discard them: Since bone is a poor conductor of heat, tie them back onto the roast to guard against overcooking.

1. Using sharp knife, remove roast from bones, running knife down length of bones and closely following contours.

2. Trim surface fat to ¼ inch and score with crosshatch slits; rub roast with sugar mixture and refrigerate.

3. Sprinkle roast with pepper, then place roast back on ribs; using kitchen twine, tie roast to bones between ribs.

---

herbs balanced beautifully with the meaty roast. This was a dish that I'd be proud to serve at any special occasion. And only I would need to know how dead simple it was to prepare.

SLOW-ROASTED BONE-IN PORK RIB ROAST
SERVES 6 TO 8

This recipe requires refrigerating the salted meat for at least 6 hours before cooking. For easier carving, ask the butcher to remove the chine bone. For other tips on shopping for the pork rib roast, see page 30. Monitoring the roast with an oven probe thermometer is best. If you use an instant-read thermometer, open the oven door as infrequently as possible and remove the roast from the oven while taking its temperature. The sauce may be prepared in advance or while the roast rests in step 3. For our free recipes for Cider–Golden Raisin Sauce and Orange-Cranberry Sauce, go to CooksIllustrated.com/dec13.

1	(4- to 5-pound) center-cut bone-in pork rib roast, chine bone removed
2	tablespoons packed dark brown sugar
1	tablespoon kosher salt
1½	teaspoons pepper
1	recipe sauce (recipe follows)

1. Using sharp knife, remove roast from bones, running knife down length of bones and following contours as closely as possible. Reserve bones. Combine sugar and salt in small bowl. Pat roast dry with paper towels. If necessary, trim thick spots of surface fat layer to about ¼-inch thickness. Using sharp knife, cut slits, spaced 1 inch apart and in crosshatch pattern, in surface fat layer, being careful not to cut into meat. Rub roast evenly with sugar mixture. Wrap roast and ribs in plastic wrap and refrigerate for at least 6 hours or up to 24 hours.

2. Adjust oven rack to lower-middle position and heat oven to 250 degrees. Sprinkle roast evenly with pepper. Place roast back on ribs so bones fit where they were cut; tie roast to bones with lengths of kitchen twine between ribs. Transfer roast, fat side up, to wire rack set in rimmed baking sheet. Roast until meat registers 145 degrees, 3 to 4 hours.

3. Remove roast from oven (leave roast on sheet), tent loosely with aluminum foil, and let rest for 30 minutes.

4. Adjust oven rack 8 inches from broiler element and heat broiler. Return roast to oven and broil until top of roast is well browned and crispy, 2 to 6 minutes.

5. Transfer roast to carving board; cut twine and remove meat from ribs. Slice meat into ¾-inch-thick slices and serve, passing sauce separately.

PORT WINE–CHERRY SAUCE
MAKES ABOUT 1¾ CUPS

2	cups tawny port
1	cup dried cherries
½	cup balsamic vinegar
4	sprigs fresh thyme, plus 2 teaspoons minced
2	shallots, minced
¼	cup heavy cream
16	tablespoons unsalted butter, cut into ½-inch pieces and chilled
1	teaspoon salt
½	teaspoon pepper

1. Combine port and cherries in bowl and microwave until steaming, 1 to 2 minutes. Cover and let stand until plump, about 10 minutes. Strain port through fine-mesh strainer into medium saucepan, reserving cherries.

2. Add vinegar, thyme sprigs, and shallots to port and bring to boil over high heat. Reduce heat to medium-high and reduce mixture until it measures ¾ cup, 14 to 16 minutes. Add cream and reduce again to ¾ cup, about 5 minutes. Discard thyme sprigs. Off heat, whisk in butter, few pieces at a time, until fully incorporated. Stir in cherries, minced thyme, salt, and pepper. Cover pan and hold, off heat, until serving. Alternatively, let sauce cool completely and refrigerate for up to 2 days. Reheat in small saucepan over medium-low heat, stirring frequently, until warm.

Italian Beef and Onion Ragu

We knew that the meat in this Neapolitan gravy would add big savory flavor. What we learned in the making was that the other key player—the onions—would, too.

⇒ BY ANDREA GEARY ⇐

There are those who have the best of everything, and there are those who make the best of everything. The residents of 16th-century Naples fell into the latter category. Faced with a population explosion that caused severe food shortages, they created a thrifty yet supremely satisfying gravy of beef and aromatic vegetables known, ironically, as *la Genovese*. (The provenance of the name is unclear: Some theorize that Genovese cooks brought it to Naples; others believe that the name references the reputed frugality of the people of Genoa.)

Later in the 19th century, onions took center stage, and the dish became one of the region's most beloved. The classic preparation is straightforward: A piece of beef, usually from the round, is placed in a pot and covered with approximately twice its weight in sliced onions, along with chopped aromatic vegetables, salt, and perhaps some herbs. Then several cups of water and a bit of wine go into the pot, and the mixture is simmered for anywhere from 3 to 6 hours, until the liquid has evaporated, the beef is tender, and the onions have cooked down into a soft, pulpy mass.

Traditionally, frugal cooks served the beef-flavored onion gravy—notice that I didn't mention tomatoes; the dish predates the introduction of tomatoes to European kitchens—as a sauce for sturdy tubular pasta like rigatoni. (Incidentally, the sauce doesn't include garlic either.) The meat itself was typically reserved for a second meal, or at least a second course, with a vegetable. But in these comparatively prosperous times, the beef is more likely to be shredded and incorporated into the sauce for a substantial single dish—exactly the kind of pasta sauce I love to make in cold weather months.

Humble Beginnings

I started with a very traditional recipe, but since I was making just one meal, not two, I immediately cut down the amount of beef and onions to a more

Our ragu contains chuck-eye roast for both its beefy flavor and—as a nod to this dish's parsimonious roots—its relatively low cost.

practical size—1 pound of trimmed beef round and 2½ pounds of thinly sliced onions, which I hoped would produce six to eight servings. To those key players I added a finely chopped carrot and celery stalk, plus some chopped marjoram and salt, all of which I put in a Dutch oven with 8 cups of water and 1 cup of white wine (the meat is not usually seared). I let the pot bubble away for a good 2½ hours, giving it an occasional stir to keep the contents cooking evenly. By that point, the beef was fully cooked; I removed it to let it cool before chopping it (its texture was too tight to shred) and adding it back to the sauce. In the meantime I reduced the oniony cooking liquid.

Perhaps not surprisingly, this early version did not produce the succulent, deeply flavorful ragu I had envisioned. The lean round was not the best cut to be using in a moist heat environment; it lacks fat and collagen, which keep meat tasting tender and juicy, so it cooked up dry and tight. Also, reducing the sauce itself took too long—almost 40 minutes. Lastly, the color of the sauce was an unappealing beige.

What did impress me was the deeply savory flavor

of the onions. They weren't sharp and sulfurous like fresh onions, nor did they have the sweetness of the caramelized kind. They were just plain beefy-tasting. In fact, one taster observed that the onions tasted beefier than the actual beef. I'd come back to this discovery once I'd nailed down the basics of the sauce—for starters, the meat.

Testing the Water

Beef round's tight grain makes this cut a good candidate for slicing, but since I was in pursuit of more tender meat that I could shred and return to the sauce, I moved to our favorite braising cuts: short ribs, blade steaks, and chuck-eye roast. The latter won for its beefy flavor, tenderness, and (in homage to the thrifty nature of this dish) relatively low price tag. The only glitch? Cooked whole, it took upwards of 3½ hours to turn tender. Cutting it into four chunks reduced the cooking time to 2½ hours and allowed me to trim away intramuscular fat pockets. I also seasoned the roast with salt and pepper before cooking and moved the braising to a low (300-degree) oven, where the meat would cook more evenly.

And I cut way back on the water—down to 3 cups—hoping to drastically shorten the reduction time. But even with that little amount, it still took about a half-hour of stovetop reduction to turn the onions and cooking liquid saucy. I wondered: Did I have to add water at all?

In the next batch I omitted the water and simply nestled the beef in the onion mixture and sealed the pot tightly with foil (to lock in steam) and then the lid. This worked well; the meat braised to perfect tenderness in the released juices, and the sauce required less stovetop reduction time—just 10 minutes. But strangely, this version tasted less savory.

To ramp up meatiness, I turned to innovations that started to show up in later Genovese recipes: pancetta and salami (which I finely chopped in the food processor) and tomato paste. They all made the ragu more savory, particularly the *umami*-rich tomato paste when I browned it in the pot before adding the onions. The tomato paste also warmed up the color of the formerly drab-looking finished sauce. But while this batch tasted meatier than the previous one, it still was not as savory as the first version. I was baffled. I had not only added meaty ingredients but also taken away the world's most neutral ingredient: water.

Savory Secret

A consultation with our science editor solved the mystery. Astonishingly, it was the water that was the key to extracting the meaty flavor that was locked inside the onions. That meatiness is due to a water-soluble compound known as 3-mercapto-2-methylpentan-1-ol (MMP), the byproduct of a reaction that occurs when onions are cut and then heated in water. (For more information, see "A Surprising Formula for Meaty Flavor.")

By eliminating the water, I was severely limiting the development of savory flavors, so I added back 2 cups—just enough to cover the onions but not so much that the sauce's reduction time would be lengthy. I also switched from slicing the onions to chopping them in the food processor—a timesaving technique that would also lead to the creation of more MMP. This time the sauce regained the meatiness of the original batch, and then some, with the pancetta, salami, and tomato paste. Even better, I found that I could cook it in the oven with the lid off, which encouraged evaporation and saved me some reducing time at the end. The sauce was a bit sweet, so I reserved half of the wine for adding at the end for extra brightness.

One last tweak: I found that when I vigorously mixed—instead of just lightly tossed—together the cooked pasta and sauce and a bit of cheese, the starch on the surface of the pasta pulled the components together, helping keep the liquid from separating out from the solids.

I had to hand it to those thrifty 16th-century Neapolitans. This was a true ragu—humble at its roots but as savory and satisfying as the meat-and-tomato-heavy versions that would follow. My 21st-century tweaks would make it a staple in my wintertime pasta sauce rotation.

RIGATONI WITH BEEF AND ONION RAGU
SERVES 6 TO 8

If marjoram is unavailable, substitute an equal amount of oregano. Pair this dish with a lightly dressed salad of assertively flavored greens.

- 1 (1- to 1¼-pound) boneless beef chuck-eye roast, cut into 4 pieces and trimmed of large pieces of fat
     Kosher salt and pepper
- 2 ounces pancetta, cut into ½-inch pieces
- 2 ounces salami, cut into ½-inch pieces
- 1 small carrot, peeled and cut into ½-inch pieces
- 1 small celery rib, cut into ½-inch pieces
- 2½ pounds onions, halved and cut into 1-inch pieces
- 2 tablespoons tomato paste
- 1 cup dry white wine
- 2 tablespoons minced fresh marjoram
- 1 pound rigatoni
- 1 ounce Pecorino Romano cheese, grated (½ cup), plus extra for serving

1. Sprinkle beef with 1 teaspoon salt and ½ teaspoon pepper and set aside. Adjust oven rack to lower-middle position and heat oven to 300 degrees.

2. Process pancetta and salami in food processor until ground to paste, about 30 seconds, scraping down sides of bowl as needed. Add carrot and celery and process 30 seconds longer, scraping down sides of bowl as needed. Transfer paste to Dutch oven and set aside; do not clean out processor bowl. Pulse onions in processor in 2 batches, until ⅛- to ¼-inch pieces form, 8 to 10 pulses per batch.

3. Cook pancetta mixture over medium heat, stirring frequently, until fat is rendered and fond begins to form on bottom of pot, about 5 minutes. Add tomato paste and cook, stirring constantly, until browned, about 90 seconds. Stir in 2 cups water, scraping up any browned bits. Stir in onions and bring to boil. Stir in ½ cup wine and 1 tablespoon

marjoram. Add beef and push into onions to ensure that it is submerged. Transfer to oven and cook, uncovered, until beef is fully tender, 2 to 2½ hours.

4. Transfer beef to carving board. Place pot over medium heat and cook, stirring frequently, until mixture is almost completely dry. Stir in remaining ½ cup wine and cook for 2 minutes, stirring occasionally. Using 2 forks, shred beef into bite-size pieces. Stir beef and remaining 1 tablespoon marjoram into sauce and season with salt and pepper to taste. Remove from heat, cover, and keep warm.

5. Bring 4 quarts water to boil in large pot. Add rigatoni and 2 tablespoons salt and cook, stirring often, until just al dente. Drain rigatoni and add to warm sauce. Add Pecorino and stir vigorously over low heat until sauce is slightly thickened and rigatoni is fully tender, 1 to 2 minutes. Serve, passing extra Pecorino separately.

TASTING Gluten-Free Spaghetti

Gluten is the protein matrix that gives wheat noodles their structure and chew. The challenge for gluten-free pasta manufacturers is to achieve similar texture with grains that lack those proteins. We tasted eight products made variously with rice, corn, and quinoa, first tossed with olive oil and then with tomato sauce.

Most samples were "mushy" or "gritty"; worse, they tasted "bland" or even "fishy." But one standout was "clean" and "springy"— impressively close to regular spaghetti.

After reviewing labels and doing research, we made two discoveries. First, thanks in part to its use of brown rice flour (which includes bran), our favorite product contained a relatively high combined total of fiber and protein (the combined total matters more than the amount of either fiber or protein alone). Protein and fiber keep the noodles intact during cooking, forming a barrier around the starch molecules, which prevents them from escaping and leaving the cooked pasta sticky and soft. Second, a low temperature is used to dry our winner's strands, which helps preserve flavor and ensures that the proteins coagulate and provide structure for the starch. Those two factors helped account for why Jovial Gluten Free Brown Rice Pasta, Spaghetti tasted "pretty close to the real deal." For more information, go to CooksIllustrated.com/dec13. –Lisa McManus

STELLAR STRANDS
JOVIAL Gluten Free Brown Rice Pasta, Spaghetti
Price: $3.99 for 12 oz (33 cents per oz)
Comments: These strands were "springy" and "clean"-tasting with none of the gumminess or off-flavors that plagued other brands.

Secrets to Foolproof Pizza at Home

Producing a perfect parlor-style pizza is almost entirely about getting the dough right. We take you inside the recipe to show you why ours works every time.

BY SHANNON FRIEDMANN HATCH

THIN-CRUST PIZZA

MAKES TWO 13-INCH PIZZAS

3   cups (16½ ounces) bread flour
2   tablespoons sugar
½   teaspoon instant or rapid-rise yeast
1⅓ cups ice water
1   tablespoon vegetable oil
1½ teaspoons salt
1   cup tomato pizza sauce
1   ounce Parmesan cheese, grated fine (½ cup)
8   ounces whole-milk mozzarella cheese, shredded (2 cups)

1. In food processor fitted with dough blade, pulse flour, sugar, and yeast until combined, about 5 pulses. With food processor running, slowly add ice water; process until dough is just combined and no dry flour remains, about 10 seconds. Let dough sit for 10 minutes.

2. Add oil and salt to dough and process until dough forms satiny, sticky ball that clears sides of bowl, 30 to 60 seconds. Transfer dough to lightly oiled counter and knead briefly by hand until smooth, about 1 minute. Shape dough into tight ball and place in large, lightly oiled bowl. Cover bowl tightly with plastic wrap and refrigerate for at least 24 hours or up to 3 days.

3. One hour before baking, adjust oven rack 4 to 5 inches from broiler element, set baking stone on rack, and heat oven to 500 degrees. Transfer dough to clean counter and divide in half. With cupped palms, form each half into smooth, tight ball. Place balls of dough on lightly greased baking sheet, spacing them at least 3 inches apart; cover loosely with greased plastic and let sit at room temperature for 1 hour.

4. Coat 1 ball of dough generously with flour and place on well-floured counter (keep other ball covered). Use your fingertips to gently flatten dough into 8-inch disk, leaving 1 inch of outer edge slightly thicker than center. Using your hands, gently stretch disk into 12-inch round, working along edges and giving disk quarter turns as you stretch. Transfer dough to well-floured pizza peel and stretch into 13-inch round. Using back of spoon or ladle, spread ½ cup sauce in thin layer over surface of dough, leaving ¼-inch border around edge. Sprinkle ¼ cup Parmesan evenly over sauce, followed by 1 cup mozzarella. Slide pizza carefully onto baking stone and bake until crust is well browned and cheese is bubbly and beginning to brown, 10 to 12 minutes, rotating pizza halfway through baking. Transfer pizza to wire rack and let cool for 5 minutes before slicing and serving.

5. Repeat step 4 to shape, top, and bake second pizza.

WHY THE FORMULA WORKS

Here's a behind-the-scenes look at why each ingredient and step adds up to the ideal parlor-quality crust, which is thin, crisp, and spottily charred on the exterior and tender yet chewy inside.

Why Bread Flour?

Bread flour contains 12 to 14 percent protein by weight (our favorite, from King Arthur, contains 12.7 percent protein), compared with 10.5 to 11.9 percent for all-purpose flour. The more protein in a flour the more readily the individual proteins link together to form gluten, leading to a denser, chewy crust.

How Sugar Helps

The browning temperatures of sugars are as much as 100 degrees lower than those of the starches and proteins in flours. We found that a recipe with 4 percent sugar, or 2 teaspoons per cup of flour, guaranteed quick browning in the time that it took the crust to cook through without adding noticeable sweetness or affecting the dough's rising time.

Use Enough Water—and Make It Iced

The hydration level of the dough—or the weight of the water in relation to the weight of the flour—affects how easy the dough is to work with as well as its final texture. After testing a range of amounts, we settled on 65 percent (or 10.66 ounces of water to 16.5 ounces of flour), for a dough that was neither too stiff nor too sticky and retained moisture in the hot oven. Why does the water need to be iced? It prevents the dough from heating up in the food processor, which would cause it to ferment too quickly and produce overly strong flavors.

What About Oil?

Just a tablespoon of oil coats some of the gluten strands, allowing them to stretch and slide past one another, ensuring that the crust, while chewy, isn't too tough.

Knead in a Food Processor

A food processor kneads dough in about a minute, while a stand mixer takes 8 to 10 minutes. Besides saving time, this limits the dough's exposure to air, and curbing oxidation adds up to better flavor.

Rest Before Adding Salt

After processing the dough just until it comes together, we give it a 10-minute rest and then add the salt (and oil). This rest is called an autolyse, and it gives enzymes in the wheat time to snip into smaller pieces the long strands of gluten that have initially formed. These shorter chains more readily link together to form a stronger gluten network with subsequent processing. Because salt inhibits the enzymes that make autolyse possible, we hold off on adding it until after the dough has rested.

24 Hours in the Fridge

Most recipes call for letting pizza dough rise at room temperature for a few hours after it's kneaded. During this rest, yeast first converts the dough's starch into sugars, alcohol, and acids, which then convert into carbon dioxide, expanding the bubbles created in the dough when it was initially mixed. Resting the dough in the fridge makes the yeast behave differently. Fermentation is slowed, which triggers the creation of more flavor compounds that are pleasing and complex and fewer that are sour. The texture of the finished pizza is also improved. Because it spends more time fermenting and less time producing bubbles, the chilled dough bakes up with a finer, less bready crumb.

A Nap Before Baking

In bread dough, a second rise after shaping is necessary for dough to expand to the optimal volume. Here we rest the dough to bring it up to room temperature and to relax the gluten network, both of which make for a more pliable dough that's easier to stretch.

Tomato Pizza Sauce
For our free recipe, go to CooksIllustrated.com/thincrustpizza.

GETTING A HANDLE ON HANDLING DOUGH

Shaping pizza dough can be a cinch—if it doesn't snap back. Following these tips will make it easy.

To Stretch Dough Evenly, Use Counter Intelligence

This draping method uses gravity to pull the dough into a perfectly round shape.

1. Drape dough (pressed into 8-inch round with outer inch left thicker to create a "handle") over edge of counter. Lift up top half, with hands at 10 and 2 o'clock.

2. Rotate dough clockwise, using left hand to feed dough to right hand, meeting at 12 o'clock. Continue until gravity has pulled dough to 12-inch diameter.

If Dough Contracts, Relax

Our method of cold fermentation followed by an hour rest at room temperature slows gluten formation and creates a more relaxed dough. But if yours still retracts when flattened into a disk, give it a 5-minute rest on the counter to help it relax.

Shake Before You Bake

After placing the dough on the peel, give the peel a quick shake over the counter (rather than halfway into the oven). A quick swipe of the bench scraper under the dough will release any sticky spots and redistribute the flour underneath. Also, be sure that the peel is dry—dollops of sauce could cause sticking.

HOW TO FREEZE DOUGH AND REHEAT LEFTOVER PIZZA

Freeze Extra Dough Before Shaping

Our recipe yields enough dough for two 13-inch pies. Although the dough is best used fresh, you can freeze whatever you don't choose to bake right away. Follow the recipe as directed, letting the dough proof in the refrigerator for at least 24 hours. Then, instead of shaping it, wrap it in plastic wrap coated with vegetable oil spray, place it in a zipper-lock freezer bag, and freeze it. Thaw the dough in the refrigerator for 24 to 48 hours before dividing and shaping.

Bring Leftovers Back to Life

You might think you have only two options: a soggy, leathery slice from the microwave or an overly crisp, dry piece from the oven. Try this method, which guarantees a tender crust, melty cheese, and juicy toppings.

1. Place cold slices on rimmed baking sheet, cover sheet tightly with aluminum foil, and place it on lowest rack of cold oven.
2. Set oven temperature to 275 degrees and let pizza warm for 25 to 30 minutes.

BEST BAKING STRATEGIES

Pizza parlor ovens have a distinct advantage over home ranges: blazing heat. Here's how we imitate.

Superheat the Stone

Preheating the baking stone for a full hour at 500 degrees may sound like overkill, but it's not. In tests, we found that 30 minutes of preheating produced an anemic-looking bottom crust, and even 45 minutes wasn't sufficient to produce the ultracrispy, well-browned bottom crust created by an hour of preheating.

Aim (the Stone) High

Placing the baking stone as close to the ceiling of the oven as possible—instead of its usual orientation on the lowest rack—means that heat will hit the top of the pie and brown the toppings before the crust overcooks.

What If You Don't Have a Pizza Stone?

Use an inverted baking sheet. You'll still need to preheat it, but 30 minutes in a 500-degree oven is ample time for its lesser mass.

ESSENTIAL TOOLS

BAKING STONE

Old Stone Oven Pizza Baking Stone ($38.69)
This ceramic slab produces beautifully bronzed crusts and offers plenty of room for standard-size pies. Plus, its elevated feet lift the edge and allow for a comfortable grip.

BAKING PEEL

Super Peel by EXO Products, Inc. ($55)
What sets this wooden peel apart is the attached pastry cloth, which works like a conveyor belt to transfer the dough to the stone without any sticking.

PIZZA WHEEL

OXO Good Grips 4" Pizza Wheel for Non-Stick Pans ($12.99) and **OXO Good Grips 4" Pizza Wheel** ($11.99)
Both wheels offer comfortable thumb guards and large, soft handles that absorb the extra pressure needed to slice through a chewy crust.

ILLUSTRATION: JOHN BURGOYNE

Black Olive Tapenade

After fine-tuning every element in this rich, lusty Provençal spread, we still hadn't managed to tame its saltiness. Finally, we found inspiration across the border.

⇒ BY DAN SOUZA ⇐

When I'm not snacking on olives by the handful, I'm often turning them into tapenade. The cured fruits form the base of this rich, pungent Provençal paste, which typically includes capers, anchovies, garlic, and a few glugs of olive oil. Because all those ingredients are pantry staples, tapenade is my first thought when I need a bruschetta topping, a no-cook sauce for boiled potatoes or pasta, or a vinaigrette picker-upper. (Whisking just a little tapenade into the oil and vinegar beefs up the dressing's flavor and body.) Best of all, the hands-on work required for this soft spread is practically nil: A few seconds in the food processor and you're done.

But despite its ease and countless applications, good tapenade is hard to come by. It should spotlight the olives but also round out their assertiveness with rich, savory, and subtly sharp background flavors, but just about every jarred condiment I've tasted and every recipe I've followed has been flawed. The tapenades are either too sharp, too fishy, or too salty—sometimes all three—not to mention greasy. I was convinced that the secret to producing bold but balanced tapenade was in the details. I'd have to look closely at the condiment's short ingredient list and fine-tune each component.

Two Are Better than One

My supermarket's olive aisle was an obvious, if confusing, place to start. I wasn't just choosing among olive varieties; more significantly, I was choosing among harvesting and curing methods, which largely determine the differences that we see and taste in olives. The most traditional tapenades are made from black olives, and partly to help narrow the field, I decided to stick with these. Other than flavorless lye-cured canned black olives, I still had two styles to choose from: brine-cured and salt-cured (often

This bold spread pairs nicely with crusty bread, but it functions equally well as a sauce for pasta or vegetables or as a base for a vinaigrette.

referred to as oil-cured—a misnomer). I scooped up a couple of varieties within the two curing categories and processed 2 cups of each olive with 3 tablespoons of capers, an anchovy fillet, and a clove of minced garlic. I then drizzled in ⅓ cup of extra-virgin olive oil, hoping that these bare-bones tapenades would make apparent the best olive for the job. A dozen batches and an overnight rest (to meld flavors) later, tasters weighed in. No one olive made a perfect spread: Though tasters favored the bright tanginess of kalamatas over the other brine-cured black olives, niçoise and Sicilian, the tapenade was one-dimensional. With their earthy richness, salt-cured black olives had complexity in spades (not to mention creamy texture), but that quality was overwhelmed by their heavy saltiness and bitterness.

If one style of olive wasn't going to cut it, why limit myself? I started mixing and matching kalamatas and salt-cured olives until I figured out the right balance for complex flavor: 3 parts brine-cured olives to 1 part earthier, more intense salt-cured ones.

Supporting Players

Satisfied with my olive base, I sifted through a stack of tapenade recipes for suggested amounts of capers, anchovies, garlic, and oil, as well as any other potential additions. Those sources—and several more tests—confirmed that I'd been right with 3 tablespoons of capers. (Tapenade actually takes its name from *tapeno*, the Provençal word for caper, but the briny buds almost always play a supporting

Tapping into Two Kinds of Olives

The two common olive-curing methods affect the flavor of the fruit (and our tapenade) very differently.

BRINE-CURED: TANGY

Brine-cured black olives (made with mature fruit) undergo natural fermentation over a period of months in a strong salt brine, much like naturally fermented pickles. During fermentation, sugars in the fruit convert into acetic and lactic acid, providing the characteristic sour flavor.

SALT-CURED: EARTHY

Salt-cured black olives (often misleadingly labeled oil-cured) are packed in salt when fully ripe, left to dehydrate and soften over a month or two, and then briefly plumped in oil. The intensely flavored results have soft flesh, little acidity, and a good bit of their original bitterness.

THREE TO ONE

For a balanced tapenade, we use a 3:1 ratio of punchy brine-cured olives to the richer salt-cured kind.

PHOTOGRAPHY: CARL TREMBLAY

role.) I minced and added a second anchovy to amp up the spread's background meatiness and stepped down the garlic to half a clove and the oil to ¼ cup, heeding my tasters' complaints about sharpness and greasiness, respectively. I also switched from processing the oil with the rest of the ingredients to stirring it into the puree by hand, since whirring the oil causes its bitter-tasting polyphenols to separate and disperse throughout the mixture.

Slowly the strong flavors were evening out, and yet the ingredients hadn't quite coalesced into the superior result that I'd hoped for. My tapenade was still bluntly salty, and something was missing. I tried other additions, some off-the-wall: citrus zest and juice, brandy, mustard and mustard powder, cooked egg yolk, yeast extract—even canned tuna. My traditionalist tasters rejected all but the Dijon. Its subtle kick was a keeper.

(Nut) Butter Up

Saltiness was another matter, since almost every ingredient was loaded with sodium. Rinsing the capers and anchovies helped, but not enough. What I needed was a buffer, and fat immediately came to mind since we know that it has a dulling effect on our taste receptors. My tapenade couldn't hold more oil, so I went back to my research for other clues and found an unlikely idea: butter. A Romanian recipe for tapenade added it for creaminess; I figured butter would also temper the salt without separating out and turning the olive paste greasy. (Unlike oil, butter remains emulsified in the tapenade.) Indeed, when I added a few tablespoons to my tapenade, the spread's soft, silky texture was convincing, and the sodium was mellower. But the butter's dairy flavor? It just wasn't the right fit.

But butter wasn't a bad idea, I thought as I spied a jar of unsalted peanut butter in the pantry. It, too, had plenty of emulsified fat to keep the spread from breaking, so I processed it in my next batch. While I was at it, I tried unsalted almond and cashew butters, too. These tapenades looked great—rich, soft, and not at all oily—and the salt was in check. But I hadn't solved the flavor problem; in fact, the nuts' flavors were more distracting than the flavor of regular butter.

Just then I spotted a fellow cook tossing pine nuts into a food processor to make pesto, and the gears in my head started turning: Why couldn't I do the same and simply process these mild nuts (untoasted to keep their flavor quiet) into a butter before adding the rest of my ingredients? Grinding ⅓ cup of them into a sticky, smooth butter took all of 30 seconds, and just as I'd hoped, they blended seamlessly into the background.

This was the tapenade I'd envisioned: robust, rich, just salty enough, and faintly sharp with garlic and mustard. I thought I'd keep the stuff on hand, just in case I needed a quick pasta sauce or an impromptu spread for bruschetta (tapenade keeps well for up to two weeks), but the way my colleagues kept snacking on it I knew it wouldn't last long.

BLACK OLIVE TAPENADE
MAKES ABOUT 1½ CUPS

The tapenade must be refrigerated for at least 18 hours before serving. It's important to use untoasted pine nuts in this recipe so that they provide creaminess but little flavor of their own. We prefer the rich flavor of kalamata olives, but any high-quality brine-cured black olive, such as niçoise, Sicilian, or Greek, can be substituted. Do not substitute brine-cured olives for the salt-cured olives. Serve the tapenade as a spread with sliced crusty bread or as a dip with raw vegetables.

- ⅓ cup pine nuts
- 1½ cups pitted kalamata olives
- ½ cup pitted salt-cured black olives
- 3 tablespoons capers, rinsed
- 2 anchovy fillets, rinsed and patted dry
- 2 teaspoons Dijon mustard
- ½ garlic clove, minced
- ¼ cup extra-virgin olive oil

1. In food processor fitted with metal blade, process pine nuts until reduced to paste that clings to walls and avoids blade, about 20 seconds. Scrape down bowl to redistribute paste and process until paste again clings to walls and avoids blade, about 5 seconds. Repeat scraping and processing once more (pine nuts should form mostly smooth, tahini-like paste).

2. Scrape down bowl to redistribute paste and add olives, capers, anchovies, mustard, and garlic. Pulse until finely chopped, about 15 pulses, scraping down bowl halfway through pulsing. Transfer mixture to medium bowl and stir in oil until well combined.

3. Transfer to container, cover, and refrigerate for at least 18 hours or up to 2 weeks. Bring to room temperature and stir thoroughly before serving.

SPAGHETTI WITH BLACK OLIVE TAPENADE
SERVES 4 TO 6

Any long, thin pasta can be substituted for spaghetti.

- 1 pound spaghetti
- 1 tablespoon salt
- ¾ cup Black Olive Tapenade
- ⅓ cup pine nuts, toasted
- 1 tablespoon lemon juice
- 2 tablespoons chopped fresh parsley
  Parmesan cheese

1. Bring 4 quarts water to boil in large pot. Add spaghetti and salt and cook, stirring often, until al dente. Reserve 1½ cups cooking water, then drain spaghetti and return it to pot.

2. Add tapenade, pine nuts, lemon juice, parsley, and ¾ cup cooking water to spaghetti and toss thoroughly to combine. Add remaining ¾ cup cooking water as needed to adjust consistency. Serve immediately, passing Parmesan separately.

A Nutty Solution to Saltiness

Given that tapenade is built on olives, capers, and anchovies, it can be tricky to keep the spread's saltiness in check. We adjusted ingredient ratios and rinsed away excess salt before we found our real fix in an Italian pesto–inspired trick: grinding pine nuts into paste. The mild-flavored (untoasted) nuts, which, like the other tapenade ingredients, are a staple in Mediterranean cuisine, temper the saltiness without adding much distracting flavor of their own.

PILE OF PINE NUTS
Adding pine nuts (ground first) to the tapenade tames its saltiness.

BOILED POTATOES WITH BLACK OLIVE TAPENADE
SERVES 4 TO 6

Use small red potatoes measuring about 1½ inches in diameter.

- 2 pounds small red potatoes, unpeeled, halved
- 1 tablespoon salt
- ⅓ cup Black Olive Tapenade
- 1 tablespoon lemon juice
- 1 tablespoon chopped fresh parsley
  Extra-virgin olive oil

1. Bring 6 cups water, potatoes, and salt to boil in large saucepan over medium-high heat. Reduce heat to medium-low and simmer until potatoes are just tender when pierced with knife, 10 to 15 minutes.

2. Reserve ¼ cup cooking water. Drain potatoes and return them to pan. Combine tapenade, lemon juice, and 2 tablespoons cooking water in bowl. Add tapenade mixture to potatoes and fold gently to incorporate. Add remaining 2 tablespoons cooking water as needed to adjust consistency. Transfer potatoes to serving bowl, sprinkle with parsley, drizzle with oil, and serve.

BLACK OLIVE TAPENADE VINAIGRETTE
MAKES ABOUT ½ CUP

Serve on salad greens or with grilled swordfish, halibut, or sea bass.

- 3 tablespoons Black Olive Tapenade
- 4 teaspoons lemon juice
- ½ teaspoon honey
- 3 tablespoons extra-virgin olive oil

Whisk tapenade, lemon juice, and honey together in medium bowl. Slowly whisk in oil until combined.

Rich Chocolate Tart

Most chocolate tart recipes have similar ingredients, but why do some turn out dull and others shine? We set out to solve the mystery.

⇒ BY DAWN YANAGIHARA ⇐

Inflated descriptors like "unbelievably decadent" and "death by chocolate" are de rigueur when it comes to chocolate tarts. But for me, the real draw of the dessert is its pure, uncomplicated profile: The best versions boast a flawlessly smooth, truffle-like texture; unadulterated chocolate flavor; and a sophisticated polish. With the holidays approaching, I decided that there was no better time to uncover what makes an exceptional chocolate tart.

I stocked up on high-quality bittersweet chocolate, heavy cream, eggs, and butter—the building blocks of just about every filling recipe I had found—and prepared to start testing. It quickly became clear that, while the filling components were more or less identical for all the recipes, the way in which those ingredients were treated separated the tarts into three unique styles. The first, a baked, egg white–aerated dessert, turned out slightly souffléed and brownie-like—not quite the suave, satiny dessert that I had in mind. The other two styles started out on the same course, by calling for melting chocolate into hot cream, and then they went their separate ways. One style got a rich addition of whisked-in butter and was simply popped in the fridge to chill until set—it was essentially a very rich ganache. The other style traded butter for eggs, baked in a moderate oven for about 30 minutes, and then chilled for a few hours until nicely set. Both styles had merits. Lots of butter made the ganache filling taste great—for about two bites. The custard-style tart was more velvety and less greasy, and the clear favorite among my tasters.

And yet I still had plenty of testing ahead of me. Without the butter, the custard-style filling tasted flat. It also emerged from the oven with a rather drab matte finish—too underdressed for my holiday table.

Getting My Fill(ing)

To nail down the basics, I tested varying ratios of chocolate and cream before landing on 9 ounces and 1¼ cups, respectively. With those amounts, the filling was intense but not cloying, and silky without turning runny. Two whole beaten eggs (I tried one and two—the range that most recipes suggest—as well as one and two yolks) lent the filling just enough body without turning it rubbery. Trouble was, with eggs in the mix,

To dress up this baked tart for the holiday table, we cover it with glossy dark chocolate ganache and garnish it with chocolate curls or flaky sea salt.

the edges of the tart baked up ever so slightly curdled.

It occurred to me that perhaps the 350-degree oven I'd been using was too hot for this custard-style filling—after all, eggs curdle when overcooked. So I prepared several more tarts and staggered their baking temperatures at 25-degree intervals from 350 down to 250 degrees. The differences were astounding. The 350-degree tart was predictably stiff, but with each reduction in temperature the texture improved, and the 250-degree tart had the ethereal quality that I was after. It wasn't just curd-free; it was downright plush.

If only the filling didn't taste—and look—so dull and one-dimensional. The ganache-style filling's buttery foundation may have been too rich, but dull it was not, which got me thinking: What if I strayed from the typical custard-style tart and added a moderate amount of butter? Using my working recipe, I compared fillings made with 8, 6, 4, and

Low and Slow

Baking the tart at 250 degrees—about 100 degrees lower than in most recipes—might sound like a mistake, but we found that heating this custard-style filling very gently is the key to producing a texture that's silky smooth, not curdled.

2 tablespoons of butter and found that 4 tablespoons nicely rounded out the chocolate flavor without overdoing the richness. A touch of espresso powder, dissolved in the cream with a bit of salt, added an echo of bittersweetness that highlighted the chocolate.

Over and Under

As for looks, my tart needed a makeover—or at least some cover-up. In the heat of the oven, its surface formed tiny fissures and took on a matte finish. I wanted this holiday-caliber dessert to boast a glossy sheen and figured that a simple chocolate glaze would do the trick. I played with a few formulas and settled on a bittersweet chocolate ganache spiked with a little corn syrup for shine. Pouring the glaze over the baked and chilled tart created the polished look that I wanted.

With the filling perfected at last, I test-drove pastry options for the crust, pitting a basic *pâte sucrée* (butter, flour, sugar, egg yolk, and heavy cream, all pulsed in the food processor) against versions dressed up with cocoa powder and toasted nuts. The cocoa pastry made for a dramatic-looking dessert (dark crust, dark filling), but a third chocolate component felt like overkill. Replacing ½ cup of the flour with ground toasted almonds (my tasters' choice over walnuts and pecans, although hazelnuts made a fine substitute) turned out a rich-tasting, pleasantly nubby dough—an ideal match for the lush chocolate filling. The only downside to the nut pastry: Because it contained small bits of almonds, the dough was quite tender and fragile. After some experimenting, I adopted an old test kitchen technique for transferring and fitting tart dough into a pan without tearing it (see "Fitting Delicate Pastry into a Tart Pan").

A dollop of lightly sweetened whipped cream plus either a sprinkle of coarse sea salt or a pile of chocolate curls produced a stunning presentation. I prepared myself for handing out the recipe—often. Anyone who tasted this luscious chocolate tart was going to want to make it him- or herself.

This novel method works with any tart dough, but it is especially helpful when working with this higher-fat, more fragile pastry.

1. Remove top layer of plastic from dough. Invert tart pan on dough. (Removable bottom will drop.) Press pan to cut dough.

2. Invert baking sheet and pan, then set down pan right side up. Remove sheet; peel off and reserve bottom layer of plastic.

3. Roll over dough edges with rolling pin to cut (dough will slip into pan). Gently ease and press dough into pan, reserving scraps.

4. Roll dough scraps into rope (various lengths are OK). Line fluted wall of pan with rope(s) and press into sides.

5. Line pan with reserved plastic. Using measuring cup, press dough to even thickness. Sides should be about ¼ inch thick.

RICH CHOCOLATE TART
SERVES 12

Toasted and skinned hazelnuts can be substituted for the almonds. Use good-quality dark chocolate containing a cacao percentage between 60 and 65 percent; our favorites are Ghirardelli 60 Percent Cacao Bittersweet Chocolate Premium Baking Bar and Callebaut Intense Dark Chocolate, L-60-40NV. Let tart sit at room temperature for 30 minutes before glazing in step 6 and then at least another hour after glazing. The tart can be garnished with chocolate curls or with a flaky coarse sea salt, such as Maldon. Serve with lightly sweetened whipped cream; if you like, flavor it with cognac or vanilla extract.

Crust
1	large egg yolk
2	tablespoons heavy cream
½	cup sliced almonds, toasted
¼	cup (1¾ ounces) sugar
1	cup (5 ounces) all-purpose flour
¼	teaspoon salt
6	tablespoons unsalted butter, cut into ½-inch pieces

Filling
1¼	cups heavy cream
½	teaspoon instant espresso powder
¼	teaspoon salt
9	ounces bittersweet chocolate, chopped fine
4	tablespoons unsalted butter, cut into thin slices and softened
2	large eggs, lightly beaten, room temperature

Glaze
3	tablespoons heavy cream
1	tablespoon light corn syrup
2	ounces bittersweet chocolate, chopped fine
1	tablespoon hot water

1. FOR THE CRUST: Beat egg yolk and cream together in small bowl. Process almonds and sugar in food processor until nuts are finely ground, 15 to 20 seconds. Add flour and salt; pulse to combine, about 10 pulses. Scatter butter over flour mixture; pulse to cut butter into flour until mixture resembles coarse meal, about 15 pulses. With processor running, add egg yolk mixture and process until dough forms ball, about 10 seconds. Transfer dough to large sheet of plastic wrap and press into 6-inch disk; wrap dough in plastic and refrigerate until firm but malleable, about 30 minutes. (Dough can be refrigerated for up to 3 days; before using, let stand at room temperature until malleable but still cool.)

2. Roll out dough between 2 large sheets of plastic into 11-inch round about ⅜ inch thick. (If dough becomes too soft and sticky to work with, slip it onto baking sheet and refrigerate until workable.) Place dough round (still in plastic) on baking sheet and refrigerate until firm but pliable, about 15 minutes.

3. Adjust oven rack to middle position and heat oven to 375 degrees. Spray 9-inch tart pan with removable bottom with vegetable oil spray. Keeping dough on sheet, remove top layer of plastic. Invert tart pan (with bottom) on top of dough round. Press on tart pan to cut dough. Using 2 hands, pick up sheet and tart pan and carefully invert both, setting tart pan right side up. Remove sheet and peel off plastic; reserve plastic. Roll over edges of tart pan with rolling pin to cut dough. Gently ease and press dough into bottom of pan, reserving scraps. Roll dough scraps into ¾-inch-diameter rope (various lengths are OK). Line edge of tart pan with rope(s) and gently press into fluted sides. Line tart pan with reserved plastic and, using measuring cup, gently press and smooth dough to even thickness (sides should be about ¼ inch thick). Using paring knife, trim any excess dough above rim of tart; discard scraps. Freeze dough-lined pan until firm, 20 to 30 minutes.

4. Set dough-lined pan on baking sheet. Spray 12-inch square of aluminum foil with oil spray and press foil, sprayed side down, into pan; fill with 2 cups pie weights. Bake until dough is dry and light golden brown, about 25 minutes, rotating pan halfway through baking. Carefully remove foil and weights and continue to bake until pastry is rich golden brown and fragrant, 8 to 10 minutes longer. Let cool completely on sheet on wire rack.

5. FOR THE FILLING: Heat oven to 250 degrees. Bring cream, espresso powder, and salt to simmer in small saucepan over medium heat, stirring once or twice to dissolve espresso powder and salt. Meanwhile, place chocolate in large heatproof bowl. Pour simmering cream mixture over chocolate, cover, and let stand for 5 minutes to allow chocolate to soften. Using whisk, stir mixture slowly and gently (so as not to incorporate air) until homogeneous. Add butter and continue to whisk gently until fully incorporated. Pour eggs through fine-mesh strainer into chocolate mixture; whisk slowly until mixture is homogeneous and glossy. Pour filling into tart crust and shake gently from side to side to distribute and smooth surface; pop any large bubbles with toothpick or skewer. Bake tart, on baking sheet, until outer edge of filling is just set and very faint cracks appear on surface, 30 to 35 minutes; filling will still be very wobbly. Let cool completely on sheet on wire rack. Refrigerate, uncovered, until filling is chilled and set, at least 3 hours or up to 18 hours.

6. FOR THE GLAZE: Thirty minutes before glazing, remove tart from refrigerator. Bring cream and corn syrup to simmer in small saucepan over medium heat; stir once or twice to combine. Remove pan from heat, add chocolate, and cover. Let stand for 5 minutes to allow chocolate to soften. Whisk gently (so as not to incorporate air) until mixture is smooth, then whisk in hot water until glaze is homogeneous, shiny, and pourable. Working quickly, pour glaze onto center of tart. To distribute glaze, tilt tart and allow glaze to run to edge. (Spreading glaze with spatula will leave marks on surface.) Pop any large bubbles with toothpick or skewer. Let stand for at least 1 hour or up to 3 hours.

7. Remove outer ring from tart pan. Insert thin-bladed metal spatula between crust and pan bottom to loosen tart; slide tart onto serving platter. Cut into wedges and serve.

Look: Perfect Tart Technique
Video available FREE for 4 months at CooksIllustrated.com/dec13

ILLUSTRATION: JOHN BURGOYNE

Florentine Lace Cookies

The easy part about these cookies is that most of the work takes place in a saucepan. The harder part? Perfecting their delicate lacy shape and glossy chocolate coating.

> BY ANDREA GEARY

You may think you don't know what Florentine cookies are, but chances are that you do. Remember those slim, lacy disks of ground almonds bound with buttery caramel and gilded with bittersweet chocolate that you see in upscale pastry shops? The ones that you probably eat first whenever they appear on a cookie platter? Those are Florentines. Any lack of familiarity with the name probably derives from the fact that most people don't make them at home, so the name doesn't get repeated much.

That's because Florentines have a reputation for being fussier and more unpredictable than the average cookie. They start out like candy: Butter, sugar, cream, and either honey or corn syrup are cooked in a saucepan until the mixture reaches 238 degrees, the temperature at which most of the water has evaporated. Then they veer into cookie territory, as flour, almonds, candied citrus, and sometimes dried fruit are stirred in to form a loose, slippery dough. Spoonfuls of dough are then deposited on baking sheets and baked until each forms a crispy, thin, perfectly browned disk—or, if things don't go well, a mottled, chewy, amoeba-like blob. Factor in the uncertainty of whether the chocolate is going to set up firm and shiny or remain sticky and dull, and it's no wonder that most people leave this cookie to the pros.

But here's the thing about Florentines: While producing bakery-quality specimens does require a careful formula, they're actually less work to make than many more conventional cookies because the dough doesn't require beating in a stand mixer—just

A small zipper-lock plastic bag, snipped at one corner, makes an easy stand-in for a traditional piping bag.

a brief stir in a saucepan. Plus, these confectionlike cookies are stylish and keep well for several days, making them ideal for holiday baking. As for coming up with a careful formula, that would be my job.

Covering the Spread

Setting aside the chocolate issue for the moment, I concentrated on the cookie itself. Following a typical method, I melted butter with cream, sugar,

and corn syrup (which I chose over honey for its more neutral flavor) in a saucepan and cooked the mixture for 6 to 8 minutes, until it reached 238 degrees. I admit that I wasn't keen on breaking out my thermometer for cookie making, so as the caramel mixture cooked, I kept my eye out for visual indicators that might allow me to leave the device in its drawer. Happily, I noticed that the mixture turned a distinctive creamy beige color and started to catch on the bottom of the pan just as the temperature approached 238 degrees—exactly the kind of cue I had been hoping for. (No need for that thermometer after all.) After I took the mixture off the heat, I stirred in chopped almonds, flour, a bit of vanilla, and a good amount of candied orange peel to give the cookies a citrusy brightness to offset their richness. I scooped 1-tablespoon portions of dough onto baking sheets and baked them for 12 minutes.

This early batch was, in a word, disappointing. The cookies hadn't spread sufficiently, so they were chunky instead of thin and delicate, and their surfaces sported tight fissures instead of the fine, lacy holes that are characteristic of Florentines. Their texture was also tough and a bit chewy. Finally, instead of enhancing flavor, the candied peel didn't taste like much of anything.

It occurred to me that finely grinding, rather than chopping, the almonds might give the cookies a flatter profile, and upping the cream might encourage them to spread more. Those changes did indeed move me toward a thinner Florentine, but I didn't produce the crispiness and delicate filigreed appearance of bakery-quality cookies until I had made a

---

STEP BY STEP | HOW CONFECTION AND COOKIE BECOME ONE

I. MAKE CARAMEL
Heat cream, butter, and sugar in saucepan until thick and brown at edges.

2. MAKE DOUGH
Off heat, stir in ground almonds, marmalade, flour, vanilla, orange zest, and salt.

3. DROP AND SHAPE
Spoon dough onto parchment paper–lined baking sheets and press into circles.

4. BAKE AND COOL
Bake cookies until uniformly brown; transfer on parchment paper to cooling racks. Let sheets cool for 10 minutes; repeat.

5. "TEMPER" CHOCOLATE
Microwave some chocolate at 50 percent power, stirring frequently, until two-thirds melted. Stir in remaining chocolate.

6. PIPE AND CHILL
Pour chocolate into zipper-lock bag, snip off corner, and pipe onto cookies. Refrigerate for 30 minutes to set chocolate.

PHOTOGRAPHY: CARL TREMBLAY; ILLUSTRATION: JAY LAYMAN

few more adjustments. Three extra minutes in the oven allowed the cookies to crisp and turn deeply golden brown from edge to edge, and a touch less flour helped them spread even thinner. Since more spreading also encouraged my neat rounds to bleed into amorphous shapes, I took a minute to pat each mound of dough into a flat circle. Bingo: These thin, round, crispy wafers looked like prime pastry shop offerings. If only there was a way to boost that backbone of orange flavor.

Pump Up the Jam (and Chocolate)

Swapping the candied orange peel for freshly grated orange zest (and adding a bit of salt) helped, but it wasn't enough. Adding more zest wasn't an option—the little bits became too noticeable. But there was one bakery cookie that I'd tasted as part of my research that I knew had exactly the orange profile I was after. It came from the Lakota Bakery in Arlington, Massachusetts, and proprietor Barbara Weniger generously divulged her secret: orange marmalade.

When I added ¼ cup of marmalade to my working recipe (swapping it for the corn syrup, which contributed similar viscosity), the difference was incredible. Thanks to the marmalade's concentrated flavor, my Florentines finally had the bright, citrusy, and faintly bitter taste that I wanted, and the jam provided a contrast to the rich, sweet caramel base. Satisfied with my thin, crispy, orangey cookie, I moved on to the final hurdle: the chocolate.

The classic Florentine has a thin, smooth coat of bittersweet chocolate on its underside, an elegant effect achieved by dipping the entire bottom surface of each cookie into a large container of melted chocolate. This approach presents two problems for the home cook: First, you wind up with loads of leftover chocolate. Second, to ensure that the chocolate retains an attractive sheen, you have to either temper it (a painstaking process of melting and cooling the chocolate to ensure that it stays within the optimal temperature range) or get your hands on special coating chocolate, which contains a small amount of a highly saturated vegetable fat that extends the temperature range at which the chocolate can safely melt. I needed to come up with an easier, more practical alternative.

After some trial and error, I devised a great faux-tempering method that involved melting part of the chocolate at 50 percent power in the microwave and then stirring in the remainder—a very gentle approach that kept the chocolate glossy when it resolidified. (For more information, see "Helping Chocolate Keep Its Temper," page 31.) To apply the method to the cookies, I tried spreading a small bit of chocolate onto their undersides with a spatula, but that looked messy. The chocolate seeped through those lacy holes that I had worked so hard for, and it was difficult to get the skim coat that I wanted, which meant that the chocolate flavor overwhelmed the delicate cookies. In the end, I took a different but not uncommon approach: piping decorative zigzags over the top of each cookie. (In lieu of a pastry bag, which not all home cooks have, I poured the melted chocolate into a zipper-lock bag and snipped off the corner.)

With Florentines as crispy, flavorful, and elegant as these, I know exactly what I'll be giving for holiday gifts this year.

FLORENTINE LACE COOKIES

MAKES 24 COOKIES

It's important to cook the cream mixture in the saucepan until it is thick and starting to brown at the edges; undercooking will result in a dough that is too runny to portion. Do not be concerned if some butter separates from the dough while you're portioning the cookies. For the most uniform cookies, use the flattest baking sheets you have and make sure that your parchment paper lies flat. When melting the chocolate, pause the microwave and stir the chocolate often to ensure that it doesn't get much warmer than body temperature.

- **2 cups slivered almonds**
- **¾ cup heavy cream**
- **4 tablespoons unsalted butter, cut into 4 pieces**
- **½ cup (3½ ounces) sugar**
- **¼ cup orange marmalade**
- **3 tablespoons all-purpose flour**
- **1 teaspoon vanilla extract**
- **¼ teaspoon grated orange zest**
- **¼ teaspoon salt**
- **4 ounces bittersweet chocolate, chopped fine**

1. Adjust oven racks to upper-middle and lower-middle positions and heat oven to 350 degrees. Line 2 baking sheets with parchment paper. Process almonds in food processor until they resemble coarse sand, about 30 seconds.

2. Bring cream, butter, and sugar to boil in medium saucepan over medium-high heat. Cook, stirring frequently, until mixture begins to thicken, 5 to 6 minutes. Continue to cook, stirring constantly, until mixture begins to brown at edges and is thick enough to leave trail that doesn't immediately fill in when spatula is scraped along pan bottom, 1 to 2 minutes longer (it's OK if some darker speckles appear in mixture). Remove pan from heat and stir in almonds, marmalade, flour, vanilla, orange zest, and salt until combined.

3. Drop 6 level tablespoons dough at least 3½ inches apart on each prepared sheet. When cool enough to handle, use damp fingers to press each portion into 2½-inch circle.

4. Bake until deep brown from edge to edge, 15 to 17 minutes, switching and rotating sheets halfway through baking. Transfer cookies, still on parchment, to wire racks and let cool. Let baking sheets cool for 10 minutes, line with fresh parchment, and repeat portioning and baking remaining dough.

5. Microwave 3 ounces chocolate in bowl at 50 percent power, stirring frequently, until about two-thirds melted, 1 to 2 minutes. Remove bowl from microwave, add remaining 1 ounce chocolate, and stir until melted, returning to microwave for no more than 5 seconds at a time to complete melting if necessary. Transfer chocolate to small zipper-lock bag and snip off corner, making hole no larger than 1/16 inch.

6. Transfer cooled cookies directly to wire racks. Pipe zigzag of chocolate over each cookie, distributing chocolate evenly among all cookies. Refrigerate until chocolate is set, about 30 minutes, before serving. (Cookies can be stored at cool room temperature for up to 4 days.)

TESTING

French Press Coffee Makers

The French press (or *cafetière à piston*, as the French call it) uses a piston-like mechanism to force ground coffee through hot water, sending the spent grounds to the bottom of the pot and leaving a full-bodied brew on top. Oily and thick from minute particles of the grind suspended in the brew, French press coffee is impossible to confuse with drip coffee. But there are potential drawbacks: The mass of steeped coffee creates pressure, making it hard to push down the filter, sometimes shattering glass pots. Also, heat escapes glass pots quickly. Some people dislike suspended coffee particles in their brew. And wet, compressed grounds can be hard to dislodge.

HOT POT
The Bodum Columbia French Press Coffee Maker, Double Wall, brews "rich" coffee and stays hot.

Several new models promised to address these issues, so we rounded up six 8-cup pots priced from $26.43 to $119.95, to see if any could displace our previous glass winner, the Bodum Chambord French Press, 8-Cup ($39.95). Our runner-up, the Espro Press Coffee Maker ($119.95), was notable for a double filter ringed with a silicone gasket to keep fine sediment out of the coffee. A few tasters bemoaned its "thin" texture, complaining that it wasn't much like real French press coffee. As for heat retention and cleanup, insulated all-steel pots kept coffee hotter than glass (and eliminated the risk of shattering), and pared-down pieces simplified washing. In the end, our top pick was the insulated stainless-steel Bodum Columbia French Press Coffee Maker, Double Wall ($79.95). It delivers hot, full-bodied coffee and is dishwasher-safe. For complete testing results, go to CooksIllustrated.com/dec13. –Lisa McManus

---

Watch the Laciness Happen

Video available FREE for 4 months at CooksIllustrated.com/dec13

Introducing Caldo Verde

Everything about this classic Portuguese soup, from the smoky sausage to the tender potatoes and greens, is hearty and satisfying—except for its thin body.

≥ BY LAN LAM ≤

My fondness for caldo verde started in my friend Sam Paterson's kitchen. He grew up in a Portuguese community in Gloucester, Massachusetts, where this soup of sausage, potato, and hearty greens was a staple in many households, and he often invited me to dinner when his grandmother was serving her version. After sautéing onion and garlic in extra-virgin olive oil, she added cubed russet potatoes and a couple of quarts of water, brought the pot to a boil, and let the soup simmer until the potatoes were tender. As that was cooking, she browned pieces of smoky, garlicky linguiça sausage in a skillet and finely shredded a large bunch of kale as a stand-in for *couve tronchuda*, the traditional greens used for the dish. After about 10 minutes, she gave the pot a stir to break down the potatoes and introduce body to the broth; then she added the sautéed sausage and kale. The greens softened during the last few minutes of cooking and gave the soup its generally verdant appearance—and its name.

What I like best about this dish is that, while the flavors are rich, it's not a heavy soup. In fact, my friend's family serves it as a starter. Without changing the soup's essentially light character, I wanted to create a slightly heartier result—something that could function as a main course.

To start, I replaced the hard-to-find Portuguese linguiça sausage with widely available Spanish-style chorizo, which boasts a similar garlicky profile. I also sautéed the sausage right in the Dutch oven—no need to dirty a skillet. The ¼ cup of extra-virgin olive oil that many recipes suggest for cooking the sausage seemed excessive, so I reduced it to just 1 tablespoon. One more tweak: I split the water with an equal amount of chicken broth for deeper flavor.

While the soup simmered, I dealt with the greens. The problem with shredded kale, I'd noticed, was that the wilted strips dangle from the spoon, making the soup messy to eat. I also wondered if kale was really the best option: Several caldo verde recipes that I found call for collards to replace the traditional couve. One side-by-side test settled things: My tasters preferred the collards, which offered a delicate

Look: A Soup to Savor

Video available FREE for 4 months at CooksIllustrated.com/dec13

Blending a few tablespoons of oil with a bit of the broth and potatoes adds richness and body.

sweetness and a meatier bite. Chopping the leaves into bite-size pieces made them more spoon-friendly.

So far, my caldo verde was shaping up nicely, save for the broth itself, which was too thin. I also didn't love how three separate layers developed as the soup sat: a thin film of flavorful chorizo oil on top, broth beneath it, and a bed of grainy potato bits on the bottom of the pot. I wanted something with creamier, more even body.

Until now I'd been vigorously stirring the broth once the potatoes had softened so that they broke down. But it was becoming clear that using this mixing method would never produce the smooth body I wanted: I realized that I should just puree some of the softened potatoes into the liquid. This way, the broth would thicken up and become uniformly silky. I blitzed ¾ cup of the russets with an equal amount of broth in a blender. The resulting puree was definitely smooth-textured. The problem was that by the time the soup was simmering with the greens and the sausage, the unpureed potato pieces (which I wanted to remain intact) were completely blown out. Switching to lower-starch Yukon Golds, which hold their shape even during long cooking, was the easy solution.

And yet the broth was not quite as silky as I wanted it to be, which made me think of those 3 extra tablespoons of oil that I'd vetoed early in my testing. Maybe emulsifying that fat in the broth would be just what the soup needed. I drizzled the oil into the blender with the softened potatoes and broth, and as I'd hoped, a brief whirl left me with

a uniform, velvety puree. I added the greens to the broth and then stirred in the chorizo a few minutes later. When the greens were tender, I poured my potato-oil emulsion into the soup along with a bit of white wine vinegar to brighten the pot.

Here was just the hearty soup I wanted, with all the flavors that I loved in the classic.

CALDO VERDE
SERVES 6 TO 8

We prefer collard greens, but kale can be substituted. Serve this soup with hearty bread and, for added richness, a final drizzle of extra-virgin olive oil.

- ¼ cup extra-virgin olive oil
- 12 ounces Spanish-style chorizo sausage, cut into ½-inch pieces
- 1 onion, chopped fine
- 4 garlic cloves, minced
  Salt and pepper
- ¼ teaspoon red pepper flakes
- 2 pounds Yukon Gold potatoes, peeled and cut into ¾-inch pieces
- 4 cups chicken broth
- 4 cups water
- 1 pound collard greens, stemmed and cut into 1-inch pieces
- 2 teaspoons white wine vinegar

1. Heat 1 tablespoon oil in Dutch oven over medium-high heat until shimmering. Add chorizo and cook, stirring occasionally, until lightly browned, 4 to 5 minutes. Transfer chorizo to bowl and set aside. Reduce heat to medium and add onion, garlic, 1¼ teaspoons salt, and pepper flakes and season with pepper to taste. Cook, stirring frequently, until onion is translucent, 2 to 3 minutes. Add potatoes, broth, and water; increase heat to high and bring to boil. Reduce heat to medium-low and simmer, uncovered, until potatoes are just tender, 8 to 10 minutes.

2. Transfer ¾ cup solids and ¾ cup broth to blender jar. Add collard greens to pot and simmer for 10 minutes. Stir in chorizo and continue to simmer until greens are tender, 8 to 10 minutes longer.

3. Add remaining 3 tablespoons oil to soup in blender and process until very smooth and homogeneous, about 1 minute. Remove pot from heat and stir pureed soup mixture and vinegar into soup. Season with salt and pepper to taste, and serve. (Soup can be refrigerated for up to 2 days.)

The Last Mixer Standing

A stand mixer is one of the most expensive appliances in your kitchen, so it had better do it all—from whipping a single egg white to kneading thick pizza dough.

⋟ BY AMY GRAVES & LISA McMANUS ⋞

Kneading wet, heavy bread dough by hand is hard work. So is mixing together thick cookie dough. Thus, when KitchenAid debuted the first stand mixer designed for home cooks in 1919, it caused a big stir. For households that invested in one of these machines—and at $189 a pop, the equivalent of about $2,551 today, they were an investment—the chore of making breads and baked goods was gone with the flip of a switch.

As their relative cost has dropped considerably over the years, the appeal of stand mixers has only grown, and these days the appliance is a fixture in many kitchens. But deciding which one to buy has never been more complicated. KitchenAid still makes the majority of stand mixers, but other manufacturers now offer small commercial-grade machines that promise to knead, whip, and mix with even more ease and efficiency. Improvements range from bigger bowl capacities and more horsepower to timers with automatic shutoff and easy-to-use splash guards.

Given the dizzying range of features and still considerable cost of stand mixers, we shop carefully—and test exhaustively—before we commit. Our last round of evaluations singled out two winners: the KitchenAid Professional 600 Series 6-Quart Bowl-Lift Stand Mixer and the Cuisinart 5.5 Quart Stand Mixer, both originally priced at around $400 (their prices have since changed). What made them stand out was their ability to perform a range of core tasks—to muscle through stiff bread dough as confidently as they beat egg whites. But how do they stack up against newer machines that boast more power and (supposedly) more convenience? And, more important, does the home baker need all that added bling? We ordered nine models, priced from nearly $230 to a jaw-dropping $849, to find out.

Attachment Disorders

All but one of the stand mixers came with three standard attachments: a whisk for whipping cream and egg whites, a paddle for creaming and incorporating cake and cookie ingredients, and a dough hook for kneading bread and pizza dough. However, every manufacturer designed its parts a little differently. Whisks were bulbous or narrow and tapered, and they had as few as 10 tines and as many as 24; the "fingers" within some paddle frames were Y-shaped while others were Z-shaped or even splayed in concentric arcs like a menorah; dough hooks were generally molded in the shape of a C—think Captain Hook's weapon—or as loose spirals. We assumed that one particular design within each category would prove to be the best, and in some cases it did. But as we put each model through a battery of tests, we noticed that the relationship between the attachment and the bowl usually mattered more than the design of the attachment itself.

Consider whipping a pair of egg whites. This test, which involves only a small quantity of liquid, made it obvious which bowls and attachments had been carefully designed together for maximum contact between the whisk and the food and which hadn't. The best combination came from KitchenAid: The 7-quart Pro Line model features a wide, shallow bowl that raised the whites relatively close to the attachment and a 22-tine whisk, the outer layer of which featured elbow-bent tines that almost grazed the walls when the whisk circled the bowl.

Conversely, whipping was a struggle for the Vollrath, Waring, KitchenAid 600, and both Cuisinart machines because their bowls and whisks didn't align closely enough for the whisk to engage all the whites. As a result, these machines took longer to whip small quantities and in some cases left an untouched pool of liquid beneath the cloud of silky peaks.

The same principle of bowl-to-attachment proximity applied when we used the paddles to cream together butter and sugar. In most cases, the lateral reach of these flat beaters wasn't enough to grab food that had clung to the sides of the bowl, forcing us to regularly scrape down the unincorporated portions of the batter and remix. Only the Breville came with a beater that specifically addressed this problem: an extra "scraper" paddle with silicone extensions that continually swiped the sides of the bowl. As a result, it reduced the need to scrape, shaving minutes off mixing times. (KitchenAid sells scraper blades separately; we tested included attachments only.) What's more, the Breville paddle, as well as those included with all three KitchenAid mixers, featured a distinct design advantage: the aforementioned Y-shaped webbing inside its frame. Because the angles between the "fingers" are relatively wide, cookie dough didn't become clogged in the crevices as it did with the sharper-angled Z-style paddles that came with the Cuisinart models, particularly the smaller one.

The Powers That Be

Attachment issues followed the 7-quart Cuisinart and the Bosch mixers into kneading tests, too. Their dough hooks made limited or no contact at all, respectively, with the ingredients when we added enough for a single batch of pizza dough but capably mixed the ingredients when we added twice as much flour and water for double batches (though both machines needed extra time to finish the bigger job).

However, the shape of the bowl and the dough hook were secondary factors when it came to kneading. For one thing, we had successes and failures with both C- and spiral-shaped hooks. More important, heavyweight tasks like kneading are more affected by the machinery itself than by the attachments.

During kneading, dough develops more gluten and becomes stiffer; the stiffer it gets the more it pushes back against the machine and increases the "load" on the motor. If a machine has enough power, it can keep moving and mixing at its set speed despite that load; if it doesn't, the mixer will slow, which causes the motor to heat up and potentially burn out. So what makes a stand mixer powerful?

Initially, we thought it boiled down to horsepower—that is, the force that the mixer exerts. But that wasn't the whole story: Several machines

Mix Masters Through the Ages

1885
First mixer with electric motor introduced in U.S.

1914
Debut of first commercial stand mixer (80-quart capacity).

1919
First stand mixer designed for home cooks introduced under brand name KitchenAid.

1930
First smaller, more affordable KitchenAid rival, the Mixmaster, by Sunbeam, introduced.

1936
Joy of Cooking is first major U.S. cookbook to include "rules" for mixing cakes "with an electrical mixer."

1937
Smaller, cheaper KitchenAid introduced; design hasn't been substantially tinkered with since.

A Stand(out) Mixer

Here's why we think the pricey KitchenAid Pro Line Series 7-Qt Bowl Lift Stand Mixer ($549.95) is worth shelling out for.

POWERFUL ENGINE
Plenty of torque made this the only mixer that kneaded double batches of pizza dough and stiff bagel dough without flinching.

HEAVYWEIGHT BUILD
At 27 pounds, this mixer's die-cast frame stays anchored to the counter.

CRANK IT UP
Bowl lift models like this one allow you to access the bowl by cranking it up and down rather than tilting the mixer's entire head up and down—a perk if your mixer lives under low cabinets.

BROAD BOWL, BIG HANDLE
A wide, shallow bowl keeps contents within easy reach of attachments. Its long vertical handle provides plenty of leverage and control for pouring.

PERFECT PADDLE
Open Y-shaped branches in this paddle's frame thoroughly incorporate ingredients without trapping them in tight crevices.

WIDE-ARMED WHIP
The tines making up the outer layer of this whisk's 22 tines are bent at near-right angles, enabling them to reach food near the bowl's sides and bottom.

SPLASH ON, SPLASH OFF
Unlike most splash guards, this C-shaped one slides on just as easily as it slips off for instant access to the bowl.

with relatively high horsepower, such as the Waring (1.07 HP), performed either inconsistently or markedly worse than mixers with less than half as much oomph, like the KitchenAid Classic Plus (0.37 HP).

We later learned that a mixer's power depends on a combination of factors—horsepower, yes, but also the machine's torque. Torque, or rotational force, provides leverage: The more torque a machine has the more effectively it will not only push on dough but also rotate it in the bowl. "Abundant torque availability allows [the mixer's] speed to be held constant over a wide load range, while the beater of an underpowered mixer will lose speed as ingredients are added or dough stiffens, resulting in inconsistent mixing batch to batch," explained Michael Borgen, lead mechanical engineer at Metis Design Corporation in Boston, Massachusetts. From the manufacturer's point of view, it's not always cost-effective to provide plenty of power, he added. "There is a balance to be struck. A motor with superfluous power will unnecessarily increase the cost, size, and weight of a mixer." But an underpowered mixer doesn't just deliver bad dough: When it slows or stalls, this strain makes the motor more likely to burn out, explained Ruqiang Feng, professor of mechanical and materials engineering and an American Society of Mechanical Engineers fellow at the University of Nebraska–Lincoln.

See Why It Won
Video available FREE for 4 months at CooksIllustrated.com/dec13

No mixer exemplified this more clearly than the Breville, a front-runner until the kneading tests. Not only did it shudder and lurch as it churned a single batch of dough but it became very hot (its top surface reached 100 degrees), emitted fumes, and from that test on rumbled angrily during both light and heavy tasks. A second brand-new copy failed similarly, struggling to knead for several minutes before finally shutting down. The bigger Cuisinart also struggled: Its dough hook actually ripped off the shaft when it became overworked mixing super-stiff bagel dough, our most demanding test. Suddenly, beefy-looking machines were boxing above their weight class—and a stand mixer that can't do anything more than a hand mixer is not worth the investment.

Sibling Rivalry
But what was even more surprising than those machines' failures were the impressive results put up by the seemingly low-power KitchenAid Classic Plus ($229.99), the company's smallest and cheapest model. (An earlier version of this machine won our inexpensive stand mixer testing.) This mixer outperformed almost every challenger, producing billowy egg whites as capably as it did a double batch of pizza dough. In fact, its only real competition was its sibling: the KitchenAid Pro Line, a machine with more than three times as much horsepower, nearly twice the capacity, and a much heftier price tag ($549.95). The only time the Classic Plus faltered was in an abuse test: a KitchenAid versus KitchenAid standoff between these two models, our overall top performers, to see which could mix 10 batches of bagel dough and 10

batches of pizza dough (with 30-minute rests between batches) without flinching. After finishing the pizza dough, it was only on the sixth batch of bagels that the latch locking down the tilt head on the Classic Plus stopped working—a result that indicated more about the potential disadvantage of tilt-head mixers than it did about this machine's motor, which, by the way, carried on just fine if we held the mixer's head in place.

Besides a bowl-lift rather than a tilt-head design, we had a few wish list items for the Classic Plus: a bowl handle, preferably a vertical one to help us control the weight of the vessel and keep our other hand free for scraping, and a splash guard (one that could slip on and off easily, such as the one on the Pro Line). And for all three KitchenAid models, an easy-to-set timer with automatic shutoff would be nice. (Notably, a larger bowl capacity is not something we missed, as evidenced by its strong performance with a double batch of pizza dough. What's more, we measured each mixer bowl's usable capacity—the volume of the space between the top of the attachment and the bottom of the bowl—and discovered that no model actually made use of its bowl's total volume; some used barely more than half. Bottom line: A stand mixer's stated capacity may not only be misleading but it also may not be a good indication of the machine's ability to handle large loads.)

Thanks to its power, heft (at 21.5 pounds, it's one of the heaviest mixers we tested), compact size, simple operation, and relatively wallet-friendly price, the Classic Plus earned our Best Buy status. But if you do a lot of heavy-duty baking, you'll want to save up for the Pro Line, a stand mixer whose range of ability and durability make it truly worthy of investment.

Don't Judge a Mixer by the Size of Its Bowl
Just because a stand mixer comes with a 7-quart bowl doesn't mean that all 7 quarts are available to use. When we measured how much water we needed to pour into each mixer bowl to reach the top of each mixer's attachment and compared that figure—the usable capacity—with the bowl's stated volume, we discovered that there were dramatic discrepancies. In fact, no mixer used its bowl's full volume, and some, like the Cuisinart 5.5 Quart Stand Mixer, used barely more than half.

SPEAKS VOLUMES
The usable capacity of the Cuisinart 5.5 Quart Stand Mixer is only 3 quarts.

More important, most larger-volume stand mixers didn't perform better than "smaller-capacity" models. The KitchenAid Classic Plus, the mixer with the smallest stated capacity that we tested (4½ quarts), handled double batches of pizza dough at least as well as mixers with larger stated capacities.

TESTING STAND MIXERS

We tested nine stand mixers from leading brands, focusing on the key tasks of whipping, creaming, and kneading and also rating them on design and ease of use. Mixers appear in order of preference. Prices shown were paid online; sources for the winners appear on page 32.

WHIPPING: We whipped average and very small amounts of ingredients, including two egg whites, four egg whites plus hot sugar syrup for meringue, and 1 and 2 cups of heavy cream. High marks went to machines that quickly and easily handled all quantities and tasks.

CREAMING: The best mixers quickly and thoroughly creamed butter and sugar for sugar cookie dough and reverse-creamed yellow cake batter, and required minimal scraping of the bowl or paddle.

KNEADING: We preferred mixers that could handle both single and double batches of glossy, elastic pizza dough and also knead stiff, heavy bagel dough into a smooth, cohesive mass without jamming or struggling. Mixers that failed at these jobs were downgraded significantly.

DESIGN: We evaluated the weight, shape, controls, and operation of each mixer and its parts, including the whisk, mixing paddle, dough hook, and splash guard (when included). We also assessed the usable capacity of each model by measuring how much water we needed to pour into the bowl to reach the top of each mixing attachment, and we compared those results with the stated capacity.

EASE OF USE: The best mixers were intuitive to set up, use, and clean.

HIGHLY RECOMMENDED

	CRITERIA		TESTERS' COMMENTS

KITCHENAID Pro Line Series 7-Qt Bowl Lift Stand Mixer 
Model: KSM7586P Price: $549.95
Stated Capacity: 7 qt
Actual Capacity: 5¾ qt
Weight: 27 lb
Horsepower: 1.3 Style: Bowl-lift

Whipping	★★★
Creaming	★★★
Kneading	★★★
Design	★★★
Ease of Use	★★★

This powerful, smartly designed machine made quick work of large and small volumes of food. The bent tines of its whisk fit the bowl's shape perfectly, its Y-shaped paddle creamed quickly without allowing butter to bunch up in the crevices, and the model handled batches of stiff dough without flinching. Testers liked the bowl-lift design and large vertical bowl handle that aided pouring.

RECOMMENDED

KITCHENAID Classic Plus Series 4.5-Quart Tilt-Head Stand Mixer 
Model: KSM75WH Price: $229.99
Stated Capacity: 4½ qt
Actual Capacity: 3¼ qt
Weight: 21.5 lb
Horsepower: 0.37 Style: Tilt-head

BEST BUY

Whipping	★★★
Creaming	★★★
Kneading	★★★
Design	★★½
Ease of Use	★★★

This basic, compact, heavy machine's across-the-board performance knocked out many competitors that were bigger and much more costly (although its tilt head broke on an extreme abuse test). We wish that its bowl had a handle, and a bowl-lift (rather than a tilt-head) design would have been nice, but those are small concessions given its affordable price.

KITCHENAID Professional 600 Series 6-Quart Bowl-Lift Stand Mixer 
Model: KP26M1X Price: $449.95
Stated Capacity: 6 qt
Actual Capacity: 5¼ qt
Weight: 25.4 lb
Horsepower: 0.8 Style: Bowl-lift

Whipping	★★½
Creaming	★★★
Kneading	★★½
Design	★★½
Ease of Use	★★½

Compared with its siblings, our former favorite stand mixer wasn't quite as impressive. Runny egg whites didn't turn into stiff peaks until we cranked the speed to create a vortex. It was also relatively noisy, and as it jerked slightly on tough kneading tasks, the bowl briefly popped out of place. But the results were nonetheless excellent.

RECOMMENDED WITH RESERVATIONS

WARING Commercial Professional 7-Quart Stand Mixer 
Model: WSM7Q Price: $564.65
Stated Capacity: 7 qt
Actual Capacity: 4½ qt
Weight: 19.25 lb
Horsepower: 1.07 Style: Tilt-head

Whipping	★★½
Creaming	★★½
Kneading	★★★
Design	★½
Ease of Use	★★

This powerful machine performed particularly well when kneading. Design and user-friendliness were its weak points: The narrow bowl required repeated scraping; its tilt head flew up during mixing unless we were extra careful to secure it; its close-fitting, horizontal handles were unwieldy for pouring batter into cake pans; and its bowl guard was hard to attach.

CUISINART 5.5 Quart Stand Mixer 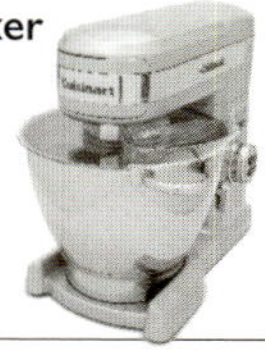
Model: SM-55 Price: $349
Stated Capacity: 5½ qt
Actual Capacity: 3 qt
Weight: 17.8 lb
Horsepower: 1.07 Style: Tilt-head

Whipping	★★
Creaming	★★
Kneading	★★★
Design	★½
Ease of Use	★½

Our former cowinner was outmatched by the competition. Its loose speed dial made it hard to pinpoint settings; the jumpy timer raced past the numbers we wanted; and its small, horizontal bowl handles made pouring awkward. It produced fine dough, but whipping cream and egg whites took extra time, and cookie dough repeatedly stuck in its dinky Z-shaped paddle.

NOT RECOMMENDED

VOLLRATH 7-Quart Countertop Commercial Mixer 
Model: 40755 Price: $849
Stated Capacity: 7 qt
Actual Capacity: 5¼ qt
Weight: 43.9 lb
Horsepower: 0.87 Style: Bowl-lift

Whipping	★★
Creaming	★★★
Kneading	★★★
Design	½
Ease of Use	★

We struggled to move this 43.9-pound behemoth, and its 19.5-inch-tall body didn't fit under our cupboards. Cake batter and larger volumes of cream and egg whites were no problem, but the ill-designed bowl and attachments meant that it struggled with smaller amounts of food. The attached bowl guard began to separate from the bowl by the end of heavy kneading (and doesn't detach for cleaning).

CUISINART 7.0 Quart 12-Speed Stand Mixer 
Model: SM-70 Price: $449.90
Stated Capacity: 7 qt
Actual Capacity: 4½ qt
Weight: 19.25 lb
Horsepower: 1.3 Style: Tilt-head

Whipping	★★
Creaming	★★★
Kneading	½
Design	★½
Ease of Use	★

This mixer's deep, narrow bowl limited testers' view of mixing progress and let cream and egg whites pool out of reach of the whisk. Its motor was loud and shrill. When kneading bagel dough, the dough hook separated from a bolt at its base and had to be rethreaded.

BOSCH Universal Plus Mixer 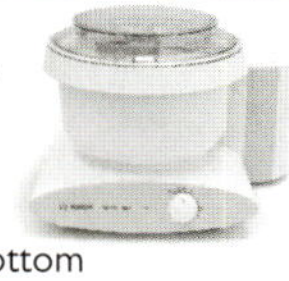
Model: MUM6N10UC Price: $399.99
Stated Capacity: 6 qt
Actual Capacity: 4¼ qt
Weight: 12.1 lb
Horsepower: 1.07 Style: Motor on bottom

Whipping	★★
Creaming	★★½
Kneading	½
Design	★
Ease of Use	★★

Shaped like a tube pan and with the motor beneath (rather than above) the mixing action, this model whipped and creamed quickly, except with small quantities of ingredients in the bowl. Kneading was its downfall: For single batches of dough, the flour never made contact with the dough hook.

BREVILLE Scraper Mixer Pro 
Model: BEM800XL Price: $280.95
Stated Capacity: 5 qt
Actual Capacity: 3¾ qt
Weight: 16.5 lb
Horsepower: 0.74 Style: Tilt-head

Whipping	★★★
Creaming	★★★
Kneading	zero
Design	★★
Ease of Use	★★★

This model's fast, quiet whipping and creaming and user-friendly features (scraper paddle and timer) advanced it to the lead—until it utterly choked during kneading. A second copy also failed. We can't justify spending nearly $300 on a machine that's no better than a hand mixer.

The Best Dark Chocolate

It's easy to find a great snacking chocolate. But cooking is different: Choosing the right dark chocolate can make the difference between a dessert that's flawless and one that's a flop.

In the past decade, Americans have gotten serious about dark chocolate. Rich, complex, and even bitter, its flavor transcends the mild, sugar-laden milk chocolate that many of us grew up with. As a result, ever-climbing cacao percentages are now posted prominently on packaging, and chocophiles have come to describe bars with the same level of detail that they'd use for a fine Cabernet. "Bean to bar" is hot, as artisanal chocolatiers take control of every aspect of chocolate making, from sourcing to production. Single-origin bars are trendy, too, showcasing distinct regional characteristics such as the intensely floral flavor of beans from the mountains of Peru or the dried mint overtones of bars made from the beans from Trinidad.

But almost all these pricey chocolates are meant to be eaten plain, savored by the sliver, rather than used for cooking. It seems wasteful to cook with them, as many of their more delicate notes won't survive a hot oven. (You know that unmistakable fragrance that pervades the kitchen when you're baking chocolate cake or brownies? Those are flavor and aroma volatiles driven out of the baked goods by the heat.)

To find a great everyday dark chocolate, we focused on national supermarket brands; after all, we want to be able to pick some up whenever the

Proof's in the "Pot"

The percentage of cocoa solids in a chocolate helped determine whether it would produce *pots de crème* that were runny or properly thick and dense.

DRIPPY
Its relatively low range of cocoa solids explained why Nestlé Semi-Sweet Baking Chocolate Bar made runny pots de crème.

VELVETY THICK
An ideal percentage of cocoa solids in the Ghirardelli 60 Percent Cacao Bittersweet Chocolate Premium Baking Bar translated to a dense, velvety dessert.

need for a brownie strikes. The U.S. Food and Drug Administration (FDA) doesn't set a standard of identity for dark chocolate except that "bittersweet" and "semisweet" chocolate must contain at least 35 percent cacao—and it doesn't differentiate between the two terms. (The cacao percentage is the portion of the chocolate made from the cacao bean and includes both cocoa solids and cocoa butter; the rest is mostly sugar.) In the past we've focused on products with about 60 percent cacao, but this time, to truly evaluate all the supermarket options, if it met the FDA's 35 percent cacao minimum, we considered it for our lineup. We found nine nationally available chocolates, priced from $0.47 to $1.43 per ounce, and included our winner from a previous tasting, Callebaut Intense Dark Chocolate, L-60-40NV, which is available in most Whole Foods Markets and via mail order.

We conducted three blind taste tests, evaluating the chocolates' flavor, sweetness, texture, and overall appeal. We sampled them plain and also in brownies to see how well the chocolate flavor endured heat. Finally we melted them in *pots de crème*—a creamy application where textural differences are laid bare. After the results were tallied, we had to ask: Was there such a thing as a great-tasting, easy-to-find dark chocolate that works well in recipes? Happily, yes. But buyer beware: It's stacked on supermarket shelves right next to products that can ruin a dessert.

The Dark Side

Dark chocolate is made of three primary ingredients: cocoa butter, cocoa solids, and sugar. Across the board in the chocolates we tasted, we determined that fat levels were relatively consistent, with cocoa butter making up about one-third of the total composition of each chocolate; the remaining two-thirds is a tug-of-war between sugar and cocoa solids— more sugar means fewer cocoa solids and vice versa. Sugar amounts ranged from 36 to 57 percent; in the plain and brownie tastings, products with more than 50 percent sugar sank to the bottom of the ratings, coming off as "sickeningly sweet," with a "faint" chocolate presence. In the same tastings, we weren't surprised to find that low-sugar, high-cocoa-solids products rocketed to the top, scoring points for intense chocolate flavor.

But it wasn't until we made pots de crème that we realized that the wrong ratio of sugar to cocoa solids could actually ruin a recipe: Our 10 custards—each made exactly the same except for the chocolate that we used—ran the gamut from loose and drippy

to dense and decadently creamy. Previous tastings taught us that more cocoa solids make firmer pots de crème, and in this lineup the solids ranged from 13 to 30 percent. Indeed, when we organized our pots de crème from runniest to firmest, we noted that those made with products with less than 20 percent cocoa solids failed to set up, dripping off our spoons. Chocolates with 22 to 25 percent cocoa solids hit the sweet spot, turning out consistently dense and creamy. At the extreme, the two products with the most cocoa solids, Callebaut and Baker's Bittersweet (both at around 30 percent), sometimes caused the custard to break and turn clumpy, a result of cocoa particles bonding with themselves instead of with the limited amount of free water in the mix. But thanks to the natural variability of water in eggs and even minor differences in heat and stirring rates, clumping didn't always happen.

Bar Brawl

In the end, two 60-percent-cacao chocolates that we've singled out in the past topped our charts, but they weren't identical: Tasters raved about Callebaut Intense Dark Chocolate, L-60-40NV, calling it "complex" and "luxurious." Its downside is that it can be a little hard to source and is sometimes finicky in creamy applications. On the other hand, Ghirardelli 60 Percent Cacao Bittersweet Chocolate Premium Baking Bar always produced texturally flawless desserts that were "luscious" and "subtly fruity"; plus it's available in supermarkets nationwide. In addition, Ghirardelli 60 Percent is supremely easy to work with when it's melted (such as when we are glazing a cake or tart) because it has the highest fat level of all 10 products. (More fat means better flow when the chocolate is melted, since fat creates a liquid base that transports the other ingredients.) The type of fat is important, too. Ghirardelli contains milk fat (along with cocoa butter); Callebaut doesn't. In fact, six of our 10 products add milk fat, an ingredient that has been used increasingly in recent years for its softening effect. Milk fat has a lower and wider melting range (85 to 94 degrees) than cocoa butter (90 to 93 degrees), so chocolates containing milk fat melt faster and stay liquid longer, giving a wider window of liquidity that can come in handy if you're making, say, truffles or trying to smooth the top of a chocolate tart.

For effortless performance across all applications and easy availability, we're naming the Ghirardelli 60 Percent Cacao Bittersweet Chocolate Premium Baking Bar our go-to dark chocolate.

COOK'S ILLUSTRATED

28

RATING DARK CHOCOLATE

We tasted 10 nationally available supermarket brands of dark chocolate that met the FDA minimum of at least 35 percent cacao, sampling them in three blind tastings—plain, in brownies, and in our Chocolate Pots de Crème recipe—and rating them on flavor, texture, sweetness, and overall appeal. Fat and sugar levels were taken from nutrition labels and are expressed in a serving size of 42 grams. We learned approximate cacao percentages from manufacturers and calculated approximate cocoa solids with the help of chocolate experts from the Penn State University Cocoa, Chocolate, and Confectionery Research Group and the MIT Lab for Chocolate Science; levels are plus or minus 2 percent. Scores were averaged and the products appear below in order of preference.

HIGHLY RECOMMENDED

	CRITERIA		TESTERS' COMMENTS

GHIRARDELLI 60 Percent Cacao Bittersweet Chocolate Premium Baking Bar
Price: $2.99 for 4 oz ($0.75 per oz)
Cacao Percentage: about 60% Cocoa Solids: about 22%
Sugar: 16 g (38%) Fat: 16 g (38%)

Plain ★★★
Brownies ★★½
Pots de Crème ★★★

This bar rated the highest for eating plain, with a complex flavor that combined the tart fruitiness of cherries and wine with a slight smokiness. Its high—but not too high—level of cocoa solids made this bar easy to work with in creamy desserts, turning out exceptionally "satiny, gorgeous" pots de crème with "dark, bold" flavor that "screams chocolate."

CALLEBAUT Intense Dark Chocolate, L-60-40NV
Price: $8.39 for 1.05 lb ($0.50 per oz)
Cacao Percentage: about 60% Cocoa Solids: about 30%
Sugar: 15.12 g (36%) Fat: 12.6 g (30%)

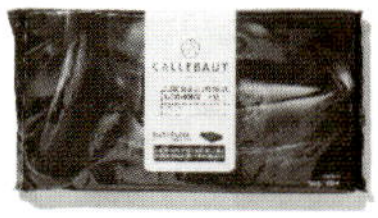

Plain ★★★
Brownies ★★★
Pots de Crème ★★½

Our previous winner was again "rich," "intense," and "earthy," with notes of "coffee," "a balanced bitterness," and "just the right amount of sweetness"—attributes that made their way into the brownies. With a high level of cocoa solids, this product sometimes made silky pots de crème that were a bit grainy.

RECOMMENDED

DOVE Silky Smooth Dark Chocolate
Price: $3.20 for 3.3 oz ($0.97 per oz)
Cacao Percentage: about 55% Cocoa Solids: about 22%
Sugar: 19 g (45%) Fat: 14 g (33%)

Plain ★★½
Brownies ★★½
Pots de Crème ★★★

This fudgy mass-market bar lacked bitterness but still offered pleasing complexity: boozy notes of Kahlúa and rum with a "nutty, mocha flavor." But a few tasters found it too sweet in desserts—more "like a candy bar" than like baking chocolate. It was notably smooth, with tasters calling it "lush" and "melt-in-your-mouth."

SCHARFFEN BERGER Semisweet Fine Artisan Dark Chocolate
Price: $4.29 for 3 oz ($1.43 per oz)
Cacao Percentage: about 62% Cocoa Solids: about 25%
Sugar: 15.6 g (37%) Fat: 15.6 g (37%)

Plain ★★½
Brownies ★★½
Pots de Crème ★★½

Many detected "intense" grown-up flavors in this chocolate, which boasted hints of berry and a "background smokiness." Others found it "pleasant but generic," impressions that carried over to brownies and pots de crème.

RECOMMENDED WITH RESERVATIONS

BAKER'S Bittersweet Baking Chocolate Squares
Price: $4.99 for 6 oz ($0.83 per oz)
Cacao Percentage: about 66% Cocoa Solids: about 30%
Sugar: 15 g (36%) Fat: 15 g (36%)

Plain ★★★
Brownies ★★★
Pots de Crème ★

In both the plain and the brownie tastings, this basic supermarket product was a hit with tasters, earning praise for a "rich," "intense" chocolate flavor that had notes of coconut and coffee. But with high levels of cocoa solids, it consistently made "gritty" pots de crème.

BAKER'S Semi-Sweet Baking Chocolate Squares
Price: $3.79 for 8 oz ($0.47 per oz)
Cacao Percentage: about 56% Cocoa Solids: about 24%
Sugar: 18 g (43%) Fat: 13.5 g (32%)

Plain ★★
Brownies ★★★
Pots de Crème ★½

Though in the main tasters found this chocolate "uninteresting" for snacking purposes, it excelled in brownies, where it was dubbed a "good little workhorse," with a nice balance of cocoa and sugar and with hints of "roasted pecan." In pots de crème, it exhibited an unwanted coconut aftertaste.

GHIRARDELLI Semi-Sweet Chocolate Premium Baking Bar
Price: $2.99 for 4 oz ($0.75 per oz)
Cacao Percentage: about 52% Cocoa Solids: about 19%
Sugar: 20 g (48%) Fat: 14 g (33%)

Plain ★★
Brownies ★★½
Pots de Crème ★

The enjoyable bitter and dried fruit flavors in this bar were muted by a milky sweetness. This product was "enjoyable" in brownies, but with low cocoa solids, it made disappointing pots de crème that were too loose.

NOT RECOMMENDED

HERSHEY'S Semi-Sweet Chocolate Baking Bar
Price: $2.49 for 4 oz ($0.62 per oz)
Cacao Percentage: about 42% Cocoa Solids: about 13%
Sugar: 24 g (57%) Fat: 12 g (29%)

Plain ★½
Brownies ★½
Pots de Crème ★½

Far too sweet and milky, this high-sugar, very low cocoa solids bar was "like being attacked by a Tootsie Roll." Its strong notes of hazelnut, caramel, and butterscotch overwhelmed its feeble chocolate flavor so much that the brownies "might as well be blondies," one taster said. The pot de crème was runny.

HERSHEY'S Special Dark Chocolate Bar
Price: $2.19 for 4.25 oz ($0.52 per oz)
Cacao Percentage: about 45% Cocoa Solids: about 14%
Sugar: 21 g (50%) Fat: 13.2 g (31%)

Plain ★
Brownies ★½
Pots de Crème ★

Despite its name, this bar was too much like milk chocolate, a "cream bomb" with just a touch of caramel and roasted nuts. Texturally, it was "bendy," with "no snap." It made "loose and runny" pots de crème and its brownies rated "on the bland side."

NESTLÉ Semi-Sweet Baking Chocolate Bar
Price: $3.31 for 4 oz ($0.83 per oz)
Cacao Percentage: about 43% Cocoa Solids: about 14%
Sugar: 24 g (57%) Fat: 12 g (29%)

Plain ★
Brownies ★½
Pots de Crème ★

Sampled plain, this bar was flat-out sweet, like "cheap Halloween candy." Brownies were its best application, though it was still overly sugary and weak on chocolate flavor. In pots de crème it was "runny, like bad pudding."

KITCHEN NOTES

⇒ BY ANDREW JANJIGIAN, LAN LAM & DAN SOUZA ⇐

SHOPPING Bone-In Pork Rib Roast

When making our Slow-Roasted Bone-In Pork Rib Roast (page 13), you'll want a 4- to 5-pound center-cut roast with a fat cap that's ¼ to ½ inch thick. But you might have to go one step further at the butcher counter, as some roasts come with the chine bone attached. Ask the butcher to remove as much of this bone as possible to facilitate carving. –A.J.

WITH CHINE BONE   WITHOUT CHINE BONE

Yes, You Can Freeze Cheese

By wrapping hard and soft cheeses such as cheddar and Brie in parchment paper followed by a loose covering of aluminum foil, we've successfully stored them in the fridge for as long as a month. But we've always wondered whether cheese could last even longer in the freezer or whether the ice and fat crystals that form would rupture their protein network, leading to breakage and weeping upon thawing. To find out, we wrapped a variety of cheeses (extra-sharp cheddar, Brie, fresh goat cheese, and Pecorino Romano) tightly in plastic wrap, sealed them in zipper-lock bags, and froze them for six weeks. Then we let them defrost overnight in the fridge (a 2½-hour rest on the counter also works). To our surprise, all samples were essentially identical to never-frozen controls. The frozen cheddar even melted properly. As long as you wrap the cheeses extremely well (or vacuum-seal them) to prevent freezer burn, it's fine to freeze cheese for up to two months. –D.S.

Better French Press Coffee

Even devoted fans of the simplicity and convenience of using a French press (see page 23 for our new recommended press) know that the coffee made in it can be a bit bitter and lacking in complexity. But 2007 World Barista Champion James Hoffmann has popularized a break-and-clean method of preparing French press coffee designed to fix some of its shortcomings.

Ordinarily, with a French press you pour nearly boiling water over coarsely ground coffee, stir the grounds into the water, let it steep for 5 minutes or so, and then push down the plunger to separate the grounds from the coffee. The problem is that the raft of grounds creates back pressure against the filter, which can force unwanted compounds from the beans, resulting in an overextracted, bitter flavor.

The break-and-clean method circumvents this entirely by removing most of the grounds prior to plunging. Here's how it's done: First, once the steeping is complete, you "break" the raft of grounds by gently stirring it up with a large spoon. Then you use a spoon to clean out most of the remaining grounds floating on the surface before using the plunger to filter those that are left behind.

When we gave it a whirl, the majority of our tasters agreed that the technique produced a cup of coffee that was distinctly rounder, sweeter, and more complex. (If you find your coffee not quite as strong as you like, try extending the brewing time by a minute or two.) –A.J.

Carryover Cooking in Fish

We often talk about carryover cooking in meat—how a roast, for example, will continue to cook even after it's been removed from the oven, the result of heat migrating from the outer portions of the meat toward the center. This is why we often take a roast out of the oven before it's fully cooked. But carryover cooking can also have a dramatic effect on fish and its loosely structured flesh.

To quantify the effect of carryover cooking on salmon, we cooked three batches of 1-inch-thick fillets on a wire rack set in a baking sheet at various oven temperatures until they were 125 degrees at the center. We then watched how that number rose as the fish sat outside the oven for 5 minutes. The salmon cooked at 250 degrees carried over an average of 7 degrees, just above the ideal 130 degrees for serving. The salmon cooked at 325 degrees rose 9 degrees at its center after 5 minutes, while the fish cooked at 350 degrees rose 15 degrees. And at 450 degrees? The salmon's temperature rose a whopping average of 27 degrees after 5 minutes.

Though the extent of carryover cooking will vary depending on the type (and width) of the fish, these tests underscore why a low oven temperature can work best for fish, since the hotter the oven the more dramatic the effect of carryover cooking. A low oven temperature will help ensure that the flesh is evenly cooked from edge to center and stays near the ideal doneness temperature until the fish is served. –L.L.

Quick Microwave Kale Chips

If you've somehow missed that kale chips are a "thing," with recipes flooding cooking sites and packages of commercially made chips now turning up even in ordinary supermarkets, trust us: Tossing torn leaves of kale with oil and salt and baking them until crispy is a worthwhile endeavor. The slightly browned leaves take on a nutty, sweet taste and a pleasing, brittle texture. But the standard oven approach isn't perfect: It's hard to get the leaves evenly browned; plus, it's difficult to drive off enough moisture so that the chips stay crispy when stored for more than a few hours. So when we noticed a few blogs promoting a microwave method, we were eager to give it a try. We found that the microwave dehydrates the leaves evenly and thoroughly, so they stay crispy longer—and the chips cook a whole lot faster than they do in the oven. (Note: For the best texture, we prefer to use flatter Lacinato kale. We also found that collard greens work well, but we don't recommend curly-leaf kale, Swiss chard, or curly-leaf spinach, all of which turn dusty and crumbly when crisped.) Here's our take on the technique. –D.S.

1. Remove stems from 5 ounces kale (about ½ bunch). Tear leaves into 2-inch pieces; wash and thoroughly dry, then toss well with 4 teaspoons oil in large bowl.

2. Spread roughly one-third of leaves in single layer on large plate and season lightly with kosher salt.

3. Microwave for 3 minutes. If leaves are crispy, transfer to serving bowl; if not, continue to microwave leaves in 30-second increments until crispy. Repeat with remaining leaves in 2 batches. Store chips in airtight container for up to 1 week.

Perfectly Round Cookies

We love refrigerator cookie dough—the kind that is chilled in a log shape and sliced before baking—because it can be made ahead; plus, we can bake off only as many cookies as we want at a time. But shaping the dough into an even, round cylinder is hard to do just by rolling it back and forth on the counter, as most recipes instruct. Here's a more effective method. –A.J.

1. Place cookie dough in center of large piece of parchment paper and use your hands to shape it into rough log. Fold parchment in half over dough.

2. Grasp bottom half of parchment. With your other hand, press bench scraper into crease that forms between dough and parchment. Move scraper back and forth along length of dough to even out cylinder.

3. Roll parchment into cylinder and firmly twist ends together to form tight seal. (Refrigerate cylinder on bed of raw rice to prevent flat bottom from forming.)

Eggnog: Better—and Safer—with Age

The usual approach to making eggnog is simple: Mix together eggs, sugar, cream, and hard liquor, and then enjoy. But when we heard of a way to improve on the appeal of this drink—and at the same time dispel any concerns over using raw eggs—we had to give it a try. The idea? Make a batch of eggnog and let it age for at least three weeks in the refrigerator before drinking. The rest period supposedly drives off eggy taste while giving the other flavors a chance to meld. At the same time, the alcohol has a chance to kill any potential pathogens in the mix.

This latter benefit was conclusively proven by microbiologists Vince Fischetti and Raymond Schuch at New York City's Rockefeller University. They deliberately added salmonella bacteria to a batch of eggnog and analyzed the bacteria content over a three-week period. By the three-week mark, the alcohol had rendered the eggnog completely sterile. When we tried their recipe, we indeed found it smooth and drinkable, though at 14 percent alcohol it packed quite a punch.

Satisfied with the sterility of the drink, we set out to produce an equally safe (but less potent) nog. Our solution? Waiting until serving time to add the dairy. This way, we could use enough alcohol to properly sterilize the eggs during storage and then temper the booze-egg base with dairy for serving. We stirred together a dozen eggs, 1½ cups of bourbon, ½ cup of cognac, and ⅓ cup of dark rum; added 1½ cups of sugar; and refrigerated the 18-percent-alcohol mixture in an airtight container. After three weeks, we poured the base through a sieve to remove any egg solids and then mellowed out the mixture with 6 cups of whole milk and ½ cup of cream, bringing it down to about 8 percent alcohol. The unanimous verdict: Alongside a fresh batch, which tasted comparatively boozy and harsh, our aged nog went down more smoothly. To age your favorite eggnog recipe, be sure to use 1½ ounces of 80 proof liquor for every egg, and leave out the dairy until serving. –A.J.

New Pie Protocol

To avoid the risk of the glass shattering, we know not to put a hot Pyrex baking dish on a cold surface, but we have often recommended the opposite situation when baking pies in our favorite pie plate from Pyrex: We typically chill the dough-lined pie plate before transferring it to a preheated baking sheet, which helps ensure proper browning of the bottom crust. World Kitchen, the company that now owns the U.S. Pyrex brand, doesn't specifically warn against such a practice, but we recently decided to confirm with them that it was safe. As it turned out, the company cautioned against putting cold (or even room-temperature) Pyrex pie plates and baking dishes onto hot baking sheets because they conduct heat so efficiently that they could shatter.

Our new recommendation is to place the pie plate on an unheated metal baking sheet before sliding it into the oven. The metal pan still helps conduct heat to the bottom of the pie but without risk of cracking the Pyrex plate since it heats up gradually. To apply this new approach to any of our existing recipes calling for a preheated sheet, bake the pie 5 to 10 minutes longer to guarantee a crisp, browned bottom. (Times will vary depending on the moisture of the filling and whether the pie has a single or double crust.) –A.J.

SCIENCE Helping Chocolate Keep Its Temper

Good chocolate right out of the wrapper has an attractive sheen and a satisfying snap when you break it in two. But if you melt the chocolate to use as a coating or for drizzling and try to use it immediately, it will set up into a soft, blotchy, dull-looking mess that melts on your fingers. Why the difference? The short answer is that the crystal structure of the cocoa butter in the chocolate has changed. Cocoa butter can solidify into any of six different types of crystals, each of which forms at a specific temperature. But only one type—beta crystals—sets up dense and shiny and stays that way even at warmer temperatures well above room temperature. When a chocolate is made up of beta crystals, it is said to be in temper. So how do you put melted chocolate back in temper?

IT'S A SNAP
Chocolate that's been tempered is glossy and breaks cleanly if snapped.

LOST ITS TEMPER
Chocolate that is melted and cooled without tempering will look dull and bend instead of breaking.

FUSSY, OLD-FASHIONED ROUTE

The traditional way is a painstaking process known as tempering. First the chocolate is melted so that all its fat crystals dissolve. It is then cooled slightly, which allows new "starter" crystals to form. Finally, it is gently reheated to a temperature high enough to melt the less stable crystals and allow only the desirable beta crystals to remain (these handily melt—and form—at around 88 degrees), triggering the formation of more beta crystals that eventually form a dense, hard, glossy network.

EASIER, UPDATED APPROACH

For our Florentine Lace Cookies (page 23), we used a far simpler approach: We microwaved three-quarters of the chocolate (first chopped into fine shards) at 50 percent power until it was mostly melted. We then added the remaining chocolate and stirred it until melted, returning it to the microwave for no more than 5 seconds at a time to complete the melting. While not quite as shiny as traditionally tempered chocolate, this chocolate had a nice luster and decent snap. This method works because it keeps the temperature of the chocolate close enough to 88 degrees so that mostly stable beta crystals form and act as seed crystals. It's a great method when taking the time to carry out true tempering is too much trouble. –D.S.

The Science of Cooking: Tempering Chocolate
Video available FREE for 4 months at CooksIllustrated.com/dec13

EQUIPMENT CORNER

⋙ BY AMY GRAVES, SARAH SEITZ & TAIZETH SIERRA ⋘

UPDATE Oven Probe Thermometer

An oven probe thermometer transmits meat temperature data to a digital console via a thin cord attached to a long probe that is inserted into the cooking meat. The ThermoWorks Original Cooking Thermometer/Timer ($24) is a particularly user-friendly model, with simultaneous time and temperature displays on a large readout. But in 2008, we could only halfheartedly recommend the tool because its probes were sometimes defective. ThermoWorks has since updated the thermometer, so we checked its accuracy by plunging multiple copies of the probe into boiling water (212 degrees) and then into ice water (32 degrees) before using them to chart the temperature of a roast that cooked for 2½ hours. The probes were spot-on in the water temperature tests and gave readings for the roast that were nearly identical to those of our favorite (and accurate) instant-read thermometer, the Splash-Proof Super-Fast Thermapen ($96), also by ThermoWorks. The new button layout was clear and easy to use, and the numbers display as large as ever. Since the wires inside the probe's cord can wear out, we recommend occasionally checking its accuracy with a water temperature test. The new model is an improvement over its predecessor. –T.S.

TIME AND TEMPERATURE
An updated version of the ThermoWorks Original Cooking Thermometer/Timer offers more accurate readings and easy-to-use controls.

UPDATE Cookie Presses

A cookie press works like a dough "gun": You put a perforated disk for the desired cookie shape on the barrel, fill the tube with dough, and squeeze the trigger to release a spritz of dough. We tested five models priced from about $13 to $30, including our previous favorite and an updated version. Two were immediate failures, either producing irregular cookies or refusing to release them at all. Of the rest, certain features proved handy, such as a nonslip base for holding the press steady while you squeeze, which helps keep cookies uniform. We also liked models that had an indicator showing when the plunger was engaged and ready to press after loading. The OXO Good Grips Cookie Press with Disk Storage Case ($29.99) had both of these features and was the only press to make perfectly shaped cookies with each of its dozen disks. –T.S.

READY, AIM, PRESS
The OXO Cookie Press releases cookie dough in consistent shapes with each of its dozen disks.

NEW Folding Proofer

If you have a cold, drafty kitchen and need a way to control the temperature at which your dough proofs (rises), the Brod & Taylor Folding Proofer ($148) offers a solution. This 10½-inch-tall box provides a 12 by 15-inch surface large enough for a bowl of dough or two loaf pans. Its enclosed heating element lets you regulate the temperature while a small water pan creates a humid environment. We made a batch of bread dough and divided it in two, leaving half in the proofer and half in a cold oven with a pan of boiling water, the test kitchen method for replicating a proofer box. The oven temperature started at 95 degrees and then dropped to 80 degrees over 2 hours and 15 minutes, while the proofer held at 85 degrees (the temperature we set). The dough was equally well risen using both methods. The folding proofer offers two advantages: It allows you to use your oven for other purposes while your dough rises, plus it gives you precise temperature control. Hard-core bakers may want to splurge; the rest of us can simply use our ovens. –T.S.

PRECISE PROOFER
The Brod & Taylor Folding Proofer lets dough rise at precise temperatures, but a home oven works just as well.

UPDATE Adjustable Measuring Cups

We've relied on the KitchenArt Adjust-A-Cup Professional Series, 2-Cup ($12.95) since 2008 for measuring sticky ingredients like honey and peanut butter, so we wondered if a new adjustable cup from OXO's Good Grips line ($11.99) offered any advantages. Like the Adjust-A-Cup, OXO's cup consists of a clear plastic barrel with measurement markings and a plunger insert. The plunger is drawn back to the desired marking, filled, and then pushed forward to eject the ingredient. OXO's cup sports a twisting track that guides the plunger and holds it steady for precise measuring. Unfortunately, this feature complicated things; while the Adjust-A-Cup uses an easy pull-push motion, the OXO plunger stubbornly stuck to the track as we muscled through twisting it up and down, occasionally sending the plunger flying out of the tube. We also nearly knocked the measuring cup over as it teetered on its wobbly base, making us miss the large, solid foundation of the Adjust-A-Cup. For our sticky measuring needs, we're sticking with the Adjust-A-Cup. –S.S.

STICK WITH IT
The Adjust-A-Cup makes measuring sticky ingredients a snap.

NEW Silicone Food Covers

Flexible silicone covers, priced from $14.95 to $40 and sold singly or in sets of three to four sizes, are designed to replace plastic wrap and turn any bowl into an airtight, leakproof, microwave-safe container for storing and reheating foods. Some lids stretch tightly over the bowl; others are flat and rest on the bowl's rim, forming a suction seal when you tug gently on the tab or knob on top. Most were leakproof: When we sealed bowls of soup and tipped them over, all but one model prevented dribbles. However, flat lids made more airtight seals, we discovered, after we loaded bowls with Drierite moisture-reacting crystals, covered them with the lids, and left them for three days. Flat lids also stayed put during microwaving, while stretchable lids inflated from the warming air and popped off. Our favorite, the sturdy Top This! Silicone Lid Set by Rachael Ray ($19.95 for three), stuck firmly, keeping contents under a moistureproof, airtight seal. –A.G.

DON'T GET CLINGY
When clear plastic wrap won't do, the Top This! Silicone Lid Set by Rachael Ray keeps foods under an airtight, leakproof seal.

For complete testing results for each item, go to CooksIllustrated.com/dec13.

Sources

Prices were current at press time and do not include shipping. Contact companies to confirm information or visit CooksIllustrated.com for updates.

PAGE 23: FRENCH PRESS COFFEE MAKER
• Bodum Columbia French Press Coffee Maker, Double Wall: $79.95, item #1308-16, Bodum (800-232-6386, **bodum.com**).

PAGE 27: STAND MIXERS
• KitchenAid Pro Line Series 7-Qt Bowl Lift Stand Mixer: $549.95, item #KSM7586P, Amazon (**amazon.com**).
• KitchenAid Classic Plus Series 4.5-Quart Tilt-Head Stand Mixer: $229.99, item #KSM75WH, KitchenAid (800-541-6390, **kitchenaid.com**).

PAGE 32: OVEN PROBE THERMOMETER
• ThermoWorks Original Cooking Thermometer/Timer: $24, item #TW362B, ThermoWorks (800-393-6434, **thermoworks.com**).

PAGE 32: COOKIE PRESS
• OXO Good Grips Cookie Press with Disk Storage Case: $29.99, item #1257580, OXO (800-545-4411, **oxo.com**).

PAGE 32: FOLDING PROOFER
• Brod & Taylor Folding Proofer: $148, item #FP-101, Brod & Taylor (800-768-7064, **brodandtaylor.com**).

PAGE 32: ADJUSTABLE MEASURING CUP
• KitchenArt Adjust-A-Cup Professional Series, 2-Cup: $12.95, item #694297, Cooking.com (800-663-8810, **cooking.com**).

PAGE 32: SILICONE FOOD COVERS
• Rachael Ray Top This! Silicone Lid Set: $19.95, item #403723, Cooking.com.

INDEX
November & December 2013

AMERICA'S TEST KITCHEN COOKING SCHOOL

Let us help you become a better cook. Offering more than 100 courses for cooks at every level, our school combines personalized instruction from America's Test Kitchen test cooks with leading-edge technology to provide a unique and effective learning experience. Start a 14-day free trial at OnlineCookingSchool.com.

COOK'S ILLUSTRATED IS NOW AVAILABLE ON iPAD!

Download the *Cook's Illustrated* app for iPad and start a free trial subscription or purchase a single issue. Issues are enhanced with recipe videos, full-color step-by-step slide shows, and expanded reviews and ratings. Go to CooksIllustrated.com/iPad to download our app through iTunes.

Follow us on Twitter: twitter.com/TestKitchen
Find us on Facebook: facebook.com/CooksIllustrated

Julia Child's Stuffed Turkey, Updated, 7

Rich Chocolate Tart, 21

Best Chicken Stew, 11

Twice-Baked Sweet Potatoes, 9

Slow-Roasted Bone-In Pork Rib Roast with Port Wine–Cherry Sauce, 13

Rigatoni with Beef and Onion Ragu, 15

Black Olive Tapenade, 19

Florentine Lace Cookies, 23

Caldo Verde, 24

PHOTOGRAPHY: CARL TREMBLAY; STYLING: MARIE PIRAINO

Meyer Lemons

Mandarinquats

Calamondins

Oro Blancos

Ojai
Pixie
Tangerines

Tangelos

Grapefruits

Uniq
Fruits

HYBRID CITRUS